D0935145

A Brand Plucked From the Fire

The Life of
Herman E. Schaalman

A Brand Plucked From the Fire

The Life of
Herman E. Schaalman

Richard Damashek, PhD

KTAV Publishing House, Inc.
Jersey City, New Jersey

Copyright © 2013 Richard Damashek

All rights reserved
No part of this book may be used or reproduced in any manner whatsoever without
written permission from the publisher, except in the case of brief quotations embodied
in reviews and articles.

Manufactured in the United States of America

KTAV Publishing House, Inc.
888 Newark Avenue
Jersey City, NJ 07306
Tel. (201) 963-9524
Fax. (201) 963-0102
www.ktav.com
bernie@ktav.com

Printed in the U.S.A.
First Printing February, 2013

ISBN 978-1-60280-227-8 (hardcover)

Library of Congress Cataloging-in-Publication Data

Damashek, Richard, 1941-
    A brand plucked from the fire : the life of Rabbi Herman E. Schaalman / Richard
Damashek.
        pages. cm
    ISBN 978-1-60280-227-8
    1. Schaalman, Herman E. (Herman Ezra), 1916- 2. Rabbis--Illinois--Chicago--
Biography. 3. Reform Judaism. I. Title.
    BM755.S2493D36 2013
    296.8'341092--dc23
    [B]
                                                                    2012043633

Dedicated to my loving and lovely wife,
Jane A. Thomas,
my companion on our life's journey

Contents

Acknowledgments

First, to my wife, who has so graciously given up so much of our time together to allow me to work on this book over the last eight years, usually in the morning six days a week and with time off on Saturday for Shabbat. Even those mornings, I was off to attend Schaalman's Torah Study. How she let me take this book on our vacations and sacrifice mornings six days a week is almost a mystery to me. I think she liked to see me working on a project that she too considered important, and, though she was not able to spend nearly as much time with the Schaalmans as I did, she came to love them as much as I do. Near the end of the project, she became one of my most diligent and competent editors.

Then, there is Bindy Bitterman, an angel who appeared almost out of nowhere. I barely knew her when she volunteered to be a reader of this biography, not only a reader, but a superb editor. For the last several years, she has been reading and commenting on the manuscript, never failing to say when I asked if she would be willing to read another chapter: "I'd love to, if you can stand my carping." Stand it? I welcomed it.

And then there are Herman and Lotte Schaalman. I cannot even begin to thank them enough for allowing me into their home these many years to probe and question them about their lives. For most of these sessions, Lotte played the gracious host. Before I arrived, she prepared tea or coffee for me, some of my favorite chocolate chip cookies, and occasionally fresh fruit or cheese and crackers. When she was not available, the Rabbi took charge and made sure I was fed and properly plied with caffeine to make it through the interviews. Of course, in listening to him, I was always sitting on the edge of my chair, hanging on every word and hoping I copied it down accurately. As a backup, I always had my trusty digital recorder to ensure that I did not miss anything.

Other people also need to be acknowledged, particularly members of the Schaalman family who provided information and insight into my subject: daughter and son, Susan and Michael; grandchildren Keren, Johanna, and Jeremy; brother Freddie Schaalman; and, of course, Lotte.

Friends and students also chipped in with information and evaluations of what their Rabbi has meant to them. The first to allow me to interview them: Frank Metzger and Mel Abrams. Then, other members of the "Class of Schaalman," his students and friends: Bernie Rozran, Barbara Steinberg, Charlotte (Charli) Hart, Robert Edwards and Neil Rest. Add to this list his friends who gave me their time: Col. James Pritzker, Bob and Audrey Morris, Bill Schindler, Steve Melamed, Beverly Falstein, David Fleischman, Bob Cooper, Ruth Terrill, Alice Fript, and Jane Ramsey.

The list of Schaalman's rabbinic friends and colleagues who were kind enough to allow me to interview them include Rabbis Michael Zedek, Robert Marx, Irwin Fishbein, Charles Kroloff, Marc Berkson, Peter Knobel, Hillel Cohn, Michael Weinberg, Joseph Edelheit, Stephen Hart, David Sofian, John Friedman, Mark Weiner, and Richard G. Hirsch.

Also helpful to me were other Schaalman friends and colleagues: Jerry Kaye, Dr. Michael Kotzin, Dr. Thomas Baima, Dr. Leo Lefebure, Dirk Ficca, Fr. John Pawlikowski, PhD, Sr. Mary Christine Athans, BVM, PhD, Sr. Ann Ida Gannon, BVM, PhD, and Sr. Carol Francis Jegen, BVM.

Then, there were the libraries and librarians without whose help this book could never have been written: Elise Nienaber at the American Jewish Archives and her boss, Ken Proffitt; and Camille Brown and Kathy Bloch at Spertus Institute.

Another thank you is owed to Carolyn DeClue, Office Administrator of Temple Judah, Cedar Rapids, Iowa, for copying documents and pictures that have made an invaluable contribution to this book.

A special thanks to the readers I solicited to review this book, who helped correct factual, stylistic, grammatical, and, yes, even typos and spelling errors: Fr. John Pawlikowski, Fr. Alphonse Spilly, Rabbis Marc Berkson, Hillel Cohn, Barry Marks, and Edward Zerin.

A note about documentation and sources. I have tried to cite all print sources used to complete this biography. I have not cited most of the interviews with the Schaalmans that I recorded on audio tape and in digital format. I need to offer special thanks to the trailblazers who came before me. The first is Esta Star in her series of nine extensive interviews with Schaalman conducted over a year and a half from 1987 to 1988. Then there is Sheila Novak-Rodin who covered some of the same ground as Star but brought the history up to 2001. In her 2007 rabbinic thesis at Hebrew Union College, Rabbi Ann Folb produced the first, and so far the only, thesis on Schaalman. Whether he was talking to Star, Novak-Rodin, Folb or me, his recounting of the events of his life is largely consistent and, for that reason, I have cited their work only when they include information he did not tell me. In 2006, on his ninetieth birthday, Schaalman made a DVD with his family present so that he could tell them the story of his life. As I watched the program, I was astonished that the stories he told were almost word for word the same he had given me in our interviews and that he had given to Star, Rodin-Novak and Folb. A complete Bibliography appears at the end of the book, and readers so inclined can track down my sources.

Then there is Andrea Liss, the graphic artist who digitized the Schaalman family pictures that appear in this book.

And finally, I would like to extend special appreciation to Marc and Gail Fenton, and Karen Pritzker and husband Michael Vlock without whose efforts publication of this biography would not have been possible.

Preface

When the president of Hebrew Union College, Julius Morgenstern, officiated at his students' ordinations and while they stood together in front of the ark, his habit was to speak some special words of encouragement quietly to each of them. For Schaalman, he chose the text from Jeremiah 1: 17–19: "The Lord said to Jeremiah, 'Get yourself ready! Stand up and say to them whatever I command you. Do not be terrified by them, or I will terrify you before them. Today I have made you a fortified city, an iron pillar and a bronze wall to stand against the whole land—against the kings of Judah, its officials, its priests, and the people of the land. They will fight against you but will not overcome you, for I am with you and will rescue you.'" Morgenstern could not have known how aptly these words would characterize his student's life. Whether these words fortified Schaalman or not, his life revelas that he has lived them.

The title of this book, *"A Brand Plucked from the Fire,"* comes from Schaalman's acceptance speech delivered before his rabbinic colleagues after they elected him president of the Central Conference of American Rabbis. At that moment, he took on the most prestigious role a Reform rabbi could aspire to in the world of the Reform rabbinate. He saw this ascent as both a vindication of the fact that he had been saved from the Holocaust and an opportunity "to prove to [himself] and to the God Whom I seek to serve that it *might have been worthwhile to rescue this brand from the conflagration* [italics added]" (Schaalman, H. E., 2007, p. 166). The "might have been" is so typically Schaalman. It reveals a humility he has expressed at every stage of his life whenever he received recognition for any of his many accomplishments. He might have been consciously echoing Abraham Joshua Heschel (1966), a Holocaust survivor and one of the greatest twentieth-century Jewish theologians. He, too, saw himself as "a brand plucked from the fire" (p. 282). Alternatively,

Schaalman might have had in mind Zechariah 3:2 where God speaks of Joshua (who represents Jerusalem) as "a brand plucked from the fire."

Appreciation

This book is, above all else, the product of the skills and faithful devotion of my student and friend professor Richard Damashek. Its origin lies in his most thoughtful and uninterrupted attention and response to a Torah study group, which meets regularly each Shabbat morning in my study at Emanuel Congregation.

The usually most stimulating and wide-ranging thoughts and commentaries of the women and men who attend with astounding regularity are most frequently the background for my own thoughts and discoveries of the text and its implications for my understanding and insights.

Almost every week I experience the surprise of understandings and their articulation of which I had not been aware before. These sessions are to me "revelatory."

Since I do not keep notes or use mechanical devices to be available for later review, I have come to rely on Richard, as occasionally only on one or two others, to furnish a faithful, consistent record of the proceedings. Some of, to me, the most significant and important paragraphs and chapters in this book are the result of these Shabbat morning Torah Study.

I am most deeply indebted to Richard for these recollections, as I am for countless hours that he spent over about seven years in most diligent, widespread research, and for many, many precious hours of conversations between him and me.

There is no way that I can thank him adequately; his love of learning, disciplined attention to a most difficult task, and his unflagging friendship are priceless. To Richard and his Jane, I hope for endless blessings.

Herman E. Schaalman
August 28, 2012

Foreword

To me they were theological giants: Rabbi Herman F. Schaalman, Fr. John T. Pawlikowski, and Rev. Clark Williamson, representing respectively Jewish, Catholic, and Protestant perspectives on the state of Jewish-Christian relations. Rabbi Barry Marks had invited them to Springfield, Illinois, to participate in a panel discussion on interfaith issues. The two-day event took place May 11, 1986. Initially, I did not know them, but they quickly became reference points for the theology of Modern Judaism, Catholicism, and Protestantism. Although I have only vague memories of the event, one sticks out as a defining moment in my personal, religious, and spiritual development. A member of the audience asked Rabbi Schaalman, "Where was God during the Holocaust?" and without hesitation, he answered, "God was in the concentration camps suffering with his people." His answer penetrated my psyche and has remained as clear to me today as it was then.

I had been struggling with the same question. Six million Jews had been murdered, one million of them children under the age of ten. How could I justify the existence of such a God under those circumstances? My only recourse was to conclude that God did not intervene in the affairs of humanity. Schaalman's response put the whole issue of the relationship of God and the Jews in a completely new perspective. I had never considered the idea of a suffering God. I thought of God as omniscient and omnipotent, compassionate and loving. Schaalman proposed a God that was neither omniscient nor omnipotent, a vulnerable God powerless to prevent the tragedy that befell the Jews. For me, this postulation had the ring of truth, and I have never forgotten it. Indeed, the Rabbi's words seared themselves into my brain.

I did not see Schaalman again until 1998 at an annual lecture sponsored by the Cardinal Bernardin Center on Catholic-Jewish relations. By then, I was a faculty member at Calumet College of St. Joseph in Whiting, Indiana. I learned about the lecture from Fr. Alphonse Spilly, a colleague and former assistant to Cardinal Bernardin. When I noticed Schaalman and his wife in the lecture hall, I introduced myself and told him that I had been in the audience when he came to Springfield to participate in the interfaith conference. I reminded him of his remark that God was in the concentration camps suffering with His people and the profound effect it had had on my thinking. He seemed pleased to hear what I said but appeared otherwise puzzled.

I had no further contact with Schaalman for another five years until I knew that I was relocating to Chicago from the suburbs. I asked my rabbi in Temple Chai, Stephen A. Hart, where in Chicago I might find a rabbi as caring and compassionate as himself. Without hesitation he said, "Schaalman. He's at Emanuel Congregation on North Sheridan." I was delighted with the news, first to find out that I could become a member of Schaalman's congregation, and then that it was only five blocks from where I lived. I joined the congregation and came to feel as if Schaalman and his wife, Lotte, adopted my wife and me as members of their family. Over the last nine years, I have attended almost every Torah Study that Schaalman held. During that time, I developed a deep attachment for the Rabbi and have had the pleasure of participating with him in discussions of the Torah and to witness his theological evolution.

None of those sessions provided as clear and succinct a statement of his beliefs as a session held on April 30, 2005. His remarks were a response to a challenging question presented by the Emanuel Congregation's new rabbi, Michael R. Zedek. Not long after he arrived, he was an occasional visitor to Schaalman's Torah Study. Some of the members of the small but dedicated group had been Schaalman's students for more than four decades.[1] On that memorable morning of April 30, 2005, Zedek asked Schaalman to discuss his own personal theological views on the portion we were reading. Schaalman told him that he believed that God is a mystery, as are God's interventions in the life of humanity. The God of creation, too, is a mystery. If we accept the theory of the Big Bang as the beginning of our universe, we have no way of knowing what role, if any, God played in it. Nor do we know what role God played in the formation of the biblical nation of Israel. The Torah tells us stories, but how do we know that the stories were not written to account for the wonders that happened to the people and as a means of providing the laws and the moral and religious principles of Judaism? Furthermore, if

God is responsible for leading the Israelites out of Egypt and guiding them to establish a nation, where was God when the nation was in peril throughout history? The only satisfactory answer, he told Zedek, is that God is a mystery.

After the session, I thanked Rabbi Zedek for asking the question and told him that I was still reeling from the response. In fact, the response may have had something to do with crystallizing my decision to go ahead with my plans to write this biography. I had been contemplating it for at least a year when the idea first occurred to me, but recently had begun to doubt not only my ability to take on such an enormous task, but whether I would have the stamina to complete it. During a weeklong spring break before the beginning of summer session and one year away from retirement, I made the decision that I should make the effort. If nothing else, I knew I would enjoy the research and the writing. The biography was born out of my desire to give back to him a small portion of the great gift he has given me: his learning, his inspiration and his love. It is also my way of giving his family, friends, and colleagues the opportunity to have access to the details of his remarkable and exemplary life.

My first contact was Rabbi Barry Marks in Springfield, Illinois, who had been my rabbi for seventeen years and whom I deeply admired and respected. I considered him a friend. In addition, Rabbi Marks has a superb memory, and I knew I could count on him for information about my first encounter with Schaalman. As it turned out, he remembered the event more fully than I and offered to help by sending me a package of material from that event, including Schaalman's presentation. When I expressed my hesitation and anxiety about whether I could write this biography (after all, almost all of my writing experience was academic, and I had never taken on a task of this magnitude), he expressed his confidence in me and offered to be a reader of the manuscript.

After that conversation, I mustered my courage and called Schaalman to let him know that I planned to write a book about him. He said he was "overwhelmed" that I would want to take on this project. I detected a sense that he was not sure his life deserved so much attention. I told him that I planned to begin the book with an introduction that would explain how the book came to be written and then to write a chapter on his theology. "Someone else," he said, "was writing a book on his theology, and it was supposed to be finished this summer and ready for him to read. The author, Anita Rifkind, was a Christian woman, who was likely to take a different perspective." At that point in the discussion, I realized that I should write a biography that not only explored his theology, but also sought to discover the experiences, the people, and the thinkers that helped shape who he is, as well as what he thinks. The biography would be my testament to my teacher, an expression of my love for all he has given to me. To that end, I dedicate this book.

Introduction

"You are the rabbi's rabbi. ...We your colleagues, cherish your sweet friendship, your profound scholarship and your never-failing leadership in our lives and in our sacred work."

Rabbi Joseph B. Glaser, Executive Vice President, the CCAR

Jeremiah 1:17–19: *"Get yourself ready! Stand up and say to them whatever I command you. ... Today I have made you a fortified city, an iron pillar and a bronze wall to stand against the whole land—against the kings of Judah, its officials, its priests and the people of the land. They will fight against you but will not overcome you, for I am with you and will rescue you. ..."*

Dr. Julian Morgenstern, remarks to Schaalman on his ordination

"When we came to Chicago thirty years ago, you were spanking new ... [and] in those years you have made a monumental contribution which I am sure will be adequately remembered and extolled."

Rabbi Hayim Goren Perelmuter (1986)

To understand Herman E. Schaalman is to recognize that the *Shoah* became the defining experience in his life. It became the "shadow" at his "heel" that he wishes were not there. So powerful is the *Shoah* in his life that it reshaped his religious thinking. In the face of the overwhelming and unjustified suffering of his people, Schaalman was compelled to conclude that the God of the Hebrew Bible and of the rabbinic tradition had "failed totally to protect Jews in the *Shoah*." Schaalman was forced to deal with an unthinkable reality and to find a way to continue believing in God. Because he cannot make peace with that reality, he concludes that God is not omnipotent, but "needs our

1

help" to make this a better world. To accomplish this goal, Jews, as well as the rest of humanity, must enter into a partnership with God to make the world the kind of place envisioned by the Prophets.

One of the German Jews to survive the *Shoah*, he is one of the foremost rabbis in the Reform movement with honors and testimonials from political, cultural, and religious leaders and institutions around the country. His fame extends internationally as well with recognition and awards from his home country of Germany.

Here, at home in Chicago, Schaalman is one of the most respected rabbis to serve the Jewish community in the more than sixty years he has been here. Perhaps his most significant contribution in the public domain has been his focus on intermarriage issues. So powerful has been his work and presence in this area that he became a close friend and confidant of the Cardinal Joseph Bernardin from Chicago and his successor Cardinal Francis George. His friendship with Cardinal Bernardin resulted in a new dimension of mutual respect and tolerance between Catholics and Jews in Chicago.

Within the Reform movement, he became the "Rabbi's Rabbi" in part because he became a major facilitator in cross-denominational dialogue and because for nearly a half century he has been an educator and source of inspiration for rabbis throughout the movement (Hart, 2006).

On his ninety-fourth birthday, Schaalman found himself reflecting on his life and the remarkable events that brought him to this point. Every development was a mystery to him. Throughout his career, he believed that things happened to him that he never envisioned. When he was the rabbi at Temple Judah in Cedar Rapids during the 1940s, he thought he would be there for life. However, fate, or whatever you want to call it, had a different plan. Soon, he was "called" to Chicago where he began by taking on a professional leadership role in the Union of American Hebrew Congregations. Only a few years later, he became the rabbi of one of the most famous Reform synagogues in America. As the years passed, he found himself taking on greater responsibilities—in the community where he lived, for Reform Judaism nationally and internationally, and on the world stage of interfaith relations. Although he did not seek it, he became a celebrity in the sense that his reputation and good works earned him the respect and admiration in every avenue of his personal and professional life. This is his story.

Chapter 1

The Early Years
Germany 1916–1935

*"Age was not a factor; we were all young together.
These were the days of innocence, simplicity."*

Herman E. Schaalman, 2006

*"'Gentlemen, you have 15 minutes to decide which three will go.
When you have made your decision, knock on the door, come in my study,
and close the door.' All of a sudden, destiny was knocking on the door."*

Herman E. Schaalman, 1987

Germany and the Jews at the Beginning of the Twentieth Century

By the end of the nineteenth century, Germany was beginning to experience a new sense of its own power and a strong desire to become a more dominant player on the world stage. It had produced two of the most influential thinkers in the twentieth century: Marx and Einstein. Marx's insight into class struggle and Einstein's theory of relativity had enormous cultural, and, through Marx, economic and political repercussions that helped shape the twentieth century. In Russia, Marx gave meaning and purpose to the rising revolutionary spirit of the time, as millions of Russian workers and peasants sought to free themselves from the desperate poverty and political despotism that was their life. Joining forces with the Bolshevik Party in 1917, they seized power from the reigning Czar, Nicholas II. In the process they set about to create the first Communist state in the history of the world. During the next thirty years, the Communists took possession of most of Eastern Europe, spread around the globe—most notably to China—and became a strong influence in the internal politics of most of the Westernized world, and, ultimately the second most powerful country in the world.

Simultaneously, the discoveries of Albert Einstein revolutionized modern physics and gave scientists the tools to develop the most powerful military weapon ever known, the atomic bomb. In 1905, he published a series of four papers that turned the study of physics on its head and upended the way the world understood itself.

Another Jew, Sigmund Freud, although not a German but rather an Austrian, helped revolutionize thinking about the function and structure of the mind. He argued that our conscious mind is deeply rooted in an unconscious reservoir of primordial sexual longings that exercise control of human behavior. Out of these discoveries he developed a psychoanalytic method to heal damaged minds. It was a revolutionary therapy that changed the modern view of how the mind functioned.

All three names—Marx, Freud and Einstein—entered common parlance, becoming part of the lexicon of educated and not-so-educated people. Nevertheless, none of these figures was ever discussed in the Schaalman household, despite the fact that Schaalman's father was a university graduate, a teacher of mathematics, a scientist, and a well-educated man of his time. (Sometime later, his father did admit to him that he never understood Einstein.) Nor were they discussed when Schaalman was a student at Hebrew Union College in Cincinnati.[2]

In at least one respect, though, this scientific revolution had penetrated the Schaalman household. Schaalman identifies his upbringing as *Liberale Judentums* (Liberal Judaism), which was one of the two strands of German Reform Judaism, an outgrowth of nineteenth century rationalism. Jewish thinkers, rabbis, and lay people were eager to apply to Judaism the new rationalist principles that provided so much excitement and energy behind the latest scientific discoveries. Reason, they argued, was superior to faith and provided a defense against magic and superstition (Borowitz, 2002). A key premise of these reformers was that Judaism was constantly evolving to fit the changed circumstances brought about by time and culture. The new rationalism meant that many of the liturgical practices and beliefs of traditional Judaism were outmoded and unsuitable for a modern, culturally sophisticated congregation. As a result, German Reform made major changes in traditional liturgy, including the substitution of German for Hebrew, the introduction of the organ to accompany the prayer service, significantly shortened services and, in some congregations, Shabbat services held on Sunday. The reformers also did away with the kippah, the tallit, and phylacteries. When German Reform was imported to America by German immigrants, it became what would eventually be called "American Classical Reform Judaism."[3]

Until Herman was nineteen, he was deeply "enmeshed" in German culture and "knew nothing else, didn't want to know anything else." Partly, he claims, this attraction was based on a desire to explore the depths of human experience, reflecting the German proclivity for ponderous works in the arts and philosophy. In certain areas of Judaism, Schaalman found a similar interest, particularly in Kabbalah, where there is a similar search for the depths of human experience, "ordinarily unseen and unspoken, which you only find if you dig in a kind of monastic penetration." In German culture, there is always the assertion that it is the best in the world. The German national anthem asserts "Deutschland uber alles" (Germany above everybody in the world). Schaalman recited this anthem almost every day. Yet, he claims, "Everybody would know it, so what is the need to proclaim it?" The reason is the doubt that the statement might not be true; therefore, one needs to repeat it to reassure oneself.

Tracing Family Roots

Herman Ezra Schaalman is not really Herman Ezra Schaalman. When he came to America and enrolled in the Hebrew Union College, one of his student friends advised him that in America, he did not need the double "n" at the end of his first and last names: Hermann Schaalmann. According to Schaalman, he has seen the family name spelled in various ways, including "Schaalman," which is a corruption of "Schlomo."[4] He speculates that the name may be derived from "*Shin lamed mem*," or paymasters. It could also be derived from "*shalom*," meaning peace, the peace that comes from paying one's bills, a reconciliation, or from a Babylonian emperor named Schalman-Ezer.

Thanks to Edward Strauss, a family friend and historian, Schaalman has been able to trace his family history to the sixteenth century. The earliest known record comes from 1519 in the Bavarian town of Regensburg. According to Schaalman, it states that a rich Jew named Schaalmann was driven out of Regensburg. Schaalman believes that his ancestor was "driven out" by a pogrom.[5] With a grin on his face, he remarks, "This ancestor was the last rich Jew in the Schaalman family." Although Schaalman has no further information about the family until the nineteenth century, he knows that his paternal grandparents lived in the Regensburg area, where his grandfather, whose first name was Hermann (his Hebrew name was "Naphtali") taught Hebrew to children.[6] Schaalman's parents named him "Hermann" to perpetuate the memory of his deceased paternal grandfather.

Schaalman thinks that this paternal grandfather may have been born around 1845 or 1846. He had four sons—Marcus, Samuel, Joseph, and Adolf—and 2 daughters—Sophie and another whose name Schaalman no longer remembers. The only birthdates he is certain about are his father's, 1890, and his uncle Marcus's, 1870. Adolf, the youngest of the six children, was born in Franconia. Like all the other Jews in Franconia, the Schaalmans were Orthodox Jews.

Although details are scarce, this much is known: by the time they were adults, Adolf's brothers and sisters had moved to different parts of Germany. According to an unpublished manuscript by one of Adolf's students, Marcus, who was a famous professor of mathematics, lived in Nuremberg (Adolf Schaalman, n.d.). Another lived in Frankfurt and the third in Baden-Baden, a well-known health resort in Southwest Germany. Sometime between 1910 and 1912, Adolf and his older brother Marcus were both at the university in Munich, Adolf as a student and Marcus as a professor. This was no small achievement. Although Jews had been attending German universities for several decades, in Imperial Germany their entry into academic careers was still a challenge. Many graduates became "*Privatdozenten*"—a title that allowed them to be part of the academic community but without compensation, rank, and tenure or other faculty rights. Discrimination of this kind was even more severe for women. Nevertheless, on Schaalman's mother's side, both her brothers, Pinchas and Julius Wanschel, became physicians—Pinchas, the younger, a surgeon; and Julius, the elder, a general practitioner.

Uncles Samuel and Joseph went into business. Neither Marcus nor Samuel had children. Marcus died sometime before he might have been sent to a concentration camp. Samuel's wife, Melania, nee Roos, born January 20, 1885, was one of 112 Jews from Baden-Baden, Karlsruhe, Baden, Germany, who were deported to Gurs, a concentration camp in southern France. When the Germans occupied the region in November 1942, they began deporting Jews from prison camps like Gurs to extermination camps in Poland (Yad Vashem, The Holocaust Martyrs' and Heroes' Remembrance Authority, 2006). On August 10, 1942, Melania was transported to Auschwitz, where she died either in 1943 or 1944.[7]

Tante Sophie had six children and Schaalman's other aunt three, a total of nine cousins. Schaalman remembers that Sophie visited once or twice a year, that she married a man whose family name was Gruenbaum and lived in Bad Kissingen, a small town in southern Bavaria. She made a living selling clothes and notions in her own store. Because she was *shomeret Shabbos*, meaning she observed the commandment not to perform any work on the Sabbath, she closed her store on Saturdays. Herman's other aunt on his father's side married a man named Kahn and lived in the Palatine. Both aunts and their families died in the *Shoah*.

Uncle Joseph had one son, Edward or Eddie, who eventually made his way to New York City. In his first marriage, Eddie had a son named "Siggy" (possibly "Sigmund" or "Siegfried"), whom Schaalman believes is living in Richmond. He has had only one contact with Siggy, which did not result in a meeting. Schaalman confides, "The fact that my knowledge of my family background is so sketchy is the result of my early training that taught me not to ask questions of my parents. Even later, after my family had been in Brazil for many years, I never inquired about their relatives and their backgrounds." In retrospect, he realizes that he made a major mistake, a mistake he hopes not to make with his own grandchildren.

On his mother's side, Schaalman has fond memories of the Becker family. They lived in Munich after having immigrated from the same town as his maternal grandparents, Asalia, Ukraine. Mrs. Becker (Schaalman no longer remembers any of their first names) was the sister of his maternal grandmother. He remembers that as a young boy, he was impressed with his bearded Uncle Becker's "deep, rumbling voice" and smell of tobacco. This olfactory memory is as available to him today as is his grandmother's brisket and chicken, which he can still taste. Friday night was social night for the Beckers. When they had no other engagement, they came to the Schaalman home for Shabbos dinners. However, when Shabbos services started later in the late spring and summer, and the Schaalmans did not get home until 8:00 or 8:30 p.m., there was not much time for a meal or a social gathering with the Beckers.

When the Beckers visited, they brought with them their chubby son, affectionately nicknamed the "rubber elephant." He loved his name, and unlike his parents who struggled with German, the boy had become very German and no longer spoke the Yiddish of his parents. In addition to this son, the Beckers had a daughter, who was an occasional visitor.

During Herman's childhood, the Schaalman household was the center of family social life. Despite the fact that Adolf was the youngest member of his family, most family events took place in his home, including Shabbos meals, holiday events, and the B'nai Mitzvot of his three sons. However, whenever other family members had B'nai Mitzvot or weddings, the Schaalmans went to their homes. Casual visits, on the other hand, were infrequent because travel was difficult.

Uncle Edward, or "Eddie" as he was known, was one of Adolf's nephews and a welcome visitor. Schaalman remembers him fondly, "Everyone loved him. He was a successful Schwinn bicycle salesman, who also owned a car at a time when few people could afford one." Because he was a businessman, he brought with him the values and ideas of the outside world. His semi-annual visits were like a breath of fresh air in the Schaalman house, saturated as it was with an air of high culture. His energy and outgoing personality created a kind of vitality and festivity that his parents and their friends did not have. His visits were eagerly anticipated, not least because the family got to ride in his car any place they wanted to go. Usually, they chose the country because it was an opportunity to get away from the city. "Another treat," Schaalman remembers, "was the ices he bought as a sort of special gift." This seemingly trivial event was important to the young boy because the Schaalmans did not have extra money for treats.

The *Shoah*,[8] however, wreaked havoc on the Schaalman family. Many of them perished, but a few of the younger ones escaped to Shanghai, and some now live in France. The Becker-Katz branch of the family from Kolmar in Alsace-Lorraine was nearly wiped out, except for a few survivors. Their descendants still live there or in Strasbourg. Other family members include sons of a first cousin. The cousin and his wife died in a concentration camp; the sons, however, were rescued. Schaalman thinks a few of them may be living in the United States and one may be in Israel.

Adolf also had an uncle on his father's side, Max Samfield. Born in 1844 in Bavaria, he immigrated to America at the age of twenty-three and began what became a distinguished rabbinic career. His first congregation was in Shreveport, Louisiana, and, later, he took a post as senior rabbi at Temple Israel in Memphis, Tennessee. By the time he died in 1915, he had been president of the Central Conference of American Rabbis (CCAR) and a national leader in the Reform movement (positions his great nephew would later hold). Samfield became such an important figure in Memphis that, when he died, nearly every business closed and every streetcar came to a halt for a brief acknowledgement of his death (The Goldrin Woldenberg Institute, 2006). Herman did not discover this side of his family until he was a student at Hebrew Union College.

On Herman's maternal side, his mother, Regina Wanschel, was the youngest of three children and only six months old when her family fled the Ukraine to escape a pogrom. Her family was part of a larger Russian-Jewish community that sought shelter in Germany from the frequent pogroms in Russia and the Ukraine. Until the outbreak of World War I, his mother's parents, Rebecca and Ernst, lived in Nuremberg. Their three children were bright and curious and defied the popular stereotype of the poor and alien East European immigrant. Regina's brothers, Julius and Phineas (known in the family as "Jux" and "Pix"), became part of the success story for the Eastern European Jews. Although they did not get to stay in Germany, they managed to climb into its highly prized professional class. Through her marriage to Adolf, Regina, too, moved into the respected middle-class German society.

By the time Regina met her future husband, her father was dead, and her mother was remarried to a man named Minikes. Schaalman remembers him not as "grandfather" but as "Mr. Minikes." Although Rebecca did not live long enough to attend Herman's Bar Mitzvah,[9] he remembers her fondly as "absolutely wonderful, embracing, caring, and

Max Samfield

sweet … [a woman] that could make a brisket that I can taste today. She did not say much, but she was a warm and affectionate woman, who conformed to the Old World pattern of non-assertive women who were more seen than heard."

In 1923, recognizing that Germany was not a safe place for Jews, Regina's oldest brother, Phineas, now an ophthalmologist, immigrated to Argentina to live in the Baron Maurice de Hirsch colonies. Established to facilitate mass emigration of Jews from Russia, the colonies were intended as a safe refuge for Jews who would find new opportunities to engage in agricultural, commercial and other enterprises. Once in Argentina, however, most of the settlers left the colonies to live in the towns and cities (Baron Maurice de Hirsch, 2008). When life as a settler did not work out for Phineas, he moved to São Paulo, Brazil, where he set up a thriving business and prospered.

Because Herman was only seven years old at the time, he did not have as much contact with this Uncle as with his Uncle Julius, a frequent visitor in the Schaalman home. At the time, Julius was a struggling student and getting help from his sister. During these visits, Herman grew to be very fond of him. Julius remained in Munich a few more years until he got his degree before immigrating to Brazil to join his brother. Once there, he set up a successful medical practice in Rio de Janeiro. In a twist of fate that no one could have predicted, in less than two decades most of the surviving Schaalman family also would immigrate to South America, where a major part of the family lives today.

When Regina's Ukrainian family came to visit, she and her husband spoke Yiddish in order to accommodate their guests. Speaking Yiddish was no imposition on Adolf because, unlike most German Jews who were horrified by Yiddish, he loved it, and it helped his in-laws feel welcome and accepted. This acceptance was a relief because, in their other contacts with Germans, they were embarrassed by their speech. From this warm family connection through Yiddish, and perhaps because of his father's influence, Herman developed a special "fondness" for the language.

How Schaalman's parents first met is unclear. He knows that his father's oldest brother, Marcus, was a professor of mathematics in Nuremberg, and speculates that when Adolf visited him he may have met some of his brother's students. One of them might have been Regina's brother Phineas, who may have studied in Munich and at the university in Nuremberg. As the elder brother, Phineas may have been instrumental in Adolf meeting his sister. Another possibility is that after Adolf's parents died, he may have met Regina when he and his brother moved to Nuremberg.

Adolf was twenty-four when he married Regina, three years his junior. Getting married, however, turned out to be a complicated ordeal. Because World War I had already begun and Germany was at war with

Russia, which controlled half of the Ukraine, Adolf and Regina were not allowed to marry. Another complication was the fact that the Schaalman family was patriotic and did not want to be suspected of associating with the enemy.[10]

A larger obstacle confronting the newly married couple was that Adolf's family would not accept the marriage. Their opposition was based on several apparently insurmountable issues. They held Russian Jews in contempt and despised their Yiddish language. In that, they were typical of other German Jews who looked down on their Eastern European cousins because they were poor, uneducated, and a drain on scarce community resources (Meyer, M., 1998).[11] Many of them were seen as pariahs with their eighteenth-century dress and their long hair locks hanging down the sides of their faces. Tensions between the two communities were already high. For the most part, German Jews had assimilated into German culture: they dressed like Germans, talked like Germans, behaved like Germans, shared their values and antipathies, and were generally middle and upper class. Their Eastern European cousins, on the other hand, had few, if any, of these characteristics.

Worse, because of their perceived differences from the average German, they were an easy target for anti-Semitic propaganda (Barkai, 1998). Their German-Jewish counterparts, therefore, did not want to be identified with them for fear that they, too, would be targeted. The result of this quasi anti-Semitism coming from German Jews was social exclusion and even "spiteful prejudice" (Barkai, 1998a). The East European Jews reacted in kind, scorning German Jews whom they accused of a humiliating assimilation into an alien society. Because over one quarter of Munich's Jewish population (approximately 9,000)[12] were East European Jews, very likely Adolf's family had had some contact with them and shared these prejudices.

However, thanks to the intervention of Rabbi Fruedenthal, a Nuremberg rabbi and longtime Wanschel family friend, Adolf and Regina got the necessary permissions. The couple still had another obstacle: Adolf was a soldier in the German army and about to be shipped off to the front lines. When the couple went to get the marriage license, they discovered that they were not the only ones wanting to marry before the prospective grooms were sent off to war. Long lines of soldiers waited outside Munich's city hall to get their marriage licenses. By the time Adolf and Regina got their license, they had only two hours for the ceremony. The rushed circumstances must have been a tremendous strain for the young bride; she fainted under the huppah!

One manifestation of the Schaalman family's refusal to recognize the marriage was that they did not send Adolf a single package or postcard during the four-and-a-half years he spent in the trenches. To them, he was a "traitor" who had forsaken his family by marrying a Russian Jew. Not until Adolf became the father of three boys and a successful professor did they accept the marriage. The healing took nearly a decade.

With eventual acceptance, Adolf became the head of the family, and all the important family events began to revolve around his household. Regina, who had been rejected by the family, had the satisfaction of having the Schaalman family life center around her home. Despite the fact that he was the youngest of his siblings, Adolf won this standing because of his dominant personality and because he was far more successful and capable than his siblings. The same was true for Regina who, although the youngest in her family, proved to be more capable than the other Schaalmans. As the center of the family, the couple was accorded great respect and "even deference," perhaps in part as compensation for the way the family had treated them.

When Herman was born on April 28, 1916, Adolf was serving his four-and-a-half years military service on the front lines in France. It was during this time that Regina, and possibly her mother, moved to Munich. These years were difficult for them. The Allies had blockaded Germany's ports, and food was scarce (Barkai, 1998a). In order to find food for herself and her infant son, Regina was forced to leave the city and move to an Alpine village where, in exchange for milk and bread from local farmers, she took a job as an organist in a nearby church. She lived in this village for the first two years of Herman's life, during which he was essentially fatherless. At the end of the war in November 1918, the two-year-old Herman met his father. Hearing someone come into the apartment, he went into the foyer where he saw a strange man dressed in a uniform who was taking off his belt and fatigue cap and hanging them in the wardrobe. Having never seen his father before, he began to scream. For the next several days, father and son worked at getting to know each other.

Because his father was reluctant to discuss his war experiences, Schaalman knows little about them. He speculates that the reason his father did not talk about them was that part of the German character required that people keep their personal feelings to themselves. As Schaalman has confided, "My training and still, really, my way of handling myself to this day, is to internalize things. You manage it within yourself." He knows that his father had been conscripted to fight in the war and fought as part of a team of sappers, whose job was to cut the barbed wire and remove mines before the troops left the trenches. One of the battles in which he participated was the siege of Verdun, which, according to Schaalman, "was then the single bloodiest battle in military history. Over a half a million men died in the period of three or four years [with] a total of 200 yards changing hands." By the end of the war, Adolf had risen to the rank of sergeant and had been decorated for bravery.

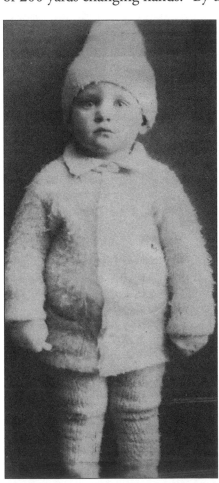

Baby Herman

In late April of 1916 when his son was supposed to be born, Adolf came home on furlough. Because the birth was late, he decided to return to his company in France and keep a few days of his furlough in reserve. When the news came that his son had been born, Adolf requested permission to go home for the bris. As he was walking back towards the rear of the line to catch a ride to the nearest railway station, the company messenger overtook him and told him that the shelter in which he had lived for two years had taken a direct hit and everyone in it had been killed. Ever after, Adolf credited his son's birth for saving his life.

Although most Jews supported the war enthusiastically, Schaalman does not know what his father thought about being a soldier in the Kaiser's army. Two days after Germany declared war on Russia, one of Germany's most influential rabbis and intellectuals, Rabbi Leo Baeck, wrote, "It is not a war over land or influence that is now waged, but a war that will decide the culture and morality of Europe, whose destiny has been placed in the hands of Germany and in the hands of those who stand by its side" (as cited in Folb, 2007). Baeck's position was part of German Jewry's identification with the German cause. The perception was that the moment for Jewish acceptance by their fellow Germans had finally arrived. Baeck was joined by Martin Buber, who was inspired to write: "Never has the concept of 'people' become so real for me as it has in these weeks [prior to the outbreak of war]. ... Among Jews in general one finds nearly everywhere a great and solemn feeling" (Mendes-Flohr, "In the Shadow of War," as cited in Folb, 2007, p. 7).[13]

Baby Herman (eight months) with mother

Whether Adolf served in the Kaiser's army reluctantly or with pride, Schaalman knows only that once the war was over, his father believed that he had served his country well and that it owed him respect and would value him as a citizen. In this belief, Adolf was not alone. After the War, Germany's Jews felt more German than ever: "They had proven their patriotism on the battlefield side by side with non-Jews" and had high hopes of being fully integrated into German society (Barkai, 1998, p. 45). After all, the Weimar constitution had given the Jews new status by enfranchising and giving them legal protections. For the first time, Jews were able to play a prominent role in German politics. Between 1919 and 1924, twenty-four Jews were elected to the Reichstag and at least six served as senior cabinet ministers in the central government, and German universities opened to Jews (Elon, 2002). Despite these advances, the post-war years 1918 to 1924 were a disappointment. As the economy worsened, Germans across the spectrum of society turned against the Jews and blamed them for the increasingly dire conditions (Barkai, 1998a).

The attempt by Jews to identify with Germany and thereby gain acceptance as full citizens backfired. The German propaganda machine promoted myths and symbols that subtly excluded Jews from recognition as part of the war effort (Folb, 2007). When Buber realized what was happening, he changed his mind about the value of the war for Jewish acceptance into German society.

When Adolf returned from the army in 1918, he moved his family back to Munich, where life in the city had so much more to offer than the village where his wife had taken refuge. With a population of about 800,000, it was the second-largest city in Germany and the capital of Bavaria. An hour by electric train from the Alps and surrounded by beautiful lakes and forests, it was a hub of cultural and artistic activity. Schaalman remembers that it had three opera houses—one of them almost exclusively for Wagner, two or three outstanding theaters, a well-known orchestra, and world-class museums. Among them were the Deutsche Museum of Science and Industry; the Alte Pinakothek, a museum of classical art; the Neue Pinakothek, specializing in eighteenth- and nineteenth-century art, and the Glyptotek, a museum totally devoted to sculpture. Munich also had a great university with several Nobel Prize winners on its faculty. In addition, the city's architecture was well known for its beauty; some of its buildings dated to the fourteenth century. In the nineteenth century, King Ludwig, renowned for his architectural indulgences and interests, built whole sections of the inner city.

The 10,000 Jews living in Munich made it the third-largest Jewish community behind Berlin and Hamburg out of Germany's Jewish population of about half a million (Laqueur, 2001). Despite the fact that they represented slightly more than one percent of the city's population, Jews played an important role in the life of the city (Yad Vashem, 2006).[14]

The Schaalmans were part of the intellectual upper crust of the city, where education and position mattered. The fact that Adolf was a professor gave the family prestige and respect. Adolf began his career as a professor of mathematics and physics at the *Luitpold Obberrealschule*, a prestigious coed high school specializing in the sciences. He decided to teach instead of pursuing the path of research because teaching paid better and provided more security for his family.

Many years later, one of his students who had developed what he described as "a personal relationship" with his teacher, wrote a brief laudatory memoir in which he described what it was like to be one of Adolf's students. [15] His teacher, he wrote, was a small man, "totally black," with a face that clearly identified him as a Jew. Although he was "no Adonis," his gestures, which were "strictly controlled," reminded everyone of Napoleon, an attribution which he did not deny" ("Adolf Schaalman," p. 1). He was known to his students as "Studienrat (in English: "secondary school teacher") Schaalman." Although he was a strict disciplinarian, he was respected for it because his discipline was "tempered by justice and humanity." His students had such high admiration for him that they would have gone through fire for him: "He stood in totally unshaken authority before us ... [and] never showed any sign of weakness" ("Adolf Schaalman," p. 1). Although the writer confesses to have been one of Schaalman's worst students, his teacher gave him help when he needed it to graduate.

The writer of the memoir remembered an outing in which Adolf took the students on a climb of Herzogstand, a mountain 75 km south of Munich in the foothills of the Bavarian Alps. Although he was ill fitted to lead a nature expedition, and seemed "comical" to his students, he insisted to the school authorities that they should be taken to "their mountains, their meadows, and to their mountaintops" ("Adolf Schaalman," p. 2).

After the Nazi takeover, despite the difficulties imposed on him, Adolf stayed on as a teacher at the *Luitpold-Oberrealschule*. When he was forced to retire, some of his students went to his home and, as a memento of their admiration, presented him with a copy of Egon Friedell's *Cultural History of the Modern World* ("Adolf Schaalman," p. 2). [16] Originally published in 1930 by Albert A. Knopf, the book was a cultural sensation in its time and contributed to Friedell becoming a target of the Nazis (Janik, 2009).

The years that Herman was in elementary school were a tumultuous time in German history, "marked by political assassinations, the abortive putsch by Hitler and his allies in Munich, and communist-inspired unrest in Hamburg, Saxony, and Thuringia" (Barkai, 1998c, p. 103). For the Schaalman family, these were the years of the birth of two more sons, Ernst in 1921 and Manfred in 1924.

After the founding of the Nazi Party in 1922, Munich became its first national headquarters and the home of Adolf Hitler. As a young boy, Herman had a near run-in with the future *fuehrer*. On their way home from school, Herman and his best friend decided to stop in at their favorite teahouse. As they were about to drink their tea, the door "flew open and six or eight of the SA cased the joint" before Hitler walked in. [17] Because Herman had no desire to be in the same room with him, he immediately "slunk around the wall and out the door."

He recognized Hitler because he had seen him on Tengstrasse, when, in his open Mercedes touring car, Hitler had arrived to visit Franz Ritter von Epp, a Nazi who was an important nobleman and military officer. [18] Von Epp lived kitty-corner across the plaza from the Schaalmans. By leaning out his window, Herman could see Hitler and Goering drive up. "I knew Hitler had arrived because, wherever the car appeared, it was surrounded by a swarm of people."

On January 30, 1933, as Herman was coming home from school, he ran into a huge celebration in front of the "Brown House," the Nazi headquarters in Munich. [19] Herman, who in contrast to his father looked like an Aryan, asked someone what was going on: "Hitler," he was told, "had just been installed as Chancellor." [20] After hearing the news, he left immediately.

Life in Munich

Herman's family lived on 37 Tengstrasse in a solidly middle-class neighborhood of tree-lined streets in a district of Munich called Schwabing. Running down the middle of their street were streetcar tracks. Because the Schaalmans never had a car and relied exclusively on public transportation when they wanted to get somewhere beyond walking distance, the nearness of the streetcar was nearly a necessity.

The Schaalmans rented an apartment in a five-story luxury apartment building with only five units, each on a separate floor. Because their apartment was on the top floor, their rent was cheaper than that of the lower floors. It was big enough to house six people comfortably—the three boys, their parents, and the maid. The entrance opened into a large foyer at the end of a long corridor, big enough to allow the boys to run around in it and even to roller skate down its length. One third of it was covered by heavy curtains, providing good cover for the mischievous brothers. From time to time, they hid behind them, waiting to jump out when others came by and scaring them out of their wits.

The curtains separated the foyer from the two main rooms, the dining room and Adolf's study containing a large bookcase with glass doors that were always locked. "The idea of locking a bookcase was part of the domestic security typical of the German home. In German culture," Schaalman explains, "nothing was kept open. Even the pantry was locked; every door had a lock with a key in it, and my mother always carried a big bundle of keys to open all the locks."

Next to the study was his parents' bedroom. It contained wide twin beds and a stove that supplemented the central heating system. Between the beds was a space called a *graebele*, or "little ditch" in English. Whenever Herman was having a nightmare and needed to feel the security of his parents, he would climb into their bed and lie in the graebele between them.

Herman's room was small and completely barren except for two beds and a desk for the three boys. Because Herman was the firstborn, he had a bed to himself; his brothers had to share the other one. Herman also had first crack at the one desk in the room, although it was understood that everybody had a right to use it. Unlike other families with similar means, the Schaalmans had a private bathroom. Schaalman explains, "Even respectable families like the Rosenfelds, my Hebrew teacher, shared a toilet with another family in their apartment building." Although the bathroom had a bathtub, it did not have hot running water. A large heater provided hot water for a bath. Unlike today, when family members can bathe or shower by themselves, in the Schaalman household all five of them took their weekly bath in the same water—first the parents and then the three boys together.

Another convenience we take for granted, toilet paper, in the Schaalman household "consisted of cut-up railroad timetables, which came in a thick book that my father brought home. Printed on thin paper, they made ideal toilet paper and also 'entertaining' reading while one sat on the stool."

Although the apartment building was solidly middle class, the Schaalman apartment reflected their lack of means. The only objects hanging on the dining room walls were a small picture of the poet Heinrich

Heine and a woolen tapestry known as a *Gobelain*, picturing a farmyard, some young people, and animals.

Despite the wealth of some of the buildings' residents, the desperate economic conditions in Germany at the time made everyone conscious of the need to cut expenses. The rapid rise in inflation meant that many Germans suffered a demoralizing loss of their all-important social status and produced a widening of the economic and social gap between rich and poor. Among the worst hit was the fixed-income middle class, which Alon (2002) claims was "annihilated." Unlike Herman's father, who was able to find employment as a teacher after he returned from the front, many discharged soldiers wandered from city to city looking for work in the midst of the increasing hyperinflation. According to Alon (2002), by the end of World War I, the value of the mark had declined by 40 percent. Herman's father was fortunate to get a job at a time when the "new" Jewish middle classes were in crisis.[21]

In an effort to counter the rising inflation, Adolf organized the building's residents into a cooperative to buy coal, a cheaper way to buy it than for a single household. In the process, Adolf developed a bond with the superintendent that enabled him to be an effective negotiator on behalf of residents' complaints. In response to his efforts, the other residents gave Adolf the respect and deference to which he was entitled as a professor. On one or two occasions, he and his family were invited to afternoon tea, the standard way people entertained in those days. This new prestige even rubbed off on Herman, who now felt he was the object of much greater respect. In part, this new status was conferred upon him by European social custom, which granted special rights and privileges to the first-born son, though not to daughters.

Education

Because his apartment building was in a gentile neighborhood, most of Herman's friends were non-Jews. Occasionally, this situation caused him problems. At first, when he began elementary school, he was able to walk to school by himself, but in a few years, it was no longer safe for him to walk the streets alone. For his protection, his parents sent their maid as an escort. When Herman entered high school, because he was the only Jewish student in his class and only one of two in the entire school, his parents were fearful of his safety.

Schaalman remembers a particularly nasty event that occurred when he was seven or eight years old. While he was on his way home from school, he was attacked by a group of his friends and badly beaten. When he finally got free, he asked them why they had attacked him: "'We just found out you killed Our Lord, and we won't play with you anymore.'" When he got home, he told his father about the beating and what the other children had said. "The children," his father replied, "do not know what they were talking about." The reason for the attack was soon forgotten. The next day, the boys were willing to play with him again. Unwilling to let them off so easily, Herman rebuked them sharply: "Either you are liars or you had been told wrong." "This response," he told this interviewer, "is part of a lifelong unwillingness to take anything lying down. I developed this combative spirit because I was the son of an army veteran."

This spirit, however, did not protect Herman from the class bullies. Because he was always either the smallest or the next-to-the-smallest kid in his class, he was an easy mark. Yet, despite his size, he was not afraid to fight, and, when attacked, he was capable of defending himself. When another boy said something disparaging and knocked him off a locker room bench, Herman grabbed the bicycle chain he had brought to school and chased the boy seven or eight blocks to his home. "When I caught up with him, I beat the boy and then collapsed, possibly from the concussion that resulted when I fell off the locker room bench and hit my head on the concrete floor." In order to protect his son from further attacks, especially after the Nazis came to power in 1933, Adolf hired a retired police captain to teach his son jujitsu. This new fighting skill came in handy. "When I was attacked in high school for being a Jew, I fought back and floored a much larger boy. I gained enormous respect from the other boys and was never threatened again."

Jewish schoolchildren, writes Barkai (1998b), were often the butt of anti-Semitic abuse. As Germany drifted toward Nazism, Jewish children in the public schools had to cope with increasing anti-Semitism from teachers and were bullied and badgered by their gentile schoolmates on a daily basis (p. 246). School life became increasingly difficult as pressures in the classroom and on the school grounds increased. Schools now set aside "isolation desks for Jews," and the school authorities modified the curriculum to include daily discussions of the "Jewish Question." While their classmates stared at them as members of a despised race, Jewish children had to sit through these discussions, no matter how demeaning and humiliating. To make matters worse, they "were often called to the front of the class in order to demonstrate the 'typical Jewish racial features'" (p. 246).

In response to this anti-Semitism, some parents tried to protect their children by removing them from school. Others chose to deny that they had any religious affiliation. This denial put them in a new protected political class called "*Confessionslos*," a term meaning that they did not believe in religion. The family of one of Schaalman's schoolmates became *Confessionslos*, though ultimately, because they had been Jewish, they were not immune to Nazi persecution. For Herman, such an option was inconceivable; he took great pleasure in being Jewish, and, despite all the turmoil, remembered his life as "idyllic."

Notwithstanding all of these difficulties, the rigorous German education system left an enduring mark on Schaalman's development. He had begun school at the age of six and attended the neighborhood grade school for four years. By the time he was nine, his parents had decided what school they wanted him to attend, and a year later, enrolled him in the gymnasium. Herman had no choice in the matter. "Children did not question parental decisions; indeed, this family code reflected the authoritarian nature of German society." Herman spent nine years in the Maximillian Gymnasium, the German equivalent of high school and a prerequisite for admission to the university. Fortunately for him, it was right around the corner from where he lived (and is still there).

Herman's school experience was not without its challenges. He recalls having frequent struggles with his teachers, particularly with his teachers of Latin and Greek.

> They would return my papers covered in red ink, and, occasionally, my teacher made mistakes in computing my grade. When I discovered these mistakes, I would raise my hand and address my teacher as 'Herr Professor.' After listening to my concerns, the teacher would take off his glasses to clean them, and then erase the grade and record the correct one. My teachers did not take kindly to correction by a student, whose primary job was obedience to authority.

In math classes, things were different: "Only one correct answer is possible: Some things are right and some things are wrong: two and two is not seven. However, in language study a given phrase translated from Greek to German was not so precise. Several possibilities were equally valid, and teachers sometimes made mistakes."

The rigor of his education is apparent in the fact that Herman took nine years of Latin, one hour a day, and six years of Greek.[22] In an effort to encourage students to take the study seriously, his teachers gave tests twice a week. Because he was such a competitive and disciplined student while he was in elementary and high school, he still had time to participate in the schools' athletic activities. "I remember taking them so seriously that frequently, I played so hard that my hands bled."

The Brothers: Ernst and Manfred

Not too many years after Herman was born, the Schaalmans had two other children: Ernst and Manfred, known as Freddie. The parents named Ernst after his maternal grandfather (Schaalman speculates that "Ernst" was a Germanization of "Ezra," his Ukrainian grandfather's Hebrew name) and gave him the middle name of "Naphtali," his paternal grandfather's Hebrew name, thus perpetuating both. Although Freddie bore the closest resemblance his father, having discharged their obligation to perpetuate their ancestors, the Schaalmans felt no sense of responsibility for naming him after anyone. Instead, his father made up a new Hebrew name to add to the Schaalman and Wanschel family tribe, "La'el." And then Freddie was just Freddie.

Early on, the family noticed that Freddie began developing a slight hunch back. At first, they thought he had a curvature of the spine. Years later, doctors discovered that he had been born with an extra rib, which was responsible for the curvature and the slightly hunched appearance. In order to contain this deformity, his parents put him in an orthopedic swing and, when he went to bed, a kind of orthopedic cast. As Freddie got older, he practiced a series of rigorous exercises that built up a muscular physique, which he maintained even into his 80s. According to Freddie, this physical problem not only caused the family a great deal of concern, but also put an extra burden on his mother. She was still a student at the university when the problem was diagnosed. Nevertheless, she made time to help him cope with his problem (Schaalman, F. L., 2008).

As the first-born son, Herman had a privileged position in the family. As the oldest son, he was not only his father's favorite, but also the most trusted and influential of the sons. Of the three brothers, Herman became the best educated and the only one to achieve international distinction. Ernst and Freddie prospered financially and, in many ways, achieved something Herman came to envy. They established large families in Brazil, where Ernst remained (currently he has three children and seven grandchildren) and in Israel where Freddie later immigrated and became the father of four children, two sons and two daughters, and twenty-one grandchildren, eight from one son and five from another. All of Freddie's children are married and live in close proximity to each other, and two of his grandchildren are already married. Of the three Schaalman brothers, only Herman and Ernst are still alive. Freddie died in November 2011.

Schaalman considers both brothers fortunate in a way that he was not. They created large and close-knit families that live near each other and visit each other often. Until his recent death, Freddie's family gathered for Shabbat dinner. One of his sons became a rabbi more Orthodox than his father. According to Freddie, "The creation of such a large family would not have been possible in Germany. Like the United States, the prevailing value in Germany is money, which limits the viability of having a large family. In Israel among the Orthodox, the primary value is leading a religious life; money in that context is only incidental. Typically, in an Orthodox family, the men study all day in the Yeshiva and the women work at home and may practice a profession. Living in Israel is by far the greatest blessing. As I told my brother, Herman, 'I live in *Gan Eden*' (Hebrew for the Garden of Eden)" (Schaalman, F. L., 2008).

Schaalman's family is much smaller: two married children, daughter Susan in Chicago, and son Michael in Milwaukee. Susan has no children of her own, though she claims two step-children and two step–great-grandchildren through her marriage to Rabbi Ira Youdovin. Michael has three children: Jo, Keren, and Jeremy, all living in Denver. Herman would have liked for Michael to have followed in his footsteps and become a rabbi. He even sent him to Israel to begin rabbinic studies but Michael's interests lay elsewhere. The Schaalmans are in frequent communication with their children. Hardly a day goes by when Susan and her mother are not on the phone with each other. Michael and his parents call each other at least once a week, and since they have been sick over the last year, more frequently. Typically, he and his wife, Roberta, drive to Chicago either Friday night or Saturday morning to spend Shabbat with their parents. The Schaalmans also see their grandchildren several times a year, usually on major Jewish holidays. In this last year, Keren and Jo married their sweethearts and grandfather Herman performed their weddings. Lotte has no surviving family. The fact that the Schaalmans do not have a large family living nearby is a source of great sorrow for them.

Money Problems

When Adolf moved his family to Munich, he found that it was difficult to live a respectable middle class life on a teacher's salary. Schaalman remembers his mother telling him that the family was so poor after they moved to Munich that to pay her tuition at the university she had to take a job delivering milk in the early morning before she went to class. She learned the work from her father, who, for a time, had been in the milk business. Despite their poverty, Adolf's academic position established the family as middle or upper middle class. Because she was the wife of a professor, Regina had the special distinction of "Frau Professor," an honorific title that normally would have precluded her from working. The one exception was her milk delivery route during their first years in Munich.[23]

Although a financial burden, the family's social status required that they have a live-in maid, a critical distinction between the middle and working classes. The job of maintaining a household of six people on a professor's salary was challenging, especially when inflation in 1923 made everyone's life miserable. The financial crisis wiped out the family's savings, forced them into debt, and made it difficult for Adolf to feed his family. Schaalman remembers one occasion when his father came home with his monthly salary in a cigar box and turned it over to his wife with the urgent instruction, "Run and buy supper." So fierce was the rate of inflation that if she did not purchase the food quickly, by the next day, the cost of the food would have been beyond their reach. "Near the end of this inflationary period, my father gave me a billion mark note, worth only a penny, which I used to buy a marble."

The family's effort to control costs for meals was part of a larger effort to manage family finances within the limitations of Adolf's modest income. For example, the purchase of new clothing, always in short supply, was more the exception than the rule. His parents stretched the clothing budget by buying Herman new clothes; his brothers wore his hand-me-downs and the maid his mother's discarded dresses. On the other hand, because Adolf was a high school professor, every five or six years he bought handmade, quality suits from a tailor who came to the house to fit him. Yet, when Adolf heard that his sister had died, while the family looked on during dinner, he took up a knife and cut his suit, as dictated by Jewish custom: "To my father, clothes in themselves were only a means to an end, and therefore were of little importance to him."

When it came to books, however, Adolf's spending habits were more liberal. His home library included hundreds of volumes: "There was never any question that if he wanted a piece of music or a book on art or Jewish matters, he bought it. On the other hand, no matter how short of funds he might have been, he always gave money to someone in need rather than improve his lifestyle or that of his family." The lack of money for family necessities was chronic. "I don't remember a single year or week when there wasn't a question whether we could afford what we did and when often it was said we couldn't."

Because of these pressing financial needs, even as a young man Herman worked to earn extra money. He took a job as a Hebrew tutor to two young people, one of them the daughter of a wealthy Jewish family. His earnings from these jobs, however, were meager, only a few pennies. One benefit, though, of this teaching experience was his discovery that he enjoyed teaching others. It was an experience that contributed to his decision to become a rabbi.

The financial challenges the Schaalmans faced were not unlike those faced by other Germans and particularly by German Jews. The hyperinflation and high unemployment for Jews were tearing at the fabric of family structure and values. Nevertheless, Barkai (1998b) writes, religiously liberal German Jewish families in the cities remained intact.

The Schaalman family was one of them. Despite its financial hardships, Schaalman remembers his family life as happy and fulfilling.[24] In no small measure, he attributes this experience to his "progressive" parents, who treated their children as "growing human beings." Nevertheless, they maintained "continuous and strict discipline," tempered with a great deal of love and affection. Because of this treatment, Schaalman never felt unloved, insecure, or unappreciated. Although his parents expected unquestioned obedience from their children, their requirements were never harsh, and he had no reason to rebel against their authority or to harbor negative feelings. When he was twelve or thirteen, his parents involved him in discussions of important, even private, matters, including the family budget. Most significant, they gave him the key to the apartment, a sign of their confidence in him.

His friends, on the contrary, had a completely different experience with their parents: "They hated them because of the fear they instilled, based in part on their neglect of their children and the vehemence of their punishments." Because of this negativity, Herman did not want to be around them. He recalls one nasty incident when they were on a group excursion. One boy said, "I hope my parents die soon so that I can be free." What troubled Herman even more was that no one objected to these remarks. Because he had no such feelings towards his parents, the remarks created a barrier between him and this group of friends, and he was no longer able to associate with them.

The Mischievous Boy and the Development of Character

Despite the fact that Herman loved and honored his mother and father, he admits to being a sometimes-mischievous child. One event from the time he was three years old is still vivid. Attribute it to guilt. The incident occurred while the family was preparing to leave for a winter vacation in the Alps. His parents' bedroom had an iron stove to supplement the central heating system. The maid often used it to keep soup hot before bringing it into the dining room during a midday or evening meal. On this day, she removed a pot of boiling soup from the stove and placed it on the floor to make room for something else. Herman ran into the room and inadvertently knocked it over and burned his foot so severely that a doctor had to be called. The doctor ordered that he be kept in bed, flat on his back and remain immobile. The vacation, of course, was cancelled.

While Herman was confined to his father's bed during his convalescence, Adolf set up his son's favorite toy, a windup train, to entertain his son and to provide a diversion from his suffering. "Next to the bed, he constructed an ingenious platform four or five feet high, supported by piles of his books so that I did not have to strain to see it. In retrospect, I think of this event as an occasion that my father turned into an opportunity to show his great love for me." The experience left an indelible impression that has remained with him ever since.

When Herman was a little older, he began sliding down the marble balustrades on both sides of the front steps of the apartment building. Although he and his friends were having lots of fun, the superintendent, who lived in the basement below the stairs, was irritated by their noisy play. Whenever he was disturbed, he came out to chase the boys. This mischievous behavior was particularly appealing because it involved Stefel, the superintendent's son, a boy about his own age. Schaalman remembers, "Stefel's misbehavior did not come without penalties; if he caused enough trouble, his father would box his ears."

But that didn't prevent Stefel from participating in other mischievous behaviors with his friend. Another naughty activity the two boys got into was climbing the narrow wall connecting their building to two or three others in their backyard. What made the feat so daring and dangerous was that the wall was seven feet high and less than a foot wide. Their daring attracted the attention of other neighborhood kids. "Not only was walking on the wall dangerous, but I competed with Stefel to see which of us could stay up the longest. Keeping one's balance under these circumstances required considerable skill."

When eight-year-old Stefel died suddenly of unknown causes, Herman was inconsolable: "I cried so hard that my parents recommended that I go down to the basement to talk to the parents. When I stammered out that I was sad that Stefel had died, his parents told me not to cry because Stefel no longer had to live in this crummy apartment. He was with Jesus and living a wonderful life." Although Herman knew that the family was Catholic,[25] he learned that day something about

Catholicism that so upset him that he needed to discuss the matter with his father. "How, I asked, could anyone be happy in the face of the death of a child? To me it was a major blow, a catastrophic experience. It took me a long time to get over the death of my friend.[26]

Herman found other ways to create mischief. He relished the opportunity to race down the five flights of his building's stairs to see if he could beat the elevator to the ground floor. Another prank was to "wrench" himself into the door in such a way that he prevented other people from getting out. "I knew better, however, than to play this trick on my father or my relatives."

One of his favorite activities was to instigate fights with his brothers. He and Freddie would gang up on Ernst. Picking on him was no accident. When Ernst was born, Herman discovered that he was no longer the *only* child and was resentful of the intruder: "I was disappointed, especially when I was told I had to take care of this baby brother."[27] To protect Ernst from the unfair advantage his brothers had over him, his mother would try to rescue him. Occasionally, wielding the carpet beater, she chased Herman around the room and hit him wherever she could: "But she had her work cut out for her because I could run very fast, sometimes faster than she." Other times she would take off her house slipper and hit him with it while he covered his head to protect himself: "Getting hit with the slipper was more painful than getting whacked with the carpet beater, but I never doubted the justice of her punishment."

Giving Herman caretaking responsibilities for his brother may not have been one of the better decisions his parents made. When Ernst was only seven or eight months old, they gave Herman, who was only five and a half, the responsibility of taking him for a walk in the baby carriage. On one of those occasions, Herman headed toward the end of their street where there was a lovely park (which is still there to this day). At its entrance was a large fenced-off flower bed surrounded by benches on all sides: "To get to the park, I had to push the buggy across a heavily traveled street. Surprisingly, my parents trusted me and knew I could do it." When he got to the park, he spotted one of his buddies, who challenged him to one of their usual races around the flower garden. Handicapped by the baby carriage, Herman accepted the dare: "A challenge is, after all, a challenge, and I could not resist it." Pushing the carriage as fast as he could, when he came to the first turn, he made a sharp ninety-degree turn and Ernst flew out of the carriage onto the gravel path. While the baby was screaming at the top of his lungs, Herman picked him up and tried to console him. "I couldn't get him to stop crying. I was terrified. My parents had trusted me, and I had damaged their baby."

Instead of trying to cover up his disgrace, he went home and told his parents what he had done. "I felt compelled to tell them because I had been taught always to tell the truth no matter what the consequences. To not tell the truth did not fit into the family's trusting relationships. Because they knew I would tell the truth right away, they never needed to interrogate me. All they had to do was ask." This trust was manifest in his parents' decision to allow him to continue to push the buggy. "They knew I would never do anything like that again."

When Herman was a few years older, he had another occasion to test this trusting relationship. He and a friend went beyond the square at the end of Tengstrasse to a place that he remembers dimly as possibly a quarry or a commercial place that ended at the former entrance to a much larger park. Next to it was an undeveloped piece of land with an alluring heap of gravel. No sooner had he and his friend sat on the pile than his friend picked up some gravel and tossed it at his own ankles. Following his lead, Herman picked up some gravel and threw it at his own ankles. After tossing the gravel at their feet for a while, the friend decided to be more adventurous and threw a handful at Herman. The gravel hit him in the head, causing him to bleed profusely. With blood covering his face and soaking his shirt, Herman ran home, his friend right behind him pleading not to tell on him. He had not meant any harm; the event was an accident: "Of course, I never told my parents who had done it. I simply said we were playing, and I got injured. Although this might not have been the full truth, it was not a lie."

As a child, Herman thought of his parents as if they were gods: "They knew just what to do. If I didn't behave, they spanked me or locked me in the bathroom that didn't have any windows." Schaalman remembers at least one occasion when his behavior so angered his father that he felt it was necessary to cane his son: "There was no question [that] … time and again I deserved to be punished." When he was seven years old and had come home late from school, his father decided his son needed to be punished severely, although the offense seems trivial. He had given Herman strict instructions to come home right after school, only two-and-a-half blocks away. That day, the city received its first snowfall, and in typical boy behavior, Herman and his friends could not resist engaging in a snowball fight. "The fight didn't last long, but it delayed my getting home by ten or twelve minutes. My father, who usually arrived home about 1:30 in time for the midday meal, was waiting for me."

The caning took place in the windowless, dimly lighted bathroom. While his son leaned over the bathtub, Adolf caned him with his walking stick.[28] Afterwards, his father turned out the light and told him not to come out until he understood why he was being punished. "I remember sitting in the dark biting my tongue and wiping away my tears." Because the experience was so painful and humiliating, the young boy was filled with vindictive anger: "I wished I could die so that I could punish my father for what he had done. Despite the pain, however, I never cried out." As he cooled down, he recognized the justice of the punishment: "I returned to the world of the living, humiliated but, nonetheless, wiser. By the time I was eleven or twelve, this form of corporal punishment was never needed again. Nonetheless, it left an indelible impression, and I can still see that on my tush. It was the only time he really beat me."

Endurance of pain was part of Herman's upbringing. In his youth, he had read a story about a young Spartan soldier who found a fox cub and adopted it as a pet. During a surprise inspection, the soldier tried to hide the fox by putting it under his tunic. Unwilling to disgrace himself, he stood at attention while the fox ate out his intestines. The soldier never uttered a cry, even though he collapsed and died. Schaalman is so fond of this story that he still tells it when he wants to make a point about endurance.

Another story he tells provides another example of this kind of stoicism that was inculcated in his youth. The story involves Countess Spee, the wife of German admiral Graf Spee who commanded the German Atlantic Fleet during World War I. Like all good German noblewomen, Countess Spee was a volunteer in a hospital for the wounded. When an officer informed her that her husband and two sons had been killed in a battle with the British fleet, she thanked the officer and continued her rounds.

Stories like these reflect the extraordinarily high degree of self-discipline and self-sacrifice that was a basic part of Schaalman's training and later played a major role in his life. In his nineties, Schaalman questions this self-imposed limitation: "Occasionally, I think I have the right to assert myself, and, I must tell you, this is really no way to keep going. Lotte, who had a similar upbringing, objects to any self-assertion that I might make. Her attitude is so totally self-effacing that she considers it her assignment, her duty, to live for others."

Father and Son

As far back as Schaalman can remember, he and his father established a close bond that became one of the most important experiences in his growth and development. One of Schaalman's earliest memories is the pleasure he got in lying next to his father on the sofa or in his bed: "I still remember his warm body and the sound of his snoring, which, as he fell into a deep sleep, resonated through the room: I loved this sound but stayed only ten or fifteen minutes before leaving his side." This privilege of lying next to his father was accorded to him as the oldest child. "My brothers had an entirely different relationship with my father, and this cuddling may have ended when Ernst was born in 1921."

Another bonding experience that helped Herman develop a sense of responsibility was his father's habit of sending him three or four times a week, no matter what the weather, to fetch a stein of beer from the neighborhood beer hall. Although he was only five or six at the time, Schaalman remembers carrying his father's heavy stein to the tavern. The bartender, who knew him well, would fill it to the brim. On the way home, he had to be extremely careful not to spill any. His father always warned him before he went that he would spank him if he spilled the beer: "My father told me, 'I don't know whether I should spank you now because you're going to spill it or after you come home and have spilled.'" Occasionally, Schaalman acknowledges, he would stumble and spill some of the beer. According to Barkai, 1998, such positive experiences between fathers and sons were not typical in this time and place; more typically, German mothers played the greater part in the lives of their children and in keeping the family together.

The practice of sending a little boy to the beer hall is not as bizarre as it may appear. In Munich, babies were raised on malt beer; it helped produce pudgy and healthy-looking children and was probably better for them than the local tap water. Beer occupied such an important part in the lives of his German neighbors that when the bock beer season arrived, Oktoberfests were held so that people might celebrate the season. "Although I did not participate in these annual 'goyish' events, I remember watching people who were climbing a local hill to participate in the beer drinking revelry falling down drunk and rolling down the hill. Drunken men would fight with steak knives, occasionally resulting in serious injuries and, sometimes, death." Nevertheless, when he was eight years old, he had a memorable encounter with the nasty effects of drinking alcohol: "While the family was on its way to visit an uncle in Frankfurt, we stopped in a café and ordered 'heurigwein,' a special preparation of freshly made wine. The drink was so powerful it knocked me out."

Another of Herman's early formative experiences was watching his father while he red-penciled student papers and exams. Because he enjoyed being around his father and loved the pleasant smell of his pipe tobacco or aromatic cigars, he would enter his father's study quietly and unobtrusively and keep him company while he worked. "Many years later," Schaalman reports, "when I became a college and university educator, I found myself performing similar tasks. Even in my nineties, I still red-pencil student exams and papers."

Home: A Rich Cultural Environment

An important part of Schaalman's admiration for his parents was their level of education and their cultural sophistication. Adolf was a university graduate, a scientist, and a scholar of Judaism and Jewish history. Possibly because of his mother's influence, his parents were lifelong devotees of culture, particularly music, an important part of their household. On special occasions, Adolf sang arias and Handel oratorios while accompanied on the piano by a colleague. He was also a great Wagnerian aficionado who so loved Wagner's music that it was not unusual to hear him sing passages at home: "I still hear those sounds today. Because he was also fond of Jewish liturgical music, hardly a day passed when he did not chant the daily prayer service into my young ears." (As a student at the university in Munich, Adolf used to organize outings for other students to attend the opera. If they were willing to accept standing-room-only tickets in the uppermost tier, students could get low-priced tickets. To get these coveted tickets, however, they had to stand in line all night.)

Like her husband, Herman's mother was also an intellectual and an avid reader. She loved poetry and was musically inclined. When she was alone, she sang and played her favorite Mozart arias. "These were special, though rare, moments for me. I used to sneak in, squat down next to the piano, and put my ear to it to hear the music transmitted through its innards."

She also took private lessons in English and French to improve her foreign language proficiency. According to Schaalman, "Because of her intellectual bent, she was one of the first girls to go to the university where she worked toward a degree in chemistry and biology."[29] However, her first attempt was unsuccessful. Herman was only two and a half when she started, and, because the family had little money, she could not afford a babysitter. Consequently, having no better choice, she took her son to school with her. "On one occasion, while she was in class, she left me outside next to a fountain with instructions not to move, no matter what happened. After she left, a large black dog came by and terrified me. I panicked despite the efforts of passersby to comfort me." When his mother returned, he was crying inconsolably. Because she was unable to make other arrangements for her son's care while she was in school, she had to drop out. Another difficulty for her was the fact that she was one of the few women to attend the university in Germany (or anywhere at that time). Some of her professors refused to teach class as long as she was in it. According to Freddie Schaalman (2008), one of her professors told her, "'Woman, go out or I will not teach!' Ironically, he was not even German, but Ukrainian!"[30]

Like other women of her class, Regina found other outlets for her talents. Her keen intellect, sense of humor, and leadership skills enabled her to become an active volunteer. Unlike her husband, who was not a good public speaker, she had a talent for public speaking. Schaalman claims, "At the drop of a handkerchief, even without a handkerchief she was able to give a talk." Because of this ability, she was elected president of the Sisterhood of B'nai B'rith, a major social honor, and she was the first non-German born woman to achieve this position, the highest social level of Jewish womanhood in Germany: "Her election to a second consecutive term was unprecedented, a significant honor, and a great social accomplishment."

On regular occasions, the Schaalmans hosted intellectual and artistic forums for Adolf's colleagues and artist friends. Because of his strong interest in the arts and the fact that he was so well respected for his astute critical judgment and support, Adolf frequently offered advice and criticism to Jewish artists whom he had taken under his wing.

In addition to cultural activities in the home, Schaalman remembers that he parents took him to the opera and the theater. When he was six or seven, his parents took him to see E. T. A. Hoffman's famous opera *Undine*. As he dressed for the event in short pants and long black stockings, he discovered that the stockings had a hole in the calf. Because this was his only pair of long stockings and because he did not want to be embarrassed, he covered his calf with black shoe polish to camouflage the hole. Despite his parents' best efforts, Schaalman never developed a taste for opera.

Schaalman remembers another event in which his mother took him to see a play. They sat in the front row of the balcony, which gave the gullible little boy ready access to the events on stage. During the performance, he became so involved in the drama that he screamed when the protagonist was in mortal danger. With Herman in tow, his mother immediately left the theater.

These rich artistic and cultural experiences helped Herman develop a strong base for his own lifelong pursuits.

Religious Life

A fundamental part of Herman's early upbringing was the intensity of religious life in his home. Shabbos was special for the family. Every Shabbos Friday evening, before dinner the father and his sons went to the synagogue or the orphanage while Regina stayed home with the maid to prepare the meal and to light the candles at the proper time.[31] His parents' strict observance of Jewish laws required that before every meal the family perform the mitzvah of washing their hands. Before the meal was served and to create a sense of holiness, "My father chanted the Kiddush while the family stood by their chairs at the table. After reciting the Motzi (the blessing over the bread), the children lined up in front of our father according to our age to receive his blessings." Following this formal blessing, their mother kissed and hugged each of them.

At the end of the dinner, the family and guests (usually, these dinners were shared with friends or family) recited the Birkat Hamazon (grace after meals) followed by the singing of zemiros (Shabbat table songs sung in Hebrew). Although Adolf typically led the singing, as they got older, the boys were allowed to lead the singing. Each had his favorite song, and, sometimes, the singing would go on for thirty minutes or more. As Schaalman recalls, "There was no limit ... no need to set a limit." When they had company, after-dinner discussions became serious, and the children were sent to bed.

The Shabbat ritual continued the next morning. While most Jewish families went back to their businesses or professions, the Schaalman family got up, ate breakfast, and went to synagogue: "No matter what the weather, we walked twenty to twenty-five minutes each way." The Schaalman family synagogue was huge with 3,000 seats, 3 cantors, and 2 rabbis. The religious orientation of the synagogue was "liberal," which resembles today's Conservative Jewish practice. The synagogue had an organ and a mixed choir of men and women. Unlike a traditional synagogue where all the prayers were chanted in Hebrew, in this synagogue, one or two of the prayers were chanted in German. Nor would a traditional synagogue have had an organ or a mixed choir.[32] Schaalman remembers how intimidated he felt when he had the honor to sing in this assemblage. Under such scrutiny, he felt his knees tremble.

When the services were over, they came home by noon to eat their main meal of the day. After the meal, Adolf would nap and, when he awoke, lead a Torah study session for the rest of the afternoon. "Study" meant that he read the Torah to his family while they sat quietly and, for the most part, attentively. Schaalman adds, "In traditional Torah study the text would be subjected to analysis and debate, but in the Schaalman household there was no discussion; my father read and everyone listened; no one asked questions, nor did they discuss the portion."[33] If he had any doubts about the validity of the Torah, of its literal veracity, he never gave any hint that he did not believe every word of the Torah was true." His practice was to read the entire Torah in a year and then began again with *Bereshit* (Genesis).

The sanctity of the day was inviolate, and nothing was allowed to intrude: "It would never, ever occur to me that there was anything to be done except to go to synagogue with my father [and] to come home and have Shabbos at home; Shabbos was always a great day." Except when it prevented him from playing or doing something else, such as playing outdoors with his friends. Nevertheless, his German discipline and his love for his father kept him from deviating from this practice.

One of Schaalman's fondest memories from this period is being in the synagogue with his father on the High Holy Days: "After I observed my father's habit of placing his Tallis bag on the floor to cushion his knees when he prostrated himself, a common practice at that time in Germany, I decided I should do it. When the time came for congregants to prostrate themselves, I was proud to place the bag on the floor for my father to kneel on."

Not all ritual practices were this easy. Fasting on Yom Kippur proved to be a major challenge for the pre-Bar Mitzvah boy. When he was ten or eleven years old, he wanted to fast, but by two o'clock in the afternoon, his hunger pangs got the best of him: "I remember nudging my father to get me something to eat. He was always prepared for this eventuality. He took me outside into the courtyard of the synagogue, pulled a chicken leg out of a bag and shielded me while I ate it." By the time Herman was twelve, he could fast the whole day: "From then on, fasting became a sport." When the family went to the orphanage for Yom Kippur, a twenty-five minute walk from home, Herman and his brothers, who by the end of the service were starving, raced each other and got there in fifteen minutes. The maid had herring and sweets ready for them, but Herman's system did not react well to fasting. After he ate, he always had a stomachache.

As Herman approached his thirteenth birthday in April 1929, he began to prepare for his Bar Mitzvah, which was not only the major event in his life up to this time, but also a defining moment for his family. As a special treat for the Bar Mitzvah boy, he got a store-bought dark blue suit with long pants, which was later handed down to his middle brother Ernst and then to Manfred. Ready-made suits had just become available in Germany (Rodin-Novak, p. 27). When the time came to study for his Bar Mitzvah, the Cantor of his synagogue coached him for six or seven months to prepare him for his participation in the service. His Torah portion was *Kedoshim*. The Cantor taught him the tropes and cantillations he needed to chant his portion. Schaalman recalls that he was trained so thoroughly that "two weeks before my Bar Mitzvah, if you had awakened me from my sleep, I could have chanted my Torah portion." Fortunately, the young boy was a gifted singer, a gift that to this day, despite the fact that he is ninety-six years old, has held up. Herman was to chant forty minutes of the service, including the Haftorah. According to Berenbaum (2007), Schaalman was only "the second boy in the Liberal Gemeinde to read the entire sidrah for his bar mitzvah" (p. 96). Because he had such a large family, many family members would be accorded honors by being called to bless the Torah.

On the day before his Bar Mitzvah, his cousin Adie Wanschel arrived from Stuttgart. (According to Rodin-Novak, 2001, after her marriage to a pharmacist, she and her husband left Germany for Peru, where they created the leading pharmacy in Lima, p. 26). Adie was the daughter of the consul to Panama and his mother's cousin. She was not only a wonderful person, but also a nationally known athlete and one of his favorite relatives. On her visit, she helped him prepare his derasha. While he paced nervously back and forth in his bedroom, she sat on his bed and listened attentively. He was tense because he was concerned that he might make a mistake in front of all the guests and disappoint his father. On the day of his Bar Mitzvah, he performed so well that everyone applauded his recitation and "oohed and aahed over this great ... smart kid" (p. 26). Now, he was free to relax and enjoy the day, which turned out to be a wonderful experience. Among the presents he received were a bicycle, some fountain pens and volumes of Goethe and Schiller, all standard gifts given for Bar Mitzvahs. No money was given because such a gift was inappropriate and would have been unacceptable.

The reception for the Bar Mitzvah was held in the Schaalman home. His parents removed the furniture from their bedroom and made it into a dining room, though it was not big enough for the sixty people who had been invited. To feed so many guests, his parents hired several cooks to help prepare the food. Live carp were swimming in the bathtub and although Schaalman loved carp, when he saw them in the bathtub, he lost his appetite. The menu included chicken, which came with all their feathers and their stubbles. Soon the apartment was full of the pleasant smell of the chickens roasting over an open wood fire, the only kind of stove the family had at the time. As part of the celebration, Schaalman had to give a derasha on his Torah portion, "How to treat a stranger." His father found a book by a Jewish philosopher who had written on the subject and its relation to the Jewish tradition. After reading the difficult book together, his father asked him to write an essay as a basis for a speech on his understanding of the subject. The speech, which he had to memorize, was to be given after dinner; as a result, the nervous Bar Mitzvah boy did not eat much of this meal.

After his Bar Mitzvah, Schaalman had the privilege of davenning with his father. Every morning they donned tallis and tefillin to recite the morning prayers. Unlike the typical congregant who customarily rattled off the prayers perfunctorily, his father recited every word distinctly so that he could reflect on their meaning. Long before his Bar Mitzvah, Mr. Schaalman had taught his son the meaning of each prayer so that he would understand it. His strategy was to translate them into German, as he did when they studied Torah on Shabbat, and then to explain them. Part of this education in Judaism included his father's warning never to make the Kohanitic sign of holding out the four fingers of the right hand separated in a "V," with two fingers forming each side of the V shape. To make this sign, which had deep religious meaning, was considered a transgression that should be avoided.

Schaalman's parents were masters of infusing Judaism with a sense of joy and pleasure and made holiday celebrations joyous, even High Holy Days. When *Shavuot* arrived, the family celebrated two days, and *Pesach* the full eight days.[34] Adolf stayed home on these days. Hanukkah was Herman's favorite. Although a minor Jewish holiday, in the Schaalman household it was always special. The event was full of suspense and surprise. "My parents locked themselves in the dining room with the menorahs and set out presents. Unable to stand the suspense, together with my brothers we took turns peering through the keyhole to see the size of the packages."

One of Schaalman's earliest and magical memories is a Passover Seder that took place when he was four or five. "While sitting on my father's lap, and after reciting the 'Ma Nishtannah' (the four questions recited as part of the Seder), I put my head on my father's warm and comforting chest and was lulled to sleep by the sound of his deep rumbling voice as he chanted from the Haggadah." Part of the wonder of the experience was his father's skill in creating "hiddur mitzvah, the beautification of the performance of the commandment." The same atmosphere that pervaded the house on Shabbos and holidays carried over to nonreligious celebrations, such as birthdays and wedding anniversaries. At these events, the family exchanged presents, ate cake, sang songs, or recited poems that his parents or his brothers composed for the occasion. Schaalman remembers the family celebrating one Passover in 1924 at a hotel in Italy. The family went there mainly because his mother needed to recuperate after she gave birth to Manfred when she was too weak to manage the Passover preparations.

Fundamental to the family's Judaism was the strict observance of Jewish dietary laws. The family "never ate non-kosher food at anytime, anyplace." That restraint included not eating in restaurants in order to avoid the possibility that they might be served nonkosher food. His mother kept a strictly kosher kitchen and even made sure that, when they went away for summer vacations, they had enough kosher food to last the entire trip.

The Judaism that was integral to family life helped establish basic household routines. Every day, when Adolf came home from school between 1:15 and 1:30 p.m., the family sat down immediately for an hour-long dinner. The main course was meat, but because kosher meat was expensive and served as the main course every day, the portions were

Right to Left. Herman, Freddie, Ernst, 1929

small and, most of the time, there were no seconds. In addition to the meat, lunch usually included soup, plenty of potatoes, and bread, all of which were inexpensive. Sometimes, Herman's mother made his favorite potato salad.[35] After lunch, Adolf took a nap while the children did their homework. Later in the afternoon, they went back to school for electives such as gym or music, or spent time with friends. Supper, except on Shabbos, was a light dairy meal served between 7:30 or 8:00 p.m.

Such an observant Jewish home life provided the future rabbi "a fine Jewish upbringing and background." In fact, his parents were so skilled in making Jewishness "wonderful" that for Herman being Jewish was a "joyous" experience: "Because both my parents had a sense of aesthetics and style, their everyday life, including holidays and festivals, was tasteful and had its own beauty." After his Bar Mitzvah, this religious upbringing led Herman to decide that he should be more observant. He made a commitment not to write on Shabbat, which meant that he could no longer attend the full six days of public school, Monday through Saturday. Because he was such a good student and his father was a professor, the school gave him permission to stay home on Shabbat.

His father, who was thoroughly competent in performing Shabbat and major holiday services, even served as a lay Chazzan (cantor) at a local orphanage where he shared the responsibility of leading *erev* Shabbat services for the eight or ten people who showed up. The orphanage was connected to the *Liberale Gemeinde* (the branch of liberal Judaism). When his father performed the entire Shabbat service or the service for Rosh Hashanah or Yom Kippur, the whole family went with him. They preferred this service to their synagogue's because of its intimacy. Adolf took pleasure in knowing that it was a mitzvah to provide services for the boys and girls who lived there. In performing the service, he had help from another Chazzan, a tenor by the name of Silverman. The two would alternate so that the job was not too much of a burden for either of them. Schaalman remembers that the service, which was recited only in Hebrew, was "beautiful, especially when the two sang together." His father knew all the melodies and traditional prayers for the entire year.[36]

On Rosh Hashanah and Yom Kippur, the two cantors performed the entire service for the congregation of sixty to seventy orphans and possibly twenty to thirty *balabatim*.[37] To prepare for his part in the High

Family gathering for Herman's Bar Mitzvah: front row, left to right, Schaalman boys: Ernst, Freddie, Herman; second row, first person, Regina; third, Uncle Marcus Schaalman; fifth Sonia Wanschel, Oscar Wanschel's wife; third row, first person, Edward Schaalman, cousin, son of Uncle Joseph; second person, Uncle Joseph's wife (name forgotten); fourth row, third person, Uncle Joseph Schaalman; eighth from left, Tante Sophie; eleventh from left, Oscar Wanschel, Regina's cousin; row five, fourth from left, Adolf Schaalman; sixth from left, Uncle Samuel Schaalman.

Holy Day services, Adolf began rehearsing weeks before. For up to an hour each day, he would seclude himself in his study and practice the entire *Mahzor* and chant prayers until he was satisfied that he knew them well. Because he did not have any music to work with, he relied totally on his memory. His sonorous and mellifluous voice carried throughout the apartment. The melodies came from southern Germany where his father had lived. The melodies, specific to the region, had been passed from father to son to grandson.

After his Bar Mitzvah, Herman had the honor of reciting small portions of the Rosh Hashanah and Yom Kippur service in the orphanage and chanted the prayers in these same melodies. Even as a young boy, he sang well enough that he was allowed to be a Chazzan in the big synagogue, and once or twice, accompanied by the organ, he chanted part of the Hanukkah service. He was not the only son who helped lead the services in the orphanage; his other two brothers had excellent singing voices and occasionally served as Chazzans.[38]

This early life was "idyllic" and helped to provide the young boy with such a strong base in Judaism that it helped shape his decision to become a rabbi.[39] Ultimately, Herman's decision to become a rabbi was based on his desire to help people and do something Jewish: "The natural combination [of these desires] was the rabbinate," he says. Other factors influencing his decision was his preparation for his Bar Mitzvah. "As a twelve year old, I was deeply affected by the experience. By the time I finished high school, I was convinced that the rabbinate was to be my life's work."

He also had positive role models provided by his father and by Rabbi Fruedenthal: "To this day, I have my father's picture by my desk, at home, [and] there isn't a day that I don't sort of wave towards him, even though he's gone now." Schaalman still finds himself evaluating his life in the light of what he remembers were his father's values. He is saddened that his father did not live to experience some joy in his eldest son's achievements and by the fact that "I could not get his opinion on issues that are important to me."[40] When Schaalman's own Rabbi Baerwald, who taught him Talmud, ignored him, Rabbi Fruedenthal, who was a friend of the family, took on the responsibility for advising the young student.

Adolf's Ambitions for His Sons

Part of every child's maturation is the process of establishing oneself as a person separate from one's parents no matter how hard the parents work to mold their children into the people they want them to become. When that happens, conflicts may develop between parents and their children. Although in many ways he was very liberal, Adolf had preconceived ideas about what he wanted his three sons to become. He believed that young Jews should have a better balance in career choices and did not want two doctors or three attorneys in his family. He also believed in the value of nonacademic and nonbusiness careers and preferred that his children be in different social strata. His plan was that his first son would be an academic of some kind, the second a merchant, and the third a craftsman. He also had definite ideas about the kind of academic son he wanted. Schaalman reports, "He wanted his firstborn to be intellectually keen … deeply observant and pious." Largely, he got his wish. Herman went to college, Ernst went to business school and became a successful businessman in San Paolo, and Freddie went to technical college and became a tool and die maker.

Regina, on the other hand, had another idea for Herman. She instilled in him the notion that becoming a rabbi was the most wonderful choice a Jewish boy could make and told him about other family members who had been rabbis: "Once I made my decision, my father made sure that I had private tutoring in Hebrew to ensure that I was competent."

The Nazi takeover thwarted Adolf's plan. When Jewish children could no longer go to public schools, Jewish parents began sending them abroad for an education. Barkai (1998c) estimates that 18,000 young people between the ages of ten and sixteen were sent to England or to Palestine. Ernst was one of them. His parents sent him to England to finish his last year. Freddie never finished high school.

Growing Up

When he was a young boy, Herman was not immune from romantic ideas about his future. "At various times, I entertained thoughts of becoming an African explorer, a streetcar conductor, or a psychiatrist. After reading about the famous African explorer, Dr. David Livingstone, I fantasized what such a life might be like." On the other hand, the job of streetcar conductor also appealed to him: "Silly as it may seem, I thoroughly enjoyed riding the trolley, hearing its bell, and the authority that came with the job. As a product of an authoritarian society, I found the absolute authority of the conductor appealing."

Because Munich had so few Jews, Jewish friends were had to find: "Only two Jews attended my high school. Most of my friends, therefore, were non-Jews, including my best friend, Albert Klein, whose parents were friends of my parents." That friendship terminated when Albert's Nazi stepbrother forbade his family from socializing with the Schaalmans and threatened to report them to the Gestapo if they persisted in visiting them. Soon, Albert, too, joined the SS. "At six feet two inches tall and very handsome, he was the perfect candidate. Nonetheless, he did not forget his Jewish friends."

An important part of Herman's development was his lively interest in sports. Not only did he enjoy them, but he excelled in gymnastics and track and field activities. Remarkably, for a boy of his small stature (he was under 5'), he was competent in high jumping, swimming—one of his favorite activities—and in throwing the javelin and discus. He also loved to ski and was particularly fond of soccer and Schlagball, a variation of baseball, both highly competitive and physically demanding sports: "My athletic ability made me one of the most sought-after people in any game."

By the age of fifteen, he had developed such a solid reputation for maturity and competence that some parents were willing to entrust their children to him to lead a group of them on a skiing trip in the Alps. This trust was based in part on the fact that he was the son of the well-known Professor Schaalman. The fact that Herman's younger brother, Freddie, was tagging along may have inspired further confidence. However, through no fault of his own, when the boys got to the Alps, their trip turned into a nightmare. They found themselves trapped in their cabin by a major blizzard. So much snow fell that it covered the cabin up to the roof. The situation was a crisis because the boys could not get out to buy food and provisions. Herman, realizing that something had to be done, climbed up to the attic and, with great difficulty, pushed open the trap door that was covered with heavy snow:

> After I pulled myself out, I struggled to walk on the snow wearing the improvised snowshoes that I knew would be necessary to hike to the village. Before I could get very far, the heavy backpack I was wearing hit me in the head and knocked me face down in the deep snow. I struggled to get my head up enough to breathe. Finally, I was able to stand upright and continue to the neighboring village.

Herman encountered another near calamity when one of the boys broke his arm. Using the little first aid he knew, Herman placed the boy's arm in a sling and, after entrusting the well-being of the boys to his assistant, "a youth with more brawn than brains, I set out on the arduous journey to take the boy home to Munich. When I got to the boy's house, I apologized to his parents, who not only proved to be forgiving and understanding, but who sent their son back a week later."

This leadership role was part of Herman's involvement in youth activities that were to play a critical role in his future development. His love of the outdoors, fostered by family vacations and by experiences as a youth leader, helped shape his adult commitment to create a camp for Reform Jewish youth. Thanks to his home life, he knew what it was like to be Jewish in an environment that was both supportive and joyous. As an adult and a leader in the Reform Jewish movement, he wanted Jewish youth to have a taste of the life lived in nature, as well as to have a joyous Jewish experience.

Another important part of his early life was the family vacations. These special times provided the children the opportunity to form deeper ties with each other and with their parents. Despite the family's limited means, every summer they left Munich for a six-week vacation on a farm at Starnberger See, a lake in the foothills of the Alps where they rented what Schaalman calls a "cottage." It was part of a settlement of two farms that hosted vacationers during the summer. Consisting of several rooms on the upper level of a garage used for storing farm equipment, the Schaalmans were happy to be there. Behind the cottage were a small brook, several orchards, and a field where the cows grazed. Unwilling to lose a single day of vacation, the family left Munich the first day of Adolf's summer vacation and did not return until the day before school began. The family enjoyed a variety of activities, including swimming, hiking, reading, and study, which they did together.

In his early years, Schaalman's vacation experiences were restful and pleasant, but when he got older, his father insisted that he work for the farmer. The farmer assigned him two tasks: first, he was to remove manure from one of the stables and, then, go into the fields to collect the cuttings of a scythe-wielding farmhand and lay them in straight rows. The first day did not go well. Overwhelmed by the August heat and by the fact that the thistles and thorns in the cuttings bloodied his arms, he fainted. Recognizing that the work was too much for the boy, the farmer sent him home. Thereafter, Herman was reassigned to work in the stable. Even that job did not last long; after only two weeks, his mother took pity on him and allowed him to quit. "Nonetheless, despite the fact that I worked only two weeks, I romanticized the experience and came to think of it as 'sport,' a test of my physical abilities, something not to be taken seriously or to complain about." Thinking back on these vacations, Schaalman remembers them as "wonderful times."

Despite the fact that the family was on vacation, the Schaalmans continued to observe their normal Jewish routines: they ate kosher meat, which they brought in an icebox, and *davenned* (prayed) together on Shabbos. However, because the Shabbos routine required that the Schaalman brothers *daven* in the morning and study in the afternoon, they did not get to play with the other children: "Even if we had wanted to, our formal Shabbos clothes prevented us from participating with the other children in one of our favorite activities, climbing trees."

On one of these trips, Herman met Lotte Strauss, the girl to whom he pledged his heart. They met when Herman was barely fifteen years old. The parents of his current girlfriend, Ruth Gusstein, owned a house on Lake Constance in southwest Germany near the Swiss border, where they spent summers with their three daughters. The house was large enough that they could rent some of its rooms. Because the lake was also a favorite of the Schaalman family, they vacationed there for six weeks during two summers.

This six-week period was a special time for the family. They could all be together without the routines of daily life. The Schaalmans and the Gussteins cooked together and ate together in the single kitchen. One of the reasons Herman had such a good time was the fact there were eight young people living in the house: the three Gusstein girls, two other teenage girls, Lotte Strauss and another young girl, and the three Schaalman brothers. Although one of Ruth's sisters was three years older and the other several years younger than Herman, the mix of ages did not prevent the young people from having a good time together. In his memory, "Age was not a factor; we were all young together."

Nearby was the tiny picturesque village of Wangen, situated on an arm of the lake. Schaalman remembers that the village had not yet been invaded by automobiles and to get there, the family had to travel by rail. One of its amenities was a tiny synagogue where Adolf and his family attended Shabbos services. Their presence infused new life into the community synagogue. Not only did the Schaalmans add four more people to the handful in attendance, but also the quality of the service improved significantly. "Unofficially, my father took on the role of cantor and chanted all the prayers in his rich cantorial voice."

Despite the fact that the Schaalmans were on vacation, Adolf made sure their days were structured and that they included study on a daily basis (a practice that Schaalman continued with his own children, when they went away for summer vacation). Herman's parents believed that part of their responsibility toward their children was to educate them.

However, for Herman, the summers were not without other pleasures. Lotte Strauss was the daughter of a prominent family in the steel business in Ulm. By the end of the second summer, she had replaced Ruth in Herman's affections. The relationship began innocently enough. They played cards together, swam, and went horseback riding. Occasionally, the entire Schaalman family, together with Ruth, her two sisters and Lotte would commandeer two or three boats and row across the few hundred yards of the lake to Switzerland, where they read newspapers that had been banned in Germany. The trip was not without some risk. Before they could leave Germany, they had to get by a policeman who might have stopped and questioned them, were it not for the fact that he had known the Gussteins for many years. By the second summer, Schaalman had fallen in love with Lotte. For him, "These were the days of innocence, simplicity."

Youth Group

During these critical years of Herman's development, Germany experienced a resurgence of national feeling, a sense of pride and superiority in being German. Its youth groups (closed to Jews) became a valuable resource for building a stronger sense of national pride and identity. Recognizing the value of such organizations, the German-Jewish community formed its own groups, including sports clubs and various youth movements. At first, the majority of Jewish youth chose apolitical activities, and some turned to escapist diversions such as "the customary array of social activities and cheap amusements ... [such as] the increasingly more permissive sexual relations in the big cities" (Barkai, 1998c, p. 70).

Herman remembers that the first group he joined was the German-Jewish Boy Scouts, which he loved. He enjoyed hiking, usually on Sundays, but did not participate in the summer camping activities because he accompanied his family on their summer vacation trips (Folb, 2007). As he got older, his teenage Jewish friends were drawn to political movements, particularly to Zionism, which had become a passion for many Jewish teenagers. The emergence of Zionism as an interest of Jewish youth may be explained in part as a response to the growing anti-Semitism that placed severe limitations on their ability to find a meaningful place in German society. Well before the exclusion of Jewish children from the public schools, young middle-class graduates encountered great difficulty getting jobs commensurate with their level of education and their social aspirations. When they could find employment, it was frequently in positions that reflected a downward mobility that pushed them into the ranks of the proletariat. Children from poor families had even more trouble finding employment and were often unemployed for long periods (Barkai, 1998c).

Some of Herman's friends became committed Zionists and immigrated to Palestine. Although Herman was sympathetic to Zionism, his friends could not convince him to go with them, despite their best efforts. Even if he had wanted to go, he would not have left his family, particularly his father, who, although he tolerated his son's Zionist leanings, was not a Zionist.

Another group Herman joined was an educational group that was studying Martin Buber, Germany's most famous Jewish scholar and intellectual. Sometimes, Buber even taught the course. For Schaalman, the experience of being in the presence of this great man was sufficient to leave a lasting mark on him and became a major influence on his life (Folb, 2007, p. 6).

A New Direction

When Herman graduated from the Maximillian Gymnasium in the spring of 1935, he was the last Jewish student to do so. Although he could not have known it at the time, the Nazis were developing their strategy for a "solution to the Jewish question." Part of that effort was to make life in Germany so uncomfortable for Jews that they would have to leave the country. One of their first strategies was to introduce an economic boycott of Jewish businesses and professionals such as doctors and lawyers (Barkai, 1998a). Already in 1935, organized terror in the form of attacks against Jews on the streets had become commonplace. In April of that year, the Nazis attacked and defaced numerous shop windows in Munich.

Prior to Schaalman's graduation from high school, he had applied to and been accepted by Berlin's renowned *Lehranstalt Für Die Wissenschaft Des Judentums*,[41] a small Liberal rabbinic school of about 150 students. He had tried to register at the University in Berlin but was told that Jews were no longer allowed to enroll officially, but he could attend unofficially (Folb, 2007).[42] By the time of Herman's enrollment in the seminary, the Nazis had stripped it of its university standing, and, as a result, the students lost their special privileges. Although Herman was unaware of it at the time, these political developments were being monitored by Hebrew Union College and, in a short time, would precipitate his premature departure from the seminary.

In May, when Herman graduated high school and moved to Berlin to begin rabbinic studies, the Nazi campaign in Munich accelerated with the smashing of shop windows and violent demonstrations. In ensuing months, boycotts of Jewish businesses and violence against Jews spread to "scores of cities, smaller towns and villages" (Barkai, 1998a, p. 209). In Berlin, the violence caught up with him. In June, the Nazi party newspaper *NS-Parteikorrespondenz* "demanded that Jews no longer be recognized as citizens" (p. 210). In mid-July 1935, it called for the death penalty for Jews who rented rooms to Aryan lodgers or hired Aryan domestic help. On July 15, violence erupted in Berlin with the result that calls came for additional measures against the Jews. In August, as part of the accelerating progression of the national insanity, Goebbels declared that marriages between Aryans and Jews would no longer be tolerated (Barkai, 1998a).

Although Herman had been enrolled in the seminary for only a few months (from the first week of May 1935 to the early part of July), by a fortuitous set of circumstances he was able to leave the seminary and escape to America. Soon after he arrived at the Berlin seminary, the Board of Governors of the Hebrew Union College (HUC) in Cincinnati invited five students from the seminary to continue their studies in the United States. HUC had a special relationship with the seminary and with German Jews (Folb, 2007). HUC founders had been graduates of the seminary, and the HUC Board of Governors was composed of men whose parents or grandparents were German immigrants. Even American-born faculty members, including the college president, Julian Morgenstern, had received their doctorates at Berlin universities and had intimate acquaintances among German Jews. For these reasons and, because HUC had sent five of its faculty members to study at the *Lehranstalt* in the 1920s, in 1935, the HUC Board of Governors decided to reciprocate by offering five scholarships for its students. Folb (2007) claims that humanitarian concerns served as a strong part of HUC's motivation. The very survival of German Jewry was in jeopardy.

The presidents of the two institutions collaborated on an arrangement to send five students of the *Lehranstalt* to HUC to continue their rabbini-

Wissenschaft des Judentums

cal studies. Part of the agreement was that, if conditions permitted, once the students were ordained they would return to Germany. If that were not possible or desirable, they would remain in the United States where they would seek rabbinic positions (Folb, 2007). To HUC's credit, despite its own financial difficulties and the lack of pulpit vacancies for its own students, the college decided to underwrite the students' expenses. Although these students were the first, in the next few years other students and faculty left Germany and came to HUC.[43]

The *Lehranstalt* faculty picked two students. Through a competitive process, four additional finalists emerged for the remaining three slots. Originally, Herman had no interest in the competition and only entered it after his father told him he should. He was reluctant to participate for several reasons. First, he had barely started rabbinic studies. A second, more formidable reason was that he had no desire to go abroad, "certainly not to America," which he thought of as "uncivilized Indian territory ... the wild west," gangster territory. Third, he had never heard of Cincinnati or Hebrew Union College. "To find out something about Cincinnati, I turned to my encyclopedia and was astonished to learn it was a city."

A key part of his ultimate decision came from the intercession of Ismar Elbogen, the *Lehrenstalt* president who was well known as one of the greatest liturgical scholars of all time.[44] Elbogen was upset when he found out that Herman had not entered the competition and asked him whether he had discussed the matter with his father. When Herman replied that he had not, the president, who knew his father, demanded that he write to him immediately. When Adolf received the letter, he was perplexed; he had never heard of Reform Judaism and had no idea what advice he should give. He wasted no time in consulting Rabbi Fruedenthal, who responded in three simple words: "*Herman muss gehen*"—Herman must go.[45]

The next day the anxious father sent an urgent telegram stating, "Apply immediately. Letter follows." The telegram had the force of a decree; his father's word was law. Although Herman was nineteen, going against his father was inconceivable.

In late June, the four finalists for the three remaining slots met with Elbogen in an anteroom to his study. Blank affidavits were sitting on a table. Schaalman remembers Elbogen saying, "Gentlemen, you have fifteen minutes to decide which three will go. When you have made your decision, knock on the door, come in my study, and close the door." Up to that point, the competition had meant nothing to Herman, but suddenly it took on immense importance. The four knew each other; in fact, three of them were in the same class. As they sat together, Herman had an awful sensation in his stomach: "All of a sudden destiny was knocking on the door." Each student tried to figure out reasons why the others should not go. They went through several rounds, when all of a sudden, one of the boys got up and announced that he was not going and walked out. The other boys knocked on Professor Elbogen's door and when the door opened, he looked at them and asked, "So, this is your decision?" The three boys told him they would accept the scholarships, and Elbogen replied, "Congratulations, you are going to America."

In addition to Herman, the finalists included W. Gunther Plaut, Alfred Wolf,[46] Wolli Kaelter, and Leo Lichtenberg. Schaalman speculates that the fourth boy, who later died in a concentration camp, must have decided suddenly that he did not want to leave his fiancée. As for the five rabbinic students heading for America, none had positive attitudes about American Judaism. Instead, they saw themselves as "crusaders" with a mission to reform the heathen American Jews by teaching them what it meant to be truly Jewish. All five of them achieved considerable fame as rabbis in the Reform movement.[47]

Sometime before leaving for America, Herman's father took him to Poppenheim, a cemetery where his grandparents and great grandparents were buried. Schaalman speculates that his father may have had an inkling that his son might never live in Germany again and wanted him to see the burial places of his ancestors from the first half of the nineteenth century. The earliest date he remembers seeing on the stones was something like 1840. One of the stones bore the name "Hermann Schaalmann," though not the Schaalman after whom he was named. In 1987, like his father before him, Schaalman returned to this cemetery with his two granddaughters, Keren and Johanna (seven and eleven respectively), to pass on this knowledge of family heritage. Both Keren and Johanna have fond memories of this event, which they say left a deep impression on them (Schaalman, K., Schaalman, Jeremy, and Schaalman, Johanna, 2006).

When Herman left home at the age of nineteen, he lost direct contact with his father as a figure of authority and support. Although initially at a loss for his guidance, Herman also found himself free of direct restraints and was now responsible for his own actions. This freedom allowed him to grow in a direction very different from that provided by his father. Asked whether this freedom allowed him to form an identity different from the one his father would have desired, he responded, "I became the person he had helped to raise."

In 1935, getting a student visa to the United States was easy because the Nazis were, as Plaut (1981) wrote, "[only] too cooperative" (p. 47).

Before Herman left for America, his father had given him a Rosh Ha-shanah New Year's card that he had received many years earlier from his uncle Max Samfield (1844–1915), who had immigrated to America. Although Adolf did not know whether the man was still alive, he told his son to try to get in touch with him.

Although getting past the Nazis was not an obstacle, leaving his parents and brothers was difficult for Herman. The psychological and emotional consequences are still with him today. In an interview in 2011 when Schaalman was ninety-five, he told an interviewer, "I will never forget hanging out of the window of the train of the Munich station and waving a handkerchief and seeing their handkerchiefs waving goodbye. And somehow or other I had an anticipation … I felt terribly lost and alone."[48] When he arrived at Hebrew Union College in 1935 as a young man of nineteen years, he had no idea that in 1966 he would return to Germany to receive an Honorary Degree of Doctor of Divinity (Berenbaum, 2007).

Chapter 2

Coming to America
Hebrew Union College
1935–1941

"If it hadn't been for America, I probably wouldn't be alive today.
I love this country."
Herman E. Schaalman, July 2, 2011

"Father in Dachau. Save him!"
Regina Schaalman, 1937

She did not look like the rabbis' wives he knew in Germany, not remotely.
I didn't know a single rabbi who had a car let alone a rebbetzin who
would be allowed to drive one. Imagine our surprise when she arrived in a
lovely large car with radio blaring! She was a buxom blonde who
looked like Jean Harlow.
Wolli Kaelter, 1997, p. 52

Culture shock best describes Herman's initial experience with America. What he knew about America came from reading Karl May's cheap novels that were full of tall tales of gangsters and Indians (Tutush, p. 1).[49] In addition to May's influence, the only other information he had about America, despite studying world history for seven years, came from one short paragraph in a textbook. All he remembered from his reading were the names of Washington and Lincoln. In contrast, "I knew a great many particulars about Germany, including every battle and the names of all the mistresses of every German emperor."

The journey to America began a month after the five scholarship students were selected and shortly before the *Nuremberg* Laws were enacted on September 15, 1935, denying Jews their German citizenship.[50] Herman and Alfred Wolf were the youngest of the five, Leo Lichtenberg and Wolli Kaelter were one year ahead of them, and W. Gunther Plaut was their senior by two years. Their plan, according to Schaalman, was to meet in Paris[51] and then depart on the *Brittanic*[52] and arrive in New York City September 5, 1935, the day before Labor Day.

When Herman left Germany with his one suitcase, he set out on a new adventure such as he had never dreamt nor desired. He remembers that the voyage by ship provided the first significant challenge to the students' entry into the English-speaking world.[53] Their inability to speak English became an immediate problem. Plaut (1981) remembered sitting at a round table in the kosher section of the dining room when a man in a yellow sweater rose repeatedly during the meal, made a German-style bow in Plaut's direction, and spoke to him in English. Plaut interpreted the behavior as the man's way of introducing himself. Taking the man's manner as his cue, Plaut "rose, bowed in return and responded, 'My name is Plaut'" (p. 50). Plaut's response provoked laughter from the man's friends. Only later did Plaut learn that the man had been asking him to pass the salt and pepper.

Herman also ran into a problem when he had to order his first meal. At breakfast, he didn't recognize anything on the menu. When the waiter suggested he order cereal, he declined, though he did not know what the word meant. "Instead, I ordered 'poofed rice,' which had just been introduced into Germany. The waiter must have realized that he had a greenhorn of the purest form in front of him. Taking advantage of the situation, the waiter brought me everything on the menu." The combination of the excessive and unfamiliar foods and the rocking of the ship, made him seasick: "Within fifteen minutes," Schaalman recalls, "it had all been sacrificed to the gods of the sea." He was sick for two days. The rest of the trip was pleasant, especially after the ship stopped off in Ireland to pick up a group of young people on their way home to New York. A fun-loving bunch, they danced and sang all night and provided Herman a good time for the rest of the trip.[54]

When the boat docked in New York, Herman was detained on board until someone claimed him. The Council of Jewish Women had been alerted to meet the other students, but Herman's family had arranged for him to be picked up by a distant relative on his mother's side. Unfortunately for Herman, she was late. Because he had no way of communicating with her, and because he was the last passenger on board, he felt abandoned: "The thought crossed my mind that I might have to turn around and go home." Finally, the woman arrived and took him to her home. Fortunately, for Herman, the family spoke Yiddish, which he had learned from his Yiddish-speaking German relatives.

As a way to introduce him to America, his host, including her son and daughter, took him by streetcar to Coney Island where she thought he would get a taste of America. Serious culture shock began to set in when the first object that attracted Herman's attention was a moving Sunkist billboard in English and Yiddish: "I was shocked by the fact that it was in Yiddish and afraid it would provoke a riot. In Germany, anything Jewish in public and with Hebrew lettering was an incitement and an open invitation to vandalism or worse. Yet no one seemed to notice this billboard or to take offense." He had hardly time to digest this first surprise, than another lay in store for him. Ahead of them, he noticed some kind of disturbance. His host's son, acting as a scout, came back and reported, "Some Jews have just beaten up a Nazi or two and sent them to the hospital." At a complete loss to understand this situation, Herman responded, "You must be mistaken; it was the other way around, some Nazis had beaten up a Jew who was on his way to the hospital. Because I had never seen Jews beating up Nazis, I could not believe the explanation."

Herman had another surprise, though on a much smaller scale, when he was treated to a root beer ice cream soda, known colloquially as a "black cow." Because ice cream was not kosher, he had never tasted it, only ices, which were kosher. Nor had he ever tasted root beer: "Nevertheless, out of politeness, I drank the soda, though I did not enjoy it. So ended my first day in the new land, which left me confused and bewildered."

The day after Labor Day, his relative took him to Wall Street to cash the vouchers HUC had sent him to purchase a train ticket to Cincinnati. "My ignorance of the city left me ill-prepared for the sight of the city's skyscrapers. These architectural innovations had not yet been introduced in Europe; by contrast, the tallest building in Munich, perhaps twelve stories, inspired awe in the people who saw it." Consequently, Herman's visit to Wall Street, where he was surrounded by skyscrapers, overwhelmed him. When he came to one of them to cash his vouchers, he reports, "I remained outside the building and gawked at it." Then, to his total surprise, "A truck pulled up, men jumped out and ran into the bank with guns drawn. They came out with sacks of money, threw them in the back of the truck and sped away. I inched my way into the building and told my friends that I had witnessed a holdup. They stormed out to inspect the scene, but, by then, it was over." They recognized that what he had seen was not a robbery and explained to him that the men had come to pick up money from the bank. The young greenhorn could not believe it: "Because no one paid any attention to the 'robbery,' I concluded that such events must be commonplace and did not merit peoples' attention." The experience reinforced his culture shock and negative attitude toward America.

In order for the young rabbinic students to learn more about America, HUC had arranged that on their way to Cincinnati they would take a detour and make a brief visit to the nation's capital. After a one-day visit, they traveled overnight on a B & O train to Cincinnati. The journey turned out to be an unexpected delight. Though he had ridden on trains in Germany, he was not used to riding in luxury. The coach class, where he was sitting, had upholstered seats. In Germany, coach meant you sat on wooden benches, the only way the Schaalmans could afford to travel. His cushioned seats were the equivalent of second class, more luxurious than coach.

Another surprise occurred the next morning when he saw a man at the end of the car davenning in tallis and *tephilin*. So traumatized was he from his experience with the Nazis that Herman feared for the man's life. He said to himself, "Don't you understand you're going to be killed the next moment? However, no one seemed to take any notice of the man; even the conductor walked by without saying a word. I, on the other hand, was terrified." As he thought about the situation, he realized that "something was going on" that he did not understand.[55]

Although America seemed to the young immigrant to be benign and free of anti-Semitism, at least the virulent kind he experienced in

Germany, he was oblivious to the fact that anti-Semitism was deeply imbedded in American society. He did not know, for example, that Cincinnati was heavily German and that many pro-Nazi German-American organizations were active in the city (Sarna and Klein, 1989). Among these groups were Father Coughlin's Social Justice Movement, William Dudley Pelley's Silver Shirts, the German American Bund, and Rev. Gerald B. Winrod's Protestant fundamentalist organization, Defenders of the Christian Faith. These and other groups were responsible for the growth of anti-Semitism that reached its peak in 1944 (Wyman, 1998), about the time of the awakening of the world to the horrors the Nazis were inflicting on the Jews.

Because they knew little of their new American environment, the five young German rabbinic students were deeply susceptible to first impressions. When they arrived in Cincinnati, their first impression of HUC helped confirm their negative view of the seminary and American Judaism. They were met at the train by Professor Nelson Glueck, Professor of Bible, who later became famous as an archaeologist and president of HUC. Schaalman reports that the professor, who spoke perfect German, took them to breakfast at the home of his mother-in-law, Mrs. Ranshoff, the daughter of a prominent Cincinnati family.[56]

When the five students sat down to eat in the dining room, they discovered that they were being served bacon and eggs. Despite the fact that the students were famished, Plaut (1981) thanked their hosts and told them that they were not hungry and had already eaten (p. 52). When Glueck realized that none of them would eat nonkosher food, he was "mortified" and immediately ordered that the food be taken away (Kaelter, 1997). According to Schaalman, "The food that was served next was either new eggs without the bacon or the old eggs with the bacon removed from their plates." Not to offend their host, they ate the breakfast.

A half hour later, reporters from a local newspaper arrived to interview them. The students, however, said nothing; they were afraid that what they said would get back to Germany and jeopardize their parents, who might be accused of revealing harmful information about Germany through their sons. They gave the reporters only their names and did not allow them to take their pictures.[57]

Hebrew Union College: 1935–1941

When the five refugee students arrived at Hebrew Union College in the fall of 1935, they found themselves part of a very small seminary with only about sixty students enrolled. It was a relatively new campus, having been built in the 1920s. Comparing it to the modest building of their seminary in Berlin, which was located in "squalid surroundings," Plaut (1981) described it as "unreal in its splendor and extravagance" (p. 52). Located across the street from the large campus of the University of Cincinnati, it appeared to him to be "a series of castles set in spacious grounds" and a reflection of American opulence. In addition to an administration building, which housed the classrooms, the complex included a dormitory, gymnasium, swimming pool, and two outdoor tennis courts.

HUC provided the refugees full financial aid, including tuition, room and board, and all fees. According to Plaut (1981), this beneficence was part of an "ancient custom" of relieving aspiring scholars of financial worries, a practice even for scholars in European *shtetls* and one that had been transplanted to America (p. 54). Because the Nazis had devastated their families' financial resources, the young men would not have been able to accept the offer without this assistance. When the students arrived without any money, the college gave them a loan of twenty dollars, which they were required to repay when they left the college (p. 57). In order to repay this loan and to have some spending money for himself, Schaalman took a job working for a professor ten hours a week, for which he earned $5. When the college was on summer break, in the summer of 1937 he worked as a counselor for sports at Camp Tel Chai in Michigan. Another summer, he was hired at a camp in Osceola in North Carolina: "They had heard that I played tennis and hired me as a tennis counselor."

At the time Herman enrolled in HUC, the college was strictly a male institution. The only women on campus were two secretaries, two cooks, and Lillian Waldman, the dorm matron. Both Plaut and Schaalman were extremely fond of Lillian, whom Schaalman described as "wise, gentle, [and] charming." She lived with her daughter on the first floor of the dorm and served as a surrogate mother. Schaalman remembers her as "a good sounding board; because I was far from home and parents and

Herman Schaalman, 1937
Counselor at Camp Tell-Chai

utterly alone, I confided in her and asked questions I could never ask anybody else."[58]

Herman was not the only one feeling isolated and alone. Plaut (1981) wrote that the refugee students felt "rootless" and like aliens in a strange new land (p. 57). They compensated for this feeling by sticking together and creating a shared fraternity with a common language and culture, sharing memories and stories of their past lives. They found comfort in their teachers, most of whom had been educated in Germany and spoke fluent German.[59]

Part of the students' education included learning how to mingle with the wealthy members of Reform society. In order to prepare them for the foods they were likely to encounter, the president's wife introduced the freshman to artichokes, a delicacy they would likely be served. Modern ideas and contemporary events, however, were not part of their education. Although they had heard of Freud and Einstein, they did not discuss them, nor did they know about the horrors the Nazis were perpetrating against Jews. Although the refugee students were anxious about the war cables and the safety of their families, Schaalman reports, "We did not feel engaged in the war. We felt protected and sheltered from the world."

Next to the influence of his father, Schaalman's experience at HUC must be considered the most profound influence on his growth and development. Within six years of his arrival at HUC, not only did he become Americanized but also a Classical Reform Jew. In Germany,

The Gang of Five, 1935
Left to right: Alfred Wolf, Leo Lichtenberg, W. Gunther Plaut,
Herman Schaalman, Wolli Kaelter

Hebrew Union College, Cincinnati, OH

although Schaalman identifies his upbringing as Liberal, his father practiced a much more traditional Judaism.[60]

At first, the young refugee had difficulty adjusting to this new religious world and to American customs and values. In that, he was no different from other immigrants, Jewish and non-Jewish, arriving in America:

> We saw ourselves as coming to a new world that called on us to radically reshape our entire existence. It is the Promised Land full of hope and opportunity for individual prosperity and happiness. We had to adapt to this new world in ways we could not have imagined. Intellectually and emotionally, this radical adjustment was confusing and disorienting.

Compounding their adjustment difficulties was their growing awareness of what was happening in Germany and the danger these events posed to their parents and families: "Our inability to do anything about these dangers," he states, "produced a profound sadness."

One of the transformations the students had to make was to their cultural stereotypes. They came with the stereotype that Americans, including Jews, were hunters and owned guns. Traditional Judaism frowns on hunting or any other activity that causes pain to living creatures. The Jews Schaalman knew before coming to America did not own guns or hunt or fish; the Jew who did was the exception. When one of his fellow rabbinic students brought out a gun and boasted about its use, Herman was surprised and put off.

Another paradigm shift occurred in the discovery that Americans, unlike Germans, gave their children middle names. As part of his effort to adopt the customs of his new country, Herman adopted his Hebrew name "Ezra" as his middle name, the Hebrew name he had been given to perpetuate the memory of his maternal grandfather "Ernst Ezra." He even had to change the spelling of his name. Soon after his arrival in America, he was advised to use an American spelling, which required that he drop the double "n" (Folb, 2007, p. 36).[61]

Their difficulty of adjusting to the ways of American Reform Judaism confronted them on the day after their arrival at HUC. It was Shabbat and Rabbi David Philipson, one of the foremost rabbinic scholars of his time and a teacher at HUC, invited them to attend services at his

Rockdale Temple in Rockdale, a Cincinnati neighborhood. According to Kaelter (1997), Philipson's assistant, Rabbi Morton Cohen, dispatched his wife to pick them up.[62] Imagine the young men's surprise when she arrived in a "lovely large car with radio blaring ... a buxom blonde who looked like Jean Harlow ... in short skirts" and not much older than the students themselves (pp. 51–54). "Nor," Plaut (1981) added, "did I know a single rabbi who had a car let alone a rebbetzin who would be allowed to drive one" (p. 54). Herman was similarly impressed.

When she got out of the car, she introduced herself as Sally Cohen, wife of Rabbi Mort Cohen, and she was there to drive the students to the temple. Although none of the young men had ever ridden to Shabbat services, as captives to their new surroundings they got in the car and drove off with her to the temple. Sensing their embarrassment, Mrs. Cohen responded, "When in Rome, do as the Romans do" (p. 54). The rabbi's wife may also have been surprised by the students' appearance. They must have looked like pariahs with their formal German synagogue clothes, replete with their broad-brimmed hats. (According to Schaalman, no respectable German Jew would be seen in a German synagogue without a top hat.) One can only guess at her amusement.

When they arrived at the temple, an usher escorted them to the front row. As was the custom in a Liberal synagogue, men and women were seated together, but the sanctuary was nearly empty. This new fact of life took the students by surprise. In Germany, synagogues were packed and served as the center of Jewish life.[63] The prayer books were another surprise. They were thin books that opened from left to right and were largely in English. On the bimah sat two men in black robes. Plaut (1981) assumed one of them was the cantor but found out later was Rabbi Cohen, the assistant rabbi. The other man, his senior, was silver-haired, the famous Rabbi Philipson. Another surprise for the rabbinic students was that he was not wearing a kippah or prayer shawl and that the service he conducted was almost entirely in English. It was also apparent that the congregation knew next to no Hebrew. The students had entered the strange new world of American Reform Judaism.

In the meantime, Philipson had his own issues with the greenhorns. He was seventy-three years old and had been serving as Rockdale Temple's rabbi since 1888 and was in no mood to tolerate the students' outlandish attire. As a founding member of the Central

Conference of American Rabbis and its president from 1907 to 1909, he was regarded as a leader of "classical" Reform Judaism and a staunch advocate of Americanism, which meant that he had devoted his life to the assimilation of Jews into American life (David Philipson Papers: Manuscript Collection No. 35, n.d.).

Philipson had a clear view of the refugees, and, as the service proceeded, became increasingly irritated. Kaelter (1997) described him as "close to apoplexy" (p. 53). The custom of wearing hats in a Reform service was strictly taboo. As Kaelter (1997) tells it, "he could barely get through the Kaddish before summoning us to his study" (p. 53). In Plaut's (1981) account, the Rabbi "glowered" at them and lectured them in "stentorian tones well within the hearing of the other congregants" (p. 55). Then, he ushered them into his study and demanded to know why they did not remove their hats. "The first thing you have to learn," he reprimanded them, "is manners. In our temple we have long given up the wearing of hats" (p. 54). Then he turned nasty: "If you ever appear here again with those things on your heads, I will have you physically removed" (p. 54). Plaut (1981) speculated that to Philipson, "the chief exponent of [Reform's] classical expression," the immigrants must have represented "the antithesis of his ideals" (p. 56). With their butchered English, they must have reminded Philipson of the Old World from which Reform Judaism had tried to distance itself.

In their attempt to defend themselves, the students told him that they had cleared wearing hats with HUC's president, Dr. Julian Morgenstern. Philipson was not mollified: Morgenstern might have given them permission to wear their hats during services at HUC, but not in Rockdale. In separate accounts of the incident, Schaalman and Kaelter reported that, when they objected, Philipson gave them the same response as Sally Cohen, "When in Rome, do as the Romans do" (Kaelter, 1997, p. 53). Herman, the brash and quick-witted young seminary student, fired back, "I thought we were in Cincinnati" (Folb, 2007, p. 27). Plaut (1981) vowed that he would never "set foot in Rockdale Temple again as long as Dr. Philipson was the rabbi" (p. 56).

Soon after their arrival at HUC, the students attended their first High Holy Day services. The experience was a real eye-opener. Held in Cincinnati's famed Plum Street Temple, the synagogue was crammed wall to wall.[64] According to Kaelter (1997), the entire service was conducted in English, and the women were dressed in "party-like" dresses, "too showy, too extravagant" (p. 51). He also objected to the music, which, to him, sounded "totally goyish"; he couldn't recognize a single tune.[65] The sermon proved to be another obstacle for the new students. Kaelter (1997) reported that not only could he not understand it, but he was so distraught that he left the service "in tears and vowed never to return or to participate in such a service" (p. 51). Ironically, he did return many years later to give the ordination speech to the 1985 graduating seniors. Schaalman also returned to give the ordination speech to the graduating class of 2007.

Not all of the adjustments Herman made to his new life were problematic. When he enrolled in the Berlin seminary, he had been responsible for finding his own housing and providing for his own meals. Not so at HUC where his room and board were provided. He loved his dorm room and the fact that all his meals were included. The food, however, was a problem: "Because I had been brought up in a strictly kosher home, the thought of eating non-kosher food was at first repugnant, though later it proved to be liberating." He had to get past the fact that, although HUC did not serve pork or shellfish, "it did not observe the commandment to keep milk and meat separate. Giving up that commandment proved to be the easiest of all."

More astonishing for him was the fact that he did not have to clean up after himself: "Every day, a man showed up to make my bed and clean my room. Like all the other serving help at the college, this man was African American, the first I had ever met. Although all of these amenities were 'foreign' at first, I soon got used to them, though I felt like I was living in a 'Never Never Land.'"

Not only were the customs strange, but because Herman had not mastered the language, trouble started on his second day when he found himself the butt of an upper classman's practical joke. When his dorm matron invited him to introduce himself to a group of women visiting the college, he readily accepted. The upperclassman, however, exploiting the fact that Herman knew very little English, told him to address the women with a word that Schaalman later learned was "foul and sexually perverted." When he greeted the women with the "word," they turned all shades of red and looked very uncomfortable. When this writer asked Schaalman to identify the word, he refused to reveal it: "The episode was so demeaning that I have never used the word again.[66]

Newspapers also proved to be a challenge for Herman. When he read a headline on the sports page, "Webber died on third," he pondered what it might mean. What was "third"? Who was Webber? How did he die? Learning English was a continuing challenge: "I still remember to this day how difficult it was for me." Plaut (1981) relates a similar experience. The headline of the Cincinnati paper read: "REDS MURDER CARDINALS." He thought that it meant, "the revolution had come to Rome" (p. 58). In time, Schaalman claims that his command of German began to slip: "Now my German is street German, but my vocabulary for curses remains strong, particularly Bavarian curses." Referring to his friends, he says, "We were really masters, experts in swearing."

At first, the refugee students were not well received by the other students. Kaelter (1997) described them as "suspicious and standoffish." Plaut (1981) thought that at first they were "leery" (p. 59). "This response," Schaalman adds, "was based, in part, on their perception that we huddled together to talk about them in German and because we introduced rituals (such as the *birkat hamazon*) in the dining hall that were not been part of the seminary's practice."

Fortunately, a group of eight or ten classmates with similar religious beliefs formed a support group for the refugees. Kaelter (1997) identifies them as Lou H. Silberman, Myron Silverman, Dudley Weinberg, Morton Fierman, Malcolm Stern, Bernie Rosenberg, Abe Shaw, and David Schor. Schaalman describes them as "sensitive," "gentle," and understanding: "They helped us learn English and served as a buffer against other students who might otherwise have made fun of us." [Plaut (1981) described Weinberg as "one of the most sensitive and beautiful human beings it has ever been my privilege to know" (p. 59). Kaelter (1997) wrote that because Silberman befriended the Germans, he became known to his American classmates as the "sixth German" (p. 48).][67]

Another of Herman's American friends, William Silverman (1986), remembered his first impression of the young refugee: "I thought [he] was some kid who was being tutored for his Bar-Mitzvah. Instead, the kid turned out to be my classmate who had come fresh from Germany. … He wore high shoes (I believe they were buttoned down) and with his ruddy complexion, he looked as though he was getting ready to hike through the mountains of Bavaria."

Despite the best efforts of their friends, some unfortunate incidents did occur. A classmate, whom Schaalman declines to identify, who later became a professor at HUC, referred to the Germans as "Heinies," a derogatory term coined during World War I: "He never spoke of anything else and enjoyed announcing when they arrived at an event, 'The Heinies are here,' or 'Hi, Heinies.'" Although spoken in jest, the Germans sensed an insult.

His teachers, many of whom were also foreigners who had had to learn the language when they arrived in America, were largely sympathetic. Not all, however. Some of them who were wedded to the school of biblical criticism thought the Germans were not convinced that HUC's methods and conclusions were valid. Schaalman believes that these faculty members were frustrated because they didn't get the enthusiastic response they desired: "When it did not happen, they chose to ignore us." Professor Sheldon Blank and his wife, Amy, were among those who were sympathetic. Schaalman has fond memories of their cordial treatment and their hospitality: "No treatment of my student days would be complete without paying genuine tribute to them."

Schaalman remembers with reverence and affection Rabbi Samuel S. Cohon and Professor Feinsinger. Cohon, who was professor of theology, served as his thesis advisor and, when Lotte Strauss died unexpectedly, Cohon helped him through the crisis with humanity and compassion.[68] Schaalman describes Feinsinger as the most supportive of all during his early years at HUC.

One of the immediate challenges the refugee students faced was an entrance examination. According to Kaelter (1997), "the news really shook the five of us" (p. 48). Why would such tests be necessary when so many of the HUC faculty had studied at the *Hochschule* in Berlin? Because the refugee students considered Hebrew Union College inferior to their Berlin seminary, they had expected that shortly they would be asked to teach in the institution, but they were rudely disappointed. In their second week, they were told they had to enroll at the University of Cincinnati to earn undergraduate degrees. Although they did not know it at the time, they were not singled out as exceptions: some of the American-born students entering HUC had come directly from high school and were required to get an undergraduate degree from the University while at the same time pursuing a BA from HUC. Typically, students would spend five or six years in rabbinic training before they were ordained. Half of their studies consisted of graduate work leading to rabbinic degrees. Herman was no exception; he did not graduate until 1941.

The five refugee students were advised to make the rounds of the various academic departments of the University of Cincinnati to find a major that would accept them and whether any of their prior education could be parlayed into college credits sufficient to earn a degree. With the help of an HUC student, Herman went from department to department for an evaluation of his transcript from his days at the Gymnasium. His first stop was the Latin Department where he thought he could get credit for his nine years of Latin and parlay his B+ GPA into a degree. The professor, who examined the record, passed him with full credit for Latin, but he still lacked sufficient credits for a degree. Because Herman had had six years of Greek, his next stop was the Department of Greek Language Studies. The faculty advisor also gave him full credit. Next on Herman's list was the French Department. Because his parents always spoke French when they did not want him to understand what they were saying, he knew enough French to pass the professor's inspection. When he asked Schaalman to speak in French, he gave the professor an account in French of how the five rabbinic students had made their trans-Atlantic odyssey, how they had met in Paris and arrived in Cincinnati by train. He also named various Paris boulevards and streets that they had passed in their taxi ride to their hotel, the Tres Charmant. "The Tres Charmant," the professor responded quickly, "Monsieur Schaalman! Tres Charmant!!!!" Not realizing what he had said, Herman discovered, "I had told the professor that I had spent the evening with three young girls rather than my four friends. Despite this embarrassing mistake, I passed the French oral test."

By the end of the day, Herman had amassed the 124 credits required for a BA without having spent a day enrolled in the university. The last requirement was English. When the English professor looked at his 124 credit hours, he was astonished: "Can't be! You can't even speak English." He told Herman to come back the next day. Before he returned, the college administrators must have conferred and concluded that the university would give him the credits, but not a degree. They awarded him senior class status and required him to enroll in two years of English and a major and two minors.[69]

According to Kaelter (1997), all the Germans majored in German— what else? His account of the experience gives us a sense of what it must have been like for students fluent in German to major in their native language. When they found themselves in a class with a professor who had a doctorate from Yale in German but knew very little, these brainy rabbinic students "drove him crazy." The professor retaliated by putting them in a separate group and assigning them to read "all the boring German literature that [they] had managed to escape in Germany" (p. 49). Kaelter (1997) described the literature as "junk," but they had to read a "mind boggling" amount of it to complete their major. Although he had never earned anything less than "A"s in German in Germany, Kaelter now found himself with a B– in Cincinnati.

All the refugees satisfied their minor requirement with minors in philosophy and German. After Herman learned that all the chairs were taken in his preferred minor, psychology, he enrolled in philosophy, the only other minor still open. Although not his first choice, philosophy, by broadening his thinking, proved to be excellent preparation for his rabbinic studies and for the development of the radical theological positions he adopted later in his career. With all the refugee students taking a minor in German, there were bound to be problems for their professor. After about two weeks into the course, he summoned them into his office and told them, "I don't want any of you ever to come to my class again." Apparently, he was insulted when they corrected his German grammar, this despite the fact that he was a Yale graduate. He gave them all passing grades, but not an "A."

Although attending the University of Cincinnati was a major obstacle, Herman's philosophy teacher, Howard D. Roelofs, became one of the important people in his life. Roelofs, who was the department chair, loved philosophy and the classics and took a serious interest in Herman. Roelofs introduced him to Plato, Aristotle, and Plotinus. Schaalman comments, "The importance of reading Plotinus, I learned later, was that so much of the Kabbalah and the Zohar are totally indebted to him. Roelofs provided the intellectual grounding of whatever goes for mysticism." After Herman graduated with a BA, Roelofs helped him get a fellowship in philosophy, which Herman says enabled him to "discover the need for critical examination."

As much as he loved philosophy, he was not above tormenting his philosophy teacher and, later, his thesis advisor, Professor Diesendruck. He became the butt of his students' pranks when they discovered that he could easily be derailed from the course of his lecture by asking him totally unrelated questions. Schaalman describes the game they played with him as "football." "Before class, my fellow students and I took turns making up questions to absolutely be sure to distract him from teaching philosophy. We always succeeded, and these digressions frequently monopolized the entire class time." Their questions were as inane as "why the Cincinnati Reds would not win the pennant this year? or why the French had negotiated with the Nazis who had defeated them?"

Though he admits to learning a lot in his English course, it was not easy. One of the professor's idiosyncrasies was his love of Haiku. To a native English speaker, Haiku is difficult enough because it does not tell a story and depends on a juxtaposition of images, not necessarily related, to create meaning or a new awareness that otherwise cannot be spoken. The meaning depends on a sophisticated understanding of the language that is a translation from Japanese, at best only a rough approximation. Another of the professor's interests was his sense of the majesty of a well-written English sentence, particularly its structure. He knew that for his German students, sentence structure was critical to understanding the meaning of a sentence. In German, the verb, for example, is always at the end. For Schaalman as a German speaker, introducing the verb early on in the sentence proved to be very difficult: "The notion that you introduce the verb early, I can't even begin to tell you how difficult all this was." To read philosophy in English required that he read and reread passages: "Had I thought of it, I might have read the texts in German or Greek before attempting to read them in English." He still owns his text book, *The History of Philosophy* (1914) by Dr. W. Windelband.

Together with his courses at HUC, Herman was taking five or six courses a day, a total of ten or eleven hours of class a day in a language he did not understand. On top of that were all the cultural and religious adjustments he was struggling with. In retrospect, Schaalman remarks, "How we got through those first two years before we were finished in the university I will never understand."

HUC provided its own set of challenges. Reform ritual practice was the first hurdle. So novel were the Reform practices of the day that Schaalman called them "a revolution," to which he needed to adjust. One example was the wearing of a *kippah*. When he chanted in the choir at the college, he felt "naked" without it. His training told him he was sinning against God, yet the administration chastised him when he wore the *kippah*. One day he overslept choir practice and had to race to the chapel to get there on time and barely made it. While he was fumbling around for his *kippah*, the organist started playing the opening cords for Herman's initial solo. When he couldn't find his *kippah*, he panicked. "I was convinced God would strike me dead. I thought wearing a *kippah* was something God wanted." As he told his Torah Study many years later, "I was in misery. I even expected to die that morning. When I didn't, I came to the joyous conclusion that God didn't care whether I wore a *kippah* or not. That was the environment in which I had grown up as a Jew." By the time he left HUC, he only wore his *kippah* for special occasions.[70]

For Schaalman, this experience was a major event in his religious life. From that time forward, he says, "I came to the conclusion that God was much too busy to be concerned over such little things as a *kippah*." Eventually, he realized that wearing a *kippah* was a Jewish custom, a Jewish means of identification, not a commandment. It was a means of expressing reverence in the presence of the divine. "The culture of ancient Judaism," he adds, "may also have produced this custom because people were used to covering their hair in the presence of a superior. In the cultures of that time, hair was a sign and assertion of virility and power, so you covered your hair as a sign of submission."

Such an adjustment to Reform practice helped prepare Schaalman to accept the ideological foundation of Reform Judaism, its unique insight into God's relationship with humans and Jews. He learned to apply reason as a test for the validity of ritual and liturgical practice. "Reason," Schaalman states, "is one of God's great endowments [and] gifts." At the same time that he recognized the importance of reason to validate practice, he concluded,

> There are whole sections of human experience that transcend reason and that are of no use to it, particularly in one's religious life. The failure to recognize this dimension of human experience, particularly in the religious aspect of one's life, is a grave deficiency. This experience of the transcendent is exceedingly precious and unique and, like reason and intellect, a highly significant and unusual gift, an endowment of the human. Not to

use the metaphysical dimension as a tool by which to arrive at liberty and value is a serious deficiency.

"Ultimately," he claims, "recognition of this dimension of human experience is the heart of the Reform position." "Nonetheless," he argues, "most Reform Jews see Reform ideology or theology as a negation, a rejection of this metaphysical component, a stripping away." This position is the result of the "process of intellectualization" that comes with Reform. For Schaalman, what is gained by "intellectualization is a totally new basis if, in fact, through it one can establish a value, a validity for a given statement or practice." In its essence, Reform Judaism "is not merely one of the developments that come out of, or the assimilation of Western rationalists. It is an indispensable acceptance of the totality of human beings' response to the mystery of God. I became a Reform Jew by conviction, in other words, not by accident or by inheritance."

The young rabbinic students had to make other adjustments at HUC. In Germany, prayers were recited in Hebrew, whether one knew the meaning or not. In contrast, Reform Judaism chose to use English translations so that congregants could understand the prayers they were chanting. Not only did Herman have difficulty understanding the English translations, but he recognized that they lacked the sense of ritual language he was used to.

Foreign to the seminary were traditional religious practices such as the *birkat hamazon*, the prayer recited at the conclusion of a meal, and the laying on of *tephilin*. When Herman attempted to introduce the prayer at the end of a meal in the student cafeteria, Plaut (1981) recalled that the students left the room "jeering" (p. 59). In later years, Schaalman realized, "The students very likely were offended not by the practice, but by their perception that we were attempting to impose our own religious practices on them." To reintroduce the practice of laying *tephilin* for morning prayers, Herman started a *Tephilin* Club. "After about six months," he remembers, "attendance dropped off and I gave up. Soon after, even I stopped laying *tephilin*. To continue this practice and to wear a *kippah* and tallis meant that inevitably my friends and I were the foci of conflict."[71]

In fact, he was called into the president's office to answer for these actions. For Herman, this was a particular embarrassment because he revered Morgenstern and considered him his savior. "Morgenstern chewed me out so thoroughly, that I was reduced to tears. It was one of the few times I cried as an adult." Schaalman concluded that Morgenstern's reprimand was based on his dislike of him. Among the chastisements, Morgenstern doled out was, "That as long as I was in Rome, I should do as the Romans did" (not the first time Herman had heard these words). Morgenstern objected to the recital of prayers after the meals in the dining hall. He was particularly irate that the young rabbinic student had no idea what the prayers meant. He told Herman, "Your version of the prayer thanks God for the good land that He has given us. You need to realize that you are in America and that this is *the good land*" [italics added].[72] He recommended that Herman avail himself of a *Haggadah* written by one of the faculty that excised these passages and contained an acceptable version of the *birkat hamazon*.

Morgenstern called Herman into his office on two other occasions to read him the riot act. He reminded Herman that he was a scholarship student and that "he should know his place" (Folb, 2007, p. 27). "I understood these remarks as a warning not to make waves. The memory of the encounter is still vivid to me today." Without malice or forethought, Herman had established himself as the "bad boy" on campus![73]

Several factors could have accounted for Morgenstern's sharp reaction. Herman's apparent unwillingness to adapt to his new environment was a profound embarrassment to Morgenstern. He was, after all, the college president and may have thought that Schaalman and his fellow refugees were testing his authority by introducing Jewish practices they knew were not acceptable. These actions would have been perceived as provocative and in need of stern rebuke, especially coming from refugees who were scholarship students and whom the college had rescued from Hitler's oppression. Yet, they had the audacity to challenge the college's administration, faculty, and student body.

Although Schaalman believed that Morgenstern disliked him, letters that Morgenstern had sent him from 1947–1950 are full of expressions of warmth and care. After being presented with them by this writer, Schaalman was deeply moved and realized that he might have been mistaken. He remembered that, at his ordination, Morgenstern had whispered into his ear a passage from *Jeremiah* 1:17–19:

> "Get yourself ready! Stand up and say to them whatever I command you. Do not be terrified by them, or I will terrify you before

them. Today I have made you a fortified city, an iron pillar and a bronze wall to stand against the whole land—against the kings of Judah, its officials, its priests and the people of the land. They will fight against you but will not overcome you, for I am with you and will rescue you," declares the LORD.

When asked what Morgenstern might have meant by these words, Schaalman explained, "Morgenstern must have seen me as a man of principle, willing to defy authority in the support of his own convictions."

Morgenstern and Schaalman came from very different universes. They had vastly different religious upbringings and engaged in religious practices that were worlds apart. According to Folb (2007), until he was ordained in 1902, Morgenstern had never attended a Passover Seder (p. 25). David Komerofsky (1999) writes that because of Morgenstern's nonobservant background, "He would always feel slightly uncomfortable in traditional Jewish settings" (as cited in Folb, 2007, p. 33). Among the HUC faculty, Morgenstern was not alone. His minimalist ritual practice was also the practice of "most of the faculty, and nearly all of the students" (p. 33). Only a few of the HUC faculty and students "kept the laws of Sabbath or of Kashrut; worship in the HUC chapel was conducted without head covering or prayer shawl, most students coming regularly on Sabbaths (when attendance was required), but rarely to the daily services" (as cited in Folb, 2007, p. 33).

This clash of religious cultures between the president and the German refugee students proved to be the first round of the impact they had on the college and an early sign of the transformative effect they would have on Reform Judaism. At first, they wore *kippot* to services and chanted the complete *birkat hamazon* alone. Later, however, reciting the prayer became customary in the dining hall. Because Morgenstern was known to have held tight rein over the college and its internal affairs, Folb (2007) asserts, "it is fair to say that he gave his tacit consent to these new behaviors" (p. 33).

Although Schaalman claims that he and his refugees colleagues had no intention of overthrowing or rebelling against traditional Reform, nevertheless, their attempt to introduce more traditional practices in the seminary was the first sign of the profound impact they would have on Reform Judaism. At the same time, they, too, were radically transformed by their training as Reform rabbis, a transformation that allowed them to become part of the Reform establishment, as well as agents of change.

The early 1980s were an extraordinary point in the history of Reform Judaism when all its leadership positions were filled by rabbis who were refugees from Nazi Germany: Rabbis Alexander Schindler, head of the Union of Reform Judaism (formerly the UAHC); Herman Schaalman, president of the CCAR; and Alfred Gottschalk, president HUC-JIR (Weiman, 2006). Schaalman cites Plaut, in particular, as having a major impact on Reform through the publication of several books, the most important, *The Torah: A Modern Commentary* (1981), which Schaalman calls "the outstanding reference work of its kind in English." Other German refugees who played a major role in this transformation, included Emil Fackenheim and Rabbi Leo Baeck.[75]

Studying to Be a Rabbi

One of Herman's classes was a Bible study class that was unlike anything he had experienced before. In those days, the Reform movement approached the Bible clinically and trained its rabbinic students accordingly. Before enrolling in HUC, Herman had never thought to question the Torah: "The experience of critically analyzing and interpreting it was totally alien to me." In one class, the professor told the students that for their next class they should bring an English Bible along with scissors and paste. During the class, he had the students cut and paste sections of the prophetic literature in a way that allowed the text to read more naturally and logically.

This rearrangement of text using textual critical methods was meant to prove that the text had been written by different authors. This approach violated the storytelling aspect of Torah in favor of logical progression. Schaalman comments, "For me and my refugee colleagues, this method seemed a violation of the traditional texts. I think we sometimes exchanged both thoughts and ideas about how this [approach] didn't seem right. On the other hand, other colleagues were fine with it."[76] Eventually, he developed a deep respect for the knowledge of some of his professors. They were very good scholars and knew not only modern scholarship, but were intimately acquainted with the original sources.

At the time of Herman's enrollment in the HUC, it was the citadel of American Reform Judaism. Its ethos was a rational approach to Judaism that had its origins in the tradition of German rational philosophy

(Borowitz, 2002). The Jewish reformers of the nineteenth century elevated reason over faith and, in the process, discarded many of the religious practices and beliefs of traditional Judaism, which they thought were outmoded and based on superstition. A Reform movement that was not based on reason could not be justified (Borowitz, 2002). This intellectual and religious environment at HUC was an entirely new experience for Herman and shaped his religious thinking and practice for years to come.[77]

Although HUC was the citadel of Reform Judaism, the movement paid little attention to theology. Borowitz (2002) writes, "Even a cursory examination of the history of the movement shows that Reform, like traditional Judaism, has been occupied mainly with the practical problems of 'living a Jewish life'" (p. 14). These problems included social justice, anti-Semitism, and Zionism. The movement was skeptical of theology and discussion of God, which were considered "pie in the sky."[78] "A better education," Schaalman said many years later, "should have included instruction in theology that provided a systemization and a coherent structure of belief, both completely lacking in my education." Schaalman felt cheated because he would have liked to have a grasp of theological issues:

> In retrospect, I missed that particularly with the one professor to whom I was probably the closest, Dr. Samuel Cohon, professor of liturgy and well, really Jewish knowledge. He was a wonderful repository of sheer knowledge and information [who] … either didn't want to, or never thought of, linking things together so that they became a coherent traceable sequence or some kind of structure.

Instead, theology was taught as a separate subject and by lecture. Even if he wanted to, asking questions was not part of the learning process. Not unlike his experience in German schools, he was not given the opportunity to question, nor did he think he had the right to do so. In his prior training and in his new environment, respect for authority was a given. "At the same time, I was alone in a foreign country participating in a new religion that was totally foreign to me.

Other life-changing challenges surfaced when, in his freshman year, he read Mordecai Kaplan's new book, *Judaism as a Civilization: Toward a Reconstruction of American-Jewish Life* (1934). The book was a theological reformulation of Judaism, which profoundly altered Herman's thinking about Judaism. At the same time that Reform Judaism found its justification in the strict exercise of rationalist thinking, Kaplan provided an alternative rationalist perspective. He proposed that the rational understanding of Judaism had room for Judaism's "particular folk feelings and associations" that gave "full scope to man's emotive as well as his rational capacity" (Borowitz, 2002, p. 49). By allowing for this emotive component, Kaplan's Judaism had more appeal to the young rabbinic students than the more austere classical Reform.

Moreover, unlike the classical Reform with its German roots taught at HUC, Kaplan's rationalism had an American flavor, meaning that scientific methodology could be used as a way to approach theology. The methodology transformed the supernatural God of traditional Judaism into a "process of nature," thereby depersonalizing and demythologizing God. Apparently, this depersonalized God appealed to Herman and many of his contemporaries, as did Kaplan's attack on the idea that God chose Israel, which he considered nothing more than a folk-conceit. Israel, Kaplan maintained, chose "the idea of God" (Borowitz, 2002).

Kaplan's seminal idea, soon reinforced in the publication of *Judaism in Transition* (1936), was that Judaism in the modern age was in transition and would not survive with an outdated attachment to a transcendent being. Neither traditional nor Reform Judaism "can help the Jews formulate a program of collective action that might save Jewish life from disintegration" (p. vii). Such an idea no longer vitalized the Jewish people who were in search of a new view of themselves, a central core based on the reality of their condition in the modern world (Jewish Virtual Library, "Rabbi Mordecai Kaplan," 2008). Stripped of its supernaturalism and reduced to its essence, Judaism, he maintained, was first and foremost a civilization, a people. Far from advocating a pared-down Judaism, Kaplan wrote that Judaism is robust, an "organic totality" that includes all of Jewish life. In one quick stroke, Schaalman maintains, Kaplan had substituted for Judaism's belief in God a belief in the reality of Judaism as a people, a civilization with a long and proud heritage. Despite the fact that he was an observant Jew, Kaplan argued that God did not play a role in history or in personal lives; God was more of an idea, a concept. Kaplan relegated God to a footnote to history.[79]

It is not difficult to understand how such a radical theology would not only turn on its head traditional and Reform concepts, but prove to be a rallying call to young students like Schaalman, seeking ways to counteract the influence and control of their elders. Kaplan's views captured the imagination of Herman's fellow students and helped mold their religious and theological perspectives for years to come: "I found comfort in Kaplan's views," he says in retrospect.[80] Kaplan's argument that Jewish peoplehood was the core value of Judaism provided Schaalman a coherent and organic view of reality. For the first time in his life, he began to develop new and radical ideas about Judaism. Kaplan's book, which was a serious challenge to the Judaism they were being taught, also captivated the imagination of his friends.[81]

Schaalman explains that he could become a disciple of Kaplan because, at this point in his life, the lack of theological instruction at HUC necessitated that he, along with the other students, choose whatever theology made sense at the time. One exception to this scarcity of theological instruction was the annual address of HUC's president, Julian Morgenstern, who would raise fundamental theological issues. Schaalman adds, "In general, however, because the students were typically resentful of authority, they were not receptive. In fact, they felt that the faculty treated them as if they were high school students, and they resented what they perceived as paternalism."

Despite the limitations of theological instruction at HUC, its faculty had a major impact on Herman's development. Previously, he had not had what he calls "high-level instruction" in Judaism. What he learned in his early years was "conformity," not so much in what you did, but in what you thought. At HUC, he was confronted with an entirely different approach, one that was critical of the biblical text. He learned that the Bible did not come from a divine source but was a human document derived from various sources. This revelation was not only difficult for him to accept, but actually physically painful. What made the experience of reading the Bible critically so difficult for him was that his prior training conditioned him to be obedient, to accept what he was told. "In fact," he maintains, "I only began to become an independent thinker in the last half of my life when I began to question what up to that time I considered certainties. I think this happened only in the last thirty, forty, fifty years of my life." As he was growing up, nothing theological was ever brought to his attention.

Whatever he may have thought in later years, his immediate objective was to get through his classes and graduate. For that, he needed to know what his professors expected of him. He spent six years at HUC under their tutelage, from the time he was nineteen until he graduated at twenty-five. A few of them left an indelible mark on him, especially his professor of Liturgy and Ritual, Samuel S. Cohon, who was more a "historian than a thinker." Schaalman describes him as having "an awesome effect" on him. Partly that effect was based on his awareness of Cohon's breadth and depth of knowledge, his comprehensive and profound grasp of sources and text. His limitation, according to Schaalman, was that he was more an explicator of those texts than a critical evaluator. It is on the personal level, however, that Cohon had his deepest impact on Herman. After the death of Lotte Strauss, Cohon was the first to come forward to help him "particularly [on] those [first] nights after I had found [out] about Lotte's drowning in Palestine. He was the one who took me into his home and I never forgot."

Cohon also came to his rescue when his thesis advisor, Professor Diesendruck, died suddenly from a heart attack brought on by the news of the Nazi victory over France. At the time (1940), Herman was at the beginning of his senior year and had just begun working on his thesis, "Die 'Dialoghi d'amore': Leone Ebreo." His subject was an obscure fifteenth-century philosopher in the Italian Renaissance. Although Cohon agreed to take over for Diesendruck, he was not much help because he had no interest in Herman's topic. Neither did Schaalman, "I just wrote a thesis in order to fulfill the requirement. I have no idea what I said; never reread it, don't want to."

Another of his professors who left an indelible imprint was his professor of music, Eric Werner. He was a Professor of Musicology, whom Schaalman remembers as "a fine singer" and "the most stimulating" of his professors. His special talent was to involve his students in learning, rather than employ the more typical approach of I talk, you listen. Schaalman also remembers a professor Abraham N. Franzblau, Professor of Education. Although he had only one class with him, Schaalman remembers him as a "modernist," and a "thinker." In retrospect, he wishes that he had been "smart enough to take more of his classes, even as electives. Had I done so, I might have had the opportunity to get closer to him as a person and to have woken up earlier than I did."

Initially his HUC grades were only fair, as one might expect from an English-as-a-Second-Language student, but, over the next few years, they improved significantly (Folb, 2007, p. 33). The faculty minutes of May 28, 1936, report that his advisor, Dr. Finesinger, believed Herman was a good student but was not working up to his capacity. Several other faculty members—Glueck, Cohon, and Englander—agreed with Finesinger and supported a motion that Schaalman be told "that he can do better" (p. 33).

By 1939, his grades had improved sufficiently that the faculty approved his request to work on an MA in Philosophy at the University of Cincinnati while he continued his studies at HUC. At the time of his ordination in 1941, Herman had been awarded a BA and MA from the University of Cincinnati. Although he thought of himself as an average student, Kaelter (1997) wrote that next to Plaut, of the five German immigrants, Herman was the best. (To understand the value of Kaelter's assessment, it is important to know that Plaut went on to become the foremost Reform Jewish scholar of the last half of the twentieth century.) One of Schaalman's best friends at HUC, Rabbi William B. Silverman (1986, May), described his first impression of the young man who had just arrived: "It didn't take long before his fellow students began to appreciate his spirituality, dedication, and scholarship."

Herman's German refugee colleagues were another important influence on his development. All of them were brilliant students who went on to become major figures in twentieth century Judaism. One can only imagine what it might have been like to have "bull" sessions with the likes of W. Gunther Plaut, Alfred Wolf, Wolli Kaelter, and Herman's roommate, Leo Lichtenberg.[82] According to Schaalman, "We discussed a lot of things … simply because we felt we had a different experience, came from a different background. Yet, despite the fact that we thought that what they were learning at HUC was 'strange,' we were not opposed to it." Because these young Germans had been brought up not to question authority, it is reasonable to assume that Schaalman (and possibly the others) accepted the Classical Reform practices and beliefs, even though they were at odds with their own backgrounds.

In addition to his refugee friends, Herman's two American-born friends—Lou Silberman and Dudley Weinberg—not only helped him adjust to the college and to life in America, but also helped nourish him intellectually.[83] After they tired of studying, usually around 10 p.m., the three of them used to go out together for a sandwich and a Coke (no alcohol, not even a beer) before returning to their studies, which continued until after midnight. Because Silberman and Weinburg had independent minds, both were critical of the new ideas they were learning. Schaalman thinks that had he grown up in American universities, he, too, might have had a critical cast to his thinking and that his search for selfhood and independence might have come sooner.

It is a well-known saying that all study and no play makes a dull Jack. During his early years at HUC, Schaalman learned to improve his tennis game, which became a life-long passion. Someone told him he had a "sense of the ball" that would give him an edge: "Instinctively, I knew where the ball would land." Although he had been given a tennis racket when he was thirteen, because there were no public tennis courts, he never had a chance to use it: "The only courts were private and Jews were not allowed." Plaut, who had been one of the best players on the German tennis team, gave him half a dozen lessons and even allowed him to play with him on one of the two HUC tennis courts. At HUC, according to Kaelter (1997), tennis was the game of choice: "The entire student body played, but especially the Germans" (p. 57).

Because of his fluency in English, Plaut was socially active and, according to Kaelter (1997), a lady's man. Unlike his German friends who didn't go out at night, Plaut frequently left the dorm for a date or social events. One night when he left the dorm, his friends decided to play a prank by changing his room number and everything else in the room. When he came back he was completely disoriented and "had no idea where he was" (p. 50). Another prank involved Leo Lichtenstein, who slept a lot and very deeply. On one occasion, his friends picked him up, bed and all, and carried him into the shower (Kaelter, 1997). "At first," remembered Rabbi Silverman (1986), "[Herman] was most reluctant to participate in the pranks occasioned by the boredom that would punctuate the long hours of learning grammar, Torah and Mishna. After a while he caught on."

Despite his difficulties with English, Schaalman published a book review of Solomon Goldman's *The Golden Chain: Torah and the Earlier Prophets* (1937) in the May 1938 issue of the *Hebrew Union College Monthly*, a student/faculty publication (Folb, 2007, p. 34). Although

HUC class of 1941: first row, left to right, first person, Alfred Wolf; second person, Herman Schaalman; fourth person, Lou Silverman; second row, last from left, Malcolm Stern; third row, second person from left, standing, Sylvan Schwartzman; first person to Schwartzman's right, sitting, William Silverman; last row, fifth from left, Asher Gordon; last person, row three, behind Stern, Dudley Weinberg.

not important in itself, the review represents the beginning of Schaalman's attempt to have his voice heard beyond the confines of the college. Schaalman's review reveals how far he had come in his acculturation as a Reform Jew. He is critical of the author's negative attitude toward the scientific approach to the Bible. For a German refugee who knew no English when he came to America three years earlier, Schaalman's review is a remarkable piece of writing and an early indication of the outstanding prose of his mature years.

At the end of the academic year when all the other students went home or off to other places, Herman spent his first summer alone in the dormitory. Unlike his refugee colleagues who had made outside connections, Herman had none. At nineteen and never having been away from his family and friends, he felt intensely lonely. Because the dormitory was locked at night, he had been given a key to the building and, when he returned to the dark interior, he whistled just to hear a sound. Although he did some work for Dr. Jacob Marcus, it was Lillian Waldman who made his life more bearable.

To alleviate his loneliness, Schaalman decided to follow up on his father's recommendation that he contact the Samfield family. From the postcard his father had shown him, he knew that his great uncle, Rabbi Max Samfield, lived in Memphis, Tennessee. More than twenty years had passed since his death in 1915, and, when Schaalman contacted his family, they sent word that they would be happy to meet him. Samfield was survived by his wife and four children, two sons and two daughters, none of whom were married. Although Schaalman was delighted to find family members in America, neither he nor the Samfield family followed up this first contact. They did not meet until the early years of the 1950s.

Only a year after beginning his rabbinic studies at HUC, a series of events began to unfold that laid the foundation for his later career. Schaalman claims that none of them was planned nor were their future outcomes predictable. In 1936, he received an invitation from the Secretary of the Union of American Hebrew Congregations, Rabbi Louis Egelson, to come to Chicago to lead High Holy Day services for a new congregation of German refugees.[84] Schaalman accepted the offer and led that first service in the German Liberal tradition he and they had grown up in (Ner Talmid Ezra Habonim Congregation of Northtown, 2007). Apparently impressed by the young rabbinic student, Dr. Louis L. Mann, Chicago Sinai's rabbi and one of the most famous Reform rabbis in America, requested that Schaalman come once a month to lead services for the German congregation (Folb, 2007, p. 33).[85]

This experience of conducting a service in America was a first for Schaalman. He had never written a sermon, but within three weeks, he would be conducting a service at one of Chicago's most prestigious congregations.[86] "I was scared to death because I was only half way through my rabbinic training and did not consider himself qualified or capable. Even now I can still feel my stomach turning somersaults when I think of it."

Arthur Strauss, the president of Sinai's Men's Club, wanted to provide an enjoyable Rosh Hashanah service for his mother and sister, whom he had brought over from Germany. He invited Schaalman to dinner on the two nights of Rosh Hashanah and persuaded him to lead a special service for his mother and sister. During the dinner, Strauss surprised Schaalman by telling him that, as an indication of the importance of the service, "At this very moment, an announcement was being made as part of a radio program that was being broadcast from an airplane flying over the city." Schaalman was even more surprised when Strauss told him that the announcement included his name as the leader of the service. The reader can imagine how this new information only compounded the rabbi's anxiety.

The service was held in the Emil G. Hirsch Annex building of Chicago Sinai Congregation on South Parkway and 47th Street. Rabbi Mann introduced Schaalman to the congregation of about 800 refugees. "I had never seen that many Jews together, except in Munich, where I was a worshipper, not an officiant." He could take comfort in the fact that, like his father, he had an excellent cantorial voice, and that the cantor was the famous opera singer, Madame Sonia Sharnova, a star of the Metropolitan Opera in New York City.

Officials, anticipating that the congregation would respond better to a service conducted in their native language, instructed Schaalman to conduct the service in German. They made available the Einhorn prayer book, a nineteenth-century prayer book, originally written in German by one of the earliest Reform rabbis in America, and later translated into English. Schaalman remembers that this translation, which was in plentiful supply at Sinai, "turned out to be a total failure." At the end of the first day of services, the congregation requested that Schaalman use a Hebrew prayer book, like the one they had used in Germany. Instead of the traditional blowing of the Shofar at the end of the service, a cornet player performed the traditional melody from behind a curtain. For the refugees, this substitution for the blast of the Shofar, considered the most solemn and inspirational moment in the High Holy Day service, was distasteful. Schaalman remembers that "the High Holy Day service as a disaster for the refugees."

Little did he know at that time that the experience in Chicago was to become the launching pad for his professional development. He had barely begun rabbinic school, when he was already officiating in Chicago. Rabbi Mann had identified Schaalman as an outstanding choice for an assistant rabbi. He pointed out to his secretary that a second desk in his office would be for Schaalman. Although at the time Schaalman was flattered with the comment, he had no idea that it was prophetic of his long career in that city. Nor did he have any idea of the tragedy that was awaiting him that would also transform his life. In retrospect, as if looking at his life from a distance, Schaalman remarks, "This trajectory of my life is astounding. I never planned it. It just happened."

Return to Germany: 1937

Before he left Germany, Herman had promised his family he would come home in two years to attend Freddie's Bar Mitzvah. After HUC agreed that he would be allowed to return to the seminary, in 1937 Herman and two of his refugee friends returned to Germany (Folb, 2007, p. 29).[87] Plaut (1981) was one of them. He had been warned by one of his professors not to take the chance of going home because the Nazis might not let him return to America (p. 71). Like Schaalman, he had promised his family that he would only stay away for two years and come home to attend his brother William's high school graduation. Plaut characterized his decision to make this risky journey as "one of the most stupid chances I have ever taken" (p. 72).

In his decision to return home, Herman was not as much worried about his safety but about how his father would view the new Judaism he had adopted. He was surprised to learn that his father did not object but wanted to know only whether his son was "getting a good education ... was he able to pray" and "was he on good terms with God?" Nor did he mind that his son's lifestyle was changing and becoming different from his own. Nevertheless, when at home with his father, Herman reverted to the liturgical practices he had been taught. (Ten years later after his parents had immigrated to Brazil and he had not seen them during that time, he reverted to davenning with his father as he always had before. As a clear sign that his father accepted his son's new ways, he bragged about him to his Brazil friends and never challenged his authenticity as a Reform rabbi.)

A second reason Herman wanted to go home was to see his girlfriend. He had promised her they would become engaged when he returned. Looking back at the decision, he commented, "Returning to Germany at that time, was foolish, foolhardy ... in fact things happened then that really underscored how hare-brained it was." According to his brother,

Freddie, the family thought he was "crazy" to take such a risk. "Many people cried, including friends of the family. They could not understand why Adolf allowed his son to come home. The Nazis were putting many young people who had returned to Germany from America in concentration camps because they thought they were spies for America."

By this time, most of the infamous anti-Semitic laws and government actions had been put in place. State governments had stopped issuing licenses to Jewish doctors, veterinarians, and pharmacists. Jews were no longer allowed to sit for professional exams, and a ban was in place to prevent anyone related by marriage to a Jew to teach in a vocational or agricultural school (Barkai, 1998). Mixed marriages had been outlawed, as was the ability to hide one's Jewish identity by changing either one's first or last name. The schools had been racially segregated, and the *Nuremberg* Laws had been enacted to protect Aryan blood, including a prohibition of marriage or sexual relations between Aryans and Jews (Barkai, 1998). A German who had Jewish grandparents four generations removed was still a Jew, though only considered one quarter Jewish; a German two generations removed from Jewish grandparents, was one-half Jewish. Half-Jews were to be treated as Jews, and quarter-Jews were not allowed to marry Aryans but only other Jews (Barkai, 1998).

Because of these political developments, Schaalman was almost trapped in Germany. To return to America, he needed a student visa. At the time, he did not consider emigration an option. Even if he had wanted to, given the fact that large numbers of German Jews were fleeing the country, emigration was risky. He would have had to take his chances by subjecting himself to America's tight immigration quotas.

The only way he could get the visa was to pull strings. His mother's cousin in Stuttgart, Oscar Wanschel, a commercial consul to the Republic of Panama, came to his rescue. Wanschel knew the American consul who had helped Herman get his first student visa. In order to get the visa, you had to prove that your English skills were sufficient to benefit from study in the United States. The American council's wife, who was German, had the responsibility of certifying the young man's English skills. When Schaalman met with her over tea in her home, they spoke to each other in English: "I could barely speak," Schaalman recalls, "but she couldn't either." When she reported to her husband that the young man had the requisite skills, he issued the visa.

Herman and mother, São Paulo, 1958

Having accomplished his mission of attending his brother's Bar Mitzvah, Schaalman was eager to cut his vacation short and return to America. Having lived the United States for two years, he could see the dangers Nazi Germany posed to the Jews and the fragility of Jewish life, but he still hadn't visited his girlfriend.

The Schaalmans had already felt the first of the direct impact of the Nazi takeover. According to Stern (1983), in April 1933, most Jews "were deprived of their civil service jobs—their university, clinical, or judicial appointments—simply on the basis of race" (p. 15). The Law for the Restoration of the Professional Civil Service ordered "the immediate forced retirement of all 'non-Aryan' government employees" (Barkai, 1998, p. 201). President Hindenburg, however, appealed to Hitler to exempt combat veterans. As a result, Adolf, a decorated veteran of World War I, was allowed to keep his job until 1936 and his pension for life. By this time, the situation for German Jewry was deteriorating rapidly. The aim of the Nazis was to make life in Germany intolerable for Jews and to drive them out. The effort covered all aspects of German life, economic, political, and social. By 1936, one report[88] estimated that 20–22 percent of the Jewish population was now dependant on welfare and that another 20–25 percent was living off their savings (Barkai, 1998, p. 241).

One example of the effort to humiliate the Jews was the vicious signage that popped up throughout the country. Uncle Eddie, the Schwinn salesman, who lived in Frankfurt on the Main, reported that when he drove through German villages in 1937, he saw banners proclaiming "Jews Enter at Their Own Peril." By that time, also, restaurants and inns posted signs: "No Dogs or Jews served." In response to these developments, Schaalman tried to convince his parents to leave, but his father obstinately refused. He believed passionately that he had a right to remain in his country. After all, he had sacrificed too much as a four-year veteran serving on the front line during World War I. Moreover, he could trace his ancestry back four hundred years, and his family had always been loyal citizens. He became even more stubbornly German: "Mother and the boys can go, I'll never leave. I'll get a gun and, if I have to, I'll die shooting a few of them. I will not leave!" His mother's response was equally definitive, "It's out of the question. I'm staying with father." This question of whether to stay or to leave was being asked at dinner tables of Jews throughout the country.

Adolf decided to remain because he was not convinced that his situation or that of the Jews was hopeless. He thought it prudent to "wait and see," and, if need be, to "tough it out." In this, he had lots of company. Barkai (1998) notes that, dire as the situation had become for Jews, by 1937 the German economy was improving dramatically, and the political climate had stabilized. These two conditions, especially the economic one, which allowed "numerous economically active Jews" to benefit, "raised Jewish hopes that they could somehow survive the difficulties in Germany" (p. 205).[89] People who lived through this period reported retrospectively that compared to the excesses of the initial Nazi triumph and horror of subsequent events, and despite sporadic anti-Semitic incidents, this period was generally tolerable. Moreover, men were reluctant to leave in part because they were "attached to their professional identities [and] needed more time to adjust to the idea of emigration" (Barkai, 1998c, p. 250). They realized that they would have to find new, and, probably, less prestigious means of making a living. However, in the final two years leading up to the War, all doubts about the need to get out of the country vanished. In order to purge the country of its still large Jewish population, the Nazis instituted a more radical policy of interring Jews in concentration camps (p. 250).

When it was clear to Herman that he could not change his father's mind, he decided to leave as quickly as possible. He realized, too, that had his parents wanted to go, he was in no position to pay for their transportation or for their support in America. Although he had a scholarship to attend school, he had no money of his own. To travel to Germany he had had to borrow his travel expenses and now lacked the money to return to America. He wrote to his cousin in Stuttgart to ask for help and was so anxious about being trapped in Germany that he hand-carried the letter to the post office. As he was leaving the post office, he noticed the clerk examining the letter and holding it up to the light. It occurred to Herman that perhaps his father's mail (his father's return address was on the envelope) was being searched or opened and read. When he recounted this event to his father, his father said immediately, "I'll tell you what; tomorrow we go on a vacation, you and I. We'll go mountain climbing. We'll go away for three or four days."

The next morning the bell rang sometime between 4:30 or 5:00 a.m., the hour the Gestapo used to come by. Adolf told his son, "Lock yourself in the closet while I open the door." Seized with fear and dread, "My whole life passed before me." To the family's immense relief, the person at the door was delivering a telegram from his cousin stating that everything was in order and that Herman should proceed to Stuttgart. Why the telegram had to be delivered at that time remains a mystery, but it ruled out the vacation; Herman left for Stuttgart as quickly as he could.

Yet, he had one more mission to complete. He had not yet visited his girlfriend, Lotte Strauss. He took the train to Ulm[90] and spent the night at her home. Now that he was twenty-one, he was old enough for the couple to be formally engaged and to plan their marriage the following year. Because Lotte was less observant than he, while he was away, she went to Würzburg to study with an Orthodox rabbi to prepare herself for a more traditionally religious life (Folb, 2007, p. 20). The next morning, while he was getting ready to leave, Lotte's parents asked him to take some valuables, including a pure gold cigarette case and a large tube of toothpaste from which the toothpaste had been removed and replaced with a large sum of currency. Because he was fearful of the consequences of being caught with the money, he refused to take it.[91]

In order to return to America, Herman needed someone to vouch for him. The president of HUC provided the necessary documentation.

Interesting in this regard is the fact that the HUC Board of Trustees was aware that Schaalman's return was not guaranteed; they knew his visit to Germany was a risky enterprise. Nonetheless, HUC absorbed most of the cost. When Schaalman returned to America, neither he nor his family had any idea that they would not see each other again for ten years.

Death of Lotte Strauss

After returning to HUC, Herman and Lotte kept in touch by mail. In one of her letters, she informed him that she and her parents were leaving for Palestine to live near one of her brothers, a Zionist and a founder of the city of Nahariya. At the time, they were one of a relatively small number of German Jewish families to leave Germany for Palestine (Alon, 2002, p. 379).

Sometime later, Lotte wrote again to tell him that her father had died but that she and her mother had decided to remain in Palestine. Instead of getting married in the United States where she had an older sister, Herman and Lotte decided to marry in Palestine and then return together to Cincinnati. When it was time for the wedding, Schaalman arranged passage on a steamer to Haifa on a Sunday in June of 1938. He arranged to meet Lotte's sister in New York. His plan was to take a sleeper the night before his departure and arrive in New York by noon on Sunday before the ship departed in the afternoon. His German refugee friends sponsored a farewell luncheon. That morning, Herman received a cable from his parents urging him to "be strong." At the time, he did not realize the import of the cable. While waiting for his friends to arrive, Herman felt that something was amiss. "I found myself completely alone and concluded that my friends were planning to surprise me. Then, Wolli Kaelter, came in as white as a sheet and handed me a cable announcing that Lotte had drowned in Nahariya." The telegram from his parents, he realized, indicated that they knew about Lotte's death before he did.

News of Lotte's death wiped out a vital part of Schaalman's life. "Yet, despite my grief, I took the train to New York to meet Lotte's sister because I felt that we could comfort each other. To this day, I still grieve for Lotte. During my many trips to Israel, I always make time to visit her grave in Nahariya." For more than sixty-five years, he has maintained a friendship with her family, which, incidentally, "became the largest ice cream and butter manufacturer in Israel."

Fortunately, his friends rushed to his aid to help him survive the most difficult challenge of his life. While he was in New York, they made plans to take care of him during the summer so that he would not be alone. Their plan was to take him during the summer months to various cities where they had friend or family connections. Rabbi Bernard Rosenberg would take him on the first leg of the journey. Rosenberg had just been ordained and had been assigned as the assistant of Temple De-Hirsch in Seattle. When Herman had arrived at HUC, Rosenberg, then an upperclassmen, befriended the young man at a time when he was in great need of help. The two drove to Seattle, where Herman would begin his summer odyssey. In preparation for the trip, Rosenberg went to Flint, Michigan, to pick up a new car and then drove to Chicago to pick up Schaalman who had arrived there by train from Cincinnati. "For me the trip was an exciting adventure. Not only would I get to see a substantial part of America, but also have a chance to ride in a new car!"

Rosenberg decided to make his first stop Cedar Rapids, Iowa, partly because it was a comfortable drive of five or six hours from Chicago, but mostly because his Aunt Tillie lived there. For the cash-strapped young men, the likelihood of the aunt putting them up for the night and feeding them was an important consideration. They arrived late in the afternoon and spent a delightful evening with her before leaving the next morning. To Herman, Rosenberg's aunt was "a character." "During dinner, she defamed virtually every member of the Jewish community in Cedar Rapids … because she and her somewhat deranged brother, who lived with her, had apparently run afoul of the congregation. She called them swindlers and criminals, the dregs of the earth." As they drove out of town the next morning, Schaalman turned to Rosenberg and said, "Boy, this is sure the last place I would ever want to go to." Two years later, HUC's president gave him his first rabbinic assignment at Temple Judah in Cedar Rapids.

After spending part of the summer in Seattle recovering from his grief, Schaalman moved on to San Francisco and roomed with another classmate and friend, Lou Silberman. The next stage on this journey of recovery was Los Angeles, where Silberman took him when he went to visit his grandmother. From there, Herman was sent to Dallas, where he spent the remainder of his summer with another of his seminary friends, Rabbi David Shor. The trip proved to be therapeutic: "My friends' extraordinary efforts rescued me from my grief and helped me readjust to life and to some semblance of normalcy."

The Nazi Terror and the Schaalman Family

When the Nazi took over Germany in 1933, Germany's Jews were not prepared for the aggressive measures taken against them. As they were gradually stripped of their civil and political rights, "they passed their days strung out between hope and desperation, making an endless chain of painful decisions or postponing them. ..." (Barkai, 1998b, p. 231). At the same time, the Nazis' consolidation of their political hold on Germany not only affected the Jews, but anyone who opposed the Nazis, including unionists, socialists, and Christian clergy who might have, and actually did, speak out against them. Yet, Schaalman recalls,

> Germany was a police state even before the Nazis came to power. When guests stayed three or more days in your home, the host had to go to the police station to fill out a special form acknowledging that guests were present. This requirement applied even if the guests were relatives such as cousins, or grandparents. In this way, the government was able to keep track of its citizens. Their location was part of the police record.

Herman's hometown of Munich had the less-than-honorable distinction of being one of the most volatile regions in the country, and perhaps because of that, it became the launching pad for the rise of the Nazi party. In 1923, the Nazis launched an abortive coup in Munich. According to Barkai (1998), the effort reflected "the depth and virulence of popular antipathy to the Jews" (p. 49). Long after the end of World War II, survivors still struggle with the trauma the Nazis inflicted, reparations in terms of stolen property are still being made, and a new generation of Germans is attempting to heal the wounds created by their parents. The Schaalman family is still living with its effects.

Once the Nazis achieved national power in 1933, the Schaalman family was changed forever. In May of that year, the Nazis began a reign of terror. Almost immediately, they confiscated the property of fifty

Jewish organizations, and, soon after, members of the Storm Troopers (SA), Hitler Youth (Hitlerjugend), and employees of the Nazi newspaper, *Der Stürmer*, began to attack Jewish-owned businesses and beat up Jews they found in the streets (Yad Vashem, 2006). Their objective was not only to destroy the Jewish economy, but also to send a clear message that Jews were unwanted and would not be tolerated. Their tactics included pressuring Jewish business owners to close their businesses, and discouraging Germans from patronizing those that remained open (Yad Vashem, 2006).[92]

Over the next five years, conditions for Germany's Jews continued to deteriorate. On November 9 and 10, 1938, the Nazis unleashed their most devastating attack to date. The pretext was the assassination by a Jew of a German official in Paris on November 7, 1938. Goebbels, Nazi Minister of Propaganda, seized on the event as an opportunity to attack international Jewry and Jews living in Germany (Barkai, 1998). Billed as a means to avenge the murder, a well-organized effort was launched from Munich throughout Germany and Austria. The night of terror, known as "Kristallnacht," was carried out by German SS and SA units, some dressed in civilian clothes.[93] The 400 synagogues that had not yet been destroyed were burned to the ground (Barkai, 1998). Another 7,500 Jewish-owned stores were looted and destroyed. Approximately 30,000 Jews, many of them wealthy and prominent members of their communities, were arrested and deported to Dachau (Yad Vashem, [n.d.], "Kristallnacht"). Adolf Schaalman was one of them.[94]

As part of the crackdown, the Nazis passed a law forbidding Jewish children from attending public schools. Freddie Schaalman remembers that when he showed up to school the day after Kristallnacht, November 10, 1938, he was told he could no longer attend the school. This event turned out to be the last day of Freddie's formal education. Although he took some private lessons with a Jewish professor, as he remembers it, "There was no learning. The lessons were only a way to fill the time."[95] Ernst, on the other hand, was more fortunate. His parents had sent him to a finishing school in Berlin, where he lived in a Jewish "kinder home." After he graduated in July 1938, they sent him to England to finish high school.

Another consequence of the rampant official and unofficial anti-Semitism was that Freddie was no longer able to play with his Aryan friends. Because there were no other Jewish children in the neighborhood, he remained at home with his mother; travel in the city to other neighborhoods was simply too dangerous for a Jewish child. Freddie remembers occasions when his father had to take him to school because he was liable to be set upon by Hitler Youth. When he was not with his father, they threatened and even attacked him. "They were cowards, who would only attack in numbers. I never ran from them out of fear. When I was attacked in school, usually between classes, I defended myself and earned some respect from the other boys." Like his oldest brother, he never backed down from a fight, no matter what the odds. In some of these fights, his brother Ernst came to his defense. "Had my 'big' brother Herman not been away in Berlin attending the seminary, I would have been able to count on his assistance as well."

Herman, on the other hand, while he was in grammar school, had some protection because his father was a teacher. When Adolf visited his sons' schools to meet with their teachers, typically they were his friends, and, although they were wearing Nazi uniforms, they treated him with respect. The only way they could keep their jobs was to wear the uniform. No matter what their politics, they had to become at least *de facto* Nazis.

Teachers were not the only ones to wear Nazi uniforms, but children wore their Hitler Youth movement uniforms to school. Schaalman reports that in his school one or two students dressed in SA uniforms and intimidated the professor who lost his authority. Schaalman also remembers when the Nazi flag raising became a fact of life in his school. "It was a demonstration of the power and authority the Nazis had over the education system." The first time the flag was raised in the schoolyard, one of the tallest boys in the class accused Herman of "slandering it." He had not said anything, but he knew he was in trouble. Although he knew who made the remark, he was not about to tell. While his teacher stood by helplessly, his accuser "pulled out his watch and said, 'I'll give you ten seconds to retract what you have said or else I'll go the Gestapo." When the thirty seconds had passed, he closed up his grandfather's watch and hauled off to belt the little boy. The next moment, the attacker found himself flat on his back, the result of a jujitsu move that Schaalman had learned. From that moment on, no one dared to touch him for the next two-and-a-half years he spent in the school.

According to Barkai (1998c), this kind of intimidation was not un-usual for Jewish schoolchildren, who were frequently bullied and intimidated by non-Jewish children. The Jewish children experienced this harassment in classes, on the playground, and on the way to and from school. Harassment was also meted out by teachers and school administrators, though not by all. Some of them were sympathetic and aware of the psychological and physical burden their Jewish students were experiencing. While at school, the Jewish pupils would be forced to participate in the daily opening ceremonies that included raising the Nazi flag, the Nazi salute, and participation in compulsory "racial studies" programs (Barkai, 1998c). As time went on, however, in order to keep their jobs, more and more teachers sought to harass their Jewish students as a way of demonstrating their Nazi zeal.

The Schaalman boys had frequent anti-Semitic encounters both in and out of school. One of them, which might be considered humorous, involved Herman Schaalman as a high school student. Among the indignities Jewish students had to endure were lessons about their own inferiority and denunciations of Jews as criminals and subversives (Barkai, 1998c). Because the Nazis were fanatically concerned about the dilution of the superior Aryan gene pool, they developed a specious science of physical characteristics to identify an Aryan and a non-Aryan. A key measure was physiognomy. When specialists in the new science came to the schools, Jewish children were required to sit through their virulent anti-Semitic propaganda while their classmates stared at them as models of the despised race (Barkai, 1998c). Schaalman recalls that one of these "experts" on racial theories and profiles came to his school to teach the students how to identify Jews. Ironically, he picked out the handsome young Schaalman as an example of the second-best Aryan racial type. "When my teacher whispered in his ear that I was the last Jewish student in the school, he fled and never returned."

Although the students were being propagandized to despise and reject Jews, they did not entirely reject Schaalman, who, we must assume, was well liked. Together with the school administration, they invited him to the graduation dance. Unwilling to give them the impression that he was afraid to go, he took his Jewish girlfriend to the dance. They did not stay for the whole event, just one dance to show them he was not afraid. He knew full well, however, that the presence of this Jewish couple was a stain on the others, most of them Nazi sympathizers or Nazis.

This Nazification had been under way for some time and was manifested in anti-Semitic remarks made in class, though never directly to Schaalman, who escaped untouched. Nonetheless, he found it difficult to avoid anti-Semitic confrontations. A near miss for one of them occurred when he and his father were riding on a streetcar. His father, who thought of himself as the epitome of the Jewish stereotype (in his own words, "My dark hair and prominent nose makes me look like a whole synagogue") deliberately took out his Jewish newspaper and began to read it. Schaalman remembers, "I was sitting close to him and was ready to spring on the first attacker." Remarkably, no one bothered them.

Adolf felt entitled to his place in Germany; after all, his family's roots went back to 1519 in Regensburg, and he had spent four-and-a-half years in the trenches fighting for Germany. Like so many other German Jews, his family had lived in Germany for centuries. This history was also the reason he did not want to emigrate. Nevertheless, when Herman returned in 1937, he begged his father to leave. Having lived in the United States for two years, he had developed a perspective on events in Germany that his parents lacked: "They were blind to the dangers because the loss of their liberties was incremental and not sudden. They learned to live with each loss by rationalizing, 'Okay, we can live with that.'" Or, "We can make an adjustment to that.'"[96] They learned to live with such indignities as banners hung in villages declaring, "Jews can enter only at their own risk," and inns and restaurants that would not serve Jews. Even park benches in Schaalman's neighborhood had signs like, "No Jews allowed to sit on this bench." Schaalman remembers election posters that read, "Jews are our misfortune. Germans, protect your wives and daughters against Jews."

Still, Jewish people dismissed the significance of these signs as trifles, an annoyance, but something they could live with; nobody believed these civil rights infringements would last. Stern (1983) points out that this belief was based on the thought "that in time the National Socialists would moderate, that anti-Semitism had had a long history in Germany that these new manifestations were but the old anti-Semitism revisited …" (pp. 19-20). Because acts of spontaneous anti-Semitism in early 1933 were few, Jews believed that the official boycott did not have much effect. Moreover, during the first few years after Hitler's election, Germans continued to use Jewish doctors and lawyers and, to some extent, maintained social relationships with Jews (Stern, 1983). In retrospect, the belief that these events were only temporary was, at best, naïve and, at worst, catastrophic.

The ascendancy of the Nazis naturally affected Jews attending synagogue services on the High Holy Days. When Jews went to services on Rosh Hashanah and Yom Kippur, they wore opera hats as part of the required holiday uniform. If a man came to services without one, the *shamas* would provide one. Without the hat, you could not be called to the Torah. Schaalman remembers walking to services during the Nazi period with his father and feeling as if the hat was a "provocation of the worst kind," although nothing ever happened to them. Other Jews, however, were assaulted, though not necessarily for wearing the opera hat. Schaalman remembers that one of his Jewish friends, Franz Weil, was beaten regularly, and, to spare him further harm, his parents sent him to Switzerland to finish school.

Schaalman also had a narrow escape from a situation that might have turned into a violent confrontation. He had taken the train to visit his girlfriend, Lotte Strauss. When he took the train home, he found himself in a car filled with drunken SA men who were returning from a mass rally with Hitler. "They were shouting and singing and when they noticed me, a teenage boy who didn't look Jewish, they put their arms around me and sang and danced with me. One of the songs they sang was 'When Jewish blood spurts from the knife, then everything goes good.'" This revelry went on for over an hour until the train arrived in Munich. Schaalman reflects, "If they had known I was Jewish, the outcome might have been a catastrophe." He had heard rumors of Jews being beaten to death in the streets (Rodin-Novak, 2001, p. 33).

One of those rumors was about one or two attorneys who had defended communists, socialists, and labor leaders and who were murdered in cold blood. Still, people said to themselves, "This is Germany … the land of Goethe, Schiller, Beethoven, Mozart"—how could such things happen here? It must be a temporary illness that the nation will get over in a few months, perhaps a year or two."

During the Nazi era, the Schaalman family lost almost all their gentile friends. This experience was common and a source of great disappointment, especially for those who thought of themselves as successfully assimilated (Barkai, 1998c). To be friends with a Jew or a Jewish family was dangerous and required great courage. Not only you, but also your entire family might have to bear serious consequences. Jewish men and women experienced this ostracism as they were gradually excluded from organizations, associations, and clubs (Barkai, 1998c). Only one of his father's colleagues kept in occasional contact with him. The loss of gentile friends, however, was not the family's greatest loss. Most of the family perished in the *Shoah*.

On Kristallnacht when Adolf was rounded up and sent to Dachau, a concentration camp only ten miles outside of Munich, the Schaalman family found itself in desperate straits. Herman, of course, knew nothing of this event. On November 9, 1938, he was in Cincinnati conducting the wedding service of his friend Gunther Plaut. As Herman was chanting the service under the huppah, he was called out and presented with an urgent cable sent by his mother: "'Father in Dachau. Save him!" Although he could do nothing himself, he was fortunate that attending the wedding were people with political clout: Professor Englander, the officiating Rabbi, and Dr. Julian Morgenstern, the President of HUC. As soon as he concluded the service, he showed the cable to Morgenstern, who immediately made a phone call to Senator Alfred Cohen, a man with considerable influence. He was the Chairman of the Board of the College, the International President of B'nai Brith, and a State Senator. Cohen got in touch with the State Department and within a few hours, Schaalman was told not to worry because the roundup was a mass action not directed at his father.

One hope for Herman was that prisoners could get out of a concentration camp if they could obtain a visa and pay for their own transportation.[97] In an effort to do all he could to secure his father's release, he tried to get his father a position as a cantor in a small congregation in Hamilton, Ohio, where he taught Sunday school. Cantors and rabbis did not have to wait in line as part of the emigration quota because they had priority status. Schaalman described the quota as deadly because it took so long: "People committed suicide, often in the consulates, waiting, hoping for a quota." After the congregation's board deliberated for several days, they decided against offering Adolf the position. Hebrew Union College, despite its political connections, was unsuccessful in getting the family out of Germany.

Unable to wait for a response from her son, Regina knew she had to get to Stuttgart where her cousin was a consul and could provide protection for a few weeks until things calmed down. (Consulates provided a safe haven because they were extra-territorial, and so far, the Nazis had not touched them.) She appealed to Herman's childhood friend, Albert Klein, who agreed to help. Dressed in his SS uniform, he escorted her with her sons Freddie and Ernst to the train station. In Stuttgart, she found the protection she sought. Her cousin secured the release of her husband, who already had spent six weeks in Dachau, and helped arrange for the family to get to Brazil.

Regina's next move was to cable her brother Phineas in São Paulo. When the cable arrived, Phineas' wife, Ollie, took charge. In the late 1930s, Brazil accepted only Catholics and farmers, not professors of mathematics or physics who were Jewish. Because of that restriction, there was little chance they could get Adolf and his family into Brazil. Tante Ollie, however, was a resourceful woman with a great deal of personality. It did not take her long to concoct a plan.[98] It was simple, but audacious. She would pay a personal call on the Secretary of State in Rio, the seat of the government.

After arriving by train, she scoped out his office for several days, observing his habits. She discovered that he took a daily siesta at noon. When she was confident that she could rely on this schedule, she waited outside his office for him to leave for his siesta and then promptly "fainted" in front of him. Because the Secretary was a true Portuguese aristocrat, she counted on him coming to her rescue. Without hesitation, he picked her up and carried her into his office. When he "revived" her, he asked whether there was anything he could do for her. Without hesitation she replied, "'You can save the lives of my darling brother-in-law and his family.'" He responded by asking her what she needed, to which she responded "four immigration certificates for Brazil." The Secretary promptly wrote them out and went home for his siesta.

Even with the visas, the Schaalmans had a difficult time leaving Germany. Freddie remembers the long lines of people waiting to get a number for approval from the immigration authorities. To be sure they would get a number, he went to the immigration office at 3:00 a.m. so that, when his father arrived at 8 a.m., he would have a position near the front of the line. The immigration office closed at 1 p.m., and, if

Herman and Regina, 1937

your number were not called that day, you were simply out of luck and were told to come again tomorrow and take another number. One of the advantages the Schaalmans had in being processed by the immigration authorities was that because Adolph was collecting a pension for his military service during World War I, he had a clear paper trail for his income. The authorities quickly determined that the family had no financial problems that might prevent them from leaving the country.

They left on August 24, 1939, a week before the start of World War II. This harrowing experience destroyed Adolf's illusions about his value as a German citizen. Later, he told his son, "I found out that I was not beloved by them." Schaalman understood these words as his father's way of admitting that he had been wrong all along.

On their way to Brazil, the family went first to England to meet up with Ernst, whom they had sent there as a way to use every possible means to get the family out of Germany. When the family arrived in Brazil, they had only twenty German marks in their pocket. They moved in with Regina's brother Phineas, who had emigrated to Brazil in the 1920s and had become well off. To help the family survive, Freddie had to go to work immediately and was not able to continue his education, though he was only fifteen at the time. We may assume, too, that Ernst, who was eighteen at the time, had to find work as well. Happily for the family, Adolf found a job as a mathematician for an architectural firm founded by a refugee from Vienna. Adolf's mathematical skills allowed him to perform calculations related to engineering and architectural problems related to the various structural projects of his employer. In addition to his earnings, Adolf had his pension from the German government that allowed the family to live decently. After he died in 1957, Regina continued to receive his pension until her death.[99]

Once Adolf was making a comfortable living, the family sought quarters of their own. They moved twice before Adolf built a house. Partly, it was financed by his son Herman, who sent him the money to buy a large 150-foot deep lot in a decent residential neighborhood. Because he was working for an architectural firm, the company built the house. Regina lived in it until she died in 1986 at the age of ninety-three, when it was sold by her son Ernst, now known as "Ernesto."[100]

Although physically cut off from each other, the family maintained a lively contact by mail. Nevertheless, the radical change in environment for the family resulted in a major unintended consequence. One of Schaalman's nieces married a Sephardic Jew. For an Ashkenazi family, particularly a German Ashkenazi family, this development posed a significant challenge to family cohesion. Perhaps because his parents remembered the difficulty they encountered from his family when Adolf married a Russian woman, or because of the adjustment to the great changes, they had already experienced as immigrants in a foreign land, they were able to accept this new reality.

Possibly the greatest impact of the Nazis on the Schaalmans was the traumatic separation of their family. As a result, Herman had only occasional contact with them. Not only did he not see his parents for ten years after his short visit home in 1937, but, he has commented, "I had to live by myself and go through every major stage of my life without anybody with me. Not until I found Lotte [Stern] in 1940 did things begin to fall in place." The family's immigration to Brazil created not only a geographical but also a religious divide with long-term consequences for the family's cohesion. In Germany, the family had been Liberal Jews, but in Brazil, Schaalman's family became more religiously observant, while he, due to circumstances largely beyond his control, became a Reform Jew. Of his two brothers, Ernst remained more "liberal" than Freddie, who adopted traditional Jewish Orthodoxy and, in 1972, made *aliyah* to Israel.[101] One of his reasons for moving his family to Israel was that he did not want his children to marry Brazilians.

The theological divide between Schaalman and his youngest brother has had profound consequences for both of them. Schaalman considers his brother's "conversion," a case of "arrested religious development." Freddie is so religious that, when he moved to Jerusalem, he would not take the elevator during Shabbat to his apartment in his thirty-story building. In the heat of the summer, because he could not climb the stairs to his tenth floor apartment, he was forced to move. Schaalman deplores what he considers the Orthodox value system. To him, Orthodoxy is based on a sense of guilt that one is never good enough to live up to the commandments. To be holy in the eyes of one's neighbors and to please God, one must lead an exemplary life that fulfills the commandments. "This need creates a basis for anxiety because one is never fully capable of wholly fulfilling all the commandments. Orthodox Jews are forced to judge their every action against the actions of their neighbors. If one perceives that a neighbor is more observant, then one may feel less than adequate. This attempt to emulate and outdo one's neighbors produces a further increase in behavioral restrictions. My choice is to be free to engage in a relationship with God that is based on gratitude to God for who He is, rather than attempt to fulfill what is virtually an impossible set of commandments." Instead of locking himself into a set of beliefs and religious practices required by the Orthodox, Schaalman has kept himself open to new ideas and considers himself a work in progress.

Freddie, on the other hand, has no sympathy for his brother's Reform Judaism. To him it is not Judaism as he knows and understands it. The brothers kept the peace by not discussing their religious beliefs. During his years in Israel, Freddie established a large Schaalman clan, all

Orthodox, and two of his offspring are Orthodox rabbis. Sadly, his oldest brother, his children and grandchildren have almost no contact with the Israeli side of their family.

"The real tragedy of the family," according to Schaalman, "is that it is scattered in various cemeteries in foreign lands; my grandmother is buried in Munich, my father-in-law in London, my sister-in-law in Israel, my parents in São Paulo, and my wife's mother in Chicago." The result is that the family lacks roots: "Graves have always been symbolic and tending them is a sign of relationship between generations. Not to have that relationship suggests fragmentation, 'tornness' in the lives of Jews, the consequences of which are only beginning to become apparent." Schaalman links this fragmentation to the question of what it means to be a Jew today. Before modern times, it was not difficult to tell who was a Jew because "the parameters of being one were pretty firm. In America today, marriage, for example, is a reflection of the times. A Jew may marry a non-Jew and raise children who are part Jewish or not Jewish at all. One can even choose not to be Jewish at all."

Student Rabbi: 1938–1941

While his family was settling in Brazil, Schaalman was interning as a student rabbi. One of his assignments was to an Orthodox congregation outside of Cincinnati. His friend and student colleague, Ernst Lorge, also a German refugee, served as student rabbi and Schaalman as cantor, a role for which he was admirably suited. The assignment proved to be an important learning experience for them as they were exposed to another variety of American Jew. After ten minutes of the service, one of the congregants stood up, stretched and spit on the floor. One can only imagine the reaction of the young fastidious German at the sight of a congregant behaving in such an irreverent, not to say obnoxious, fashion.

Lotte Stern: Courtship and Marriage

In October of 1940, during the last year of his studies at HUC, Schaalman met Lotte Stern, the woman who was to become the love of his life and life-long companion. It was an event that transformed his life.

"Before meeting her, I was like a zombie. I went through the motions doing whatever was expected of me and to the best of my ability. Once I met her, everything began to change." Both refugees from Nazi Germany, they had been in America only a few years and were still learning to adjust to their new country.[102] Once he met her, he had no doubt that she was the woman who would be the perfect life companion and wasted no time in winning her. In three or four dates (depending on which of the two you ask) the young rabbinic student asked Lotte to marry him. Her acceptance opened "a new chapter" of his life and changed it forever (Folb, 2007, p. 41).

Like her future husband, Lotte was a war baby. She was born January 13, 1915, during World War I, in Karlsruhe, the capital of the state of Baden-Baden and lived there until she left for America in 1936 at the age of twenty-one. She was the first of two children of Herman and Gussie (Augusta) Stern. She and her sister Ilse were born one year apart. During their childhood, their father suffered serious health issues brought on by an injury he sustained during the war. As a result, their mother took on the job of supporting the family. She became a partner in the family shoe business and was largely responsible for its success. The business thrived under her guidance, allowing the Sterns to have a lovely home with servants.

The Stern's home life was typical of the assimilated German Jewish family. Lotte remembers that her home was more Christian than Jewish.[103] The family always had a Christmas tree, though Gussie must have felt enough guilt to claim that the tree was for the benefit of the help. Contributing to this non-Jewish environment was the fact that the girls were raised by a Protestant governess. Maria (referred to by the sisters as "Miele") was a graduate of Froebel, an exclusive training school for governesses. She took good care of her charges and even made the Stern sisters part of her family. A sense of the privileged status of the Stern children may be understood from their reception at their governess's village. Whenever she took them to visit her home city of Ungstein, her family and their neighbors treated them as little princesses. When, in 1926, Gussie and her sister took a vacation in America, Maria took care of them. According to Lotte, Miele was "almost" more of a mother to them than their own.[104]

When Lotte was in her teens, her parents sent her to Neuchatel, a finishing school in Switzerland for daughters of wealthy European families. The college not only provided a solid education, but also taught her to speak French fluently. Her student friends were the children of diplomats and nobility from across Europe. Occasionally, she spent weekends in their castles and chalets. She loved to ski and take long hikes. As a smart, outgoing, attractive young woman from a wealthy family, she had excellent prospects of landing a husband and leading a good life in Germany. However, because of increasing anti-Semitism, her parents realized that their daughters had no future in Germany and encouraged them to leave the country.

In 1935, Ilse immigrated to Palestine. She was a Zionist and trained social worker, and later, during World War II, served in the British Palestinian Corps; she drove a tank as part of a unit that supported the Allied attack against the Nazis in Italy. After the war, she was in charge of social work in the Cyprus concentration camp where the British interred the illegal immigrants they caught in Palestine. Eventually she became one of the leading social workers in the country and taught at the University of Jerusalem. Never married, she later served with distinction in the Israeli Demographic Bureau, a subcabinet position. Her job was to certify the number of children in an Orthodox household. The job was important because each family received a government stipend based on the number of children in the household. By the end of her life, she had become a well-respected member of Israel's subcabinet. Whenever the Schaalmans took groups on tour of Israel, they visited her and, after she died, whenever they went to Israel, they made sure to visit her grave.

Schaalman admitted that Ilse's academic and professional success contributed to Lotte's feeling of regret that she did not pursue higher education. One of her disappointments was that after coming to America the family she lived with in Danville did not give her the opportunity to further her education. The family put her to work immediately. After her marriage, she assumed full-time responsibilities as the rabbi's wife, and two years later, had her first child. After that, she never pursued a university education, though, according to her husband, she realized she had made a mistake. In fact, many years later she took him to task for not encouraging her to seek further education. When she was in Cedar Rapids, she could have attended Coe College or the University of Iowa, a half hour away by car. Schaalman tried to assuage her disappointment by reminding her that she had touched the lives of so many people and now had two accomplished children, and three grandchildren. One of her most significant achievements is that she has devoted her life to helping her husband become the superb rabbi he is.

Part of Lotte's family had already come to America and prospered. Six or seven of her grandmother's siblings had come to the United States in the 1860s and '70s. One of them, Amy Weiler, Gussie's first cousin, was the wife of Simon Lazarus, who was the head of the Lazarus Company in Ohio; in 1929 it became the Federated Department Stores.[105] Her brother, Morris Weiler, kept in touch with the Stern family and, along with his friend Jules Strauss, visited them in their home in Karlsburg, Germany. In 1927, Morris arranged for Gussie and Ilse to visit him in Portland, Indiana, a bold and daring expedition for two unaccompanied women.

When her family decided that she should come to America, Lotte sent several letters to Uncle Morris asking him to sponsor her, the only way she could get a visa to come to America.[106] Weiler did not respond to the letters, and, in frustration, Lotte sent him a final letter informing him that this would be her last effort to contact him. Apparently, this letter had an impact. Weiler wrote back saying he would be her sponsor. The situation became complicated for Lotte when she arrived because Weiler's wife objected to her living with them. Weiler turned to his friend Jules Strauss for help. According to Lotte, Jules's wife, Jenny, did not want her to stay with them either, but, at her husband's insistence, acquiesced (It is reasonable to assume that Mrs. Strauss, who was in her eighties, may have been reluctant to take on the responsibility of caring for the young girl.) During the next four years, Lotte lived with them in Danville, Illinois. They gave her a room in their attic and put her to work as an unpaid employee in their elegant, boutique-style dress shop. When they realized that she had a nice figure and was attractive, they used her to model the new styles and fashions brought to them by manufacturers.

Although she was now safe, Lotte worried constantly about the safety of her parents and tried desperately to get them out of Germany. Soon after she arrived, she asked the Weilers to sponsor her parents so that they could get a visa to travel to America. The Weilers, however, did not want to take on the responsibility of two more dependents and told Lotte that they would not vouch for her parents. They rationalized that

Lotte with Jules Strauss, Danville, IL, 1938

her parents were very comfortable in Germany where they could lead a better life. If they came to America, they would be handicapped because they did not know English and would not be able to bring any of their money with them.[107]

After a few years, Lotte saved enough to sponsor her parents. However, there was a quota on German immigrants, and her parents had to wait for their number to come up. When they finally left Germany in 1939, they travelled first to London, where they waited a year before they were able to get visas to travel to America. In that interval, Lotte's father died and was buried in London.[108] According to Schaalman, Gussie woke up one night and found that her husband had rolled out of bed and was dead. Alone and a widow, after the visa finally arrived, Gussie came to America in 1940 and settled with her daughter in Danville.

Because Lotte was young, attractive, and single, friends of the Strausses had tried to fix her up with suitable dates. Aunt Jenny, as Lotte called her, also felt responsible for finding Lotte a husband, and she had excellent connections. She came from a prominent Jewish family in Springfield, Illinois, the Myers family, and tried, unsuccessfully, to fix her up with one of her nephews. Other friends of the Strauss's also tried to fix her up with suitable dates. Lotte remembers dating a son of the Mies family, one of Danville's prominent families that had emigrated from Strasbourg. As Lotte tells the story, she was incapable of going on a date because she was so worried about her parents' safety. She describes herself as being "totally overwhelmed with grief and anxiety."

Perhaps it is not surprising that soon after she arrived, Lotte's mother realized that finding a Jewish husband in that small Midwest city would be impossible. She told her daughter, who was already twenty-six years old, "We're getting out of here; you'll never get a husband here." They decided to go to Cincinnati where they already had family connections through Uncle Morris. Morris had already contacted the Lazarus family and reported that Lotte had done an outstanding job in Danville. With that recommendation, Lotte had no difficulty landing a job in the women's wear department of Shillito's, the family-owned department store.

Fortunately for Lotte and her mother, Lotte knew a man named Ben Singerman who had moved from Danville to Cincinnati. Singerman had an apartment that was large enough that he was able to rent them a room. As Schaalman tells it, the story gets "even more weird" because Singerman was Lillian Waldman's boyfriend. Singerman called her up and told her that a nice German girl had just moved to town and was looking for a date. Apparently, he had heard about the five German rabbinic students and asked her to send one of them to a dinner party he was hosting for Lotte and her mother. According to Schaalman, Waldman, knowing of his background, told him about this young woman and asked him whether he would be willing to meet her at dinner at Singerman's house. Schaalman understood that Lillian was asking a favor, which he could not deny her. He also knew Singerman from his contacts with him during dormitory meals and understood that he was doing him a favor as well. Soon after, Schaalman met Lotte and her mother, Gussie, for dinner at Singerman's home. The dinner was a complete success; Schaalman was smitten.

Lotte also must have seen something in the young rabbinic student that she liked. By the time the party ended, she expressed interest in seeing him again. He reasoned: "Okay, she wants to see me again. I'd better call her to find out when she was available on a Saturday."[109] The eager and lonely young man asked her for a date to go with him to the art museum (Folb, 2007, p. 34). Lotte accepted what for him was a perfect date because he had no money, but he realized that he had failed to impress her with his knowledge of art history. His efforts collapsed when he discovered that his identification of several of the painters was either incorrect or that she knew more about them than he did.

Afterwards, they went to a restaurant, because, as he said, "it was the right thing." Understanding that he was broke, Lotte ordered a salad. By this time, Schaalman was hopelessly in love. Not only was he attracted by the commonality of their backgrounds, but by her beauty and grace. He could not resist asking her out on another date. The week after that second date, he met Lotte at a cultural event sponsored by the refugee group he chaired. He remembers sitting in the choir loft directing the production when he spotted Lotte sitting with a young attorney. The sight "went through me like a knife." When he got home that evening, his only thought was that he "had to have a date with this young woman immediately." Again, she agreed to see him, and on this date, the impetuous young man proposed to her. He explains that he was encouraged by "signs of affection on her part."

They had another date on a cold and snowy day and, on the way home, Lotte, who did not have gloves, put her hand in his coat pocket to keep warm. Schaalman describes the touch as electric. When they passed a bench, Lotte asked if they could rest for a while. Schaalman remembers brushing off the snow, and they sat down and talked for a while. The date proved transformative for Schaalman. He knew that something had happened.

To understand the complexity of this situation, it is necessary to know that this was the first time since coming to America that he had this kind of relationship with a woman. As he explains, previously he had no "female companionship." The catastrophe of his engagement to Lotte Strauss had left him traumatized in matters of the heart. He felt that he could not even look at a girl without feeling guilty. Nevertheless, he had had a few dates during his five years in America. At a faculty member's suggestion, he dated a young woman because, he confessed, he "was very polite, you know, and obedient." The experience meant nothing to him. The other experience he remembers was with a high school girl whom he had met in the choir in which he was singing. He remembers taking her out a few times. Dating her gave him a kind of comfort, especially because everyone else was going out on dates. In the end, she proved to be too young for him.

When he proposed to Lotte after only three dates, she was startled. The idea of marriage had not occurred to her. He remembers that in response to this peremptory request, "she kind of gently pushed me off." Not to be deterred, his next move was, as he describes it, "a real mistake" and almost ruined any prospect he entertained about marrying this extraordinary woman. He invited her to come with him to a Shabbat service at Beth Israel, an Orthodox synagogue in a nearby suburb, where he served on alternate weekends as a student rabbi. The assignment provided him a small income, five dollars a week, and, in order to spend time with Lotte, he took her with him. Schaalman had been officiating as a student rabbi for the last year because the synagogue could not afford a full-time rabbi. He shared the pulpit with another student, Laurence Huberman, who was also a German refugee enrolled at HUC. Unlike Schaalman, who came as a scholarship student, Huberman had come on his own. Schaalman was pleased to share the pulpit with someone sufficiently acquainted with traditionalism to conduct the service.

The mistake, as it turned out, was taking Lotte to a congregation that, as Schaalman describes it, was "uncouth … really a rough bunch." Lotte was disgusted with what she saw. On the way home, she was so upset that she refused to sit next to him on the streetcar. Schaalman knew that something was desperately wrong. When they arrived at her home, he attempted to get off the streetcar with her, but she told him not to bother. Recognizing that he had made a mistake taking her into such an unpleasant environment, and unwilling to give her up, he persisted and walked with her to her apartment. Immediately she told him, "No way … no way can I be your wife if this is the way your life … if this is going to be your life, this is impossible for me. Forget it. I like you as a person. … If you want to quit your rabbinic studies to become a doctor, psychiatrist, or a lawyer, anything, I'll work to put you through school, but I'll never be a rabbi's wife." The whole idea contradicted everything she thought about herself and that she hoped for in marriage. She was brought up in a family that was only marginally Jewish and had no pretensions to, or interest in, becoming more observant. Nor did she want the responsibilities that went along with being the wife of a rabbi.

When they arrived at her home, she said goodbye and told him that she did not think she would see him again. Unwilling to let the situation rest, Schaalman persuaded her to allow him to come inside. Her rejection was entirely unacceptable to him; he stayed until 2:00 a.m. trying desperately to convince her that this congregation was not typical. He told her that the only reason he served this congregation was the $5 per week he earned, and he desperately needed the income. "The reason Lotte did not want to marry a rabbi," Schaalman explained, "was that she came from a home that was barely observant." Nevertheless, the family was "observant enough," probably kept kosher, though not necessarily when they went out for a meal. Schaalman speculates, "On the high holy days, they probably did close their big shoe store in Karlsruhe, as was the custom in all Jewish establishments."

Inevitably, he won her over; Lotte promised she would think it over. She escorted him to the door, shook hands, and said, "Hope to see you again." He went home feeling as if he had escaped a near calamity. By now it was so late there was no transportation running, and he had to walk from Avondale to Clifton, a twenty-five minute walk. He described it as the longest walk he had ever taken. By the time he got home, he concluded that this was the woman he wanted to marry and with whom he would live the rest of his life. He would not accept "no" for an answer.

He decided on a desperate gamble and designed an ingenious stratagem. He printed a wedding invitation and presented it to her on their next date. The invitation stated that they would be married May 25, 1941, the day after his ordination. He told her, "And I'm sending this out to our friends. What's your list? I had faked it of course … but at that point Lotte understood that there was no going back … for me." Schaalman speculates that very likely she had never been "wooed quite that ardently and quite so absolutely." Moreover, he was able to meet one of her chief concerns. As a dutiful and loving daughter, Lotte felt responsible for her mother, whose well-being was as important to her as her own. By the fourth date, Schaalman promised Lotte that her mother would always have a home with them. This promise cleared away any obstacle to her decision. Schaalman had left her no room for argument or for equivocating, and she accepted. Elated by her acceptance of his proposal, at the first opportunity, Schaalman took her to the college and introduced her to his friends and colleagues (Folb, 2007, p. 35).

During the time that Schaalman and Lotte dated, Schaalman was also a student rabbi in Henderson, Kentucky. To get to this assignment in time for Friday services, he had to leave on Thursday and stay over in Louisville. On Friday morning, he took the early morning train to Henderson in order to conduct Friday night services. After the services on Saturday morning, around noon he took the train to get back to Cincinnati by eight or nine o'clock in the evening. Frequently, Lotte would meet him at the station and ride the streetcar with him back to her apartment where, sometime, she would have prepared him a meal.

They married May 25, 1941, the afternoon of his ordination. HUC had a strict policy forbidding rabbinic students from marrying before their ordination. As it turned out, they were married in the same chapel as the ordination and were able to use the same flowers. A second couple was also married with them. The groom was a colleague of Schaalman's named Malcolm Stern. Because Lotte's surname was also Stern and since the weddings were only a half an hour apart, guests who came for the first Stern wedding stayed for both. As it happened, the guest list for both weddings largely overlapped, and most of the guests for each wedding were the same friends and colleagues from the college. In attendance at Schaalmans' wedding were Sy Lazarus and his wife, Amy. Lazarus, whose signature is on Schaalman's diploma, was the president of the HUC Board of Trustees and Lotte's relative. Fortunately for the Schaalmans, the Lazaruses paid for the wedding dinner. They recognized that the Schaalmans had nothing and could ill afford to pay for a dinner for thirty guests.[110]

From Schaalman's perspective, marrying Lotte was the best decision he could have made: "She's been the best rabbi's wife ever." Their marriage is still as vibrant and affectionate as it must have been at the beginning. It is a testament to the longevity of the marriage that even in their nineties the couple unself-consciously embraces each other in public.

Chapter 3
Cedar Rapids: 1941–1949

"'Can I be saved?' asked Schaalman. The minister stopped abruptly and blurted out, 'Damn it, there's got to be a way; you're such a nice fellow.'"

Herman E. Schaalman, 1999, pp. 18–19

"We finally have a rabbi who can represent the Jewish community."

Howard Hall, 1941

*"The message is not the sermon, but the man himself. …
The Rabbi must not deliver a message, he must deliver himself."*

Leo Baeck

Plaut (1981) reported that the original invitation from HUC inviting five rabbinic students to come to Cincinnati included a warning that the students should not expect to get rabbinic jobs in America. He wrote, "Congregations which yesterday had flourished were today on the brink of bankruptcy and many of them were getting along without a permanent rabbi" (p. 57). Instead, they brought in students for short stints. Despite hard economic times even before Schaalman's marriage and ordination, events were taking their course that would soon transform his life. In the spring of 1941, Temple Judah, a Reform congregation of thirty-two members in Cedar Rapids, Iowa, was making plans to hire a new rabbi.[111] Although members of its Board expressed concern that they might not be able to find a rabbi willing to work for so little, the Board approved a motion to hire a rabbi at a salary of $2,000, a low salary even for that time (Temple Judah, April 25, 1941).[112] Because the Board wanted a new rabbi as soon as possible, it wasted no time in contacting Morgenstern, who recommended Schaal-man. (In those days, rabbinic graduates did not apply for positions; congregations did not seek out graduates from a pool of qualified students. Instead, the power to place them was the sole prerogative of the college president, the influential Dr. Julian Morgenstern.)

At a meeting held on May 9, 1941, the Board approved a motion to invite "Rabbi Schollman [sic] for an interview" (Temple Judah, May 9, 1941). Soon after this meeting, Schaalman got a call from Morgenstern's secretary. "Herman," she said, "Dr. Morgenstern wants you in his office at three o'clock." Schaalman understood that Morgenstern wanted to discuss his placement in his first rabbinic assignment. Because Schaalman believed he was not one of the top students, he concluded that he was not one of the first to be called in. However, out of the small class of fourteen, only two or three other students had done better. To make himself presentable, Schaalman bathed, shaved, and put on his best suit. As he describes it, "You wore a tie; I mean you really decked yourself out." Even though the president knew him from the five-plus years he had been a student at HUC, Schaalman wanted to make a good impression.

At the appointed time, Morgenstern invited Schaalman into his office and asked him to sit across the desk from him. After a brief conversation about the fact that Schaalman was approaching his ordination, Morgenstern informed him that it was time for him to be assigned to his first congregation. On his desk was a box containing 3 × 5 cards. Playfully fingering them, as if he were deciding Schaalman's fate, Morgenstern pulled one out and announced, "Herman, you are going to Cedar Rapids, Iowa." Schaalman was stunned. "If the ground had been opening up and allowing me to sink into it and make me disappear into nothingness," he claimed, "it would have been the best for me." He felt as if he were being sent to rabbinic Siberia, and that Morgenstern was trying to "bury him."[113] Instead of his first rabbinate being a launching pad for a career in the rabbinate, Schaalman concluded that Morgenstern wanted him "to get off there." His only response was to stammer, "If that's where you want me to go, I'll go there, Dr. Morgenstern." Sixty-five years later, he remarked, "You don't need much imagination to understand how desperate I was about his choice. Well, there was nothing that could be done. It was a déjà vu experience of the most peculiar and distressing kind."

Why this extreme reaction? The posting was the one he had dreaded when he passed through Cedar Rapids in 1939 on his way to Seattle.

Now, he felt completely alone and at the mercy of the president's decision. As a stranger and alien in America, without family, friends, or influential rabbis to promote his interests, he had no recourse but to accept the assignment. HUC notified the congregation that its new rabbi would be coming shortly.

Morgenstern's selection of Schaalman was only the first stage of the placement process. Because the final choice of rabbi belonged to the congregation, Schaalman would have to audition for the position. He had heard negative reports about the Cedar Rapids Jewish community and had no confidence that they would hire him. Even if they did, he was aware that the new position would not begin until fall. In the meantime, he needed money, especially because he was about to be married. He had already arranged a full-time good-paying summer job as a lifeguard at the Jewish Community Center's pool in Cincinnati. The money was enough for the young couple to rent an apartment from one of Lotte's friends, who happened to be away for the summer.

Schaalman did not wait for a job offer to get married. Since December of 1940, he and Lotte had been planning to marry the day he was graduated and ordained. They married May 25, 1941, as they had planned, and that evening left by train for their honeymoon in Indiana's Spring Mill State Park. On their way, they stopped in Louisville, Kentucky, and spent their first night in a hotel that Schaalman had used previously for his weekend rabbinic assignments in Henderson, Kentucky. He planned to take the train the next morning to Spring Mill State Park. Before their departure from Cincinnati, Schaalman had received an invitation from Rabbi Joseph Rauch to be his summer replacement at his Louisville synagogue. Rauch had heard from congregants in Henderson and from people Schaalman had met in Louisville that he was an "all right speaker." Because the assignment that Rauch offered him was a weekend position, Schaalman was eager to get it and knew he could easily fit it in with this job as full-time lifeguard. The two rabbis had arranged a breakfast on the day after the Schaalmans arrived in Louisville and before they took the train to the state park. The purpose of the meeting was for Rauch to brief Schaalman on his duties. When Rauch, who had not been told of Schaalman's marriage, learned that the young rabbi had married, he was "smitten" and embarrassed. Had he known in advance, he would have been prepared to acknowledge the *simchah*. As the Schaalmans were about to board the train, Rauch ran up to them and handed them a box of candy.

Schaalman had chosen Spring Mill State Park because it was inexpensive and far enough away from Cincinnati that they were unlikely to run into anyone they knew—and there were no phones to disturb them. To their surprise, one of the seminary faculty members, Professor Blank, dropped by with his wife to see how they were doing. Another intrusion followed almost immediately. Barely had they begun their honeymoon when a telegram arrived from Morgenstern informing Schaalman that the congregation in Cedar Rapids was expecting him by Friday, only two days away. Morgenstern was able to locate the couple because Schaalman had left word where he was going (most likely in the event a job offer came through while he was away). Schaalman felt he had no choice but to comply with Morgenstern's order. Recognizing the importance of the moment, Lotte did not hesitate and began packing. Only a few days into their honeymoon, they returned to Cincinnati.

The next day, Schaalman took the train to Chicago and then took an overnight train to Cedar Rapids where he arrived Friday morning in time to conduct the Shabbat service that evening. He was met at the station by Dr. Morris Katzoff and Zig Salit, who took him to Temple Judah (Schaalman, H. E., Cedar Rapids History, 1999, p. 1). That evening, he found himself leading a service for thirty-two families, almost the entire congregation. Schaalman was nervous because he had never auditioned for a position as full-time rabbi and had never submitted himself to the judgment of total strangers. His immediate future for himself and his new wife was at stake. Failure would mean that he would have to go back once again to Morgenstern, only this time hat in hand and "face the powerful, fear-inducing president of Hebrew Union College" (p. 1). Would Morgenstern give him another chance?

Another source of his anxiety was the fact that he was uncomfortable with his sense that he was German-born and had not grown up in this quintessential Midwest American environment. Not only was he uncomfortable, but he projected a similar discomfort onto the congregation. How would they perceive him? Would they accept him? Would they see him as inexperienced and unsuited for their needs? For a full-time rabbi, he was a complete novice. Another, possibly more dreadful fear came over him. Because of the suddenness of the invitation, he had not had time to prepare. The service itself was not the problem. He felt fully competent to lead one, but the sermon, that was a different story.

He had no confidence in his ability to find "proper words without a complete manuscript committed to memory" (p. 2). He had had only two days to compose "the sermon which would determine my young wife's and my own immediate future" (p. 2). On top of these pressures, he had the additional pressure of breaking off his honeymoon, hurrying back to Cincinnati, getting on a train to Chicago and then traveling by train to Cedar Rapids.

To get through the service, he had to learn the customs and adjust to the fact that the choir was composed of non-Jewish singers who were responsible for chanting many of the Hebrew passages. For his part, the prospect of conducting the prayer service was something he savored: "I had always loved to pray [and] was profoundly conscious of the sacred privilege of leading a congregation's prayers" (p. 2). He speculates that the conveyance of "that sense of the sacred" may have been perceived by the congregation.

Following the service, the congregation held a reception in the home one of its leading couples, Ceil and A. L. Smulekoff (p. 3). To his surprise, Schaalman found himself in the company of women only. Apparently, the men had gone off to another room. Not long after, the congregation's president came out and invited Schaalman to join the male members of the congregation. He informed Schaalman that the twenty or thirty men in the room had met and decided that he should be their rabbi. Schaalman was delighted and overwhelmed. He had not expected to make that kind of impression. Before he accepted the assignment, he told them he would have to call his wife. When he told Lotte about the offer, she said, "Take it!"

He accepted the assignment without inquiring about his compensation or the congregation's expectations. They told him, however, that a committee would meet with him the next day to work out the details. On June 6, 1941, the Board approved a motion to hire him at a salary of $2,000 (Temple Judah, June 6, 1941). Schaalman accepted the salary "without as much as batting an eyelash or without realizing that it was only $38 a week."

The new assignment did not begin until September. In the meantime, the congregation offered to find him housing but told him he would have to pay for it himself. In August 1941, the Schaalmans packed their bags and headed for Cedar Rapids. It was a world away from the devastation and nightmare of the world at war. It was also the city in which Schaalman made his formal entry into the rabbinic world.

On September 1, 1941, Schaalman began his new life as a rabbi at Temple Judah. He was fresh out of rabbinic school, newly married, uncertain of his future, unaware of his enormous potential and, apparently, unaware of the historic events reshaping the world and his future. Only a few years before, he had arrived in America knowing nothing of its culture, its customs, or its language. By the time he left Cedar Rapids eight years later, he had become one of the community's foremost citizens as both a religious and a civic leader. Not long after he arrived, he held leadership roles in many of the city's most important civic and social service organizations.

However, the beginning was difficult. At the time of his ordination, Schaalman had very little confidence in himself and, as a result, had only modest expectations. For one thing, he was insecure about his ability to speak English, and, for another, he felt inadequate as a rabbi: "I was intimidated by the prospect of being a rabbi, and, because I held myself to uncompromisingly high standards, I was anxious at the thought of writing sermons. Because of the high expectations I placed on myself, I have always been plagued by the sense of impending or possible failure."

His rabbinate in Cedar Rapids gave him the opportunity to know the Midwest and its people. It was also his first experience with a diverse religious community. Up to that point, he had never known a Methodist, an Episcopalian, or a Baptist. As in most small Midwestern cities, the churches exerted a powerful influence on the lives of the city's residents: "It was simply expected that one belonged to a religious community. Church affiliation was a significant part of the social structure and fabric" (Schaalman, H. E., 1999, pp. 5–6).

In 1941, the population of Cedar Rapids was approximately 62,000, and, when Schaalman left in 1949, it had increased by about 16 percent to 72,000 (City Data). By the end of the twentieth century, it was the second-largest city in Iowa. As early as 1858, about 1,000 Jews, almost all of them German refugees, had settled in Iowa near its rivers, the Mississippi, the Des Moines, and the Missouri (Iowa Pathways, 2005, p. 1). Undoubtedly, some of them settled in Cedar Rapids. In 1907, Cedar Rapids had a population of fifty Jews out of a population of 24,000.

Five years later, the number had risen to seventy-five, most of them Russian immigrants (Rockway, 1998, pp. 44–45).

At the beginning of the twentieth century, Jews from Eastern Europe and Russia began arriving in Cedar Rapids and brought with them different customs than their German predecessors (Iowa Pathways, 2005, p. 1). These new immigrants spoke Yiddish and were more orthodox than their German cousins, who sought to assimilate and become Americans. The Eastern European Jews, however, were not as immediately interested in Americanization; they wanted to keep their culture and maintain their language. World War I and increased anti-Semitism in Europe caused more Eastern European and Russian Jews to settle in Iowa. By 1916, Iowa's Jewish population had risen to 9,000 (p. 1).

Cedar Rapids was a major Midwest industrial center and a hub for railroad traffic (Henry and Hunter, 2005, p. 9). Train traffic in and out of the city, including the downtown, was so heavy that 130 passenger trains and another 130 freight trains passed through each day (p. 9). The city's economy was based on the manufacture and processing of agricultural and food products, steel fabricating, tool and die making, and radios and electronics.[114] Cedar Rapids also had a rich cultural tradition. It housed the Museum of Art, the Paramount Theatre for the Performing Arts, the Cedar Rapids Symphony Orchestra, and the Cedar Rapids Opera Theatre (City-Data).[115]

Although Schaalman had dreaded the thought of coming to Cedar Rapids, this midsized Midwest City satisfied his desire to lead a normal life. It was not Berlin or Cincinnati, but it provided a safe place where he and Lotte could establish roots, find acceptance as newly minted Americans, make new friends, and start a family. At night, they could leave their doors open, and they could count on the support of their neighbors. Cedar Rapids was a haven from a world in turmoil.

While the Schaalmans were attempting to embark on a new life, the Axis powers were waging war in Europe, the Far East, and Africa. In September of 1941, soon after they arrived in Cedar Rapids, Germany invaded Russia and expanded its efforts to exterminate world Jewry. Although the young couple had barely escaped the immediate threat to their lives, the Nazis shattered the lives of their families. To save themselves, the Schaalmans and the Sterns fled Germany with little more than the clothes on their backs. The most critical effect of this dislocation for the Schaalman and Stern families was the destruction of their family cohesion and the loss of most of their relatives in the death camps. For Lotte and Herman, the loss of family would affect them for their rest of their lives.

By December 7, 1941, only a few short months after the Schaalmans arrived in Cedar Rapids, Japan attacked Pearl Harbor and changed the course of world history. The United States declared war on Japan and subsequently Germany and Italy. The loyalty of Germans and Japanese living in America was immediately called into question. Whether citizens or visitors, they came under suspicion as potential foreign agents. Even Schaalman was required to register as an "enemy alien." Immigration of Jews from throughout Europe was also severely curtailed. From 1939 to 1941, the number of Jews who immigrated to this country was 42,424, but in the last six months of the year, June 1941–1942, only 3,600 were admitted (*American Jewish Year Book, 1942–1943*, p. 146). Japanese Americans suffered the most. Those living on the Pacific coast were uprooted and sent to internment camps. Although spared this fate, German Americans had to contend with the inevitable conflict of loyalties resulting from living in their adopted country, which was at war with their homeland.

The day the Japanese attacked Pearl Harbor, Schaalman was on his way to deliver a speech at a B'nai B'rith meeting in Oscaloosa, Iowa. M. J. Frankel, one of his congregants and an active member in the organization, was driving when an announcement of the attack came over the car radio (Schaalman, H. E., 1999, p. 14). The next day, after President Roosevelt declared war on Japan, a wave of patriotic fervor swept the country. Subsequently, virtually all of Temple Judah's young men either enlisted or were drafted. The government introduced rationing of basic food supplies and local Ration Boards were established around the country. Although not yet a citizen, Schaalman was appointed to serve on one. Citizenship for an alien required a five-year waiting period, which for him would not be up until 1943. "Technically, I was an enemy alien who had to register as such and had to obtain permission to leave the city. Fortunately, in the few months after my arrival in Cedar Rapids, I had become well known by the Chief of Police, who treated me with unvarying civility, and my involvement in civic activities cleared me of any suspicion and gave me considerable public standing" (p. 15).

In the first two years of the war, the Allies experienced a string of defeats, but slowly the fortunes of war began to change, and the Axis powers were put on the defensive. Throughout the war, Schaalman shared the anxieties of families, especially those in his congregation, who had sons and daughters in the armed forces. When the surrender of the Axis powers was announced, he participated in the wild celebrations. However, as the reports of the devastation of European Jewry became public, his elation faded. The horror of these events cast such a dark shadow over his life that it would eventually lead to a radical reformulation of his religious thinking, but this evolution took years to mature. As it was for so many of his generation, the full scope of the attempted extermination of world Jewry did not sink in at first, and nearly two decades would pass before he came to grips with its full impact.

Jewish Life in Cedar Rapids

When the young rabbi and his new bride arrived in Cedar Rapids, they found that there were two Jewish congregations, one Orthodox, Congregation Beth Jacob, and the other Reform, Temple Judah (Murray, 1950, p. 120). The fact that they were on opposite ends of a theological divide with their own rabbis meant that inevitably there would be frictions between them. The two congregations also represented different age groups. Beth Jacob's congregation tended to be older; Temple Judah's, younger. A few families were members of both congregations (p. 10). Traditional members of the Jewish community resented Reform Judaism for its "minimalist orientation" (Schaalman, H. E., 1999, p. 10). They also resented the fact that their children tended to gravitate to the Reform congregation. Schaalman describes the reaction of the more traditional Jews as fearing that the "older, more traditional ways and values were succumbing to the powerful pull of modern America and that they were conducting a less and less successful holding action against the seeming irresistible trend away from a cherished past" (p. 10). These frictions created an "unwholesome competition" between them and, in some cases, divided families.

In part, the resistance was, in Schaalman's words, "personal" (p. 12). He characterized some of the older members of Beth Jacob as "opinionated and stubborn" and lacking in-depth knowledge of Judaism.

This situation made them defensive when they were confronted by the Reform views of the young rabbi who was barely out of rabbinic school. Occasionally, his conversations with them "nearly turned bitter," putting to the test his patience and personal communication skills. The frictions died down at the beginning of the war when almost all the young men entered the armed forces.[116] Fortunately, none of them were killed, but when they returned, they tended to align themselves with the Reform congregation. Schaalman speculates that his more traditional background, which was so much more like that of the younger generation of Beth Jacob, served as a bridge between the two congregations and facilitated the transition of the younger generation to his Reform congregation. This movement helped to bring the two sides of the Jewish community together. Occasionally, Schaalman attended services at Beth Jacob and that, too, may have helped Beth Jacob's younger congregants make the transition (p. 11). By the end of the war, the tensions in the Jewish community had "evaporated."

Beth Jacob had been the first organized congregation in Cedar Rapids. Founded in 1906, the members of this small Orthodox congregation were largely elderly, and, as they died, the congregation began a slow decline. Within a few years after Schaalman's arrival, some of its younger members had become his friends, and they began to migrate to Temple Judah. One of them even became its president. A year after Schaalman's arrival, Beth Jacob's Rabbi Ralph DeKoven left and the tensions subsided sufficiently that the two synagogues began discussing the possibility of merging (p. 12). They recognized that a merger would insure their survival and strengthen the Cedar Rapids Jewish community (McQuiston, 1989). The merger, however, did not occur until 1949, after the Schaalmans had already left for Chicago.[117]

Temple Judah had been established in 1922 by a small group of younger members of Beth Jacob who decided to form a synagogue of their own. According to McQuiston (1989), they wanted a more liberal service that used English rather than Hebrew. Although they purchased a plot of land on Washington Avenue, they were not able to complete the temple until 1927[118] because of poor economic conditions. The building, though only a modest stucco bungalow, was an important milestone in the history of Cedar Rapids Jews that now had two "thriving" Jewish communities (McQuiston, 1989).

During its first two decades, Temple Judah struggled to meet its financial obligations but by 1944 was able to retire the balance of its original $22,000 mortgage. Despite its small size, it hired full-time rabbis. Prior to Schaalman's arrival in late August 1941, four other rabbis preceded him: Rabbi Joseph L.,Baron, its first rabbi, Max Schenk, Albert Goldstein, David Polish,[119] and Hirsch Freund (McQuiston, 1989).

Schaalman tells an interesting story that provides insight into the financial condition of the Temple and of its members when he arrived. When the movers arrived from Danville at the house that the congregation had rented for the rabbinic couple, they confronted Schaalman with a bill twice as much as they had originally estimated. Their story was that they had "grossly underestimated" the weight of the furniture, which Lotte's parents had sent from Germany. The Schaalmans had saved the prearranged amount but lacked the money to pay for the bill they were presented. They needed another $120. Although he was deeply embarrassed, Schaalman turned to the Temple treasurer, Harry Carney, to ask for an advance on his salary.[120] Carney told him that the Temple's treasury did not have that much money. Not to leave the rabbi in the lurch, Carney came up with a plan to raise the funds from other congregants with downtown businesses. He recommended that Schaalman come downtown with him so that he could take the young rabbi around to other congregants to come up with the funds. The plan worked, and Schaalman had the money to pay the movers. He was humiliated, however, that he had to put himself and the congregation into such a tight financial bind.

That afternoon, the Sisterhood paid an unannounced visit to the Schaalmans to inspect their "belongings" and to ensure that their new home was set up properly. (One can imagine that the Sisterhood took pity on the two young newlyweds and wanted to help them get settled.) Determining that the unloaded furniture had been placed haphazardly in the living room, the ladies set about arranging it to suit their own tastes. Not to offend their guests, once they left, the Schaalmans placed the furniture where they wanted it. That night, two of the congregants, Mini Kushner and her daughter, Meretta, took the Schaalmans to dinner at the prestigious Amana Colony.

Lotte, 1940s

In coming to Cedar Rapids, the Schaalmans faced two daunting challenges. First, Herman had no experience as a rabbi, and second, neither of them had experience as a husband or a wife. Describing himself and Lotte as "greenhorns," Schaalman confessed that they had to learn to adjust to each other both mentally and sexually, how to relate to each other and to "discover each other in all ways." This early period was an "adventure with its ups and downs." When they first moved to Cedar Rapids, Lotte, who had never cooked before, gradually learned to become an excellent cook.

Because they brought with them the old world value that having a child was necessary to be a legitimate family, they decided to have a child as soon as possible.[121] At the same time, the couple was terribly aware of how alone they were and felt like outcasts without friends or family. The isolation from their families was the most difficult part of their adjustment. Schaalman had been used to relying on his family for advice and emotional support. He missed them terribly and "the conversations that made sense."

Lotte, too, had to make major adjustments, first to being a rabbi's wife and then to living in a community of strangers. In a short time, however, Cedar Rapids and Temple Judah provided her many opportunities to participate in community life. She was elected president of the Cedar Rapids chapter of Hadassah, taught in the temple's Sunday school, and became a member of the temple sisterhood. Through her involvement in these activities, she helped her husband build strong social ties to the Jewish community. She had a knack for entertaining and attracting people. She lavished her natural generosity of spirit and affectionate nature on the congregants and anyone else her husband brought home.[122]

The Schaalmans rented a two-story house with an unattached garage, a basement, and an attic, all for only $45 a month. It was located conveniently on 19th St., S. E., two short blocks from the Temple. The garage was not of much use until 1944 when the congregation bought them a car, a secondhand Plymouth that had been used as a taxi and barely had survived an accident. At the time, Schaalman had never driven before, but, in his own words, he was "delirious" at the thought of learning how to drive. The only memories he had of the pleasure of riding in a car were from his childhood rides with Uncle Eddie.

The congregation quickly embraced the young couple and helped them make the difficult transition from relatively new immigrants to Midwesterners. Because of this warmth, many of the congregants became Schaalman's life-long friends. Despite the fact that he found a

The Schaalmans at their Cedar Rapids home on 19th St., S. E., 1943

welcoming and grateful community, his new congregation, however, could not replace completely the sense of attachment to home and family. He found two congregants with whom he could have "tangential conversations in this regard," and who provided intellectual companionship. One of them was Dr. Morris Katzoff, a dentist who was involved in dental research and had a scientific mind. Together, they had many stimulating intellectual discussions, a vital necessity for this rabbi who was isolated in America's hinterland. The other friend was David Thaler, a young Polish doctor who came to Cedar Rapids after the war and with whom he became best friends.

The origin of that friendship began early one Sunday morning when Schaalman received a call from a man with a heavy European accent who was looking for the rabbi. Schaalman assumed that he was one of the indigents who passed through the town and sought financial help from the rabbi. Because Cedar Rapids was a rail junction for trains heading to San Francisco and St. Louis, Schaalman encountered poor Jews who were on their way to the Mayo Clinic in Rochester, Minnesota. When they arrived in Cedar Rapids, they would seek help from the Jewish community. In those days, Mayo Clinic charged patients according to their ability to pay, and many of these Jews were treated free. To manage the requests of these indigents, the Jewish community had established a fund that Schaalman administered. Two or three times a month, he would get a phone call from an indigent Jew who needed a few dollars to buy a bus ticket get to Rochester.

Schaalman invited the man to come to his home to discuss his needs. Soon after, while Schaalman was outdoors washing his car, a black luxury car drove up and out stepped a handsome young man who asked Schaalman where he could find the rabbi. Schaalman said, "You may not realize it, but you are speaking to him." The man was David Thaler who told Schaalman that he was looking for a place to establish himself and wanted to know if there was a Jewish community in Cedar Rapids. Schaalman was overjoyed. He invited the doctor to a B'nai B'rith dinner that evening so that the doctor would be able to meet the Jewish community. The connection between the two was almost instantaneous. They were about the same age, and, because they were both refugees, they shared a good deal of experience. Before coming to Cedar Rapids, Thaler had established a successful medical practice on Park Avenue in New York City.

The Thalers decided to stay in the community and found a house next to the Schaalmans. The two families remained close friends until Thaler died many years later. Thanks to Schaalman's contacts and Thaler's skill as a physician, he had patients from the highest levels of Cedar Rapids society. Because neither Katzoff nor Thaler knew much about Judaism, they looked to Schaalman for answers to their religious questions.

The Schaalmans soon learned that an important part of life in Cedar Rapids was the social pressure to affiliate with a religious community. Although not part of the city's mainstream, Jews were not immune from this pressure (Schaalman, H. E., 1999, p. 6). In their efforts to assimilate, Jews tended to model their behavior on their Christian neighbors' and affiliated with one or the other of the synagogues. Unlike their Christian counterparts, they were not, however, as diligent in attending services. Some of his congregants even "prided themselves on being nonbelievers" and usually turned up only for social events. In the urge to assimilate, for example, most of the homes of his congregants had Christmas trees and did not observe Hanukkah. In an effort to counter this situation, Schaalman developed a Hanukkah decoration contest for the most beautiful and ingenious decorations displayed in the home. Soon, he had the satisfaction of knowing that most of the trees disappeared from the homes of his congregants.

He discovered that the other clergy were "doing the kinds of things that I enjoyed … and felt it necessary to do because they were theologians." These colleagues, with whom he became good friends, gathered monthly to discuss books or listen to talks by invited speakers. Perhaps because he was so likeable or because his Christian counterparts wanted to show their Midwest hospitality, they invited him to become a member of their clerical group. However, they had no idea what it meant to be Jewish or a rabbi. When it was Schaalman's turn to make a presentation to the group, one of his clerical friends introduced him as a "fine Christian man." To Schaalman's dismay, the assembly broke out in a chorus of "Onward Christian Soldiers." Although there was virtually no Jewish forum to promote his growth and development, Schaalman credits this group with helping to nurture his intellect.

When Schaalman took over the duties as rabbi at Temple Judah, he was just twenty-five years old, though he looked to be nineteen, a youngster, by his own admission. As his pictures of the time reveal, Schaalman was a decidedly handsome young man, with strong facial features reflecting his inner strength and strong personality. Those features are still evident, though he is ninety-six. If his current personality can be taken as a guide to what it was like when he was a young man, it is likely that he exuded warmth and compassion and was open and tolerant of others, even of their faults. When you met him, he immediately put you at ease and inspired a sense that you were important to him.

Nevertheless, he found that he was expected to function at a level for which he did not feel prepared or that he merited. His whole training had been to prepare him to be a "gentleman rabbi, venerated and respected." HUC had not equipped him for the practical matters of serving as a pulpit rabbi. Because it considered itself a school for producing scholars, HUC's focus was entirely on scholarly pursuits and subject matter.[123] Despite these handicaps, Schaalman concludes that one reason for the reverence his congregation showed him was the fact that most of them had only the shallowest idea about Judaism.[124] Most joined Reform congregations because little was expected of them and membership had no preconditions.

Apparently, Schaalman's career as a pulpit rabbi began with a huge success. "Thirty-two families, sixty to seventy people turned out for my first service, a massive attendance for a community of this size. The average Friday night attendance in the first few years might have reached as high as thirty, though that number was a lot higher than for my predecessors." By the time he left eight years later, the congregation had increased from thirty-six to eighty-three families, mainly from young members of the Orthodox synagogue, who came over to Temple Judah.

Most of his congregants were businessmen and homemakers. Three were professionals, two were lawyers, and one was a dentist. Some had gone to Harvard or the Wharton School of Finance. Cedar Rapids also had wealthy Jewish businessmen, some of whom were part of Schaalman's congregation. Other Jews in the community also lived comfortably. The income level of his congregation reflected the spectrum of the financial status of the Cedar Rapids community: "Although a handful could be considered wealthy, the bulk was middle class, and some were poor." He discovered people who had traveled worldwide, others who had visited Chicago for theater and took vacations in Florida. To his surprise and pleasure, some of his congregants were highly cultured and in good standing in the community. There was also "considerable human talent and value lodged in a surprisingly large number of congregants" and a strong desire to be active members.

Because Temple Judah was his first rabbinic assignment, Schaalman spent a great deal of time in preparation for this new job. He had been a student for the last six years and had led "a very sheltered life." Initially, the congregation's president, Jack Gasway, who became a life-long friend, became his guide to learning about what it meant to lead a congregation. Schaalman knew nothing about temple boards or their finances, and nothing about administering a congregation or religious school. Gasway, whom Schaalman described as "congenial … good-humored, witty … keenly intelligent, and wise in the ways of the world," took him under his wing and taught him the basics of his job. Schaalman's contribution to this learning process was his "youthful energy, his willingness to learn, [his] feeling for people" and what "he had learned about Judaism in [his] studies." He credits Gasway for molding "this raw material into a functioning congregational rabbi." Through his knowledge of the congregation, Gasway helped Schaalman understand the intricacies of individual congregants and their complex relations to each other. Such guidance kept him from "making egregious mistakes."

Gasway and his wife, Miriam, took an immediate liking to the young rabbinic couple. At the end of their first week in town, the Schaalmans were invited by the Gasways to a Shabbat dinner in their home. Schaalman reported arriving "promptly at six," part of a lifetime pattern of always being on time. Their hosts had not yet come downstairs, probably assuming that their guests would be late. The Schaalmans "were ushered into the living room" (by the maid?) and were soon surprised by the appearance of "a young boy in full Indian regalia." "With pistol strapped to his thigh," he took one look at the Rabbi and shot out, "Are you the new rabbi?" When Schaalman indicated that he was, the boy responded, "Are you going to have Sunday school?" When Schaalman answered "yes," he "spat out 'phooey' and ran from the room." That, according to Schaalman, was his introduction to the challenges he would face with the Temple's children.

One of his challenges was to write and deliver sermons in English. His practice was to write them out and memorize them so that he would never have to read them to the congregation. Because he was extremely conscientious and wanted to assure himself that he would be perceived as articulate and competent, he devoted an "extraordinary" amount of time to writing these sermons.[125] The more experience he had, the more sure he became of himself. He welcomed "thoughtful responses" and critiques by some of his more active congregants (Schaalman, H. E., 1996, p. 5). Quickly, he learned that if he talked too long, he would interfere with his congregants' Friday night party time. If he ended services "in time to catch the last movie downtown," he realized that more people would come to his service (p. 5). Afterwards, the moviegoers would take the Schaalmans to the movies and, later, they would all go out for coffee and snacks.

Preaching was his main work, an important opportunity to educate his congregation. While they looked to him as their teacher and spiritual advisor, he had doubts about whether he could do the job. He thought he did not know enough to provide a variety of topics and, therefore, devoted as much time as he could to study and reading.

While his sermons took a great deal of time to prepare, he had few other daily responsibilities. He taught Hebrew school and Sunday school to about thirty children and Confirmation class for a handful of teenagers. Running the school had its challenges. Because the faculty was made up of volunteers, he could not always depend on them to show up. On such occasions, "substitutes had to be found, often on short notice" (p. 7). Another challenge with volunteers was their limited knowledge of the elements of Judaism that were part of the curriculum. As a result, it was not unusual for Schaalman to have to tailor the curriculum to what the teacher knew. To compensate for these gaps in teacher preparation, Schaalman found himself giving private lessons to help prepare teachers for their assignments.

Schaalman also took on the job of school principal. Although he had no experience in this role, it provided him "on the job training." Once the school was running satisfactorily, he turned over the responsibility to Ruth Licht, whom he credits for the school's ongoing success. Originally from Chicago, she was a "flaming Zionist" and competent in Hebrew. According to Schaalman, she was "absolutely capable and very beautiful, an engaging woman." Before he arrived, she had helped solidify the congregation and the whole Jewish community. After his arrival, she gave him considerable help in getting established in the community. She also provided support for the school and Jewish education in general.

When Schaalman left Cedar Rapids, she and her husband moved to Chicago and became members of Emanuel Congregation. Subsequently, she divorced her husband and remarried. After her second husband died, she moved to Israel to be near her sons. She died in 2008. For more than half a century, the Schaalmans remained in contact with her.

To become proficient in his new role as principal, Schaalman sought help from the Union of American Hebrew Congregations, which supplied him with curricula and educational materials. In addition, he queried other rabbinic colleagues with whom he came in contact. In time, together with his teachers, he was able to implement a consistent and effective curricula "that made their mark" on his students. In the end, he discovered that there were advantages to a volunteer faculty. They loved what they were doing and respected their students, most of whom were their own children or the children of family or friends. Schaalman was delighted that they could convey a sense of excitement and respect for the sacred.

His major responsibility was to lead Shabbat and holiday services. Because his congregation was so small, he did not have to officiate at many funerals, weddings, B'nai Mitzvot, or visit many sick people. In order to enrich the lives of his congregants and to help them learn about Judaism, he initiated an adult education program, with classes held in the homes of his congregants. The informality and social nature of this arrangement undoubtedly contributed to its success.[126] Nonetheless, because he had no prior training or experience in this type of educational offering, his preparation time was far greater than if he had been trained or had been brought up in an American congregation. Although Cedar Rapids was off the beaten track for speakers and officials of Jewish organizations, Schaalman would corner them to speak at Temple Judah. He also invited intellectually challenging speakers from the University of Iowa, as well as Coe and Cornell Colleges. However, speakers were rare, so his congregation expected him to provide intellectual stimulation.

A measure of Schaalman's success during his first year may be seen in the renewal of congregational commitment and strength. A sign of this new vitality is apparent from the minutes of a Board meeting held on April 15, 1942. The Board discussed a motion to pay off "immediately" the balance of its mortgage, an ambitious decision for a congregation of thirty-six members (Temple Judah, April 15, 1942). The motion was amended and approved to read "that instead of paying off the mortgage, the Board of Directors be authorized to remodel the Temple basement" to make necessary repairs and to build classrooms. At that time, the Temple was a small house with an unfinished basement. This new investment in the Temple's building indicates the congregation's recognition of the need to expand services to its members, and, it is reasonable to assume, that Schaalman's rabbinate stimulated this development. In Schaalman's view, the expansion of the Temple reflected confidence in its future, and, at the same time, a shrewd investment that could be sold as a home if the congregation failed. The remodeled basement housed his office and new classrooms.

One of the changes Schaalman stimulated in the congregation was the awareness of the need for increased opportunities for learning for all age groups. In order to fund these improvements, the Board approved a motion to institute a special assessment of each member. Members who objected to the amount of the assessment were entitled to appeal, but if the appeal was denied, and the member refused to pay it, the individual's membership would be cancelled.

At the same meeting, the Board passed a motion to extend Schaalman's contract for another year without a raise but with a "parsonage" allowance. One Board member proposed an amendment to increase Schaalman's salary to $3,000, but the amendment died for a lack of a second. The Board approved a motion to thank the Sisterhood for its financial support of the rabbi. Later that year, the Board approved a rabbinic pension plan proposed by the Central Conference of American Rabbis (CCAR). The plan required the congregation to pay 7 percent of the rabbi's salary into a pension plan and the rabbi to contribute 3 percent of his salary. In 1943, the Temple board renewed Schaalman's contract for another year with a $600 increase provided by the Temple Sisterhood and a parsonage stipend of $600. He was now making a total of $3,200 for the year 1943–1944. Although not discussed in the Board minutes, the extra funds may have been a response to the young couple's increasing financial needs. Lotte was due to have a baby—their first child was born May 28, 1943—and Lotte's mother had come to live with them to help care for it. The rabbi's meager salary was due to the limited resources of the tiny congregation and its low annual dues of less than $50. During the eight years Schaalman remained Judah's rabbi, the congregation's support of its

Temple rose significantly to meet its needs, though there were never more than eighty-three families. Schaalman also credits the Temple's economic limitations to the fact that the country was just coming out of the Depression and the war, and most people did not have much money.

When the war ended, the congregation changed dramatically. Some of the veterans who had taken advantage of the GI Bill returned as doctors, dentists, and other professionals. They wanted to get married and settle down. As Schaalman recalled, "there were weddings and babies." They took on leadership roles and infused the congregation with a new vitality. The brothers Abbott and Norman Lipsky and their wives, Jean and Belle, were responsible for a good part of this change in leadership. Others who had returned or had gone to college introduced a new worldliness. Their educations and experiences "had widened their horizons" that "drastically" changed the community. They had returned with a new concern for the future of their city and Jewish community. Fortunately, most of them chose to stay.

As a result, the Temple's social organizations—Sisterhood, B'nai B'rith, and Hadassah—"flourished." Although Schaalman's efforts to promote adult education went nowhere, he remembers that lunches at May's Drug Store[127] served as an "almost daily informal meeting for concerned members of the congregation." Owned by Lou Feldman, one of Temple Judah's congregants and a close friend of the rabbi, May's was known as "Feldman's congregation." Schaalman attempted to attend as many of the meetings as his schedule permitted. While enjoying inexpensive lunches, they engaged in stimulating conversation about issues ranging from Temple to world affairs. Sometimes, the lunches turned into mini-Board meetings. A small group even joined Toastmasters to improve their speaking skills and used their new skills to critique the Rabbi. They took notes during his sermon, gave each other knowing looks and whispered comments. Schaalman never let this parsing of his sermons bother him, and, occasionally, "took their critique seriously." The tone of the critiques was nonthreatening and served all, including the Rabbi, as good fun.

Schaalman Enters Cedar Rapids High Society

To understand Schaalman's success in Cedar Rapids' non-Jewish community, it is important to know the situation of Jews in this community and in the country. Although not as virulent as in Germany, anti-Semitism was an unpleasant fact in America and deeply ingrained in its culture. In hindsight, Schaalman acknowledged that it "was a widely accepted form of social behavior ... sometimes open and even violent" (Schaalman, H. E., 1999, p. 13). The Nazi-inspired Black Legion, the KKK, and the German Bund were among the most active and danger-ous of these hate groups. The German Bund blamed the Jews for the war and posed America's greatest internal danger (*American Jewish Year Book, 1942–1943*, p. 151). One of the most prominent Americans of the time, Charles A. Lindbergh, had attacked Jewish control of the media and the government for promoting U.S. involvement in the war. Bigots like Lindbergh and these Nazi-front groups had actively supported Hitler's actions against the Jews (Cole, W. S., 1974, pp. 73–74).

Another form of anti-Semitism was polite, the kind that shows up in Ernest Hemingway's depiction of attitudes toward Robert Co-hen in *The Sun Also Rises*. This form of anti-Semitism was embodied in restrictions on admission to social clubs, prestigious colleges and universities, employment, corporate boardrooms, and neighborhoods. Accustomed to this discrimination, Jews responded by forming their own clubs and society.

When the Schaalmans arrived in Cedar Rapids, they found that the country club had accepted only one Jewish member and that social rela-tions between Jews and non-Jews were almost nonexistent. Schaalman remembers, "The five o'clock shadow, which signaled social separation even for those who had business relationships during the day." "Jews," he recounts, "were subject to innuendo and racial slurs, whether overt or subtle, and found themselves questioning why they were not accepted. They did not know what the gentiles expected from them."

The government recognized that anti-Semitism was a threat to na-tional unity. In an effort to stave off efforts to undermine the unity that was critical in time of war, the government closed down some of the most virulent pro-Nazi publications and radio stations. Less extreme anti-Semitic media, when they were exposed publically, stopped broad-casting and publishing for fear of antagonizing the authorities (*American Jewish Year Book, 1942–1943*, p. 140).

The end of the war brought about a new sympathy for Jews and the crumbling of some social barriers to their full inclusion in American life.

In large part, that sympathy developed from the public awareness of the concentration camps and the murder of six million Jews. The pictures of emaciated camp survivors and the piles of decaying corpses raised public awareness of the Jewish catastrophe. So, too, did the testimonies of the U.S. troops who had entered the camps. Newsreels shown in movie theaters all over America brought the horrible images into the lives of the common American. Hundreds of thousands of Jewish soldiers fought side by side with their gentile comrades for whom this contact was their first experience of Jews. When the millions of troops returned, many of them, Jews and gentiles, took advantage of the GI Bill to go to college or graduate school. This experience allowed for further mingling and the development of greater understanding and tolerance.

The effect of this new awareness was to alter the social relationships in Cedar Rapids.[128] Now, as never before, young Jews on college campuses met their future mates, who frequently were gentiles. Intermarriage became more common. Relations between business neighbors improved. Unfortunately, religious leaders did not change as quickly. Many of them had difficulty changing their traditional doctrinal and personal biases against Jews. Schaalman remembers a Ministerial Association meeting to which he had been invited, the first rabbi in its history. After the meeting, while he was walking with a Methodist minister, he turned and asked, "Can *I* be saved?" At first, the minister did not respond. As they walked along silently, the minister stopped abruptly and blurted out, "Damn it, there's got to be a way, you are such a nice fellow."

The city of Cedar Rapids had a rich social life that the young couple soon became part of. Some of the city's wealthy and powerful elite invited the Schaalmans to their homes at a time when no other Jews were invited. Schaalman's various community involvements opened other doors that allowed him entrée to the city's elite society, one that had been closed to Jews before him. He began speaking in churches and became the vice president of the War Allocation Board, a wartime organization that was responsible for the distribution of ration coupons.

One of his most important and influential friendships was with Howard Hall, a wealthy industrialist and the owner of the Iowa Manufacturing and Iowa Steel & Iron companies. Hall was a major figure in Cedar Rapids social and business world. Their friendship began when Hall attended a funeral at which Schaalman gave a eulogy. Schaalman had only been in town for two or three months and had never given a eulogy before. The funeral was for a Jewish scrap dealer named Esaac Cohn, a leading citizen in Cedar Rapids, who had business dealings with Hall. Cohn was a member of the Orthodox synagogue and Schaalman barely knew him. His children, on the other hand, were members of Temple Judah and insisted that Schaalman conduct the funeral. Because there was only one funeral home in town, Schaalman conducted the funeral in a Christian funeral home.[129]

When Schaalman finished his eulogy, he was accosted by the temple's treasurer, Ruth Miller, who told him that he made the man out to be a saint, "but he was such a bastard." Schaalman was stunned by her comment and has never forgotten it. He was expecting something else because, as he put it, he had "pulled out all the stops" but, still, the eulogy was wrong. Not blaming himself entirely, he recalled that he was working from the family's input, and they "deified the man." Whenever he now does a funeral, he hears Ruth Miller in the background and re-members not to say anything untruthful in a eulogy. He has admitted, on the other hand, to "gilding the lily" and not telling the whole truth.

Soon after the funeral, Cohn's oldest son, Harry, called to tell Schaal-man to hurry up and get dressed: "Howard Hall wants to see you." As Schaalman reported, "If anyone in that part of the country got a call from Howard Hall to come, you did not walk, you ran." Hall was not only president of the Iowa Steel and Iron Works but had established the Iowa Manufacturing Company (present day "Cedarapids, Inc.") He was also chairman of a number of banks and a director of such companies as Amana Refrigeration and The Quaker Oats Company. Not coinci-dentally, his wife, Margaret Hall, was the daughter of George Douglas, the son of one of the founding partners of Quaker Oats. Hall was also a catalyst for Cedar Rapids economic development. On many Sunday mornings, the city's business elite gathered in his home and, around his swimming pool, informally planned the city's future. These sessions were referred to as the "Sunday School" (Brucemore, 2005).

Cohn and Schaalman headed for the steel mill. When they arrived, they walked through the factory and then were ushered into an office as big as a house. Once inside, they were met by Hall's bodyguards, two large German shepherds. Schaalman, who had not yet met Hall, was pleasantly surprised when he came from behind his desk to shake the young rabbi's hand. Hall told him that he wanted to meet him after hearing the most magnificent eulogy he had ever heard. He invited Schaalman to sit with him, and, in the next fifteen minutes, Hall talked about himself and told Schaalman what an asset he would be to the community. "We finally have a rabbi," he said, "who can represent the Jewish community." In the meantime, Harry, intimidated by this wealthy and successful man, merely nodded and said "yes" to everything Hall said. At the end of the interview, Hall handed Schaalman a photograph of himself with his head in the mouth of his pet lion, and wrote, "From one lion tamer to the other," and then signed it.

Not long after this meeting, while the Schaalmans were at home, the doorbell rang. When Lotte opened the door, she was met by a uniformed chauffeur, who had driven up in a big Cadillac limousine. The chauffeur handed her an envelope that contained a formal invitation from Mr. and Mrs. Hall, requesting the pleasure of the Schaalmans' company the following Sunday. The young couple looked at each other and laughed at the thought they had been invited to visit one of the most powerful men in the community, and, though they did not know it at the time, the country. Lotte drafted a response, which they delivered to the servants at Hall's residence. The palatial home was situated on approximately twenty acres in the middle of town.

At one o'clock that Sunday, Howard Hall himself drove up in his Cadillac. His wife Margaret was sitting in the back and their two German shepherds were sitting in front. Hall invited the Schaalmans to get in. Their initial meeting with Margaret was a complete surprise. She was the daughter of the founder of Quaker Oats and as charming and graceful a woman as they had ever met. Hall drove them to their luxurious "cottage" overlooking the Cedar River, where they lived while their magnificent new home was being remodeled. Known as "Brucemore," it was a twenty-one room Queen Anne-style mansion surrounded by a twenty-six acre park-like estate in the heart of Cedar Rapids (National Trust for Historic Preservation, 2009).[130] To the Schaalmans, the cottage looked like a Hollywood set. They marveled at the huge picture windows looking out over the river and the beautiful landscape spread out behind it.[131] Schaalman remembers the cottage as a magnificent place with copper ceilings and hand-laid floors. The Halls had a pet lion named Leo, one of three with the same name.

To put his guests at ease and to allow the four of them to spend time alone, Hall had dismissed the servants. After they had a chance to be acquainted, Hall instructed his wife to take Lotte into the kitchen to cook steaks while he and the rabbi took a ride on the river in his large Chris Craft boat. Because his cottage bordered on a two-mile stretch of the river bounded at both ends by waterfalls, they could ride only about two miles before they had to turn around. As soon as they were out on the river, Hall remarked, "Those Goddamned Jews. If it were not for the Jews, we would not have those goddamn labor unions, because it is the Jews that make all these agitations. Those goddamn communist Jews." The war had not yet started and Hall was fighting with his unions. Surprised by the outburst, Schaalman realized he needed to take a stand. Hall had not only antagonized him, but also aroused his combative spirit. "Mr. Hall," he parried, "if it were not for the goddamned steel barons who do not pay their workers a decent wage, there would not be any unions, there would not need to be any agitation." Not expecting to be challenged, Hall changed the subject and never brought it up again. From then on, he referred to the young man as "Herman." Despite this unpleasant experience, the rest of the visit was pleasant, and the Schaalmans left feeling that they had had a wonderful time.

This visit was the first of many. The Halls had fallen in love with the Schaalmans, especially with Lotte, whom Margaret loved almost on first sight. Schaalman remembers an invitation from the Halls to meet their friends, including Roy Fruehauf[132] and Walter Chrysler, two of the most powerful industrialists in America. During the visit, Hall told Fruehauf and Chrysler not to leave until they had an opportunity to meet his rabbi. To Schaalman, they were notorious anti-Semites from Detroit.

An indication of how strongly Hall felt toward Schaalman was his decision to become a member of Temple Judah. Although he was not Jewish, Hall became the single largest contributor; his annual gift of $1,000 was three times greater than that of any other congregant. No doubt because of Schaalman's influence, Hall even contributed $1,000 to the "Jewish Fund," one of the largest gifts the fund received. When Schaalman was hospitalized after an automobile accident in early 1945, Hall had meat delivered to his house for the entire twenty-two weeks of his hospital stay, at a time when "meat could not be had."[133] Another measure of their friendship was Hall's decision to accept Schaalman's recommendation to take on Dr. David Thaler, then newly arrived in Cedar Rapids, as his physician ahead of all the other top doctors in Cedar Rapids. Even after he left Cedar Rapids for Chicago, the Rabbi and the industrialist remained friends. A year later, while the Schaalmans were vacationing in Miami Beach at the Saxony Hotel, they ran into Hall, who happened to be in his Florida beach home. Somehow, he discovered that the Schaalmans were there at the same time and invited them to dinner. This was not the first time that Hall had invited the Schaalmans to visit him in Florida.

Community Involvement

Part of being a rabbi in a small Midwestern town meant that he had to become active in local community affairs. Although just out of rabbinic school and not much more than twenty-five years old, Schaalman was drafted to play a significant role in the community. Community leaders sought him out and involved him in various activities. Various factors contributed to this development. For one, Schaalman was recognized as an impressive and competent religious leader; for another, this genial Midwestern small city was willing to extend its good will toward Jews, especially now that Schaalman was its representative. So popular and renowned a figure did he become, that after a few years, he was invited to cohost a radio program together with two other community leaders. The format for the program featured special guests and time for listeners to call in to comment or ask questions.

A speech Schaalman gave at the Kiwanis Club provided his entrée into the life of the community. Kiwanis was a venue for the city's social elite, including owners of local business and the city's major industrial complexes. As a newcomer to the city and not yet thirty, he was invited to speak because the Club was always looking for new programs. Kiwanis rules required that members stand while the speaker was brought in, yet the occasion was informal enough so that on a later occasion when Iowa's Governor, Bourke B. Hickenlopper, spoke, one of the members stood up and said jokingly, "Hurry up and sit down! We want Herman to speak." Schaalman was embarrassed at receiving so much attention. Although a joke, this remark was an acknowledgement of the prestige accorded him. Schaalman's initial speech was so well accepted that he was invited to join the organization.

Soon, he felt very much at home and was regarded affectionately. He became familiar with several of the city's leading men and even received invitations to their homes and invitations to join other organizations and boards. (One consideration specific to the time was the fact that so many men were away in the war that there must have been an acute shortage of members to attend these meetings.) He could walk into "any bank and see the president just by sahing, 'I am here.'" There can be no doubt that because of his many gifts—his acute mind, his verbal felicity, and his cheerful and optimistic personality—he was considered an asset to the community. His popularity with Cedar Rapids elite carried over into the community at large, and he became a popular local figure. His popularity allowed him to become a spokesman for the Jewish community. More than simply teaching Judaism to their children, the Jewish community appreciated the fact that Schaalman was opening doors for them in the gentile community.

A sign of his growing stature and acceptance by the local business, professional, and religious community was an invitation to join the Freemasons. Schaalman progressed through the first three stages of initiation: "Entered Apprentice," "Fellow Craft," and "Master Mason."[134] Before long, Schaalman became a Mason and the single most sought after speaker in churches and civic organizations in that part of Iowa. His stature as a significant public figure began to grow even before he became an American citizen, which did not occur until 1943.[135] Reflecting on his acceptance by the community from hindsight of more than sixty years, he claims that because he was "never quite sure of himself," he had no idea of what he might be capable.

In 1947, Schaalman became a radio personality. Together with two friends, Harry Boyd, the editor of the *Cedar Rapids Gazette*, and the president of Coe College, Byron S. Hollinshead, he cohosted a successful weekly radio program on station WMT (AM). Because of the excellent rapport among the three men, Schaalman thought it would be a good idea to initiate a weekly radio program based on current issues. They decided on a talk show format and named the program "The Three Men on a Limb" (*Cedar Rapids Gazette*, January 4, 1948, p. 11). The program was modeled after a popular national radio program,

Information Please, which also used the three-person co-host format to dialogue with a guest on a wide variety of topics (Schaalman, H. E., 1999, p. 20). To ensure that the program would be interesting, the hosts collared important visitors to Cedar Rapids as guests on the program. Schaalman remembers that Henry Wallace and Paul Robeson were two of the guests.

In October of 1947, the hosts held a round-table discussion on the subject "Do Women Have Equal Opportunity for a Career in a Man's World" (*The Coe Cosmos*, 1947). The topic must have pleased Schaalman, who believed in the equality of women. According to an article in the *Cedar Rapids Gazette*, the program became so popular in eastern Iowa that Schaalman became a household name. The paper described Schaalman as riding "the precarious branches of current problems with ease" (Meek, 1948, p. 11). When guests were not available, because it was wartime and the Roosevelt era, the program hosts found plenty to talk about among themselves. In the midst of conservative Republican territory, the three hosts spoke from a decidedly liberal bent and raised significant controversy. The young German-Jewish rabbi had become a well-known radio personality in the Midwest heartland.

After several years in Cedar Rapids, Schaalman had become "one of the public figures of that community. When, in 2008, he was shown newspaper accounts of his many community involvements, he was completely surprised. He had not remembered having played such an important role in such a large number of community and civic organizations. The list of these involvements in the eight years he spent in Cedar Rapids is formidable. Among the organizations in which he played a major role were: chairman of the Associated Jewish Charities for Linn County and the Jewish Welfare Fund; vice president of the YMCA, chairman of the Council of Social Planning, member of the Linn County Red Cross Board of Directors, member of the Public Welfare Bureau, chairman of the Community Chest drive and a member of its Board, member of the War Resources Board, chairman of the Associated Jewish Charities for Linn county and chairman of the Family Agency (Meek, 1948, p. 11). In 1947, this commitment of time and energy in the community earned him the Distinguished Civic Service Award (Gerald Hiland, 1949). As late as June 1949, only two months before leaving Cedar Rapids, he was still taking on new civic responsibilities. On June 16, he was introduced at a dinner event at the local YMCA as a new member of the executive committee of the Cedar Rapids Radio Council and as its new vice president (Radio Council Committee, 1949).

Among the many contributions to the Jewish and non-Jewish community were his frequent speaking engagements. As a member of the Jewish Chautauqua Society,[137] he spoke in many local venues, including the YMCA, business groups such as the Kiwanis Club, Coe and Cornell Colleges, and Christian summer camps.[138] Considering the fact that he was not a native-born speaker and was insecure in his use of the language, his frequent ventures in public speaking were a testament to his budding self-confidence, intelligence, and ability.[139]

Another major contribution to Cedar Rapids was his support for its mental health community. Shortly before Schaalman left Cedar Rapids for Chicago, *The Cedar Rapids Gazette* (May 1, 1949) reported that Schaalman took a lead role in advocating for additional financial aid to set up a county mental hygiene clinic (Financial Aid, 1949, p. 1). Schaalman argued, "Both social and financial benefits would result from such a mental hygiene clinic" (p. 1). It would reduce the number of juvenile delinquents and help people in the first stages of mental illness before they became "incurable." Such an investment would help to "salvage the lives of many persons who might otherwise be committed to institutions" and thereby save the county money that it would otherwise spend to keep the individuals in state institutions (p. 4). Referring specifically to the benefits the community could expect from the clinic, Schaalman offered as an example that many of the psychiatric patients might receive treatment on an outpatient basis. Most of these patients, he told the supervisors, could not afford to leave their jobs and families to travel back and forth to a hospital in Iowa City. The appeal for funds for the new clinic was a partial success; although the clinic opened December 15, 1949, it had to rely heavily on private funds to do so (Foto Facts, 1949).

Interfaith Activities

One of the lessons Schaalman derived from the Holocaust was that positive interfaith relations were critical to Jewish survival and to creating a more harmonious world. He believed that if positive interfaith relations had developed in Germany, the Holocaust might never have occurred. At this early stage of his career, Schaalman began his lifelong effort to form close bonds with the Christian, and later, the Muslim community.[140]

One of his earliest experiences of the need for his involvement in interfaith activities came early in his rabbinate in Cedar Rapids. It was also another significant encounter with American anti-Semitism. In 1943, the Jewish Chautauqua Society (JCS), an organization sponsored by the National Federation of Temple Brotherhoods (now, "Men of Reform Judaism"), invited him to participate in a nearby Methodist camp in Clear Lake, Iowa. The objective was to expose the campers and its ministerial faculty to Jews. That summer, he packed up his wife and daughter and drove off to the camp. The camp was huge, hosting about 800 youngsters and 120 ministers. Although Schaalman felt welcome, he noticed that some of the ministers and campers were wary. They came from small Midwestern towns where they had never seen a rabbi nor had any contact with Jews.[141]

Schaalman taught two classes on Jewish history for seventy campers. When Schaalman asked them to list on paper three Jews they had heard of, most of them listed "Roosevelt." To his surprise, none of them listed Jesus. He concluded that at least in Iowa "Jews were virtually unknown. … They were caricatures or myths, mostly starkly negative. It was not unusual to hear adults venting their contempt for that 'Jew' Roosevelt," he remarked, "or to voice the well-known canard, 'Jews have all the money.' Jews were also labeled 'Christ killers' and unjustly condemned to suffer as a result." By the end of the summer, he was convinced that he and his wife had made an impact on the community and helped to dispel some of the negativism toward Jews. He and Lotte also knew that the camp had had a major impact on them.

To make better use of his time and to supplement his income, Schaalman sought other opportunities to make constructive contributions to the community. When teaching positions opened up at Coe College and neighboring Cornell College, he grabbed them. His first assignment was at Coe College where he taught an adult education course in the Great Books, a study of fiction and non-fiction works that contributed to the forming of the Western mind (Meek, 1948, p. 11). Because the course was popular and many of Cedar Rapids' leading figures enrolled in it, Schaalman taught it for several years. According to the Coe College newspaper, the course enrolled thirty students in 1948, the second highest of the evening courses that were offered (Layton Announces, 1948).

In 1946, the JCS funded a teaching position at Cornell College, founded as a Methodist college in Mt. Vernon, Iowa, and selected Schaalman to fill it.[142] His appointment was part of the JCS's national rabbinic scholars' program, supporting faculty appointments at Christian colleges and seminaries to promote interfaith understanding. By exposing future ministers and priests to Jews and Judaism and the contributions they have made to world civilization and Christianity, the JCS's expectation is that from this exposure, these future ministers will develop more positive and informed opinions about their Jewish colleagues and neighbors and communicate them to others. The institutions select the subjects to be taught and the JCS appointed speakers deliver lectures and conduct forums and classes for small and more intimate group discussions (*American Jewish Year Book, 1942–1943*, pp. 118–119).

The college offered Schaalman a course in Comparative Religions, including Buddhism, Hinduism, Islam, and Judaism. Because he had no background in religions other than Judaism, he had to do a great deal of preparation, but he had an understanding with the college that he would spend more time on Judaism than on the other religions. The atmosphere at the college was supportive, and he credits this experience as the basis for his special feeling toward Methodist colleges. As he explained, "I became hooked on Methodists."[143] Because the students were very bright, Schaalman considered this one of his most exciting teaching encounters. Schaalman's developing rapport with Methodists was the basis for his later teaching in Chicago at Garrett-Evangelical Theological Seminary. These two college teaching assignments led to a life-long second career as faculty member at various colleges and universities.

Although he had been an invited speaker in various high schools and churches both in and around Cedar Rapids, the earliest record of his participation in a formal interfaith event appears in the May 15, 1947, edition of *The Cedar Rapids Gazette*. The newspaper reported that Schaalman participated in a forum to discuss "Practical Solutions for World Peace" ("Baha'i groups," 1947, p. 1). Held two years after World War II and sponsored by the Cedar Rapids Baha'i, the interfaith discussion of how to achieve world peace was one of the most pressing topics of the day. The fact that Schaalman was invited to speak at numerous interfaith events suggests that at least one city in America's heartland was ready for interreligious change and cooperation.

Becoming Parents

When children become adults, it is not unusual for them to create their own family life based on their experiences as children. This is especially true when the experience of childhood was a good one. By their own reports, Herman and Lotte had ideal childhoods and happy home lives, which proved to be excellent models of family life. Their parents had given them complete and unconditional love, support for their life choices, the gifts of educational opportunities, and the freedom to make their own decisions. These experiences also gave Herman and Lotte the tools to leave home and establish a new life in an alien country, and that led to their success in the new world.

Although they came from radically different backgrounds, Herman and Lotte had one thing in common: the experience of happy childhoods, which they drew on when they set up their home in Cedar Rapids. Not only were they a loving and openly affectionate couple, but they also adored their children who were loving and supportive in return. Fundamental to the Schaalman family life was the observance of religious holidays and lifecycle events, which nourished it and gave it structure. Susan, their oldest child, refers to these events as "milestones." Even when she and her brother Michael returned to school in the fall, the occasion was marked by a "special *b'racha* in which everyone participated." The family celebrated not only birthdays but also "annual cake and ice cream parties with the children's friends."[145]

Two years after arriving in Cedar Rapids, the Schaalmans had their first child, which they considered a blessing. Having a child meant an "authentification" of their marriage, but raising a child is something else and proved to be a major challenge. Not only were they young and inexperienced, but the pregnancy was difficult for Lotte. Thanks to the fact that the War had drained off many of the local doctors, the Schaalmans had trouble finding a competent obstetrician. After ruling out the doctors in Cedar Rapids, they found a doctor named Gerstein in Marion, a small suburban town five miles from Cedar Rapids. Like them, Gerstein was a Jewish refugee. Because he came from Vienna, they trusted him; they knew that Vienna had an excellent reputation for its medical education and practice. Moreover, they could talk to him in German. Because neither of them could drive and they had no car, getting to Gerstein's office for checkups was a challenge. The only way to get to Marion was by bus. The trip was difficult for Lotte. Because of the poor condition of the road, she experienced a great deal of discomfort, which, Schaalman speculates, may have been responsible for the complications that developed during her pregnancy.

Susan's birth was not an easy one. Lotte's labor was long and difficult, and she was sick the whole time. After she had spent Thursday night in the hospital, Dr. Gerstein told the expectant father he could guarantee the life of the baby, but not the mother's. By Friday afternoon, the situation improved dramatically. Because Lotte was no longer in danger and there was no indication that the birth was imminent, Schaalman left the hospital confident that there was time for him to fulfill his congregational responsibility of conducting Friday night services. Not that he had much of a choice: Lotte insisted that he go. Fulfilling that obligation was more important to her than having her husband with her in the hospital. It so happened that while Schaalman was leading the services, out of concern for the young couple the president of the congregation had gone to the hospital in time to discover that the baby had been born. He rushed back to the temple and announced that Lotte had given birth to a baby girl.

Not only were the Schaalmans delighted to become parents, but Susan's birth was also a cause for celebration for the congregation. Apparently, this birth was a first for a rabbinic couple employed by the congregation. It was supportive of the Schaalmans and delighted that they were now parents. The congregation showered them with presents and brought them food during Lotte's hospitalization and her recuperation at home. Giving food in the middle of the war was no small sacrifice. Many items could only be purchased with ration coupons for minimal amounts of food items.

Fortunately for the Schaalmans, Lotte's mother came to live with them. Because Gussie had considerable experience as a caretaker and nurse in various homes in California, she was an enormous help and a

wonderful companion. Where some husbands might object to the extended presence of a mother-in-law, Schaalman welcomed her into his
home. According to Schaalman, she was a remarkable woman, vigorous,
intelligent, and capable.

When Gussie came to live with them, she was in her late forties
and a widow. Schaalman thought of her as a proper German-Jewish
matron, a strong and independent woman, a lady never seen without
makeup and always well groomed. Before the First World War, she and
her husband had owned a well-respected and successful shoe business.
Because they were financially able, she always had servants in her home.
During the war, her husband served in the German army and returned
home seriously ill. When he did not regain his health, Gussie took over
the business and became its driving force. When she came to America
as a refugee, she was forced to give up her independence and work in
other peoples' homes as a caretaker and baby nurse. Typically, when a
mother and her baby came home from the hospital, Gussie moved in to
take care of them. She assumed these new responsibilities without any
hesitation or loss of self-respect or status.

A few months after Susan's birth, the Schaalmans had an opportunity to take a summer vacation in the country. Though they had no
car, one of the Rabbi's congregants offered to let them use his summer
cottage in the woods. The man drove the family to the cottage and told
them he would return in a week to pick them up. Quickly, they realized they had no food, nor was there any place nearby where they could
purchase some. Fortunately, a nearby neighbor—there were a few other
cottages in the vicinity—told them that he would take them shopping.
The first day in the cottage, the family was delighted with their situation.
August in Iowa can be brutally hot and this wooded retreat provided a
welcome respite.

Their satisfaction at having gotten away from Iowa was soon wrecked
when their precious infant fell out of bed. When Susan fell asleep, they
placed her on a bed in one of the bedrooms and went into the living
room to relax. Shortly after, they heard a loud thud and rushed into the
room to find her on the floor crying her heart out. They thought the end
of the world had come. Had they been more experienced, they would
have known that they should have placed cushions or pillows around her
to keep her from falling. Another miscalculation was not to realize that

Susan was an active baby who was likely to turn over and roll off. Had they had access to a doctor, they would have gone to him immediately. Instead, they spent the day fretting over their child and inspecting her to see whether there might be some kind of damage. Fortunately, there was none, but they were plenty scared.

Thanks in large part to Lotte's outgoing personality and her generous nature, the Schaalmans entertained frequently. In Schaalman's terms, they "didn't want to be only takers, but givers" and, therefore, "opened their home to their congregants." On one of those evenings, when Susan was probably a year and a half, a congregant brought her a toy puppy. Her father turned to her and remarked, "You have a beautiful girl pup." The brash little girl responded, "This is not a girl pup." The guests were stunned and got very quiet. When the Rabbi asked her how she knew the pup was not female, she smiled knowingly, "No lipstick!" In retrospect, Schaalman recognized that this precocious remark was an indication of her sophistication at a very young age.

By the time Susan was two, she had a mind of her own. One day, as the family was walking to buy groceries, she decided she was not going any further. Her father thought a "little potch on her tuchas" would get her going. Not so. She sat down on the sidewalk and refused to move. Her parents decided to keep walking, fully expecting their daughter would follow. People began to gather around the child and began cooing over her, exactly what Susan wanted. Their looks implied criticism of her heartless, neglectful parents. The parents turned on their heels and came back to try to persuade their unruly daughter to get up. The admiring group of five or six adults was impressed that this tiny girl would dare to do exactly what she wanted.

A year later, the Schaalmans learned another lesson, only this time not about basic parenting skills. They learned firsthand about American anti-Semitism. The event began innocently enough when the Schaalmans went on a month-long vacation in Minnesota. They rented a cottage on the lake where members of their congregation spent their summers fishing. In addition to the well-needed rest and the time alone with his family, Schaalman planned to use the summer to prepare for his course at Cornell College in Comparative Religions. When the Schaalmans arrived, they were told that the cottage was available for only two weeks. Then, they would have to move to another cottage for the remaining two weeks. During the first two weeks, they had a visitor from their congregation, their dentist, Dr. Maury Katzoff and his wife, Bernice. He was a fisherman and had told them about Minnesota where many of Temple Judah's congregants spent their summers.

The sight of the Katzoffs apparently alerted the resort owner to the fact that the Schaalmans were Jewish. The day after they moved into their new cottage, the owner came by and placed the Schaalmans' deposit on the table. "I'm returning your deposit," he stated. "I didn't know that you were Jewish, and I've worked hard to get my resort going, and I just can't afford to have you stay there." The owner told them there was a resort nearby that they could go to and that he would be "glad to make the arrangements [at a place] where you people go." The moment posed a crisis for the young German immigrants. "Here we were on vacation in our newfound country and found ourselves victims of anti-Semitism right in the middle of the war." He realized there were many sympathizers for Fascists and Nazis in the United States, especially in Minnesota where there was a lot of anti-Jewish sentiment.[146] After a moment's reflection, the Rabbi said, "I'm not taking my money back, but I'll make a deal with you. My wife, my daughter, and I will … remain for three days, and, if after those three days you still feel that it would be to your advantage to have us leave, we will leave." Although the owner was not happy, he accepted the deal without protest.

Two or three days later, the Schaalmans moved to the other resort where their experience was the polar opposite. It had eight or nine lakefront cottages, though only one was vacant. The first morning, they set about pursuing their usual activities, which meant they went outside where Schaalman took up his reading, and Lotte busied herself with her knitting. In the meantime, Susan, who had become an adorable toddler with long golden locks, played in the sand nearby. "While we were absorbed in own activities, we did not notice that she had been attracted by the neighbors' small children and had toddled over to the next cottage." When they realized that Susan was now playing at their neighbors, Schaalman got up and went over to the parents to offer an excuse for his child. He picked her up and brought her back to their cottage. Not content to play by herself, in a few minutes Susan again toddled over to the neighbors' cottage. Again, the Rabbi went over and offered an excuse for his daughter. As he tried to pick her up, the woman asked, "Is your daughter sick?" "No," he replied, "we just don't want her to bother you, to intrude." "She's no bother," the woman replied. "Leave her here! She and our children can play with each other."

He left Susan there, and after a while, the Schaalmans decided to go inside their cottage. When the neighbor brought Susan back, she noticed that the Rabbi was reading a stack of books, several about Islam. When she asked what he was reading, he told her about his interests but did not reveal that he was a rabbi. She remained curious and asked, "Why are you doing this?" At that point, he decided "to spill the beans": "I'm a rabbi, and I'm about to teach at a college."

When word got around that there was a rabbi in their midst, the Schaalmans became the center of attention. "Unlike the snub at the other resort, here I became a celebrity. The fact that I had become such a prominent member of Cedar Rapids society may have influenced our reception." During the next two weeks the Schaalmans stayed there, they were frequent guests for dinner in the other cottages.

Soon after the Schaalmans returned to Cedar Rapids, they were forced to move out of the house they were renting. When their landlord informed them that he wanted to use the house for a relative, they rented a house in another part of town. One afternoon when the parents were coming home from the temple, they noticed what they thought was a cute little naked girl playing in the fountain across the street from their home. Another look and the Rabbi realized that this cute little girl was their independent minded three-year-old Susan sitting in the fountain and washing her hair. Even though she had been told not to leave the house, she did as she wished.

Susan

Sometimes, the joy of parenthood is overshadowed by a child's health issues. As a young child, Susan developed a severe case of asthma. Although in many respects Cedar Rapids was an ideal town to raise a child, its air was polluted from two factories that spewed harmful particulates into the air. Schaalman blames this pollution for the fact that Susan's asthma required constant vigilance and was a source of great anxiety to her parents. They would never know in advance when she would suffer an attack, nor its severity. Later, the Schaalmans discovered that Cedar

Rapids was known for its high level of asthma victims and had a relatively large number of allergists who practiced there.

The Schaalmans learned that they could comfort their daughter during one of her attacks by placing her on her father's chest where he would hum to her in his lowest baritone voice. The remedy worked wonders, and soon Susan would fall asleep curled up in his lap. One of her attacks was so severe that they took her to a hotel that had air conditioning, which they knew would help relieve her asthmatic symptoms. Curiously, Susan's pediatrician advised that she could be cured by eating bacon. From that point on, although she continued to have asthmatic attacks throughout her childhood, her parents, more concerned about her health than Jewish dietary prohibitions, followed the doctor's advice. As a result, Susan grew up eating bacon.

Another early event in the life of the new parents—this one humorous—occurred when Susan wanted a dog. The Schaalmans bought her a Golden Retriever puppy, which they called "Snippy." One afternoon as they were coming home from the temple and approaching the front steps to their screened in porch, they heard a huge commotion coming from inside. When they opened the door, they found Susan and the dog tangled together, and, to their complete surprise, Snippy was biting Susan's ear while she was biting his paw. Soon after, Susan had an asthmatic attack. Given this development, the Schaalmans concluded that they had no choice but to get rid of the dog. The asthmatic attacks, however, continued even without the dog.

The Accident

On Sunday, January 25, 1945, the Schaalmans drove out to a rural church some 30 miles outside of Cedar Rapids where Schaalman was scheduled to speak. It was a cold evening when they started for home. As they approached a bend in the road, suddenly he heard a "roar" and saw a "big light," and his car, which had been a gift from the congregation, was rammed head on at high speed by a drunken driver. The car, which previously had been a cab and constructed of sturdier materials than the average car, probably saved their lives. Nevertheless, the accident resulted in serious injury to both Schaalman and his wife. "Lotte's whole face," he recounts, "was molded into the windshield." The impact broke her arm and jaw, the effect of which still lingers. The force of the collision pushed the steering wheel to the roof and the front wheel into his lap. He noticed that the car was smoking and turned off the ignition. Then, he pushed open the door and, as he began to crawl out, his right leg would not follow him out of the car. He realized that it was broken. When he dragged himself free of the wrecked car, he lay on the roadway in excruciating pain. The driver of the other car, which had turned over into a ditch, climbed out of his car and began yelling at Schaalman. Incensed, Schaalman threatened to beat him up even though he was lying on the ground and could not move. The drunk got back in his car. In desperate shape, Schaalman succeeded in flagging down a speeding car. The driver did not see him until the last minute and nearly ran over him. The driver, who had stopped twenty feet from Schaalman's head, took one look at him and drove off to the nearest farmhouse to call for an ambulance.

A half hour later, an ambulance arrived and took the Schaalmans to St. Luke's Methodist Hospital in Cedar Rapids, where Schaalman spent the next twenty-two weeks recovering from his injuries. At the time of the accident, the only doctor Schaalman knew was Gerstein, who had delivered his daughter and was now serving in the Army. Schaalman did not know what to tell the ambulance driver when he asked Schaalman what doctor to call. When the driver called for a doctor, the one who responded was Dr. Phil Crew, one of the biggest anti-Semites in town.

Both Schaalmans were hospitalized, though Lotte's injuries were less severe. Nevertheless, when her best friend, the wife of their dentist, Dr. Katzoff, saw her in the hospital, she almost fainted. Not only did Lotte have a broken arm and jaw, but also she had lost seven teeth and her jaw needed to be wired together. Her arm was not set for several days. Because they desperately wanted to be close to each other, the Schaalmans "drove the nurses crazy until they finally broke every rule and put [them] in the same room." In the meantime, the Cedar Rapids community was so concerned about their welfare, that the hospital issued medical bulletins almost daily.

Schaalman considers the experience of the accident and his subsequent hospitalization "a watershed" in his life. Because he discovered what it was like to be hospitalized for a long term, he developed empathy for people suffering long-term hospitalization. "The experience, however, took a terrible toll on my psyche. By the time of my birthday in

April, had someone put a gun on the table, I think I would have used it. I was that desperate." Part of the problem was that the leg was improperly set. Schaalman developed excruciating pain and, when he told his doctor, Crew responded, "You Jews cannot stand pain. You are all alike." Nevertheless, he ordered injections of morphine every four hours. The pain intensified and a few hours later, Schaalman found himself gripping his bed. "To keep from screaming, I asked that towels be stuffed in my mouth. The pain was so excruciating that I chewed them to bits."

The pain went on for at least two days. When the doctor came to visit him, Schaalman pleaded with him, "Dr. Crew, I don't care what you think about Jews. I want you to cut a window [in the cast] and take a look." Although the doctor was disgusted with him, he cut open the cast and was stunned by what he saw. Apparently, he had wound the bandages so tight that they cut into in Schaalman's flesh, which, as it dried, had become infected. He told Schaalman that the infection might have become gangrenous, and he could have lost his leg. Crew immediately cut off the cast, inserted a Kirschner wire[147] through his bones, and then attached it to a weighted device to keep the fragments aligned. "I was hung up in this manner and unable to get out of bed for twenty-one-and-a-half weeks." He was ordered to lie flat on his back and to be careful not to move.

Another consequence of the accident was that it prevented him from entering the military chaplaincy to which he had applied after becoming a citizen. Schaalman's desire to enter the military was part of his desire to serve his newly adopted country and to respond to the "vastly increased need for Jewish chaplains in the army and navy" (*American Jewish Year Book: 1942–1943*, 1942–1943, p. 97). When the appointment came through in January of 1945, it was just days after the accident, which disqualified him from service.[148]

Although Schaalman believed Crew's anti-Semitism had caused him harm, in the end they became friends. As a byproduct of this friendship, the doctor changed his attitude toward Jews and became friends with other Jews in the community. "Crew eventually turned out to be a human being, though I never felt completely comfortable with him." Because of his new relationship with the Jewish community, Crew did not object to the new Polish refugee doctor, David Thaler, settling in his domain and actually helped integrate him into Cedar Rapids' medical community.

During their convalescence, Lotte's mother took care of Susan, who was only a year and a half. Once Lotte was released, she, or occasionally her mother, brought Susan to visit her father. Schaalman remembers that she came every day and made good use of the opportunities the hospital provided for her enjoyment. "She would bound down the hallway and poke her head into the six rooms she passed on her way and greet everyone she met in her little girl sing-song voice, 'Hello, Hello, Hello.' When she came to my room, she would jump up on my bed, but was careful not to disrupt my fracture."

By the miracle of broadcast radio, which was set up in his room, he was able to speak to the congregation and participate in its worship services. When President Roosevelt died on April 12, a large memorial was held in Cedar Rapids attended by thousands of people. "I was asked to make a speech to the assembled crowd. Once again, a microphone was put in front of my face so that I could broadcast outside. The community and the hospital could not think of holding such a public event without my participation."

During his convalescence, his good friend Howard Hall visited him frequently and provided assistance to his family. In addition to the fresh meat he had delivered to the Schaalmans, he sent him "buckets full of gardenias" to give to the nurses to ensure that he got the best treatment. Schaalman was convinced that Hall's attentiveness to him undoubtedly influenced the care he received. As Schaalman describes the situation, "The Halls took care of us. Nevertheless, for the rest of the year, I had first to use crutches and then a cane to get around but was never completely free of pain."

Schaalman left the hospital in late June. Unable to walk, he left in a wheelchair, and for the next few months walked on crutches. By the time the high holidays came, the congregation had built him a ramp so that he could wheel himself onto the pulpit. "During the months that I was hospitalized, the congregation provided its own leadership for services and took care of itself and maintained their school." Help also came in the form of occasional assistance from visiting rabbis, as well as local clergy who came to his rescue.

While Schaalman was recovering in the hospital, Abe Bass, the only Jewish lawyer in town and a member of his congregation, came to visit. Bass told Schaalman that he had taken the liberty of visiting the accident site and taking pictures of the skid marks and told Schaalman that he was going to investigate the kind of person who caused the accident. That afternoon, Bass returned with a report on the unsavory character of the other driver, who had emerged from the accident unscratched. He was not alone in the car but with a woman who appeared to be dead, though she woke up two days later and walked out of the hospital. Luckily for Schaalman, the driver had an insurance policy that would enable him eventually to recover the cost of his hospitalization and the replacement of his car.[149]

By November, Schaalman was able to walk with a cane and was concerned that the case had not yet been settled. Not long after he came home from the hospital, his lawyer called to tell him he had received an offer for settlement. Schaalman was willing to accept it, but his attorney was not. Bass set up a meeting with the representative of the insurance company to discuss a new settlement offer and told Schaalman to be prepared to walk out if the new offer was too low. When the attorney packed up, Schaalman got up with him and went home. "I had barely gotten home when Bass called to tell me that he had received a better offer and that I should accept it." When the Schaalmans found out that the offer was much greater than the one that had been offered previously, they were delighted. It allowed them to travel to Brazil to see his parents and to make a down payment on a new co-op apartment when they came to Chicago in 1949.

Michael (A.K.A. Mickey)

In 1944, Schaalman attended a Hadassah convention in Atlantic City, and, for the first time, heard an account of the horrors of the concentration camps. Up until that time, he had heard about the concentration camps and that Jews were being killed in them, but not about the conditions in the camps and the treatment of their inmates. "I was so overwhelmed by the vivid descriptions that I ran to the bathroom and threw up. When I went home and shared this information with Lotte, we realized that the slaughter of millions of European Jews made having another child more urgent." They also felt that they had a responsibility to restore their families, so many of whom had died in concentration camps. Their awareness of this terrible tragedy became a "shadow" on their lives: "It became the motivation for changing the world to ensure that another event like this could never happen again."

Having another child, however, turned out to be an ordeal neither of them expected. Lotte had three miscarriages, presumed by the couple to have been related to the automobile accident. When they signed the settlement papers in late 1945, they did not realize it contained a section absolving the insurance company of further liability. When the couple finally realized that the failed pregnancies might have been the result of the accident, they had no recourse but to pay their own medical costs. Nor could they sue the insurance company for additional damages. Their new gynecologist, Dr. Thaler,[150] convinced them that once Lotte had healed, they should attempt to have another child as soon as possible. After a fourth miscarriage, the Schaalmans concluded that it was unlikely, or perhaps impossible to have another child.

One of the miscarriages occurred while Schaalman was in Toronto attending the annual CCAR conference. At the time, because there was no air travel to Toronto from Cedar Rapids, he traveled by train, a long and tiring journey. When he arrived at the conference hotel, he called Lotte to find out how she was feeling. She confessed that she had known from a visit to her obstetrician several days earlier that the fetus was dead. She kept the information secret because she was certain he would not have gone to the conference had he known that shortly she would have to undergo surgery to remove the fetus. That day, she had had a D and C. "The news devastated me as I considered what I thought was the dereliction of my marital duties. Although Lotte opposed the decision, the next day I took the train to Cedar Rapids to get home as quickly as possible. I knew I had made the right decision." He also realized that there would be times when he would have to make decisions he thought were right, even though Lotte did not approve.

Sometime in 1946 or '47, the Schaalmans moved into a bigger house, an older home on 1411 Washington Avenue SE, a few blocks from their previous home and within walking distance of the Temple. Although Schaalman now had another car, he tried to avoid unnecessary driving because the memory of the accident was still fresh. "We moved because we needed more space not only because of Susan, but because we anticipated that we would have at least one more child."

In August of 1947, either shortly before, or soon after the Schaalmans traveled to Brazil to see his family (Schaalman is not sure), Lotte conceived again. This time, Dr. Thaler advised the couple to consult an internationally famous doctor in Iowa City as a means of getting the best possible medical advice. The doctor came to Cedar Rapids to examine Lotte and then ordered her to stay in bed for the next eight months. "The last three months of the pregnancy was a critical time for us and a source of great anxiety not only for us, but also for our extensive circle of friends."

Her confinement was an embarrassment to Lotte. She thought the congregants looked down on her because she was bedridden. Although she thought they saw her as sickly, she was only following the doctor's orders as the best way to save the baby. "As the rabbi's wife, I was expected to be part of his ministry." To the extent that she served in that role, she gave up her own independence in order to be the ideal rebbetzin, an asset to husband's rabbinate. Although she spent much of her time in bed, she was able to get up and do some of the less taxing chores of maintaining a home. Had they been able to hire help, life would have been much easier for them, but that was not possible on his meager salary.

On April 25, 1948, five years after Susan's birth, Michael was born, a healthy, perfect baby. The birth came three days before Schaalman's birthday and must have been a special present for the proud father. From Lotte's perspective, "The birth was much easier than Susan's, which had taken more than twenty-four hours. Michael came quickly, so quickly that the doctor raced to the hospital in his house slippers, a feat made possible because the town was so small." Two days later, however, the doctor told Schaalman that his son had contracted a yeast infection of the mouth called thrush, a highly contagious disease. As a result, Michael was quarantined for several days, and his parents were not allowed to come near him. Schaalman was appalled when he saw his son crying, his mouth a deep purple, the consequence of having been coated with gentian violet (the treatment of the day). To Schaalman, "The sight of my baby crying and his mouth dark purple was pitiful."

Once the thrush was under control and no longer infectious, the Schaalmans were able to have a bris for Michael. They hired a mohel, probably from Des Moines.[151] Despite what must have been a joyous occasion, Schaalman no longer remembers anything about the event. "The stress of the high-risk pregnancy, coupled with Michael's scary illness overwhelmed me at the time, and I remember very little about it." The bris was held in his home and with most of his congregation, by now about eighty members, in attendance. The birth of a male child was a source of great joy to them. "Michael's birth was for us an affirmation of the hope for Jewish survival and its eventual triumph over Nazism."

By now, the Schaalmans had had enough experience as parents to know what to expect and were a lot less anxious. In contrast to Susan, who was difficult to raise because of her parent's inexperience, Michael was much easier. Susan's allergies proved to be a formidable health issue for her and her parents. Michael, on the other hand, did not suffer any unusual health issues. Lotte describes him "as easy-going, happy, and contented."

To the delight of the family, Lotte's sister Ilse arrived to help with the new baby.[152] Her arrival coincided with the birth of the State of Israel, which declared its independence on May 14, 1948. This "mysterious visitor," as Ilse seemed to Susan, turned out to be a blessing for the five year old. Although she had come to help with the baby, Susan reported, "she wound up being the personal companion-psychologist every first-born needs in adjusting to the intrusion of an uninvited newcomer" (Schaalman Youdovin, S., 1986, p. 260). As the only child, Susan was accustomed to receiving the exclusive attention of her parents. Now this "intruder" was the center of attention. Nevertheless, Ilse helped soothe her sense of abandonment. Among her various contributions, she taught Susan how to make a paintbrush by snipping locks of her own hair. The new and "wonderful" paintbrush helped usher her into a "short-lived (but significant) career in art" (p. 260). Susan remembers Ilse as bringing excitement into her life and, in future years, looked forward eagerly to her visits. When the children became adults, they enjoyed arguing with Ilse over her "definitive view of world and human affairs" compared with their more liberal views (p. 260).

The Future Calls

As early as 1945, elements of Schaalman's eventual departure from Cedar Rapids were beginning to take shape. Unknown to him at the time, Des Moines would soon play a deciding role in determining his future. Sometime during his recuperation, Schaalman received a visit from Rabbi Eugene Mannheimer, a prominent Des Moines rabbi. During his tenure, Mannheimer's congregation, Temple B'nai Jeshurun, became one of the Midwest's leading Jewish congregations (Donation documents, 2007). Mannheimer offered Schaalman a position as his assistant rabbi, with the prospect of becoming his successor when he retired. Given the prominence of the temple and its rabbi, this offer was a testament to how, in a few short years, Schaalman's reputation as a competent rabbi had spread beyond Cedar Rapids. "The timing, however, was bad for me. I was in no position to make long-term commitments. At that point in my recovery, I did not know whether I would be able to keep my leg, so I declined the offer."

Des Moines would play another role in the development of his future. Although Schaalman was convinced that Morgenstern had sent him to a rabbinic outpost that would be a career dead end, four years later their paths crossed again. "In the summer of 1945, I heard that Morgenstern had given an inspiring and successful seminar on Judaism in Des Moines. I invited him to come back to Cedar Rapids to conduct a seminar on Judaism for an Institute on Judaism that I was sponsoring for local Christian clergy." A week after Schaalman sent the invitation, Morgenstern wrote that he was unable to accept because he was about to engage in a multi-million dollar fundraising campaign for Hebrew Union College. In his place, he recommended several of his faculty who could fill the role. At least two of them had been Schaalman's professors, Drs. Cohon and Marcus (Morgenstern, J., June 8, 1945). Schaalman agreed to the substitution and Morgenstern sent Marcus. This Institute was the first in series of annual Institutes Schaalman sponsored while he was in Cedar Rapids and the beginning of his lifelong effort to bring together Christians and Jews to promote understanding and tolerance of each other.

Two weeks before the event scheduled for February 1, 1946, Schaalman asked Morgenstern to allow Dr. Marcus to stay another two days to conduct an institute for the Sunday school teachers in his congregation (Schaalman, H. E., January 15, 1946). The institute was a huge success. When it was over, Schaalman wrote to Morgenstern that Marcus had "won the whole congregation by storm and had helped raise the esteem in which HUC was held more than any previous event" (Schaalman, H. E., February 8, 1946). Prior to the institute, the congregation had not had a speaker from HUC in more than twenty years. In an attempt to build on this success, Schaalman planned to invite a speaker from HUC for an annual program.

It is reasonable to infer that this event was part of Schaalman's effort to put his tiny congregation on the map of contemporary Reform Judaism and that he was not content to let Cedar Rapids remain a sleepy backwater. Although he claims that he harbored no ambitions beyond Cedar Rapids, his actions to bring his congregation into the Reform mainstream suggest otherwise.

At the same time that he and Morgenstern were communicating about speakers for Cedar Rapids events, they were having another conversation about the upcoming UAHC biennial convention to which Schaalman planned to send several of his congregants as representatives. Morgenstern wanted them to attend a dinner where he planned to make a pitch for the HUC endowment fund. When Schaalman realized Morgenstern's intentions, he told him that his congregation's president was out of town and that it would be difficult to get anyone to attend the convention. Nevertheless, though he needed more time, Schaalman promised to "make every effort to secure the right persons for this project" (Schaalman, H. E., January 22, 1945).

Schaalman, however, was not able to deliver. On February 8, 1946, he wrote to Morgenstern that he couldn't find anyone to attend the March convention on such short notice (Schaalman, H. E., February 8, 1946). Morgenstern did not give up; a week later he stepped up the pressure. In a note to Schaalman, he stated that sending a member or members to the biennial convention of the Union "will mean a great deal for the health and progress of [your] congregation" (Morgenstern, February 15, 1946). Morgenstern understood more fully than Schaalman the importance of raising the visibility of his congregation.

Visibility of his congregation, however, was not an issue for Schaalman, who was now seeking greener rabbinic pastures. In 1947, a newly formed congregation in Los Angeles offered him a position (Star, E., November 13, 1987).[153] He learned of the job through Alfred Wolf, a former classmate, who at the time was director of the Union in Los Angeles. Schaalman accepted the position on the condition that he would not leave Cedar Rapids until he found a successor. The Los Angeles congregation wanted him to take the position by January 1, but Schaalman told them they would have to wait another month or two. In that time, he began a search for a successor but could not find a suitable replacement. After several months of fruitless effort, he told the congregation in California that in all good conscience he could not leave the congregation that had stood by him during his accident and recovery. "Subsequently," in the same interview, Schaalman told Star, "this Los Angeles congregation became one of the major congregations in Los Angeles. The rabbi who accepted the position was still there thirty years later. In retrospect, I might have missed an excellent opportunity."

A year later, Schaalman got a letter from Congregation Adath Israel in Louisville, Kentucky, notifying him that it was seeking an assistant for Rabbi Joseph Rauch. Schaalman describes Congregation Adath Israel as huge and that it could accommodate 1,600 people. "Compared to the small congregation I was currently serving, a position in a congregation of this size would be a huge step up in the Reform rabbinate." Schaalman speculates that the congregation may have remembered him because they knew him from the time that he substituted for Rauch in either the summer of 1941 or 1942. Schaalman was able to take on the assignment because his own temple did not have services during the summer.[154] "Little did I know at the time that five years later I would be applying for a position as senior rabbi for this congregation. I had reason to be optimistic that I would get the position because I had friends in the congregation and among its leaders."

Schaalman had serious concerns about his lack of professional or family contacts that would help promote his career. Because Morgenstern was the clearinghouse for all rabbinic assignments, Schaalman had no recourse but to appeal to him. Schaalman, however, believed Morgenstern did not like him and carried a grudge. The history of their relationship began with his arrival at HUC. Schaalman found himself totally dependent on Morgenstern: "He made no bones about the fact that I was a scholarship student and therefore had to conform to whatever tone and values he set as the head of the seminary." Nevertheless, that warning did not stop Schaalman from engaging in actions that antagonized him. Together with his fellow refugee colleagues, not only did Schaalman espouse radical ideas about the direction of the Reform movement, but he also attempted to introduce more traditional Jewish practices at HUC. Schaalman considered himself the leader of this rebellion: "I admit that I was a thorn in Morgenstern's side, especially, but not only, about my emerging view that Classical Reform no longer met the needs of Reform Jews. It was sterile, unengaging, too restrictedly intellectual, and without appeal to the Jewish masses."

He also objected to the Classical Reform position on Jewish identity. The movement's stance was that Jewish identity was a matter of individual choice. Morgenstern, who was one of Reform's most prestigious leaders, was one of its proponents. Schaalman's position was more traditional: "Jewishness was conferred by descent and by the fact of one's being part of the Jewish community, part of the Jewish people." Although this view was unacceptable to Reform when Schaalman entered HUC, the movement soon adopted it. In 1937, at an historic meeting of the CCAR, the Reform movement took a dramatic turn when it issued what became known as the Columbus Platform, the first revision of the original 1885 Pittsburgh Platform, which denied the concept of Jewish peoplehood. The Columbus Platform presented Reform Jews with a new vision of themselves, particularly with its emphasis on the oneness of the Jewish people and the recognition that, although the individual could choose to be a Jew in practice and belief, the individual was, nevertheless, a Jew by descent. According to Schaalman, "Reform was moving in this direction before I and my fellow German refugee students arrived at HUC. We only helped push the change forward."

Schaalman wanted the Louisville position and Morgenstern was his best hope for getting it. On January 4, 1947, he wrote to Morgenstern to let him know that he had already notified the congregation that he was interested and wanted to know what Morgenstern thought of the whole matter. He particularly wanted to know what Morgenstern knew about the opening (Schaalman, H. E., January 4, 1947). Two weeks later, Morgenstern responded that the hiring committee, including Dr. Rauch, had consulted him a few weeks earlier and suggested that Schaalman was their man. Morgenstern told them he was happy to "endorse everything which they said about you" and that his "chances for getting the post [were] excellent" (Morgenstern, January 17, 1947). He added that should Schaalman be selected he could expect to succeed Rauch in "that very large and distinguished pulpit." As an indication of his regard for Schaalman, Morgenstern told him that he was confident that he would serve the congregation with "high distinction." In closing, Morgenstern added a personal note expressing his sadness and grief for the loss that Lotte's miscarriage had caused them and was pleased to know she was making a good recovery.

When Schaalman did not get the position, he wrote to Morgenstern to tell him he was bitterly disappointed. Although he had not sought the position, once it was offered to him, he found it "most attractive" and wanted to know from Morgenstern "what went wrong" (Schaalman, H. E., March 10, 1947). "As you know best yourself," Schaalman complained, "there seemed to be reason to believe that matters had gone rather well. Letters from the Louisville committee seemed to confirm this impression." He wanted to know that if he had made some mistake how to avoid it in the future. In closing, he thanked Morgenstern for his friendship and his advice and his "sincere efforts" to help him.

Morgenstern wasted no time responding. A week later, he wrote Schaalman that he was well aware of the decision not to hire him and offered his sympathy. He also tried to comfort Schaalman by sharing his own experience of seeking a job as a rabbi. On two occasions, although he was certain he was the right person for the job, he had been "greatly disappointed" when he was rejected. However, better opportunities opened up for him. One of these jobs proved to be a stepping-stone for his current position as president of Hebrew Union College. As if foretelling Schaalman's future, Morgenstern proposed that Schaalman might have a similar experience. He counseled, "There is no accounting for the tastes and decisions of congregations, or their committees in the selection of rabbis" (Morgenstern, March 17, 1947). He advised Schaalman to be patient and not to be discouraged or to think less of himself. In time, something better was bound to materialize. When he was asked to make a recommendation about Schaalman for this job, he told the congregation that he had "complete confidence in his ability to do the job" (Morgenstern, March 17, 1947).

Three months later, Congregation North Shore Israel in Glencoe, Illinois, contacted Schaalman about a job opening. The contact came about through a complex set of circumstances. One of Schaalman's friends and a member of Temple Judah's board recommended him to a friend on the board of the Glencoe temple and encouraged Schaalman to apply for the position. Aware that any Reform congregation would have to alert Morgenstern of its decision to hire a new rabbi, Schaalman thought that Morgenstern might have additional information and sought his advice. He told Morgenstern that, although he was happy in his present situation, he was "anxious to change to a pulpit that seems to offer such a wide and distinguished field of activity" (Schaalman, H., E., May 20, 1947). Three days later, Morgenstern wrote to advise Schaalman that if he received the offer, he should pursue it. Morgenstern offered this encouragement: "that you are worthy is beyond question" (Morgenstern, May 23, 1947). On the other hand, because he had not been notified that the congregation was searching for a successor to its current rabbi, he did not know what qualifications they are seeking for their next rabbi. If the congregation notified him that it was seeking a new rabbi, he would "deem it a privilege to recommend [Schaalman] very highly to them" (Morgenstern, May 23, 1947).

In the same letter, Morgenstern turned his attention to another matter, his disappointment that Schaalman would not be able to attend the testimonial dinner sponsored by the Board of Governors of Hebrew Union College in Morgenstern's honor. Morgenstern also wrote that he was deeply "touched" by Schaalman's compliment that he, Morgenstern, "had been an inspiration and source of continuing support … and was pleased to have had the privilege to play an important role in [Schaalman's] life and professional career" (Morgenstern, May 23, 1947).

To his disappointment, however, Schaalman did not get an invitation for an interview for opening at Congregation North Shore Israel. In 1948, he had another opportunity for a job at South Shore Temple, on Chicago's south side. The congregation's rabbi, who was about to retire, knew Schaalman and liked him. Although members of the hiring committee came to Cedar Rapids to interview him, Schaalman did not get the position. In what must surely be considered sour grapes, Schaalman claims they were impressed by the appearance of the candidate they eventually hired: "He was tall and handsome. I, on the other hand, was short and not handsome enough for this congregation."

Within a year, the new rabbi was gone. In the meantime, Schaalman had moved to Chicago to take a full-time job with the UAHC. This time, South Shore Temple offered him the position. They invited him to a meeting at the Standard Club[155] in Chicago, "where they locked me in a room and told me they would not let me out until I said yes. I turned them down; my pride had been injured when they had not chosen me the first time."

Visiting the Family in Brazil

Before leaving Cedar Rapids, Schaalman took his wife and daughter on their first trip to visit his family in Brazil. Because he had not seen his parents in ten years and because all of their lives had changed so dramatically, he was not sure how they would respond to each other. He had been out of touch with his family when his father had been in Dachau, and he was now a Reform rabbi, a husband, a father, and an American. "Moreover, I had no idea what kind of reception Lotte would receive. It was also the first time that she would meet her in-laws and their first time to meet their grandchild."

Although the settlement from the automobile accident made the visit possible, the trip itself was not easy. The first of a series of complications was with their visa, which did not arrive until the day before they were to fly to New York City on the first leg of their journey. With visa in hand, Schaalman sent a cable to his parents to inform them of their travel plans and imminent arrival. They left New York on August 30, 1947, on Pan American Airways. In those days, an international flight was not an easy trip, especially with a four-year old child. They flew on a DC-4 in an unpressurized cabin with no air conditioning. "At high altitudes, we were so cold that we needed to cover ourselves with blankets. Yet, when the plane landed for a lunch stop in Kingston, Jamaica, the outside temperature was 120°!" Totally disoriented by these changes and by the exhaustion, Susan got sick.

When they finally landed in Brazil at 1:00 a.m., health officials were on hand to take their temperature to ensure that they were healthy. This checkup was a source of concern because the family had been flying for twenty-four hours and they all felt sick. Nonetheless, they passed the physical and flew on to Rio de Janeiro. Prior to their departure from the states, Schaalman had asked his mother to notify her brother, Julius, to meet them at the airport. But Julius, who had immigrated to Rio in the 1920s where he set up a medical practice, was not there to meet them. Rio has two airports, and he was told to go to the wrong one. The Schaalmans never saw him.

They arrived in Rio at 6:00 a.m., exhausted from their journey. Because nothing was open at that time, they waited an hour for someone to open the lounge so they could have breakfast. After breakfast, the family boarded a small plane and flew to São Paolo, their final destination. The ride was so bumpy that even the flight steward got sick. When the plane reached the airport, it was covered in clouds. The pilot announced that he had no choice but to return to Rio. "At the last moment," Schaalman remembers, "he spied a break in the clouds and, in a very steep dive, made a dash for the airport." They landed in the middle of a severe rainstorm and were met by the ground crew in hip boots who had come to carry the women and children off the plane. The luggage, which had been thrown on the ground, had broken open and it lay in puddles of water.

As Schaalman sloshed his way towards the arrival gate, he spied his parents and his two brothers. "The moment I saw them, my anxiety melted away; they were just as I remembered them." Lotte was an instant hit, and so was Susan. "Everyone was excited, and the family began speaking to each other in German, a language that we had refused to speak in our home." Susan could not understand a word. Because Schaalman's parents and brothers knew a little English, they interspersed their conversation with English. Susan, ever the precocious child, told her grandfather, "You learn my English, then we can talk." During their stay, she learned one phrase in German, "Bitte, gib mir meine Milch!" (Please, give me my milk!)

When they arrived at his parents' home, Schaalman discovered that their standard of living was very different from what it might have been in America. By American standards, Brazil was primitive. "Vegetables, for example, had to be treated chemically before they could be eaten. Water and milk had to be boiled. The culture, too, was alien." The years that Herman and Lotte had spent in America had changed them. "We were no longer the Europeans, the Germans we once were. Now, we were Americans and Reform Jews." For the rabbi, this change meant that he had given up the strict Shabbos observances of his parents' home.

Part of the transformation of the family once they moved to Brazil was that they became more strictly observant Jews than they had been in Germany. Schaalman's father, however, retained his liberal orientation and was still tolerant of others' views. His liberalism was particularly helpful in reestablishing his relationship with his son whose religious behavior had changed dramatically.

Schaalman's family had invited a large number of friends to meet them. They had heard that Professor Schaalman's son, the rabbi and his family, had come to visit. A sign of the religious distance that had developed between the son and his father's family and friends was the terrible *faux pas* he made by turning on a light on the Shabbos afternoon. "I remember a collective gasp, as the visitors were stunned that the Rabbi turned on the light on Shabbos. The moment I heard the gasp, I understood my mistake. Orthodox Jews believe that lighting a lamp on the Sabbath is a sin." The company quickly recovered, and the anxiety he provoked was diffused by laughter: "I laughed too and realized that my awkwardness had become a joke to everyone."

Another challenge for the Schaalmans, particularly for Lotte, was the Orthodox practice of separating the women from the men in their synagogues. Nevertheless, when she accompanied her mother-in-law to services, she conformed to the custom. Her mother-in-law was proud of having her daughter-in-law and grandchild sitting with her.

The Schaalmans speculated that this family reunion was a vindication of all the pain that the family had suffered. Sadly, one of the effects of the protracted suffering inflicted by the Nazis was that his father was no longer the jovial and humorous man who loved to tell jokes and stories. "His experience in Dachau along with the loss of his heritage and status in German society had left an indelible scar. In Brazil, he was a newcomer and was never comfortable with his new language. His wife, however, became fluent in Portuguese in no time. Moreover, the family's finances were on shaky foundations even though Germany continued to pay his pension." As with their experience in Germany, Brazil, too, suffered from "rampant" inflation.[156]

During their stay, the Schaalman family had so much to talk to each other about that they stayed up late during the evenings to catch up on all that happened in their lives. Freddie was an apprentice in a factory making dental instruments and soon became foreman. Later, he bought out the owner and expanded the business. By 1988, he had 100 employees. Ernst was a salesman, who made a good living selling glass products for a local firm. He had a girlfriend Eva whom he later married.

During Schaalman's visit, a rabbi by the name of Pinkus, who had a large congregation, suggested to him that he needed help and wanted to retire soon. He offered Schaalman a job as assistant rabbi.

"The opportunity to join with my family and do the work I loved there was something I had not anticipated. During the next few days, Lotte and I agonized over the decision that was one of the most important of our lives." They were acutely aware that they had no family other than her mother and sister, who was living in Israel. Nevertheless, Schaalman decided that he could not accept the offer:

> The prospect of having to learn another language was too daunt-ing. I was conscious of the fact that it had taken me years to become sufficiently comfortable with English to communicate accurately and effectively with my peers and in public forums, whether teaching or preaching. I anticipated that it would take me many more before I would be as fluent in Portuguese as I had become in English.[157]

The decision was not an easy one; his parents desperately wanted him to relocate. In previous years, they had made the suggestion, but this time more forcefully. "They told me about the prospect that Rabbi Pinkus would soon retire and that they had an excellent relationship with him and with the leadership of the congregation. Although disap-pointed, my father understood the decision though the consequences of this decision have troubled me ever since."

As late as 2010, he and Lotte complained that the lack of family had been the single greatest defect in their lives. Lotte's sister Ilse's first visit in 1948 was a sad reminder for the Schaalmans of the fact of their fam-ily's dispersal (Schaalman Youdovin, S., pp. 260–261). Not until some-time in the 1950s after Gussie had moved to Chicago did the surviving members of the Stern family reunite for a short visit. It was the first time the three of them had been together since Ilse left home in 1935. The only other times Lotte saw her sister was when she visited her when the Schaalmans led tours to Israel for Emanuel congregants and when she went to stay with her during the last month of Ilse's life.

1947: A Turning Point

The year 1947 was a pivotal year that radically altered Schaalman's life. Not only was it the year Lotte conceived their son Michael and the year Schaalman got to see his parents for the first time since he left Germany, it was also the year he attended his first annual meeting of the CCAR. The young rabbi could not have known then that this conference would prefigure a major milestone in his career. It was the year that the CCAR passed a resolution declaring its objection to rabbinic officiation at mixed marriages.[158] Although the issue continued to be a source of concern to the Reform rabbinate, another twenty-five years passed before the CCAR decided to reconsider the matter. When it did, the CCAR appointed Schaalman to chair its Committee on Mixed Marriage.

Another event that year had more immediate consequences when Schaalman experienced a crisis that shattered his religious beliefs. The crisis very likely was the result of a debate with his old friend Emil Fackenheim at the 1947 CCAR conference.[159] They were contemporaries and born two months apart. In 1935, they met as rabbinic students at the *Lehranstalt für die Wissenschaft des Judentums*. This propitious meeting was the beginning of a lifelong friendship.[160] In Schaalman's mind, the friendship was never of equals; Fackenheim was hands down his intellectual superior. Once Schaalman left Germany, he lost sight of his friend and assumed he had died in the *Shoah*.[161] When they met again in 1947, Fackenheim was already on his way to becoming internationally known as a philosopher and theologian.

The outcome of the debate shook the young rabbi to his core. The two argued from the opposite sides of a wide theological divide about the nature of God and the importance of prayer. As discussed earlier, when Schaalman was a student at HUC, he had fallen under the influence of Mordecai Kaplan, as did most of the other Reform rabbis and students in the seminary. Until he met Fackenheim in 1947, Schaalman considered himself a Kaplanite and a Reconstructionist. To be a Kaplanite did not mean one had to abandon traditional ritual and practice. Throughout his life, Kaplan practiced the Judaism in which he had grown up. Like Kaplan, Schaalman remained ritually observant after his ordination and, following Kaplan, identified himself as a "humanist." He argued that God was not a supernatural Being but was a "process of nature." The idea that God had chosen Israel was nothing more than a folk-conceit. Israel, Schaalman (2007) argued, chose "the idea of God." To survive in the modern age, Judaism needed to strip itself of its supernatural trappings and to see itself as a civilization, a people.

Fackenheim presented a radically different view. He argued that God had a central place in the world and was the locus of meaning and value. Especially powerful for Schaalman was Fackenheim's argument that Judaism not founded on the centrality of God was hollow. In order for prayer to have meaning and purpose, it must be directed to a caring God.

When Schaalman returned home, these arguments swirled in his head (p. 46).[162] "Bit by bit," his own views collapsed, and he considered quitting the rabbinate (p. 46). Finding himself alone in the sunroom of his home in Cedar Rapids, he noticed on his bookshelf a copy of Martin Buber's *I and Thou*, which he had not read since he was a teenager. Now, he was drawn to it again. When he began reading, he could not put it down. It was so fascinating that he stayed up most of the night until he had read "the entire 110 pages." The next day, he began to feel restored. Buber had given him a new way of approaching Judaism. *I and Thou* allowed him to see clearly what he must do: "It was as if a curtain had rolled away." What he discovered was a system of belief that was "whole, firm and clear … one that has sustained him with only minor variation, throughout his life" (p. 47). Nonetheless, he admits to having periods of continuing doubts and questions about whether he was on "the right track." At the time, however, he did not reveal these struggles to anyone, not even to Lotte. He knew that she had faith in him and he could not rock that boat: "We were young," he explained, "and she had a child already."

He also chose not to share his doubts with his congregation, despite the fact that he felt inauthentic leading prayer or talking about God and teaching Torah. A certain element of fear and uncertainty contributed to his decision not to reveal his doubts. Partly, his feelings may be attributed to the fact that he was so young and inexperienced as a rabbi. He remembers being "thrown into Cedar Rapids a few weeks after [he] got married." To destroy their beliefs, as his were destroyed, was too difficult for him to consider. It might even have been irresponsible.

Buber provided him new hope that he could indeed have a relationship with God, but to do so required a whole new way of interacting with others. He learned that it was possible to respond to reality in two distinct ways, the I-It and the I-Thou. The first is controlling, manipulative and predictable, the way we relate to things. I-Thou means to establish a relationship by giving oneself totally to the surprise of the experience of the "Other," as in a first encounter with the unknown. To do the latter, meant shedding preconceptions, prejudgments [possibly, "stereotypes"] that prevent direct experience of the other (pp. 131–132). Engaging with reality in this manner is no less true of an attempt to experience God: "all the certainties, all the words, all the frozen images begin to dissolve." This unconditional openness means making oneself vulnerable to the "Other," accepting all the risks of such openness. An authentic relationship with another requires that we wholeheartedly listen and respond to the other, the "thou" of the relationship. Schaalman realized that to be fully human and to enter into an I-Thou experience with God meant to engage in a "dialogic relationship with the world, its people, and its objects" (p. 48). Heretofore, Schaalman had experienced the world as the "Other," Buber's term for I-It, a depersonalized and unsympathetic relationship in which the Other is experienced as object rather than subject. When he emerged from his religious crisis, Buber's *I-Thou* gave him a new theological understanding, which he began incorporating into his sermons and teaching at Temple Judah.

Difficult as it is for him to admit, he confesses to his shame and embarrassment that this new thinking had no effect on his understanding of the Holocaust, which had not yet become a part of his thinking. Although the Holocaust certainly affected his life, it had not yet had the profound and transformative effect that it would have in later years. In the first few years of the war, like so many others, he had difficulty believing the stories of the atrocities. Their scale defied the imagination and, he admits, "I probably didn't want to believe it, and I didn't" (University of St. Thomas, 1992, p. 17).[163] In fact, as late as 1948 he was optimistic about the post-war Jewish situation. He told a reporter, "Despite the fact the Jewish people experienced in Europe under Hitler the greatest shock in their history of persecution, I still believe that they have made more progress in their relation with their environment in the last 25 years than in all the long years previously" (Meek, 1948, p. 11).

Part-time Regional Director, UAHC

Sometime around 1945 or 1946, Schaalman met Rabbi Maurice Eisendrath, the new president of the Union of American Hebrew Congregations (UAHC), the national organization representing American Reform congregations. Eisendrath was sufficiently impressed by the young rabbi to offer him a part-time job as Midwest Regional Director of this prestigious organization. Schaalman gratefully accepted it. In this role, he provided services for two to three dozen Reform congregations in his region, including Colorado, Nebraska, Missouri, Minnesota, Wisconsin, and Iowa.[164] He served as their direct liaison to the Union's headquarters.

His main responsibility was to acquaint synagogues with the services of the Union and to bring them into its fold (Schaalman, Report, 1949, p. 249). He conducted "teachers' seminars, regional meetings, and information sessions with boards of congregations" (p. 249). Because approximately two-thirds of the congregations ranged from small- to medium-size, they lacked sufficient resources to offer their congregants a full range of services, particularly religious school education, youth work, synagogue music, and adult education. He was able to give them some help, but the size of the territory and the fact that he was only part-time made it impossible to provide the region the full service it needed (p. 249). He recommended that the Union give consideration to hiring a full-time staff person to strengthen the region's Reform congregations and to help the Union financially "from an area very well able to give it" (p. 249). One of the benefits of this job that would stand him in good stead in later years was the opportunity to develop relationships with two of Chicago's most prestigious rabbis, Louis Mann and Louis Binstock. A recommendation from one of them could be very helpful to a young rabbi's career, especially one who was a refugee and had no family in America.

In 1948, soon after Michael's birth, Rabbi Samuel Mayerberg, a well-respected rabbi in Kansas City, offered Schaalman a job as assistant rabbi at congregation Bnai Yehudah, one of the leading Reform synagogues in America. Rabbi Mayerberg had become acquainted with Schaalman through his visits as Midwest Regional Director of UAHC. Uncertain about whether to accept the position, he discussed it with Eisendrath. Eisendrath had already taken notice of Schaalman's exceptional abilities as part-time Regional Director for UAHC and had other plans for him. He told Schaalman, "Under no circumstances [should you take the job]. This is just an overgrown Cedar Rapids." The job, he explained, would only lead to another posting in the Midwest where his talents and abilities would not be fully realized. He would have something better to offer him.

Schaalman claims that he did not intend to leave Cedar Rapids and was quite content to spend the rest of his life there. His tiny congregation of thirty-three members had grown over the years to eighty-three, nearly three times the original number. Not only had the congregation grown in numbers, but in stature as well. Nevertheless, the fact that Schaalman remained in Cedar Rapids for eight years became something of a personal problem for him. One of his best friends, a leader in the congregation, told him that people were questioning whether he was as good as they thought he was because nobody seemed to want him. Schaalman told his friend that he and Lotte were very happy in Cedar Rapids and had no intention of leaving.

However, his thinking changed after he turned down the offer of a rabbinic post in Los Angeles. He decided to challenge the congregation to prove it wanted him to stay. Although he had never asked for a raise in salary, he asked the board to build him a house on a piece of ground on the outskirts of town. "If they did that, I would stay for the rest of my life. When the board refused, I knew it was time to go." He began an active search for a new position and, in the fall of 1948 when Schaalman told them that he was leaving, the board hastily convened a meeting and offered to build him a house. However, it was too late. Perhaps because he recognized that his future now lay elsewhere, Schaalman declined the offer. "I assured the board that I was not using the new job offer as a means to extort financial concessions. I had never done that in the past and did not intend to do it now."

Eisendrath had already invited him to come to Chicago and take on a full-time position as the Midwest Regional Director of UAHC. Schaalman welcomed the offer; it was an opportunity for a young rabbi to play a more important role in the Reform movement. His move to Chicago was the beginning of his rise to leadership in the Reform movement and to participation in contemporary global moral and religious issues. Even Temple Judah's offer to build him a house could not change his mind. A few other matters also may have influenced his decision. In 1946, his salary was a paltry $3,000, and he was not given a raise for the next year (McQuiston, 1989).[165] Although the board was at first unwilling to provide him with a home of his own, it was moving forward with a plan to build a new auditorium. At a board meeting in May 13, 1947, Temple Judah's building committee reported that $25,000 of the required $30,000 was in the bank (McQuiston, 1989). Moreover, at the same meeting, board members discussed limiting Schaalman's right to speak "to outside groups on controversial issues." Because he had friends on the board, it is likely he was aware that this discussion had been raised before. By his own confession, Schaalman had been, and still is, a feisty and combative rabbi. Then, as now, he cherished his freedom and was secure in his judgment.

Accomplishments

In his own accounting, Schaalman considers that one of his major accomplishments as a rabbi in Cedar Rapids was to gain the respect of the gentile community for the Jewish community in its midst. Prior to his arrival, the non-Jewish community was either indifferent or hostile. By the time he left, new friendships and business partnerships had developed between the Jewish and the non-Jewish community. He also claims credit for the growth of his congregation from thirty-three to eighty-three members; according to Schaalman, "That was all of the Jews that could be gotten." Schaalman also takes credit for the improvement of relationships between the Orthodox and Reform Jewish communities.

For Schaalman, the eight years in Cedar Rapids was "an enormous growth experience." Not only did Cedar Rapids provide experience and initiation into the rabbinate, but it was also his first exposure to the non-Jewish world. His involvement in the community brought him into his first contact with various Protestant groups and with Catholics. Moreover, the opportunity to teach at both Coe and Cornell College gave him an academic outlet and provided an intellectual challenge that he had not known previously.[166]

Another sign of the respect he earned in Cedar Rapids was his friendship with Byron S. Hollinshead, president of Coe College. When Schaalman moved to Chicago to take on the full-time job as UAHC Midwest Regional Director, Hollinshead delivered the principal address at his installation. Before traveling to Chicago, Hollinshead (1949) offered "to carry felicitations from any individual or organization in Cedar Rapids to Schaalman at his installation."

Five years after Schaalman left Cedar Rapids, local groups were still inviting him back to speak. On February 16, 1954, he participated at a forum sponsored by Coe College on interreligious understanding (One World Religion, February 16, 1954, p. 2). The panel included speakers representing Judaism, Catholicism, Protestantism, and Islam. Schaalman advocated for a Parliament of the World's Council on Religions[167] that would complement the United Nations. The Parliament, he maintained, would provide an opportunity for representatives of the world's religions to meet and discuss issues of importance and have the opportunity to get to know each other. Through this forum, they would "achieve a feeling of the contribution each could make to the establishment of one world" (p. 2). He proposed that people of faith could accomplish this goal because they believe that problems can be solved without resorting to violence. Schaalman urged his colleagues to work actively to achieve that goal (p. 2). The other panelists agreed with him, including Dr. Marcus Bach, professor and associate director of the State University of Iowa School of Religion.[168]

For the next two decades, *The Cedar Rapids Gazette* continued to remind its readers of Schaalman's contribution to the community. In its November 17, 1954, column "This Day 10 Years Ago," the newspaper reported that ten years earlier Schaalman had been elected vice president of the Linn County Veterans' Service and Information Center. That same year, 1944, Schaalman had become an American citizen ("This Day, 1954"). How ironic his election must have been for the young German refugee who was now part of the war effort against his native country.

On June 1, 1956, the column reminded readers that ten years earlier Schaalman had been elected president of the Cedar Rapids Council of Social Agencies. In the December 18, 1967, column "This day 10-20-30 years ago, 1967," the *Gazette* reminded readers that in December of 1947 Schaalman participated in the Fellowship Festival sponsored by the Cedar Rapids Council on Social Planning. At the time, Schaalman told the newspaper that his appearance on the program was "probably the first time in Cedar Rapids those denominations participating in a single observance included Catholics, Jews, Protestants and a Moslem" ("This day 10-20-30 years ago, 1967," p. 6). In addition, newspaper records reveal that Schaalman participated in an Institute on Judaism in 1951 and 1954 and was a member of the Cedar Rapids Rent Advisory Board ("Religion in life week, 1954;" "This day 10-20-30 years ago, September 2, 1968").

In 1961, *The Cedar Rapids Gazette* reported that Schaalman would participate in a lecture series at Northwestern University on the connections between Jewish and Christian liturgies. His topics included the history of Jewish liturgy and modern major Jewish liturgical patterns ("Schaalman to lecture, 1961, p. 3"). The purpose of these lectures was to expand "the church music program at the University and to give Protestant Christian musicians an opportunity to learn the background of music which has come into Protestant use from Jewish sources" (p. 3). Schaalman remembers teaching this course for four or five years.

On June 5, 1963, the newspaper reported that Schaalman had returned once more to Temple Judah to speak at its annual dinner ("To speak, 1963," p. 16). Two years later, February 13, 1965, the *Des Moines Register* reported that Schaalman had returned to Cedar Rapids to speak at the annual Drake University Convocation Religious Emphasis Week. The focus of the event was interfaith understanding ("Drake to hear Malcolm Boyd, 1965," p. 6). The last record of Schaalman speaking in Cedar Rapids was a speech he made on April 2, 1972, at Temple Judah.

Long after he left Cedar Rapids, Schaalman was called on to conduct weddings and funerals for old family friends. In 1954, the Schaalmans returned to attend the wedding of the daughter of their good friends, Dr. and Mrs. Morris B. Katzoff ("Audrey Katzoff married to Burton Donald Cohen," 1954, p. 8). Again, on March of 1959, he co-officiated at the wedding of Nancy Gasway and Alvin Malmon ("Miss Gasway," 1959, p. 10). The young woman's father was president of Temple Judah when the Schaalmans arrived, and her parents became their good friends.

Occasionally, he was called back to conduct funerals. In early March of 1951, he conducted a funeral service for Elmer Freud, president of Hawkeye Rubber Manufacturing Company ("Deaths," 1951, p. 8). Years later, in 1971, *The Cedar Rapids Gazette* reported inaccurately, as it turns out, that Schaalman co-officiated with Dr. Theodore G. Lilley at the funeral of Howard Hall ("Many corporate officials," 1971, p. 3). Most likely, the article had been submitted before Schaalman notified Mrs. Hall that he had just returned from a trip to Israel and was too exhausted to come.

In spite of his significant accomplishments, Schaalman believed that some work was incomplete, particularly adult education. He tried for a few years to begin such a program within his congregation, but it was not successful, despite the fact that his Coe College adult education class for a non-Jewish community was a great success. He was also dissatisfied with the results of his youth education.

In hindsight, he laments the fact that he was remiss in not drawing the community's attention to the *Shoah*. He describes this omission as painful and embarrassing. Prior to 1944, he has no recollection of his giving thought to the plight of European Jewry, which had not yet penetrated his life. He can only assume that he was repressing it. The only memory he has of the effect of becoming aware of the horrors of the *Shoah* was a presentation at the Hadassah meeting in Atlantic City near the end of 1944. Although there must have been other sermons and speeches that he may have given, he remembers none of them. On the other hand, he remembers two refugee families that the community helped to resettle. They kept to themselves and remained on the margin of the Jewish community.

An article in *The Cedar Rapids Gazette* reveals the extent to which Schaalman had become part of the community and how much it would miss him (*The Cedar Rapids Gazette*, July 17, 1949). The column begins: "Iowa and Cedar Rapids are losing a most valuable citizen in Rabbi Herman E. Schaalman of Temple Judah" (p. 1). While lamenting the community's loss, the newspaper wisely noted, "It was inevitable that someday he would be called to a position offering an opportunity for broader service. Now that the day has arrived, his outstanding work in the community would be an inspiration for other young men" (p. 10). Schaalman, the paper continued, "is the kind of a person some communities never are blessed with … he is at once a thinker and a doer" (p. 1).

Elaborating on the qualities Schaalman brought to the community, the newspaper commented on Schaalman's success in practicing the democratic values of his new home in America in a way that exceeded that of many native-born citizens. Praising Schaalman's devotion to freedom and to its promise for the future, the paper referred to his independence of thought: "He despises the kind of thinking that leads men to think in grooves worn down through the centuries [and took] positions with a forthrightness, a firmness and a convincing logic that leads us to think whether or not we want to" (p. 1). The newspaper referred also to his various accomplishments in the community, including his efforts as chair of the Family Service Agency to establish a mental health clinic and his participation in the civic, cultural, social, educational, and intellectual life of the city. In its final praise, the newspaper quoted Schaalman's own words about other Cedar Rapids citizens to whom he gave public praise: "'He is the kind of a person who makes Cedar Rapids a better place to live" (p. 1).

Chapter 4

Chicago: 1949–1955

"Unlike the sleepy backwater of Cedar Rapids, Chicago was a dynamic and vibrant new world. In Cedar Rapids, I was never sure of myself and had no idea what my potential might be."

Herman E. Schaalman, 2006

Transition to the Big City

Leaving the security of Cedar Rapids and resettling in Chicago meant that Schaalman would be starting over. He would have to build new friendships, establish himself as a presence in Chicago's Jewish community, and adopt a new lifestyle for himself and his family. No longer would he be able to walk to work or leave the door open in his home. Living in Chicago meant being cautious about whom he allowed into his home and whom his children might talk to outside the home. He also had to be aware of potential threats of physical violence and threats to the security of his property. In addition, not only was there the problem of discovering modes of transportation, but of locating and purchasing housing in a safe neighborhood with quality schools for the children, and the very fact of finding one's way around in a huge metropolis. He would be a stranger in a new environment. Whom would he call to help him get established? Whom would he call in case of a medical emergency? Who were the best doctors? Where should he shop? What were the best neighborhoods, the best schools?

While still in Cedar Rapids, by coincidence, Schaalman was performing a wedding for a Cedar Rapids girl and a young man from Chicago. To impress his fiancée, the prospective groom had brought with him a catalog that included a prospectus of a new building going up in

Chicago. Because he knew the Schaalmans were intending to move to Chicago, the young man left the catalog with Schaalman, who took it home to show his wife. On one of their visits to Chicago, the Schaalmans drove to Hyde Park on the city's south side where they thought they might find an apartment.[169] They were not impressed by what they saw and turned instead to a new north side co-op building under construction on Lunt Avenue in Rogers Park. They were struck immediately by the fact that the building was on Lake Michigan and had its own beachfront. One of Schaalman's great fears in leaving Iowa was that he might end up living in some urban "stone canyon." The couple was excited by the prospect of living next to the beach. They purchased a three-bedroom co-op on the sixth floor with a clear view of the lake. Their front window also allowed them to see the sunrise and the sand abutting their building. They even had money for the down payment. Although Schaalman did not know it at the time, the location, which was less than a mile north of Emanuel Congregation, turned out to be "ideal."

While they waited for their new home to be completed, the Schaalmans lived in a small two-bedroom apartment at the Piccadilly Hotel in Hyde Park. It was owned by one of the members of Temple Sinai whom Schaalman knew through his work as UAHC Regional Director. They lived in these crowded quarters for nearly eight months, from the time of their arrival in Chicago on Labor Day in September of 1949 until April 1950 when, to their great relief, they were able to move into their new home. The rooms, however, were small and did not allow much space for a family of four, nor did it have a study or office for Schaalman. Their first summer was extremely hot and, because their new co-op had no air conditioning, they would take their bedding out on the beach and sleep under the stars.

Not long after they moved in, Lotte's mother arrived from California, where she had moved after the Schaalmans had recuperated from their automobile accident. Because she wanted to be near her daughter and grandchildren, she rented an apartment around the corner from them. This closeness was a blessing, not only for Herman and Lotte, but for their children as well. Gussie was a loving mother, mother-in-law, and grandmother and a great help with the children. When they could not sleep at night, she took turns with her daughter staying up with them.

An inevitable fallout of the move to Chicago was the transformation of the Schaalman family life. They were now living in what to them was the "Big City." Because Schaalman had taken on greater professional responsibilities, most of the time he was not around when the children came home from school. Frequently, meetings kept him out late, and he was often out of town attending meetings and conventions. Not only was he thoroughly involved in the Jewish community, but also his new responsibilities involved social events that required Lotte's attendance. A few years later, when Schaalman took on the responsibilities of rabbi for the large Emanuel Congregation, the children saw even less of them. They also missed the small town where people knew them and where they could feel special as the Rabbi's children.

In Chicago, no one knew them, their school was not down the street, and they had to be careful about to whom they talked. Shadowy characters walked the streets, sat on buses and trains, and begged for help on the streets. People of all nationalities, religions, and skin colors were in their schools, their neighborhood, and their building. Danger lurked everywhere for children outside the house who were not accompanied by an adult. Compared with Cedar Rapids, everything in Chicago was strange, if not threatening.

Life also changed dramatically for Lotte, who threw herself without reserve into helping her husband succeed as Emanuel's new rabbi. She assumed much of the social responsibility that was incumbent upon a rabbi's wife, and she became the "rebbetzin par excellence." If her current activities in her nineties are any indication of how much she worked as his partner before he retired, then her contribution to his success is incalculable. One example witnessed by this writer includes her role as her husband's "pitchman" and social secretary. When Schaalman held New Year's Retreats and Lehrhaus sessions in the summer at Oconomowoc, Lotte made calls to people she thought would be interested in attending. If they gave the slightest hint that they might not go, she turned on her charm and persuasive powers. As anyone who knows her can testify, "It is impossible to refuse Lotte."[170]

Even though she is ninety-six, Lotte does not sit still during Emanuel's social events. If she is at a dinner, without being asked she helps clear tables. Her husband long ago gave up trying to stop her. She even works the room, a function she must have carried out from the beginning of her husband's rabbinate. Until the arrival of Rabbi Zedek, if the congregation needed a *minyon*, she made phone calls. If the library needed to be reorganized, she reorganized it. At home, she helps keep his social and professional calendar. She does not make appointments for him, but she keeps track of them.

If these activities in her nineties are any indication of what Lotte must have done in her forties, it is no wonder that the children "felt neglected" and let their parents know it (Schaalman Youdavin, S., p. 261). Undoubtedly affected by these complaints, the parents did their best to involve the children in as many of their activities as they could. As a result, they felt that "we, too, were somehow contributing to the well-being of the Jewish community. In small, but meaningful ways, we 'worked' alongside our parents" (p. 261). On Friday afternoons, the children were assigned the task of maintaining "the pre-Shabbat tranquility" of their home. To shield their parents "from having to deal with the outside world, [they] took turns answering the telephone" (p. 261). They enjoyed the opportunity to be "protectors" of their parents.

They also "participated" in their father's work in establishing the Union Institute, the summer camp that was so much a part of Schaalman's life in these early years in Chicago. During 1951, when her father was exploring possible sites for the Reform movement's first summer camp, Susan went with him. She quips that in some small way the Schaalman kids contributed to American Jewish history. When the camp was established, she and Michael were "the first faculty brats" before other rabbinic faculty started bringing their families (p. 261). They even helped with the arduous task of readying the camp for its opening in the summer of 1952. She remembers the work of cleaning out dust and mildew from the campers' mattresses and eavesdropping on the conversations of the camp counselors and learning "things [their] parents would never have taught [them]" (p. 262).

For Susan, the move to Chicago was traumatic. In the small town of Cedar Rapids, her father had been an important person, and his reputation was reflected in the life of the family and in the special attention she received from friends, neighbors, Temple Judah congregants, and the social elite of the city. When the family arrived in Chicago, however, her father was unknown, and no one came to their home. She missed this special attention. In Cedar Rapids, the Temple was only a block away from her home, and she could run over to see her father whenever she wanted. Everyone knew her and gave her special attention. She was the Rabbi's little girl. In Chicago, on the other hand, she could not visit her father's office, which was downtown. Another, more difficult transition, involved her schooling. Though school was only a block away from their apartment, for the first time in her life Susan found herself in the presence of black children. Her lack of exposure to them proved to be a difficult adjustment. At first, she was frightened, and it took many years for her to get over her fear.

Although the experience of moving to Chicago proved to be traumatic for Susan, for Michael it was a blessing. He was only one year old and, in part because his parents were more experienced, much easier to raise than his sister. Unlike his sister, who suffered from severe allergy problems, he was a healthy, easy-going, and contented child. With Susan out of the house and at school, his mother was able to spend the entire day with him.

Because of Susan's negative experience in public school, the Schaalmans enrolled their children in the Anshe Emet Synagogue day school, which they described as a "pricey private school." Because Schaalman was a rabbi, he was able to get scholarships for his children: "Otherwise, I could not have afforded the tuition." The children spent eight years in the day school. Susan, however, had a difficult time adjusting. The small-town girl found herself competing with sophisticated and wealthy big-city girls with whom she never made friends.

Schaalman reserved Thursday afternoons for time with his son, "Everything else was off limits." When Michael was a student at Anshe Emet, his father took him swimming every Thursday afternoon, an activity that became the basis for bonding between father and son and, as well, for Michael's later devotion to swimming as a sport. Not only did he swim in high school, but also was an outstanding swimmer in college. Father and son would swim together at the Standard Club and play ping-pong and basketball. One of the perks of a rabbi in Chicago was an honorary membership in the Standard Club, the key to which was sponsorship by one of the club's members. In Schaalman's case, sponsorship came through his friend Sam Hollender.

Saturday afternoons the family studied Torah together, modeled after the Shabbat Torah study that Schaalman experienced as a child.

Maintaining a weekly schedule of Torah study turned out to be a challenge, however, mainly because of the children's many social and athletic activities.

By the time the children went off to college, Susan in 1961 to the University of Wisconsin and Michael to Grinnell in 1968, they began to notice that their father's name and picture was appearing in the Chicago press (Schaalman Youdovin, S., 1986, p. 263). One article that Susan recalled involved a racial incident at a nearby high school. Her father had been called in by the school's principal to try to reduce tensions between blacks and whites and Jews and Chicanos. She also became aware of his growing prestige among Chicago's rabbinical colleagues, which led eventually to his becoming a leader of Reform Judaism. Her mother never allowed any of this success to go to her father's head. When he was awarded an honorary doctorate from Hebrew Union College-Jewish Institute of Religion, Lotte jokingly asked him "whether the new doctor was entitled to prescribe headache remedies" (p. 263).

Despite any sacrifices the children may have made on behalf of their father's calling, they came out of the experience fully appreciating their parents as "special," "unique," and "undeniably" authentic. Herman and Lotte's "profound depth and [the] genuineness of their ideals" became a model for their children and, as well, a guide to living an ethical and moral Jewish life (p. 263).

It did not take Schaalman long to make a friend in the building. Because it was co-op, the owners of each unit were part of an association that governed the building's maintenance and upkeep. At one of the first meetings, Schaalman met his neighbors, Mr. and Mrs. Albert Mecklenburger, who lived on the second floor and became friends with the young rabbinic family. The Mecklenburgers had a large family and frequently invited the Schaalmans for dinner. Other times, the Mecklenburgers would invite them to share their leftovers from one of their family dinners. "There was no question," says Schaalman, "that there was good chemistry between us."

Albert Mecklenburger was also a key member on Emanuel's Board of Trustees. Through him, Schaalman also met Albert's brother-in-law, Samuel Froelich, treasurer of the congregation. "These two were the sort of key people around whom the congregation revolved. At the end of the year, when the board met to consider its finances, together with a few friends they would write checks for $5,000 each to cover any deficit, sometimes as much as $25,000 to $30,000. "In those days," Schaalman added, "that's how congregations were run." Five years later, when Schaalman was being considered for the position of senior rabbi to replace Rabbi Levy, these early connections came in handy.

In 1952, Schaalman's parents made their one and only visit to Chicago. They stayed a month and got to meet "Mickey," as he was now called, now the same age as Susan when they first met her. One of the challenges for Schaalman's father was the fact that his son was a Reform Jew who belonged to a Reform synagogue. "The difficulty was overcome, however, when my father found a small Orthodox shul near where we lived. Not willing to let him go alone to Saturday morning services, I went with him. On a few occasions, I drove him to services." This was a significant concession for an Orthodox Jew, who otherwise would never drive on Shabbat. To accommodate his parents' kosher practices, Schaalman purchased kosher meat and new kitchenware, including pots, pans, and dishes.

The visit to America was a revelation to Adolf, who was "utterly awed" by American civilization. On one level, plastic food containers fascinated him. He bought cheese from a local supermarket simply because he was so impressed with the containers, and he took them back to Brazil to show his family and friends what civilization was like in a technologically advanced country. In Brazil, food was still wrapped in newspaper or placed in bags that you brought yourself. Another fascination for Adolf was downtown Chicago. "Because my father spoke very little English, I usually wrote out instructions to prevent him from getting lost. One of his favorite destinations was the museums, particularly the Rosenwald Museum, the original name of the Museum of Science and Industry."

In 1955, the Schaalmans made their second and last trip to Brazil, only this time they left from New Orleans on a passenger freighter. Susan and Michael quickly learned to enjoy the amenities of ship travel. They loved the pool, and no sooner than they woke did they put on their bathing suits and jumped in for a swim. They loved the pool so much that they even ate their breakfast and lunch in it. Along the way the ship stopped in the Virgin Islands, and eventually in Rio and finally in Santos, where they met their family who had come to pick them up.

Schaalman brothers and mother. Right to left, Ernst, Freddie, and Herman, São Paulo, 1955

By that time, his parents had built a new house, in part with money that Schaalman had given them to acquire a piece of land. Schaalman's father, who worked for an architectural firm, designed the house, which his employer helped build. Schaalman remembers the house as small "with a lovely garden that was overgrown like a jungle. Orchids grew out of pieces of bark that hung on the wall. Bananas hung from a tree nearby, which the children picked from their grandparents' tree." During the visit, Schaalman accompanied his father, who was then sixty-five, on a visit to his doctor for a thorough checkup. "The doctor declared my father 'fit as a fiddle' and predicted that he would live for many more years. The next year, he died of a heart attack."

Sometime during the 1950s, Schaalman reestablished contact with the Samfield family. The reconnection occurred when Schaalman received an invitation from Rabbi James A. Wax to give a lecture at Samfield's former temple. Wax had been a classmate of Schaalman's and knew of the family connection between Schaalman and the surviving Samfields. He thought that he might make a connection between Samfield's history with the congregation and its present membership. Schaalman accepted the invitation on condition that Wax arrange a meeting with the surviving Samfield family. Wax agreed to Schaalman's request and, after picking him up at the airport, drove into the heart of the city's black ghetto where two surviving sisters of the Samfield family lived. Schaalman was stunned by the squalor and neglect of their neighborhood. The ancient spinster sisters seemed to be lost and alone. He was uncomfortable, and so were they. He noticed some pictures of younger people on the mantle and asked who they were. The sisters told him that there were two married brothers and that the pictures were of their families. He asked for their addresses so that he might get in touch with them.

When he returned to Chicago, he contacted both brothers. One of them sent him a polite response, but, to his surprise, he received an enthusiastic letter from Polly Sloan, a niece of Rabbi Samfield. She and her husband, Sol, lived in a beautiful home in San Bernardino, California.[171] Her letter included a warm invitation to visit the next time he was in California. Schaalman was delighted to establish relations with this branch of the family.[172]

Midwest Regional Director of UAHC

During Schaalman's rabbinate in Cedar Rapids, major changes had been taking place in the world. Nazism and Fascism had been defeated, the Nuclear Age was being born, and the Cold War between the Soviet Union and the United States had begun in earnest. With the creation of the State of Israel, Jews worldwide began to have new hope in their future, but, at the same time, the reality of the Holocaust and its consequences were slowly becoming part of the American Jewish consciousness. The effect of these events on American Judaism was profound.

When Schaalman arrived in Chicago in 1949, life for Jewish Americans was undergoing a remarkable transition. After years of struggle to be accepted in American society, Jews were making huge strides in becoming part of an assimilated middle class (Borowitz, 2002, p. 62). In part the result of public sympathy for the Holocaust, Jews found they were more accepted socially. Colleges and universities were admitting more Jews, and Jews had begun to assume more prominent roles in the professions, in business, in government, the arts, and science and technology. As they became more affluent, they bought more expensive cars and homes and began the exodus to the suburbs (Borowitz, 2002, p. 62).

Along with these material changes came a new awareness of the meaning of being Jewish. The new life of freedom and opportunity, so different from the financial and social limitations of their fathers and mothers, led many Jews to seek a theology better suited to their improved circumstances (Borowitz, 2002, p. 62). These newly liberated

Jews found a fresh basis for religious involvement in social action and *mitzvot.* The centuries-old social awareness of their ancestors turned into a strong desire to correct injustices and promote the common good. Thus Jewish money and "manpower" poured into various social causes such as civil rights, economic justice, and, during the 1960s, anti-war and feminist causes. This was the American Jewish world that Schaalman stepped into when he came to Chicago.

Unlike the sleepy backwater of Cedar Rapids, Chicago was a dynamic and vibrant new world. In Cedar Rapids, Schaalman was never sure of himself and had no idea what his potential might be. Moreover, the kinds of religious questions that were soon to reshape his thinking and his rabbinate never came up. Chicago changed all that. It was an exciting place to live, alive with culture such as he had known in Munich and Cincinnati. Chicago had museums, theaters, concert halls, an opera house, universities, intellectuals, artists, and baseball.[173] Next to New York City, Chicago also had the second largest Jewish population in America. That fact alone provided the fertile soil for Schaalman's talents and abilities to blossom. Given his personal charm and his presence, everywhere perceived as distinguished, not only did he fit right into the new society, but soon was recognized as an important part of it.

As Midwest Regional Director of UAHC, Schaalman now had the opportunity to interact with major "players" on a national level and in the Chicago metropolitan Jewish and non-Jewish communities. He had no difficulty cultivating friendships and working relationships with some of Chicago's most successful Jewish businessmen, including J. S. Ackerman, Albert Mecklenburger, J. Logan Fox, Sidney Hollender, Sidney Robinson, Robert Max Schrayer, and Samuel Froehlich. Happily, three of his new friends were leaders in the national UAHC: Ackerman was its vice president, Hollender its president, and Schrayer a board member.[174] Another part of his job was to serve as liaison for the organization's interfaith activities. Not only did he speak before various lay and church groups, but he also served on various nondenominational civic and religious committees.

Chicago proved to be an incubator for Schaalman's talents and abilities and led eventually to his national and international renown. When Schaalman came to Chicago, the Chicago Federation of the Union membership consisted of only fourteen congregations (by 2005, the number had risen to thirty-five). Because his territory was the Midwest, he made contacts with rabbis and congregations as far west as Colorado and north to Michigan. These contacts and his participation in various civic and Jewish organizations contributed to his personal and professional growth and to his growing reputation as a competent and effective Jewish leader. Not incidentally, his many speaking engagements could only work to improve his English.

The Midwest Regional director's position opened up because its director wanted to move to Los Angeles to take on the leadership of the new office the Union had just opened. When Schaalman was offered the job, he laid out one condition: that he would be allowed to develop a summer camp for Reform Jewish youth. According to him, convincing the officers of the Chicago Federation of the Union to accept his condition was difficult; he believes his idea "was received most coolly, if not with indifference and rejection by most." Schaalman thinks Rabbi Eisendrath "humored" him because he wanted him to accept the job and so did the leadership of the Chicago Federation of the Union.[175]

On October 27, 1949, Eisendrath presided over Schaalman's installation as Midwest Director of the Union of American Hebrew Congregations. The principal speaker of the event held at the prestigious Standard Club in Chicago was Schaalman's friend from Cedar Rapids, Byron S. Hollinshead, the president of Coe College. The event was important enough to include Chicago's mayor, Martin Kennelly, and Rev. George A. Fowler, president of the Church Federation of Greater Chicago ("Hollinshead to speak at installation," 1949; INSTALL RABBI, October 28, 1949).

As Midwest Regional Director, travel between cities and congregations in his geographically disparate territory would be a large part of the job as well as settling disputes and helping to establish new congregations. Despite the travel burden, the job also gave him new freedoms that he did not have as a congregational rabbi. For one, he no longer had to conduct Shabbat services, and most of his work was done during regular business hours. In the beginning, he had Saturdays to himself. Occasionally, he was asked to speak and lecture.[176] However, as the responsibilities increased that free time disappeared. He now had the responsibility to help develop new congregations and to substitute for rabbis who were sick or on vacation. One of the most important responsibilities of his new job was to interact with the highest level of the Jewish philanthropic community, its socialites, and its prominent members in business and finance. "What I discovered in working and socializing with these people was that they liked me and supported my work as the Union Director." Undoubtedly, these connections with wealthy laymen would serve him well in his new rabbinic role at Emanuel Congregation where, later, he was able to attract financial support, as well as new members from Chicago's Jewish elite.

He also interacted with the other Reform rabbis in the Chicago metropolitan area. Not only did he have the opportunity to visit their synagogues and attend their services, but he also worked with their boards as a troubleshooter and problem-solver. If a congregation was experiencing difficulty, or if two congregations were engaged in controversy with each other, his job was to assist in remediation and/or reconciliation. He even found himself in the middle of one of these conflicts. When he began offering adult education courses for the Jewish community, local rabbis objected. He remembers an unpleasant visit by three rabbis who came to his office to complain because they thought he "had no business conducting adult education," a function they considered their exclusive province. They warned him to stay away from their lay congregants and their lay leadership. "Of course," he remarked, "I didn't listen." One of the qualifications for this job was the ability to negotiate effectively between hostile parties, and Schaalman had a natural instinct for this kind of activity.[177]

Occasionally, he walked into congregational conflicts and quarrels that made his first year "really terrible." The first of these conflicts had to do with the President of the Chicago Federation of UAHC, Max Robert Schrayer, who was also president of KAM (Isaiah Israel) congregation.[178] Schrayer, whom Schaalman described as a "creative layman," believed that congregants had little motivation to be involved in temples that they had no part in running. Consequently, they felt little attachment to them and attended services only occasionally. Typically, the same people ran congregations for years and became a self-serving coterie that was not open to new membership. Schrayer concluded that the remedy for this alienation was greater involvement of the laity in congregational decision-making.[179] His model was based on his conviction that "ordinary" people should be involved in almost every aspect of the congregation.[180] KAM became his laboratory. His strategy was to develop a committee structure to oversee the various aspects of temple operation. Events in KAM so polarized the congregation that in 1949 the congregation split into KAM and Beth Am. For Schaalman, the new UAHC regional director, "this situation exploded right in my face."

For Reform temples in Chicago, a committee structure to manage temple affairs was a radical departure from previous practice, a revolution in temple affairs. Nor were Schrayer's innovations accepted by Chicago's rabbinate. Up to that time, they had total charge of liturgy and were untouchable. "They acted as they pleased," Schaalman recalls. "Nobody had anything to say. The exception might have been the president of the congregation, or a small group of wealthy people who controlled temple finances." Schaalman, however, was quick to recognize the value of Schrayer's innovations and incorporated them into his work as Regional Director and then, later, in his own work at Emanuel.

One of Schaalman's more pleasant responsibilities was to help establish new congregations. One of them was Temple Judea in Skokie, Illinois. In 1954, Skokie experienced an influx of veterans returning from the Korean War and World War II veterans who were finishing college on the GI Bill. Many of them were Jews, who were leaving Chicago's south, west, and near north neighborhoods. They sought good schools for their children and a modern Jewish community that was "attuned to their spiritual and social needs" (Temple Judea Mizpah, 2008). For many of them, this new temple met their needs. Schaalman "lent his avid support to the launching of the new congregation." To help the congregation get off to an impressive start, he officiated at the first Shabbat service on April 2, 1954. His official status added prestige to the fledgling congregation.[181] He also played an important role in the founding of several other congregations, one in Park Forest, South Suburban Jewish Liberal Reform Congregation, and B'nai Torah in Highland Park. Other newly formed temples sought his advice, among them Beth Am, Menorah, and Beth Emet.

Schaalman's work also included fundraising for the national UAHC, an effort organized through the "Combined Campaign," the fundraising arm for local activities and the national organization. The fundraising was not as successful as he had hoped, mainly for a lack of qualified and effective lay leadership. A troubled economy had a direct impact on congregational contributions, particularly on large givers, who made sizable cuts in their giving (Schaalman, H. E., 1956, p. 423). Nonetheless, because of the addition of five new congregations, total contributions increased by more than 10 percent in the five years during Schaalman's service as Midwest Regional Director and more than compensated for the decrease in contributions from existing sources.

In addition to working with the Combined Committee, Schaalman had responsibility for several other committees. One of the most important was the Youth Committee, which developed education programs and was the cauldron in which the first ideas of establishing a summer camp were developed. Schaalman also had responsibility for three other committees: Education, Synagogue Activities, and New Congregations. These committees had begun to make significant progress in improving education programs in the area's congregations, and they made plans to develop a citywide Adult Education program and materials and suggestions for their use. He looked forward in the near future to working with the Synagogue Activities Committee to create a citywide cooperative program for the study of Torah, and, with the help of the New Congregations Committee, to establish additional suburban congregations to reach out to unaffiliated Jews.

Among his other achievements, Schaalman is especially proud of the work he did with the Chicago Symphony Orchestra when, in 1950, he coordinated a five-day festival to honor the seventieth birthday of the world-renowned Jewish composer, Ernest Bloch (Pablo Casals called him "the best composer of our time" [Belknap, 2003]).[182] The event, which required months of strenuous work, was a great success for the Union.

Despite these achievements, however, Schaalman reported that he was frustrated by a sense that he had failed to fulfill the assignment he had been given. The job of serving the Union's entire Midwest and Great Lakes Regions in addition to the Chicago area was impossible. He simply did not have the time to provide adequate service to forty-five congregations in so large an area.[183] Nevertheless, during his tenure as Regional Director, he took credit for the growth of the Union's Midwest Region, and, as we shall see below, at least one achievement that he considered "spectacular."

Zionism and Israel

In the summer of 1951, Schaalman served as a faculty member at a two-week UAHC Youth Training Institute at Haverford College. The event was part of the Union's ongoing initiative for training youth leaders. Although apparently benign, the Institute sparked a major controversy between the Union and the American Council for Judaism, an anti-Zionist group of Reform Rabbis.[184] In Eisendrath's account of the incident, Leonard Sussman, a staff person for the Council, wrote an article for its newsletter (*The American Council News*), condemning the event as the Union's effort to inculcate Jewish youth in a "rabid Jewish nationalism and to orient them exclusively to the State of Israel rather than to America …" (Eisendrath, M. N., October 24, 1951, p. 98).[185] Sussman was particularly brutal to Schaalman, branding him "warped in mind and soul." The American Council on Judaism followed up the article with a letter to all American Reform rabbis that attempted to discredit the Union. The letter alerted the rabbis to the Union's leadership Institute and the "villainous antics of a Faculty [sic] who 'cram our religious school textbooks with extreme nationalist bias'" (p. 100).

Eisendrath had been warned by rabbis from other parts of the country that the Union was under attack, but, until he saw a copy of Sussman's article, had no concrete basis to respond to it. Now, he was ready to repudiate the article, which he called "libelous" (p. 98). Its claims threatened to undermine "one of the most laudable undertakings in the whole program of the UAHC" (p. 98). As part of the Union's response, he assigned its Youth Director, Rabbi Sam Cook, to prepare an extensive report on the Institute and invited Schaalman to respond as well. Eisendrath felt particularly bad for Schaalman, a survivor of Nazi Germany, for the "unfair and unsportsmanlike manner" in which he was attacked.

To counter Sussman's charges that the Institute was teaching "fierce nationalism," Eisendrath quoted parts of the written responses from participants that told a very different story. One of them stated that the twice-daily religious services created and conducted by the boys and girls attending were filled with "youthful hopefulness and spirituality." One participant reported that evening services were held outdoors under "a huge tree" that, for him, "symbolized the spirit of Judaism." For Eisendrath, these remarks, and others like them, demonstrated that the Institute "was suffused and saturated with spirituality—more spirituality, we may be certain, than any other Jewish agency in America, including the Council" (p. 100). Schaalman was so impressed with this aspect of the event that he made spirituality a fundamental part of the summer camp he helped launch in the summer of 1952.

Seizing on this theme, Eisendrath asserted that this spirituality was a sign of the times and a reflection of a turn in American Reform Jewish life. Reform Judaism was *"turning back to the synagogue, back for new religion* and new life," a turn from remembrance to *"hope for the future. Hope for mankind"* (p. 100–101). For Eisendrath, this hope and the spiritual needs that propelled it were major factors in the Union's effort to establish its own summer camps. He urged his colleagues to accept and "zealously" approve the establishment of the two camps proposed for the Midwest and West Coast Regions.

Sussman's attack on the Union for promoting Jewish nationalism and Eisendrath's vigorous denial highlight one of the major conflicts in the Jewish community at that time, namely how to relate to the new state of Israel. Since Biblical times, Jews had lamented their forced removal from their homeland. They longed for the coming of the Messianic Age that would allow them to return. This desire became a central part of the Passover ritual where it was enshrined in the refrain, "Next year in Jerusalem." At the end of the nineteenth century, a serious rift developed in the Jewish community when a strongly secular and largely socialist Zionist movement took root. The Zionists were convinced that Jewish survival depended on establishing a Jewish homeland in their own time. Their religious counterparts were convinced that this event depended on the arrival of the Messiah. During the first half of the twentieth century, Reform Judaism strongly opposed the idea of a separate Jewish homeland. In his defense of his youth leadership training, Eisendrath noticeably did not comment on the value of supporting Israel or on its importance in the life of American Jewry.

This conflict in world Judaism had a direct impact on Schaalman's early life and the peace in his household. As discussed in the first chapter, "The Early Years: Germany 1916–1935," Zionism had become part of the German-Jewish youth movement and a strong force in German-Jewish life in the 1930s. When some of Schaalman's Jewish friends were planning to immigrate to Palestine, he refused to join them, although he sympathized with their decision. Very likely, his strong family ties and the fact that his father was anti-Zionist influenced his decision. Soon, however, Schaalman was faced with the fact that his first love, Lotte Strauss (not Lotte Stern, whom he later married), immigrated with her family to Palestine.[186] Although she was willing to come to the United States to be his wife, like Schaalman, she too would be split off from her family.

After the Holocaust, however, the mood began to change. Jews worldwide, and especially in America, looked to their Judaism with new interest and fervor and the Jewish state took on a new importance. The Schaalman family that had so narrowly escaped the Holocaust sought to hold onto and preserve what was left of European Judaism in their new Brazil home. Although they had been "Liberal" Jews in Germany, they now turned toward tradition to find their spiritual footing.

In 1953, the American Reform Jewish community was still struggling to understand its relationship with the new state and what it meant for Diaspora Judaism. Eisendrath told his Executive Board, "the Union as an institution and our Reform movement as an organization ... have [not] been quite sufficiently sensitive to or sympathetic with the problems and the plight of our brethren in Israel. I include myself in this category" (Eisendrath, M,. Annual Report to the Executive Board: 1953, p. 259).[187] He decided to take a delegation of congregational leaders on a pilgrimage to Israel to discover firsthand what this relationship might mean. The congregational leaders who went with him were from the Chicago Federation of the UAHC and included Joe Ackerman, Michael Newberry, and their wives. To his great delight, Schaalman was able to go with the group after the Chicago Federation of the Union voted to take him along and pay his expenses.

The experience of the trip had a profound impact on the delegation. Eisendrath spoke of it as "the most deeply stirring experience of our respective lives" (Eisendrath, M. N., 1956, p. 258). Even those who were not sympathetic to Zionism or to Israel, he wrote, "were so genuinely moved by the unfolding challenge of Israel ... that none of them returned but with quickened hearts and new or renewed sympathy for and appreciation of what our brother Jews are achieving in the Holy Land." Part of Eisendrath's "religious" conversion to the need to support Israel may have been what he described as an extraordinary spiritual experience of praying in the Holy Land. He credited the Shabbat services conducted by

Schaalman and his rabbinic colleague, Rabbi Jay Kaufman, for helping to create this deeply moving experience. Another part of his conversion may be attributed to the fact that his administrative assistant, Rabbi Kaufman, was an "ardent Zionist," who was married to an Israeli. Schulman (1993) claims that Kaufman "convinced Eisendrath of the importance of Hebrew and Zionism in Reform Jewish education (p. 43).

Upon his return, Eisendrath proposed opening a "new chapter" in the Union's relationship to Israel." Zionism, which had been such a sticking point for the Union, was no longer an issue. Nevertheless, he acknowledged, they would have to contend with the "fanatical opposition to anything and everything that would link us with our brethren in Israel." Among his proposals for this new chapter was an exchange program for "Israeli and Reform Jewish youth in a mutual youth camp program," and tangible support for struggling Liberal and Progressive Judaism in Israel. The future of Israel, he declared, was dependent on "a moral and spiritual resurgence which only Reform Judaism can provide." For Eisendrath and Reform Judaism, this new awareness was a complete turnaround in Reform's attitude toward and approach to Israel.

The trip to Israel also had a profound effect on Schaalman. He had the sense that he was walking in the land of Isaiah and Jeremiah. Even the stones on the road had special meaning. He remembered visiting Megiddo and, while he was sitting on a piece of rock, was told by the guide that the rock was thought to be a windowsill in King Solomon's bedchamber. The experience gave him a sense of a physical connection to the Bible that he had not had before. One of the highlights of his trip was a meeting with Israel's Prime Minister, David Ben-Gurion, who was surprised that Schaalman could speak to him in Hebrew. Ben-Gurion asked:

> "Oh, you speak Hebrew? How come?"
> "I read the Bible."
> "That is a good history book."
> "Well, it is not a history book."
> "What do you mean? That is all it is."
> "I thought there were more things in it than history."
> "We would have to discuss it. I do not really take it that way."

Very likely, Ben Gurion did not expect a Reform Jew to know Hebrew. His response is an indication of the cultural divide and the igno-

Left to right. Schaalman, Eisendrath and
Israeli Prime Minister, David Ben Gurion, 1953

rance of each other that existed between Reform Judaism and the State of Israel.

Another unique experience awaited the young rabbi during his two weeks in Israel. An official from the Foreign Office took the Chicago group into the desert to meet with a local Sheikh. Upon entering his tent, Schaalman found himself in the presence of a tall, good-looking man with an imposing dagger stuck in his belt. When they sat down together, Schaalman told the Sheikh that he thought the camels outside were beautiful. The Foreign Office official poked Schaalman in the ribs and whispered, "He'll have to give you one." In the customs of the Bedouins, such praise might require the Sheikh to give Schaalman the camels as a gift. As he thought about the absurdity of taking a camel home with him, Schaalman dropped the subject. He also took advantage of his trip to pay a visit to the grave of Lotte Strauss and to visit her family, with whom he had kept in close contact.

Israel was beginning to exert a hold on Schaalman; he could not help but be affected by the sense of excitement and youthful enthusiasm that permeated the society. Despite the Holocaust, Israelis were overwhelmingly positive and optimistic. He was profoundly attracted to some of the kibbutzim he visited. As mini-Socialist societies, they offered a sense of a life built on mutuality and a complete system of security. These positive experiences led him to consider making *aliyah*. However, he was held back by his sense of the work that needed to be done in the Diaspora that was critical to Israel's growth and security.

Many years later when he retired, he did consider making *aliyah* but didn't follow through because of the distance it would put between him and his children and grandchildren. Instead, he chose to make frequent visits. On one of them, he took his grandchildren so that they, too, might develop an interest in Israel.

Instead of returning home at the end of the visit, Schaalman accepted an invitation to visit Paris as guests of some friends from Chicago, Mike and Vivian Newberry. As sophisticated art collectors, they took him around Paris to see the sights and treated him to restaurants and nightclubs "the like of which [he] had never seen." He flew to Paris on El-Al, Israel's new airline. Sitting next to him was a young man who revealed that he was on his way to Paris to buy arms. Later, Schaalman learned that the man was none other than Shimon Peres. He was given this assignment because of his ability to read and write French. In later years, Schaalman had other contacts with Peres, but this first contact was the most significant.

Chapter 5

Reform Jewish Camping
OSRUI

"There can be little doubt that Schaalman's tireless work as both the regional director of UAHC and camp director contributed to the success of the Union Institute during its fledgling years."

Michael Lorge and Gary Zola, 2007, p. 64

"We still remember the early years when we took our young people to a Salvation Army camp in Northern Illinois before your foresight caused the UAHC to invest in the Union Institute in Oconomowoc, Wisconsin, the forerunner of all the youth camps in our movement."

Rabbi Karl Richter (1986)

UAHC Youth Programs

Now that Schaalman was the Union's Midwest Director, he made his most important priority the establishment of a summer camp for Reform youth. His motivation came in large part from his participation in the Methodist summer camp in Iowa in the summer of 1943. His participation in this camp gave him new insight into the possible impact a religious summer camp could have on children. He experienced firsthand the fervent commitment to Christian values and learning that was evident in almost every aspect of camp life. This encounter convinced him that Jewish children should have a similar experience with a focus on Judaism. On the drive back to Cedar Rapids, he and Lotte discussed the experience and concluded that he should be teaching Jewish, rather than non-Jewish, children. He knew that Jewish parents sent their children to camps such as Kawaga and Agawak, camps that stressed nature lore and sportsmanship. Schaalman concluded that a camp stressing Jewish content was a necessity.

He must not have been aware of the extent to which the UAHC was already committed to setting up a camp for Jewish youth or the efforts of others to establish Jewish camps during the first half of the twentieth century.[188] Prior to World War II, the UAHC had recognized the potential of such camps to develop Reform Jewish youth and had set aside $5,000 as seed money (Lorge and Zola, 2006, p. 54). In 1943, Eisendrath, as the president of the UAHC, set as one of his first priorities to establish "one pilot Youth Camp with several other regional camps to follow" (UAHC, *77–80th Annual Report*, p. 64).[189] The war, however, caused the collapse of the Union's Youth Program and made that objective impossible. After the war, Eisendrath used his "State of the Union" address at the UAHC biennial in Cincinnati in 1946 to advocate for an expanded youth program, including the establishment of a summer youth camp. A year later, he asked his Executive Board "to consider" the idea of a camp that would be used as a summer camp for youth but also year-round for institutes for adult retreats and teachers (p. 65).

In Chicago, Jewish leaders had been considering the idea of establishing a summer camp since the early 1940s, an idea that lay dormant for the rest of the decade. Lorge and Zola (2006) speculate that the reasons might have been the lack of a lead person and/or that the War and the fate of European Jews became higher priorities. According to extant documents from the first few months of 1951, the effort to establish a summer camp for Chicago area youth began to solidify soon after Schaalman took over the job of UAHC Midwest Regional Director. Working closely with J. S. Ackerman, president of the Chicago Jewish Federation of the UAHC and vice president of the UAHC, and other lay leaders and rabbis, Schaalman held meetings to establish the camp with area rabbis and lay synagogue leaders (Sarna, J. D., 2006, p. 43). Support also came at the national level when the Union established the Committee on Youth Camps to develop a nationwide network of summer camps.

A critical element in establishing the camp was the need to raise funds from local Jewish organizations and congregations (Ackerman, October 4, 1951). Schaalman was in a unique position to rally that support.[190] Within two years of his arrival in Chicago, he contacted all the

Jewish organizations and Reform temples in the metropolitan area and could readily enlist their support for this new venture. In Schaalman's recollection, his effort to get the Chicago Jewish community to adopt and support the idea of a Jewish summer camp was a major challenge and required a great deal of his time.

On March 29, 1951, working in close cooperation with Ackerman, Schaalman called a special meeting for youth and lay leaders from Chicago area Reform congregations (Chicago Federation UAHC, 1951). Thirty-five of Chicago's most prestigious Reform Jewish leaders representing ten Reform synagogues attended the meeting.[191] Support for the project came from Rabbi Ernst Lorge, Rabbi Arnold Wolf, and Bernard Sang, a young Chicago attorney, who had been the second president of the National Federation of Temple Youth. When the meeting was over, Sidney I. Cole, a leading supporter of the effort, wrote to Rabbi Lorge to compliment him on the event. Cole told him that "when you or Herman or the others speak, the cause is won" (as cited in Lorge and Zola, 2006, p. 59-60). When Harry Lawner, UAHC's national Camp Committee chair, learned of the positive outcome of the meeting, he sent an enthusiastic letter to the leaders of the effort praising them for the work they were doing and expressing his optimism that they would be successful.

A "Special Committee," referred to as the "Chicago group" in UAHC correspondence, led the effort to find a suitable campsite. According to Schaalman, Ackerman would scan the Sunday *Tribune* for suitable real estate offerings. After consultation with the other committee members, he would call Schaalman to ask his opinion of the possible sites. When they identified a site that seemed like a good possibility, Ackerman would pick up Schaalman in his Cadillac, and off they would go to Wisconsin. The ride in the Cadillac was a "special treat" for Schaalman, who was not used to riding in such luxury.

In July, they found a site in Oconomowoc, Wisconsin, a private Jewish boys' camp called Briar Lodge (Lawner, September 6, 1951, p. 78).[192] The moment he saw it, Schaalman said, "Joe, this is it." Ackerman wanted to know why Schaalman was so certain. Schaalman fired off three quick responses: it was north of Chicago; the Edens, connecting Chicago and Milwaukee, had just been completed; and Chicago Jews were moving north. Another attraction Schaalman saw was that the camp included a large estate on the edge of a lake that could be used in winter for adult education, as well as for a camp in the summer.[193]

Because of her advancing age, the owner of the camp, a woman named Garland, wanted to get rid of it. The camp included a forty-five-year old residence that served as the main lodge with enough bedroom and bathroom space to accommodate fifty-five to sixty people and eight cabins that could house eighty to eighty-five campers. In addition, it had a recreation hall, a completely developed waterfront with bathhouse, dock, sundeck, and boats, two tennis courts, and two baseball diamonds. After a team of architects had surveyed the site and reported its suitability as a camp for the Chicago region, the Special Committee, working with Schaalman, began the process of acquiring the camp, settling various legal matters, and raising the funds. On July 9, 1951, Schaalman sent a detailed memo to Ackerman explaining that the original terms for the purchase were $63,000 with $20,000 down and the balance to be paid in a ten-year mortgage of $48,000 including its four percent interest.[194] On June 17, 1951, the UAHC approved the purchase of the camp, allowing the Chicago Federation of the UAHC to proceed with the purchase.[195]

Finding the funds to purchase the camp was a story in itself. Schaalman took the lead in raising funds for the down payment (Lorge and Zola, 2006, p. 60). His objective was to come up with three $5,000 contributions. Ackerman gave him $5,000 and told him, "Go back and raise the rest.'" Upon his return to Chicago, Schaalman contacted his friend Bernard Sang, who donated an additional $5,000. With this gift in hand, Schaalman had to raise another $5,000 and did not have to wait long. He remembers that he was sitting at his desk on the sixth floor of the Union office when he received a call from the president of a small congregation. The president, aware that Schaalman needed to raise another $5,000 for the camp, told him that he had the money. The donor, however, wished to remain anonymous. When Schaalman asked why the donor did not want to be identified, the president responded, "'He says, 'anonymous!'" Not only did this response pique Schaalman's interest but also made him suspicious. He asked the president why "someone wouldn't want to have their name connected with an institution which teaches Judaism to young people and adults?" After a brief pause, the president responded, "It just has to be anonymous." Despite the fact that he was in need of the money, Schaalman would not accept the gift without knowing the donor. After a brief pause, the president told him the donor was Jake Guzik, a member of his congregation. Schaalman recognized that he was part of the Al Capone gang and in charge of brothels with all their white slavery issues.[196] Schaalman told the president that he had to refuse the donation "because he could not build a Jewish camp on the bodies of prostitutes." Nevertheless, the conversation and his refusal to accept the money weighed heavily on Schaalman.

The story does not end here. Several days later, Schaalman was on his way to his office on Michigan Avenue and, while waiting for the light to change, bumped into an old friend. Surprised and pleased to see him, Schaalman asked, "Sidney Robinson, what are you doing in Chicago?" Just as surprised as was Schaalman, Robinson wanted to know what Schaalman was doing there. After filling him in on the developments in his life, Schaalman told Robinson about his recent disappointment in raising money for the camp. Robinson asked him how much he needed. When Schaalman told him that he still needed $5,000, Robinson invited him to his office only a few doors away and wrote a check for the remaining $5,000. Schaalman knew he had his camp.

With the down payment secured, the camp was on its way to becoming a reality. Ackerman wrote to Lawner that they still needed another $20,000 to winterize the buildings and provide working capital for the first year's operations (Ackerman, J. S., October 4, 1951). He suggested that Lawner proceed immediately "to get approval for the purchase of the property … so that as soon as we have the money lined up, we can go ahead."

On October 11, 1951, Schaalman wrote to Rabbi Lorge to ask for "help" and "advice" on the camp project.[197] He told Lorge that he was making "slow but steady progress" and needed his help to raise additional funds and help recruit campers (Schaalman, H. E., October 11, 1951). He planned to hold meetings during the coming weeks to garner support for the project. Because Lorge had been involved in youth conclaves over the past several years, Schaalman wanted him to speak at the meetings "to demonstrate the need to create such a camp." Although "a good bit of money [had been raised] for a down payment, there was still a need to pay for repairs." Schaalman urged Lorge to invite potential financial backers to these meetings.[198]

By mid-winter of 1952, the process of acquiring the camp jumped into high gear. On February 26, Schaalman sent a memo to "All Rabbis in the Midwestern, Rocky Mountain, & Great Lakes Regions of the Union" inviting them to send their young people to the new camp (Schaalman, H. E., February 26, 1951). The memo indicated that the land had been purchased in southern Wisconsin. The camp offered two two-week sessions for young people, both male and female, of Confirmation age or older. The memo stated that the first session began June 30, and the second, July 14. The cost was $75 per camper for each two-week session.[199]

Two days later, Schaalman wrote to Eisendrath that he had the down payment for the camp and that a contract to purchase the camp had been "executed" (Lawner, H., March 25, 1952).

The Camp Becomes a Reality

On May 22, 1952, the camp was legally incorporated in Wisconsin as the Union Institute (Lorge and Zola, 2006, p. 52).[200] In his June 1952 Semi-Annual Report to the Union's Executive Board, Eisendrath called the establishment of the camp a "historic milestone" for the Union (Eisendrath, M. N., 1952, p. 153). He complimented Ackerman and Schaalman for their work in securing the camp and for developing its "comprehensive program" (p. 153).[201] Nevertheless, in the aftermath of the Sussman article, misrepresentations about the camp movement persisted, and Eisendrath wanted to assure the board that the camps were having a positive impact on its campers.[202] Already, he had received "a myriad" of testimonials to the "unparalleled religious impact" the camps were having on the young people who had attended them (p. 154). Their experience would "prepare them for their future role as congregational members and leaders. Most important, and a cause for celebration, was the fact that "at least a dozen, perhaps sixteen or seventeen young people who had attended the NFTY Camp-Institutes planned to enter the rabbinate" (p. 155). He was so enthusiastic about the fact that the Union now had the camp in Oconomowoc that he proposed the board meet there in October of 1952 for a "spiritual retreat" (p. 154).

Because the Union wanted the camp to open that summer and did not have time or funds to hire a director, Schaalman took on the

OSRUI first Summer 1952. Right side, Herman Schaalman (standing) and on the left, Lotte Schaalman (seated) holding Michael, first row, third from right, Susan

assignment in addition to his full-time regional director responsibilities. Although he had no experience running a camp, he had excellent managerial skills and a hardworking and practical wife who helped get the camp ready for opening. Lotte cooked, cleaned, painted and generally did whatever was necessary right alongside her husband to bring to fruition her husband's dream.[203] They drove up to the camp on weekends to get it in shape for the opening.

During the first summer, the Schaalmans lived in one room with their two children. They felt like pioneers or kibbutzniks. Together with staff, they spent many evenings preparing curriculum for the next day. Some days, they did not go to bed until two or three in the morning, barely enough time to get a few hours of sleep before the campers woke up. Fortunately, the Schaalmans had compa ny and support from Rabbi Wolli Kaelter and his wife, whom Schaalman had invited to help set up the camp. Kaelter (1997), who had been one of the five rabbinic students who came to America with Schaalman, remembered how excited he was by the prospect of working with his friend and "jumped at the chance" (p. 117). The Kaelters stayed for three weeks. In return, Schaalman recommended him to Eisendrath, who was then recruiting a director for the new UAHC summer camp in Saratoga, California.

Schaalman's policy was that work and study should be integral parts of the campers' day. He remembers establishing work crews at 10:00 a.m. for one hour of work time. He divided the campers into groups, depending on what needed to be done. Part of the hour would be taken up in getting ready to work. The actual time for work shrunk to twenty to thirty minutes. "It never really worked well," Schaalman remembers. "Had I known anything about camping, I would not have done that. It was not a workable situation. In those days, I knew nothing. My only experience in the camp had been as a counselor."

At first, finding rabbis willing to give their time to teach in the camp was a major challenge. However, as the reputation of the camp spread, rabbis were eager to come. Then, as now, they served without pay. However, in exchange for their service, whether a week or a month, they could bring their families free of charge. Most took advantage of this benefit.

Partly in recognition of the impossibility of one man shouldering the responsibilities of two jobs and doing both successfully, by the end of the summer the camp's board began a search for a new director. However, finding a suitable replacement for Schaalman turned out to be a challenge. At the beginning of the camp's second year, the Union hired Rabbi Gerald Raiskin as director. Raiskin, a recent HUC-JIR graduate, reported directly to Schaalman and served as camp director for the 1953 camping season (Lorge and Zola, 2006, p. 65). Two other directors followed in quick succession: Rabbi Daniel E. Kermin and Rabbi Irwin Schor, each holding the job for only one year (pp. 67–70). As late as 1955, the Union had not hired a full-time camp director. That year, the camp's Evaluation Committee reported that the camp needed to hire a "trained group leader" with camp experience.

The Camp Becomes a Success

Within a year of launching the Union Institute, Eisendrath (1953) reported that the camp was a success and the beginning of the "long-delayed" nationwide Union camp program (p. 544). He was particularly proud that the camp movement had begun in Chicago where he had his own roots. He noted further that the camp had been "nurtured" by Rabbi Felix Levy of Emanuel Congregation and Chicago was the home of

OSRUI Board Meeting 1952: Left to right: Row 1, Eli Blumberg; fifth from left, Rabbi Schaalman, Executive Director of OSRUI; seventh from left, Robert Cooper, first President of OSRUI Board; Row 2, seventh from left, Rabbi Karl Weiner; eighth from left, Sid Cole, second president of OSRUI board: ninth from left, Rabbi Joseph Buehler.

Left to right. Rev. W. Sterling Cary, Chairman, Council of Religious Leaders; Bishop Paul Erickson, President, Illinois Synod, Lutheran Church of America; Rabbi Schaalman and Cardinal Joseph Bernardin.

Dr. Sidney S. Hollender, UAHC's current chair of the Executive Board (pp. 544–545). He credited Schaalman for his "vision and vigor" and for being largely responsible for making the camp a year-round program. He also affirmed Schaalman's evaluation that the camp provided a "'priceless opportunity for worship and Jewish study [that was] changing the whole tone of our religious life and the quality of participation in congregational activity'" (as cited in Eisendrath, 1953, p. 546).[204] Eisendrath was so pleased with this aspect of the newly emerging camps, that he recommended the creation of a National Commission for adult "retreats" that would be based on the model of "this notable and noble Chicago pattern" (p. 547).

In his annual report to the Union's Executive Committee, Schaalman wrote that the camp's success was unparalleled "in Chicago history or, for that matter, anywhere else in the country" (p. 423). In the first few years of its existence, the Union Institute was already having a positive effect on the area's congregations and the Union's committees. It was being used year-round for adult meetings and retreats and, more importantly, the camp was having a great influence on the entire Reform movement's efforts to establish camps around the country (p. 423).

Lorge and Zola (2006) credit Schaalman for his leadership in steering the camp successfully during these first few years: "There can be little doubt that Schaalman's tireless work as both the regional director of UAHC and camp director contributed to the success of Union Institute during its fledgling years" (p. 64).[205] In acknowledgement of his founding work and ongoing support of the camp, members and friends of Emanuel Congregation donated funds to renovate a lodge that had been built in 1961 to make it more attractive to house visiting rabbinic faculty. It was rededicated on July 12, 1997 as the Herman and Lotte Schaalman Lodge.

Over the next half century, Schaalman continued to play a major role in the camp's development. Jerry Kaye, who became camp director in 1969 and continues to this day, provides a good window through which to view Schaalman's ongoing participation in the camp's affairs. According to Kaye (2006), he was hired in 1969 by a small group of rabbis including Schaalman. At the time, it was not clear to Kaye whether Schaalman was chair of that committee or merely one of its members.

Although it was apparent to him that these rabbis ran the camp, Schaalman never imposed his views, but gave advice when Kaye asked him.

Kaye (2006) notes that Schaalman could also be receptive to new and contemporary musical arrangements of traditional Jewish music. In some small way, this receptivity may have contributed to the reform of Jewish liturgical music that evolved over the last three decades of the twentieth century. In 1972, while Schaalman was holding one of his annual New Year's Retreat weekends, Kaye brought to camp an unknown young singer, Debbie Friedman, to audition for the job of camp song leader. When Schaalman heard her sing, "He fell in love with her immediately, as she did with him" (Kaye, 2006).[206]

This reciprocal admiration helped propel Friedman into the major figure she later became in Reform Jewish liturgical music. Because of the success of her audition at Schaalman's New Year Retreat, Kaye hired her to be the camp's song leader. In the ten years she served in this position, she wrote many of the songs that made her famous. By the early part of the twenty-first century, as campers nurtured on her music matured into rabbis and cantors, her music had become the music of choice in Reform camps and synagogues and helped transform Reform liturgy.[207]

The success of the Union Institute allowed it to become the prototype for the development of a network of UAHC camps in other parts of the country. J. D Sarna (2006), Brandeis University Professor of American Jewish History, maintains that this development may be understood as a response by the Jewish community to the Holocaust which destroyed Europe's centers of Jewish learning (p. 28). American Judaism recognized a need to compensate for this loss by establishing a vibrant Jewish culture in America, and because of their ability to educate and provide an immersion experience in Judaism, the summer camps were one way to do that (p. 36).

Schaalman considers his contribution to establishing a summer camp for Jewish children the most important achievement of his long and distinguished career. Rabbi Richard G. Hirsch (2010) offers a similar assessment, "The most important thing he did was establish the camp, which, along with the establishment of the Religious Action Center, had more impact on Reform Judaism than anything else in the last half of the twentieth century." Rabbi Karl Richter (1986) wrote that the camp was responsible for bringing "forth so many young leaders and stands as a monument to [Schaalman's] courage and wisdom." At the age of ninety-six, Schaalman continues to work on behalf of the camp. As a member of its board, he helps raise funds and teaches as one of its rabbinic summer faculty.

Chapter 6

Emanuel Congregation and Leadership in Reform Judaism: 1956–1986

"I am a brand plucked from the fire from among the dozens who were equally prepared, equally worthy (perhaps more so). I have been given the gift of life, to prove to myself and to the God Whom I seek to serve that it might have been worthwhile to rescue this brand from the conflagration."

Herman E. Schaalman, 1981

"In the rabbinic calling, one has to make one's peace with the fact that one is never done. And not just never done because there is so much, but because the kinds of things you do just don't have an end."

Herman E. Schaalman, 1988

"The real problem for someone like me as a rabbi is how do I live in the community? How do I find people who will listen? How do I conduct the service with my way of thinking? The opportunity to talk to you like this is my form of praying."

Herman E. Schaalman, 2008

Background

Although Schaalman loved his work for the Union, by 1953 he began to feel that he missed the experience of working with a congregation. In part, he was motivated by the thought that

213

a congregation would provide a social context for his family and a community in which he could establish lasting ties. As Union director, he dealt almost entirely with the leadership of congregations in his region. Even though he established close ties with many of them, he was aware that their primary affiliation and responsibility was to their own congregation and rabbi and that he had to be careful not to interfere in that relationship.

When he told Eisendrath his misgivings about continuing in his role as Regional Director, Eisendrath proposed that he come to New York to be the head of the Education Department, or, if he preferred, the head of Adult Education. The offer was tempting; it would have given Schaalman the opportunity to exercise his creativity and to be in contact with some of the most important leaders in the national Jewish community. Nevertheless, he had already moved several times—first from Cincinnati to Cedar Rapids and then to Chicago—and the idea of moving his family one more time was not appealing. Moreover, although he always enjoyed his visits to New York City, he felt that the city was simply too big. (In later years, he realized that he might have become Eisendrath's successor. When Eisendrath died suddenly just before he was to speak at his final UAHC conference, Rabbi Alex Schindler moved up from his position as head of the Education Department to take his place. In this role, he became one of the outstanding leaders in American Jewish life.)

By this time, Rabbi Levy had reached retirement age and was expected to retire soon. Eisendrath, who had grown up in Emanuel and become good friends with Levy, knew of the impending retirement and told Schaalman that if Levy were to retire, he could understand that Schaalman might seek his position. Because he had done such good work for the Union, Schaalman did not take Eisendrath's words as a sign that he wanted him to leave.

Schaalman's connection with Emanuel had begun years before he ever had any idea that someday it would become his home. He had known Rabbi Felix Levy since 1936 when, as a student rabbi, Schaalman had come to Chicago to conduct services for a German refugee congregation on Chicago's south side. During that brief stay, Schaalman came to know the young Paul Basinger, a future leader in Emanuel, who, at the time was courting Rabbi Levy's daughter, Suzanne. Through his friendship with Basinger, Schaalman was invited into Rabbi Levy's home. The two rabbis quickly became friends, and the Levys invited him to room with them and sleep in their study. The offer was too good to refuse.

After his stint as student rabbi in Chicago, Schaalman kept in close touch with Levy, who became his closest rabbinic contact and friend. Mostly, they met at CCAR annual conferences, but when Schaalman came to Chicago to take the job with the UAHC, he and Levy had more frequent contact. Whenever Schaalman did not have to speak at other services and had the time, he attended Saturday morning services at Emanuel. Other times, he attended services at Temple Mizpah, which was only a few blocks from where he lived on Lunt Avenue, and where he had enrolled his kids in religious school. Nevertheless, he preferred Emanuel, largely because Rabbi Levy's sermons were "always quite deep, quite erudite."

Another factor that may have played a part in the bond between the two rabbis was the fact that Emanuel Congregation had begun as an Orthodox German-speaking congregation and many of its early rabbis and members were German immigrants, or children of German immigrants.[208] During its formative years, all of its congregants spoke German and, for that reason, until 1901 all sermons, board meetings, and school classes were conducted in German. Before the end of the nineteenth century, however, the congregation discarded its Orthodox orientation in favor of what it saw as the newer and more liberating Reform Judaism. It switched to English and abandoned yarmulkes as head coverings for services ("History of Emanuel Congregation," 2009).

The congregation had hired Rabbi Levy in 1907, in part because he spoke fluent German. Under his leadership, the congregation flourished and quickly outgrew its several homes. During his years at Emanuel, Levy became well-known for his scholarship and leadership ability, serving as president of the CCAR from 1935-1937. According to Rabbi A. Stanley Dreyfus (1986), during his presidency Levy helped steer the Reform movement away from "its universalistic creed" bordering on Ethical Culture and Unitarianism and reminded Jews of their history, their peoplehood, and the richness and sanctity of their religious heritage. Dreyfus (1986) asserts that Levy was "the prime mover in the ratification of the 1937 Columbus Platform and the architect of Neo-Reform Judaism," which helped restore a balance between traditional Judaism and modern notions of Reform.

By 1950, Emanuel had grown to 500 members and needed a building with more space. Plans were developed to build a new synagogue on Lake Michigan that would be large enough to accommodate its congregation. When it was completed in 1955, the congregation moved into its new building at 5959 N. Sheridan Road, the building it currently occupies ("History of Emanuel Congregation," 2009).

In 1954, Levy, who had been Emanuel's rabbi for forty-seven years, announced his intention to retire at the end of 1955. Following the announcement, Emanuel's Board created a rabbinic search committee to hire a new rabbi. The committee met throughout 1955 in a protracted effort to find a replacement for their esteemed and prestigious rabbi. They interviewed candidates from all over the country but could not find anyone of Levy's caliber. Then they approached Schaalman. One of his considerations in becoming an applicant was the fact that his position as director of the Union was temporary; typically, rabbis remained in that position for a year or two before returning to their congregations. Schaalman, however, had no congregation to which he could return, and Emanuel, one of oldest and most prestigious Reform congregations in the nation, was the only congregation in Chicago that interested him.[209]

The Selection Is Finalized

The search committee picked Schaalman, whom they already knew from his last five years as the director of the Union and his occasional guest speaking appearances. It did not hurt that he attended services at Emanuel and that he had become good friends with several of the board members. Schaalman is not sure whether it was Mecklenburger or Sam Froelich who put his name in the hopper. Of one matter, he is completely certain: had Rabbi Levy not wanted him as his successor, he would never have been hired. The outgoing rabbi had veto power over the choice of successor.

In October of 1955, Emanuel's Board put their choice of Levy's successor to a vote of the congregation and got its endorsement to hire Schaalman. In November, the board made him a formal offer of a contract that would be effective January 1, 1956. Schaalman was delighted to accept the offer. Because he did not want to leave UAHC without a replacement, he remained in a caretaker role as Regional Director for the UAHC until the arrival of his successor. In the spring of 1956, the UAHC hired Rabbi Richard G. Hirsch, who had been one of Levy's assistants, as its new Regional Director. Schaalman, however, did not relinquish his sense of responsibility for the Union Institute but remained a member of the Board of Governors and served on the Union's National Camp Committee.

For Schaalman, acceptance of this new position was the stepping stone that catapulted him into the national spotlight of Reform Judaism. It was the beginning of a steady climb in growing recognition by his colleagues of his potential as a national and international leader of Reform Judaism. Levy left behind a legacy of dedicated and accomplished leadership not only of his congregation but also of the Reform movement. The fact that he served as president of the movement's rabbinic governing body, the CCAR, was a testament to him and greatly increased the prestige of Emanuel Congregation.[210] Filling his shoes would be a major challenge for Schaalman, who had no expectations of ever achieving Levy's stature.

Although his official duties had not started, Schaalman remembers that he began assuming rabbinic duties for Emanuel in October of 1955. Not only was he the new rabbi, but he took over the pulpit in a modern attractive building on the shore of Lake Michigan.[211]

The Challenging Transition

On January 6, 1956, Rabbi Levy installed Schaalman as Emanuel's new senior rabbi. Levy had been Emanuel's rabbi for half a century and the job of filling his shoes was a major test of Schaalman's personality and resources. Levy was well liked by his congregation and highly respected as a writer and scholar in the national Jewish community as well. When he retired, some of his friends and family members were initially hostile to Schaalman; in his first few years at Emanuel, those who did not accept him as Levy's successor clustered around the congregation's cantor, Robert Handwerger, who had been there for many years.

The chief grievance of this group was the fact that Levy's assistant rabbi and nephew, Rabbi Arnold Wolf, did not get the appointment. Because he was convinced that he had earned the job, Wolf had no doubt that he would be his uncle's successor. Like his uncle, he was an intellectual and on friendly terms with the congregation. Moreover, Wolf was well known to them. He had grown up in the congregation, and influential family members were part of it. However, for whatever reasons, the board did not hire him. Schaalman claims that he did not "enter the picture [as a candidate] until the congregation had made up its mind not to take Arnold." Wolf blamed Schaalman for the board's decision not to hire him and never forgave him.[212] This rejection, however, did not prevent Wolf from becoming one of America's distinguished Reform rabbis.

Arnold Wolf's mother, the sister of Rabbi Levy, was a member of the congregation and very unhappy with the turn of events. In addition, Levy's daughter, son-in-law, and some of their friends who were influential leaders in the congregation were hostile to Schaalman. This prominence of one family in the congregation meant that Schaalman had a difficult time becoming part of its culture. The Schaalmans struggled for many years to gain acceptance and respect from this faction. The effort was costly; it was a source of deep hurt and frustration for them, and, to this day, they still have the scars of the struggle of these early years.

Schaalman also ran into difficulties with Emanuel's board. Many of its members were major figures in their own worlds and had a long history of association with Emanuel. Among them were David M. Riff; Herbert Decker; A. L. Fader, president of Emanuel's Board of Trustees; Kurt Goldsmith; Sam Froehlich; and Albert Mecklenburger. They were not only outspoken board members, but also they were decision-makers who had a strong commitment to managing the temple's affairs. Often the board's meetings were contentious and difficult for the new rabbi. When he got home, he would be so upset that Lotte would take him out for a walk to calm him down. At one point, a friend on Emanuel's board told him that he would have less difficulty if he did not speak so often at meetings. Schaalman was frustrated in part because, as the UAHC Director, he was used to having his way with temple boards, as he did with his board while he was rabbi in Temple Judah. As the Director of the UAHC, his recommendations to its board of prestigious rabbis were generally accepted.

In addition to the board, Schaalman ran into resistance from the Couples Club. Emanuel had established this Club under Levy because it knew that its strength lay in the strength of its families, particularly its young families. Led by Levy's assistants, Rabbis Hirsch and Wolf, the Club was very active in temple affairs. During Schaalman's first two years, he remembers that Hirsch made him feel unwelcome.[213] After a few years, as younger members began to drift away to the suburbs, the Club died out. Schaalman speculates, "It may have ceased to function because some of its members could not accept my leadership." As a way to bridge the gap between Club members who remained in the congregation, Schaalman established a study group that met in the homes of group members. As late as 2011, with additions and subtractions, the group continued to meet with Schaalman several times a year.

Schaalman speculates that another reason he was not immediately accepted by many in the congregation was the fact that he had a German accent and may not have been as competent a speaker as he later became. "It took me a decade to win over the congregation and gain their full support." "From then on," Schaalman asserts, "my rabbinate was peaceful, and I was never challenged again. There was a wonderful sense of partnership that made my rabbinate an almost unsullied joy."

Rabbinic Contract

Schaalman's first contract was for one year at a salary of $20,000, a substantial increase over his meager $3,000 salary in Cedar Rapids. Schaalman maintains that a renewal of his first year contract was by no means a certainty. In fact, given the resistance to him by some board members and congregants, he had reason to be concerned. Had the board been dissatisfied, it had the option of terminating him the following year. Although board minutes record each of Schaalman's contracts prior to their renewal dates, Schaalman does not remember ever signing a contract. In fact, he has very strong views about a rabbi having a contractual relationship with a congregation. He believes that when a rabbi accepts a rabbinic post, the rabbi is entering into a marriage with the congregation. Contracts, Schaalman maintains, are business arrangements and totally inappropriate for a rabbi and a congregation. Nonetheless, although he does not remember signing a contract, one was issued by the board and a copy is available in Emanuel's Board Minutes for November 19, 1955. Because he was unwilling to think of his rabbinate in monetary terms, he gave no thought to negotiating contracts and accepted whatever he was given. In retrospect, he now thinks that the congregation took him for granted. During his first five years, he did not get a raise.

One sign that Schaalman was having a positive impact on Emanuel was the recommendation of its Rabbinic Committee to extend his one-year contract for another three years from July 1, 1958 to June 30, 1961 (Emanuel Trustee Minutes, December 10, 1957, p. 1). The recommendation for renewal was presented to the Board of Trustees in the form of a glowing endorsement of the rabbi's services and abilities.[214] The contract provided for an annual compensation and expense allowance totaling $20,000 plus a payment by the congregation of its share of the Rabbinic Pension Fund. The contract also stipulated, "All emoluments received by the Rabbi for services rendered to be remitted to the Congregation" (p. 2). What that stipulation meant was that as long as the congregation was paying Schaalman's salary, the time he took from temple duties for which he received payment was legitimately owed to the temple. Although the board did not give Schaalman a raise in his 1959–1961 contract, it approved a substantial housing allowance (Emanuel Congregation, May 24, 1960, p. 1).

One of the benefits of his rabbinic contract was that he had summers off. Because the temple did not have air conditioning, the congregation closed down for three months of the summer. In the brutal Chicago summers, the hot and humid building was not conducive to holding services, and a sizable portion of the congregation was away on vacation. Closing down for the summer gave the rabbi a respite from his daily obligations and an opportunity to study and travel. For Schaalman, however, the summers had special meaning. It was the time he could get away to participate in the Union Institute. Although he was no longer its director, he and his family would spend much of their summer in residence at the camp where he served as camp rabbi and spiritual leader.

Membership Issues

By 1957, Emanuel Congregation's membership had grown from 620 to 849 members (Emanuel Board Minutes, February 26, 1957). Most of them were German Jews and many were the descendants of Emanuel's founders. This huge increase can be attributed to the excitement over Schaalman's new and dynamic leadership that made Emanuel the "happening place." As a forty-year-old, he was much younger than his predecessor and brought renewed energy and innovative ideas. In the early years of Schaalman's rabbinate at Emanuel, its Hebrew School flourished. Enrollment rose to over 400 students. A small but significant part of that enrollment included forty-four students in the first Confirmation class.

Despite this initial growth in membership, the demographics of Emanuel's congregation were beginning to change. In 1956, its membership included between seventy and eighty young couples, but that number began to erode as families with financial means to do so left Chicago for the greener northern suburbs (Skokie, Evanston, Winnetka, Glencoe, Glenview, Highland Park, and Northbrook). The decline was gradual, but relentless. By 2010, the 400+ students enrolled in the Sunday school and Hebrew School in 1957 had shrunk to 165 with deep and lasting financial consequences for Emanuel.[215]

In a board meeting held on September 24, 1957, the Conservation Committee reported that in the recent period there had been seventy-seven resignations or "drops." The number was alarming and the board decided to take action to try to stem the tide of declining membership. Recognizing that the membership decline could be offset by improved efforts to hold on to existing members and to encourage new membership, Ronnie Harlow, an executive with an independent telephone company and an expert in communications systems, proposed that a committee be established to help integrate new members into the congregation and to improve communication with members.[216] The board accepted his recommendation and established an Integration Committee to help new members become part of the Emanuel family. As the head of the Integration Committee, Harlow, who was a close friend of Schaalman, created the Schochen Program that took on the challenge of organizing local neighborhood groups of congregants. These groups were responsible for helping to keep track of eight or ten new members in their neighborhood. In such a large congregation, new members could easily feel isolated and insignificant. The job of these committees was to keep in touch with them so that they would know that the congregation cared about them. Contact was sometimes made by phone, or new members might be invited to a dinner. One of the groups was in West Rogers Park, another in Evanston, and another south of the Loop.

Harlow proposed another method to try to hold on to members. His proposal involved improving transportation services to bring suburban

```
            O U R   S C H O C H E N   P R O G R A M


        A remarkable new project has quietly gotten under way in our Congregation.
    As far as we know, it is the first such effort in this general area and possibly
    anywhere.  The first few "trial runs" have proven its inherent value and benefit
    to the Congregation and we are looking forward to its progress with eager antici-
    pation.

        I am talking about the Shochen (pronounced sho-chayn) sponsor project which
    has gotten under way under the most capable leadership of Ronney Harlow and his
    Committee.  Shochen means neighbor.  The project thus aims at bringing together
    those members of our Congregation who live in given neighborhoods, to make them
    acquainted with each other and to strengthen the feeling of community and belong-
    ing one with the other.

        A moment's reflection will indicate to you the size and scope of this
    undertaking.  Between 80 and 90 individual members of our Congregation will be
    asked to open their homes to their neighbors.  Innumerable phone calls will have
    to be made, hundreds of people will have to be accommodated and allowances made
    for the available free time of hosts and guests.  The project will run for several
    months and possibly for as long as a year, until the entire membership has been
    contacted.  If, therefor, you hear of one of these Shochen parties and have not
    been invited to yours, please be patient.  You're on someone's list and will be
    called sooner or later.

        It is a big project and those working on it are devoting a great deal of
    their time and effort to it.  But we think it's most worthwhile, for it will re-
    sult in an Emanuel strengthened by ties of friendship and renewed devotion to
    its inspiring program and sacred purposes.

                                            Rabbi Herman E. Schaalman
```

Emanuel's Schochen Program, November 1958

children to religious and Hebrew school. With the aid of the Couples Club, the temple launched an ambitious busing program that allowed families who had moved to the suburbs the opportunity to maintain their membership and to allow their children receive a quality Jewish education. On Sundays, two or three buses picked up children from the suburbs to bring them to Sunday school and then returned them safely to their parents when school was over.[217] The program, however, had only limited success since this new affluent Jewish core in the suburbs had begun to build their own temples and to worship where they lived.[218]

Another of Harlow's proposals was to revive regular "Meet the Rabbi" parties, which allowed congregants to meet the Rabbi in an informal setting and each of them to become more familiar with each other. During the year of the rabbinic succession, this activity had fallen by the wayside; the board and Schaalman agreed that it was now time to reinstate it.

The Children

Schaalman's work as the Midwest Regional Director of UAHC and his role as Emanuel Congregation's rabbi came at a critical time in the lives of the Schaalman children. They were in the process of growing up and becoming real people, shaped by their extraordinary parents and their role as children of a renowned father. In this pressure-cooker of a life, Schaalman's family time was under constant pressure from his ever-increasing professional responsibilities. Nonetheless, he worked hard at being with his family and making sure they had the unforgettable and nourishing childhood his father and mother had provided him. Schaalman remembered the pleasures of his childhood family vacations and recognized how important they could be in creating lasting and loving bonds between children and their parents and between each other.

In 1959, as part of a tour for Emanuel congregants, Schaalman took his family on a four-month trip to Israel, including stops in Germany and France. Michael was now twelve and Susan sixteen, both old enough to appreciate the trip (Rodin-Novak, 2001, p. 95). Schaalman does not remember much about the Israel part of the trip, other than that they visited the major tourist sites. They would have visited Lotte's sister Ilse, but she was studying in Paris, where they would meet her on the last leg of their journey.

One of Schaalman's objectives for this trip was to give his children some experience of the world in which he and Lotte grew up. Returning to Germany, however, was not easy for him. He was still smarting from the blows of the Holocaust and found that he was "edgy" in the presence of other Germans. One incident is particularly vivid in his mind. The family stayed over in an old German hotel. At check-in, Schaalman requested two rooms, one for himself and Lotte and another for Susan and Michael. When the clerk put the children in a room at the opposite end of the hall, Schaalman bristled. Always on the defensive while in Germany because of all the hurt he and his family had suffered at the hands of the Nazis, he asked the clerk why he had done that. The clerk came back with an indirect anti-Semitic remark. Schaalman, who even as a child was ready to defend himself against anti-Semitic slurs, was enraged: "If you want, let's go outside and I will beat the hell out of you."

Munich and the house on Tengstrasse was the first stop in this sentimental journey. To Schaalman's surprise, the janitor who lived there when he was a child still lived in the same basement apartment. When Schaalman knocked on his door, the janitor recognized him immediately and greeted him with, "Der Hermie," his way of addressing Schaalman when he was a child. After introducing his family and asking about the janitor's health, Schaalman told him that he would like to visit his old apartment. The janitor, whom Schaalman remembered was either a socialist or communist, told him that it was not a good idea. The building was filled with Nazis.

From Munich, they traveled to Paris and decided to take advantage of an offer that had been made to them by Louis Vaudable, the owner of Maxim's restaurant, one of the best-known restaurants in the world. The Schaalmans had met him in Chicago at a banquet he was hosting. When Vaudable heard that the Schaalmans planned to visit Paris, he invited them to visit his restaurant. Soon after they arrived in Paris, Schaalman called the restaurant to make a reservation for dinner. Upon their arrival at the restaurant, the doorman, who had been anticipating their arrival, escorted them inside and told them that a man they remember only as Colonel Picard, a veteran of the French-Indochina war, would meet him at the bar. He took the Schaalmans to an upstairs dining room, the same room used in the film *Gigi*, which Susan recognized immediately.

Susan ordered lobster for dinner, her favorite meal, but the waiter soon returned with the bad news that they were sold out. Colonel Picard said something privately to the waiter and—voila!— a lobster appeared. The dinner, which included wine and after dinner drinks, was an extravagant feast far beyond anything the Schaalmans had ever experienced. Toward the end of the meal, Schaalman began to sweat over the likely cost; now that they were near the end of the trip, his money was running out. Picard, however, proved to be an excellent host and picked up the check. When the dinner ended, he had a cab waiting to take them back to their hotel.

By the time they reached their room, the Schaalmans were feeling the effects of drinking alcohol and ordered seltzer water to calm their stomachs and alleviate their thirst. When Michael and Susan, who had their own adjoining room, were alone, Michael decided that the best use of the seltzer was to pour it over his sister's head. She got soaked and so did the bed she was sitting on. Schaalman let Michael off the hook because it reminded him of the pranks he and his brothers played on each other when they were children.

Eagle River and the Pritzkers

The four-month international trip was only part of Schaalman's effort as husband and father to spend quality time with his wife and children. Soon after he was engaged by Emanuel Congregation, he established a routine of taking his family to Eagle River, Wisconsin, for summer vacations. They were so happy there that they returned off and on for the next ten to fifteen years. It was not unusual, however, for this vacation time to be interrupted by a death of a congregant or crisis at Emanuel. Schaalman remembers several occasions when, immediately after his arrival in Eagle River, he received a call that someone in the congregation had died. He turned right around and drove the six hours back to Chicago and, then, after the funeral, drove six more hours back to Wisconsin.

Susan describes the time at Eagle River as "idyllic" (Schaalman Youdovin, S., 1986, p. 262). It was a special place for the family and a time when many of the conventions of daily life were suspended. Getting there, however, was a challenge. The problem was fitting the four of them and their luggage into the car. There simply wasn't room for each of them to have a suitcase and for the books, which were essential freight for her father (p. 262).

Not only was it a time for family play and leisure, it was a time of intense learning. Like his father before him, Schaalman maintained a rigorous schedule for the family of reading books aloud. One of the reading events involved a series of books about art history published by the Metropolitan Museum of Art. They also "schlepped along" a record player and dozens of classical records. One suitcase was full of books that mother and father were reading and another of books for Michael and Susan. Undoubtedly, Schaalman's intention was to recreate the environment that his father had provided in their summer vacations in the Bavarian mountains.

The books were by no means children's books. One that Schaalman insisted they read was by Father Teilhard de Chardin, a Catholic theologian and perhaps one of the most abstruse twentieth-century thinkers. The reading became a family joke. Susan's former husband, Rabbi Ira

Youdovin, used to tease her when they were preparing to go on vacation: "Did you remember Teilhard de Chardin?" It was an outrageous subject for a teenager, and to this day, Susan doesn't pretend she understood it.

Usually, one of the first activities in the morning was an hour—at least—of Torah study, as his father had done on family vacations. Instead of the expectation that there would be no discussion of the reading, however, Schaalman made discussion as important as the reading itself.

Not all the family's time was spent in study and reading. Susan remembers water skiing, swimming, and boating. Her parents were strong swimmers and liked to swim across the lake. Like their parents, both Susan and Michael became expert swimmers. Michael even swam competitively in high school and college and passed his love of swimming on to his children, who also swam competitively in college. The family also liked to play Scrabble for hours on end. Their father was an excellent player who was able to maximize the point value of all the letters. The children learned a great deal from playing with him and, because they played frequently, created their own rule, which they called the "Eagle River Convention." Their rule was that you couldn't add an "S" to someone else's word but could only extend the S left or right to make a new word. As the children's skill improved, the game became very competitive. Although Susan and Michael were at a handicap, their parents never deliberately allowed them to win. Occasionally, they beat their parents. Once they were away from the game, however, the competition ended.

During these summers, the Schaalmans became good friends with the Pritzker family, one of the richest families in America and well known for their philanthropy. When he met the Pritzkers in the 1950s, Abram Pritzker (A. N. Pritzker, as he preferred to call himself) together with his brother Jack, had launched the family empire that in the coming years was to amass a fortune from investments in real estate and small companies. According to Susan (1986), her father's relationship with the Pritzkers developed accidentally (p. 262). The Schaalmans had rented a cabin down the road from the Pritzkers' summer home, known as "Jabodo," named after A. N.'s three sons, Jim, Bob, and Don. It was during these early years that the Schaalmans developed close friendships with both Robert and Audrey Pritzker, and, many years later, it was Audrey and her second husband, Albert Ratner, who were supportive of the Schaalmans when they were having difficulty taking care of themselves.

When Susan developed an allergy to the algae in the lake, her parents arranged for her to use the Pritzker's pool. From then on, the Schaalman children had an open invitation to swim in the pool, and their father formed a lifelong friendship with the Pritzker family.[219]

The Pritzkers were among several Emanuel families that vacationed in Eagle River, mostly women and their young children because the husbands remained in Chicago managing their businesses. On weekends, the husbands would fly in on private or small commuter planes. During the week, there wasn't much for the women to do other than sun themselves or play golf on the nine-hole course. The weekends were party time with the same people and the same food. Susan speculates that the wives must have been terribly bored.

To their surprise and delight, the Schaalmans were eagerly accepted in this world of wealthy Jews, among the elite of Chicago's commercial world. Susan speculates that the reason was because they were "sweet, educated, knowledgeable, articulate oddballs," and they read books. It didn't hurt that the women loved ("luuuuvvvved") her father.

While the Eagle River crowd tried to divert themselves during these summer months, during the week their children, including Susan and Michael, "frolicked on the boats and played with other expensive toys the women made available" (p. 262). In retrospect, Susan remembers the summers as "a time of unrelieved happiness—which of course cannot be the way it really was."[220] Her description of her experience at Eagle River sounds like a Jay Gatsby world.

Mother-in-law Comes to Live with the Schaalmans

Common wisdom says that if you want to know what kind of a husband a man will make, look at how he treats his mother. Stretching the point, we might add, if you want to know how good a husband a man will be, look at how he treats his mother-in-law. In 1967, when the Schaalmans moved to their new condominium at the Tiara on Sheridan Road, they took Lotte's mother with them. The condominium included a large master bedroom with adjoining bath and dressing room, which the Schaalmans gave to her (p. 74). They moved into their guest bedroom and converted the third bedroom into a study. They also helped integrate Gussie into the life of the synagogue. She had no trouble making friends and basked in the glow of the congregation's admiration of her son-in-law. Although her daughter and son-in-law insisted that they would provide for her financial needs, she worked part-time to provide extra money to maintain herself. She also received money from the German government that was restitution for the loss of her family's property. With the addition of this money and the fact that she did not have to pay rent or provide for necessities, she was able to live comfortably. After she died, the Schaalmans kept the master bedroom for their guests.

Innovations at Emanuel

During Schaalman's tenure as the Midwest Director of the UAHC, a large part of his job had consisted of visiting Reform congregations in the Chicago area. As a result, he was able to observe ritual practices and temple activities that were innovations or simply good methods for carrying out temple activities. These observations gave him ideas of how best to function in a rabbinic capacity when he took a pulpit assignment. Soon after he became senior rabbi at Emanuel, he introduced a major reform, the expansion of the role of lay leadership in the congregation. This concept was a radical departure for the congregation and for Reform Judaism in general. Typically, congregations placed their rabbi on a pedestal and gave him full decision-making power in matters relating to ritual and nothing else. As Schaalman put it, "The rabbi's word was gospel." At the same time, lay leadership took charge of most matters related to the running of the temple. At Emanuel, this leadership provided a functional hierarchy made up of prominent professionals and businessmen. It made sure the temple operated in a businesslike fashion and that it was solvent.

Schaalman was convinced that no part of temple life should be outside the participation of lay leadership. The temple's well-being, he thought, required that it move from having a passive to an active and participating body and that Emanuel should be a vibrant and fulfilling part of its congregants' lives. "Under Rabbi Levy," Schaalman notes, "there were few committees to conduct other temple business and little opportunity for congregants to participate in the various aspects of temple life. Temple life centered on Rabbi Levy." One of the reasons why attendance was sparse may have been Levy's perceived intellectual superiority to the congregation. "As an intellectual and a scholar, his sermons were frequently over their heads; it was not unusual for Levy to tell the congregation that they would not understand what he was going to talk about."

Schaalman changed that. Taking his lead from Robert Schrayer, who led the transformation of participation in temple life at KAM (Isaiah Israel), Schaalman set about to create a congregation, which allowed as full congregational participation in temple affairs as possible (Folb, 2007, p. 50). The first committee Schaalman created was an Usher Committee. The role of the Committee was to help congregants find their seats during services, particularly when the temple was crowded on the High Holy Days, and to inform them of the page on which the service was being read. For Shabbat services, the role of the ushers might be nothing more than to hand out programs and to act as greeters. Another committee he established was a Ritual Committee that would serve as a "sounding board for his ideas," to test them with congregational involvement and consent.

The Board of Trustees responded to this new direction by holding an all-day seminar to set the temple's direction for the coming year and for its future. Several committees, including the Conservation, Membership, and Temple Families Committees, made dramatic long-range recommendations to reach out to members and to increase their involvement in congregational activities. The Conservation Committee came up with a ten-point list of proposals including that Emanuel organize neighborhood hosts and sponsors; reorganize the "Meet the Rabbi" parties so that they were regionally based; and create a "true" hospitality committee to function for Friday night Shabbat services.[221]

The Membership Committee recommendations were as extensive and equally creative. Perhaps the most radical and directly in line with Schaalman's objectives, it proposed that temple members should become "participating" members and outlined several critical responsibilities of membership. First was the members' financial obligation to support the temple by contributing as much as they could. Next, the Committee recommended that members participate regularly in all of the temple's religious activities and contribute time and effort to all temple projects. The Committee's final recommendation was that members should be encouraged "to lead a Jewish life" by becoming more knowledgeable about Judaism through participation in Jewish education programs and by participating in the secular life of the community. Convinced that the temple could handle as many as 950 members, one member of the Committee, Hal Abrahamson, proposed the temple undertake a membership drive that should include not only areas around the temple but also "areas adjacent to the lake" (Emanuel Congregation, November 30, 1957).

By March 1957, slightly more than a year after Schaalman became Emanuel's senior rabbi, the congregation had created thirty-two committees (Emanuel Congregation, March 27, 1957). When apprised of this fact during an interview in 2007, Schaalman responded, "It amazes me. I could not have remembered that there were so many committees.[222] You see, that was the new structure. It was almost a revolution."

In the early years, board members were not comfortable with this proliferation of committees and congregational involvement. The addition of several hundred members in the administration of temple life diluted the board's power. It also led to resentment of the rabbi. Occasionally, the board and the committees had serious disagreements that spilled over into the congregation and caused dissension. Not all trustees, however, were upset by this development. In his role as president of the UAHC, Dr. Hollender had worked with Schaalman when he was the Midwest Director of the UAHC and considered this democratization of the power structure a positive development. Schaalman concludes that he must have had some "real champions on the board or else this change would not have worked." In retrospect, he muses, "My rabbinic colleagues had bets off that I would last only three years, the length of my contract."

By 1971, Jewish organizations had begun a national campaign to attempt to arrest the projected assimilation of American Jews. Their concern was not only in the declining numbers of people who would identify themselves as Jewish but also in the loss of commitment to the goals of organizations, and most importantly, to Israel. American Judaism, and Reform Judaism in particular, which felt the threat to its survival more acutely, became aware of the huge need to promote Judaism among the young. Reform Judaism began an aggressive campaign to promote Jewish awareness among Jewish youth. In the summer of 1971, through its youth affiliate, NFTY (North American Federation of Temple Youth) thousands of young people were sent to Israel.

No less concerned about its own future and the future of Judaism, Emanuel's Board of Trustees decided to work harder with its own youth to promote awareness of and commitment to Judaism. The board established a fund to allow children of member families to travel to Israel. The fund, known as the Lewis Fund in honor of its principal donor, enabled the temple to send to Israel one or two young people a year.[223]

Schaalman thought that it was important that his congregation be in the forefront of the discussion of Reform Jewish life in America and that it have a connection to international liberal Judaism. He wanted the congregation to have a reach and influence beyond its Chicago Edgewater boundaries. In addition, he saw this participation as a way to get more lay involvement in the temple. When the UAHC held its annual meeting in April 1957, almost 5,000 members attended, and Schaalman made sure that Emanuel sent a large delegation. In fact, the congregation sent ten delegates, more than any other Reform congregation. In later years, Emanuel sent even larger delegations. If a delegate could not attend a specific conference, Emanuel had alternates to fill their places. Once Schaalman retired, this national and international involvement was no longer a priority of Emanuel's life. In part, that involvement suffered from a lack of financial support. As the congregation began to shrink and the temple's revenues declined, that relationship, of necessity, declined as well. However, in its heyday, Emanuel was a major player in the Reform movement.

Because at the beginning of his rabbinate at Emanuel Schaalman was still not sufficiently secure in his oratorical abilities, he took considerable time to prepare his formal sermons, which, as he had done at Temple Judah, he wrote out in advance. He contrasts this need to write out his sermons to his rabbinic practices today, which he characterizes as less formal. The service itself began with a brief silent meditation. When he appeared on the bimah, he would sit on one of the ceremonial chairs and say nothing. His aim was to give the congregation time to set aside their profane thoughts of their everyday lives and enter into a sacred space.

High Holy Days services, particularly Yom Kippur, posed other challenges. The afternoon service to commemorate the dead, the Yiskor

232   A Brand Plucked From the Fire

Service, *the* most solemn service of the entire year, was a time when many in the congregation would walk out. "Typically, these are people who either have not experienced a personal loss, or adults with children who do not want them exposed to such a deeply moving service." Schaalman remembers congregants asking him earlier in the day what time they could expect Yiskor to begin so that they would know when to leave the service. Recognizing that the break in the afternoon service and the announcement of the beginning of the Yiskor service gave congregants a convenient time to leave, he eliminated the break, making the service continuous. Schaalman claims that over the years, more and more people stayed through the Yiskor Service.

At the beginning of his rabbinate, Schaalman introduced the habit of wearing clerical robes. Rabbi Levy did not wear robes, or a yarmulke, or a tallis, all signs of what Reform considered at the time Orthodox garb. Schaalman himself had been trained at HUC to officiate without these garments. Reform congregations in the 1950s and for many years after expected their rabbis to appear in business suits without traditional religious trappings. Schaalman wanted to wear a tallis and rabbinic robe. However, to make these changes, he had to get the approval of Emanuel's Ritual Committee and Board of Trustees. They approved his request, and Schaalman began what was one of the first of his rabbinic innovations that helped move Emanuel Congregation away from the Classical Reform model that he inherited toward a form of worship that included elements that are more traditional.

Another of Schaalman's innovations was to keep the temple open throughout the year. Typically, during the months of June, July, and August, Reform temples closed down, and many congregants took vacations during these hot summer months. Schaalman decided that once Emanuel was air-conditioned, it would remain open during the summer and provide its congregants with a full schedule of religious services. He told them, "We don't give God a vacation." Services were provided Friday night and Saturday morning. This commitment was unusual for Reform congregations, which tended to hold only one Shabbat service, either on Friday night or on Saturday.[224] Under Schaalman's leadership, services for all traditional holidays, major and minor, were held, as he says, "on the right day." For example, Emanuel had Confirmation services on the day of *Shavuot* no matter what day of the week it fell.

The youngsters who were being confirmed had to take a day off from school to participate in this service. Schaalman promoted the practice that, along with the children's parents and families, the congregation should attend as well. Despite protests from congregants, this practice remained in place for decades. Many Reform congregations, because they did not get much of a turnout when holidays fell out during the week, would hold services for minor festivals as part of Shabbat worship. This is still the practice in some Reform congregations.

Apparently, the congregation enjoyed coming to Schaalman's services. He estimates that as many as 235 people would attend his Friday night services out of a congregation of 950 families. Nonetheless, Schaalman considered that he had failed in so far as "the vast majority didn't need it, didn't care about it, had other things to do that were more important. On the High Holy Days, Emanuel could barely contain the 1,600–1,700 people who attended. The only way to fit them into the sanctuary was to have seating on the bimah." For Schaalman, the letdown after Yom Kippur with the drop-off of attendance was a problem. In order to steel himself against the sense of desertion, he would come out of the room at the side of the bimah where he put on his robes with the expectation that no one would be there. "When there were congregants, I would be pleasantly surprised. I had to live with the recognition that the appeal of coming to Shabbat services was minimal. To cope with this recognition, either one had to be indifferent or non-caring."

One of his efforts to attract the congregation was to introduce discussion of controversial subjects, some of which he claims were "really hot." Issues included Israel, abortion, the death penalty and the Vietnam War. He thought that if he talked about such subjects, the congregation had a right to respond, and respond they did. Schaalman concluded that this opportunity to respond to these controversial issues gave congregants an incentive to come to services. He is convinced that they enjoyed this form of sermonic discussion. Occasionally, he found himself challenged for his unorthodox and unpopular opinions. The result was lively interchanges. Although he would not announce his sermon topics in advance, congregants would find out through the grapevine. "When they would ask my secretary what the sermon would be, she was likely to let the cat out of the bag. When there were controversial issues facing the community, congregants would come out to hear what their rabbi had to say about them."

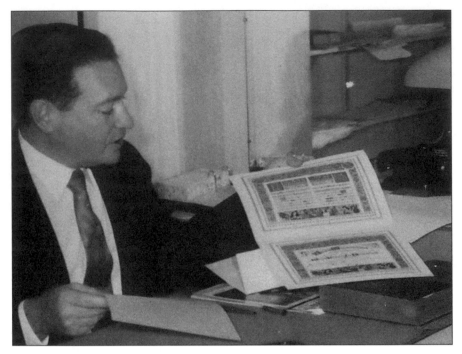

Schaalman reviewing a Ketuba with married couple, 1956

When Schaalman took over at Emanuel in 1956, the practice at the Yom Kippur Yiskor service was to read aloud the names of all the loved ones congregants wished to remember. Schaalman noted that he was "scandalized" at the reading of this extensive list. Consequently, he introduced the use of a booklet of names, an idea he had picked up as Director of the Union when he traveled to various congregations in the Chicago area. In addition to this innovation, he established a Ritual Committee, which did not exist under his predecessor, part of his effort to increase lay involvement in the ritual life of the temple.[225]

Schaalman also changed the relationship of the cantor to the congregation. Traditionally, cantors were placed with their choirs, not infrequently out of sight, and usually not on the bimah as a partner with the rabbi.[226] Schaalman brought Cantor Handwerger down to the bimah so that he could have a more interactive role in the service. Not only was this a change for Emanuel but for the Reform movement as well.

During the 1950s, Reform Judaism adopted B'nai Mitzvah ceremonies as part of its rites of passage.[227] During Schaalman's first year as

Emanuel's rabbi, his daughter Susan, who was now thirteen, was the first girl to have a Bat Mitzvah at Emanuel. All 800 seats in the sanctuary were filled with congregants and friends. When she turned sixteen, she was confirmed.[228] In 1961, the Schaalmans held a Bar Mitzvah for their son Michael. As with Susan's Bat Mitzvah five years earlier, the entire congregation turned out, along with friends and neighbors.

Another of Schaalman's innovations was to invite congregants to the Torah during the month of their birthdays or for other upcoming or recent special occasions. He felt it was important that people actually see the inside of the Torah because too many congregants never had. If it was your birthday, anniversary, or other special occasion, you were invited to come up to the bimah and stand right beside or behind him as he read the portion of the week. Afterward, the rabbi recited a blessing for you. This practice was well received by the congregation, and it became part of standard practice in Emanuel.

The Rabbi as Teacher

Before the end of the twentieth century, rabbinic scholars were arguing for a more learned rabbinate, one that was capable of bringing the lessons of Judaism to the often complex and sometimes painful and disappointing lives of their congregants. The teachings of Torah and Rabbinic commentary, as filtered through the experience of the rabbi, had become an indispensible part of the rabbinic assignment, thus making study and learning a key part of their life (Karff, S. E., 1990). None of these challenges was new to Schaalman. In his first rabbinic assignment in Cedar Rapids, Iowa, he launched adult education classes and lectured to various religious, educational, and civic groups. Despite his youth and his challenges with the English language, he earned the community's respect and admiration. Long after he left Cedar Rapids, the major daily newspaper, *The Cedar Rapids Gazette*, and Coe College's newspaper, *Coe Cosmos*, were reporting his guest appearances at community and college forums on interfaith issues and lectures on Judaism.

Since 1947, Schaalman has been a lecturer and adjunct professor through the sponsorship of the Jewish Chautauqua Society's (JCS). Founded in 1893 to promote Jewish education it was taken over by the North American Federation of Temple Brotherhoods[229] in 1936 to promote interfaith understanding through a national rabbinic scholars' program.

When Schaalman moved to Chicago in 1949, he continued his work for JCS at Garrett Theological Evangelical Seminary in Evanston and the Chicago Theological Seminary (CTS) on the campus of the University of Chicago. He estimates that during these many years he must have taught several thousand students, most of them preparing for the ministry (JCS Programs, 2008). He taught such courses as Liturgy of the Synagogue, Introduction to Rabbinic Judaism, and Modern Jewish Life and Thought. One measure of his success over the years is the fact that many of his former students have come to Emanuel to visit with "'their rabbi,' to view the Torah and to share in worship" (JCS Programs, 2008). Most important to Schaalman is that all of his students had an opportunity to study Jewish traditions, learn about Jewish belief and practices, both traditional and contemporary (JCS Programs, 2008).

When Schaalman retired from Emanuel, Garrett's president, Neal F. Fisher (1986), sent him a letter in which he praised Schaalman's "spiritual depth," his "gracious personal manner," "the intellectual depth of [his] work," and for exposing the seminary "to a heritage that helps define who we are." Fisher went on to say, "We are mindful of the far-reaching influence which your ministry has had throughout this nation."

In the early 1970s, Schaalman taught courses in Judaism at Beloit College in Beloit, Wisconsin, nearly 100 miles from Chicago and easily a two-hour trip each way. According to Rabbi Marc Berkson (2007), a student there at the time, a quarter of the student body was Jewish, some 300 to 400 students. Schaalman got the job because Beloit's chaplain, who once had a pulpit in Evanston, Illinois, invited Schaalman to offer a course for the Jewish students. Schaalman would make the long drive on Monday afternoons to teach a three-hour course in Modern Jewish History, one of a few Judaic studies courses at the college. Rabbi Berkson, one of several students who later became rabbis, described the class as "incredible." Schaalman so captured his interest and that of a small group of other Jewish students that, when they graduated, they went off to rabbinic school. The group included Marc Berkson, Bennett Greenspon, Deborah Hirsch, and Michael Weinberg, who later became Schaalman's assistant (Berkson, M., 2007). Prior to Schaalman's arrival,

Beloit had produced only one rabbinic student in the ten previous years. After Schaalman's departure, the Religious Studies department developed several other courses in Judaism (Berkson, 2007).

Schaalman had a deep and lasting influence on these future rabbinic students. Berkson (2007) recalls that he and several of his young rabbinic colleagues created their own rabbinic Torah study modeled after the one Schaalman had been carrying on with another rabbi for over twenty years. When Berkson became a rabbi in the late 1970s, he introduced Torah Study to his congregation, a practice, he says, that was not common in those days: "If this was something Rabbi Schaalman was doing, then it was something I should be doing also" (Berkson, 2007).

On September 1, 2008, Emanuel Congregation's Temple Brotherhood, together with the Jewish Chautauqua Society, recognized this contribution to JCS at a special ceremony in the home of Robert Morris, one of Schaalman's oldest friends.[230] Each year, Emanuel's Brotherhood holds an annual "kick-off" event at which it gives an award to an Emanuel staff member or congregant who has made a significant life-long contribution to the congregation. The lifetime achievement award was presented to Schaalman by the Brotherhood co-chairs, David Fleischman and Barry Glaser, and by Phil Arendt, the Brotherhood chairman of the JCS Chautauqua Society Award Selection Committee.

Sermons provide Schaalman a vehicle for teaching. Early on, he chose controversial issues such as the McCarthy Hearings, civil rights for minorities, and the Vietnam War. In the 1950s, Senator Joseph McCarthy led a crusade to identify and denounce Americans who were in any way connected to the Communist Party no matter how tangentially or how long before (Hepburn, M. A., 1990). He targeted Hollywood personalities, including famous writers, directors, and actors, many of whom were Jews. In his committee hearings, broadcast live over national TV, he denounced them for their earlier participation in Communist Party activities. Many had merely attended rallies or meetings, signed petitions, or participated in Communist organized demonstrations. Once they came before the committee, all were tarred with the brush of un-American activities and frequently blacklisted from their professions (Hepburn, M. A., 1990).

In his self-righteous zeal, McCarthy even attacked high-ranking Republican administration officials, including Eisenhower himself.

Schaalman, along with many other Americans, considered Eisenhower a "hero of World War II"[231] and rejected this "witch hunt" and what he considered was McCarthy's anti-Semitic emphasis on Jews in Hollywood. He thought McCarthy a threat to Jews and to the nation and condemned him in sermons and speaking engagements.

By the start of the Korean War, Schaalman had become critical of the use of war to settle international disputes, a position he still holds today. During the Vietnam War, although originally uncertain about the validity of the U.S. involvement in Vietnam, by late in the war he took a strong stance against it. At the end of Shabbat services, he gave talks about the war—his own version of the "teach-ins" popular on college campuses.

Although sermons have always been an important part of Schaalman's sense of his role as teacher, he was not always comfortable in that role: "There was rarely a time when I was preaching regularly when I was not really worried about what I was going to say. I mean deeply concerned." For those who have listened to his sermons, this admission may come as a surprise. They know he has no notes or written text and that he has not memorized them. The sermons appear to be spontaneous reflections delivered with a fluency and tone that is inspirational. Yet, Schaalman has never been sure that his message has been heard as he intended it:

> Nevertheless, I am in awe at the amount of time people have given me over the many years of my sermonizing. Multiplying the twenty minutes some two hundred fifty, five hundred or a thousand people have given me over the course of my career, the number is astronomical. My awareness of this precious gift that people have given me makes me strive to do my level best, to give the utmost of which I am capable at any given moment. To do less is a betrayal of their trust and my responsibility as a rabbi.

Schaalman's challenge was to find something that was worth hearing. Sometimes, he felt, "There was really something there and that it was good to let out. Those moments, however, were relatively rare. More frequently, I was deeply concerned that what was given was worth receiving." Comparing himself to his younger colleagues, he commented, "All too frequently I would hear one of them boast of the great sermon he had delivered, or what a great sermonizer he was. Such comments are inappropriate." He has never thought that nor said that about his own sermonizing: "That's one of the things a rabbi has to learn to do to turn off what is obviously an exaggerated flattery that his people like to shower on him. That, incidentally, was part of my wife's duties." Whenever he finished giving a sermon, the look on Lotte's face told him whether he had been successful. "If she had a wan smile on her face ... I said to myself, 'Boy, I didn't get to her, anyway.'" No matter what anyone else said about the sermon, her response was definitive. "To this day, whenever Lotte is anywhere near where I speak, when I see her, her face will tell me immediately what it was and sometimes she'll make up a sign with her two fingers and I know it went alright [sic]."

When Schaalman teaches in the seminaries, he begins his classes by asking his students whether they have any questions: "If they have no questions, I take that as a sign that either they have not read the material or that they have no interest in the subject." He admonishes them gently that there is no sense in continuing the class: "The learning experience must be a dialogue between teacher and student, student and student."[232]

Schaalman's teaching has also taken other forms, including scholar-in-residence at many synagogues around the country, guest lectures in college classes and for various Jewish and non-Jewish religious and civic groups. He has also served on panels as part of symposia and been an invited guest on a variety of radio and television programs.

Publication is another form of teaching for Schaalman. Although he has been reluctant to commit his ideas to print, his earliest traceable publication is one he edited and wrote the introduction for: the CCAR's 1963 *The Goals of Jewish Religious Education: A Symposium*. During the brief period from 1982 to 1985, he published several articles in *Judaism*, a major academic publication: "An agenda for Reform Judaism in Israel," "The Key is the Covenant," and "History and Halakhah." From the early 1990s, he wrote weekly columns commenting on the weekly Torah portions for the *The Sentinel*, a local Chicago Jewish publication.

His first efforts to put in print his developing ideas on the Holocaust came in 1991 when he published "God of Auschwitz?" (cf. *Threescore and ten: Essays in honor of Rabbi Seymour J. Cohen on the occasion of his seventieth birthday*). In 2001, together with Fredrick C. Holmgren, he edited *Preaching Biblical Texts: Expositions by Jewish and Christian Scholars*. That same year, he published another theological essay, "God of the Future" in W. D. Edgerton's *The Honeycomb of the World*, his second effort to reveal important developments in his theology. The crowning achievement, however, was his publication in 2007 of *Hineni*, the only full-length exploration of his theology.

Schaalman's most joyous teaching experience comes from teaching Torah. Every Saturday morning, barring illness or commitments that take him out of town, he holds Torah Study sessions in his office at Emanuel. Because they form one of the most fertile grounds for the development of his theology, they are discussed in detail later.

Adult Education

One of Schaalman's great achievements as Emanuel's rabbi was to develop various adult education programs. In Iowa, he would have liked to develop similar programs, but lacked the resources. Schaalman believed then and believes now in the value of creating an educated congregation. Under Rabbi Levy, a scholar in his own right, Emanuel had a long tradition of quality adult education; Schaalman's contribution was to expand the offerings. He viewed adult education as a way to enliven the intellectual life of the temple and to promote Jewish learning among his congregants. Through his influence on wealthy members of the congregation, he was instrumental in creating funds to subsidize a number of adult education programs. Because of his friendship with many of the leading intellectuals and religious leaders in America (among them Elie Wiesel, Emil Fackenheim and Yitz Greenberg), when he called them, they usually came.[233] An indirect benefit to him of inviting these intellectuals was that they stimulated his own thinking in ways that otherwise might not have occurred. This expansion of adult learning opportunities gave Emanuel a reputation as a place where things were happening.

Schaalman was so committed to adult education that his commitment became a family joke. If something prevented him from holding his regular Tuesday morning study session, he would bump it to Wednesday and then bump the Wednesday Public Affairs Forum to Thursday morning. Then, he would bump the Thursday morning Bible Class to the afternoon in place of the Thursday afternoon Holiday Workshop, which could meet Friday before breakfast (Schaalman Youdovin, S., 1986, p. 262).

Because Schaalman believed that it was a mitzvah to take groups to Israel, in 1968 he began to lead groups of his congregants there every other year. Organizing these trips was not easy; it involved meeting with the group for as many as eight sessions to teach them basic facts about Israel and to discuss housekeeping and administrative details. Fortunately, Schaalman had the help of his friend Mel Abrams who served as his trip coordinator and travel agent. Typically, these trips, which lasted three weeks, involved side trips to other places such as the Greek islands, Rome, Paris, London, or Amsterdam. Two of the weeks would be in Israel and the third week somewhere else.

From the beginning of his rabbinate at Emanuel, Schaalman played a direct role in the education of its youth. This should not be surprising, following his success in developing OSRUI. Among adults, he was a model of decorum, and, because he had a natural affinity for children, he knew how to get "down and dirty" with them. In that respect, according to Mel Abrams (2007) who was one of these youngsters, Schaalman was the exact opposite of Rabbi Levy. When the congregation sponsored a hayride for its youth, the Schaalmans rode the wagon with them. Here was a group of young people with their hormones pumping, making out and groping each other while the rabbi and his wife served as chaperones (Abrams, 2007).

Schaalman also taught the Confirmation class of older teenagers who were approaching their sixteenth birthday. Reform Judaism placed a strong emphasis on this education as a way of holding onto these youths beyond their B'nai Mitvah and as a vital component toward maintaining their Jewish identity. This additional education was particularly important for Reform households. Often, parents knew very little about Judaism and, consequently, did not observe religious customs in their homes or represent good models of Jewish observance. Even today, at Jewish lifecycle events such as B'nai Mitzvot, many family members are embarrassed because they do not know what to do when they are called to the Torah and asked to recite a blessing in Hebrew, to dress the Torah, or even to open the Ark. These relatively simple rituals are second nature to a more observant Jew.

To say that Schaalman was busy is an understatement. He worked long days serving a congregation of more than 900 families, gave frequent lectures, and was often out of town for days at a time attending meetings and conferences. His frenetic pace took its toll. Unbeknown to the congregation and only to his family and a few close friends, every year before the High Holy Days, Schaalman would develop a high fever, which by Rosh Hashanah "blossomed into a raging virus." On Yom Kippur, the most holy day in the Jewish calendar, because Jewish law mandates that no food or drink should be ingested, Schaalman refused to drink water "to soothe his burning sore throat" (Schaalman Youdovin, S., 1986, p. 262). His daughter, Susan, believes that this reaction was the result of her father's extreme sensitivity to the "enormity of both the challenge and the opportunity" presented by the High Holy Days "to reach hundreds of Jews who were unreachable during the rest of the year" (p. 262).

Raising the Children: Susan

For the Schaalman children, their father's important position in the Reform movement meant that they had to shoulder responsibilities most children do not have. As they grew up, Susan and Michael could not help but be conscious of the fact that their behavior was a reflection on their parents and that they needed to act in a manner that would be a credit to them. On the other hand, they were also children, with all that it implies and had needs that often conflicted with those of their parents'.

As the older child, Susan had more advantages than Michael. Like her father, she was the first child and invested with its special status and privileges. Not only as the first child but also as a daughter she was heir to the special relationship that daughters typically have with their fathers. She was "Daddy's girl." Among her earliest memories of her father is wondering why other fathers did not have the same demands on their time and why their children did not have the same privileges. As she grew older, she never felt anything but pride and delight that her father was on the bimah. As a child, she thought it was "cool."

The Schaalmans like to tell the story of her childhood when she entered into religious school. A special "consecration ceremony" was held

Herman and Lotte Schaalman at Emanuel Congregation Jubilee
and Herman's 75th birthday

to induct the children into the school. One by one, they mounted the bimah to receive a blessing. When Susan went up, someone who came into the sanctuary late sat in her seat. When she came down from the bimah and discovered that the seat was taken, she went back up, tugged on her father's robe and said, "Daddy, there's someone in my seat."

One of the challenges of being a rabbi's daughter was that many of her friends were the children of members of the congregation. Throughout her life, people have felt free to tell her what they thought of her father, both good and bad. While she likes to hear the one, she doesn't like to hear the other. She prefers not to hear either. To be a rabbi's daughter also meant that your parents always expected you to be in the synagogue with them on important and not-so-important occasions: Shabbat, holidays, and temple functions such as social gatherings, study groups, and lectures. Because she was older, Susan was more involved in the temple than her brother and aware of its undercurrents, its rumors, sniping, and complaints. If Emanuel's Board or members of the congregation had a bone to pick, it might be highly legitimate or ridiculous.

Susan was exposed to much more of the temple's politics than the other rabbis' kids she knows. Most of them were never as involved with their parents' congregations. When she was a child, after Saturday morning services, her father took her with him while he visited the sick in the hospitals. Her job was to sit in the driver's seat (all twelve years of her), so if a policeman came by, she could say that her father was a rabbi visiting patients. The explanation was sufficient to keep officers from writing a ticket. Nor could they tell her to move the car: she could barely see over the top of the steering wheel!

This time together helped father and daughter to form close bonds and provided Susan an opportunity to have deep conversations with her philosophical and learned father. He was also a wonderful storyteller; he told her fascinating and wonderful Hasidic tales, with the message that inner beauty was more important than outer. When he found time, he helped his daughter learn Hebrew, as well as Torah, and how to read and understand Hebrew prayers. In the process, he instilled in her a deep sense of relationship with the prayer book.

Although the Schaalman family has assimilated into American culture, the Jewish part of them was never separated from their presentation of themselves to the world. The dichotomy of the inner self and the public self that seems to be part of many peoples' lives was never a factor in theirs. This is not to say that Susan accepted everything else about her life and the world around her. Like so many other middle-class children in the 1960s, she rebelled against Jewish tradition and just about everything else—dress, fashion, politics, social mores, and her parents. In fact, the Schaalmans encouraged her rebellion and nonconformity. She behaved as her father could not and would not. He had grown up at a time when he never felt the need to rebel, and therefore didn't.

Encouragement, however, did not necessarily mean acceptance of specific aspects of her rebellion. "Efforts to justify my actions with 'everyone is doing it' was the kiss of death. 'You're not everybody,'" they reminded her (Schaalman Youdovin, S., 2006). As a Schaalman, her parents taught her, she had an obligation to examine her behavior, understand why she was doing it, and ask whether it was a good fit for her. Her father admonished her "not to let other people determine how you behave. If someone is rude or mean to you, you have three choices: (1) to respond to it; (2) respond to it in kind; and (3) to ignore it. The choice is yours. The best choice is to not allow other people to dictate your behavior" (Schaalman Youdovin, S., 2006). It is an approach to confrontation that has stood Susan in good stead throughout her professional career.

When Susan did act out, her parents became "nicer." She could easily spoil precious family time by throwing "a hissy fit." Her father's way of responding to unacceptable behavior was to soothe her with the words: "'Take a breath; we're going to start all over. This hasn't happened, and we're going from here.'" According to Susan the approach always worked: "The horrible things I could have said or done were gone. His approach was an amazing way to treat a hissy fit (Schaalman Youdovin, S., 2006).

Despite Schaalman's busy schedule, he and Lotte worked hard to create an environment in which Susan felt included and, to the extent possible, empowered. "They were good listeners and made me feel that they valued what I had to say. That did not mean that they were not critical in the positive sense of helping me improve my speaking and writing" (Schaalman Youdovin, S. 2006). When the time came for her to be confirmed at Emanuel, Schaalman asked her to write her own speech as part of the ceremony. "My initial draft contained colloquial phrases such as 'and so on' and 'up and out.' Dad took one look at it and said, 'What errant nonsense is this?'" (Schaalman Youdovin, S., 2006) He cautioned her against using trite phrases, and she took them out. His counsel became a guide to her future writing.

As parents, the Schaalmans made sure to include discussions about meanings of words. Susan reports, "Instead of contradicting me, my father offered his own interpretation, and then I'd ask myself why I didn't get it? As an adult, I adopted his method in my own teaching" (Schaalman Youdovin, S., 2006).

Because a major goal for the Schaalmans was that their children should be educated and cultured human beings, they made time for visits to museums. "To this day," Susan recalls, "I can hear Dad's voice commenting on paintings and various artists, an experience that aroused in me a lifelong interest in art and art history" (Schaalman Youdovin, S., 2006). Although her parents did not share this interest, they believed it was something an educated, cultured human being ought to know. Susan has doubts that they would have gone on their own. "Now, when I invite them to go with me, I think they go along to humor me. Though they have always purchased art, they have little interest in art beyond a very personal appreciation" (Schaalman Youdovin, S., 2006).

A Family Wedding

In 1961, Susan enrolled in the University of Wisconsin-Madison where she majored in speech therapy. When she graduated in 1965, she married her college sweetheart, David Laber, a philosophy major, whom Schaalman describes as a brilliant and likeable young man. They both enjoyed each other's company, so much so that even after the marriage broke up, David kept in close touch with him. "Curiously," Schaalman told Esta Star (April 5, 1988),

> For my daughter, the only aspiration I had was that she should find a fine human being to be married to, and that did not quite turn out that way in her first marriage. ... I've always felt that there was such profound fulfillment possible in that kind of role and function, and nothing that one could do would exceed that. (p. 24)

His comments are surprising in the context of modern American Jewish families, which today, are more likely to want their daughters to excel in some area of professional or business life. However, Schaalman came from a different world. Born near the beginning of the twentieth century and heir to the idea that a woman achieved fulfillment in the home, and having seen his mother and his wife fulfilled in their role as wives and mothers, it is perhaps understandable that Schaalman held such views. Times, however, have changed, and so has the rabbi. He would never wish that his granddaughters be housewives. Already in 1988, his ideas had changed so radically that he could say, "The development of humankind has been compromised by the denial of one half the population to the same advantages as its men" (Star, E., April 5, 1988).

Long before Susan's marriage, the Schaalmans had been looking forward to their only daughter's wedding, and they took great care in planning it. According to Susan, over the years, "They had talked about what they liked and didn't like about weddings they attended, almost all of them where Dad had officiated" (Schaalman Youdovin, S., 2006). When their turn came to plan a wedding, they picked the music selections, the reception format, and invited the entire congregation of 975 people—from her perspective, "everyone in the known world." Susan did not challenge any of these decisions. "All I got to choose was the colors for the dresses" (Schaalman Youdovin, S., 2006). The fact that her parents made most of the decisions was a reflection of the times.

Because the Schaalmans wanted to show other congregants that the temple was a good venue to host a quality affair, they decided to hold the wedding reception in Emanuel's social hall. Despite their normal frugality, they pulled out all their financial stops and went into debt to make their point and to give their daughter an unforgettable wedding. According to Lotte, "They had been guests at so many extraordinary, creative, and elaborate weddings that they had a pretty good idea of what they wanted and hired a company called Weddings Incorporated to help them with the planning" (Schaalman, L. Aug. 16, 2007).

As both officiating rabbi and dad, Schaalman walked his daughter down the aisle. For both of them, it was a very special moment. As they approached the point where they would be met by the groom, the back of her full-length veil snagged on flowers that decorated the entrance to each row of seats. Schaalman was unaware that his daughter had been hooked, and the two of them, arms entwined, kept walking. When Susan realized what had happened, "I froze because I couldn't act quickly enough to alert him to my predicament." With each step, the veil, which was attached to my hair, forced my head backwards until a quick-thinking honorary usher yanked the fragile veil free" (Schaalman Youdovin, S., 2006).

The marriage to David Laber did not work out. After eight years of marriage, Susan decided that she had had enough. Schaalman advised her to "stick it out," which he later admitted was bad advice. Instead of considering her needs, he thought of the divorce as a stain on the family, which, until then, had never experienced a divorce. Indeed, popular opinion at the time held that divorce, which was relatively rare in Jewish families, stigmatized them.

Once the bills started rolling in for the 975 dinner guests, Lotte decided, and her husband agreed, that she should find a job although she had never worked during her marriage. She got a job at a market research firm owned by one of Emanuel's congregants interviewing business executives. Her earnings, though, were not enough to pay for the wedding; the couple also had to liquidate an investment worth $5,000

Michael

What are Michael's happiest childhood memories of being with his father? "When my father was most a father, not when he was being honored, or doing a particular ceremony." Michael is well aware of the compromises his father made in his busy schedule to be with his son. One of their enjoyments was to attend baseball games together. In those days, Schaalman was an avid Cubs fan and enjoyed their opportunities to go to a game together. One story stands out in Michael's memory, the time he and his father were at a Cubs game and Tony Taylor, the second baseman, came up to bat. When he crossed himself, as was his habit, "Dad turned to me and said, 'Now, what happens if the pitcher crosses himself?' As the son of a rabbi, I was expected to know the answer. That's the price you pay for being a rabbi's son."

When Michael was in middle school, his father established a weekly afternoon ritual: Thursday handball sessions. Schaalman would pick him up after school from Anshe Emet Day School and drive downtown to the Standard Club to play handball. They played a competitive game, but his father was the better player and always won. He played hard and without gloves. They played at least one full game before taking a swim and a shower. Afterwards, they headed to the café for refreshments. The experience was an opportunity for father/son bonding. His father was scrupulous in keeping those afternoons; they were their private "Shabbat," a very special time for both of them. When they weren't playing handball, they played ping-pong together. His father won most of the time, but Michael was busy calculating when his turn would come.

At the end of his Thursday afternoon sessions with his father, Michael's and his mother's paths would cross each other. Thursday was Symphony night, and she would be a few blocks away coming for the concert and dinner, a few blocks from the Standard Club. Michael reports that on occasion he was invited to go with them. Like his parents before him, Schaalman loved music and had season tickets. One of his jokes, according to Michael, was that, if the Jews stayed home, there wouldn't be a symphony program!

After middle school at Anshe Emet, Michael transferred to Senn High School where, in addition to racking up an excellent academic record, he also proved to be an outstanding swimmer on the school's swim team and competed in citywide swim meets. During one of the city championship finals, his father brought Michael's Uncle Freddie, who was visiting from Brazil, to see the swim meet. The outcome was that Michael qualified for the state championships, an achievement no one from his school had done in forty years. The preliminaries, however, were held on Friday night (fortunately, his Orthodox uncle had already gone home), and Michael knew his father would have difficulty accepting the fact that his son would compete on Shabbat. To his surprise, Schaalman gave his son permission; Michael knew it was not an easy decision but a difficult compromise of his religious values.

Although normally Schaalman did not attend his swimming events, Michael remembers the time his father rushed over to the school to show him the acceptance letter from Grinnell College that had just arrived. Schaalman was so excited by the letter that he wasn't even bothered by the fact that Michael lost the meet.

Before attending Grinnell, Michael was not particularly religious, but, to his surprise and that of his family, all that changed. During his freshman year, he asked the college for permission to go home for Passover, but the college refused. Because he was trapped there anyway, Michael decided to organize a Seder for Grinnell's many Jewish students. He called area rabbis to ask if they would officiate, but no one was willing to come. As a last resort, he called his father who agreed to come on the condition that the Seder would have to be held on Thursday so that he could return to Chicago in time for his own Friday night service at Emanuel.

The event was a huge success, Michael reports: "Students who never turned out for anything Jewish turned out. It was standing room only." Jewish students, who made up twenty percent of the 1,200 student population but were generally invisible, came "out of the woodwork."[234] Even the kitchen staff was thrilled to participate in a ritual they had never been part of before. To Michael, "It was wonderful, and I was touched by the fact that [my father] made such an effort to come."

Michael was a student during the Vietnam War years, and as a student activist, was instrumental in getting the school to invite his father to share his views on the war. At that time, Michael supported the war, and, to his excruciating embarrassment, Schaalman told the two hundred students who showed up that he was against the war. After hearing his father, however, he was sufficiently rattled that his position began to crumble.

While he was at Grinnell, Michael met and fell in love with Roberta Jones, another student there. As he tells it, it was love at first sight. A big problem, though, was that she was dating one of his friends and showed no interest in him. In fact, in her account, she took no notice of him at all, although they were in several of the same classes. Her impression of him was formed by what she observed in one of their classes together. Michael sat in the front of the room; she was in the back. The regular professor was sick and a TA was substituting for him. Unfortunately, he didn't know what to do and merely read the assigned readings from the textbook. Occasionally, he would pause and ask a question and then Michael's hand shot up. Every single time! Bobbie was embarrassed for him. From where she sat, he looked like a "suck-up." Michael claims that he was merely attempting to help the teacher get through the class.

Soon, however, Michael got up his courage to ask her out on a date. Although she wasn't excited by the idea, she agreed. She had a rule that if she were asked out on a date, she would more or less give the guy a chance. Although she didn't want to go out with him, she did. To her surprise, she "fell in love with him right away." Asked what was it about him that caused her to change her mind, she said, "He was so full of ideas, and passionate about them. We could and did talk for hours. That was huge. That was beautiful."

Their falling in love, however, raised a major complication: Bobbie was not Jewish. Michael knew that the only way he could marry her and get his parents' blessing was for her to convert. When Bobbie realized that she was in love with Michael and wanted to marry him, she decided to do so. During the next year, she studied with an Orthodox rabbi in a nearby town and asked her future father-in-law to complete the process of conversion.

In the meantime, other forces were at work attempting to direct Michael's future. His parents' dream was that he would become a rabbi. According to Schaalman, "My greatest single achievement as a rabbi would be for my son to follow in my footsteps." The Schaalmans thought that if they sent him to Israel in his junior year, he would come away with a better understanding of what it meant to be a Jew and would decide to become a rabbi.

Michael loved being at Grinnell and did not want to go to Israel: "To this day I wonder how they got me to do it. I was frightened by it, and I'd be a long way away, and it would interrupt my swimming." Although he hasn't said so, it is reasonable to assume that leaving Bobbie was not an easy decision. His sense of obligation to his parents, however, tipped the scales, and he never regretted going. It "turned out to be a wonderful experience."

When he enrolled in Hebrew University in Jerusalem in 1968, he was pleased to discover that that the school had a swim team and that he did not have to give up his beloved swimming. He also met "some of the most interesting people [he had] ever met. His three roommates were extraordinary young men. One was a student from Princeton and the son of an Orthodox rabbi. Another was from Georgetown, and the third, from Long Island (later he became Rabbi Marc Gellman of the God Squad).[235]

Jerusalem worked its magic on Michael. Little did his parents know that the experience of being in Israel might turn Michael into an

Orthodox Jew. When he began to feel that his knowledge of Judaism was inadequate, he enrolled in a yeshiva, an academy of intensive Talmudic study under Orthodox auspices. Because he knew his parents would not let him drop out of college, he attended only at night several times a week. It was enough to get him hooked. The Orthodox understood the spiritual hunger of American students and targeted them. Not long after a meeting with an Orthodox rabbi in a bombed-out building in East Jerusalem, Michael decided to make a radical change in his life. He would drop out of Hebrew University and enroll in a yeshiva as a full-time student. Imagine his Reform parents' reaction; the threat of such a decision must have been a nightmare! They sent off a telegram: "Do not drop out of Hebrew University, do not join the yeshiva. We'll meet you in Rome." The Schaalmans reasoned that, if they could get their son out of Israel, they had a better chance to convince him he was making a serious mistake. (In retrospect, Schaalman reports, "Had his Aunt Ilse been in Israel, she would have made sure he didn't join the yeshiva.")

Unlike some children of the 1960s who dropped out of the mainstream culture despite their parents' wishes, Michael was a dutiful son and met his parents in Rome. During the next week, the Schaalmans tried desperately to convince him not to enter the Yeshiva. By week's end, the three of them had reached a compromise. To his parents' relief, Michael agreed that he would stay in school and would only attend the Yeshiva at night. The experience challenged the kind of Jew Michael was and wanted to be. The outcome was that, instead of turning toward Orthodoxy, he remained a Reform Jew. After he and Bobbie married, they raised their children as Reform Jews and joined a Reform temple in Milwaukee, where they now live.

After getting his degree from Grinnell in 1970, Michael enrolled in Northwestern University Law School. His decision was a major disappointment for Schaalman. "At first," he reports, "I was both surprised and hurt and let Michael know it. In time, however, I came to accept Michael's decision. After all, rabbis need good lay people, and Michael turned out to be one of them." Schaalman confides, "In many ways maybe he's doing something that from his point of view is equally, if not even more, effective than had he become a rabbi." Schaalman became "totally adjusted" to Michael's decision and speaks with pride of his son using his gifts to do good work and that he (Michael) is at peace with his choice. When Susan married Rabbi Ira Youdovin, at least he had a son-in-law on whom he could lavish the kind of professional support he might have given his son.

During his first year in law school, Michael and Bobbie lived with the Schaalmans in their two-bedroom apartment. The house was crowded: Grandma Gussie occupied the back bedroom, the Schaalmans had the second bedroom, Bobbie slept in the den and Michael on the living room couch, an arrangement that did not please Grandma (Schaalman, R., October 29, 2011). Michael and Bobbie were married June 12, 1971, and by this time, the Schaalmans were financially better off than when Susan got married. They hosted four- to five-hundred people, including relatives and friends of both families.

When Michael graduated in 1974, he accepted a prestigious two-year position of clerk for the Chief of the Federal Appellate Court in Milwaukee, where in 1977, he and Bobbie moved. Not long after, Michael joined the prestigious law firm, Quarles & Brady, where he is still employed.[236] It might be asked, to what extent is Michael a reflection of his father? Damien Jaques (2005), one of Michael's close friends, offers this comment, "When Michael talks in our Torah Study, I chuckle to myself because when I hear Michael, I hear his father. He is so much his father's son."

In assessing his influence on his children, Schaalman is pleased that both of them are "irretrievably Jewish" and, because they are well grounded in Judaism, are able to draw on it for guidance in how to live. He also knows that Michael and Susan learned from their parents' example what it means to share a married life and to be obligated to a spouse, and that this sense of obligation extends beyond the family to the needs of others and to the communities in which they live. As a result, both children have a strong sense of family, not just in the present but also in the continuity of generations, the importance of ancestry and of their own descendants, their children and grandchildren. In addition to this impressive list of values, Schaalman is pleased that he has passed on to his children the love of books and music.

Another virtue Schaalman attributes to his children is that they have developed a deep understanding of the need to avoid hurting others. Schaalman explains: "They would rather be among the hunted than the hunters." The reader might wonder that Schaalman, who is painfully aware of the ultimate price of being the hunted, might make such a statement. "Yet, the choice of being a victimizer or a victim," he said, "is a Hobson's choice.

The Schaalmans are also extremely proud of their daughter-in-law, whom they consider an extraordinary person. Not only is she an excellent wife and mother, but she has embraced Judaism wholeheartedly. One of the ways in which she demonstrated her commitment was to teach in the Milwaukee Jewish Day School. She is the mother of three children, all confirmed Reform Jews: Johanna, born in 1977, Keren in 1981, and Jeremy in 1985.

A Prophetic Dream

The 1960s were a time of intense and often violent events in the civil rights struggle and in the reaction to the Vietnam War. The period was marked by an unprecedented number of political assassinations of major political leaders in the United States.[237] For Schaalman, as for so many others, these events were reshaping the face of America and profoundly troubling for him. On the day Martin Luther King, Jr. was assassinated (April 4, 1968), Schaalman and Lotte were in Tel Aviv at the end of a tour they had led with a group of Emanuel congregants. Accompanying them was his mother-in-law, who slept together with her daughter while he slept on a cot. On this last night in Israel, Schaalman had a dream that Martin Luther King, Jr. had been shot. He woke up about 5:00 a.m. and could not go back to sleep. He dreamt that he saw a car in a cloud of dust going over a hill and disappearing into the future. When Lotte awoke and while his mother-in-law was still asleep, he whispered to her the account of his strange dream: "You know that is absolutely so ... so unusual ... so stupid a dream! I don't know how that relates to me."

That morning they took a cab to the airport, and, as it drove away from the hotel, Schaalman heard on the cab's radio the announcement: "Martin Luther King, Jr. has been assassinated." Hearing the news, Schaalman turned to his wife and said, "Remember my dream?" Lotte did not respond. "I did not know whether she heard me and did not want to talk about it, but the subject never came up again. Only when the anniversary of King's birth was announced on television on January 15, 2006, did she recall that they had been in Israel when King was shot." Her remark triggered his memory of the bizarre experience. What made this dream so strange was that he never before (or since) had a dream that prefigured or foretold an event, either trivial or major. This preternatural experience changed Schaalman's views on the nature of reality. No longer could he deny that whatever is not known does not exist. He now allows for the existence of events, experiences, and states of being that have not yet been discovered and "of which we now have only the faintest kind of inklings."[238]

Social, Ethical, and Political Action

When Schaalman took on the role of rabbi at one of Chicago's most respected Reform temples, his commitment to social justice and his sympathy for the less fortunate had an opportunity to blossom. He found that he could not ignore the major issues affecting his new country. Only five years after the end of World War II, America was in the throes of intense uncertainty over the threat of international communism. It had good reason to believe that the Soviet Union was out to spread communism around the world and to destroy capitalism (Diemert, B., 2005). The perceived threat was cast in terms of freedom or slavery, between Christianity and a godless communism. It was also the beginning of the Korean War, a war of communist North Korea against capitalist South Korea. In short order, the war was seen in Western countries as an effort by insidious international communism to spread beyond its current borders. The war "confirmed" the "domino theory" articulated by President Dwight D. Eisenhower to describe Soviet expansion (Diemert, B., 2005).

Added to the hysteria produced by this war was the Soviet success in developing an atomic bomb and the fear of communism at home whipped up by spy accusations and the Congressional hearings of Senator Joseph McCarthy. For the Jews, this issue of subversive activity through communist affiliation became an immediate threat. Since the end of World War II, America had become more generous and accepting of Jews. However, that new status was jeopardized by the spy trial of Julius and Ethel Rosenberg and the revelations of the McCarthy hearings exposing Jews in the federal government and the entertainment industry as communists. In one of the most famous   and infamous—espionage trials of the twentieth century, two Jewish Americans, Julius and Ethel Rosenberg, were arrested as spies for the USSR. After a brief trial in the spring of 1951, despite many protests and efforts to save them, the Rosenbergs were found guilty of espionage and executed.

During this extremely tense time, Schaalman's sympathies were with the U.S. government. As a refugee from Nazi Germany, he felt he owed his life to America, and he could not abide any perceived threat to its existence. Therefore, he accepted the official line with those who thought the Rosenbergs were guilty and was not opposed to their execution. The fact that they were Jews was an additional embarrassment to him. Their trial and execution reminded him of his experience under the Nazis and the fear of any kind of negative Jewish publicity or association. The Rosenberg trial became for him, as it had for many American Jews, a threat to the progress Jews had made in America toward full acceptance as citizens and to tolerance of Judaism as a religion in what was then a predominantly Protestant nation. Although public controversy over their guilt has continued for more than half a century, Schaalman today does not question the verdict. From his perspective, the crime of espionage and an apparent conspiracy involving other Jews associated with the Rosenbergs was intolerable. It was a crime against the country that had become the most hospitable and friendly toward Jews ever in any place and at any time.

Although generally not active in this national struggle, Schaalman could not avoid facing the problems on his doorstep and in his city, and he felt compelled to get involved in the local struggle over Chicago's social issues.[239] There is no doubt that his work as Regional Director for the UAHC helped shape his awareness of social issues in America. Rabbi Maurice Eisendrath played a pivotal role in helping Schaalman identify the great social needs of America. Schaalman had the greatest respect for Eisendrath who, during the thirty years of his tenure as UAHC President (1943 to 1973), committed the organization's resources to ameliorate injustice in America.[240]

In his involvement in the local struggle for social justice, Schaalman was following in the tradition of Reform rabbis who had always been in the vanguard of social reform. For the Reform rabbinate, ethical action and social justice were a way of doing God's work, *tikkun olam*, a lesson it had learned from prophetic teachings (Kroloff, C., 1990, p. 93).[241]

In order to take an active role in local issues of social justice, Schaalman had to win his congregation's approval, an objective that threatened to be an uphill struggle. A significant and vocal portion of the congregation was still loyal to Rabbi Levy, and they did not yet accept him as their rabbi. He was, therefore, reluctant to engage in activities that might provoke further opposition to his leadership. However, once he felt secure, he began to play an active role in promoting social justice.

One of the first issues that proved to be a formidable challenge early on was the issue of race. He used his pulpit to promote social justice and the rights of minorities, particularly of African Americans, to live in peace and harmony not only in Emanuel's neighborhood, but also in the nation.

In the 1950s, Emanuel's neighboring community of Edgewater was beginning to undergo a demographic transformation. Black families began moving into what until then was a predominantly white neighborhood. Residents were unhappy with this development because they feared that blacks would have a negative influence on property values and increase the potential for crime. Some residents were outright racists and could not abide the thought of living among blacks. Edgewater began to suffer from the "white flight" that had become a plague in neighborhoods around the country as whites fled the movement of blacks into previously all-white neighborhoods. Property values declined because other whites did not want to move into integrated neighborhoods. As whites moved out, blacks moved in, and the flight to white areas switched into high gear. Soon, previously all-white neighborhoods became largely, if not entirely, black.

White flight also took a toll on Emanuel's membership. Worried about the changing neighborhood, some congregants moved north to the suburbs. This transformation did not always occur peacefully. One incident that provoked fear in the congregation occurred on Yom Kippur when one of the congregants while walking to his car was hurt by a chair-wielding teenager.

Not long after the first black families moved into Edgewater, some of their neighbors began a campaign of harassment. They organized meetings and demonstrations to protest the presence of a black family. The hostility was not limited to adults. Black and white schoolchildren, particularly high school students, engaged in frequent insults that occasionally erupted in fights. As more and more black teenagers moved into the neighborhood, they formed gangs to protect themselves. Whites, as the established majority, met them with their own gangs. This, after all, was the era of *West Side Story* and *Blackboard Jungle*.

The issue of race, the segregation of blacks, and the injustices they had experienced throughout American history were beginning to become part of America's consciousness. In the 1960s, fed by a combination of a more socially conscious student population and a responsive black community, the civil rights movement gathered momentum. Blacks took action against years of injustice and injuries that continued long after the end of slavery. In 1963, not far from Emanuel Congregation, clergy from around the country came together at the National Conference of Religion and Race to discuss race in America (Kimelman, R., 1983). According to E. J. Lipman (1990), the CCAR sent a large delegation to the conference, though the actual number is unknown. Schaalman was one of them. Also present were two of the great religious leaders of the twentieth century, Reverend Martin Luther King, Jr. and Rabbi Abraham Joshua Heschel, the renowned Jewish theologian and teacher.[242] Respected not only in the Jewish community but also by religious leaders around the world, Heschel gave one of the key addresses and one of the most important of his career.[243]   His speech on the urgency of action to secure the civil rights of minorities in America helped galvanize the clergy and became a springboard for the 1963 March on Washington (Lipman, E. J., 1990).

Edgewater Clergy and Rabbinic Association (ECRA)

To carry out his commitment to social justice, Schaalman helped establish the Edgewater Rabbi and Ministerial Association, later renamed the Edgewater Clergy and Rabbinic Association (ECRA), to reflect a wider range of religious affiliation. The organization consisted of the local Edgewater community clergy, including Schaalman, the only rabbi. Formed in 1961, according to Dean P. Rice (1986), the Association was the first in the country to bring together clergy of the Jewish and Christian communities. The Association worked together with neigh-

borhood churches, synagogues, and social service agencies to address issues of social justice affecting the community. Kenneally (1986) credits
Schaalman not only for bringing the clergy together but for helping
them realize that "as people of God in the community we had an interdependence and mutual responsibility" to work together to address the
community's problems.

Schaalman remembers two events in trying to calm the passions of
the gangs in the community. During an outbreak of violence at Edgewater's Senn High School, he and a minister of the Bethany Lutheran
Church headed off a "rumble" by inserting themselves between two
groups of angry students and got them to back down. To promote peace
in the neighborhood, Schaalman invited local gang leaders to meet at
Emanuel to try to resolve their differences. Lotte cooked for the event.
The point of these meetings was that the gangs did not have to fight to
be heard; they could learn to resolve their differences though dialogue.

To Reverend William G. Kenneally (1986), Schaalman was "the
Rabbi to the ECRA congregation." In his nearly thirty years of working with ECRA, Schaalman earned the respect of his colleagues for "his
leadership, his gentleness, and good council." According to Kenneally,
through all the changes in Edgewater during those years, Schaalman
"stood as a pillar of strength ... a religious leader who always fought for
the good of everyone."

When Schaalman retired in 1986 as Emanuel's rabbi, Kathy Osterman (April 25, 1986), a Chicago Ward Alderman and President of
ECRA, summed up what to her was his effect on the community:

> We are proud of being part of the dream you had for a viable
> community organization. As you look around Edgewater, you
> will see better housing, new trees, cleaner Lake Michigan, a rec-
> reation center, a library, a food pantry, a cultural center, but most
> important, beautiful people from all ethnic, cultural, racial, and
> religious groups living harmoniously together. This was your
> dream, Rabbi Schaalman. Thanks for letting us all be part of it.

Schaalman's work in this and other areas of social concern was recognized in 1963 by the Immigrants Service League. One of the city's oldest
social service organizations, the League presented him its award for Outstanding Foreign Born Citizen of Chicago. The award, which came as a

complete surprise, was given in recognition for his work in the Edgewater community and in the city. Schaalman could not figure out why he got it: "How I could have drawn the attention of this organization after only fourteen years in Chicago, and how I had been chosen from among the thousands of foreign-born citizens in that pool, remains a mystery to me." This early award no doubt testifies to the impact Schaalman had already made on the community and may explain why by the 1960s there was hardly a prominent Jewish family in Chicago that did not have a member in Emanuel. This external recognition and Schaalman's increasing prestige in the community helped convince its leadership to support his efforts.

In 1971, together with ECRA and under Schaalman's direction, Emanuel established the Care for Real Program. The program collected and distributed food and clothing to impoverished elderly living in Edgewater. At the same time, at Schaalman's urging, Emanuel took on additional social action projects that included drug abuse counseling and other forms of assistance for Edgewater's elderly. These activities were part of a full agenda developed by Emanuel's Social Action Committee, which worked to keep its social concerns in front of the board. Generally supportive of the committee's efforts, the board's major concern was money. Board minutes indicate that board members were concerned about taking on new financial commitments when it was operating on an ongoing deficit (Emanuel Congregation Board Minutes, January 30, 1971).

It is in this context that Schaalman's efforts to bring racial peace and harmony to Edgewater needs to be understood. When asked why he did not participate in the Selma march and other demonstrations in which rabbinic colleagues participated, Schaalman speculates that he might have been put off by the harsh tone of the radicals and their willingness to engage in violent confrontation. Nonetheless, this decision did not prevent him from meeting with radical Jewish groups and with other clergy pushing for integration. His contact with them resulted in his attending some local meetings in Rogers Park, a nearby Chicago neighborhood also feeling the effects of integration, and in local storefronts.

When Schaalman retired, one of his colleagues in Edgewater, Reverend William Johnson (1986) of the Church of the Atonement, wrote a glowing testimony to Schaalman's impact on him:

You have been a true inspiration to me to work for justice. You have taught me that justice is a word that refuses to be encumbered by any qualified restrictive clauses. It stands alone as the zenith of all human relationships, and that it is God-given. I thank you profoundly for sharing that gift with me.

Rabbinic Assistants

During Rabbi Levy's long tenure as Emanuel's senior rabbi, he had two rabbinic assistants, Richard G. Hirsch and Arnold Wolf. Yet, for the first fourteen years after Schaalman succeeded Levy, Emanuel's board would not hire an assistant for him.[244] Although the cantor was paid full time, according to Schaalman, he worked only ten to twelve hours a week, which meant that many of the religious responsibilities were left to Schaalman. Moreover, the temple needed a full-time school administrator but had only one person working part time. The only other full-time employee was the temple administrator.

Schaalman's first formal request for an assistant appears in Emanuel's Board Minutes of May 24, 1960. In response, the board appointed an Assistant Rabbi Committee. Because of the projected budget shortfall for the following year, the committee recommended and the board accepted its recommendation that the decision to hire an assistant rabbi be put off until the following year. Another ten years passed before the board hired a rabbinic assistant. As a result, Schaalman had the daunting responsibility of ministering to nearly 900 families. The workload was simply too much. Many years later, he confided to his Torah Study, "There was not a night that I went to sleep when I could have said that I had completed the tasks necessary to support a congregation of 900 families."

In 1970, Emanuel hired an assistant rabbi, and, from then until he retired, Schaalman had a total of four. Without their help, he would never have been able to take on the responsibilities of national leadership in Reform Judaism. This role began in 1972, when he was appointed to chair the CCAR's Mixed Marriage Committee, and later with his election as the organization's vice president in 1979 and president in 1981. During this time, his assistants played an important role in supporting him. They filled in for him by conducting services, weddings, funerals, and bar and bat mitzvahs.

For the most part, Schaalman had excellent relationships with his assistants. Rabbi David Mersky (Emanuel Congregation, 1986), his first assistant who served from 1970 to 1973, considered those three years "the most important years of [his]life." His association with Schaalman helped him grow and mature into a more caring and sensitive human being. After he left Emanuel, when confronted by various challenges, he found himself asking, "What would Herman do in these circumstances?" Invariably, he found that he knew the answer, and, as a result, realized that Schaalman continued to be a guide for his life. He remembered an occasion when the two of them were driving together to pay a sick call on some congregants in Michael Reese Hospital. As they were driving in Schaalman's blue four-door Thunderbird, Mersky began complaining about one of his assignments that required him to travel two days a week to the northern suburbs to tutor three children who could not get to the temple for their mid-week Hebrew lessons. Schaalman responded with a "gentle" reproof that Mersky considered "the most valuable lesson of [his] life: 'When it comes to transmitting values and teaching Torah, there is nothing that is menial or beneath one's dignity.'"

Mersky was followed by Rabbi Joseph A. Edelheit, who served from 1973 to 1976. During the years of his apprenticeship Edelheit, a young and very bright rabbi, formed a deep spiritual and personal bond with Schaalman, one that later dissolved when Edelheit was hired as Emanuel's senior rabbi. Edelheit was followed by Rabbi John Friedman, who served from 1976 to 1980 and then by Rabbi Michael Weinberg, who worked with Schaalman from 1980 to 1985. Folb (2007) reports that both Weinberg and Friedman came to love and respect Schaalman. As part of the respect he showed his assistants and as part of their training, Schaalman worked with them as if they were equals and shared with them his rabbinic responsibilities. From his standpoint, they were in no way his "assistants," but fully functioning rabbis in their own right (Folb, 2007, p. 53).

Rabbi Friedman recalled that as a seminary student, he considered himself a "hotshot, a whiz at Hebrew text and student politics" (Emanuel Congregation, 1986). His first assignment after graduating HUC, on the other hand, intimidated him: "Still single, moving to a large city to be the assistant Rabbi in one of the great congregations of America, to one of America's greatest Rabbis, was, to say the least, off-putting." After only a few years of working with Schaalman, he was able to write,

Among all the outstanding accomplishments and tributes which undoubtedly will be written and spoken about you … the one I believe characterizes your Rabbinic life is your skill at making peace. To be sure, those whom you have led and taught will agree that you have brought peace to the homes, business lives, Jewish lives and community lives of hundreds upon hundreds of people, Jew and non-Jew, throughout your decades as a Rabbi.

Speaking for his rabbinic colleagues who also served as Schaalman's assistants, he added, "You have brought that element of 'Shalom,' of fullness of confidence, through your love and through the model of your life."[245]

Fund Raising: Emanuel 1970–1986

In the 1970s, to assist Emanuel with its ongoing budget deficits and to help establish its long-term financial stability, Schaalman embarked on various fundraising activities. Robert Morris, a longtime friend of the rabbi, a major contributor to Emanuel and a former board president and treasurer, speaks highly of Schaalman's commitment to fundraising. Unlike so many other rabbis Morris has known who avoid fundraising, Schaalman considered it an important part of his job.

Because of his enormous prestige and friendship with wealthy congregants, Schaalman was able to raise substantial funds. As the congregation's chief fundraiser, he solicited funds on the basis that they were a "gift to the Temple, a gift to God, and the performance of a Mitzvah." Schaalman comments, "When people made substantial contributions, I told them the gifts were not only good for the congregation but also for themselves, something worthwhile of which they could be proud."

One of the means of raising these funds was to hold Sunday brunches for wealthy congregants. The invitation informed the invitees that the purpose of the brunch was to raise funds. Schaalman drew up lists of invitees and enlisted Beverly Falstein, one of the most able of his congregants, to handle the details. She prepared the food and took care of the arrangements, including mailing the invitations and managing attendance. The seven or eight brunches raised substantial funds, contributions in small amounts of $200, much larger donations of $10,000, and, occasionally, $40,000 to $50,000. According to Falstein,

"Rabbi Schaalman set unobtainable fund-raising calls, or goals that seemed impossible, but were always achieved." Typically, these goals were over $100,000.

Another of Schaalman's fundraising activities included the establishment of the Heritage Fund, eventually valued at 1.5 million dollars. The income from this fund alone, with an annual return of five percent, would more than cover the temple's annual deficits, rarely more than $25,000. In addition to the Heritage Fund, at Schaalman's urging, Arthur Hershey, a congregant, established a million dollar endowment fund. According to Schaalman, "Had the funds not been squandered by successive boards, this 2.5 million dollar endowment would have secured the temple's long-term financial security."

Schaalman, who worked hard to acquire these funds, enjoyed the activity and was thrilled that people responded so generously. He recalls how he visited prospective donors in their homes or offices or in the temple. The income from the funds helped balance the budget and relieved the congregation of financial stress. It also enabled the congregation to provide additional programming it could not otherwise afford. Moreover, the congregation was able to maintain a dues structure that was considerably less than that of suburban congregations. This situation created a sense of well-being that lasted until he retired. "Because of this financial cushion," notes Schaalman, "even board meetings became more pleasurable."

The fundraising was a particular strain but an essential activity. It was an ongoing process that needed constant attention and, he notes, to be "nourished day in and day out. You can never let go … it needs to grow, to be alive." Fundraising, however, got to be a chore and became part of his decision to retire at age seventy. Not long before he retired, he had used his influence to establish two endowments totaling nearly 2.5 million dollars, which would have been sufficient to subsidize the congregation's debt in perpetuity, had it withdrawn only its income. A conservative estimate is that the funds, properly invested, would likely have grown at a rate greater than inflation and, over the years, would have risen in value, as would the income. However, his successors squandered the funds by using the principal to subsidize operations. According to Schaalman, in the years following his retirement, the rabbis who succeeded him, together with their boards of trustees, did not continue to raise funds, but chose instead to spend the money in their endowments. Even though a good friend took on the responsibility for managing one of the funds, Schaalman could not convince him that the fund should not be used to supplement the operational budget.

Central Conference of American Rabbis: 1971–1991

In his mid-fifties, Schaalman began to branch out from Chicago and take on leadership roles in national and international Jewish organizations. The most important was his rise to leadership in the CCAR, which represents the organized rabbinate of Reform Judaism both in America and internationally.[246] Long before it was popular in liberal circles, the CCAR had a long history of strong, progressive social action. In 1902, it opposed the teaching of religion in public schools; in 1920, it called for radical social change, including equitable distribution of industrial profits, a minimum wage, an eight-hour workweek, workmen's compensation and universal health insurance. In 1967, it announced its opposition to the Vietnam War (Lipman, E. J., 1990).

When Schaalman joined the CCAR at the beginning of his career, these actions undoubtedly reinforced his commitment to social justice and helped raise his awareness of America's most troubling social issues.[247] His participation in the CCAR's annual meetings allowed him to connect with his colleagues and feel part of the national movement. More than a quarter of a century passed, however, before he began to take on leadership roles. During this time, when the winds of change whirled around Reform Judaism, Schaalman found himself in the center of its major controversies. By the 1970s, the CCAR was confronting two major issues: mixed marriages and patrilineal descent, issues that had been simmering for decades and now demanded attention.

When the CCAR turned to Schaalman to provide leadership to address them, he was suddenly thrust into the limelight. His appointment as chair of Mixed Marriage Committee was the beginning of his unanticipated and unplanned ascent into the leadership of the largest and most influential rabbinic organization in the world. For the next twenty years, he held the most important positions in Reform Judaism.

From 1971 to 1973, he served as chair of the Committee on Mixed Marriages. Then, in 1979, he served as chair of the Committee on Patrilineal Descent, and, in the same year, he was elected CCAR vice president. Two years later, he was elected president. During his presidency, he continued serving as chair of the Committee on Patrilineal Descent (1979–1983). Thanks to his efforts, these committees produced positions that transformed the Reform movement and prepared the groundwork for its advancement into the twenty-first century. At the end of his presidency, Schaalman took on the additional responsibility as chair of the Ethics Committee, a position he held until 1989.

Mixed Marriage Committee: The Background

The social upheaval of the 1960s contributed to the growing uneasiness among many Jews, particularly Jewish youth. Lacking a commitment to the Judaism of their parents, they rallied around a variety of liberal causes including new freedoms of self-expression and the long-standing issues of segregation, poverty, and social justice.

The new freedoms meant, too, that intermarriage had also become more common. Interfaith marriages and the weak ties of many Jews to their religion were depleting the ranks of the American Jewish population. As the number of Jewish males marrying non-Jewish women increased, so, too, did the number of families who were drifting away from the Jewish community and were likely to be lost to Judaism. At stake was no less than the survival of Judaism in America. Frightened by these developments and the projected decline in the Jewish population, lay and religious leaders across all branches of Judaism developed position papers and programs to arrest, if not reverse, this trend.

The issue of mixed marriage was one of the frontiers in this struggle and was particularly problematic for Reform Judaism. Although a small minority of Reform rabbis had been officiating at mixed marriages even as early as the late nineteenth century, the majority of Reform rabbis were opposed to it. They saw it as contributing to the decline of Judaism, and Reform in particular. Nevertheless, pressures from its congregants and their rabbis forced the CCAR to tackle this issue head on. Over the years, it passed several resolutions prohibiting the practice, but it could not prevent a growing number of its members, albeit still a minority, from performing interfaith marriages. These rabbis believed that it was better to officiate than not, arguing that half a loaf was better than no loaf. The refusal to officiate at these weddings, they argued, would further alienate the Jewish spouse from his or her already tenuous attachment to Judaism and the Jewish community. This is not to say that many of them did not impose conditions. According to D. E. Kaplan (2003), during this time a majority of Reform rabbis who officiated at interfaith marriages insisted on the condition that couples agree to maintain a Jewish home and raise their children as Jews (p. 178).[248]

The CCAR leadership was also troubled by the fact that its rabbis who refused to perform interfaith marriages were encountering difficulties getting positions in congregations that expected them to do so. Some rabbis reported feeling pressure not only from their boards, but also from individual congregants to allow mixed marriages. Sometimes influential and not-so-influential congregants wanted their rabbis to officiate at mixed marriages for a family member or for themselves. This situation put the rabbis in a difficult position. Some were willing to perform mixed marriages but were reluctant to violate the CCAR's policy against officiating at such marriages.[249] As a result, they found themselves in the uncomfortable position of refusing to accommodate congregants who needed their help. Nor were they able to assist other Jews who had no synagogue affiliation.

Schaalman was not immune from the difficulties of the situation. One of his best friends and major contributor to the congregation, Robert Morris, asked him to suggest another rabbi who would perform an interfaith marriage for his son. Morris understood Schaalman's position on interfaith marriage and respected him for it. In Morris's account, he then said to Schaalman, "All these years, I've never asked you for anything, but now I need your help. My son is marrying the daughter of a Lutheran minister, who has agreed to participate in the service. Since you don't perform interfaith marriages, I need you to recommend someone who will" (Morris, R. and Morris, A., 2007). Schaalman recommended another rabbi who performed the service.

Later, Morris discovered that Schaalman had agreed to perform an interfaith marriage for another member of the congregation. According to Morris, and confirmed by Schaalman, he made one exception to his position on performing interfaith marriages. One of his good friends, a man in his sixties and an active member of the congregation, wanted to remarry after his wife died. Schaalman performed the marriage, and, when Morris asked him how he could explain his decision to marry this couple, he responded that because of their age—the couple was in their sixties—they would not have children. "I was not happy with this explanation but I accepted it and did not allow it to mar my friendship with my rabbi" (Morris, R. and Morris, A., 2007).

Faced with a small, but persistent radical rabbinic rebellion in the ranks, the CCAR decided it had to try again to issue binding policy to address the issue. Although the CCAR had a Committee on Mixed Marriages that had been working on the issue throughout the 1960s, mixed marriage threatened to polarize the organization and shatter its cohesiveness. To respond to this threat, the CCAR concluded it needed to reconstitute the committee so that it represented the diverse views of its membership and appoint a new chairman.[250]

In 1971, the CCAR appointed Schaalman, then fifty-five years old, to chair of the Committee on Mixed Marriage in the hope of finding a solution. Although he had been a member of the CCAR since his early years in Cedar Rapids, he had never held a role as a committee chairman. Because the issue of mixed marriage created a highly emotional and political controversy that threatened to rend the fabric of the organization, the CCAR needed someone who had the respect of his colleagues to deal with this fractious issue. Schaalman was also a member of the old guard, and the CCAR, knowing his opposition to officiation at mixed marriages, expected that he might be able to influence the committee to support its current policy.[251]

Another factor in his selection may have been that in the same year of his appointment, Schaalman had written that officiation in interfaith marriages would drive a wedge between liberal and traditional segments of Judaism. "Whatever endangers the survival of the Jewish people," he wrote, "whatever fragments it further is intolerable today. Our officiating at marriages between Jews and non-Jews is a divisive element widening the gap irretrievably between the torn fragments of our people."[252]

Schaalman was convinced the committee could produce a policy recommendation that represented the diverse views of its members and would be acceptable to the membership as a whole. After two years of deliberation, he presented the committee's recommendation at the 1973 annual conference. The committee had reached a consensus that reaffirmed CCAR's policy of opposing rabbinic officiation at mixed marriages but yielded some ground to rabbis who wanted to do so by softening the language and phrasing it as an admonition "to refrain" from officiating at mixed marriages.

To Schaalman's complete surprise and displeasure, Rabbi Irwin Fishbein, one of the committee members, defected from the official committee position and launched a floor fight to amend the proposed resolution. Fishbein and his supporters sought to change CCAR official policy in order to allow rabbis to officiate at mixed marriages. By the end of an acrimonious and tumultuous session, they won a major concession that partly opened the door: In place of the language directing rabbis "to refrain" from performing mixed marriages, the Convention approved the following statement: "The Central Conference of American Rabbis recognizes that historically its members have held and continue to hold divergent interpretations of Jewish tradition." For Schaalman, this development was a major defeat; in a single morning, the committee's hard work over two years to create a delicate compromise had been undone!

The Outcome of the Committee's Action

Now that the committee had fulfilled its mandate, it was disbanded, but the issue of mixed marriage remained a source of contention among the rabbis and would come back to haunt Schaalman later when he was asked to chair the Committee on Patrilineal Descent. In commenting on the outcome of the conflict, Rabbi Alan Fuchs told Folb (2007) that the CCAR leadership sought to bury the issue and sabotaged the committee (p. 71). Whether or not this assessment is correct, Schaalman concluded that the committee's work had been in vain and that he had been betrayed (p. 71).

Although Schaalman's work on this issue did not produce the result he wanted, his work on the committee was not a total loss. One of its outcomes was that his rabbinic colleagues came to recognize him for his excellent leadership capability and, in the words of colleague Rabbi Alan Fuchs, "[his] diligence, strength and [the] enormous amount of integrity in conducting the business of the committee" (Folb, 2007, p.71).

Despite his own feelings about this issue, Schaalman did not allow them to subvert the committee's full and open deliberations. Although he had been appointed because he was known to have a position on the subject, Rabbi Joe Glaser (1983), CCAR's Executive Director, said in his evaluation of Schaalman's leadership, "We never saw as fair a way to treat a subject as the way Herman chaired that committee" (p. 87). His painstaking attempt to give justice to all sides of the issue was frustrating, according to Glaser, but the result was that "we came out with something that was fair and decent and with which we can all live" (p. 87).

Unresolved Issues

Within the Reform movement, the outcome of the Resolution on Mixed Marriages created several related issues: the Jewish status of children of mixed marriage; the inclusion of large numbers of non-Jews and their extended families in the Jewish life of mixed marriage families and their congregations; and how mixed marriage families might participate in religious ceremonies such as B'nai Mitzvah and High Holy Day services.[253] The most important challenge for mixed marriage families was how to promote the Jewish identity of their children in the context of their non-Jewish extended families, issues that were not addressed at the 1973 convention. The 1973 Resolution on Mixed Marriages had, at its core, the priority that rabbis reach out to these families and "be creative and consistent" in their efforts to cultivate involvement in the Jewish community.

The magnitude of the problem was reaching critical mass. According to Sarna and Golden (2000), by the end of the twentieth century, the American Jewish community was "at a crossroads in its history. Demographically, the community was stagnant. It had not grown appreciably since 1960, [and] comprised a smaller percentage of America's total population than it had in 1920. The researchers went further in making the dire prediction that the numbers of Jews would decline in the decades ahead. Already in 1990, nearly fifty percent of young Reform Jews had married non-Jews, and only one third of intermarried couples were raising their children as Jews (Cohen, S. M. & Wertheimer, J., 2006). A recent demographic study published in 2009 found that in the two preceding decades, while the Jewish population had nearly doubled, the proportion of American Jews who identify themselves as religious had dropped by more than twenty percent. The shift away from Jewish identification was the result of "a combination of disaffection from Judaism and intermarriage" (Kosmin, B. A., 2008).

As of 2012, intermarriage remains a major challenge for Reform Judaism. It entered the twenty-first century with the recognition that it had to respond in new ways to support the growing number of rabbis performing interfaith marriages. At its 2008 convention, Rabbi Peter Knobel (2008), CCAR president, announced that the CCAR was abandoning its previous policy of issuing resolutions, which had been divisive and unproductive, and adopting a new direction, which would provide Reform rabbis the means to lead more effectively on the issues arising out of interfaith. In what amounts to a sea change from its earlier positions, Knobel (2008) stated, "The CCAR will allow rabbis the freedom to act in relation to interfaith as their consciences require and not on the basis of a ruling from the CCAR." The times had surely changed, and the CCAR was attempting to catch up with them.[254]

This is the strange new world in which Schaalman finds himself. Until recently, his position had been that he would not perform an interfaith ceremony, even for his grandchildren. To do so would violate a basic principle of his religious belief and his responsibility as a rabbi. In 2005, he said, "I cannot see myself as a functioning rabbi if I were to marry someone who was not Jewish."[255]

Deeply troubled by the trends of increasing interfaith marriage and the lack of commitment to Judaism of the second generation of children from these families, Schaalman raised the issue in a 2005 High Holy Day sermon, "Where are we?" He sought to encourage his listeners to think about their own commitment to, and practice of, Judaism. The following year, he also challenged his congregants to consider the question, "Where are our children?" Unknown to most of them was the fact that he, too, was struggling with these basic questions.

Schaalman's reluctance to perform interfaith marriages had become an agonizing and contentious issue in his marriage. Lotte, who was more in tune than her husband with the position of the CCAR, believes passionately that her husband should bend with the times and agree to marry his grandchildren and that it is more important to try to help young couples remain part of the Jewish community than to alienate them. She contends that rabbis are stuck with traditions that compromise their humanity.

True to its history, Reform Judaism was in the process of reinventing itself, and, Herman Schaalman, who throughout his rabbinic career had undergone several metamorphoses, would not be left behind. By January of 2010, Schaalman was beginning to have serious doubts about the legitimacy of his position of not performing an interfaith marriage for his grandchildren. The sticking point for him was how to get around the language of the marriage vows requiring both partners to accept the Laws of Moses. In August 2010, he told his Torah Study that they would be surprised to learn that he had decided to perform interfaith marriages. He explained,

> Although in 1973, I had led the Reform movement's opposition to rabbinic participation in them, the world had changed dramatically since then and so have I. I now understood that the prohibition of rabbinic participation in interfaith marriages has been ineffectual and, not only unnecessary, but wrong. The survival of progressive Judaism in the United States depends on inclusion, not exclusion, inviting instead of rejecting, opening instead of closing. Judaism has been enriched by the recognition and acceptance of other groups' values and truths. The new openness that is so appealing to young Jews, and which would have been impossible a few generations ago, is a guarantee that Judaism will survive.

Realizing that he was now contradicting one of his most valued positions, he declared defiantly to his students, "Do me something!" His commitment to these new understandings and the growing pressures in his family were forcing him to reevaluate his position on rabbinic officiation in interfaith marriages. On May 27, 2012, he performed an interfaith marriage ceremony for his beloved granddaughter, Keren, and her non-Jewish fiancé.

Patrilineal Descent: The Background

CCAR's attempt to find an approach to work with the increasing reality of mixed marriage brought into focus another, equally pressing issue, patrilineal descent. In traditional Jewish law, *Halakhah* is unambiguous on the issue of who is a Jew: to be Jewish is to be born of a Jewish mother. Nothing else is required. As the number of interfaith marriages increased, the problem of the Jewishness of the offspring of a non-Jewish mother in a mixed marriage became a major obstacle for Reform Judaism. The offspring of these marriages were at risk of being raised as gentiles. Deeply committed to outreach, Reform Judaism had been working hard not to alienate Jews in mixed marriages. The CCAR discovered that the issues of mixed marriage and patrilineal descent could not be separated (Lipman, E. J., 1990, p. 47).

The issue had been swirling around the CCAR for years and was related directly to the 1947 resolution on mixed marriage, which stated categorically that the child of a non-Jewish mother is not a Jew. Despite the categorical nature of the resolution, many rabbis ignored it. They considered the promise of the parents that the offspring of such marriages would be Jewish an acceptable substitute for formal conversion. They also accepted as Jews older children of mixed marriages, as long as the children attended religious school and were confirmed. Although this position had been adopted for the 1961 *Rabbi's Manual*, it still was not recognized as official policy.[256]

The issue continued to fester. As the number of rabbis who were performing interfaith marriages increased, they sought an official ruling from the CCAR that validated their practice. By 1979, the issue came to a head at the UAHC Biennial Convention in Toronto. The UAHC's president, Rabbi Alexander Schindler, made headlines in both the Jewish and mainstream press by proposing that Reform Judaism should accept the child of an intermarried couple as Jewish whether the mother was Jewish or not. "The issue," he argued, "had reached a point of crisis" and the Reform movement needed to address it (CCAR, 1982).

Schaalman Appointed Chair of the Committee on Patrilineal Descent

Schindler had laid down the challenge, and the CCAR could no longer avoid the issue: the CCAR had to decide whether it was willing to accept as Jewish children who did not have a Jewish mother. In 1979, it established a new and controversial Blue Ribbon Committee on Patrilineal Descent, charging the committee with the task of studying the issue of the growing number of children who were born into marriages where the mother was not Jewish. Although he was only one year away from becoming president, Schaalman was asked to serve as its committee chair, the CCAR executive apparently assuming the committee's deliberations would be completed by that time.

The problem of patrilineal descent, however, proved to be as contentious as mixed marriage had been, with the result that the committee's deliberations lingered on during Schaalman's presidency. In 1981, as both the chair of one of CCAR's most important committees and its president, Schaalman was poised to play a critical role in the modern history of Reform Judaism.

Schaalman's committee recommended and the CCAR approved a new policy to achieve equity between men and women. In a radical departure from tradition, the organization overturned Jewish law and traditional practice by affirming that if certain conditions were met (namely that the parents promised to raise their children as Jews), the offspring of a mixed marriage in which only one partner was Jewish, *either* the father or the mother, would be Jewish. The process required that the children attend religious school, become Bar or Bat Mitzvah, and be confirmed.

Like its decision on mixed marriage, this decision deeply offended Conservative and Orthodox Judaism, especially the Orthodox rabbinate in Israel. Another source of opposition came from the World Union of Progressive Judaism headquartered in Jerusalem. Rabbi Richard G. Hirsch (2010), its president during those years, told this interviewer that he was disappointed in Schaalman: "I thought he had caved in on the issue. How could a guy so strongly opposed to officiating at an interfaith marriage support such a position on patrilineality?" The decision created enormous problems for progressive Judaism worldwide where it was fighting to achieve legitimacy. Unlike mixed marriage, this issue was more intractable. According to Folb (2007), "[Patrilineal Descent] was a different kind of issue than mixed marriage. With mixed marriage, there were grey areas where remedies were possible. ... The CCAR position on patrilineality 'created an irreversible condition'" (p. 78).[257] Hirsch (2010) claims, "Everybody in the World movement was opposed to it."

Presented at the 1981 CCAR annual meeting in Pittsburgh, the resolution was hotly debated. After many hours of deliberation, the original motion was amended and sent back to committee. The CCAR had to wait another two years before it could hear the committee's revised resolution.

The 1981 Conference proved to be a test of Schaalman's ability to lead Reform Judaism in dealing with this contentious issue and to manage a passionately divided Conference. Afterwards, Glaser (1982) wrote to tell him of his "unbounded admiration for the manner in which you presided over the convention. ... Although I had seen some masters at work under very difficult conditions, I had never seen anyone do as good a job." The success of the conference, he wrote, was the result of Schaalman's "forcefulness, fairness, diplomacy and grace," qualities that made him "a real and rare leader," a view that "seems to have been held virtually universally throughout the Conference."

At the next convention in 1983, the CCAR approved the Committee on Patrilineal Descent's revised resolution:

> ... the child of one Jewish parent is under the presumption of Jewish descent. This presumption of the Jewish status of the offspring of any mixed marriage is to be established through appropriate and timely public and formal acts of identification with the Jewish faith and people. The performance of these mitzvot serves to commit those who participate in them, both parent and child, to Jewish life. ...
>
> Depending on circumstances, mitzvot leading toward a positive and exclusive Jewish identity will include entry into the covenant, acquisition of a Hebrew name, Torah study, Bar/Bat Mitzvah, and Kabbalat Torah (Confirmation). For those beyond childhood claiming Jewish identity, other public acts or declarations may be added or substituted after consultation with their rabbi. (CCAR, 1983, pp. 159–160).[258]

Managing the convention was Schaalman's last official act as CCAR president. The issues relating to the status of children of mixed marriages, however, continued to surface. The CCAR's new president, Rabbi W. Gunther Plaut, reconstituted the Committee on Patrilineal Descent and reappointed Schaalman, his long-time friend, as its chair.

Because Schaalman was no longer the CCAR president, conflict of interest was no longer an issue.[259]

As committee chair, his leadership ability was sorely tested when a previously unidentified issue came before it. The Union of American Hebrew Congregations brought pressure on the committee to affirm the Jewish identity of the Soviet Jews it was resettling in America. The critical problem for the committee was how to establish whether the immigrants were Jews. It was complicated because many of the refugees were Jews in name only, or claimed to be Jews but had no evidence to prove it. Some were offspring of mixed marriages in which the mother was not Jewish. Others had Jewish ancestors, though they, themselves, were not practicing Jews. Schaalman remembers that the discussions of the issue were long and contentious.

To make matters worse, Schindler, UAHC's president, put Schaalman under enormous pressure. As the Union's president, Schindler was responsible to powerful lay people who had worked tirelessly for two decades to free Soviet Jewry. No doubt, Schaalman and the committee members felt the urgency of the situation. The question before them was not *whether* to accept this massive infusion of people into the Jewish fold, but *how*. Eventually, the committee granted the Union's wishes and ruled that immigrants who had a Jewish parent were Jews (Folb, 2007, p. 71).

Ongoing Unresolved Issues

Despite the CCAR's efforts to deal with the twin issues of mixed marriage and patrilineal descent, they did not go away. Not all Reform rabbis were pleased with the decisions. A minority opposed them, and some of them were working to have the decisions rescinded. The issues were most acute in Israel, where Reform rabbis, already struggling for acceptance by the Orthodox rabbinate, opposed the change. Their fear that it would further alienate the Orthodox was well founded, but the CCAR would not back down.[260]

By 1991, the problem of interfaith had reached critical proportions: more than a third of Jews had intermarried, more often Jewish men than women. As a result, an estimated 220,000 children in the United States were born to non-Jewish women married to Jewish men (Telushkin,

1991). From 1985 to 1995, intermarried couples made up a third of the members of Reform congregations and, by 1998, their numbers had increased to thirty-six percent. Perhaps more problematic was the report that forty percent of Reform congregants ages eighteen to twenty-four "would support interfaith" (Raphael, 2000, p. 52).[261] The ongoing question for the CCAR today in 2012 continues to be the same as it was when Schaalman chaired the Mixed Marriage Committee in 1971 and the Committee on Patrilineal Descent in 1981: how to insure the future of Judaism in America.

President of the CCAR

Although Schaalman never had any intention or desire to become president of the CCAR, his friend and rabbinic colleague, Rabbi Karl Weiner predicted it. During the 1950s, when the two rabbis met to study Talmud, occasionally their conversations veered to other subjects. At one of those sessions, Weiner said, "Herman, someday you will be president of CCAR." "You must be crazy," Schaalman responded, asking "what have you been drinking?" Weiner did not live to see his prophecy fulfilled.

In 1979, the CCAR appointed Schaalman chair of its Nominating Committee, the largest and most important of its committees. It nominated not only officers and members of the board, members of joint commissions, and liaisons to other organizations, but also its presidents and vice presidents. In his first meeting as chair, Schaalman asked the seventeen members to nominate candidates for these positions. When it was time to nominate candidates for vice president, his was one of the twenty-five whose names were proposed. In order to whittle down the list, on the second round he called for a secret ballot. His name still appeared on this pared down list of thirteen. At this point, uncomfortable with the possibility of a conflict of interest, he called for the election of a vice chairman who could preside. He left the meeting and went to await the results in another room. When the phone rang, Rabbi Joe Glaser told him that he had been nominated by unanimous consent as the organization's new vice president. Schaalman knew that this position led automatically to president.[262]

Although he was excited and pleased, Schaalman did not share this information with his wife until he returned to Chicago. When she met him at the airport, he told her, "Just incidentally, you are walking with the next vice president of the Central Conference of American Rabbis … I hope you don't mind." Lotte, surprised by the news, was thrilled.

Two years later, Schaalman, who was sixty-five and only five years from retirement, was installed as president of the CCAR. It was the highest honor that his colleagues could bestow upon another member. For Schaalman, it was "the single most coveted honor that has come to me," and he and Lotte were overwhelmed. His election had occurred exactly forty years after his ordination. It was the capstone of his career.[263] In accepting this new role, Schaalman was following in the footsteps of his immediate predecessor at Emanuel, Rabbi Felix Levy, who had been president of the CCAR in the 1930s and his great uncle, Max Samfield. The fact that two of Emanuel's senior rabbis became presidents of the CCAR is a testament not only to its distinction but also to its impact in shaping the direction of Reform Judaism. The fact that two members of the Schaalman family had been elected to the most prestigious position in Reform Judaism is even more remarkable.

According to the CCAR Executive Director, Rabbi Joseph Glaser, Schaalman's selection was attributable to his colleagues' respect for him as "a man of great intellect," a scholar, and a rabbi with "unshakable integrity." He was a man who could be counted on to stand up for his beliefs and who would not shrink from controversy. It was these qualities that landed him the appointments to chair the Committees on Mixed Marriages and Patrilineal Descent, "two of the toughest, backbreaking jobs ever faced by a conference committee," commented Glaser, which Schaalman performed with great "discernment and sensitivity" (Emanuel Congregation, 1986).

His work on these committees led inevitably to his selection as vice president, which carried the responsibility to plan the next annual meeting in 1981 in Jerusalem.[264] According to Glaser, the 1981 Annual Meeting "was one of the two best conventions within anyone's memory." Having demonstrated his integrity and proved that he was capable of effectively managing such a difficult project, Schaalman was ripe for the presidency.

Schaalman's election was a development that he had not envisioned; as he has said many times, "Things happened to me that I could never have predicted nor expected." Because he knew the position would make great demands on his time, he needed to be sure that Lotte would accept this intrusion into their marriage, and she did not hesitate in giving him permission. She had always supported him and was pleased and proud to see him advance his career.

Since his days as a rabbinic student, Schaalman believed that Reform Judaism had neglected theology and spiritual experience. Now, his new position as the CCAR president gave him the opportunity to speak to this issue from a bully pulpit. The time appeared to be ripe for such a discussion. The Reform movement's evolution toward more traditional observance had been going on at least since its 1937 Pittsburgh Platform. The desire for reform was bubbling up from younger rabbis and from congregations around the country (Plaut, 1981, p. 212). In response to this need, the CCAR issued two major publications—*A Shabbat Manual* (1972) and *The Gates of Mitzvah* (1979). When more classically oriented Reform rabbis criticized this new emphasis as a move toward orthodoxy, their criticism "unleashed a counter-movement within the Conference" by progressive rabbis (p. 212). By 1980, according to Rabbi Samuel E. Karff (1990), a number of influential Reform rabbis had prevailed on the CCAR to sponsor a series of workshops to explore issues of spirituality (p. 72). Before he was installed as the CCAR president, Schaalman attended several of them.

Schaalman, however, did not plunge into this issue in his inaugural speech during his installation in 1981. Instead, he focused on his debts to those who had helped him achieve this remarkable position. He spoke affectionately of Lotte and her support over the last forty years that gave him the sense that he was never alone in anything he had done or thought, "Whether in sorrow or joy, pain or exaltation." In a loving tribute, he quoted Proverbs 31:29: "Many daughters have done valiantly; thou excellest them all" (p. 165).[266]

Next, he credited his father as "the single greatest influence in my growing and adult years with whom he had kept up a "silent dialogue" that helped shape his thoughts. Both his parents provided a loving and supportive environment, which allowed him to grow into the person he had become. He spoke also of his sense of the "great miracle and mystery of [his] life," having been spared from "among the dozens who were equally prepared, equally worthy (perhaps more so), who were then at the *Lehranstalt* or who then lived in that society of which I was a part."

The wonder of it all made him conscious of the great debt he owed not only to HUC-JIR for the scholarship that allowed him to come to America, but also for his life. He was impelled by this gift to justify his existence by using his talents and abilities to give back to society something of what it had given him. In his new role as CCAR president, he saw both a vindication of the fact that he had been saved and an opportunity "to prove to myself and to the God Whom I seek to serve that it *might have been* [italics added] worthwhile to rescue this brand from the conflagration."[267]

About the same time as he was being installed at the CCAR's new president, Schaalman met his future son-in-law, Rabbi Ira Youdovin, who had come to Chicago to recruit new members for the Association of Reform Zionists of America (ARZA).[268] Prior to coming to Chicago, Youdovin had made inquiries in the city's rabbinic community about whom he should talk to about his organization. After receiving the unanimous recommendation from Schaalman's colleagues that he was the rabbi who had "the greatest influence with his local colleagues," Youdovin decided to meet with him (Youdovin, I., 1986, p. 251). As a Reform rabbi, Youdovin was well aware of the significance of meeting with the most powerful and influential rabbi in the Reform movement. Schaalman had been elected president of the CCAR and was about to become the next president of the Chicago Board of Rabbis.[269]

Their first meeting did not go well. Schaalman was leery about joining ARZA. "Reform Judaism," he told Youdovin (1986), "was already in serious conflict with Israel's Orthodox establishment and did not need to get further involved with thorny political issues" (p. 251). As the new president of CCAR, he thought the movement's greatest need was to address the profound theological questions at the heart of the movement's relationship to Israel. Despite his reservations about ARZA's political emphasis, however, Schaalman convened what Youdovin described as "a very successful meeting" of Chicago area rabbis (p. 251).

In the events which followed this initial meeting, Rabbi Youdovin and Susan Schaalman became acquainted, fell in love, and married.[270] The Schaalmans in America were now a two-Reform-rabbi family. Schaalman's brother, Freddie, having made *aliyah* to Israel, had also produced a rabbi, who, like his father, was strictly Orthodox, which meant that the American and Israeli Schaalmans were as far removed theologically and ritually as two Jewish families can get.

Issues Facing the New President

In 1982, a few weeks before the next CCAR convention in 1982, Schaalman, as a leader of international Reform Judaism, found himself in the delicate and difficult position of having to take a moral and political position on the war that had broken out on June 6 between Israel and the PLO. As the militant wing of the stateless Palestinians, the PLO had taken over Lebanon where, for the last several years, it had launched attacks on Israel. After sustaining many casualties and much damage, Israel invaded Lebanon and fought a brutal and bloody war that took a heavy toll of Israeli soldiers, PLO fighters, and Lebanese civilians. By August, after nearly three months of fighting and massive destruction of Lebanon's urban centers, the war had become a moral issue for Jews in America and Israel and for Schaalman in particular. In search of an understanding of the Israeli mind on the issue, in August, Schaalman traveled to both Israel and Lebanon.

In the September 1982 issue of the *CCAR Newsletter*, Schaalman wrote that the war challenged everything he believed about the Jewish community. He questioned whether Israel's ancient mission to promote peace and justice had given way to "the harsh reality of hostility and the imperative need to answer brute force with force." He was profoundly disturbed by the need to reconcile the reality of this war with the need to ensure the survival of the Jewish state. It raised for him the question of whether it is possible for Jews to have a state of their own and, at the same time, uphold the vision of a just and peaceful society. Israelis, he discovered were as conflicted as he was, "asking the same questions and finding no immediate answers." The war had raised the central issue of what it means for a people to have political power and how they could hold onto it. He concluded that it was premature to pronounce judgment on Israel, a state barely out of its infancy, and its use of its new power to ensure its security. The issue, however, continues to trouble him (cf. Chapter 11, "Schaalman on Modern Israel").

For his second presidential address in July 1982, Schaalman used the occasion to lay out his own theological positions and to urge his colleagues to make theology the center of the organization's concerns, an issue that had been neglected over the course of his forty-one years in the rabbinate.[271] He identified three planks vital to the health and

well-being of Reform Judaism that were the foundation of his own beliefs: Torah, God, and Israel, which he considered "cornerstones of Judaism and Reform Judaism" and "markers" that his colleagues could use
to evaluate themselves and their direction. He was critical of the idea
held by some rabbis that Jewishness is based on "radical personal freedom" rather than on the collective nature of Judaism (*klal Yisrael*). The
CCAR's 1937 Columbus Platform had reestablished "our link to the totality of Israel" and delegitimized attempts by other branches of Judaism
to declare themselves the only "authentic Judaism."[272] Rabbis committed
to "radical freedom" as the touchstone of their beliefs denied the oneness
of the Jewish people and jeopardized "those bonds [sic] which it took
decades and generations to reshape."

Perhaps reacting to his own former youthful acceptance of the
arguments of Mordecai Kaplan, Schaalman offered his most scathing
criticism for rabbis who define Judaism merely in terms of ethnic characteristics—folk songs, lore, and mores. Such thinking constituted "a
remnant of ghetto mentality or a rejection of the true covenantal and
corporate nature of Jewishness. "The Jewish people," he declared passionately, "are not like all others. … We have not persisted from a tear-
and blood-stained past to be reduced now to a mere folk." The Jewish
people have a special role in the world as God's "covenant people." No
other way of thinking about Jewishness is "legitimate" or "worthy" of
our past or of our future. The Torah represents a *ketubah*, a solemn "marriage" between the *Yisrael* and God. The revelation on Sinai and the gift
of the Torah, he asserted, is the "bedrock" of traditional Jewish experience and the foundation of Jewish life.[273]

At the same time, Schaalman warned against the idea that the Torah
is a human document, subject to criticism for its many scribal errors,
duplications, contradictions, and disjointedness of time sequences and
settings. If Torah were written by humans, he contended, it lacks guidelines for its use as the "matrix of Jewish life" and is open to the judgment
of any reader and interpreter.[274] At best, such a view makes the Torah
"questionably fictive, at worst a fossilized relic unworthy of the enlight-
ened … ." Torah needs to be seen and understood as the word of God:
"God is in the Torah for us to find, to hear, to search and probe for …
to understand and *to obey* [italics added].[275]

After addressing the effects of modern life on belief, he brought up
the subject of the *Shoah* and its impact on Judaism. As the most traumatic

event in modern Jewish life, it had "upended certainties about God" and the destiny of the Jews. The *Shoah* raised the question how God could have allowed it. Taking advantage of the opportunity to share his own thinking on the subject, Schaalman told his colleagues that the reason God did not prevent it was because He lacked the power to do that. The *Shoah*, he maintained, challenges the idea that God is omnipotent and suggests, instead, that God has a "weakness ... a failure, a defect" and is not self-sufficient. Because God is not omnipotent, He could not save His people.[276]

This explanation for Schaalman was the only way to resolve the struggle to understand the tragedy. Accepting such a view, Schaalman acknowledged, requires "a revolutionary shift, a radical realignment of the understanding of human-divine relationships [that] will take generations to understand and to work through." (This idea of a vulnerable and limited God Who needs our help became one of the central ideas in Schaalman's theological development.)

In his last presidential address at the 1983 CCAR annual convention, Schaalman spoke about his concerns with Israel. He acknowledged that the creation of the State of Israel represented a major achievement for the Jewish people, but it brought with it policies and actions on the part of its government that deeply troubled him. Dominated by the Israeli Orthodox establishment, the government was considering actions against Reform Judaism and its rabbis. (He must have understood that the recent actions on the part of the CCAR in its radical decision on patrilineal descent was a major factor in this development.) He also shared his deepening skepticism that the establishment of the State of Israel might not be positive in the long-term. At the same time, he did not want to be misunderstood as failing to recognize that the achievement of statehood was anything less than a "historic achievement and marvelous source of strength for contemporary Jewish life."

Schaalman's view of Jewish biblical history is that statehood had been a disaster for the Jews. Idolatry was the rule rather than the exception; its priestly and royal politics were corrupt and, as a political entity, it attracted the jealousy of its neighbors with whom it engaged in numerous wars, usually ending in its defeat. He cautioned that statehood should not be allowed to confer a sense of exclusivity "in forming the condition in which the Jewish people exists today" nor its long-term survival. Perhaps responding to the Israeli Orthodox establishment's rejection of the validity of Diaspora Jewish life, he asserted that other modes of "rightful, authentic Jewish living" exist in addition to that created by statehood. The Orthodox were arguing that because Jews once again had a homeland, it was incumbent on them to return, as they had been vowing to do at every Passover Seder for the last 1,500 years. Authentic Jewish life, they maintained, was impossible outside of Israel. This denial of the exilic existence, according to Schaalman, may once have been valid "in Zionism's ideology ... [but] is unwarranted and even useless today. Most Jews do not consider themselves exiles, and the attempt to deny the value of their Jewish existence is a historic blunder and untruth." Jewish survival depends not only on Israel but also on the survival of the Jewish people worldwide.

In his concluding remarks, Schaalman called attention to what he saw as "careerism" in the rabbinate. He offered his own view that to be a rabbi means to respond to a "call," to be a "vessel of the sacred, a doer of mitzvot, a container of the holy, a living incarnation of Torah, and a guide to the priceless treasures of our tradition. And then God's *kedusha* and *kavod* (holiness and glory)—entrusted to us, dependent on us, flowing through people and rabbi—will be present and we will restore and heal our world" (p. 8–9).[277] Having concluded his speech, Schaalman handed over the reins of the presidency to his friend W. Gunther Plaut.

During his two years as president, Schaalman's role was to represent the Reform rabbinate worldwide. In this capacity, he attended many conferences and board meetings and traveled widely as one of the foremost representative of Reform Judaism. He also represented Reform Judaism on the political stage. When Ronald Reagan called a select group of American rabbis to the White House, Schaalman was invited as the representative of the CCAR.

Before the meeting with Reagan took place, a small group of the rabbis met with the recently appointed Secretary of State George Schultz. Schaalman reports that he was "moved" by the meeting. Schultz told the rabbis that in his position as professor at the University of Chicago the most outstanding student he had ever had was an Israeli with whom he had become very close. With tears in his eyes, he told them that when the student returned to Israel, he was killed in an attack by Palestinians. Schaalman explained that after this display of emotion, the secretary could say nothing wrong.

Next, the rabbis went into the cabinet room to await the arrival of President Reagan. Vice President George H. W. Bush spoke with them while they were waiting, but the minute President Reagan entered the room, he stopped speaking. Reagan went around the room greeting his guests and handing out his famed jellybeans. When he presented his formal remarks, he surprised the rabbis by telling them, "Before I say anything else, as commander and chief of the United States Army, I want to tell you that the Israeli air force is the best in the world."

Schaalman's presidency of the CCAR required a lot of time away from his full-time job as Emanuel's rabbi. The Reform rabbinate is spread out all over America, as well as in the Caribbean, Canada, Europe, and Israel, and, from time to time, he would be invited to speak at synagogues in these countries. His competent assistants were there to fill in for him, and, what the congregation lost in having Schaalman's full attention, it made up in national and international prestige.

Ethics Committee, the CCAR

Schaalman had one more official duty as a member of the CCAR. In the early 1980s, the CCAR recognized that it needed to tighten its ethical standards and the sanctions that it might impose. In March of 1983, it reconstituted the Ethics Committee and appointed some of its most prestigious rabbis to serve on it with Schaalman as chair.[278] Established in 1920, the committee addressed a variety of issues, including, but not limited to, allegations by rabbis against colleagues of "commercialism, occupying other rabbis' pulpits, or officiating without consultation at life-cycle events for those belonging to colleagues' congregations" (Stevens, E., 1990, p. 31). The more difficult cases were brought by lay members of congregations against their rabbis. The most difficult were cases alleging moral or sexual transgressions. Because the CCAR's rabbinic code was vague on these issues, the committee was handicapped by the lack of guidelines or principles with which to resolve these cases.

The twin issues of rabbinic officiation at interfaith marriages and patrilineal descent had caused wide chasms in the CCAR. At least one of its administrative regions and some of its members wanted the Ethics Committee to discipline members who officiated at interfaith ceremonies. Schaalman claims that, because of his intervention, such radical consequences did not occur. A key issue for the committee was the extent to which its findings would play a role in the future of those colleagues whose cases it reviewed. Such matters, Schaalman explains, were of the "utmost delicacy" especially when they dealt with sexual harassment, impropriety, unethical, or illegal behavior. After reviewing the codes and ethics of other religious and professional organizations, under Schaalman's leadership, the committee proposed revisions to the CCAR's Code of Ethics that would be acted on at the CCAR's 1991 Conference (p. 33).

In 1991, at the end of Schaalman's eight-year tenure, Glaser (1991) wrote to thank him for taking on what was "by far the worst job of the Conference" (July 3, 1991). He also complimented Schaalman for his patience, statesmanship, and humanitarianism in handling "some of the most difficult cases" he knew and for shepherding through to adoption the committee's new Ethics Code.

After reaching the heights as the most distinguished and important leader in Reform Judaism, even though he was an ex-officio member of the CCAR's Executive Board, his role in organized Jewish life diminished rapidly. The CCAR had no role—ceremonial, policy-making or advisory—for its past presidents. Retired rabbis were as good as having been put out to pasture, and he felt increasingly marginalized.[279] He confided to Folb (2007) that the CCAR made a mistake in not drawing on the experience of the past presidents and keeping them meaningfully involved in the organization.[280] Like so many of the rest of his retired colleagues, he directed his prodigious energy to other local, national, and international organizations where he continued to make significant contributions. There was no lack of meaningful work. (More of this in Chapter 12, "Winding Down: Reaching Ninety and Beyond.")

Rabbi Emeritus: Retirement, 1986

Despite excellent health and undiminished energy, at the age of seventy Schaalman retired from Emanuel in 1986. This decision arose from his fatigue from the continuous strain of weekly sermons, the attention to the sick, the responsibility for fundraising, and the need to attend committee and board meetings. He also recognized that he had become something of an anachronism. The modern rabbi, he observed, had to adjust to the changing demographics of congregations. In the 1980s, there was a new dynamic, the single-family household, maintained by significant numbers of divorcees and even widows with one or more children, or no child at all. Congregations were no longer populated with merchants and industrialists but mostly by better-educated professionals. This new class of congregants, although financially stable, lacked the kind of political and economic influence of their predecessors and could not support a congregation with large donations.

Technology was another of the changes affecting rabbis. At the time Schaalman retired, Emanuel had just purchased a new computer. "Not then, and not now," he insists, was he "willing or able to accept the computer as anything more than a convenience for billing and membership listing." Computers are "for strictly scientific work, and I immediately understand it and accept it." He was resentful every time he received a bill produced by a computer. He wanted to receive a bill that somebody wrote out or typed. Such a wish reflected an earlier time when there might have been a more personal relationship between the bill collector and the bill payer. For Schaalman, such a relationship means "that somebody thought about it," someone had an image of him as "somebody to whom they sent bills before." In this respect, Schaalman is an anachronism. He is proud of the fact that he has resisted every effort to bring him into the technological world of the twenty-first century, thinks of himself as a "pre-modern," and doesn't want to change. He writes by hand and lets someone else enter it on the computer. When he was asked for copies of his 2011 address to the National Association of Retired Reform Rabbis, he turned to a longtime friend and member of Emanuel Congregation, Phyllis Goldblatt, to transcribe a handwritten copy he prepared in response to the request. For these and other reasons, Schaalman is glad that he retired. As a classically trained rabbi, he found himself out of step with these new congregational needs.

When Schaalman was ready to retire, he became aware that the retirement provisions of his various contracts were not adequate for a comfortable retirement.[281] Concerned about the inadequacy of the retirement funds, one of Schaalman's friends, Stanley Owens, who was president of the board, took the issue to the board, an act which Schaalman himself would never have done. Owens convinced the board to set up a separate retirement fund to supplement Schaalman's retirement income. As Schaalman observed, "The congregation was made up of so many of Chicago's wealthy Jewish citizens and could well afford the extra retirement funds."

Schaalman also had a supplemental retirement fund that the congregation had set up but without giving him any legal right to it. His close friend, Bill Schindler, advised him to withdraw the funds from the account. His concern was that, if the temple found itself in financial difficulty, it could renege on giving him money. Schaalman decided to follow his advice, withdrew all the $300,000 as a lump sum, and gave it to his son, Michael, to invest. "The withdrawal cost me dearly," Schaalman emphasizes, "38% of the funds had to be paid in taxes and penalties." By 2007, however the portfolio had grown considerably. "It exceeds any hope I might have had for my future need. I don't need the funds for living expenses, and I expect that my children and grandchildren will be the beneficiaries." These funds, supplemented by a "consulting fee" from Emanuel, salary from his teaching assignments, honoraria from various scholar-in-residence events, speaking engagements, and Social Security allow the Schaalmans a comfortable retirement income. At the time, however, he had no idea that, a few years later in 2011, he and Lotte would develop serious illnesses that would wreck his sense of financial well-being and result in severe financial strain.

Before he retired, Schaalman had one more challenge from his past. In 1986, Emanuel's board decided not to renew Cantor Handwerger's contract. Handwerger responded by suing Schaalman and four of Emanuel's board members. He alleged that Schaalman had unduly influenced the board to exercise a contract option not to renew his contract when he turned sixty-five. Apparently, the cantor had made enemies of some members of Emanuel's board, who complained about the cantor's abilities (p. 49). Other congregants thought that he was being overpaid for the amount of time he spent with the congregation. Typically, he would spend an hour or two a day when he came to work. During his last seven or eight years, his attendance was even more infrequent. Apparently, there was resentment that, although the cantor was competent to lead the congregation in song, he did nothing else besides prepare students for their B'nai Mitzvot.[282]

Some members of the board wanted Handwerger to retire because they thought he was not able to develop a good rapport with the children. Nevertheless, Schaalman claims that he came to Handwerger's defense whenever his tenure was being questioned. He argued that such a gifted person should not be tied to the clock or measured by the amount of minutes or hours that were spent in any given week in the congregation. Although Schaalman claims to have defended Handwerger, he was concerned that if the board hired an assistant rabbi, Handwerger would "trample" the assistant (Star, E., January 27, 1998, p. 13). Folb (2007) reports that "both the Circuit and Federal Courts refused to hear the case and the cantor retired without the honors which had been planned for him" (p. 49).

When Handwerger retired in 1986, the congregation was able to transition from one cantor to another before a new rabbi was hired. This situation eliminated a problem for Schaalman's successor and for the congregation. In Schaalman's terms, the congregation would have been faced with the difficulty of adapting to two new congregational leaders (Star, E., January 27, 1988, p. 14). Schaalman speculates that Handwerger's suit was motivated by a lingering resentment among Levy family members against him. (One of Handwerger's grandchildren had married into the Levy family.)

Year of Tribute

Emanuel Congregation did not intend to let its rabbi go quietly. It designated his last year a "Year of Tribute" to honor Schaalman for his thirty years of service. The final "Tribute Weekend" was set aside as a special Shabbat service dedicated to the rabbi and his wife. The event was also a celebration of Schaalman's seventieth birthday and of the Schaalmans' forty-five years of marriage. Held on May 30–31, 1986, it commemorated the end of an era and the beginning of a new one. Not only was the Tribute Weekend a celebration for the Schaalmans, it was also the transition to his successor, Rabbi Joseph Edelheit, Schaalman's former assistant. Most of the congregation turned out for this memorable event, along with many dignitaries, colleagues, family, and friends.

The service began with a special ceremony known as Passing the Torah, symbolic of the passing of the Jewish tradition and heritage from one generation to another. This scroll had special meaning because it had been rescued from the Nazis who had taken it from a synagogue in Czechoslovakia. Eleven rabbis on the bimah, whom Edelheit described as Schaalman's "disciples," passed the scroll one to another before finally handing it off to Schaalman.[283] Edelheit explained that they had decided to give the scroll to Schaalman, in part, to acknowledge his work in founding and shepherding Olin Sang Ruby Union Institute:

> How do rabbis thank a rabbi? The *Pirkei Avot* tells us that the tradition has been passed down from Sinai by Moses even until today. One of the final praises in the *Pirkei Avot* is the instruction that "you should raise up many disciples."[284] We, his students, have decided to return some of the Torah given to us by our rabbi with a Torah. (Emanuel, 1986)

Edelheit explained that the gift was also meant as a "fitting response" to Schaalman's statement that he was "a brand plucked from the fire," that he incorporated in his acceptance speech as president of the CCAR. "This Torah," Edelheit continued, "could be seen as a 'brand plucked out of the fire'" (Emanuel Congregation, 1986).

Rabbi Joseph B. Glaser, Schaalman's long-time friend and the Executive Vice President of the CCAR, was the keynote speaker at the event. The two rabbis had worked together for the last fifteen years, during which they had developed a close bond and mutual respect. To set Schaalman's accomplishments in a larger context, Glaser noted that Schaalman was the first refugee from the Nazis to hold the position of CCAR president and that his election was a "grim and ironic triumph." "Having been *plucked from the heart of the fire* [italics added] that consumed six million of our people, he became a fist which we shook in the face of the monster and murders and the cowards who blindly followed" (Emanuel Congregation, 1986). Glaser explained that Schaalman's life had been "a vindication of your escape and of … your martyred classmates. You bore with you all of their rich promise, their potential, and you were not found wanting" (Emanuel Congregation, 1986). His life's work as a rabbi had been "a towering example of service to the Jewish people and humanity" (Emanuel Congregation, 1986). Glaser also credited Schaalman for his statesmanship that helped steer the CCAR "through the turbulent waters of American and Jewish life, leaving in our wake improvements, elevation, certitude. His orderly mind and commitment to principle were our keel when others were rendered incoherent or irresponsible by rage or fear or excitement" (Emanuel Congregation, 1986).

Schaalman, Glaser pointed out, had one more role to play in the CCAR. "Seeing in him his competence as a scholar, his uncompromising standards for the rabbinate and his unshakeable integrity," his colleagues elected him chair of the CCAR's Ethics Committee. They knew he was a stickler for proper behavior and trusted him in the role of judge, jury, and executioner, knowing that "with one stroke of the pen he could end a career" (Emanuel Congregation, 1986). They also knew that Schaalman "had a boundless capacity to love and to nurture and to understand" and that, therefore, they could trust him to carry out his duties justly and compassionately" (Emanuel Congregation, 1986).

Glaser also complimented Schaalman for his compassion and willingness to help congregants deal with their personal problems and sorrows. These characteristics had been an inspiration to his congregation and to him as well: "I don't have a *simcha* that is not rejoiced in by Herman and Lotte Schaalman. I don't have a trouble that he finds out about that he doesn't somehow alleviate in no other way but through sympathy and support" (Emanuel Congregation, 1986).

In summing up Schaalman's achievements, Glaser referred to the words of Rabbi Leo Baeck, Germany's foremost twentieth century rabbi. In addressing a 1920s ordination class in Berlin, Baeck said to them, "'the message is not in the sermon, but in the man. The rabbi does not deliver a sermon, the rabbi delivers himself.' If I were to sum up in 30 seconds, I would say that Herman Schaalman delivered Herman Schaalman and no congregation or Jewish agency could ask for anything more than the delivery of this man" (Emanuel Congregation, 1986).[285]

As Rabbi Glaser returned to his seat on the bimah, Schaalman came forward and spoke with his typical humility: "It is a good thing this is the last such service because no matter how resilient one is, when one receives such words of judgment, such evaluation, it's virtually too much. So I know of nothing better to do, in fact it's the best thing to do, not just to thank my dear, dear friend Joe for coming here, but to do what he claims I have done" (Emanuel Congregation, 1986). With that, he conducted the concluding service.

During the month before the celebration, Schaalman received congratulatory letters from many of his colleagues, who reflected on his contribution to the Reform rabbinate. Rabbi Sylvan D. Schwartzman (1986), an old schoolmate and friend from his days at HUC, wrote, "The '41 Class are genuinely proud of you and your achievements, and by your outstanding service to your congregation and the entire Reform Movement, you have honored us all." Rabbi Hayim Goren Perelmuter (1986) noted, "When we came to Chicago thirty years ago, you were spanking new in your pulpit north and I tackled the south. In those years you have made a monumental contribution which I am sure will be adequately remembered and extolled." Rabbi Hillel Gamoran (1986) offered a similar assessment: "You are truly one of the greats within our rabbinic community. Not only are you one of our intellectuals guiding us ... but also you are one who unstintingly gives himself toward our common causes."

Accomplishments

When he retired, Schaalman could look back in pride on his accomplishments. In 1970, a national survey of Reform synagogues conducted by the Union of Reform Judaism (URJ) had ranked Emanuel the number one congregation in the country. During his thirty years at Emanuel, Schaalman considered this recognition as one of his most important accomplishments. Another benefit for Emanuel was that its rabbi had earned national and international recognition for his leadership and intellect, and his friends and associates included some of the most influential figures of his time, political and cultural luminaries, and clergy of various religions. The most significant of his relationships with clergy was his friendship with Cardinal Joseph Bernardin, a friendship that resulted in major improvement in interfaith relations in Chicago and its surrounding communities.

Schaalman is also proud of the fact that Emanuel had grown from 600 to 940 households. In general, membership remained stable throughout most of his tenure. Natural attrition, however, required occasional membership drives. In the 1960s and '70s, when a large number of Chicago's Jewish families moved to the northern suburbs, membership did not suffer as badly as it did in many other Chicago congregations. Many of these congregents had a deep loyalty to their Rabbi and maintained their membership, and even sent their children to Sunday school many miles from their homes.[286] Schaalman believes that one reason the congregation held together was "a joyous sense of working together on an important sacred task."

Another of his accomplishments was to help the congregation stabilize its finances. Schaalman offers, "The Temple managed its money well, in fact, lived frugally. Part of that frugality meant that I was not paid well. However, because I did not enter the rabbinate to become rich like a CPA or a doctor, I was not concerned about my salary. I wanted only to live decently." During years when he knew the congregation could not afford a salary increase, he told the board that he did not expect a raise: "I never had a contract nor wanted one. I remember only one time in my 30 years asking for an increase." Thanks to his fundraising efforts, the congregation had endowment funds totaling over two million dollars.

During his tenure, Schaalman had introduced many changes in Emanuel's congregational life. One of his most important was to open congregational life to its members and to make them an integral part of its institutional life. One of the consequences of this involvement was that there was never difficulty in finding someone willing to take on the job of congregational president. Schaalman also takes pride in the fact that he never had any opposition to expanding and deepening Jewish programming and to making Emanuel a rich center for study, education, and religious life. An indication of the depth of Jewish learning offered to the congregation was the large number of adult education classes that were going on simultaneously by the time Schaalman retired. When Schaalman arrived, only one such program existed, but when he retired, he counted eight to ten.

Schaalman also introduced changes in the congregation's prayer services. Before he arrived, services were conducted with little attention to congregant participation. His aim was to give people the sense that prayer was important and to allow sufficient time for individual participation. He also introduced a cycle of Torah reading through which the congregation read the complete Torah in a seven-year cycle, a *parashah* every Sabbath. To engage the congregation more fully, he introduced a phrase-by-phrase translation. For the first time, congregants could hear the Hebrew followed almost immediately by an rendering in English. Moreover, he introduced the congregation to a Hebrew-English Bible that would enable them to follow along with the reading. Another innovation was to offer a sermon based on the Torah text. However, in the first few years, Schaalman, who knew all the melodies and enjoyed singing, ran into conflict with the cantor by singing along with him and encouraging the congregation to follow. This change gave his congregants a sense of participation in the services and a sense of fulfillment. On the other hand, it gave the cantor fits.

Another of Schaalman's contributions to Emanuel was to make the reading and study of Torah the center of congregational life. What that meant to the congregation was that everything it did had reference to Torah. Specifically, temple activities were held up to the scrutiny of the values of the Torah. Gambling, for instance, was not allowed. Nor were bingo, card games, or raffles, which so many other congregations used to raise money. The congregation also eliminated hard liquor at major ceremonial events such as weddings and B'nai Mitzvot, a practice that had existed for a long time.

When asked to put his rabbinic career in perspective, Schaalman commented that it was never easy or a smooth ride:

> Unavoidably, it was a descent into valley after valley … always a sense of incompleteness. And while this is maybe not a sense of failure, it is nonetheless. This view, however, is essential, especially in dealing with human beings. In those dealings, you never know. You think, for instance, you've helped teach something, really given your all, and then on the next occasion, when you think it could be applied, you find all of a sudden that either they didn't listen or they only half understood it, or having understood it, they still don't want to do it or whatever. A rabbi has to make one's peace with the fact that one is never done. This sense of incompleteness also has a positive side. It can be a spur to really get off the floor and do it again, and not be knocked down for the count, just rally again. But at some point, you have to call it quits and say, 'Enough!'

When he reached that point in his rabbinate, he retired.

Retirement did not mean withdrawal from his beloved congregation where he wanted to continue to play a role in its events and religious affairs. As Rabbi Emeritus, beloved by his congregation and a leader in Reform Judaism, he expected no less. He would have liked to have been included in Shabbat and holiday services, give occasional sermons, and carry on with his Monday night Current Events and his Torah Study.

"But to my chagrin, I was restricted by the unwillingness of my successors to involve me in congregational events and activities."

Although he felt he had been excluded from playing the active Rabbi Emeritus role he desired, he found plenty of opportunity to lead an active public life. "As a full-time rabbi, I had never been able to give as much of my time and energy to these pursuits as I would have liked."[287] His immense prestige in the Jewish community and involvement in national and world affairs gave him a platform that allowed him to become involved in a host of activities that he could now pursue with great vigor.

Schaalman came out of retirement on several occasions to fill in while Emanuel searched for a new rabbi. He also accepted Rabbi Marc Berkson's invitation to be on staff as scholar-in-residence at his Milwaukee Reform synagogue, Emanu-El B'ne Jeshurun. Berkson knew that Schaalman's participation would enhance his congregation's religious experience. Berkson (2007) also wanted his congregation to have the experience of a "beloved" senior rabbi or rabbi emeritus. "I was too young to be that rabbi, but Schaalman," he confided, "was perfect. In a very short time, the congregation came to love him." Schaalman also brought a sense of decorum, which the older members of the congregation appreciated. "Moreover," remarked Berkson (2007), "the power of his sermons helped draw members to Shabbat services. When he served as scholar-in-residence for a weekend program, the sessions tended to be filled. Even those who rarely came to services came to hear Schaalman."

Schaalman accepted this role not only because of his fondness for Berkson, but because it gave him and Lotte the opportunity to make regular visits to their son Michael and his granddaughters. "Still," he comments, "Had my family not lived in Milwaukee, I would have accepted the offer because it gave me a chance to do what I love most, to educate." Another benefit of accepting the position was that once Rabbi Zedek became Emanuel's rabbi in 2004, Schaalman comments, "Sharing the pulpit with Marc gave me the opportunity to try out sermons that I would subsequently deliver at Emanuel on Yom Kippur." Schaalman gave his sermon in Milwaukee on the first day of Rosh Hashanah and ten days later on Yom Kippur repeated it at Emanuel.

Beginning in 1999, Schaalman presented monthly guest sermon and study sessions at Emanu-El B'ne Jeshurun. In the last few years, however, due to declining health, he had to curtail his participation.

In 2011, because he was recovering from a stroke, Schaalman was not able to participate in the temple's High Holy Day services. Nevertheless, as of March 2012 Schaalman remains on the congregation's website as "scholar-in-residence" (Emanu-El B'ne Jeshurun, 2012).

Emanuel Post Schaalman

The year before Schaalman's retirement, the temple board hired Schaalman's former assistant, Rabbi Edelheit, to replace him. He was one of the three Schaalman assistants—Edelheit, Friedman and Weinberg—who actively pursued the job (Folb, 2007, p. 53). At first, the friendship and collegial relationship between Schaalman and Edelheit continued. A mark of their friendship and Edelheit's respect for Schaalman was the *festschrift* he put together in Schaalman's honor.[288] Published in 1987, *Life of the Covenant*, contained essays by such Jewish luminaries as Eliezar Berkovits, Eugene Borowitz, Irving Greenberg, and W. Gunther Plaut. Schaalman and his daughter Susan contributed personal essays; the rest are scholarly discussions of different aspects of Judaism.

Two years later, as a testament to the warmth of their relationship, Schaalman (1989) wrote a thank you note to Edelheit for accepting the B'yad Hazakah award presented at CCAR's one hundredth anniversary, which honored Emanuel's Rabbis Felix Levy, Herman Schaalman, and its current rabbi, Joseph Edelheit. The award was given in acknowledgement of their contributions to Reform Judaism and as recognition of Emanuel's donation of $10,000 to help alleviate the financial plight of retired rabbis, who lacked sufficient pensions to support a decent way of life. In the note, Schaalman (1989) explained that his participation in the CCAR as its president and chair of its Ethics and Appeals Committee demonstrated that "my CCAR service was a major and integral part of my rabbinate. The fact that my name has been included in the honor roll is very precious and meaningful. The fact that you participated in making it possible is deeply appreciated. I am genuinely grateful to you for this additional token of your friendship."

During the brief period that Edelheit was senior rabbi at Emanuel, the Schaalmans felt excluded from participation in temple life and that Edelheit had betrayed their friendship and collegial relationship. Schaalman, who was at the height of his powers and an international leader

Rabbi Schaalman speaking at a 1992 anti-casino rally with other religious leaders.

in Reform Judaism, was eager to play a role in the congregation, but was allowed only a substantially diminished role. He would have liked to be included in Shabbat and holiday services, give occasional sermons, and carry on with his Monday night Current Events and his Saturday morning Torah Study. "But to my chagrin, my successor did not involve me in congregational events and activities."[289]

In 1970, Emanuel had 905 members, a number that remained more or less stable until Schaalman's retirement. In the following years, membership suffered a downward spiral and a subsequent loss of operating funds. At the beginning of Schaalman's tenure, the neighborhood around Emanuel was populated by many younger post-war Jewish families who were seeking a community and religious school for their children. Twenty years later, these children had grown up and become more prosperous than their parents, and many had moved to the suburbs. Membership also declined because this younger generation no longer felt the same need as their parents to affiliate with a synagogue.

Another factor in the declining membership was the fact when Schaalman retired, his popular and well-liked assistant, Rabbi Michael

Weinberg, who did not get the position, left to take over another congregation (Beth Israel) in Skokie. Thirty to forty families went with him. By 1990, according to Rickie Jacobs, former president of Emanuel's board, the congregation consisted largely of elderly or very young members: "The middle mass, the support of the congregation, was gone."

Schaalman was succeeded by his former assistant, Joseph Edelheit. Unfortunately for both of them, tensions developed between them that were felt by the congregation. These tensions affected the congregation and contributed to the exodus. When Edelheit left in 1993, Schaalman took over as interim rabbi while the board searched for Edelheit's replacement. It was then that Schaalman discovered the extent of the congregation's decline (Folb, 2007). He was not only surprised, but also deeply hurt. Emanuel was, after all, "his baby." During his thirty years as its senior rabbi, he had brought the congregation national and international recognition.

Edelheit's successor, Rabbi David Sofian, who took over in 1993, was not able to repair the damage, and Emanuel's membership continued to erode. The cohesion of the congregation and the sense of a supportive spiritual community had disappeared. The decline in membership resulted in serious financial difficulties that plagued the congregation for the next fifteen years. "When I retired," Schaalman stresses, "Emanuel had several million dollars in endowment funds, largely the result of my fundraising. However, my successors, beginning with Edelheit, did not raise additional funds and, as membership declined, the board chose to dip into the endowment to make up budget shortfalls."

Rabbi Sofian served as Emanuel's rabbi from 1993 to 2002. Before taking the job, he had heard nothing but praise about Schaalman from Rabbi John Friedman, Sofian's friend since high school and one of Schaalman's assistants from 1976 to 1980. Sofian (2005) was well aware of the difficult situation at Emanuel but was drawn to it because of its prestige in the Reform movement. He knew that his major goal had to be to heal the congregation and get it back on its feet.

Sofian did not make Edelheit's mistake of alienating the Schaalmans and quickly established a friendly and collegial relationship with them, one that, as he reports, had to "be grounded in reality and had to be very public. I knew that Schaalman was a giant in the Reform movement [and] perhaps the congregation's most significant resource" (Sofian,

2005). He wanted to encourage Schaalman's involvement in any way he could. At first, that was difficult because Schaalman had taken a position as interim rabbi for a congregation in Highland Park while it searched for a full-time replacement for its former rabbi. "I wanted him back," Sofian confided, so I asked Schaalman to assist me during Friday night services and made sure that he was included in the life of the congregation" (Sofian, 2005).

Sofian made sure that the two of them were regularly together on the bimah and represented a public, positive, and cordial relationship to the congregation. On the High Holy Days, as long as Schaalman's son-in-law, Rabbi Youdovin, was in New York, Schaalman went there to assist him with High Holy Day services. However, when Youdovin came to Chicago, Sofian (2005) made sure he involved Schaalman in High Holy Day services. "I wanted the congregation to see that Schaalman was connected again" (Sofian, 2005). Another sign that the two were working together was the establishment of a mini-university with four to six Monday evening sessions taught by the staff including Sofian and Schaalman. Sofian also encouraged Schaalman to continue his monthly Monday evening Current Events program and his Saturday morning Torah Study, both of which had been going on for decades. "I also promoted the New Year's Retreats that Schaalman had been holding for nearly half a century" (Sofian, 2005). Sofian and his wife attended some of them to show that the two were on good terms. Occasionally, the sessions were interrupted by funerals that Schaalman was asked to conduct and Sofian would sub for him or would go back to Chicago to perform the service.

Schaalman proved to be extremely helpful to Sofian in his efforts to raise funds for Emanuel (Sofian, 2005). The congregation still had some wealthy members who were good friends of the Schaalmans and over the years responded generously to his fundraising efforts. For example, over the years, the Lederer family had donated large sums of money for temple improvements. Mrs. Adrienne Lederer set up a $25,000 four-year matching contribution. As a result, the congregation received $200,000 in contributions. She also made a significant contribution to the sanctuary renovation (Sofian, 2005). Schaalman set up a lunch for the three of them to help lay the groundwork for what they wanted to see happen, specifically how to improve the financial picture of the congregation.

With Schaalman's help, the deal was closed and, later, Sofian was able to approach Adrienne for a donation for the renovation, to which she made a significant contribution (Sofian, 2005). "Although I played a key role in these developments, none of them would have occurred without Schaalman's help" (Sofian, 2005).

Another important contribution Schaalman made to Sofian's fundraising efforts was to help him develop a strong connection with Robert Morris, Schaalman's long-time friend and a financial anchor for the congregation (Sofian, 2005).[290] Morris provided the funds for the middle part of the sanctuary, now known as the Morris Room. Schaalman also assisted Sofian with the transfer of leadership from the older generation to the younger generation and helped him develop new programs (Sofian, 2005).

Sofian's strategy of including Schaalman in the life of the congregation allowed Schaalman to regain his sense of an active and meaningful part in the life of the congregation that he loved and helped build. The working relationship of the two rabbis was also good for Sofian and helped him achieve his major goal of healing the rift in the congregation. Sofian commented: "If I accomplished anything while I was in Chicago, I would say that we got that previous stuff behind us" (Sofian, 2005). Nevertheless, despite Sofian's efforts to help the congregation survive, he was fighting a losing battle. Membership continued to decline, and the temple's finances deteriorated with it. The congregation survived largely because the board decided to withdraw principal from its endowment funds.

The congregation's financial difficulty was compounded by some older members of the board who were opposed to raising dues. It had a policy of "fair share" dues pegged to a congregant's ability to pay. A significant number of congregants abused the policy and, in fact, did not pay their "fair share." Rickie Jacobs explains, "Some believed that the wealthy people in the congregation would make up the deficit." This idea was a hangover from the Levy years, when, in fact, wealthy members did write checks to make up the deficit. However, most of these members were long gone. The board began tapping the Heritage Fund to make up the shortfall.[291]

In 2002, Rabbi Sofian announced that he was severing his relationship with Emanuel.[292] His announcement took Schaalman by surprise and created an immediate crisis for the congregation. Emanuel's board was in a quandary about finding a replacement, especially because the congregation was in such desperate financial straits. The membership had declined to a mere two hundred and the prospect of increasing it was dim.[293] A major concern was finding a rabbi with acceptable qualifications willing to take the position in a congregation that appeared to be on the verge of collapse and that was unable to pay a competitive salary. The board was ready to consider selling the building and merging with another congregation as a way of avoiding its approaching bankruptcy. When Robert Morris, who had been a member of the congregation for nearly half a century and a former president, heard this discussion, he reminded the board, "What do you mean you don't have a rabbi? You have Rabbi Schaalman, who could serve temporarily until a full-time Rabbi could be hired." (Morris, R. and Morris, A., 2007).

At first, the board was not ready to consider bringing Schaalman out of retirement. Some of the younger members complained that Schaalman was too old for the congregation. According to Robert and Audrey Morris (2007), "One young board member declared, 'My God, he would never relate to a younger congregation.'" The Morrises understood that most of the younger members had never seen Schaalman interact with children. Nevertheless, the board decided to bring in Schaalman while it searched for a new rabbi. When the board again brought up the proposal to merge with another congregation, Schaalman, who as the new rabbi was present at the meeting, told the board that dissolving the congregation was not an option. He had devoted nearly half a century to Emanuel and was not about to oversee its demise. The board dropped the proposal and decided on a new strategy to bring in more members. It established a new entry-level membership category with a radically altered discounted membership fee of $100. This initial rate would rise gradually over succeeding years to the full membership rate. The board reasoned that once people signed on at the discounted rate, they might become attached to the congregation and more willingly pay the increasing membership fee. This decision was a holding action designed to preserve the congregation while it sought a new rabbi who might be able to attract new members. The strategy worked, and the congregation survived.

During the year that Schaalman took over, the board member who announced that Schaalman was too old to take on the job told Morris that he had been wrong about Schaalman. He had discovered that Schaalman could relate to young people who were complete strangers to him. One of Schaalman's winning ways was to assemble the children attending a Shabbat service in the middle of the floor and tell them a story. He is a natural at telling stories. He understands pitch and timing, and, together with his deep bass voice, he is the archetypal grandfatherly storyteller. The children on the floor in front of him were fixated on the story no less than on the storyteller. They were both awed and mystified and so were their parents.

Schaalman took an active role in the process of selecting a new rabbi and in raising funds—as he is still doing in 2012. By the end of the year, the congregation had identified and hired a new rabbi who would be its salvation. Although there were several attractive candidates, the one that stood out was Rabbi Michael Zedek. Schaalman thought that he was the best choice, and Zedek had already made a hit with the board. What made Zedek appealing was his stature as a Reform rabbi, his extensive experience as a congregational rabbi in a huge congregation in Kansas City, his intellect, and his ability to make services fun for both children and families. Most of the older members also liked his manner and welcomed the lighter services. After serving as Kansas City's largest Reform congregation (1,700 members) for twenty-five years, Zedek had taken time off from pulpit duties to assume the role of fundraiser for the Cincinnati Jewish Federation. Emanuel was extremely fortunate to find a rabbi with such outstanding credentials who was willing to take a job in a congregation that was in serious decline. Indeed, Zedek (2005) made clear to the board and the congregation that the reason he accepted the position was his admiration and love for Schaalman and Emanuel's distinguished reputation for which Schaalman was largely responsible.

At the time, Zedek (2005) had no idea how dire the congregation's situation was. But when he found out before he was hired, he decided that he would work to save it as a gift to Schaalman. From the time he left the seminary, he had not only come to know and respect Schaalman, but over the years, that respect had turned into love. He thought of Schaalman as "one of the giants of his generation." "Even now," according to Zedek, "he continues to develop theologically in a way one doesn't expect from someone his age."

When Zedek came to Emanuel in 2004, the number of congregants stood at 270 members. By 2012, membership had risen to 400, and, for the first time in anyone's memory, including Schaalman's, the congregation was in the "black" and looking forward to expanding in the coming years. It's religious school had reached 200 students, an all-time record, and was bursting at the seams. Classrooms, rather than students, was now the congregation's chief concern.

Zedek made sure not to repeat the mistakes of his predecessors. He involved Schaalman so fully in the life of the temple, that to this observer, it seems that the two rabbis co-officiate in the spiritual life of the congregation. Schaalman frequently substitutes for Zedek when he is out of town, either on vacation or engaged in other professional responsibilities. Zedek also gets help from Schaalman with fundraising. Lest his friendship and influence with some of his wealthy friends and former congregation benefactors be lost, Schaalman has attempted to link Zedek to several of them. As late as July 22, 2012, Schaalman and Zedek organized a long-range planning and fundraising event for older and long-term members of Emanuel. Having Schaalman's name on the invitation was a certain draw for people who had been his congregants for as long as fifty years. When he is not helping with Emanuel, Schaalman's continues to lead a full life as teacher, lecturer, and as fill-in rabbi for Emanuel and other congregations requesting his help. His friend and colleague Rabbi Marc Berkson, has invited him once again to join him in leading his 2012 Rosh Hashanah services in Milwaukee.

Chapter 7

Post-retirement
Schaalman's Involvement
in Community Affairs

"The difference between pre-retirement and retirement is that when these things came up to me, I could say no. ... Before, I didn't feel I had a right. ... A perception of what I owed as a Rabbi was that no matter what anybody would demand, unless it was outrageous and beyond my capacity, it was my responsibility to help. ... Now I say, 'Do me something!'"

Herman E. Schaalman, 1988

"There is no question that when you hear the faith of others who are deeply convicted and convinced about their own faith, that you learn something about the faith life. I'm not claiming that I know everything about my own faith life, let alone what faith life should be like, but when I'm with others and see how they address these questions, what response they give to the question that life and God poses, then I learn something."

Herman E. Schaalman, 2002

When Schaalman retired in 1986 as Emanuel's rabbi, he now had the privilege to say no to requests for his participation in organizations or meetings. Before he retired, he believed that "no matter what anybody would demand, unless it was outrageous and beyond my capacity, it was my responsibility to help." He now had plenty of opportunity to lead an active public life. "As a full-time rabbi, I had never been able to give as much of my time and energy to these pursuits as I would have liked." His immense prestige in the Jewish community and his national and international stature gave him a platform to become involved in a host of activities that he could pursue with great vigor. There has been no letup in invitations to conduct scholar-in-residence weekends and to lecture before various secular groups, churches, and synagogues. In 1988, he commented that over the next six to eight months, he had "a whole raft of lectures" to give, which helped create for him a "very varied and richly textured kind of life. Sometimes it became overwhelming." (Even as late as 2012, he is still being invited to make major presentations.[294]) In Lotte's view, retirement has not meant retirement for her husband:

> Hardly a day goes by when he isn't off to some meeting in town or in New York or Washington or somewhere abroad. Even when he is home, he spends most of his time in study. We should be playing, but we don't have time for that. Herman is distraught if he doesn't get a chance to study for one day.

For Schaalman, retirement meant that he was now free from full-time rabbi responsibilities and could direct his prodigious energy into a large number of major organizations in which he held membership. His participation in Chicago area religious and civic life has been extensive.

The Jewish Council on Urban Affairs (JCUA)

Even before he retired, Schaalman had been active in JCUA. Created in 1964 by Rabbi Robert Marx, Schaalman's immediate successor as Midwest Regional Director of UAHC, JCUA's mission is to promote social justice on behalf of the city's most vulnerable groups, its poor and minorities. JCUA carries out its mission by mobilizing the Chicago Jewish community to reach out to local community organizations that lack the resources or power to address many of the city's social and economic needs (Jewish Council on Urban Affairs, 2008).

According to Rabbi Marx (2008), in its earliest incarnation, the JCUA focused on the issue of segregation, the most important civil rights issue of the 1960s. In large measure, this issue was brought into focus and demanded attention because of the work of Dr. Martin Luther King, Jr. and his associates in the Southern Christian Leadership Conference. In June of 1963, Dr. King issued his famous challenge to America's clergy,

"Letter from a Birmingham Jail." Two years later, Marx received a telegram from King asking him and other Chicago religious leaders to join him in what became the historic Selma to Montgomery Freedom March. JCUA responded immediately by organizing a freedom ride, a bus filled with synagogue members who wanted to support the civil rights movement (Marx, R., 2008, p. 275). Schaalman, however, was not one of them. As he explained many years later, "Although many Reform rabbis and the great Abraham Joshua Heschel joined with King, I did not."

Soon after Marx created the JCUA, he established a twelve-member Council that included well-known and influential Chicago clergy, all of them Schaalman's friends and colleagues, including Msgr. John Egan of the Archdiocese of Chicago, John McDermott of the Catholic Interracial Council, and Rabbi Irving Rosenbaum of the Chicago Board of Rabbis. Through the JCUA, the Council worked with Martin Luther King, Jr. to protest segregation in Chicago (Marx, R., October 16, 2008). Private donors from the Jewish community and Jewish agencies such as Chicago's Jewish Federation pumped money into the new activist organization. To develop a broader base of support in the Jewish community, the fledgling JCUA created a board of trustees including lay people, rabbis, and synagogues (Marx, R. October 16, 2008).

Although Schaalman did not become an official member of the board of trustees until 1984, he was supportive of JCUA's effort to promote civil rights in Chicago and to address the needs of Chicago's disadvantaged and disempowered. He recognized that the JCUA had a much wider sweep than the kinds of social justice activities he had been promoting in uptown Chicago through the Edgewater Clergy and Rabbinic Association.

Schaalman joined the Council specifically after receiving a request for help from its founder, Rabbi Robert Marx. According to Schaalman, "Sometime before I became an official member of the Council, Marx had called on me to help smooth over difficulties that had developed between him and Jewish funding sources."[295] Marx had angered Chicago's Reform Jewish leaders by criticizing as unethical the practices of Jewish slum landlords in Chicago. The attacks spilled over to affect JCUA funding. Both Marx and JCUA lost credibility in the eyes of these wealthy benefactors. According to Schaalman, "My presence at fundraising meetings added an air of respectability and stability that Marx had lost and helped reestablish the organization's credibility."

In the early years of his involvement with JCUA, Schaalman maintained a low profile in its deliberations. By 1987, however, JCUA minutes reveal an ever-increasing level of participation. At the time, he served on the Program Committee. Two years later, he was elected vice president and then president in 1991. In the period of Schaalman's involvement, including his presidency, 1987–1993, the JCUA engaged in a variety of social issues, including sponsorship of Arab/Jewish dialogue, economic development, civil rights, and social justice struggles in other parts of the country and abroad. According to Jane Ramsey (2011), Executive Director of the JCUA, "Schaalman was president during a crucial time for the agency. He was a terrific president, powerful and wise. He understood the issues, and, once he made a commitment to an issue, he never wavered."

One of JCUA's most important efforts was to assist poor people who had been displaced following the demolition of their homes by the Chicago Housing Authority. "Under Schaalman's leadership," Ramsey (2011) commented, "JCUA worked hard to see to it that the residents did not become homeless. He participated in meetings with residents, appeared in press conferences, and took their concerns to the Chicago Housing Authority."

As JCUA president, Schaalman was also in the forefront of efforts to eliminate the death penalty in Illinois. After 9/11, he helped fashion programs designed to promote tolerance of Muslims living in Chicago, to fight against Islamophobia. A specific contribution in this effort was his help in identifying local Muslim leaders with whom JCUA should meet and develop relations.

When his term as president expired, Schaalman remained on the board of directors. In 2001, the JCUA honored him for his contributions to the organization and his extensive years of working on behalf of minorities and civil rights. In his acceptance speech, Schaalman told his audience that injustice in Chicago is part of the fabric of injustice around the globe: "We've had to wake up to the fact that precisely the kind of ills, injustices, and evils we are banded together to address locally are at the bottom of the rage and violence that surges across vast reaches of the globe. To address this problem JCUA members need to be not just believers in hope, [but] … its protagonists" (JCUA Annual Report, 2001, p. 3). As of 2012, Schaalman is still a JCUA Board member.

Chicago's Commission on Human Relations

Schaalman's efforts to promote social justice are not limited to his work with the JCUA. Sometime around 1988, Chicago's Mayor Richard M. Daley appointed him to the Chicago Commission on Human Relations. "As a member for more than twenty years until 2008, I sat on its General Committee and heard cases of alleged discrimination based on gender, age, race, ethnicity and religion." Under the city's statutes, the commission has significant legal clout, including the power to levy heavy fines, as much as tens of thousands of dollars. Cases of alleged discrimination are brought before the commission by city attorneys who make recommendations to the board regarding the legitimacy of the complaints.

Chicago Board of Rabbis

Soon after his retirement, Schaalman was elected president of the Chicago Board of Rabbis (CBR), a forum on public issues of concern to rabbis and the city's Jewish religious community. Although hesitant at first, after taking several days to consider the offer, he accepted and served for the next two years, the maximum allowable under the CBR bylaws.

Before becoming a member of CBR, he had been chair of its TV production committee and participated in its programming. From this position, he was able to use the organization's TV production as a medium for outreach and education both to the Jewish and non-Jewish communities. His positive experience with radio in Cedar Rapids made him eager to utilize this more far-reaching venue to address Jewish issues and to promote positive public relations.

One of the committee's responsibilities was to create scripts on Jewish subjects, but, because the committee was composed of rabbis from different branches of Judaism, this was no simple matter. According to Schaalman, "Getting consensus for approving scripts turned out to be a major challenge." Complicating the process was the board's concern that it did not want to antagonize any of its members. After a script dealing with the latest findings about Jericho was sent out for review, Schaalman received a call from an irate Orthodox rabbi: "He was upset because the manuscript contained a statement that Jericho was 6,000 years old.

How could that be true when the entire creation was not that old?" The rabbi pressed Schaalman to remove the offensive language. Schaalman, who was put off by his colleague's narrow views, told him, "I was not about to compromise and I only succeeded in further antagonizing the rabbi." The rabbi ended the argument by confronting Schaalman: "Herman, what are you trying to do?" and hung up. "Realizing that I was risking the solidarity of the CBR and directly challenging the Orthodox community, I removed the offensive language. To do anything less would have meant to undermine the board's major purpose of enhancing its collective ability to have a strong impact on public policy."

Racial Problems in Chicago

As the president of the CBR, Schaalman was its representative on the Council of Religious Leaders of Metropolitan Chicago (CRLMC). Created by Cardinal Bernardin in 1984, at the beginning, its membership included only religious leaders representing Christians and Jews. From its inception, the CRLMC issued public policy statements on a long list of pressing local Chicago, national and international public concerns. These included racism and social injustice in Chicago; national issues such as immigration, video gambling, the death penalty, sex abuse, and gun control; and international issues such as Afghanistan, Iran, and the 1991 Iraq War. Its posture has always ecumenical and pro-peace, even in times of war.

Although he had barely begun to serve on this prestigious Council, less than a year later, he was elected its president, no doubt because Council members recognized his leadership abilities. "Before I could even get comfortable in my new role, in May of 1988 a major civil rights controversy erupted in Chicago's City Council." It centered on Steve Cokely, an aide to Chicago's African American mayor, Eugene Sawyer. Cokely had taped a series of lectures for followers of Nation of Islam leader Louis Farrakhan.[296] In the lectures, he attacked Jews, white Christians, and black leaders, including icons Harold Washington, Chicago's first African American mayor, and Reverend Jesse Jackson (Johnson, D., 1988).[297] *The Sun-Times*, one of Chicago's leading newspapers, published excerpts from the tapes, which revealed not only anti-Semitic attacks, but also the outrageous claim that some

Jewish physicians had injected black Africans with the AIDS virus (Johnson, D., 1988).

Angry community leaders, and some City Hall officials, demanded that Sawyer fire Cokely or, at least, censure him. Although nothing came of their demands, the publication of Cokely's remarks put Sawyer under a great deal of pressure to fire his aide. Part of Sawyer's difficulty was that he saw himself as a "father figure" to Cokely. Another was that he might not have wanted to be guilty of violating Cokely's First Amendment rights or be perceived by the African American community as buckling to whites.

The fallout from this controversy resulted in a breakdown in May and June of relations between blacks and Jews. Some black aldermen and ministers came to Cokely's defense and either added their own anti-Semitic statements in support or allowed that there was "some truth" in his remark. *The New York Times* reported, "Many black politicians apparently saw political currency in attacking Jews" (Johnson, D., 1988). Only three of the eighteen black aldermen called for Cokely's dismissal. The controversy became uglier when another Cokely supporter, Lu Palmer, an influential black political activist, said in a TV debate that Jews and whites "are in a conspiracy to rule the world" (Johnson, D., 1988).

The problem needed attention; racial harmony, or at least tolerance, was critical to the well-being of the city. Sawyer turned to Cardinal Bernardin, the most prestigious religious leader in the city, to form a group to help resolve the conflict. According to Schaalman, "Bernardin told him that he needed to take the matter to the Council of Religious Leaders of Metropolitan Chicago to enlist the aid of its current president."[298] Schaalman, who was no stranger to this controversy, had been convinced in previous discussions with local African American leaders that they tended to displace their anti-white feelings onto Jews. "The displacement," he speculated, "was because the only whites they knew were Jews."[299] Because Jews were despised in Western civilization, by lumping them together with all whites, they became a convenient target. This conflation of Jews and whites, Schaalman argues, contributes to the already "massive stream in Western civilization that is anti-Jewish." Schaalman embraced the challenge of restoring racial harmony in his beloved city and considered it as "potentially the most exciting thing maybe that I ever had to do in public."

Working in concert with Cardinal Bernardin and Reverend Sterling Cary, CRLMC's immediate past president and a leader in the African American community, Schaalman offered to assist the mayor. Sawyer accepted the offer, as did the City Council, which issued a statement denouncing what it called "outrageous and virulent expressions of anti-Semitism" (Johnson, D., 1988). Schaalman made it clear to Sawyer that whatever he did was on behalf of the Council, not as an agent of the mayor. To protect themselves from suspicion that they were acting on behalf of the mayor, the triumvirate held a news conference to announce that they were working independently of city government.

Shortly thereafter, the mayor "summoned" the clergymen to a meeting at City Hall (Lehmann, D. J., May 12, 1988). Because the Cardinal was out of town, only Schaalman and Cary were able to attend. When they arrived in Sawyer's office, they found themselves confronted by two other African American ministers, whom Sawyer wanted to include in the discussions. His aim, he told Schaalman, was to broaden the base to include other members of the African American community (one of whom was his own minister) who had a strong interest in the outcome of this issue. Schaalman was not happy with this turn of events. He told the mayor, "It's an abuse of your office for you to be thus used by black clergy to promote their need to become involved." Schaalman's position was that if these clergy wanted to be involved, they should have contacted the CRLMC, rather than the mayor's office. He was committed to working within the framework of the Council and was not going to make any decisions without first getting Bernardin's and the Council's approval.

Bernardin and the Council supported Schaalman's view that these other clergymen should not be included in the group's efforts. Reverend Cary also felt abused by Sawyer's action and agreed with the Council's decision. Schaalman was not averse to broadening the base of involvement, but, at this point, he thought it premature. The mayor, he concluded, was attempting to influence the outcome of the meetings through his proxies on the group.

Schaalman's group decided to reach out to the Chicago community and turned first to the city's religious leaders and then to the editorial boards of the three main Chicago newspapers: the *Chicago Sun Times*, the *Chicago Tribune* and *The Chicago Defender*, the leading newspaper in the African American community. Schaalman and his colleagues chose this course of action because they thought religious leaders and the press had the best outreach to the community.

To combat the hostilities, the clergymen set up meetings in churches and synagogues and created an interracial panel including three black ministers, seven rabbis, and leaders of other Jewish groups. The meetings in the churches and synagogues were designed to remind their audiences of the "historic ties" between blacks and Jews in the civil rights movement. The hope was that this approach would establish a base of understanding and tolerance between the two contending factions. The clergymen also sought to address what they considered the negative impact the racial conflict was having on addressing the issues of poverty, unemployment, and homelessness.[300]

While Schaalman and the CRLMC were using TV to attempt to deal with such divisive issues between blacks and Jews, they met with key players in the financial and corporate community. The message they brought with them was their belief that a major cause of the racial tensions was the lack of employment opportunities in the African American community. Better incomes, they thought would reduce tensions.

The attempted intervention by the CRLMC leaders did not work out as Schaalman had hoped. By the summer of 1988, he confessed to feeling discouraged that the project seemed impossible to complete. Schaalman was not someone who left a project unfinished. The more involved he got the more he realized the black community was so fragmented that he did not know with whom to work to have a major impact or whether it was possible to make an impact at all. Part of the problem, Schaalman recognized, was that 1.2 million African Americans were living in Chicago, and no one of them could be the spokesman for all of them.

Another problem Schaalman encountered was his own busy schedule and that of the Cardinal. Because Bernardin was committed to so many causes, he was frequently out of town, and it was difficult to schedule a meeting with him. That summer, Schaalman also was busy, spending three weeks in Europe and two in Oconomowoc. At the last minute, a meeting was scheduled in early June 1988 but without Bernardin, who was away in Mexico and not scheduled to return until the end of July. Because of these scheduling issues, the Council lost critical momentum in its attempt to deal with the problem.

Racism and anti-Semitism continued to dog the City Council. Realizing that it had not made any progress, the CRLMC decided to urge Sawyer to empower Chicago's Commission on Human Relations and make it the lead agency responsible for resolving the city's human relations issues. The letter reminded Sawyer that the city's Commission on Human Relations had done nothing while Cokely and his supporters "were spewing hate" and needed to be "visible and pro-active" ("City Council," 1988).

In November of 1988, the CRLMC issued a Thanksgiving prayer and a document that attempted to address the racial conflicts and social inequities in the city. The document, signed by Schaalman, Bernardin, and Cary, referred to Chicago as a city without "Shalom," in which the privileged live well while others are "unemployed, homeless, and dehumanized." It asked God to "deliver us from the illusion that peace can dawn when justice is absent" and to forgive the failure "to be instruments of [God's] justice" (Council of Religious Leaders, November, 1988). The document calls on Chicago to be a leader in addressing not only its own social and racial issues, but to be a model for the country. Of particular concern and the "cause of deep pain" is the outbreak of racial and religious hate and fear that have resurfaced in Chicago in recent months. If not addressed, this situation could "seriously damage the city's social fabric and blight its future." The CRLMC called on the people of Chicago to be united as a community of diverse people and to accept the responsibility "for safeguarding the rights and dignity of all, especially the weak and defenseless." Unless citizens take up that responsibility, the result will be "anger, bitterness and despair" and the persistence of racial injustice, religious bigotry, and economic and social injustice (Council of Religious Leaders, November, 1988).

Black-Jewish Relations: Farrakhan

Anti-Semitism in Chicago was being stoked by the rise of the Black Muslim movement, widely viewed by Jewish leaders and organizations as anti-Semitic.[301] For more than a half a century, the Nation of Islam's leadership has been highly critical of Jews, blaming them for everything from the slave trade to the inoculation of black Africans with the AIDS virus. Minister Farrakhan himself regularly makes virulent anti-Semitic remarks, all the while denying that he is anti-Semitic. An example is his 1996 Saviours' Day Speech:

> And you do with me as [it] is written, but remember that I have warned you that Allah will punish you. You [Jews] are wicked deceivers of the American people. You have sucked their blood. You are not real Jews, those of you that are not real Jews. You are the synagogue of Satan and you have wrapped your tentacles around the U.S. government, and you are deceiving and sending this nation to hell. But I warn you in the name of Allah, you would be wise to leave me alone. But if you choose to crucify me, know that Allah will crucify you.[302]

Saviours' Day Speech, Chicago, February 25, 1996

To the Chicago Jewish community and to the community at large, Farrakhan's anti-Semitic diatribes were and still are a major concern. The Jewish and mainstream press have attacked his statements and characterized him as a hatemonger and a bigot. Farrakhan, on the other hand, appeared to be dismayed by this hostility and made efforts to reach out to the Jewish community in an apparent attempt to mend fences. Most Jewish leaders do not believe he was sincere about improving relations, especially because he periodically professes to seek amicable relations, but, then, either he or a lieutenant makes hateful statements about Jews. Just two days before the 1995 Million Man March, Quanell X, the Nation of Islam's (NOI) national youth minister, told a cheering crowd in Washington, "All you Jews can go straight to hell. ... I say to Jewish America, 'Get ready. Knuckle up. Put your boots on, because we're ready and the war is going down'" (as cited in Magida, 1996, pp. 158–159). That same evening, the NOI's national spokesman, Khallid Abdul Muhammad, snarled that the Jew was a "parasite who comes into our community and takes out trailer and tractor loads of money on a daily basis" (Magida, 1996, p. 159). Yet, forty-eight hours later at the Million Man March, Farrakhan asked again to meet with Jews, but said nothing about the hate speech from inside his own organization.

Apparently, Farrakhan's effort to reach out to the Jews began during the period of the Cokely affair. In 1988, in an effort to correct what he considered gross misunderstandings of his position toward the Jews, he invited Rabbis Schaalman and Marx to a dinner meeting at his home.

To their surprise, they found Farrakhan charming and receptive. At one point, he even asked them to tell him the specific words that had offended Jews and pledged never again to use them. By the end of this first meeting, both rabbis felt that, "on the Jewish question, he would be honorable" (p. 159). In a gesture that was as uncomfortable as it was unexpected, as his guests were leaving, Farrakhan leaned over to the much smaller Schaalman and hugged him warmly.[303]

Five years elapsed before Schaalman had another encounter with Farrakhan. In January of 1993, they ran into each other in Chicago's Palmer House Hotel where both were attending the centennial of the Parliament of the World's Religions, a celebration designed to bring peace and harmony to the world. According to Schaalman, to his surprise, "When Farrakhan spotted me, he came up to me and gave me a warm hug." The Jewish community establishment, which knew Farrakhan only through his vicious public denunciations of the Jews, had no warmth for him. When the event's four Jewish sponsoring organizations[304] found out that Farrakhan was going to speak at the conference, they withdrew their support.

In 1993 for his sixtieth birthday, Farrakhan held a benefit concert for the Nation of Islam's private school and sent invitations to Chicago's white community. Held in Chicago's Christ Universal Temple, the event was a major departure from the separatism he had been preaching. Even more notable was the fact that Farrakhan would play the works of Felix Mendelssohn, a Jewish composer whom he loved. Farrakhan's aim was to hold out an olive branch to the Jewish community and to prove he was not anti-Semitic (Johnson, M. A., 1993).[305]

Farrakhan's public relations consultant, George O'Hare, claimed that following the concert, he planned to work with Rabbi Marx to arrange a "sit down" with local Jewish leaders. Marx was skeptical that the concert would assuage Jewish concerns. A more convincing "performance" and a concrete sign of his willingness to change would be the cessation of incendiary anti-Semitic articles in NOI's newsletter, the *Final Call.*

The "sit down" took place on May 21, 1993, in Rabbi Marx's home in Glencoe. In the interval since the first meeting, Schaalman had detected what he thought was a softening of Farrakhan's tone toward Jews. He and Marx decided that, as representatives of the Jewish community, they had a responsibility to follow up. Thanks to the Cokely affair, a meeting between the black and Jewish community was desirable, even with the man understood in the Jewish community as Chicago's most prestigious and powerful anti-Semite. For this meeting, Marx included other influential Jews besides Schaalman, including Irv Kupcinet, *Chicago Sun-Times* reporter, and Walter Jacobson, TV reporter for WFLD-Channel 32. Kupcinet described the meeting as "very friendly, very cordial, and very frank" (Weintraub, 1993). Farrakhan, on the other hand, was insulted when the rabbis asked for proof that he had repented and had changed his ways as he had promised. Nevertheless, in the discussion that followed, both sides agreed to hold further meetings on how to work together to improve the relationship and to repair the damage that had been created between blacks and Jews.

In the aftermath of this meeting, Farrakhan's public utterances continued to be unremittingly hostile to Jews. The rabbis felt betrayed. More than a decade would elapse before Farrakhan let it be known that he was interested in renewing the dialogue. He had developed a special fondness for Schaalman and sent word that he wanted to meet with him. "By this time," said Schaalman, "I had given up hope that anything meaningful would come from meeting with Farrakhan, and I thought it was time to pass the torch to my younger colleague, Rabbi Michael Zedek." Now, it would be his turn to represent the Jewish community in conversations with Farrakhan. Zedek has met with Farrakhan twice since 2008 and reports that he has nothing to report.

Interfaith: Reaching Out

A good deal of Schaalman's life has been devoted to improving interfaith relations. Having lived through the experience of the Nazi attempt to annihilate the Jews and the failure of Christian nations to come to their aid, he worries that without outreach to the Christian community there is little hope of avoiding such a tragedy in the future. The lesson he learned from the Holocaust is that history is notorious for repeating itself: "History only teaches that what has happened once will happen again, only maybe in a different way, by different means and in a different place" (University of St. Thomas, 1992, p. 16). The only hope of preventing a recurrence is to keep the event alive, to "keep dealing with the subject, no matter how personally painful and repulsive it really is, over and over again." Keeping the memory of the Holocaust alive is only one part of Schaalman's prescription for Jewish survival. For the non-Jewish world, there is a positive reason to keep Jews alive: "The world needs Jews. We have something that is unique to us that we have talked and lived and died for, and it deserves to continue" (Faith in Conversion, 2005). Judaism and Christianity are siblings, each a reflection of the other.

In making this commitment to improving interfaith relations, Schaalman stepped beyond the boundaries of his family. Freddie, his Orthodox brother, does not believe in outreach to Christians. For him, the atrocities of the *Shoah* and the murder of Jews by Christians over nearly 2,000 years are unforgivable. History has taught Jews not to want or expect anything from the Christian world. He also thinks that close involvement with the non-Jewish world makes one susceptible to becoming one of them. His brother's outreach efforts, he contends, are misguided: "All the time he spent with the *goyim*, he could have spent more time with the Jews." When Freddie found out that Chicago's Orthodox rabbis opposed his brother's participation in Cardinal Bernardin's funeral, he remarked, "I would have been one of them." To avoid family discord, he does not discuss such matters with his brother.

Freddie's remarks reflect a well-earned skepticism regarding Christianity. The Schaalman children grew up in a world in which anti-Semitism was a brutal fact of their lives. It taught them to fear and mistrust Christians. Even to walk past a Catholic church in their neighborhood was threatening. Schaalman remembers that during his childhood, when he and his father were on their way to the synagogue, they passed a Catholic church a few blocks from their home. As soon as they reached it, they crossed to the other side of the street, so powerful was their need to put distance between themselves and the church. By the time Herman left Germany in 1935, the German majority either had embraced Nazism or had done nothing to oppose it. The Nazis had set a course to persecute and disenfranchise Jews and, ultimately, to annihilate them. As Schaalman became more aware of the catastrophic nature of the *Shoah*, he came to believe that the only hope for Jews in a Christian world was to "work to narrow the gap between Christians and Jews."

As discussed in Chapter 3, "Cedar Rapids: 1941–1949," not long after he arrived in this sleepy Midwest city, Schaalman began to reach out to Christians to bridge the gap between the Jewish and non-Jewish communities. This outreach was the beginning of a lifelong effort to promote peace and harmony not only between Christians and Jews but between all ethnic and religious groups. When he arrived in Chicago in 1949, the opportunities to participate in interfaith events and organizations expanded dramatically. His job as the Midwest Regional Director of UAHC included serving as liaison for its interfaith activities, requiring him to give speeches before various lay and church groups and serving on various nondenominational civic and religious committees. However, his real work in interreligious activity began when he became Emanuel Congregation's senior rabbi. His efforts to organize ECRA helped prepare him for the interfaith activities that, in succeeding years, would extend far beyond the boundaries of his congregation.

Schaalman's commitment to interfaith dialogue was the basis for his decision in 1957 to accept a teaching assignment at one of Chicago's premier seminaries, Garrett-Evangelical Theological Seminary, a graduate school of theology of the United Methodist Church in Evanston, Illinois. He taught courses in the Hebrew Bible and Jewish theology. When he became president of the Council of Religious Leaders of Metropolitan Chicago in the 1980s, he was able to expand his interfaith outreach. After Bernardin's death in 1996, Schaalman was appointed to the National Advisory Board of The Bernardin Center, an organization established to carry on Bernardin's commitment to interreligious dialogue among the various faith communities (Catholic Theological Union, 2008).

Schaalman's ongoing involvement in interfaith activities was bolstered by radical changes that were occurring in the religious world. The Holocaust had jolted Christianity into a new consciousness. When post-Holocaust Christian theologians attempted to grapple with this unprecedented phenomenon, they discovered that it was the inevitable outcome of the history of Christian persecution of the Jews. Struck with the moral horror of this awareness, the main body of Christianity set about to repair the damage and protect against its recurrence (Zenger, 2009). Not long after Schaalman's appointment as Emanuel's rabbi, in 1959 the newly elected Pope John XXIII established the Second Ecumenical Council of the Vatican (popularly known as Vatican II). This action was meant to breathe new life into Catholicism and to help it adjust to the demands of the modern world (Zenger, 2009).

For Schaalman, Vatican II (1962–1965) was a major breakthrough in interfaith relations, an "astonishing, remarkable and totally unexpected improvement in Christian-Jewish relations."[306] It opened up new "possibilities in which no Jew had ever lived." Over the course of three years, Vatican II produced far-reaching reforms affecting almost every aspect of Catholic life. One of its most ecumenically progressive documents, *Nostra Aetate*, was, according to Schaalman, the most important document to affect relations between Catholics and Jews in the history of the Church (Faith in Conversation, 2005). It signaled the Church's readiness to make a radical departure from its traditional stand that God's covenant with the Jews had ended and been replaced by a new covenant with the Church. It affirmed that there are two covenants and that God did not go back on His promise to Israel (Faith in Conversation, 2005). Equally important to Schaalman, the document stated, "The Jews should not be presented as rejected or accursed by God, as if this followed from the Holy Scriptures" (Second Vatican Council, 2008). Instead, Church teachings should recognize its kinship with the Jewish people through its shared patrimony and that "hatred, persecutions, displays of anti-Semitism, directed against Jews at any time and by anyone" is antithetical to the teachings of the Church (Second Vatican Council, 2008).

Nostra Aetate not only improved relations between Catholics and Jews, but between Protestants and Jews as well. Protestants also were reexamining their history of relations with the Jews and seeking to repair the damage they had done. At the same time, they wanted to embrace the Jews as partners in attempting to achieve a better world (Robinson, 2004, p. 1). Today, the dialogue between Christians and Jews is not about conversion, but about the common roots of both religious traditions. Christians have made the unremarkable discovery that Jesus was Jewish and came out of a Jewish world. No longer seeking to ignore that fact, Christians now see Judaism as a "'sister religion' with whom they have much in common, and from which they have much to learn" (p. 1).

According to Schaalman's friend, Sr. Mary Christine Athans, BVM, in the aftermath of Vatican II, interfaith efforts "were bubbling" (Athans, 2010). Jews and Catholics in Chicago began an intensive exchange of ideas and formed new alliances. Suddenly, questions that should have been asked long before, and that some had long wanted to ask, were open to discussion between Jews and Catholics.[307] For Sr. Mary (2008), the discovery that Judaism and Christianity had much in common in matters of faith created "an excitement about meeting 'our long lost relatives'" (p. 48).[308] In Chicago, the Sisters of the Charity of the Blessed Virgin Mary at Mundelein College seized on the opportunity to explore new relationships.[309] At the time of the breakthrough, a group of nuns at Mundelein College, who had had positive experiences with Jews since childhood, wanted to reconnect. At their head was Sr. Ann Ida Gannon, BVM, PhD, president of Mundelein College, who had already introduced major reforms in the college. The new spirit of openness and cooperation allowed her to develop a friendship with Schaalman. [Coincidentally, according to Sr. Ann Ida (2010), they are the same age and were born in the same month. In 1981, she spoke at his twenty-fifth anniversary as Emanuel's rabbi and she attended his ninetieth birthday party in 2006, as he did hers. At the time of this interview in July 2010, the two friends were ninety-four years old, both bright and alert.]

The other nuns at Mundelein who were part of this outreach effort were Sr. Mary Christine, BVM, Ph.D., and Sr. Carol Francis Jegen, BVM. At Sr. Ann Ida's request, Sr. Carol Francis had already created a Jewish Studies program as part of the Theology Department. Mundelein was just a few blocks north of Emanuel Congregation, which seemed to the sisters the logical place to begin. The decision turned out to be more successful than they could have imagined. Once they encountered Schaalman, they established permanent friendships and worked together on a variety of activities to promote positive Catholic-Jewish relations (Athans, 2010).

The first contact took place in 1966 when the Sisters of the Charity of the Blessed Virgin Mary telephoned Schaalman to ask whether they could visit his synagogue (Athans, 2010). He was happy to oblige and, not long after, a group of 100 nuns attired in long black habits formed a procession along Sheridan Road on their way to Emanuel. The sight of a stream of nuns entering the synagogue must have been surreal for the drivers passing by. Schaalman met them in the lobby and made them feel right at home. He took them into the sanctuary and opened the ark to reveal the Torah scrolls. He removed one of them, spread it out on the bimah and encouraged them to come close so that they could see the Hebrew script (Athans, 2010). Some of the nuns were so impressed by what they experienced and by Schaalman's gracious manner that they asked whether they could attend a service. Schaalman told them they could come anytime. Several of the nuns came back for the Friday night service. The nuns were so impressed by their welcome and the opportunity to attend services, that they dubbed Emanuel "our synagogue" (Athans, 2010).

A year later, another group of nuns visited Emanuel. Among them was Sr. Mary Christine Athans, who later became Schaalman's friend. Once in the sanctuary, Schaalman removed the Torah from the ark, and, after reading a section in Hebrew, translated it and explained its significance. At the end of the session, one of the nuns asked, "What do you see as the relationship of Christians and Jews, and what do you think of Jesus?" (Athans, 2010) "We believe," said Schaalman, "that God gave a covenant with us, and, in no way do we believe that God will ever renege on that covenant" (cited in Athans, 2010). Then he smiled and added, "But, who's to say that He couldn't make another one with you" (Athans, 2010)?

Sr. Christine was so impressed with this statement that she never forgot it and used it as an epigraph in one of her books. She credits him and Rabbi Marc Tanenbaum, former Director of International Affairs for the American Jewish Committee, as sources for her devotion to the study of Judaism and her active efforts to reach out to Jews. Twenty years later, after she had been hired to direct the new Center of Jewish-Christian Learning at the University of St. Thomas in St. Paul, she invited Schaalman to be one of its first speakers. When she met him, she asked, "Do you realize that you are responsible for nearly all the theological writing I've done" (Athans, 2010)? Of course, he did not remember her; their only encounter had occurred twenty years earlier when she had been a mere student sitting in one of Emanuel's pews. They did not meet again until 2002 when she retired and returned to Chicago and joined the prestigious Catholic-Jewish Scholars Dialogue (Athans, 2010).

Catholic-Jewish Scholars Dialogue

In 1983 after listening to Bernardin's appeal for Catholic-Jewish dialogue, the Chicago Board of Rabbis asked him to establish a formal framework to realize his vision of interfaith encounter. His response was to create the CRLMC to promote positive Christian-Jewish relations. Its original membership included scholars, clergy, and lay people, who were thought to have "reached into their communities and could help facilitate improved interfaith relations." According to Michael Kotzin (2007), Executive Vice President of the Jewish Federation of Metropolitan Chicago and a member of the Dialogue, it represents "the epitome" of the positive Catholic-Jewish interfaith relations in Chicago (p. 7).

From its beginnings, Schaalman has been a member of the group and, despite the fact that he is ninety-six years old, regularly attends its meetings. He is concerned lest the views of his Orthodox colleagues be taken as sole representative of the views of the Jewish community. Their engagement in interfaith activities stops short of participating as guests in Christian religious services or, for that matter, of entering a church.[310] Because he is more accepting of Christians and more open to sharing in their religious experience, Schaalman has been a frequent guest in both Protestant and Catholic churches. Schaalman is critical of the Dialogue because it has not lived up to its potential. Despite the new understandings and positive feelings that result from the interaction of the group members, its members tend to be too polite to each other and "shy away from controversial issues. It is through confrontations," Schaalman maintains, that new understandings emerge. This kind of criticism is precisely what Sr. Christine values in Schaalman's participation, his ability to cut to the core of issues with what she calls his "astounding" wisdom (Athans, 2010).

Taking Interfaith into the Classroom

During the late 1960s and early 1970s, when interfaith relations were gathering momentum in Chicago, Schaalman was invited to teach at the Catholic seminary of the North American headquarters of the Society of the Divine Word (SVD). Known as Techny because of its location in Techny, Illinois, the seminary is the theological school of the Divine Word Order. It was created primarily to train men for the society's foreign missions and has sent hundreds of them to its missions around the world (Techny, 2008). Given its mission to serve "the poor, the neglected and the disadvantaged," it is easy to understand why Schaalman would be attracted to this group.[311] The fact that Schaalman taught there was, in his words, a "fluke."

In the early seventies, when Schaalman organized an interfaith con-ference at the University of Chicago, he created a separate group within the conference of representatives of the Christian seminaries in atten-dance. Typically, the seminaries were represented by their presidents or directors. Schaalman told them he was embarrassed that "virtually none of them [had] courses on Judaism.[312] He reminded them that the roots of Christianity lay in biblical and early Judaism. Because he had been teaching at Garrett-Theological Seminary since 1957, he felt justified in his criticism. Apparently, his remarks had an impact. Soon after the conference, Techny invited him to visit and discuss his concerns. When he convinced administrators that they needed a course on Judaism, they offered to hire him to teach in the religion department. However, they needed to get approval from their headquarters in Rome. Schaalman did not hear anything for several months. Then, to his surprise, an admin-istrator called and asked him with evident excitement "to please come." The request to hire him had been approved, and the seminary was eager to discuss schedules and other matters related to his teaching.

The first year, Schaalman taught a course on the Book of Psalms to a group of ordination students. At the end of the course, they invited him to attend their ordination as their guest of honor. This experience was the first time he had witnessed an ordination other than of rab-bis. As part of the ceremony, he witnessed his twenty-five students, all dressed in white, prostrate themselves in front of the altar before they were raised individually by the officiating priests. Schaalman described the experience as "unforgettable."[313]

His faculty appointment at Techny had a much greater reach than the rabbi knew at the time. In 1968, while he was teaching at Techny, his son, Michael, who was a junior at Grinnell, went to Israel with a group from his college. The Schaalmans decided they would link up with him in Rome. In anticipation of the trip, Schaalman mentioned to his class at Techny that he and his wife were going to Rome. To his surprise, the students immediately set about making arrangements for them through their contact with several Techny students in Rome who were working on their doctorates. At least one of them had been Schaalman's student. They arranged for the Schaalmans to stay in a convent beside the Vati-can and for the students to serve as their unofficial guides. The convent was run by the Divine Order of Sisters, a group of nuns from Germany.

When the Mother Superior called from Germany and found out that a rabbi was staying in the quarters, she asked Schaalman whether he would spend an evening with the sisters. Schaalman accepted the invitation, and, when he spoke to them, discovered that all of them were young and had never seen a Jew or heard of the *Shoah*. Schaalman told them about the horrors of the *Shoah* and its effect on him and his family. Schaalman's account reduced the sisters to tears. Schaalman reports, "They were so deeply affected, I wept too because that was, frankly, my first encounter with Germans [since leaving Germany in 1937]. The experience turned out to be surreal and very difficult for me to absorb."

During the rest of the week that the family was in Rome, the students escorted the Schaalmans to places they would never have seen without their escort. In one of their expeditions, they climbed to the roof of St. Peter's Basilica. Another unique experience for the Schaalmans was their visit "the bowels of St. Peter's" where they saw what was supposed to have been the tomb of St. Peter. Only recently discovered, the tomb was seven levels below ground. To reach it, the Schaalmans' descent on narrow stairs took nearly half an hour. The experience of the massive and beautiful building above ground and its deep underground caverns was truly awesome for Schaalman.

Also during that week, the Schaalmans happened to find themselves in front of St. Peter's on the day John XXIII had his Saints Day, the birthday of the saint after whom he had been named. They were completely surprised to find themselves near a crowd rushing into the basilica. Caught up in the excitement, they decided to follow. They were the last people let in before the doors closed behind them. They stood in the back of the church and watched as the Swiss guards carried in John XXIII on his portable throne. There they were, a Jewish family from America, positioned not more than ten feet away from the procession! Fascinating as the experience was, they did not stay for the service.

When Schaalman returned to the convent, he became very sick and asked the nuns to help him get a doctor. Just then, a busload of pilgrims, who were accompanied by a doctor, arrived at the convent. The doctor agreed to treat him for what he diagnosed was a bad cold. As it turned out, Schaalman discovered that the doctor and the busload of children came from the same town where Lotte had been born. In retrospect, Schaalman could not help remarking that the week was full of such wonderful and unanticipated events, "Incredible! And all because, you know, the chain that started that I needed to have an interfaith conference in ... Chicago."

This interfaith experience is a reflection of the larger picture of the new relationship that was developing between Christians and Jews. When the two religious groups discovered that they shared a common vision of social justice, they developed new channels of cooperation. During the civil rights struggles of the 1960s, Jewish organizations, such as the newly formed Jewish Council on Urban Affairs, the Chicago Board of Rabbis, and the American Jewish Congress, engaged in joint actions with the Archdiocese of Chicago, the Episcopal Diocese of Chicago, and the Church Federation of Greater Chicago. Together, they established the Chicago Conference on Religion and Race (CCRR) to unite Chicago's religious communities to participate in the civil rights movement. Churches, high schools, colleges and seminaries invited rabbis and Jewish scholars to lecture on Judaism. Because of the mutual interest in each other, Jews attempted to reach out to Catholics in ways they had never done before. They invited Catholics to attend synagogue services and to participate in model Seders at Passover (Baima, T., 1996, p. 9).

In 1964, in response to what it expected to be the outcome of Vatican II, the United States Conference of Catholic Bishops established the Commission for Ecumenical Affairs. The purpose of the commission was to improve relations not only with the Jewish community but also with non-Christian religions and the secular world (United States Conference of Catholic Bishops, 1968). In 1966, the commission (now the Committee on Ecumenical and Interreligious Affairs) participated in joint activities with the American Jewish Committee, the American Jewish Committee, the Anti-Defamation League, and, later, the Synagogue Council of America (United States Conference of Catholic Bishops, 1968).

During 1970s and '80s, when Schaalman began to play an increasingly important role in Chicago's interfaith and Jewish communities as president of the CBR, the CRLMC and the JCUA, in addition, he was a vice president of the American Jewish Congress and a frequent speaker in churches, seminars, and Jewish organizational gatherings. As he became more involved in local interfaith activities, his interreligious activities became global. His close friends in interfaith activities invited him to participate in organizations whose mission was to promote international peace and religious tolerance. The two most prominent of them were the International Council of Christians and Jews (ICCJ) and the Parliament of the World's Religions.

Council of Religious Leaders of Metropolitan Chicago (CRLMC)

Schaalman's election as president of the CRLMC gave him the opportunity to work within an effective organization to carry out his long-time commitment to social justice. Although the Council of Religious Leaders (CRLMC) struggled in its first years to find its focus, by 1987, it took on the issue of public housing. When Schaalman became president in 1988, he set as one of his priorities to move the Council to identify its mission and role in the community. One issue facing the organization was whether to expand its membership to include Muslims and representatives from other Christian communities. Schaalman was in favor of expanding membership and formed a committee to develop criteria for membership. He was well aware that to make such a proposal was, as he put it, "high risk," but the only way the Council could consider itself an "inclusive religious voice." In his acceptance speech as Council president, he had already told them that he "would like to see the Council become the conscience of the community."

By the late 1980s, the Council devoted its major efforts to promoting peace between the Israelis and the Palestinians. It issued a statement calling for a two-state solution, one Palestinian and the other Israeli. The statement recognized Israel's right to exist in secure borders, and the Palestinian's right to self-determination. It also called for U.S. involvement in the peace process. To promote its agenda, the Council voted to send a trio of Jewish, Moslem, and Christian clergy to churches, mosques, and synagogues to bring the message of the Council to a wider audience.

The religious leaders saw an urgent need to be proactive and to do what they could to mitigate the violence in the Middle East. For more than a decade, from 1980 to 1991, the Middle East had been racked by war. The most brutal and deadly was the eight-year war between Iraq and Iran. Between 1980 and 1988, over one million combatants and civilians died. Before this war ended, in 1987 the Palestinians began a low-grade war against the Israelis. Initially, this war, known as the First Intifada, began as a nonviolent protest against Israeli occupation. Soon, many of the protests turned violent as Palestinians attacked Israeli soldiers and civilians. Israel fought back, sometimes using harsh measures to control the violence. By the time of the Oslo Peace Accords in 1993, over 2,000 Palestinians had been killed, over half of them by other Palestinians as reprisals for what they thought were collaboration with the Israelis. In addition, more than 150 Israelis were killed by Palestinian violence. In 1990, a third major Middle East war erupted when Iraq, undaunted by its huge losses in its war with Iran, invaded and quickly occupied Kuwait, its oil-rich and far weaker neighbor. This war quickly overshadowed the Intifada in scale. Not only was Kuwait a major supplier of oil to the United States and other Western nations, but control of its oil fields by a hostile Iraq constituted a strategic threat to the United States and to the world's oil supply. Consequently, the United Nations authorized the United States and a coalition of other nations to expel Iraq from Kuwait. By the spring of 1991, in a lightning attack, coalition forces pushed the Iraqis out of Kuwait, and Iraq was forced to accept a humiliating defeat. As with the previous wars, the CRLMC was helpless to prevent the violence and injustice of international politics.

On June 21, 2010, the CRLMC celebrated twenty-five years of its existence. During that time, its membership had expanded dramatically. In 1988, Schaalman had expressed his hope that someday it should become a more inclusive religious community. The original membership had now expanded to include thirty-one local religious groups and seven religious organizations in Metropolitan Chicago. The membership list read like a who's who of Chicago and America's religious communities.[314] It had become a coordinating body representing nearly four million men, women, and children in Metropolitan Chicago (Council of Religious Leaders of Metropolitan Chicago, 2008). The CRLMC now represented the diverse faith traditions that, according to its mission statement, "share the values of respect for the beliefs of others and the desire to bring the highest values of their traditions" (Council of Religious Leaders of Metropolitan Chicago, 2008). Together, in Schaalman's terms, "They could work to transform the world and make it the place God intended."

For its twenty-fifth anniversary celebration, the Council chose Schaalman to deliver its keynote address. Held outdoors on a warm, humid evening behind Chicago's Garfield Park Conservatory, the event was attended by more than 100 religious leaders from the Chicago Metropolitan area including past Council presidents and representatives of local, state, and national political leaders. Also in attendance were Schaalman's wife Lotte, son Michael, his wife Roberta, and a small group of Emanuel congregants.

Cardinal Francis George, a close friend of the rabbi, introduced him. He told the audience that when he arrived in Chicago as the new Archbishop, he and Schaalman discovered that their interests and personalities allowed them to become friends immediately. At their first meeting, George spoke to him casually in German and used "the familiar 'du' rather than the more formal 'Sie'" (George, 2010). During the thirteen years that they have known each other, they shared "their personal joys and sorrows and those that have emerged in our Jewish-Catholic dialogues: locally, nationally, and internationally" (George, 2010). They have shared lunches at George's residence and dinners at the Schaalman home. On other occasions, Schaalman invited him to be his guest at the Standard Club. During these meetings, Schaalman "shared his often-questioning relationship with God, his love for his family, and reflections on his ever-widening encounters with other religious communities." These exchanges helped George broaden his thinking and made him "more restless and yet confirmed in my own attempts to live my faith authentically in ways that incorporate the self-consciousness of others" (George, 2010). Schaalman's selection as the keynote speaker came as the result of his "openness to change and his commitment to interfaith relations …, an anchor and a pioneer in the interfaith movement in Metropolitan Chicago and beyond" (George, 2010).

Schaalman began his talk with this question: "What's so great about twenty-five years? Why make such a fuss about such a short time?" His answer was that the existence of the organization is "a minor miracle." He knew of no other organization of similar scope in the country and expressed doubt that any such exists anywhere else in the world. Therefore, "the existence and the work of this truly unique and unparalleled organization of diverse people from every corner of the compass over the last twenty-five years deserves to be celebrated." Because of its eloquence and because it is a reflection of Schaalman's most recent thinking on the need and value of ecumenism, the rest of the speech is quoted in full:

> To live in each other's assumptions, if we could have the grace, then the real test of this Council is just beginning. Someone has to take the leadership in reshaping the intellectual and moral atmosphere of this world. And who is better situated, who has the most pressing commitments and call to attempt to do this than the so-called leaders of the religious world? If we here in Chicago have become a model of how people of the greatest diversity can find a way to each other and speak to each other and live within the other's assumptions.
>
> We are here to celebrate the establishment and work of a truly unique and unparalleled organization of diverse people from every corner of the world. The Council is a minor miracle, and, to the best of our knowledge, there is no other organization of similar scope. The Council, realizing that the idea was no longer acceptable that we are sufficient unto ourselves, needed to reach out and widen that tent to include whole sections of humanity that we, as leaders, had not recognized and included. Whoever heard of Jains, Zoroastrians, or Bahais? We realized that we needed to widen the tent in which we lived so comfortably, and that there were groups and whole sectors of humanity which are not only underrepresented but unrecognized by those who call ourselves leaders of the religious community. We have had to learn something that is not totally accepted, that we are no longer alone in this world, that we can no longer assume that it is up to us to shape this world, that there are vast sectors of humanity that walk to a different drummer, and who have their own dreams and hopes and skills.
>
> We have had to learn this, and it has been a difficult lesson to learn that we are not the heir and steward of the civilization that has triumphed and had the world all to itself for centuries. Western civilization now has to learn that it has fellow searchers in the vineyard of the Almighty, each of which is committed and capable of making a major contribution to that ultimate fulfillment that everyone will sit under His fig tree, and none will make them afraid. It is not easy to come to these conclusions.

I believe that it is the Council of Religious Leaders, this unique institution that is perhaps the most available in the world. The Council is the only laboratory in which whatever needs to be learned now will be. However, we have to understand ourselves and our relation to others who have been total strangers to us.

So, what I am really thinking of, after 25 years, is that the real task of this Council is just beginning. It is not a small task, I don't have to remind us. But I also believe, that in those years that it has been my privilege to be part of this Council, that I have come across human souls, human beings of such understanding of such breadth of willingness and such breath of commitments that, even with absolutely almost a messianic kind of a vision, doesn't seem to me to be impossible. A fantasy? It's a dream all right. But why shouldn't we have a dream? If we wish what we are here for, the dream ... to have a sense of destiny, to know that however long we are on this earth that not only can we make, but that we are intended to make a difference. My friends, this Council of ours has a call. Out of places we do not understand there comes the word to us of Someone calling, "Where are you? There is a task to be achieved. My dream of the world needs someone who believes in Me and will work for it, incessantly, no matter what the obstacles." This, I am convinced, needs to be the call that comes to us and it is up to us to say, "Here we are, send us."

Schaalman's major point was that, in the twenty-five years of CRLMC's existence, it had not only become more inclusive, but, by recognizing the value of diversity, it poses a direct challenge to Western civilization. For hundreds of years, Western society thought it had nothing to learn from other cultures. The outreach to many other faith communities in Chicago has shown how false the assumption is. Insofar as the Council has brought together so many disparate and divergent communities that have pledged to work together to make the world a better place, it is doing God's work, the work that He imbued in the traditions and belief systems of all of them and that they share through the CRLMC. Referring obliquely to Abraham's response "*Hineni* (I am here)" to God's call to him, he told his audience that the organization had a similar mission: to answer God's call with the response, "Call us."

By doing so, the organization would help God make the world He imagined, a world of peace and understanding and mutual love.

The Parliament of the World's Religions

In 1988, Schaalman became a member of the Council for a Parliament of the World's Religions and soon served on its program committees (Schaalman, 2007, p. 130). Originally created in Chicago in 1893, the Parliament is a global body representing all major religious and spiritual communities. It brings together religious leaders and followers from more than 80 countries to discuss issues of peace, diversity and sustainability within a framework of interreligious understanding and cooperation (Parliament, 2007–2010). Chicago continues to be the home of its international headquarters. In 1987, Chicago members of the Parliament created the Council for a Parliament of the World's Religions to serve as its program body and to prepare for its 1993 centennial celebration. According to Dirk Ficca (2010), Executive Director of the Council, Chicago has played a critical role in supporting the religious movement around the world. In Schaalman's estimation, "The Parliament is Chicago's gift to the world" (as quoted by Ficca, 2010).

In recognition of his national and international prominence in the Jewish community, the founders invited Schaalman to represent the Jewish community on its new Board of Trustees. The Council also created "Honorary Presidents" to represent each of the religious traditions that were members of the Parliament. As both Trustee and Honorary President, Schaalman helped plan the Parliament's 1993 centennial celebration in Chicago. Fr. Thomas Baima (2011) reports that he and Schaalman guided the whole planning process (2011). Dirk Ficca (2010), Executive Director of the Council, remembers that Schaalman brought to the process a "wider vision" (2010). He saw the Parliament as a potential force for the promotion of peace and justice around the world, two values at the core of each of the religions represented in the Council. He urged that the Parliament should be more than a commemorative event. It should be a dynamic working body representative of the world's religions and a means to evaluate the role of religion in "promoting good or ill." The Parliament adopted his vision.[315] Ficca (2010) also credits Schaalman for enlisting Cardinal Bernardin in the project. Because of his influence with Bernardin, the Cardinal "threw his full weight behind it," investing it with his enormous international prestige. He not only attended the event, but also made several presentations.

Schaalman played another important part in the planning of the conference. He was part of a small group responsible for editing the major document that came out of the conference, *The Principles: Toward a Global Ethic*. Although the full document had been written by groups of academics in Chicago and in Europe, according to Fr. Thomas Baima, he and Schaalman worked together as the two main editors. Schaalman also worked on a shorter version. Baima (2011) remembers that one of Schaalman's most important contributions to the documents was his powerful reaction to the language about the Holocaust. The original, written by Dr. Hans Küng, a Catholic priest and renowned scholar, used the word "recognized" referring to the Holocaust and genocide as subjects included in the document. Baima (2011) says he will never forget the vehemence of Schaalman's response: "You don't '*recognize*' the Holocaust, you condemn it. You don't '*recognize*' genocide, you condemn it" (as quoted by Baima, 2011). According to Baima (2011), that settled the matter; the committee adopted the stronger language and a more forceful tone for the document.

The 1993 meeting of the Parliament was an enormous success. Eight thousand people attended, and another four thousand were turned away because of the lack of space (Ficca, 2010). Schaalman served as its moderator and co-chair of the Jewish Host Committee. In this role, he was responsible for contacting several potential participants and for sending conference materials to the Jewish participants. He also made a presentation, "The Life of the Covenant." In it, he offered some of the ideas that he later developed more fully in his *Hineni* (2007) and which will be discussed in detail in Chapter 9, "Schaalman's Theology."

The highlight of the conference was a plenary address by Gerald O. Barney, a physicist and founder of the Millennium Institute. The fact that Barney was selected as the keynote speaker reflected the Council's sense of the importance of this international organization. The Institute's mission is to create a "sustainable, equitable, and peaceful world" for present and future generations (Millennium Institute). According to Leo Lefebure (1993), Barney "painted a frightening picture of increasing misery and conflict if current trends continue" (p. 887). This conclusion, Barncy told his audience, was the inevitable outcome of alarming growth in the world's populations, the failure to provide sufficient food for the earth's inhabitants, and the abuse of the earth's resources. He called on religious leaders to shape a "new dream, a sustainable faith tradition" to address the human needs of the earth's most desperate populations (Lefebure, 1993, p. 887).

Schaalman was deeply moved by the presentation, and, as one of the co-hosts, told the assembly, "Now we all know why we have come. We have heard from the soul of a man for whom all the earth is home. Now, we have been challenged as I have never heard anyone challenge me, and I dare say I'm speaking for each of us here " (Lefebure, 1993, p. 887).

One of the outcomes of the conference was a "Declaration Toward a Global Ethic," an attempt to address some of the planet's most pressing problems. It began, "The world is in agony" and went on to list some of the most challenging issues: a world plagued by war, ecological destruction, poverty, hunger, social injustice, and disease. The Declaration called for an awakening to the common core values and teachings of all religions that are the basis for the improvement of the human condition and the salvation of the planet (Parliament, 1993).

A few months after the 1993 Parliament, the Council for a Parliament of the World's Religions established a committee on critical issues that included Schaalman. This committee reviewed the early drafts of Barney's book, *Threshold 2000: Critical Issues and Spiritual Values for a Global Age*, and Barney credits Rabbi Schaalman and several others for making "especially helpful suggestions concerning the questions for spiritual leaders that appear near the end of the report." Barney also invited Schaalman to become a member of the Board of the Millennium Institute. This new role allowed Schaalman to expand his range of participation in and influence on interfaith and global issues. "I serve," he notes, "with fascinating people with whom I otherwise would not have come in contact. My role on the board was jokingly described to me as 'moral irritant.'"

By 1994, Schaalman was beginning to receive recognition for his work in interfaith relations. The American Jewish Congress gave him its coveted Richard Alschuler Award in honor of his years of service on behalf of interfaith understanding and collaboration. Although originally the award was to be presented by Cardinal Bernardin, it was presented by his close colleague and friend, Revered Thomas A. Baima. Baima referred to Schaalman's ongoing friendship with the Cardinal and to his work to promote interreligious understanding and the alleviation of Chicago's serious social issues. The following year, in recognition of the interfaith work they had done together, Cardinal Bernardin gave Schaalman one of the most important awards given by the Catholic Church to non-Catholics, the Award of Laureate in Ecumenical and Inter-religious Affairs.

In November 1995, as a Trustee of the Council of the Parliament of the World's Religions and as a member of the Board of the Millennium Institute, Schaalman helped plan and served as co-host of a joint program called the "Millennium Moment Roundtable." Held at Chicago's suburban North Shore Congregation Israel, the program brought together local, national, and international leaders in interfaith activities to discuss issues facing the Third Millennium. The organizers intended the meeting as a "gift of the "United Nations Spiritual Forum for World Peace" (Lama Gangchen Peace Times, n.d.).

A few years later, Schaalman played an important part in planning the 1999 Conference of the Parliament of the World's Religions held in Cape Town, South Africa. The planning took two years, but the payoff was significant. Over 7,000 people from around the world attended the conference, including "teachers, scholars, believers, and practitioners" (Parliament of the World's Religions, 1999, p. 1). He remained an Honorary President and Trustee of the Council of the Parliament for a few years after the Cape Town Parliament (Ficca, November 30, 2010).

In October 2004, Schaalman took part in a National Mission Symposium in Louisville, Kentucky. Sponsored by the Glenmary Home Missioners, the conference was designed to offer Catholic theologians and clergy the opportunity to discuss the idea of the Kingdom of God. Schaalman's role was to provide an interfaith perspective on this topic. After hearing the message that the mission of the Church was to acknowledge the brotherhood and sisterhood of all humanity, Schaalman responded emotionally: "For the first time, I have heard the mission of the Church not as self-contained privileged membership exclusive of others but as an outreach to every human being as sister and brother to penetrate more deeply the mystery of who we are as human beings" (Glenmary Home Missioners, 2004). Schaalman's remarks were undoubtedly the result of the heightened emotion of the moment.

For decades, he had heard and read similar pronouncements from the Church and from his friends Cardinal Bernardin and Fr. John Pawlikowski. Indeed, by the time of this symposium, this mission mandated by *Nostra Aetate* had become the new "gospel" of the Catholic Church. Nevertheless, it was obviously meaningful for Schaalman to hear it expressed with such fervor.

All of this activity emanating from Vatican II allowed Schaalman to feel "more protected" (Faith in Conversation, 2005). Vatican II served not only as the springboard for improved relations between Catholics and Jews but between and among all religious groups. Nevertheless, he is leery of the long-term viability of these improvements, and he is keeping a close eye on this Christian "reformation." He is aware that sensitive problems remain and new ones have developed in the relationship between Christians and Jews. He is aware, for example, that not everyone in the Church was happy with these changes. Some in the Catholic hierarchy perceived them as threatening and saw no need for change, especially, one that came from "inspiration." They fought against Pope John XXIII's vision because, from their perspective, the Church is a bastion against the forces of change in the world (Zenger, 2009). Modernism, its increasing secularism, its ideas of equality, democracy, freedom of choice, liberalism, and feminism was a challenge to the Church's authority, its theological positions and values. Zenger (2009) writes that, when Pope John XXIII proposed the Council, the Cardinals "did not respond with applause and enthusiasm, but rather with awe-stricken silence and amazement." Thus, the stage was set for a contest between the majority who thought reform was overdue and the minority who felt the basic positions of the Church were being compromised. These tensions within the Church did not surface immediately.

Although major improvements have occurred in interfaith relations since Vatican II, problems remain. In 1988, when Pope John Paul II visited Maidanek in Poland and Mauthausen in Austria, two of the Nazi's most infamous concentration camps, he made no mention of Jews. To Schaalman, this omission was "incomprehensible." Because he thought the Pope a "gifted person" who had had an "enormous impact on the world," Schaalman attributed his actions to his "enigmatic" character or the stance of the Church toward Jews. More recently, Schaalman and other Jewish leaders have been troubled by another development they see as backsliding on the part of Pope Benedict XVI. He has given priests discretion whether to use the Latin version of one of the prayers in the Mass, which contains a negative portrayal of Jews. Given the nearly 2,000 year history of the Church's oppression, this decision has been interpreted by Schaalman and others as a move backward to earlier practices.

Fuel was added to this skepticism when, in 2000, John Paul II issued *Dominus Iesus*. The document reasserted several key positions that had been Church dogma: (1) the Catholic Church is the sole true Church of Christ; (2) other Christian churches are not properly Churches; (3) and non-Christians do not have the same status relative to salvation as those within the True Church. To Schaalman, the document is a throwback to the Church's previous exclusivity. Rather than be discouraged by it, however, Schaalman understands that the process toward improved interfaith understanding cannot be steady and uninterrupted. From time to time, there will be regressions. The problem, he says, is that the massive community of the Roman Catholic Church has not been able to adapt so quickly to *Nostra Aetate*. It requires a completely new way of thinking about Jews and Judaism (Faith in Conversation, 2005). In order to have improved relations with Jews, "it is not necessary," Schaalman concludes, "for Christianity to give up its core convictions. It is only necessary that the tone and language might become more positive to make it easier for non-Christians to feel accepted and understood" (Faith in Conversation, 2005).

Schaalman has carried his interfaith efforts into the classroom where, for more than half a century, he has taught students heading for the ministry. Despite his busy schedule, even in retirement, he has carved out blocks of time to teach in some of Chicago's most prestigious seminaries. In doing so, he continues where he left off in Cedar Rapids when he taught adult education at Coe College and Cornell College. In Chicago, he taught at Barat College, DePaul University, the Divine Word Seminary, Mundelein College (now part of Loyola University), and North Park Seminary, Garrett-Theological Seminary,[316] and the Chicago Theological Seminary (CTS) on the campus of the University of Chicago.[317]

Since the late 1950s, Schaalman has been teaching part-time at Garrett, and, as of 2012, continues to teach one course in the fall semester. When he retired from Emanuel in 1986, he picked up another teaching assignment at Chicago Theological Seminary. He speculates that, over the last half-century, he has taught tens of thousands of seminary students. "In my teaching," he commented, "I try to emphasize to my ministerial students the fact that they are descended from the Pharisees and therefore must acknowledge this heritage in their sermons."

Schaalman's relationship with his ministerial students has had an interesting and important side effect. His students have helped him achieve new insights into his own religious experience: "My students at Garrett raised questions about areas of my belief and practice that I had never thought about before. The experience turned out to be fascinating, stimulating and provocative and inspired me to offer a new course, The Liturgy of the Synagogue, which I am still teaching." These experiences piggybacked on changes he was already undergoing in the 1950s as he began to open himself up to changes in his thinking and practice: "When I became Emanuel's new rabbi, I began to question the efficacy of prayer and the validity of particular ritual practices in the service. My students taught me to think about the purpose and effectiveness of practices that up to this point I had taken for granted."

Schaalman's involvement with CTS proved to be a perfect match. Modeling its curriculum on the Brazilian educator and activist Paulo Freire, CTS stresses, "What you learn depends on those with whom you learn" (Chicago Theological Seminary, CTS: About Us, n.d.). The seminary is a place where students and faculty "teach one another by our embodied diversity—our astonishing differences and our surprising commonalities. We teach one another by the gift of dialogue" (Chicago Theological Seminary, CTS: About Us, n.d.). Given Schaalman's understanding that knowledge is dialogic and that learning occurs through the interaction with others, as students of Schaalman's Torah Study will attest, this is precisely the method Schaalman uses with them.

His classes at Garrett and CTS are small, usually ten to fifteen students. Occasionally, his students are uncomfortable and even shocked when they hear what he has to say, particularly when he attempts to talk about what it means for him to be a Jew: "They just sit there; they don't even respond." Being a Jew means to him, "not only to have survived the *Shoah*, but to have a sense of the necessity to survive to prove to God that His people are not totally lost." Particularly shocking to his students is his unwillingness to accept Judaism as it was practiced by ancient Israel. Also, difficult for them is that he tries to "be open" to new ideas, especially new scientific ideas. "I tell them that the Pharisaic principle is to interpret and that, when they [his students] have to prepare sermons, they will all be Pharisees. As difficult as this statement is for them to comprehend, they nonetheless treat me with respect because they like me."[318]

Friends and Allies in the Interfaith Struggle

At the heart of Schaalman's interfaith activity is his willingness to engage in dialogue. Authentic dialogue involves risk and vulnerability in the partners. Schaalman puts it this way: "My willingness to listen allows me to reach out to others with different belief systems. In this way, I can understand their basic assumptions and compare them to my own." In 2002, he told a reporter, "There is no question that when you hear the faith of others who are deeply convicted and convinced about their own faith, that you learn something about the faith life. ... When I'm with others and see how they address these questions, what response they give to the question that life and God poses, then I learn something." Most important, he states in *Hineni* (2007), is that this openness to others is "ultimately necessary to make certain that the human family ... can eventually ... do away with some of the most destructive evil from which humanity has suffered. ..." (p. 263).

Schaalman's willingness to reveal his own vulnerability and to be an authentic listener is, in part, responsible for his enormous influence on and respect in the Christian community. He has made friends and partners with secular and nonsecular Christians who share his willingness to reveal their own vulnerabilities and to discuss their profound and alienating issues (Faith in Conversation, 2005). Vulnerability by itself, however, does not explain Schaalman's extraordinary relationship with Chicago's Catholic hierarchy. A key to that relationship is his ability to speak to Christians in their own language. He learned early on that the language of America and, for that matter, of Western civilization, is the language of Christianity. To engage in dialogue with Christians is to acknowledge that fact and to work sensitively within it. Terms such as "good and evil," "hell and damnation," and "Original Sin and redemption" have specifically Christian meanings that are not part of the Jewish vocabulary and are alien to Jewish theology. Yet, because they are the *lingua franca* of the society in which he lives, it is necessary to understand and accept their validity within the Christian context. To engage in meaningful interfaith dialogue, however, it is essential to help Christians understand that to a Jewish theologian, the words do not have the same meaning. Understanding this difference between the two religious cultures and traditions is the first step to meaningful dialogue.

Where the two traditions meet is in the idea of "suffering," a sadly familiar theme in Judaism. It is an idea that goes to the core of Schaalman's thinking. For him, the key to understanding the relationship of God to His humans is to know that the relationship is interdependent. In this relationship, God suffers when humans fail to live up to His expectations. In reference to the *Shoah*, the extreme manifestation of this failure, Schaalman does not ask how God could have allowed it. In Schaalman's terms, God could *not* prevent it and is as much its victim and as were His Jews.[319] This conclusion allows Schaalman to sympathize with Christianity's view that God was willing to sacrifice His son to redeem humanity. This sacrifice, Schaalman speculates, is God's expression of His utter despair for His failure to enlist the aid of His humans to redeem creation. It is an idea to which he will return in later years. Schaalman may have also been influenced by his close association with Christians, such as Cardinal Bernardin and Fr. John Pawlikowski. It is reasonable to assume that these friendships and subsequent interactions through conferences and workshops helped prepare the way for the development of Schaalman's understanding of God.

This fundamental willingness to be open to Christianity's basic beliefs, the depth of his character, his intelligence, and religious commitment have earned Schaalman many friends and admirers in the Christian community. One of them is Father Alphonse Spilly, Cardinal Bernardin's former assistant, who told this interviewer, "When I hear Schaalman speak, I feel like I'm in the presence of God." Another of Schaalman's good friends in the Christian community is the distinguished scholar Andre LaCocque, emeritus professor of Hebrew Scriptures at the Chicago Theological Seminary, and emeritus director of its doctoral Center for Jewish-Christian Studies and author of many books and articles on Judaism.[320] The two men met soon after Schaalman began teaching at CTS and, subsequently, became good friends. Because both share similar views, they were able to team-teach several courses until LaCocque retired. Together, the two professors had a significant influence on seminary students from diverse backgrounds (2000 Graham Taylor Award, 2000).

Looking back over the many years of their friendship, LaCocque wrote that his relationship with Schaalman was "a wonderful gift that has informed my whole life and is still ever afresh filling me with awe and supreme joy" (LaCocque, n.d.). LaCocque saw himself as the student and Schaalman as "the master, the rabbi," "the Giver," and himself as the receiver, the "disciple, the *Talmid raham* [sic, *chacham*]." LaCocque concluded with these extraordinary words: "In my own long teaching career—more than forty years—I consider as among its high points those times when I have been more a student than a teacher, gathering the pearls of wisdom coming from an 'angel' that is, a messenger of God. THANK YOU, HERMAN!" (LaCocque, n.d.)

Fr. John T. Pawlikowski, a leading figure in Christian-Jewish dialogue worldwide, is one of Schaalman's close friends.[321] Their friendship began sometime in the late 1960s when Pawlikowski began his work in Jewish-Christian relations. When they first met, Schaalman's friendliness and knowledge of Judaism and Christian-Jewish relations made an immediate impact on Pawlikowski, who had been teaching Holocaust studies at the Catholic Theological Union.[322] In the late 1980s, they worked together in planning the Parliament of the World's Religions 1993 centennial in Chicago. Both are members of the Holocaust Foundation and participate together in workshops and seminars on interfaith relations and on the Holocaust.

Cardinal Joseph Bernardin

The most important friendship Schaalman made in the Catholic community was with the late Cardinal Bernardin. Their friendship was possible, in part, because of the major changes that were taking place in the Catholic-Jewish dialogue. The changes began with the Second Vatican Council (1962–1965) during the reign of Pope John XXIII and, after his death in 1963, under Pope Paul VI (1963–1978). At the conclusion of the Council in 1965, the bishops approved a document known as *Nostra Aetate*, an ecumenical pronouncement that acknowledged the validity of the world's major religions and the acceptance of all peoples as people of God, made in God's image and part of God's Divine Plan for the earth. *Nostra Aetate* repudiated anti-Semitism and racism and declared: "The Church, mindful of the patrimony she shares with the Jews and moved not by political reasons but by the Gospel's spiritual love, decries hatred, persecutions, displays of anti-Semitism, directed against Jews at any time and by anyone."

These statements of a new direction for the Church represented a complete break with the past and an effort to create a new sense of brotherhood with Jews and an acceptance of their religion. The document went even further instructing Catholic clergy and educators to "see to it, then, that in catechetical work or in the preaching of the word of God they do not teach anything that does not conform to the truth of the Gospel and the spirit of Christ."[323]

Nostra Aetate was also a response to the sense of guilt and responsibility for the failure of Christians to prevent the Nazi effort to exterminate the Jews. Since 1965, the Church has engaged in a continuous effort to atone for its role in promoting anti-Semitism and its violence directed against Jews throughout the last two millennia. At the same time, through its public pronouncements and through its actions the Church has been attempting to reach out to Jews who are now seen as "brothers."[324]

Bernardin embodied the substance of this new direction. Before coming to Chicago, he had already established a reputation for his interfaith commitments. From the beginning of his appointment to the Archdiocese of Chicago in 1982, he developed a variety of programs to promote the development of the Catholic-Jewish and interfaith dialogue. One of his first actions was to establish a separate, fully staffed agency to expand his outreach to the Jewish community. Through this agency, he was able to forge new partnerships between the Archdiocese and major Jewish organizations in Metropolitan Chicago. Among them were the Jewish Federation of Metropolitan Chicago, the Chicago Board of Rabbis, Spertus Institute of Jewish Studies, and the American Jewish Committee (Pinkus, 1996).

In 1985, Bernardin sponsored a convocation of Jewish and Catholic leaders to mark the twentieth anniversary of *Nostra Aetate*. Bernardin's objective was not only to commemorate the event, but also to herald a new phase in the history of Catholic-Jewish relations in Chicago.[325] The Jewish community seized the opportunity to promote and develop interfaith relations. When Schaalman was a vice president, the American Jewish Committee organized an annual priest-rabbi retreat that allowed rabbis and priests to attend lectures, engage in group discussions, share prayer services, and join in friendship (Baima, T. A., 1996, pp. 11–12). These two-day retreats provided a unique opportunity for participants to engage in serious interfaith dialogue. Originally designed as a Catholic-Jewish dialogue opportunity, the retreats soon evolved to include Episcopal, Lutheran, and Greek Orthodox churches.

Through this outreach, Schaalman and Bernardin met and quickly developed a mutual affection that had a profound effect on interfaith relations in Chicago and beyond. The effort of the Chicago Archdiocese to establish positive relations with the Jewish community was enhanced by the friendship between Rabbi Schaalman and Cardinal Bernardin. The story of Schaalman's friendship with Cardinal Bernardin is one that likely has no precedent in Jewish history or in Jewish-Christian relations. It is not only a story of personal friendship, but also one that includes the development of Chicago's interfaith alliances, alliances not only between Catholics and Jews, but also between and among the wide diversity of the city's religious groups. As Schaalman tells it, the fact that the two men became such intimate friends is as much a surprise to him today as it was when it began: "It is astounding to me, and even to this day not totally comprehensible, that our relationship should have developed" (Schaalman, H. E., 2007, p. 240). The two became such close friends that Bernardin would discuss matters with Schaalman that he could not discuss with anyone else. These conversations helped Schaalman develop the sense that they were brothers. The relationship altered his life and, very likely, the Cardinal's as well. "His influence opened my whole being to an understanding that it was possible for someone at the highest levels of the Roman Catholic leadership to be, not just institutionally open to Jews, but to have really the ultimate interior capacity to be a brother, to be an 'other' for a Jew" (p. 241). This experience with Bernardin opened him up "to the vastness of interfaith experience" and helped Schaalman overcome his sense of being at the margin of "other people's religious practices, to become something to which I was more than just present" (pp. 241–242). Yet, Schaalman admits, no amount of openness could overcome his memories of the murderous treatment of Jews during his lifetime and his awareness of the Church's culpability in the persecution of the Jews for the last 2,000 years.

Schaalman does not recall when and how his friendship with Bernardin began. He remembers occasions when he was surprised by Bernardin's expressions of respect and liking for him. On one occasion, Schaalman had invited Bernardin to participate in a service at Emanuel to speak to the congregation. While the two men were putting on their robes in a small private room off the bimah, Bernardin said to him, "Herman, when you are in the room with me, I feel particularly at peace." Schaalman was surprised by these words. The two had met only rarely and he had no idea that he had made an impression of this kind that would engender such an "intimate disclosure." As the two religious leaders worked together on various projects, their relationship deepened.[326]

Soon after he came to Chicago, Bernardin convened a meeting of the city's civic and religious leaders as a way to introduce himself and to come to know them. As part of his introduction, Bernardin repeated Pope John XXIII's remarks to a delegation of the American Jewish Committee: "I am your brother Joseph." With these words, the Cardinal "won everybody's heart" (p. 231). The words also made clear that he was reaching out to Jews and non-Catholics not only in an official way, but also as part of his identification of who he was. Schaalman wrote that he had not encountered anyone else or anyone at such a high level of Church authority with this degree of commitment to Vatican II.

Another of Bernardin's achievements, according to Schaalman, was his creation in 1984 of the Council of Religious Leaders, later renamed the Council of Religious Leaders of Metropolitan Chicago (CRLMC). The CRLMC brought together nineteen heads of the various Christian and Jewish religious groups. They saw themselves as a public witness in the cause of social justice. When the occasion merited, they issued pastoral letters of either support or complaint for actions involving racism, abortion, gambling, and education (Baima, 1996, p. 12).

As noted above, in 1995 Bernardin gave Schaalman a plaque inscribed with the words "Award of Laureate in Ecumenical and Inter-religious Affairs." The program brochure for the presentation ceremony reads:

> If dialogue means to be changed by no other agenda than the
> depth and richness of the experience itself, then Schaalman is

the example, par excellence, of one whose life and work has both provided and been shaped by sensitive, critical, and compassionate interreligious dialogue and action. He is truly an icon of our movement, and for this I confer upon him this singular honor. Given this day, January 29, 1995, at the Pastoral Center of the Archdiocese of Chicago. (Interfaith Awards, 1995)

According to Schaalman, the award is one of his most valued possessions.

Two months later, Schaalman had the opportunity to accompany the Cardinal on a visit to Israel. The 1993 Parliament of World's Religions helped prepare the way for the trip. The inclusiveness of this international conference was a sign of the enormous progress that had been made in the last century in ecumenical relations. It set the stage for Bernardin's visit, which Baima (1996) called the most important interfaith activity for Jews and Christians in almost 2,000 years (p. 14).

For Schaalman, the trip was one of the most important events in his friendship with Bernardin. It was the result of an invitation extended by the American Jewish Committee and the Chicago Jewish Federation. Beginning in the 1980s, these organizations had been organizing and sponsoring visits to Israel for non-Jewish community leaders. Michael Kotzin (2005), one of the primary planners of these trips, asserts that Bernardin's visit "represented a fulfillment of the various programs maintained by the Archdiocese in conjunction with each of these Jewish communal organizations" (p. 7).

Bernardin, who was delighted to accept the invitation, led a small entourage of lay and clerical leaders that included eight Catholics and seven Jews. The Jewish members of the group included two rabbis and five laypeople. Three of them were from the two sponsoring organizations and two were representatives from the Chicago Board of Rabbis and Spertus Institute of Jewish Studies.[327] The rabbis were Schaalman and his friend and colleague, Peter Knobel, who was then president of the Chicago Board of Rabbis.[328] Although not an official delegate, Schaalman was included because Bernardin requested his presence. Throughout the trip, the delegation was accompanied by reporters and cameramen representing Chicago's two major newspapers and all the major television stations. Their presence helped publicize the trip and its importance as an ecumenical experience developed out of the efforts of Catholics and Jews in Chicago (Baima, 1996, p. 8).

When the Hebrew University was notified that the Cardinal was coming, the University invited him to give a lecture and informed him that it planned to confer on him its prestigious award, "Honorary Fellowship of the University." For his lecture, Bernardin prepared a major paper on the history of the Church's anti-Semitism and its current efforts to atone for it. Schaalman called it "a breakthrough paper," but before Bernardin could present it, he had to get approval from Rome. Approval was by no means a sure thing. The Vatican walked a fine line between recognition of the Jewish state and its efforts to promote better relations with the world of Islam and, specifically, with the Palestinians. It was concerned that any show of partiality to the Jewish state might provoke retaliation against Catholic communities in the Arabic and Islamic world. Because of these political concerns, Bernardin could not go only to Israel, but had to visit the Palestinians, which meant a visit to Arafat, the West Bank, and Gaza to hear firsthand Palestinian views on how to achieve peace between the two peoples (Baima, pp. 14–16). Although primarily a spiritual journey for Bernardin, the trip to the "Holy Land" became an opportunity to promote peace between the Israelis and the Palestinians (Schaalman, H. E., 2007, p. 233).

When Bernardin received the letter approving his paper and the trip, he invited Schaalman to his home to share his excitement over his accomplishment. The paper, Bernardin told him, would create further trust and understanding between Catholics and Jews (pp. 233–234). It would also provide direction for the Vatican in its attempt to repair the damage it had done to the Jewish people over the last two thousand years.

As the program for the visit was being formalized, Schaalman noticed that some of the events on the itinerary included the Cardinal's participation in Christian religious events. Schaalman explained to him that the Jewish members of the group would find themselves in a delicate and uncomfortable position as participants in these events. However, they could be "observers." The Cardinal understood Schaalman's concerns and accepted his solution (p. 234).

The delegation visited some of Christianity's and Judaism's most important shrines, including the Via Dolorosa and Yad Vashem. On Friday, March 25, 1995, in order to avoid the crowds, the delegation left their hotel at 6:30 a.m. and set out for the Via Dolorosa. The Cardinal led the way down the narrow streets of Jerusalem's Old City to walk the fourteen Stations of the Cross. It was the same course Jesus had been reputed to have walked as he carried the cross to his execution (Galloway, March 26, 1995, p. 10). Schaalman (2007) remembers that at each stage of the cross, the group stopped so that the Cardinal and the other Christians in the delegation could pray. Because he was uncomfortable in this setting and did not want his discomfort to be obvious to his friend, Schaalman "drifted" to the back of the procession (pp. 234–235).[329] "I always felt so marginal towards other people's religions," he wrote, "that I never allowed it to enter me as an experience, to become something to which I was more than just present" (p. 242). When the group reached the last stage of the Cross, before entering the Church of the Holy Sepulcher, Bernardin waited for his friend. Schaalman realized that the Cardinal was waiting for him so that he could share this very private and moving experience. When Schaalman caught up, the Cardinal put his arm around him and said, "Herman, I cannot tell you what it means to me to have gone the same street that my Savior and Lord walked" (p. 235). "To this day," Schaalman explains, "a chill runs through me when I think of these words" (p. 235). The experience helped him understand viscerally what he had known only intellectually, the profound meaning Jerusalem had for Christians and the deep faith of his friend in his Lord. Twelve years later, he wrote in *Hineni*, the experience was still powerful.

The highlight of the trip was Bernardin's history-making presentation on March 23, 1995, at the Hebrew University of Jerusalem. As part of the event, the University bestowed upon him the award of "Honorary Fellowship of the University," the first award of its kind ever given to a prelate of the Catholic Church. Bernardin's paper, *Anti-Semitism: The Historical Legacy and the Continuing Challenge for Christians*, broke new ground. It was the most powerful ecumenical speech ever made by a high-ranking Church official. Bernardin issued an apology for the Church's rejection and persecution of the Jews and called for a new era of Catholic-Jewish relationships (Baima, p. 16). In addition to exploring the origins of anti-Semitism in Catholic and Christian history, he cited contemporary efforts to repair the damage, including the Vatican Council's 1965 *Nostra Aetate* and the Holy See's 1985 *Notes on the Correct Way to Present Jews and Judaism in Preaching and Catechesis in*

Cardinal Joseph Bernardin and Yassir Arafat

the Roman Catholic Church (Bernardin, J., 1996). When the program ended, Schaalman congratulated his friend and told him the speech was "fabulous." He was particularly gratified that Bernardin acknowledged the failure of the Church to do more for the Jews during the Holocaust.

Although the speech went off without a hitch, Schaalman was disappointed by the reception Hebrew University accorded the Cardinal. He felt that the University had not been sufficiently sensitive to the importance of the Cardinal's visit. He should have been given the courtesy to make his presentation in the University's main auditorium, which had been reserved for a presentation of an honorary doctorate to Al Gore, the American vice president. The University, Schaalman thought, should have given an honorary doctorate to the Cardinal as well.

Before leaving Israel, the delegation met with Prime Minister Rabin, Foreign Minister Peres and, on the last day, with Yasser Arafat, Chairman of the Palestine Liberation Organization, and with the faculty at Bethlehem University on the West Bank. The meeting with Rabin was perfunctory, more a courtesy to the delegation. Peres, on the other hand, allowed them forty-five minutes and then extended the meeting to continue discussions. On the other hand, Schaalman reports that the visit to Bethlehem University did not go smoothly. The faculty was rude to the delegation and poured out a litany of anti-Semitic complaints, not only about the Israeli occupation, but also about Jews. Although not appointed by the delegation to do so, Schaalman was incensed, and he spoke out against them.

Meeting with Arafat

The meeting with Arafat had not been part of the original agenda, but it was added once the delegation arrived in Israel. It was an opportunity for Bernardin to meet Arafat and, as the representative of the Holy See, to demonstrate the Pope's interest in promoting peace in that troubled land. The meeting was held in Arafat's headquarters in Gaza City. Meeting with a man who had been responsible for the deaths of many Jews and Israelis did not sit well with Schaalman. He could not put out of his mind the thought that Arafat was a terrorist and responsible for the hijacking of the passenger ship, *Achille Lauro*, and the 1972 massacre of the Israeli Olympic team at the Munich Olympics.

To get to Gaza City, the delegation traveled with their own bus. Along the way, they had to pass through Israeli checkpoints, though they were not subjected to search. The difficulty of getting into and out of Gaza gave Schaalman the feeling that they were "entering enemy territory." The meeting was held in a second floor conference room in Arafat's compound. Members of Arafat's staff and Bernardin's delegation sat across from each other on opposite sides of a conference table. Schaalman sat at the far end, as was fitting because he was not a "major player" in the event.

The meeting began when Arafat entered the room to greet his guests. The two men carried on their discussion according to strict protocol. To Schaalman it seemed like a minuet: Arafat spoke, Bernardin responded, and so the conversation alternated between the two speakers. The meeting, which lasted no more than a half hour, consisted mostly of Arafat's effort to convince the delegation that he wanted peace. However, he did not mention specifics, which would have been inappropriate for such a meeting.

Overall, the meeting was polite until the end when the two leaders exchanged gifts. Bernardin presented Arafat with a crystal stand on top of which was a cross, a Star of David, and a dove of peace. He explained the gift was "a sign of our commitment to the peace process" (as quoted in Galloway, 1995, p. 3). Not at all impressed, Arafat noted that the gift did not refer to Islam. He pointed to a plaque on the wall opposite them, which he identified as "the Sunday Bible" written in Arabic. Next to it was a companion plaque with some language from the Koran. Then, he pointed out that on the adjacent wall was a framed depiction of Hebrew tablets on which the Ten Commandments were inscribed (p. 3). Unprepared for this unexpected turn of events, Bernardin tried to recover from this unintentional diplomatic *faux pas*. "The only reason there are only two here," he stated, "is because there are no Muslims in our particular delegation, but we're very much aware of them." Realizing that the excuse was lame, Arafat interrupted him with, "But in my office, the three traditions." Bernardin broke in: "But in my remarks, I mentioned the three" to which "Arafat laughed and looked around the room" (as quoted in Galloway, 1995, p. 3).

Aftermath of Bernardin's Trip to Israel

According to Baima (1996), Bernardin's visit to the Holy Land had a profound effect on him and propelled the development of Catholic-Jewish relationships. An outgrowth of this visit was the creation of The Joseph Cardinal Bernardin Jerusalem Lecture, an annual program that commemorates Cardinal Bernardin's 1995 visit to Israel and continues the dialogue he advocated between Jews and Catholics on the theological issues affecting their relationship (Archdiocese of Chicago: Office for Ecumenical & Interreligious Affairs, n.d.).

Schaalman Participates in Bernardin's Funeral

In the spring of 1995, Cardinal Bernardin was diagnosed with pancreatic cancer. At first, he kept the diagnosis secret, even from his close friend. Schaalman discovered that something was wrong when he and Bernardin were invited to "respond" to a sermon given by the Archbishop of

Canterbury at the Episcopal Church on Chicago's South Side. While the two men were waiting in the hall before entering the church, Schaalman noticed that Bernardin's robe was dragging on the floor. Schaalman quipped, "Joseph, are you shrinking or something? What's the matter with your garments?" Bernardin said, "Yes, I am shrinking, and I haven't had a chance to have all my garments hemmed properly" (Schaalman, H. E., 2007, p. 237). At first Schaalman dismissed the information, but the more he thought about it, the more concerned he became. He consulted a few members of Bernardin's inner circle of priests with whom he was good friends, but all they knew was that Bernardin was not well. Later, when Schaalman learned that Bernardin had fallen on the steps inside his home and that he had to call for help to get up, he knew something was seriously wrong. At the end of May, Bernardin revealed publically that he had been diagnosed with pancreatic cancer. He put up a courageous battle against it, but to no avail. In June of 1995, Bernardin underwent surgery for his cancer. For a while, it appeared that it was in remission. A year later in August 1996, he announced publicly that the

The Schaalmans with Cardinal Bernardin at award ceremony
for Laureate in Ecumenical and Inter-religious Affairs, 1995

cancer had returned, had spread to his liver and was inoperable. By the end of October, he withdrew from his active ministry.

Before he died, President Bill Clinton invited Bernardin to Washington to present him with the Medal of Freedom. Although the Cardinal did not know it, one of his entourage had invited Schaalman to attend the ceremony. After he received the award, Bernardin was surrounded by family and well-wishers and, when Schaalman appeared before him, his face lit up. In Schaalman's account, "He embraced me and expressed his absolute deep satisfaction that I was there for him at that time" (p. 238).

A little more than a week before he died, Bernardin invited Schaalman to visit him and told him that he knew he was close to death but that he was not afraid (pp. 237–238). Schaalman listened while Bernardin talked about his life and his anticipation of being with his God. His parting words were, "Herman, I'm totally serene because I will be with my Lord" (p. 283). His willingness to share his final thoughts about his impending death and his apparent serene acceptance of it left Schaalman with a sense of the "exceptional, splendid person he was." Before Schaalman left, Bernardin gave him a memento, a Lladro figurine known as *The Rabbi*, that had been given to him by a friend. When they parted, they embraced; Schaalman "was close to tears" (p. 240).

A few days later on November 14, 1996, one of the Cardinal's staff called to tell him that the Cardinal had died and that he was invited to come to the Cardinal's residence to see him. Schaalman went to visit his old friend and waited in line as the mourners passed by the body. He saw a young person touch Bernardin's hand and, when his turn came, Schaalman reached out to touch Bernardin's hand: "Here was the hand that I had shaken, that had always been so warm and receptive, now stone cold. Stone cold. I shudder to this day." Because he did not share Bernardin's faith in an afterlife, the figure before him was not Joseph anymore. Grieving for the loss of his friend, Schaalman could not help but ask himself, "Joseph, where are you?" (p. 283)

Before his death, Bernardin had planned his funeral down to the last detail. To Schaalman's surprise, even he had an important role in the service. On the second day of his lying in state, Bernardin wanted Schaalman to conduct a religious observance in the cathedral for the Jewish community. The request was unprecedented. As far as Schaalman knew, it had never happened in the history of Catholic-Jewish relations, and it placed Schaalman in a difficult position. He knew that to perform such a service would be unacceptable to his Orthodox colleagues. Traditional rabbis would not set foot in a cathedral, let alone perform a service there, and Schaalman did not want to upset them.

In a quandary, he consulted several of the Jewish leaders who had gone on the mission to Israel. They decided that he should make a presentation based on their trip and the extraordinary interfaith advances that came from it. One of Schaalman's concerns was to avoid the appearance to the Jewish community that he was participating in a liturgical rite. At the same time, he did not want to offend his Catholic friends and colleagues. The group decided that each of them would participate in the wake and would write something or say something about their experience of having been on the pilgrimage with Bernardin. Schaalman, on the other hand, would be free to say whatever he pleased. Despite their desire to appear not to participate in the funeral liturgy, by design, their participation "had a somewhat liturgical character" (p. 239).

When Schaalman's turn came to offer his eulogy, he told his listeners, "Never in the history of our world has an observance such as this taken place. We are today making history, which we hope will be the harbinger of the time to come. So great, so profound is this moment ... I want all of us to recognize how unprecedented this moment is" (Schaalman, H. E., November 19, 1996). Then, he added a personal note:

> In a manner that I can't really otherwise describe, he has been one of the most wonderfully loved friends of my whole life. He called me his friend so that I could in turn know that in him I found a true friend. It was not necessary for us to see each other regularly, or frequently. It was enough for me to know that here in this city there was this man. And if ever there would have been a moment when I really needed to feel supported, to be upheld, all I had to do was to ask my brother Joseph. And without fail and without hesitation I knew he would be there and would do what needed to be done. (Schaalman, H. E., November 19, 1996)

He went on to speak of the Cardinal's special gifts and his effect on others and on the world:

I want to acknowledge with special appreciation the beautiful words that were spoken and the profound feelings and thoughts of our hearts which will fill the days to come, the years to come. We know that in a manner totally surprising and perhaps un-merited, God gave us a most precious gift in the life of this, his splendid servant, Joseph Cardinal Bernardin.

He knew deeply how precious time was, and it was to be, alas, too little, but he managed to fill the time that God gave him with such splendor, with such profound love for all of us that he transformed this vast assembly of people—the metropolitan area of Chicago—by the magic of his being. Never before was there such a sense of reaching out one to the other beyond racial lines, beyond religious lines, ethnic lines, gender lines. This great soul taught us, led us, challenged us over and over again, and he taught us that this was what God expected, nay demanded from us. He knew most deeply that the royal road to God was through other human beings. Not only did he love others and know their needs, their pain, the goals and strivings of the children of that God to whom we pray and whose presence we seek.

Like few other people that I have ever known, he understood that all true life, all holy life was life with the other. So, with sadness we take our leave but with a determination not to let his work, not to allow the theme he put before us to disappear. We know, and I call on all of you, that we need to work harder than we ever did before, believe more deeply, care for each other more intensely so that thereby we will erect and live a memorial to that loving, lovable friend, that brother Joseph who upheld us with his affection and his care.

Dear Cardinal, as you prayed for us, we pray for you. Our feelings and prayers speed you on your final journey to that destiny which we cannot know yet devoutly believe. Shalom *chaver*, dear, dear friend. Remain at peace. (Schaalman, H. E., November 19, 1996)

More than 100,000 people came to pay their respects to the Cardinal. Day and night, they filed past his open coffin in Holy Name Cathedral (Steinfels, P. 1996). The funeral was so large and attended by so many civic and religious dignitaries that it looked like a major state funeral. Inside the cathedral people were standing in the aisles and lined the walls while huge crowds stood outside watching the event on large television screens. The event was broadcast worldwide. At the wake, while Schaalman was putting on his robes in preparation for his participation in the event, Maynard Wishner realized that, because this event was being broadcast around the world, Schaalman and his rabbinic and lay colleagues were likely to stir up controversy if they appeared in rabbinic garb and tallises. To the dismay of the priests, they decided at the last minute to go out in their business suits without any sign of religious affiliation.

With Bernardin's death, Schaalman lost not only a close friend whom he loved and admired, but also a colleague on "the cutting edge" of the improvement of Christian-Jewish relations. In summing up his contribution to interfaith dialogue, Schaalman credits him with the special gift to bring together people of different beliefs and backgrounds and to find in them a common basis for conciliation. Bernardin felt a special need to reexamine the split that occurred in Judaism that gave rise to Christianity so that he could understand better commonalities that united the two faiths as well as what divided them. Schaalman laments, "His untimely death did not allow him to pursue this end." This awareness of unfinished business became the stimulus for Schaalman's decision to study first century Judaism to discover the commonalities and divisions between Judaism and Christianity.

Not long after Bernardin's death, Schaalman became friends with his successor, Cardinal Francis George, who followed Bernardin's lead in developing Catholic-Jewish relations. Although he no longer had an official position in the Jewish community, it was a tribute to Schaalman that his friendship with Bernardin and his reputation as a leader in interfaith dialogue made the friendship advantageous to both. Moreover, the two clerics took an immediate liking to each other. Schaalman made the first contact, and, since then they have been meeting over lunch several times a year to discuss matters of mutual concern. A few weeks after Schaalman's ninety-third birthday in 2009, during one of these lunches, they discussed the issue of the sustainability of the earth. This issue, the primary concern of the Millennium Institute, was one of the major issues at the 1993 Parliament of the World's Religions. Schaalman told George of his concern for the earth's exploding population and its threat to human survival. Whether or not Schaalman's allusion to population control was intentional, the Cardinal did not miss the implication that birth control was the means of avoiding this catastrophe. For him, the solution of birth control was not a viable option. However, he did agree with Schaalman that some form of population control is necessary to avoid the potential calamity.

In 1999, together with 170 Chicago area clergy, Schaalman and Cardinal George signed a "Covenant" opposing street violence (CeaseFire. org, n.d.). The covenant was the work of a Chicago area community-based organization, CeaseFire: The Campaign to STOP the Shooting. Established in 1995, CeaseFire was the first initiative of the Chicago Project for Violence Prevention. It works with other "community-based organizations to develop and implement strategies to reduce and prevent violence, particularly shootings and killings" (CeaseFire.org, n.d.). Because of its documented successes, it has attracted high profile people such as Cardinal George and Schaalman to serve as members of its Advisory Council.

Jewish Community's Response to Interfaith Relations: Dabru Emet

The late twentieth century transformation in Christianity's relation to Jews had been one-sided. Since Vatican II, the Church has issued a series of documents on Jewish-Catholic relations including *Nostra Aetate* (1965), *Guidelines and Suggestions for Implementing the Conciliar Declaration Nostra Aetate* (1975), Bernardin's "Anti-Semitism: The Historical Legacy and Continuing Challenge for Christians" (1995), and *We Remember: A Reflection on the Shoah* (1998). Three popes have visited Israel, including, most recently, Benedict XVI in May 2009. Despite these positive developments, the Jewish community had not issued a major document acknowledging this change. Schaalman attributes this lack of reciprocity to the Jewish reluctance to forgive and forget the two thousand year history of Christian persecution of Jews (Schaalman, H. E., 2007, p. 243). It is the root of Jewish skepticism that Christianity has made an irrevocable turn towards acceptance of Jews. This history also makes Jews cautious that Christianity has made a commitment to live with them in peace and harmony (p. 243).

Dr. Eugene Fisher, who, before he retired, had responsibility to oversee Catholic—Jewish relations for the Catholic Church in the United States, remarked that "Jews still don't trust us. ... If I were Jewish, I wouldn't totally trust me either" (Allen, 2007). Skepticism has been expressed by two of modernity's most influential American Orthodox Rabbis, Eliezar Berkovits and J. B. Soloveitchik, both of whom were opposed to interreligious dialogue (Rosen, 2001). They were unwilling to forgive and forget the two thousand year history of Christian persecution of Jews, including facilitating, if not collaborating in, the *Shoah*. They wanted to see several generations of proof before Jews should accept Christian gestures of repentance for their actions and their new spirit of accommodation and tolerance (Rosen, 2001). Rabbi Soloveitchik went further by ruling out "theological" dialogue on the basis that Jews and Christians are "two faith communities (which are) intrinsically antithetic" (Rosen, 2001). However, he supported communication with Christians as desirable and essential in areas of mutual interest such as "war and peace, poverty, freedom, morality, civil rights, and the threat of secularism" (Rosen, 2001). According to Rosen (2001), by taking this position on non-theological issues, Soloveitchik might be "trying to give a permissive ruling to enable modern Orthodox participation in Jewish-Christian meetings."

Because of this well-deserved skepticism, a more liberal approach to the Jewish-Christian dialogue did not become public until September of 2000 when the Institute on Christian and Jewish Studies in Baltimore released "Dabru Emet: A Jewish Statement on Christians and Christianity" ("Speak the Truth"). Produced by four of the most distinguished Jewish scholars in America—David Novak, Tikva Frymer-Kensky, Peter Ochs, and Michael Signer—the document was signed initially by more than 170 Jewish scholars and rabbis. The signers included a veritable Who's Who of America's most distinguished rabbis, including Schaalman, Eugene B. Borowitz, David Gordis, Irving Greenberg, Lawrence A. Hoffman, Charles A. Kroloff, Harold Kushner, W. Gunther Plaut, Jeffrey Salkin, David Sandmel, Marc Saperstein, Arnold Jacob Wolf, David Wolpe, and Eric H. Yoffie. Schaalman's signature on the document stems from his acknowledgement that, as he wrote, "We have really never given ourselves a decent chance to examine Christianity for its own sake and in a dispassionate fashion" (Schaalman, H. E., 2007, p. 243). He was not entirely happy with the draft copy that was sent to him and, although he proposed several changes, none of them got into the document.

The authors, an "interdenominational group of Jewish scholars," assert, "It is time for Jews to learn about the efforts of Christians to honor Judaism [and] to reflect on what Judaism may now say about Christianity" (National Jewish-Christian Scholars Project, n.d.). They thought it necessary to provide a positive "Jewish" response to the efforts of the Christian community to make amends for its history of defamation of Judaism. [330] It was also an attempt to improve Jewish-Christian relations by acknowledging the validity and value of Christianity (National Jewish Scholars' Project, n.d.).[331]

Schaalman's willingness to sign this document came from his awareness that Jews needed to respond to and take full advantage of the possibilities created by the new Catholic attitude toward Jews. It required a reconsideration of his own views of the Church: "If Roman Catholics are prepared to accept a new way of looking at me," he said, "then I, too, have a corresponding responsibility to review what I think about Christians. ... Because this new outlook is so radical, I am required to respond in kind [and] compelled" to participate in Christian-Jewish dialogue (Faith in Conversation, 2005). Dabru Emet represented progress. The following year, he commented on another hopeful sign of the change. The fact that Pope John Paul II had offered prayers at the Western Wall in Jerusalem and that "Pope Benedict XVI had visited a synagogue in his native Germany conveys a lasting imprint of those changes that, while long in coming, are finally and hopefully permanent" (Schaalman, February, 2006, p. 6).

Dabru Emet did not eliminate the challenges Jews and Catholics face in their attempts to accept each other as legitimate partners in healing the world. A major issue troubling Catholic-Jewish relations is the controversy over the beatification of Pope Pius XII. Jews have been highly critical of his failure to intervene in the Nazi effort to exterminate the Jews. The Church has responded that the Pope did what he could to ameliorate the plight of the Jews and was not negligent or callous toward their fate. According to Pawlikowski (2006), scholars have documented another picture, but until the Vatican archives are opened for scholarly research, the case is not conclusive (p. 2).[332] Another challenge to the improvement in Jewish-Catholic relations occurred in 2007. Pope Benedict XVI gave Catholic congregations the option to use a

1962 version of the Good Friday Mass that contained a prayer for the conversion of the Jews. The Pope's action raised alarms in the Catholic and Jewish communities. Schaalman was sufficiently concerned to bring up the matter with Chicago's Cardinal George. Schaalman sought clarification of the meaning of the Pope's decision and whether it constituted a change in Church policy.[333]

Sadly, troubling signs of retrenchment have continued. By 2009, it was clear that the antagonism to *Nostra Aetate* by more conservative clerics in the Catholic hierarchy who had gone underground after Vatican II was now reemerging. Zenger (2009) claims that what had been a minority voice was once again the majority. Yet, he does not think that this retrenchment under Pope Benedict XVI has had a significant and negative effect on the new era of Catholic-Jewish relations (Zenger, 2009). Schaalman, however, is not so certain, and he has discussed his concerns with Cardinal George, who reassured him that the Church is not moving backward and has continued to make strong statements in support of Catholic-Jewish dialogue.[334]

Gibson's *The Passion of the Christ*

The progress of interfaith relations received a serious challenge in 2004 with the release of Mel Gibson's film, *The Passion of the Christ*. The film met with strong criticism in many quarters. In Chicago, the film was a cause of great distress in the Catholic and Jewish communities and a threat to the improved relations between them. A delegation of Jewish and Catholic leaders called on Cardinal George to make a statement denouncing the film. George wasted no time in responding. In an article published in the Chicago Archdiocese newspaper, he wrote, "Popular presentations of Christ's Passion over the centuries have been the occasion for outbreaks of verbal and physical violence to Jews, and these incidents are part of the memory of the Jewish people" (as quoted in Kotzin, 2007, p. 9). The Cardinal told his readers that the memories of these events should be honored. He acknowledged that Christians would be moved by Gibson's graphic portrayal of the Passion of Jesus, but he cautioned his readers that, as Christians "who share this society with Jews, we should also be moved by their concerns [and] condemn anti-Semitism" (as quoted by Kotzin, 2007, p. 9).

Sufficiently alarmed by the film, Schaalman participated in public discussions about its possible effect on non-Jews. In August 2007, he participated in an interfaith panel discussion on the film at Milwaukee's Congregation Shalom. The program was sponsored by the Milwaukee Catholic-Jewish Conference, a program of the Roman Catholic Archdiocese of Milwaukee, the Milwaukee Jewish Council for Community Relations and the Wisconsin Council of Rabbis. Other members of the prestigious panel were Rev. Steve Lampe, a Catholic priest and associate professor of biblical studies at St. Francis Seminary, and Rev. Steve Kuhl, a Lutheran minister and associate professor of systematic theology at the same institution.

When Schaalman spoke, he commented that the presence of such distinguished scholars and so many non-Jews in the audience should allow Jews to "rejoice in the fact that for once we are not alone" (Cohen, L., 2004). He hoped that the message of the scholars "will be an effective counterweight to the intent of this horrendous moving picture" (Cohen, L., 2004). Moreover, he stated, the last "nearly 40 years" of developments in Christian teachings—Catholic and Protestant—have enabled Jews to have a more "radically different" relationship to Christians and the Christian world than ever before. Gibson's film "is part of an attempt at least to slow down if not nullify" these developments. While "it is difficult to gauge what the impact of the movie may be," Jews can learn "how deeply the story" affects and shapes the lives and worldviews of Christians. On the other hand, Jews need to become "equally familiar" with Judaism's teachings so that they will know their own history and better understand the foundations of their religion. He cited the Talmud story in which Rabbi Hillel, one of Judaism's great sages, was asked by a non-Jew for a summary of Judaism. Hillel replied, "What is hateful to yourself, do not do to others. The rest is commentary. Go and study it." Schaalman concluded, "That is still a good Jewish program: Go and learn" (Cohen, L., 2004).

Schaalman and the Muslim Community

Although not as active in interfaith activities with Muslims in the Chicago area as he has been with Catholic and Protestant groups, Schaalman has participated in various events to promote Jewish-Muslim relations. In the summer of 2004, the Niagara Foundation, an Islamic organization with a mission to promote global fellowship, invited the Schaalmans to visit Turkey on an all-expense paid trip. The trip was offered to promote better understanding between Muslims and Jews, much as the American Israel Public Affairs Committee and Jewish Federation trips to Israel are for important non-Jewish leaders.

There was, however, a small hitch. Schaalman had made a commitment to one of Emanuel's families, Steve and Meeyoung Melamed, that he would perform their son's Bar Mitzvah. (At the time, he was filling in as interim rabbi after Rabbi David Sofian left.) He told them that this would be his last Bar Mitzvah, and they felt particularly pleased that they would have this honor. Caught in a bind over his desire to participate in the interfaith trip to Turkey and his commitment to the Melamed family, Schaalman let them make the choice for him. If they wanted him to honor his commitment, he would do so. The Melameds chose to release him from his commitment, rationalizing that, as much as they wanted him to perform the Bar Mitzvah, they should not let their own needs trump the importance of this historic event.

During the week the Schaalmans spent in Turkey, they were taken to visit key biblical sites such as Haran and had meetings with Turkish Muslims. In the course of the trip, Lotte made friends with the wife of a Turkish official. That friendship continued after the Schaalmans returned. When the Turkish family came to Chicago, the Schaalmans invited them for dinner at their home.

The next year in June of 2006, the Niagara Foundation honored Schaalman at one of its annual meetings with its highest award, the "Tolerance Award" for his many years of promoting social justice and interreligious understanding (Niagara Foundation, 2006). The gala event was held in Chicago's prestigious University Club and was attended by several hundred guests who had been active in promoting world peace and justice.

On January 27, 2005, Schaalman appeared on a Chicago Islamic radio program on WCEV, 1450 AM. The title of the show was "Commemorating the Liberation of Auschwitz." Not specifically a dialogue on Jewish-Muslim relations, the program was an effort on the part of the radio station to educate Muslims on the issues facing Jews. Schaalman discussed his personal experience in escaping the Holocaust, the long history of European anti-Semitism, and fact that the Nazis were successful in turning neighbors against neighbors. Together with the host of the program, Ms. Samira Said, Schaalman expressed the hope that the lessons of the Holocaust would lead all peoples to reject bigotry and stereotypes and to work together toward a shared life in a more just world.

More recently, he has become friends with Imam Kareem M. Irfan, a Chicago Muslim and the current president of the CRLMC. The two became acquainted through the Council. The Imam, according to Schaalman, is one of those "extraordinarily human beings that if there were more like him there is a chance for Muslims and Jews in the United States to live constructively and mutually beneficially with each other." In either 2005 or 2006, he and Lotte invited the Imam and his wife to one of their Passover Seders. Since then, whenever they meet, the Imam reminds Schaalman of the "wonderful time" he and his wife had at the event and asks about Lotte. For Schaalman this kind of experience is so different from that of the isolated world in which he grew up. Aside from German Jews and his Christian, mostly Catholic, neighbors, he had no opportunity to interact with people of other religions or nationalities. In the course of his lifetime, his world had changed dramatically.

The Promise of Interfaith Relations

A driving force in Schaalman's efforts to develop strong friendships and connections in the interfaith community is his sense that the Jews do not have exclusive rights to God:

> It is exactly because God is not singular in the sense that the covenant means some kind of monopoly. The covenant is God's reaching out for someone who will do God's work and there are many others who are searching for the same opportunity and maybe doing a better job than I, so I am totally committed to the notion that I neither have a monopoly on God or God on me. But that we are all together in a quest to try to figure out what our human, or in my instance, my Jewish responsibility is, how I am to answer the question that God is, the question that life is, and that life poses to me that every moment that I am conscious and awake. (Tichenor, L., 2002)

Schaalman does not let the matter rest there but believes strongly that whatever is special about the relationship [to God], "is really an urgent invitation for everybody to consider themselves, not only included, but on a similar quest. And those who are willing to understand themselves this way are certainly my fellow travelers."

In 2005, in recognition of his lifetime work to promote religious tolerance, the International Council of Christians and Jews (ICCJ)[335] awarded him its highest honor, the Interfaith Gold Medallion—Peace Through Dialogue. Rev. Dr. John Pawlikowski, the ICCJ president, conferred the award during the group's annual conference in 2005.

On September 21, 2006, speaking at a program sponsored by the Chicago Theological Seminary (CTS), [336] a Musical Celebration of Interfaith Connections, Schaalman told the audience that there was a great need for such interfaith encounters, which have "tremendous power for change in interfaith relations." Such events serve to counterbalance the assertion that there is only one truth about faith and God: "Each faith has only part of the truth of the puzzle of those great mysteries."

As early as 1988, Schaalman had stated, "It is possible to dream of a world, a western world, in which what had been up to now an unbroken hostility to Jews and Judaism may be replaced by an appreciation of Jews and Judaism as an equal partner in the ultimate hope of the salvation of the world." In response to Esta Star's (July 25, 1988) question about the status of Christian-Jewish relations, Schaalman told her that he thought, "Jews and Christians need to teach each other patience" (p. 3). Both religions are seeking the same end, a "perfected world," a world without war and a world with minimal pain. The vision, he remarked, is of a world transformed in all of its relations. Unfortunately, after 2,000 or 3,000 years, this vision is nowhere near attainment. He predicted that a serious debate, a dialogue on ultimate questions, would take place in thirty to forty years. Now, he stated, real dialogue is just beginning, and, even though it is taking place only in small groups, the hope is that some people will change and that this change will spread.

The need for dialogue and its critical part in the survival of humanity became even clearer for him with age. When he was ninety-four, Schaalman told his Torah Study that he had concluded that the struggle for the world's survival as we experience it today, and as it had always been, is based on exclusion—racial, ethnic, religious, and national groups defining themselves as different, unique, and privileged. The result has been strife, warfare, hatred, and genocide. "I cannot help but weep," he remarked, "over the damage we have inflicted on each other by our desire to be separate. To end this disastrous cycle of human existence, the world needs to abandon this model of exclusion and adopt a model of inclusion. And by inclusion he means that the world's religions, races, ethnicities, and nation states need to accept each other's existence not only for political reasons but to insure their own survival and that of the human race. In 2007, he made this case in his own impassioned words in *Hineni* (2007):

> We are at a beginning of the effort … and this is the major truth of our time. This may be the single greatest hope I have for the creation by our descendants of a different kind of human-ity and global community in the centuries to come. We are also under the threat of the opposite—unimaginable vast powers of destruction. I think we are at a stage in mankind's march toward whatever future it has where some of its options have narrowed. This adds urgency to the enterprise for lessening of friction quite beyond mere curiosity or hope. And there are groups, perhaps many of them, all over the world, working in that direction. It is a far-off vision, but it is the one most urgently worthy of our commitment (p. 263).

Chapter 8

The Reform of Reform

"In 1959, Reform Judaism was cool rationalism that was the essence of liberal Judaism and the hallmark of the sophisticated American."

Eugene Borowitz (2008, p. 56)

"Gradually, in the 2nd half of the 20th century Reform underwent significant reforms which brought it much closer to a more traditional flavor and mode. I was part of that turning especially in the first half of my rabbinate."

Herman E. Schaalman (1996, p. 11)

"Auschwitz represented a silent but as yet unnamed presence in the writings of Jewish theologians' postwar writing."

Zachary Braiterman (1988, p. 7)

During Schaalman's rabbinate in Cedar Rapids, enormous changes were taking place in the world. Nazism and Fascism had been defeated but only at an enormous cost: 35,000,000 military casualties, 17,000,000 dead civilians, and 6,000,000 Jews murdered, one-third of the world's Jewish population. Once the reality of this huge loss sunk in, it traumatized Jews throughout the world. Steven Katz (1992) explains that the trauma of the war and its horrific consequences for the Jews overwhelmed the ability of rabbis, Jewish theologians, and lay leaders to think about them in a way that was comprehensible and to place them in a larger philosophical context. Jewish philosophy after World War II provided little more than footnotes to the texts of Rosenzweig, Buber and Heschel (pp. 27–28). To these names, Zachery Braiterman (1998) adds noted Jewish theologians Joseph Soloveitchik and Mordecai Kaplan who failed to deal with the Holocaust, making "only haphazard and oblique reference" to it (pp. 6–7). When they did, they put forth "guardedly optimistic appraisals of God" and support of Jewish traditional religious values, beliefs, and understanding of texts (p. 7). "Auschwitz," Braiterman maintains, "represented a silent but as yet unnamed presence in their postwar writings" (p. 7). The delayed response was a kind of "psychological shock—like mourners and terminally ill patients who undergo a transitional period of denial and disbelief" (p. 7). Nevertheless, "despair, anxiety, and disillusionment had already begun to mark the theological literature in the 1950s and early 1960s" (p. 7).[337]

The rebirth of a Jewish homeland, by raising the hopes of Jews worldwide for the prospect of Jewish survival, may have been a distraction from the nightmare scenario of the Holocaust. According to Schaalman, "For many Jews, this development was a miracle that stood in stark contrast to the efforts of the Nazis to exterminate them." Michael Meyer (1998) notes that "the struggle to establish the state of Israel drew in Jews who had been on the periphery" and gave them the sense of active participation in Jewish life (p. 354). For some, largely Orthodox Jews, the new state was God's compensation for the destruction, although among the ultra-Orthodox, there were many who rejected it. More liberal-minded Jews saw Israel as proof that Judaism had indeed survived the attempt to exterminate it and might now flourish.

Schaalman's personal religious crisis in the late 1940s may be understood, in part, as a response to these events. His run-in with Emil Fackenheim at the 1947 CCAR conference caused him to begin to reevaluate his theology. When he moved to Chicago in 1949, he began to interact with rabbis and Jewish intellectuals for whom the Holocaust had caused major theological distress. Together with them, he participated in discussions that, in the next half century, challenged the assumptions of the founders of Reform Judaism. These discussions were not limited to Reform Judaism; rabbis and Jewish theologians across the branches of Judaism were attempting to come to grips with the meaning of the Holocaust.[338]

Reform Judaism: Post–World War II

When Schaalman and his rabbinic student colleagues had first come to America, they discovered a Judaism that was foreign to them. Having been brought up as "Liberal" Jews, a form of Judaism much more traditional than American Reform, they immediately sized up the situation and concluded that their mission was to reform Reform Judaism. In their naiveté, they attempted to introduce liturgical practices that they considered fundamental to their Judaism but quickly discovered that their brash attempt was met with hostility and summarily rejected. They did not, however, give up. Difficult as it was at times to adjust to their new country and the new religious environment, they made the necessary accommodations. During the next thirty years, however, as they gradually rose into the ranks of Reform's leadership, they helped transform the movement into something more closely reflecting the Judaism they brought with them.

Added to their ranks during the war were other rabbis—refugees mostly from Germany, but also from Eastern Europe—who would help change the religious landscape. In the late 1940s, two of them—Ernst Lorge and Karl Weiner, along with Herman Schaalman—began their rabbinic careers in Chicago. Later, they were joined by Wolli Kaelter, and W. Gunther Plaut.[339] Together, they represented a third of the Reform rabbinate in Chicago. Schaalman speculates that Chicago must have been "a laboratory" for the development of the new thinking about the *Shoah* and its place in Reform Judaism. He might have added, too: that it was a laboratory for the new thinking that was transforming the Reform movement.

The Institute on Reform Jewish Theology

Although serious discussion of the *Shoah* in Jewish religious circles had not yet begun, that is not to say that there was no theological ferment.[340] Reform's ethical humanism was giving way to a more traditional faith-based Judaism, which Meyer (1988) claims represented an about-face for Reform theology (p. 354). He quoted a CCAR member who at the time told him: "Our rabbis have begun to speak more fervently of a God-centered, rather than a people-centered religion and culture" (p. 354).

The challenge to the basic premises of Reform Judaism could not be ignored. In 1950, the CCAR organized an Institute on Reform Jewish Theology to address what it called major unsolved problems that had been overshadowing Reform theology in the first half of the twentieth century. For Schaalman, the Institute reflected the fact that rabbis like him were undergoing profound theological struggles that lay just beneath the surface of Reform Judaism and Judaism in general.

The Institute's participants came from two radically different camps: one held the traditional Jewish belief that God was unique, eternal, absolute, and capable of active intervention in human affairs; at the other extreme were rabbis whose faith in such a God had already been rattled by twentieth century discoveries in physics and the laws of nature.[341] The Holocaust cast further doubt on what remained of their belief in an omniscient and omnipotent God who protected the Jewish people and was capable of intervention in history.

The keynote speaker for the Institute, Rabbi Samuel S. Cohon, was one of the most respected rabbis and theologians of the time and one of Schaalman's friends and mentors. In his address, Cohon (1950) identified the major events that had led up to the Institute: the rise of Fascism and Nazism, the worldwide Depression, and "the bankruptcy of the materialistic utopias." In 1937, perhaps in response to these developments, he pointed out, the CCAR had revisited the original "Pittsburgh Platform" (1885) that had replaced traditional Jewish belief and practice with a form of ethical humanism.[342] In its "1937 Columbus Platform," the CCAR reintroduced many of the traditional beliefs and practices that the last Platform had eliminated.[343]

Another of the major contributors to the conference, Emil Fackenheim, identified the underlying reason for the conference as a crisis in belief, the source of so much angst among rabbis and their congregants. The Second World War and the destruction of European Jewry had undermined Reform's "unwarranted optimism" in human progress. He went on to argue, "The awareness of this failure and the lack of an alternative model were responsible for the crisis that had brought them together" (as quoted in Borowitz, 2002, p. 10).

Unfortunately, the Institute, which was attended by only thirty-five to forty rabbis, turned out to be a disappointment because it did not accomplish its objective of developing a consensus for a new direction for Reform Judaism. Although it ended with a sense of promise for further discussion, no follow-up was held, nor was a report of the conference ever published. In its draft form, it affirmed the mission of Israel and offered various practical tasks for strengthening Reform Judaism but did not refer to theological issues that were supposed to have been its focus. The Institute's failure to meet the expectations of its organizers indicated that the time was not yet ripe for this kind of discussion.

In hindsight, the Institute was not a total failure. Schaalman, although he was a young and relatively obscure rabbi in the 1950s, together with Rabbi Lou Silberman, his friend from his student years at HUC-JIR, initiated a series of conferences to take on the theological issues that the Institute failed to address (Plaut and Meyer, 2001, p. 41). The audacious young rabbis had as their goal no less than "creating a new theology for Reform Judaism" (Meyer, M., 1998, p. 362).

Held initially at OSRUI in 1956, the conferences gave Schaalman the opportunity to meet his fellow young rabbis who were soon to become some of the most influential Jewish thinkers in America. The first conference attracted thirty-five rabbis including Reform Rabbis Eugene Borowitz, Jakob Petuchowski, David Polish, Steven Schwarzschild, Bernard Martin, Arnold Wolf, Emil Fackenheim, and W. Gunther Plaut. Orthodox Judaism was represented by Rabbis Zalman Schacter-Shalomi, Irving (Yitz) Greenberg,[344] and David Hartman (Meyer and Plaut, 2001, p. 41).

Their early meetings revealed that the rabbis were not ready to deal with the Holocaust. Instead, they turned inward to find answers to their radical questionings. Meyer (1988) writes that they were "united in their rejection of earlier Reform theology, which they found superficial, removed from classical sources, and deaf to the voice of a personal God" (p. 362).[345] Influenced by various sources—Christian existentialism, Buber and Rosenzweig—they sought to discover the relationship of humans to God. In Buber's dialogic philosophy, they found a basis for a new theological perspective. They accepted his insight that the Revelation on Sinai, which established an irrevocable covenant and intimate relationship between God and Israel, was Judaism's foundational experience. This position was a return to the traditional understanding of the Jewish people's personal relationship with God, as if God were a being with whom one could hold a conversation.

By focusing on Buber, these young theologians had gone out on a limb. Buber's personalizing of God was not universally accepted by Reform, Conservative, and Orthodox rabbis (Himmelfarb, 1966, p. 7). Liberal Jews rejected Buber's views because they considered them a "return to older theological terms" (Borowitz, November 1959).[346] Nor were they ready to give up the Classical Reform emphasis on a more rational understanding of their religion and their relationship to God, which they saw as "the essence of liberal Judaism and the hallmark of the sophisticated American" (p. 56).

Covenantal Theology

In the next decade, all of this changed. The young rabbis proved to be in the vanguard of a current of feeling and ideas that were radically reshaping Liberal Judaism. No longer was Buber anathema but now was seen as a sage who was offering a more intimate relationship between God and His people. The noted Jewish scholar, Norbert Samuelson (2000), described this direction as an existential response to the horrors of modern life and part of an evolution toward a philosophy of "personalism." This new emphasis was a movement away from Reform's original formulation toward an understanding of the value of the individual in the context of inherited tradition.

Borowitz (1969) labeled this new direction "Covenantal Theology," a theology developed around the core belief that the relationship of Jews to their God and their acceptance of the God of Torah is *the* foundational reality of Judaism. Through the covenant, God and Israel, God and the individual Jew, are bound in an eternal bond of mutual responsibilities. This covenantal relationship, however, is not a static or a one-way communication but is relational. Because God endowed humans with freedom, autonomy, and the ability—indeed an obligation—to think for themselves, Liberal Jews are responsible for deciding what parts of the "received tradition" are relevant to their contemporary experience. This freedom to make choices within the received tradition is what distinguishes Liberal from traditional Judaism; it is a radical movement away from the Halachic and ideological authority of traditional Judaism to the supremacy of free choice (Ochs, 2000, pp. 5, 14). It is a perspective that Schaalman adopted wholeheartedly.

The prime movers in this new development—Fackenheim, Borowitz, and Plaut—were Schaalman's friends and colleagues. Together, they shared a dialog developed through their association at the workshops, conferences, and institutes they attended. As Covenantal Theologians, they were able to resist the temptation to allow the events of the *Shoah* to overwhelm them. Despite the fact of God's apparent absence, they put their trust in the belief that He would fulfill His part of the covenant by His eventual presence.

That the challenge of the Holocaust had not yet taken hold of Jewish thinking is confirmed by an extensive survey conducted in 1966, "The State of Jewish Belief: A Symposium."[347] Published by *Commentary* in its August 1966 edition, the survey posed five major questions about the respondents' religious beliefs, but not one about the influence of the Holocaust. Only two of the questions make oblique references: "Does the so-called 'God is dead' question, which has been agitating Christian theologians, have any relevance to Judaism?[348] What aspects of modern thought do you think pose the most serious challenge to Jewish belief" (p. 4). The fact that none of the respondents drew any radical conclusions about the significance of the Holocaust led Rabbi Richard L. Rubenstein to conclude that this failure constitutes an "act of cowardice" (p. 71).[349] Some of them saw the creation of the State of Israel, which seemed nothing short of miraculous, as the beginning of Jewish redemption.

According to Milton Himmelfarb (1966), the symposium's editor and one of the leading Jewish scholars of the time, the responses to the questions indicated "far less theological ferment than among the Christians and ... few new ideas about Judaism" (p. 4).[350] He drew attention to the fact that there was little evidence of the influence of the work of the great nineteenth- and twentieth-century German Jewish theologians—Hirsch, Buber, Rosenzweig, and Baeck (p.3). He was particularly critical of the lack of evidence of Buber's influence, which, he claimed, had a greater impact on Christian theology than on Jewish thinkers.

Even Schaalman, despite that fact that two decades earlier he had credited Buber with helping him get through a theological and personal crisis, makes only an oblique reference to Buber. Schaalman argued that, because humans are made in God's image and are God's children, they need to be treated with kindness and understanding. Although this view is a long way from the I-Thou relationship he learned from Buber, it is a beginning and an early indication of ideas he published later in *Hineni* (2007).

Lacking also in his response is reference to the Holocaust, which became central to his later thinking, and even a hint of his notion of a suffering God. His response, however, does include reference to a theological issue that remained a major strand in his thinking, namely the revelation on Mt. Sinai and its fundamental importance in the Jewish experience. Echoing the ideas of Covenant Theology, he declared that the "experience is so unique, overwhelming, and transforming that the human partner emerges from it reconstituted in his own being and certain of its meaning" (p. 202). It is the basis for the human-divine partnership. (Later in *Hineni*, he develops this idea of a mutually dependent partnership with a God who is limited and vulnerable and needs human help to complete the task of repairing the world.)

Another idea (developed more fully in *Hineni*) is that the Torah is a "transcript into human language of man's always limited capacity to understand what the presence of God in the encounter was to mean" (p. 202).[351] This "limited capacity" of humans and of language is our only means of understanding God. He then posits what is to become one of the cornerstones of his later thinking, that God is "wordless" (p. 207). What he means by "wordless" is that the essence of God transcends the ability of language to speak of it, or to think of it. Another idea that he returns to in *Hineni* is that our understanding of God is relative to time, culture, and historical circumstance, and, for that reason is always changing. Nor is the idea of God limited to Jews but is known and understood by different peoples through their own religious experiences. In other words, Schaalman writes, God is not the property of any one religion or people (pp. 204–205).

To the question, "Is God dead?" Schaalman asserts that it has "no relevance to Judaism" (p. 206). For Christianity, however, the death of God means, "God willed to die as transcendental Being and henceforth only to incarnate in man. 'Christ' is where life is lived to the fullest" (p. 206). His 1966 *Commentary* statement reveals an early recognition of an idea that became central to him later: because God allowed humans free will to do good or evil, He is powerless to intervene in defense of his people, or in history.

Coming to Grips with the *Shoah*

Although the survey showed little awareness of the direct bearing of the Holocaust on Jewish theology, dramatic changes were at hand.[352] The same year as the *Commentary* survey, Rabbi Richard Rubenstein, a Conservative rabbi, published *After Auschwitz: Radical Theology and Contemporary Judaism* (1966), the first major attempt to deal with the need to confront the meaning of the Holocaust.[353] He was "amazed" that Jewish theologians had nothing to say publicly about the issue. For him, however, the Holocaust had radically altered his theology: "The thread uniting God and man, heaven and earth, has been broken. We stand in a cold, silent, unfeeling cosmos, unaided by any purposeful power beyond our own resources. After Auschwitz, what else can a Jew say about God" (p. 134)? Auschwitz had destroyed his belief in an omnipotent and beneficent God. Although Judaism interpreted every historical catastrophe as God's punishment for the failings of His people, Rubenstein considered the idea unacceptable and "obscene." It meant that Hitler and the SS were "instruments of God's will" and that "the most demonic, anti-human explosion in all history [is] a meaningful expression of God's purposes" (p. 134).[354]

Although Jewish religious thinkers did not react immediately to Rubenstein's challenge, theologians such as Greenberg and Fackenheim, members of the original OSRUI group of theologians, were beginning to come to grips with the Holocaust as part of their theologies.[355] They developed their views in the rabbinic conferences at OSRUI and in the follow-up conferences Rabbi Hartman organized in Montreal.[356] It was at these conferences that Schaalman first met Elie Wiesel. Because at the time Wiesel was a young and unknown writer, Schaalman had not heard of him. Nevertheless, Wiesel awakened in him the consciousness of the grim and painful reality of the *Shoah*. Schaalman was so impressed with Wiesel that, soon after the conference, he read *Night* and then everything else Wiesel had written. Under Wiesel's influence, Schaalman struggled to understand the *Shoah* and the nature of a God who was powerless to prevent it. In the years that followed, the *Shoah* became for Schaalman *the* most important event in modern Jewish life and the basis for his compete reassessment of his religious beliefs.

The conferences also provided Schaalman the opportunity for renewed contact with his old friend, Emil Fackenheim, who continued to influence Schaalman's theological development during the 1950s and '60s. Fackenheim was himself undergoing a profound reevaluation of his Judaism. Nevertheless, Schaalman notes that, even twenty years after World War II, the *Shoah* had not become an essential part of Fackenheim's thinking. All that changed when, in 1967, the impending war between Israel and its Arab neighbors threatened Israel's existence. With the survival of the Jewish people at stake, Fackenheim made Jewish survival the core of this thinking. In a speaking engagement on the eve of the Six-Day War, he told his audience that he had developed a new understanding of Jewish law: Jewish survival became for him a new commandment:

> Jews are forbidden to hand Hitler posthumous victories. They are commanded to survive as Jews, lest the Jewish people perish. They are commanded to remember the victims of Auschwitz lest their memory perish. They are forbidden to despair of man and his world, and to escape into either cynicism or otherworldliness, lest they cooperate in delivering the world over to the forces of Auschwitz. Finally, they are forbidden to despair of the God of Israel, lest Judaism perish. (Fackenheim, 1968, p. 84)

Coming from his friend and fellow survivor, these ideas had a profound effect on Schaalman. Taken together with the impact of reading the works of Elie Wiesel, Schaalman began a difficult reassessment of the meaning of the *Shoah* for himself and for Reform Judaism. Like so many others in the Jewish community, he had not dealt with its meaning and implications.[357] The events of the war, he explains, caused such enormous grief, that it took a long time "before there was a fundamental review of what one believed." Awareness of these events and their implications, long suppressed, could have provoked in him another theological crisis.[358]

Although the Holocaust had not yet fully penetrated to the core of Schaalman's religious beliefs, the tide was turning, and he could not help but be caught up in it. It is clear from his 1967 review of a new translation of Franz Rosenzweig's *The Star of Redemption* that Schaalman was attempting to come to terms with the *Shoah*. Although the book had been published in 1920, two decades before World War II, Schaalman credits it for helping those who belonged "to the generation of the carnage and its aftermath of guilt and trauma" to understand that they could not escape its consequences. Rosenzweig had written that man must "*be* with all his fear of mortality" (Schaalman, H. E., 1967, p. 234). Schaalman understood this to mean that authentic "being" required his generation, which was "numbly trying to shake off the memory of the holocaust," to confront it in order to find a way back to life (p. 234). "Being" required facing reality, no matter how disturbing. Only a handful of his generation," Schaalman wrote, "a few poets and writers—for example, Elie Wiesel—[have] been able to form intelligible words the sounds [of] which strangle in the throat paralyzed by shock" (p. 234).[359]

In the year following Schaalman's article, Rubenstein struck again. He had meant his book, *After Auschwitz: Radical Theology and Contemporary Judaism*, to be provocative, but Jewish theologians ignored it.[360] In 1968, he lashed out in his article, "Homeland and Holocaust: Issues in the Jewish Religious Situation." According to Borowitz (1991), this time his attack opened a floodgate of pent up emotion (p. 36).[361] Although it had taken Judaism more than two decades to begin serious theological discussions about the meaning of the Holocaust, once the discussion began, it produced what Rabbi Eugene Borowitz (2002) identified as "the religious crisis of our time" (p. 7).

Reinforced by the documentation of the Nazi atrocities and the murder of millions of Jews and non-Jews that was now available to the public, rabbis (and their Christian colleagues) could no longer ignore Rubenstein's attack. Adding to the sense of urgency for an appropriate response was the awareness of the decimation of European Jewry's centers of learning.[362] According to P. J. Haas (2002), the grief and guilt for this catastrophe sparked a new interest in preserving and defending elements of Judaic life. The theological world, both Jewish and Christian, had begun a profound reassessment that culminated during the 1960s in the "Death of God" movement.[363]

Another response to the significance of the Holocaust came from Schaalman's friends and theological colleagues, the Covenant Theologians. Although profoundly disturbed by the Holocaust, unlike Rubenstein, they did not conclude that the God of Israel does not exist. Emil Fackenheim (1967), one of the movement's leaders, found common cause with him in disputing the traditional belief that God guides history as part of a Divine plan. Unlike Rubenstein, however, he chose to defend the notion of God *in* history. Fackenheim's answer to the question "Where was God during the Holocaust?" was that God suffered with the victims. He concluded that the ultimate message of the *Shoah* is that the survival of the Jews is a way of transcending the horror.

Borowitz (1996), perhaps the leading theologian and historian of this movement, also recognized that the Holocaust cast doubt on the question of whether God exists, or whether God is all-powerful and might have prevented it. Nevertheless, he argued, it is necessary for Jews to hold on to a belief (a trust) in an omnipotent God. Some Holocaust survivors were not able to maintain this "trust," while others, inexplicably, clung more tightly to their conviction in the validity of the covenant with God and the ultimate promise of redemption. Despite the experience of God's apparent absence during the Holocaust, Borowitz maintained, Jews did not abandon Him (p. 3).

Borowitz, however, does not make the *Shoah* the core of this thinking. To him, it is another of the historic calamities of the Jewish people, not a "Sinaitic event but an ineradicable part of Jewish identity" (Wyschograd, 2000, p. 62). This perspective on the *Shoah* allowed him to put aside its potential transformational theological conclusions to position himself in the line of the ongoing historical development of Liberal Jewish theology. In that regard, Borowitz was much closer to mainline Jewish thinking than Schaalman, for whom the awareness of the Holocaust transformed his theology (cf. Chapter 9, "Shaalman's Theology: The Evolution of a Radical Theologian").

This emphasis on Jewish survival must have touched a nerve in contemporary Judaism. Having survived a calamity that nearly destroyed it, Judaism in both its traditional and Reform embodiments bounced back by attempting to recapture what it had lost. In the process, it looked

hopefully to the future by absorbing new energy from the reestablish-
ment of a Jewish homeland and from the new prosperity and acceptance
of Jews in America. The mood of contemporary Judaism was decidedly
optimistic. Not for Schaalman, however; he had taken a radical turn in
the opposite direction.

The theological wrestling with the implications of the Holocaust was
only one of the forces challenging Reform Judaism. During the decade
of the 1960s, it was caught up in the fever of the social changes that
were sweeping America. The call for social justice, which included racial
equality and greater freedom, echoed the call of the Prophets and the
social justice message and commitment of Reform Judaism. One would
expect that this liberal-leaning movement would push Reform Judaism
in the same direction. Instead, younger rabbis and their congregants
who were dissatisfied with what they considered the dispassionate and
stultifying aspects of Classical Reform pushed Reform toward what they
saw as the more passionate and spiritually engaging tradition-based Judaism. As early as 1965, Plaut (1965) had observed what he described
as an emerging "pietistic" wing in Reform Judaism (p. 351). He asserted
that this "wing" was less interested in maintaining the distinction of
Reform from traditional Judaism than in moving it closer to embracing
in both spirit and practice *klal Yisrael* (the idea of the inclusiveness of
the Jewish people).

Finding itself under increasing pressure to change, the CCAR decided
it needed to respond, particularly as it related to its religious education.
In 1963, it published *The Goals of Jewish Religious Education*, a collection of essays with Schaalman as its editor, his first "leadership" role in
Reform Judaism. The collection reassessed the influence of Mordecai
Kaplan's 1934 publication, *Judaism as a Civilization: Toward a Reconstruction of American-Jewish Life*, the book that had had such a profound
influence on Schaalman and his generation.

In his introduction, Schaalman (1963) identified the deep split over
Reform's "theological pre-suppositions." The first, embodied in Kaplan's
writings, is the humanistic belief that human values derive from a "useful or impersonal force embedded in the universe" (p. 68). Rabbis who
accept this view consider the Torah "a historical record of the Jewish
people striving after self-knowledge [and] the prophets nothing more
than champions of social action... [and they] do not have room for

concepts of revelation, Messiah and immortality" (p. 68). Rabbis who are more sympathetic to traditional teachings hold the second presupposition: "God as Creator, Revealer, and Redeemer" and Torah as the product of the Jews' encounter with God. These rabbis accept the prophets as God's messengers and the Messiah and immortality as "logically consistent extensions of the dialogue of God and man" (p. 68). This fundamental difference of opinion, while far from new, Schaalman wrote, makes consistency in Reform religious education highly problematic. His hope was that *The Goals of Religious Education* would help bridge that gap.

Gates of Prayer

When the CCAR published *The Goals of Jewish Religious Education*, the humanistic strain in Reform was on its way out. At the same time, pressure was mounting for a change in the siddur, *The Union Prayer Book* (UPB), one of the first English language prayer books in America. Although its earlier editions (1892, 1922, 1941) had attempted to make accommodations to tradition, Rabbi Elliot L. Stevens (2006), Director of Publications for the CCAR, writes that by the early 1970s "it became clear that the 1941 UPB was showing its age." He identified several sources for the increasing desire for change during that period:

> Creative services with more Hebrew had gained in popularity; interest was also growing in the *Shoah* and Zionism; and Jewish pride was spiking in response to the Six-Day War, the movement to save Soviet Jewry, and a society-wide interest in exploring ethnic and cultural roots. At the same time, the practice of highly participatory and emotive styles of worship in UAHC camps was filtering into Reform congregations.

In an effort to address these new directions and to remain responsive to its congregants, in 1975 the CCAR issued *Gates of Prayer* (GOP). Stevens points out, "While maintaining traditional patterns of Reform worship," among its innovations was the use of contemporary English; "an unprecedented selection of new prayers, readings, and meditations to accompany the Hebrew text; services for Holocaust commemoration and Israeli Independence Day; and an extensive section of song texts."

The new prayer book represented the Reform Movement's growing openness to tradition and a theological diversity.[364]

Schaalman Unhappy with the New *Siddur*

Not everyone was happy with the proposed changes in the new *siddur*. Borowitz (1969), speaking for at least one faction in Reform, urged caution. He identified a trend in Reform that led Jewish leaders to conclude that to get people to attend services they must reshape religion to fit their congregants' lifestyle. Noted historian Rabbi Robert M. Seltzer (1998) observed that some in the Reform movement thought the new emphasis was moving it in the direction of becoming "Conservative Judaism Lite" (p. 23).

Schaalman, too, had his reservations. Although excited by the new prayer book's attempt to address contemporary needs, for him it perpetuated three areas of difficulty: Does the language surrounding the presentation of God have meaning today? Is the liturgy appropriate for modern times? Could modern and poetic interpolations in the prayer book stimulate more effectively the experience of the majesty of creation? He was particularly critical of *Gates of Prayer* because it continued to honor the traditional use of language presenting God as "King" or "Lord" and "master" of His subjects. The use of this language reflected a period of Jewish history when the only way to think about the power of God was to think of a king, the greatest earthly authority, and a male. "Worship in *Gates of Prayer*, he remarked,

> continued to center on the traditional Jewish model of the kingly court. The worshipper either stands before the king and petitions him for some favor, or thanks him for his kindness, justice, and love. In return for his subservience, his willingness to follow the king's laws, the worshipper expects protection. As king, God is the savior and protector of Jews in every generation.

This projection of God as savior is based on the Exodus, "the only event in the Bible," he remarks, "in which God intervenes to save Israel." For more than 2,000 years, this intervention, the basis for the covenant between God and His people, remained the touchstone for Jewish belief and the foundation of its liturgy. "But God," Schaalman argues, "did not uphold His end of the bargain, and, in the millennia that followed, did nothing to prevent the slaughter of Jews." He is particularly adamant that the High Holy Day reference to God as Father and King makes no sense. "Such a God," he explains, "is required to defend His people; God has not acted either as father or as King, ever. Despite all the calamities and the lack of evidence that God is the protector of His people, this most fervent utterance of God as Father and King shapes the entire liturgy of these two most important holy days. Remarkably, and without foundation, Jews continue to hope and to trust in their God."[365] Schaalman wanted (and still wants) the characterization of God as all-powerful and the savior of the Jews purged from the *siddur*. "Jews," he insists, "should reshape or reinvent their liturgy to reflect the reality of a God with limited powers."

As early as the 1960s, Schaalman had been unhappy with the *siddur*'s use of language and the theology it represented. His preference was for a prayer service that captured some of the mystery and excitement of the Jewish experience, particularly the experience of the Revelation at Sinai. To inspire the modern, progressive Jew and to make prayer and liturgy more relevant, he proposes that Israeli poets rewrite the prayers, much like their predecessors who created the poetry of the traditional *siddur* with its heightened sense of language and a passionate conviction that could only come from a poetic imagination. The new service would have to capture the imaginations and passions of its participants and render the experience of the *Shoah* and the relationship to God in ways that would be meaningful to Jews now and in the future.[366]

In retrospect, "I wish I had taken the liturgical question 'head on' and not been such a coward. I deeply regret that I had not made these recommendations to CCAR before I became a 'has been.' As the CCAR president, my opinion mattered; now, that's ancient history." Another concern holding him back was that, at the time, he considered himself a "traditionalist" and did not want to cause his late father pain were he to deviate from tradition: "Although my father had been dead for ten years, I had internalized his thinking to such an extent that I continued to measure my own behavior by what he might think of it." Once he and his father had reconnected after the war, whenever they were together, he conformed to his father's expectations: "He, nevertheless, understood that I was facing a different kind of community than the one that governed him. Although I am grateful that my father never criticized my religious practice, I would have liked to discuss it with him."[367]

Heading into the Twenty-first Century

Gates of Prayer was part of the change in Reform Judaism that would carry it into the twenty-first century. In 1981, as part of his presidential address to the CCAR, Schaalman had identified this change as a movement toward more traditional practice and belief, a change he resisted then and continues to resist today.[368] His concern was that changes in Reform needed to come from formal discussion of theological issues within the CCAR. According to Borowitz (2002), the time was not yet ripe for such an undertaking. Not until the beginning of the twenty-first century did Reform Judaism undergo a significant change from the days when its "rabbis rejected theology almost completely" (p. 14).[369]

A defining point in this transformation came in 1998, when, after years of study, the CCAR was ready to propose a new platform that would recast Reform in a mode to recapture old and provide new pathways to holiness and social justice. In writing about this turning point in the evolution of Reform, Kaplan (2003) credits Rabbi Eric H. Yoffie, then president of the UAHC, as one of the leading voices in the effort to "reform Reform" for the new century (p. 65). This "religious renewal" was evident in a new interest in the study of Torah, a greater commitment to meaningful worship, and "a renaissance of theological language" (as cited in Marmur, 2002, p. 292).[370]

Reflecting this new direction, in 1999 CCAR issued the "Statement of Principles for Reform Judaism." Designed to provide continuity with the original "1885 Pittsburgh Platform," it was radically different from anything Reform had ever experienced. The 1999 "Statement" looked both backward and forward, calling on Reform Jews "'to engage in a dialogue with the sources of our tradition ... . [in order] to transform lives too much in a state of *chol*, ordinariness, into lives infused with kedushah, holiness" (as cited in Haas, 2002, p. 243).

Schaalman and *Mishkan T'filah*

At the same time that the CCAR issued its new Platform, it was already at work making significant changes to its worship service.[371] In the effort to make the *siddur* more relevant, the CCAR created and, in 2007, adopted *Mishkan T'filah*. Based on a model of a divine-human relationship, it presupposes that God is experienced through authentic human relationships. To embrace such a paradigm shift required not only a new prayer book but also a major overhaul in liturgical practice. Rabbi Knobel (2002), who chaired the *Mishkan T'filah* editorial committee, claims the new prayer book included elements of what Jewish tradition has to offer and was an attempt to adapt and embrace new cultural realities.

Despite his years of seniority, Schaalman had no part in the formulation of the new prayer book. He had been retired from the rabbinate for more than a decade, and his views were very different from those of the younger generation of Reform rabbis in charge of the process. Although he and Rabbi Knobel had been longtime friends and colleagues, Knobel did not consult him when the book was being written. In 1995, when a prototype of the book was already in the hands of congregations across the country, Schaalman met with him to express his concerns, the same that he had had as president of the CCAR. He insisted, "A new prayer book required a theological base or is otherwise inadequate." "Reform Judaism," he said, "is only defensible if it is based on principle. Otherwise, it just becomes an accommodation to the people who don't know Hebrew, or who have never been trained in the traditional material [and is subject] to the prevailing culture in any given period." According to Schaalman, "Knobel told me that the Reform movement is not theologically inclined, nor was there reason to expect a comprehensive theological discussion in the near future."

Perhaps Schaalman's greatest disappointment is that the new prayer book does not make the *Shoah* the central reference point for the modern Jewish experience, which, he maintains, "is, next to the destruction of the Temple and even the revelation at Sinai, the most important experience in Jewish history and should be a foundational element of Reform liturgy."

Not to see it that way when Jews gather collectively to search for and reach out to God is either an act of total cowardice—which I think it is—or a lack of understanding of what has happened to us. [This failure] is a defense against the painful truth of what the *Shoah* might mean. It is not only profoundly disturbing, but, because it challenges our deepest beliefs, awareness of the event requires a personal transformation that few are willing or capable to undertake.

Schaalman maintains that this transformation requires that Jews no longer look to God to answer their prayers. "After the *Shoah*," he argues, the idea that God answers prayers is blasphemy: how many billions of prayers were uttered by Jews on their way to the crematoriums?"

This is my main complaint with my colleagues in the Reform movement. No one is taking the *Shoah* seriously, as if it didn't happen. Nothing has been revised, nothing has been changed, as though six million didn't die. And God didn't do anything. We should be living with a God who failed totally with the expectations our traditions had given us of God. And that's where we are at, if we really want to take the *Shoah* seriously.

The *Shoah* taught him that he needed to rethink his total acceptance of all that he had been taught and believed to be true. He had to "loosen up … to learn a new way of thinking." If many of the premises of traditional Judaism were no longer valid, then how should we live our lives as Jews? What part or parts of the tradition should we salvage as a valid guide to be modern Jews? This quandary resulted in some interesting conflicts. A more radical position, he maintains, "is—and I am totally committed to this notion—that virtually nothing that comes out of our past can be used any longer." The murder of six million Jews, a million and a half of them children under ten, forced him to question the system of reward and punishment: "What did those children do to deserve such punishment? For me, the system of cause and effect doesn't work anymore. A million and a half children stand in the way."

This failure to remember is not just a sin; it goes much deeper: "A person without memory, an indispensable part of human identity, is a mutilated person. Judaism is based on a collective memory that is incorporated in daily prayer services and annual holiday celebrations." Acceptance of the reality of the *Shoah*, according to Schaalman, horrible as it is, provides a new and "energizing insight into the relationship of Jews to God. Not to include the *Shoah*, then, as part of the Jewish consciousness is to make of contemporary Reform Judaism, "Reform lite."

Rabbi Knobel was, of course, sympathetic to Schaalman's concerns; they had been friends and colleagues since 1980, when Knobel first came to Evanston to assume the rabbinic post at Temple Beth Emet. He explained, "For my generation, the *Shoah* had not been as formative in our development as it had been in yours. Younger members of my congregation and Reform congregations around the country do not feel the same kind of identification with the Holocaust as the older generation. The same is true of the Six-Day War and the Vietnam War." This difference, Knobel explained, in understanding of the significance of these historical events for the two generations represents the cultural gap between people of Schaalman's generation and his own.

Elaborating for this interviewer, Knobel (2006) said, "Although for a brief time in the 1960s some theologians took up the *Shoah* as a theological issue, the movement disappeared soon after. Schaalman is part of a different generation of Europeans than the contemporary Jew." Today, Jews see genocide, not as an unusual phenomenon, "but a constant threat." He elaborated:

> The *Shoah*, on the other hand, is a piece of Jewish history no different from the destruction of the second Temple, the Spanish Inquisition, the revelation on Sinai, the reestablishment of the state of Israel. All of these events are a piece of our collective understanding of ourselves. One hundred years from now it is quite possible that the *Shoah* will no longer be part of the religious celebrations of our people.

> *Yom HaShoah*, Knobel (2006) adds, the Jewish observance commemorating the six million Jews who died in the Holocaust, no longer attracts a sizable turnout in the synagogue: "Mostly, the people who attend the service for the holiday are older people or Holocaust survivors. On Yom Kippur, we put out six memorial candles in memory of the deaths of six million people. We have a reading about the *Shoah*, but younger people objected and told me to cut it out. It does not speak to their sense of where we have come from."

Schaalman's meeting with Knobel did not produce the results he hoped for, nor did it silence Schaalman's criticism. Despite the fact that *Mishkan T'filah* succeeds in meeting today's standards of gender equity and eliminates references to God as King, it adopts more traditional aspects of Judaism, aspects that Reform abandoned more than a century ago.[372] Key to his criticism is the inclusion of the prayer for the resurrection of the dead in the recitation of the *T'filah*. According to Knobel (2006), "Schaalman told me, 'If Reform brings back the doctrine of the resurrection of the dead, then I will be back to haunt you.'"

Schaalman was not finished with his criticism of the direction of the Reform movement. Because of their friendship and his enormous respect for Schaalman's intellect and experience, in 2005 Knobel invited him to address his congregation. Schaalman seized the opportunity and attacked what he called "the archaic language" that had been incorporated in *Mishkan T'filah*. The offensive language was the reference to "divine rule and divine leadership."

> Our ancestors used such language because it was the highest accolade they could imagine. Because every other culture in that part of the world had a king, it was inevitable that they would project God as the King of Kings. A king's duty is to defend his people, and, in exchange for subservience, the subject is promised protection. In the case of the Jewish people, God failed to protect them. Therefore, speaking of God in this manner no longer has meaning.

On a more personal note, Schaalman added, "I believe the liturgy should be more human than only God-centered: The problem with the liturgy is that almost every *barachah* begins with *Melech Ha'Olam, King of the universe* and the fact is that we don't even realize what the words mean and that's probably the worst of it." He pointed out further, "There is a common practice in Reform congregations of reciting words they don't understand and are meaningless to them." When he finished, he got a standing ovation from the hundreds of people who came to hear him.

The movement toward traditional observance and ritual practice is a direct attack on all Schaalman believes. Although he had come from a more traditional background, once he emerged from his training at Hebrew Union College-Jewish Institute of Religion, he had been transformed into a Classical Reform Jew. To achieve this transformation, he had to shed practices and beliefs that had no place in pre-World War II Reform Judaism. He sees the reintroduction of more traditional liturgical practices as a throwback to a form of worship that is not suited to modern life. In *Hineni* (2007), he wrote, "A return in the *Siddur* of Reform Judaism to prayer forms that are antiquated and outlived in terms of language and ideas would be a terrible disappointment to me" (p. 229).

As a student at HUC in the 1930s, he was forced to abandon most of the traditional Judaism he had brought with him: the laws of *Kashrut*, the wearing of a *kippah*, donning *tefillin*, and reciting blessings before and after meals. At first, he was unwilling to abandon all of his traditional practices and struggled to maintain some of them. Together with his refugee colleagues, he fought the HUC-JIR hierarchy and, when he lost, adapted to his new surroundings. Once he was in charge of his own congregations, however, he reintroduced some of the liturgical and ritual practices he had abandoned; he wore a tallis and robe and incorporated more Hebrew into his services. It is ironic, therefore, that the once iconoclastic rabbi should condemn this new direction in Reform Judaism, a direction he would have welcomed when he was a rabbinic student.

Years later when he was president of the CCAR, he was aware of this movement toward traditionalism and warned his colleagues that they needed to guard against it. What he may not have understood is that many of the very rabbis to whom he was speaking were already engaged in rethinking how to make Reform more relevant to the needs of their congregants. Perhaps the greatest irony of Schaalman's career is that the establishment of OSRUI, which he considers his most important achievement, became "a crucible for the Reform movement nationally" and paved the way for a whole new generation of Reform lay and religious Jewish leaders (Lorge, M., 2006). Schaalman acknowledges that the camp experience he helped establish has been producing not only committed Jews, but also Jews more ritually observant than anyone of his generation, including himself.

Thanks to Schaalman, the OSRUI camping experience provided campers a deeper religious experience than they had known in their homes and synagogues. Now, when he serves as part of the camp faculty, he finds himself repulsed by their prayer services. They incorporate many traditional practices that Classical Reform threw out 100 years ago as antiquated and meaningless. His concern is that the campers are mimicking the prayer service of their more Orthodox brethren but do not know why they are davenning as they do. His attempt to woo them away from this form of worship appears to be a losing battle; Reform Judaism, to which he found so difficult to adjust when he came to America, has moved on and left him behind.

Most of these changes took place after Schaalman no longer had much influence in the movement. Having retired in 1986, though still a member of the CCAR, and a chair of one of its most important committees, he says,

> I was no longer consulted on major issues or invited to consult on policy or theological issues, and I no longer had an organizational base or a pulpit from which to criticize the changes I found objectionable. In retrospect, I regret that I did not assert my ideas before I retired, when I might have had an opportunity to influence the direction of the Reform movement and possibly some lay leaders, but that opportunity has also passed.

Now, he finds himself increasingly isolated and lonely within the Reform movement, not only theologically, but also personally. Nevertheless, his colleagues, especially those of his generation, continue to hold him in high esteem, and there has been no letup in invitations for him to serve as scholar-in-residence at Reform congregations around the country.

Schaalman on the Future of Judaism

None of this discussion should be interpreted to mean that Schaalman seriously questions Reform Judaism, to which he is strongly committed. He values the attempts of its founders, some of the most influential German rabbis of the nineteenth century, to discover the basic elements and underlying motifs behind traditional Judaism and to refashion around them a more modern Judaism. Reform Judaism was their response to the post-French Enlightenment Europe and the opportunities for living that emerged for Jews, opportunities they had never known before. "Because of the French Revolution," he adds,

Western civilization and traditional Judaism were at a crossroad that produced an enormous explosive energy, which Jews could use to address the reality of modern life. Reform Judaism was one of the only positive attempts Jews made to respond to this new world. ... Reform was the only attempt to make some kind of fusion between the heartbeat of Jewish tradition and modernity, to see if they could be related in some way constructively, and, therefore, to construct a whole new basic platform from which everything could be viewed, consulted, shaped, and reformed.

As early as 1988, despite the dramatic changes taking place around him and the dire predictions that Judaism in America was on course to total assimilation, Schaalman was skeptical about some of the long-range forecasts as far out as 2050. A major force contributing to Judaism's long-term survival in America, he noted, was the increasing movement toward tolerance in American society. Episcopalians, the Church of Christ, Presbyterians, Methodists, and Roman Catholics were much more accepting of Jews than they had been. The result was that being Jewish was less onerous and that Jews no longer needed to be as defensive. This new tolerance made it possible for them to fit more easily into the "texture of Western civilization" (p. 22).[373] Of course, one of the challenges of this new situation, Schaalman remarked, is that one of the forces that maintained Judaism over the centuries was precisely the fact that Jews lived in a hostile environment. To be Jewish in a world where Jews were not oppressed or rejected would be a new experience.[374]

One of the major arguments offered by Jewish demographers for the projection of a major decline in the Jewish population was the high rate of intermarriage. In what may be read as a surprising about-face, Schaalman argued, "Despite my opposition to rabbinic officiation at mixed marriages, I believe that mixed marriages might not result in the death of the Jewish community but could become a base for its continuity" (p. 19). Although in 1988, the rate of mixed marriage was one in three, he was not certain that experts had enough information to know its future result. The trend may mean that, although there will be a loss of Jewish identity, there may be "an addition to the sum total of Jewish life by many who adopt Judaism or ... try to raise their children as Jews" (p. 19).[375] This development, he asserted, may be no different from what indifferent Jews have been doing all along; the statistics reveal that about one-third of Jews affiliate with a synagogue. What this percentage indicates is that the majority of Jews are not affiliated with "what we consider to be or think of as the heartland of Jewish identity" (p. 20).[376]

Schaalman even challenged the very notion of Jewish biological continuity, the idea that Jews are a "restrictive" and "restricted" group and, theoretically, that Jewish families can trace their ancestry to an "original community of Jews." "This," Schaalman argued, "is not a totally accurate reading of Jewish history. [Other peoples in] small groups ... have always been absorbed in the Jewish stream" (p. 24). Judaism ought to "examine the possibility that the mixture of originally non-Jewish people into the stream of Jewish life may not ... be a disaster [but] over the longer run an enrichment" (p. 24). These possibilities for the development of a richer Judaism in America allowed Schaalman to draw the hopeful conclusion that the future of American Judaism might not be as bleak as has been projected (p. 25).

The Role of the Rabbi

From the very beginning, Schaalman believed that the role of the congregational rabbi was to be the channel for the congregation's worship life, a role he took very seriously and holds today. His views may have originated in the first years of his rabbinic training when he read Kaplan's *Judaism in Transition* (1936). In modern times, Kaplan wrote, the paramount concern for a rabbinic candidate should be to "bring to the Jewish heritage a passionate desire to help his people attain its uniqueness and express its individuality in such a way as to validate the primacy of the spiritual. ... The rabbi should be an expert in the art of living as a Jew" and should avoid what he called "careerism and professionalism" (p. 162).

Schaalman is passionately committed to his belief that the role of the rabbi is first and foremost a "calling" rather than a profession or career. Too many congregations and rabbis accept the concept that the rabbi is merely an employee of the congregation, hired and fired by its board. Such a relationship, according to Schaalman, demeans the role of the rabbi. The relationship of rabbi and congregation is a sacred trust, one that transcends the relationship of contractor and contractee. In a speech to the 2007 ordination class at HUC-JIR, he appealed to the ordainees to make a commitment to transcend careerism.[377]

In this regard, Schaalman, however, may be a voice crying in the wilderness. The issue of careerism in the rabbinate came to the fore in 1985, two years after Schaalman stepped down as president of the CCAR. According to P. J. Rubinstein (1990), new forces—including women in the rabbinate, more equitable assignment of household roles for rabbis and their wives—were moving the CCAR toward greater, rather than less, professionalization. He explained that women in the rabbinate had different values and interests than their older male counterparts. Moreover, in the past, rabbis never had to worry about interrupting their careers to bear children or to raise them. Now, however, men who are more accepting of the idea of staying home to care for their children, may wish to interrupt their advancement as rabbis to be "stay-at-home-dads," or to work only part-time.

Schaalman's life as a rabbi is the most eloquent expression of his idea of what a rabbi should be. He has been a strong influence on generations of young rabbis, and, it is hoped, his rabbinate will be a model for generations to come. More than one rabbi has noted that he is a rabbi's rabbi, and, the fact that Cardinal Joseph Bernardin sought spiritual guidance from him is in itself ample testimony to the force of his person.

Chapter 9

Schaalman's Theology
The Evolution of a
Radical Theologian

"Jewish theology is always at the hour of its creation. ... When the time is explosive, when frightening events belie the old questions and the old answers, then a new theology is needed."

Leo Baeck

"I do not know how anyone can be a monotheist. It is impossible for humans to understand and relate to a God that has no physical form and is beyond the reach of human reason. A meta-sensate God is virtually a human contradiction."

Herman E. Schaalman, February 23, 2008

"And so, this is my God, a God whose name I can spell Yod He Wav He but never pronounce. The God who for two thousand years has been unnamable, unpronounceable, nameless, the unspeakable God. This is my God, here in my very high age as always beckoning but never attained; here in nearing my end my God, mysterious, infinitely fascinating, but never owned."

Herman E. Schaalman, January 10, 2011

A ny discussion of Schaalman's theology must begin with his own understanding that he is a work in progress: "What I believe today may not be what I believe tomorrow." His whole adult life has been a continual evolution toward what he believes today. It has been a remarkable journey.

As a student at HUC, he learned that the rituals he grew up with were not only not practiced but also unacceptable. He had to shed his tallis, yarmulke, and *tephilin*. At first, the adjustment was difficult, but once he got used to it, he felt liberated. It put him on a path to becoming a Reform Jew. Ironically, his respect for authority, which was part of his German background, helped him make the transition. The faculty and administration of Hebrew Union College were now his new authorities. He learned quickly and turned their lessons back on his teachers and the institution. For the first time in his life, armed with new critical thinking skills, he found himself challenging the order in which he found himself. The effort brought him into serious conflict with the administration.

After his ordination, his new Reform theology and its liturgical practices ordered his world and created a place of comfort for him in his new rabbinic responsibilities. He became a rabbi that would make HUC proud.

His intellectual and theological growth, however, lay dormant until 1947 when he encountered his friend Emil Fackenheim at a CCAR annual meeting. As discussed in Chapter 3, the two rabbis went head to head in a debate that pitted Schaalman's Kaplanite view of an impersonal God against Fackenheim's insistence that for God to have meaning for human life, God must be personal. Fackenheim's arguments shattered Schaalman's complacency and produced in him a theological crisis. His reading of Martin Buber taught him that God is a living presence with whom one could establish a personal relationship.[378] Fundamental to this relationship was the covenant between God and Israel. Once Schaalman adopted this view, it transformed his life and gave it meaning and purpose.

In this acceptance, he was ahead of his time. As discussed in Chapter 8, "The Reform of Reform," at first Liberal Judaism rejected Buber's theology as a return to older theological terms. When that view changed in the 1960s, Reform moved in the direction of Covenantal Theology, a theological perspective taken by its major theologians—Martin Buber, Emil Fackenheim, and W. Gunter Plaut. Covenantal theology was not, however, a protection against the profound and troubling questions posed by the *Shoah*: How could a loving and omnipotent God allow six million of his people to be exterminated? Was it caprice? Malevolence? Lack of concern? Or a punishment, as some Jews, including their rabbis, proposed? Did God abandon His people, or was there another explanation? These questions became the theological monkey on Schaalman's back, or, what he prefers to call, "the shadow at my heel."

Schaalman found an answer to these haunting questions by concluding that God could not prevent this tragedy. This perspective of a diminished God is the ground on which he developed his theology. It helped him find a way to reconcile his growing unease over the meaning of the *Shoah*. In Chapter 8, "The Reform of Reform," we noted that as early as 1967, he had written that Rosenzweig's *Star of Redemption* provided guidance for how his generation might deal with the Holocaust. In his 1981 presidential address to the CCAR, Schaalman told his colleagues that the *Shoah* had "upended certainties about God" and the destiny of the Jews. It challenged the idea that God is omnipotent and suggests, instead, that God has a "weakness ... a failure, a defect" and is not self-sufficient.[379] This explanation was the only way to resolve the struggle to understand the tragedy. Accepting such a view, Schaalman declared, requires "a revolutionary shift, a radical realignment of the understanding of human-divine relationships [that] will take generations to understand and to work through."[380]

Schaalman, of course, did not have generations. In 1986, at an interfaith panel discussion in Springfield, Illinois, he answered the question "Where was God during the Holocaust?" by stating: "God was in the camps suffering with his people" (Schaalman, H. E., 1986).[381] A few years later, he published his most radical reappraisal to date of his reassessment of the God of Jewish tradition. In "God of Auschwitz?," Schaalman (1991) returns to the theme of his 1981 CCAR address: "The Shoa[382] has left nothing untouched, nothing is the same way as it was before. The interaction between all human beings, but especially between Jews and God, is deeply affected and altered" (p. 301). The God that emerges from this understanding is a limited God who suffers because of the actions of His humans:

> After deciding to become Creator, God could not be the puppet master pulling human creatures by divinely controlled strings.

Consequently God suffers human beings to be free and even increasingly powerful. God, therefore, suffers, as it were, this inevitable consequence of being Creator. (p. 300)

In Schaalman's view, God is stuck with the effects of human behavior:

Auschwitz, then, is a horrendous example of this interplay between divine surrender of the totality of power and human freedom turned wanton, cruel license. … When evil produced by human beings erupts then, as it were, God can be overwhelmed by it as are its victims. God is wounded. (p. 300)

Schaalman goes on to tell us that the "Shoa" is "God's wound," "God's pain and suffering" (pp. 298–299). This "God, as it were, is in need of healing much as the survivors" (p. 300). In order to be restored, God needs our love and support.[383]

This view of a limited and suffering God lays out his basic understanding of the meaning of the *Shoah*, a view from which he has not wavered. He argues that we need to abandon "the imagery of the enthroned Majesty commanding its subjects," an imagery that "ill fits … our post-Shoa condition" (pp. 300–301).[384] Schaalman's concept of God as limited, wounded, and suffering becomes the underpinning of the development of the theology that comes after.

In 1992, at an interfaith seminar at the University of St. Thomas, Schaalman repeated his new thesis that the *Shoah* had shattered his image of an omnipotent God, the image he had believed in since childhood and had been presenting to his congregants. God had not only failed to protect "His" people from the Holocaust, he said, but from every other major and minor disaster: pogroms, wars, dispersion (University of St. Thomas, 1992, p. 19).

This recognition resulted in other changes. Once he cast off the idea of God as King, he had to alter his approach to prayer. He could no longer bow to God, as required by sections of the daily prayer service. Such practice now seemed anachronistic and idolatrous. This change, however, was not easy. Having grown up in a culture that was the immediate successor of monarchy, the royal paradigm had been such an integral part of his culture and upbringing that it was still part of him.

Even as he approached his ninety-sixth birthday, he admitted, "I still have a twinge of something that responds to royalty."

To carry on his life's work as a rabbi, he had to find a new relationship to a vastly diminished deity. The God that emerged, as he had already written in "God of Auschwitz?," was a God who needed humans to help heal and restore the world. "My task," he said, "is not only to help heal his people, but ... to heal God as well" (p. 19). To support this idea, he alluded to Fackenheim's account of the Midrashic story in which God is depicted as "the weeping schechinah [sic]" who accompanied the Jewish people in their Babylonian exile. The Torah, Schaalman added, "continuously refers to our ability to anger God, to our being able to upset and wound God [who] is never impervious to our actions" (p. 19). This vulnerable God did not abandon His people during the *Shoah*, but suffered with them.[385] No doubt his Christian audience understood his concept of the suffering God, which had been Christianity's view from its beginning. What must have been surprising, however, was to hear it from a rabbi.

By 2001, Schaalman took another radical leap in this thinking. In "God of the Future," Schaalman wrote, "[The *Shoah*] is an event of a magnitude comparable to the covenantal revelation at Mt. Sinai; the pain, death and redemption associated with Golgotha; the need for revolutionary reconstructions after the loss of altar and sovereignty to the Romans" (p. 229). What is remarkable about this statement is not only the equation of the event of the *Shoah* with the Revelation on Sinai, but the reference to the foundational experience of Christianity. There is a clear indication of an emerging theological perspective leading Schaalman closer to identifying with the suffering God of Christianity.

Schaalman's new thinking required a dramatic shift not only from the "traditional formulations of God's being ... [but] also from the traditional liturgical vocabulary" (p. 232). He wrote that Judaism needs to purge the language of God as "Rock," "Shield of Abraham," and "Protector of the Jewish people"—language that is anachronistic. It is a vestige of a theology that no longer makes sense ("If it ever did," he adds), the idea that God is an "always reliable, secure, armor-like vestment for human life, its decision, crises, and hopes" (p. 232). Schaalman's God is not self-sufficient but exists in partnership with the humans He created and needs them to bear witness to and prove to Him that creation was not a mistake: "*Only such a God who needs me to love and pray and bring joy*" allows him to once again have faith "*after the enormity of the catastrophe*" (p. 231).

The Publication of *Hineni: Here I Am*

Schaalman's concern for the future of Reform Judaism may have played a role in his decision to go public with his theology. In the spring of 2007, he published *Hineni: Here I Am*, his attempt to share his life-long reflections on Judaism and what being a Jew means to him.[386] The book, he explains,

> is a partial record of decades of wrestling with what to me have been basic questions about God, about us humans, about me as a Jew, about other mysteries of existence and our inadequate attempts to respond to them. ... [It] is a partial summing up of decades of teaching and dialoging with Jews and Christians, and trying to answer their questions and to respond to their quandaries. It is the incomplete record of a long life as a rabbi—buffeted by doubts, inspired by flashes of insight, and driven by a never-ending need to explore further. (p. vi)

Publication was not an easy decision. Although he was ninety-one at the time, he is, as he likes to say, "a work in progress, a late bloomer." His thinking continues to grow and develop through his encounters with others, particularly with students in his Torah Study, but also with students in his seminary classes, with audiences at his speaking engagements, with colleagues, and in the privacy of his own study. Because these encounters are ongoing, he states, "I don't want to be seen as a repository of yesterday's ideas." [387]

Publication violated his basic conviction that knowledge is dialogic and, once rendered as text, subject to misunderstandings between author and readers.[388] "The written word," he writes, "is somehow so defenseless. The author is not present to the reader, and thus readers can do with the written word whatever they wish and are capable of." The spoken word, on the other hand, allows the speaker to interact with the listener and to refine and clarify one's ideas, to engage in a dialogue in which meaning and understanding are created in the interchange. Three years after the publication of *Hineni*, he confessed to his Torah Study that publication had forced him to speak publically about his views and to defend them. Before its publication, he had been much more reticent.

One positive result of this interaction with his public is the development of new insights. In a 2009 lecture on *Kristallnacht*, he told his audience that, although he was still struggling with the *Shoah*, he was on the verge of a new understanding that he hoped would allow him the peace for which he has been searching. A later event is indicative of his struggle. In September of 2011, at the conclusion of a family Shabbat dinner, his son, Michael asked his father for a blessing as he had done so many times before. It was a family tradition that Schaalman had carried over from his own childhood. Now, however, he discovered that he could no longer do it: "The *Shoah* had shattered my belief in an activist God. What could I say? One-and-a-half million children under the age of ten stood in the way, and God had done nothing to save them. Each of them must have been blessed with the same words. I can't think of God in that way anymore. What, then could those blessings mean to me?" Not willing to give up entirely, he realized, "I had an escape clause. All human language is inadequate for me to speak of God because it interferes with my desire to be open to God. Language, however, can be a *preamble*. The blessing is there to give structure to the effort." With that, he offered his blessings.

When he published *Hineni*, he had not come this far. Perhaps, the book can be understood as a preamble. Since 2007, his theology has taken new twists and, in some respects, deepened. In any case, it's not the same today as it was then. On his own, Schaalman would not likely have put his thoughts in writing; it is thanks to his friend, Anita Rifkind, that we have this eloquent volume. Schaalman met her when he gave a speech to her church group a few years earlier. So moved was she by his ideas that she decided to help him publish them. In the collaboration that developed, she interviewed him, recorded his answers, and then prepared a manuscript. Once Schaalman approved it, thanks to the generosity of two of his long-time friends and students, Mel Abrams and Bernard Rozran, the book was published privately by KTAV, a small Jewish press in New Jersey.

The question in Schaalman's mind was who would read it? His publisher advised him that 500 copies would be more than sufficient, but Schaalman wanted 1,000. Many of the books were given away to colleagues, friends, family members, and students. Some were "sold" to Emanuel congregants for a minimum donation of $18. Other new and used copies have turned up in bookstores in dozens of countries and are to be found in prestigious university libraries.[389]

The writing in *Hineni* reflects Schaalman's eloquent style of speaking and captures his genius for oral delivery. Anyone who has listened to him knows he has a gift for language that enables him to utter the most profound ideas with precision and grace. He never speaks from a prepared text or from notes. This ability to pull words out of some deep reservoir of insight and experience, words he himself has not prepared in advance, is a gift the origin of which baffles him and is the source of great admiration for his listeners. In 2009, he told his Torah Study, "[I do] not know where the words come from. I'm a vessel, an instrument."[390] When in May of 2007, he gave an address to the ordination class at Hebrew Union College-Jewish Institute of Religion, he was asked to submit a copy of his remarks. In typical Schaalman fashion, he informed the seminary that he did not have one.

On the other hand, he is perfectly capable of sitting down and dictating the presentation to a typist, as he did after delivering a keynote address in 2011 to the National Association of Retired Reform Rabbis (NAORRR). In a postscript to that text, Schaalman added,

> Some of you know that I never speak from notes. So, when I received numerous requests for a paper, I did what I had never done before—I recalled most accurately and faithfully what I had said on Thursday eve, January 6, 2011, at the opening session of the National Association of Retired Reform Rabbis (NAORRR) in San Diego. I had worked hard and long to collect my thoughts and give *hem voiv* [them]. So, here it is.[391]

Hineni reveals Schaalman's sense of awe and wonder in his encounter with everyday life. When he looks beyond the veil of appearances, he perceives a vast and beautiful world, one that stretches beyond time, miraculous and ultimately incomprehensible. In his fascination with this world, he seeks to understand it by keeping his mind open to the newest discoveries of science: biology, physics, mathematics, archeology, and astronomy. He uses its language to probe the mystery of the "unwordable," which he calls "God." Although he admits that he has only limited command of this scientific language, he is undaunted in his desire to incorporate its discoveries in his sermons and teaching. He uses it to expand the horizons of his audiences and students. Despite his challenge in understanding this language, it enables him to produce a prose that is elegant and soaring, such as his statement of his perspective on human development:

> The whole process is totally dependent on incremental progress. It is not a revolution. It is by and by, slow and slow, drop by drop, stone by stone, act by act. Of course there is also the consideration that the human race is still in its diaper stage. Archaeologists have just discovered a skull that could possibly push back the date of the earliest immediate ancestors to Homo sapiens by seven million years. Nevertheless, compared to the alleged age of the earth, not to speak of the universe, we humans are still not even toddlers. ... The hope is that as we grow up as a human race, as a phenomenon, that step by step, or sometimes maybe by a great leap forward, we will learn how to be human in a way that we have not yet even the imagination to dream about. (p. 106)

In another section, he discusses the contemporary notion of the "Big Bang" and its impact on human awareness of time:

> Of course it is also true that in modern cosmology it is almost senseless to ask what happened before the "Big Bang," because the Big Bang is the coming into being not only of the cosmos, but also of time. Thus, one cannot ask what was before time. That is inherently a nonquestion unless one posits a multiplicity of universes, one of which may have preceded the one in which we are, others waiting to come into being after this universe no longer exists, others that exist coevally with ours. We have no way of knowing which of these choices are true because our being is totally and inescapably woven into the texture of this cosmos, at least as far as we can understand it. (pp. 272–274)

Schaalman is the first to admit that *Hineni* is not systematic or an effort to make a final, definitive statement. That is not to say that the book has no structure, but rather that it is not presented as a structured whole.

Hineni may be thought of as a loose tapestry of many distinct, but interrelated, premises that represent the scaffolding of Schaalman's theology.
Because it is the product of a series of interviews conducted over a year
and a half, it lacks the kind of tight structure and a fully articulated theology that one expects from a carefully crafted treatise (p. 6). Therefore,
it should not be considered a "full" account of his thinking, nor his last
word. Indeed, over the next five years, he has continued to develop his
thoughts in some striking and unexpected ways.

Unabashedly autobiographical, *Hineni* is informed by his life experience, particularly his effort to understand the *Shoah* and its relevance
to Torah and his life. Rabbi Leo Baeck wrote that "Jewish theology is
always at the hour of its creation. ... When the time is explosive, when
frightening events belie the old questions and the old answers, then a
new theology is needed" (as quoted in Borowitz, 2002, p. 14–15). Right
from the beginning of *Hineni*, he states, "There are many years, a whole
part of my life in fact, that I lived as a sleepwalker. I operated on the ac-
cumulated intentions, motivations and impulses implanted in me from
the time I was a baby. ..." (p. 1).[392] When the theological significance of
the *Shoah* began to take hold, he questioned whether he could continue
to pray, whether he could in good conscience lead a congregation in
prayer, to "pray with them and through them" (University of St. Thomas,
1992, p. 19).

Although loosely organized, a careful reading of *Hineni* reveals fourteen interrelated and interdependent concepts or pillars of thought.
Grounded in the theology of modern Reform Judaism, these central
concepts are a significant reevaluation of God, Torah, and Judaism and a
major challenge to modern Jews, to the Reform Movement in particular,
and to thoughtful people everywhere.

Pillar #1: Language

A good starting place for understanding Schaalman's theology is his view
of language. We need to be clear, however, that the discussion about language is just an entry point and that the following discussion of the pillars does not represent a hierarchy of ideas. About language, Schaalman
(2007) wrote, "In this early stage of the human journey, words are certainly the best tool we have in our human armamentarium with which

to express ourselves. Human language can be very subtle and nuanced; however, each word also can, and needs to, carry the load of definitional precision" (p. 137). Then, too, language is "rich, subtle, and highly useful, but it also limits what we as human beings can experience and say (p. 137). Despite this limitation, language is also the ultimate creative tool, the means by which we understand ourselves and the world we live in. Not only is it a human tool, but it is also God's tool for bringing the world into existence. (God said, "Let there be light" and there was light. "Let there be a vault between the waters to separate water from water" and there was heaven and earth.) Schaalman concludes from this account that the ancient writers of Torah assumed that language was the highest form of expression, not only for humans, but also for God.

When Schaalman speaks about language, he speaks about it from his knowledge of Greek, Latin, French, German, English, and Hebrew. Hardly a Torah Study session goes by when he isn't offering etymological derivations of English or Hebrew words that deepen the students' understanding of the Torah text or their use of English as a means of interpretation. Recently, a student asked, "What's the difference between 'temple' and 'synagogue?'" Schaalman (2012) responded, "In Greek, the word 'temple' means a clear place in which all the scrubs and rocks have been removed. In Latin, it becomes 'templum' and from that comes the English word, 'temple.'" Then, elaborating on the Reform movement's adoption of the word "temple to refer to its house of worship, he commented:

> It is really too bad that the Reform movement took the word 'temple' because they did not want to talk about 'synagogue.' That was too Jewish in the nineteenth century when Reform Judaism began to bud and develop. ... On the other hand, 'synagogue' is a Greek word, not a Jewish term. It means simply 'getting together.' Today, the word means 'Jewish house of worship.' It is one of the indications of the enormous impact of Hellenic values and culture on rabbinic Judaism.

When it comes to understanding the language of the Torah, Schaalman identifies multiple problems: for one, we have no idea what the words meant to our ancestors or how they might have been used in idiomatic formulation; whether the words we see today are proper transcriptions of the "original"; whether, in fact, there was an original or urtext, rather than different texts produced in different times and places (e. g., the Septuagint, the Vulgate, or the Masoretic text); and the extent to which the translation we are reading is an accurate reflection of the Hebrew. About the latter, we know that all translations are interpretations, translators' best efforts to convey what they think they understand is the meaning of the Hebrew. In the development of the Jewish people, Hebrew, their original language, was lost as they adopted the languages of the cultures in which they were living. Schaalman (2007) states,

> The very fact that it became necessary to translate the Bible into Aramaic, Greek, and Arabic indicates that there was a need to make sacred texts accessible to people who were no longer primarily Hebrew speaking. The very fact that segments of the Jewish community of sufficient importance and numbers needed translations of the *Tanach* into the vernacular languages which they were using is a *prima facie* evidence of other cultural influences penetrating most deeply into the texture of Jewish life. Language is one of the most obvious evidences of such influence. (p. 34)[393]

In Schaalman's view, the fact that language is a symbolic system whose significance changes over time means that it can only point to the ultimate Mystery and can never express it. In the last year, he has identified this phenomenon as an insurmountable paradox: "Language is the human species' most notable achievement, but in reference to God it fails, becomes useless and deceptive. Other forms of creativity hold greater promise, such as the various forms of art, perhaps even silence."

Pillar #2: Torah Is a Human Document

Our discussion of language leads into Schaalman's second pillar: Torah is a human document, written by humans for humans. It is not the word of God, but a human record of encounters with God. ... a human attempt to express something so extraordinary that we have no other way of talking about it, a wording of the relationship between God and humans (p. 77). "The Talmud," he reminds us, "insists ... repeatedly:

'The Torah speaks human language'" (p. 136). [It] is the human account of a message that we believe originates outside of our own mind and being, and wells up within us by a trigger, a presence. ... So for me, Torah is the record, first spoken and then written, of the overwhelming encounter of the human with the divine. But Torah is not God's word; it is human language (p. 77).[394]

Later in *Hineni*, Schaalman writes, "Torah can be seen as an expression of the human groping for an understanding, a wording of the relationship between God and humans" (p. 177). For Schaalman, the story of creation is the human "response to that haunting and ultimately unanswerable question: How did everything begin?" The question can only be answered by belief: "God did it"—an answer, Schaalman explains, which is a "religious response to the mystery of creation" (p. 77).

Thus, God takes on anthropomorphic characteristics. On the other hand, "there is a danger," Schaalman writes, when we try to "correlate our humanness too closely with the divine." A greater danger in this anthropomorphic identification is that identifying "something of God from our human vantage point may be a transgression. ..." God must remain a mystery or God "may become so familiar that we will think of ourselves capable of using God," by which he means asking for God's help (p. 180). Human beings, however, cannot live long in ambiguity. Of necessity, we tell ourselves stories, the products of our imaginations. In Judaism, the familiar and the "nameable" become stories designed to express and reveal the ultimate mystery of existence. By "stories," Schaalman means biblical stories. In a surprising admission, Schaalman adds that these stories are speculations, fantasies (p. 135). [395]

However, for Schaalman there is another side to the humanness of the Torah. Using the Book of Numbers as an example, he tells us the seamy side of the story. It tells the story of the trials of the Israelites in the desert, one that

> is punctuated by a series of continuous disappointments that God experiences with these people who he had covenanted to himself in Sinai. Over and over again living in the desert, totally unknown to them in their prior existence in Egypt, is unbearable and leads at times to outright rebellion. This book is therefore rife with rebellious acts on the part of our ancestors, and it is

really amazing when you think of this book why anyone would have included it in the so-called sacred scriptures. It is astounding. (Schaalman, H. E., June 30, 2012)

Other peoples would have "cosmetized" their history to "show that [their] origins come from the nicest and best sort of people who ever lived. You don't want to show that your history comes from slavery, and secondly you want to show that you come from the best possible people that God could have picked for himself to be his covenant partners from whom He would have nothing but joy and satisfaction."

Not so the Torah. It "is brutal almost in making clear that our ancestors were none of that, that they were a continuous source of disappointment to God, and that they therefore regularly needed to be punished by God and that in fact God is so intemperate in his punishment or in His anger in response to their rebelliousness that several times He wants to eliminate them altogether." He wants to start over with a new community centered on Moses, to whom he makes the offer several times. What God wants, according to Schaalman (June 30, 2012), is "to have people who might be more pliable, more complacent with what God wants. None of this is so." What Schaalman finds remarkable about this text is that it

> is the single most sacred text on which the entire identity and history of our people is based. This is the story read in every synagogue, has been for the last 2,000 and some years, read regularly so that no one could say they never heard of it, they never knew what kind of background we came from, and who are our ancestors. It is an extraordinary record of honesty, of showing all the blemishes and defects of being the People of God, the Covenant People of Sinai. It's kind of fantastic.

Pillar #3: God Is a Mystery

Schaalman's third pillar comes out of his first. If human language is incapable of expressing the nature of God, God must be a Mystery and will always remain a mystery.[396] Fifteen years before the publication of *Hineni*, he told an audience at the University of St. Thomas, "All God-talk is risky, and we need to be continuously aware of the fact that at best we know only splinters of what God would be, or how we can grasp whatever God would be" (University of St. Thomas, 1992, p. 21). In *Hineni*, he put it this way:

> Words are inherently incapable of conveying what may really be ultimately unspeakable, ineffable. Thus, sooner or later, it becomes clear that the only way to confront that which cannot be spoken is by saying "Mystery." Mystery is the term to which we are virtually compelled to resort because we are confronted by the immensity of what is not only the unknown, but is mostly unknowable from a human point of view. It is just there and cannot be bound in the shackles of language. The moment we try to choose words, and all words define, we are attempting to constrain, set limits to the Mystery. We try to use words to deal with the ultimately wordless, unwordable, that which is beyond the capacity of a human to imprison in words, because if we could find the right words, then we would be the ones in charge. We are then defining the Mystery, giving it outline, and precision. Inherently this is not what one can do with God. All our words concerning God are, at best, hints, allusions, approximations. (p. 138)

In 2006, he told his weekly Torah Study, "Even as a Jew, I don't want to think about the mystery of God. It can drive you crazy. You become enmeshed in thoughts that indicate the enormity of all things and my insignificance. Of necessity, then, I approach the unwordable, the ineffable, in awe."[397] Nevertheless, despite our limitations, we must try to penetrate the Mystery.

In 2009, Schaalman told his Torah Study that the Hebrew name for God, יהוה, or YHVH, is the only Hebrew word that is unpronounceable and, therefore, unutterable. "Isn't it absolutely fantastic," he asked rhetorically, "that we belong to a system in which the name of God is unknown and unknowable except to two people: the High Priest and his deputy? How do you relate to such a God? How can one have an intimate relationship with a being without a name? In Jewish tradition, God is referred to as the 'Name' (*Ha Shem*). Yet, intimacy is based on recognition of the other." It is an obstacle, Schaalman admitted, that he only recently became aware of in his effort to establish a relationship with God. This struggle to put God in words, Schaalman adds, is compounded by a profound ontological problem: "God is, but God does not exist. We can say that God is a be-ing rather than that God exists. Therefore, the question 'Does God exist?' is either imprecise use of language or a false attribution ... when we talk about any of these matters, we need to keep some accuracy of articulation or else the whole enterprise of speaking about God is hopelessly flawed" (p. 163). Behind every effort Schaalman makes to express his fundamental belief in the nature of ultimate reality stands the reality of his inability to do so.[398]

Always wary of categories, Schaalman is quick to assert his conviction that rationalism cannot fully account for the human experience of divinity: "The reality is that there is a Mystery in which I find myself and which surrounds, suffuses, and in many ways determines me, to which I want to respond, to which I need to respond, simply because otherwise I would be totally insensitive and ungrateful, neither of which I want to be" (p. 269). Because the Torah reveals God's interaction with humans and His ability to affect the natural world, Schaalman concludes that this interaction is proof of God's presence in the world.

This sense of the Mystery surrounding and informing our life is a reminder of Franz Rosenzweig's early influence on Schaalman. From Rosenzweig, he learned that God is not only in the world, but God is the All, existing before creation, hidden, and, afterwards, Revealed.[399] Comparing Rosenzweig's views with Protestant theologian Paul Tillich's idea of God as "ground of being," Schaalman wrote, "Ground of Being is Tillich's term for everything that can be experienced and understood ... a phrase that is trying to paint a picture of the Mystery we must confront" (p. 137). In 1982, Schaalman had written that God is the "'Ground'" of Torah" (Schaalman, H. E., "Revelation," 1982, p. 91).[400] Schaalman takes God's statement "I the Lord your God am holy" (Leviticus 19:2) to mean that the very ground we walk on is sacred ground. The evidence, Schaalman maintains, is all around us; we need only to open our eyes to see it: "Sometimes when I look out in the morning I'm amazed and deeply moved by the enormity of where we are" (p. 91).

Pillar #4: Story of Creation

Driven by the necessity to make sense of his life, Schaalman develops his own story, his fourth pillar: Creation is God's experiment to achieve a sense of satisfaction and fulfillment. The story begins with Genesis. In Schaalman's account, for reasons that will always remain a mystery to us, God gave up His totality to establish "something" that was independent of Himself, to "break out of solipsism, out of total self-involvement" (p. 67). Taking this speculation a step further, he states, "We can conjecture that after untold eons of such solitude, God became slightly dissatisfied, perhaps eager to try a different kind or form of being who could be a joy to the Creator, who could provide an additional capacity for fulfillment, enrichment" (p. 135). God, he speculates, seems to be trying out various creative activities, which then develop into a world. Was creation part of a plan or did it evolve? With each act of creation, God looks at it and judges, "It was good." Schaalman understands God's expression of satisfaction to mean that He was trying out something new and did not know how it would work out.[401] This idea leads directly to the fourth pillar.

Pillar #5: Omniscience and Omnipotence

Schaalman's fifth pillar is his belief that God is neither omnipotent nor omniscient. As discussed previously, the *Shoah* destroyed Schaalman's belief in an omniscient and omnipotent God. Schaalman's premise is that an omnipotent God would (should) have prevented the Holocaust. The insight that God is not omnipotent sent Schaalman back to the Torah to test the idea that God is omniscient. In the story of creation, Schaalman sees an experiment that spins out of control and concludes that it is a clear sign that God had no prior knowledge of the consequences of His actions. At first, God declares his satisfaction and pleasure at the outcome of his creative acts—the creation of Earth, the sun and the moon, the stars and other planets, dry land and oceans, water creatures of all kinds, birds and vegetation, land animals, the separation of light from darkness and the waters above and below, and, finally, the creation of Man. He declares all of these acts "good" (Genesis 1:4, 10, 12, 18, 21, 25). After creating Adam, He declares, creation "very good" (Genesis 1:31).

He soon discovers, however, that His work is not finished. Adam's solitary existence is not good for him; he needs a partner. Schaalman argues that God identifies with Adam's solipsism, which was similar to

His own. An omniscient God, Schaalman argues, would have known this from the beginning. More problematic for the thesis of God's omniscience is His lack of understanding of an appropriate mate for Adam.[402] At first, God parades His creatures before Adam, the beasts of the field and the fowl of the air. Adam rejects all of them and, when God realizes that He has made a mistake, that the partner must be like Adam, He takes a rib from Adam's side and fashions a woman, apparently without awareness of the consequences of this act.

As the story unfolds, despite God's warning not to eat the fruit of the Tree of Good and Evil, Eve convinces Adam that they should do so. The act frustrates and angers God, and He punishes them severely by expelling them from the Garden, denying them immortality, making Adam work for his sustenance, and inflicting painful childbirth on Eve. Schaalman argues that this punishment is excessive: "God," he declares, "is out of order."

Nor is God capable of creating order. Each unfolding biblical story reveals not only is God "out of order," but so is the created world. When God discovers that He cannot control human behavior, he gets increasingly angry and frustrated. Not long after the expulsion, Eve gives birth to two sons, to Cain and then to Abel, who becomes God's favorite. Cain, in a fit of jealousy, kills him, with the result, Schaalman comments, "Rather than a fulfillment of the inherent purpose of the creation …, both Adam's disobedience and Cain's murder are severe interferences with, and tests of, the created order. …" (p. 83).

The story of Babel, the human attempt to invade God's heavenly dominion, is the next transgression, (p. 83). "Surprised" and "alarmed" by this rash act, God "takes drastic action to thwart" it (p. 83). By the time of Noah, human behavior has so degenerated that in anger and frustration God nearly destroys His creation. Schaalman interprets God's inability to control events as proof that He is not omnipotent. Quite the contrary, He appears to be powerless to prevent them. In the stories that follow, humans continue to defy and frustrate God.

To Schaalman, these early chapters of Genesis are the beginning of an "unbroken record of God's increasing failures with His human creatures and [His] concomitant disappointment and pain" (p. 84). Ten generations after Adam, God gives up on humanity and decides to start over. He sends the Flood to destroy everyone but Noah and his family.

His new plan is to establish a partnership and a covenant with Noah and his descendants (p. 178).

Pillar #6: God Changes

Schaalman's sixth pillar is that God is not immutable, but evolving and discovering what it means to be God. Schaalman's God differs from the traditional notion that God's nature is fixed and immutable. God, Schaalman argues, is a Being in the process of becoming, of renewing "Himself." God learns, adjusts, adapts to new circumstances, to "surprises" that result from unanticipated and unwanted human behavior.[403]

Schaalman derives this view of God from God's cryptic description of "Himself" to Moses in Exodus 3:14, "*Ehyeh asher ehyeh*," traditionally translated "I am that I am." This rendering of the Hebrew has been understood to mean that God is immutable and present in the here and now (p. 167). Schaalman points out that grammatically the Hebrew is a future tense construction. His translation is: "I am who I will be" (p. 167–168, 177).

Inherent in Schaalman's translation is his view that God is dynamic and evolving, in a continual state of becoming. God's relationship with humans is an ongoing and evolving learning experience. Before Adam, He had no experience with humans and has to learn what it means to interact with them. The story of Noah provides Schaalman insight into the nature of a changing and a self-reflective God. Genesis 8:21–22 contains an astonishing interior monologue in which God admits to Himself that He has made a mistake by setting out to destroy the earth and vows never to do it again:

> When the waters had receded and Noah found himself on dry land, he built an altar and made sacrifices to God. "And the LORD smelled a sweet savour; and the LORD *said in his heart* [italics added], I will not again curse the ground any more for man's sake; for the imagination of man's heart [is] evil from his youth; neither will I again smite any more everything living, as I have done."

Recognizing that He cannot change human behavior, God concludes that His creatures are "evil from their youth." For Schaalman, this is a particularly revealing and sad passage: "I could almost weep when I learned that God thought of his creation as a failure." He interprets God's recognition of His failure as confirmation of his own view that God is developing and in the process of becoming God. In this story, Schaalman adds, the Torah speaks of qualities of God, which later theologians totally ignored when they characterized God as omniscient, omnipotent, absolute, and unchanging. For him, these early stories present a picture of a God engaged in ongoing experimentation and the process of learning.

The second book of the Torah, Exodus, provides Schaalman additional confirmation that God continues to learn and change. Up to this point in the narrative, God only had to deal with individuals, never with communities. In a sense, He is totally lost. Despite all of His acts, including freeing the Israelites from bondage in Egypt, the miracle of the Ten Plagues, and the revelation on Sinai, only a few weeks later, the Israelites have lost the sense of God's imminence and His protective power. God learns from the incident of the Golden Calf that they need continual sensory reinforcement to maintain their belief. Schaalman points out that the Israelite community required a god it could recognize, a god similar to the gods of their neighbors and one who lives among them. Humans, he argues, cannot understand or relate to a god without physical form and beyond the reach of human reason: "A meta-sensate God is virtually a human contradiction."

According to Schaalman, when God realized that the Israelites needed a sensory confirmation of His ongoing existence and support, He commanded Moses to build a *Mishkan*, a structure that would provide a dwelling place for Him among the people. The physicality of the *Mishkan* and the sense of God's indwelling gave them assurance of God's existence. Yet, Schaalman points out, a home requires servants, so God orders Moses to establish a new form of worship. Up to this point, the Israelites had direct access to God, but now would have to approach Him through priests and by bringing gifts. Schaalman understands this development as part of God's ongoing experiment of creating a Holy People. He adds, "This form of worship lasted as long as the Temple existed, but, once it was destroyed, this entire system of worship collapsed."

Pillar #7: God's Failures

Schaalman's seventh pillar is that Torah is the record of God's failures. Human beings, made in God's image, are His first major disappointments. Adam violates God's one prohibition and eats from the Tree of Knowledge, Cain kills his brother Abel, and, in a vain attempt to reach heaven, humans build the Tower of Babel. When the behavior of His humans becomes completely intolerable, God sends a flood to wipe them out. Unwilling to give up completely his efforts to establish a partnership with humankind, God begins again with Noah. Like their ancestors, however, Noah's descendents continue to disappoint God. In an ongoing effort to shape and mold the world as He desires it, from this point on, God selects particular humans with whom to partner, humans whom He singles out to be leaders and models of human behavior—Abraham, Isaac, Jacob, Moses, and, later, David.

Nevertheless, Israel continues to disappoint Him. Schaalman argues, even Abraham failed God. First, on two occasions he "pimps" his wife[404] to save himself, then, at the urging of his wife, sends his first son, Ishmael and his mother, Hagar, off to die in the desert, and finally agrees to God's request that he sacrifice his only remaining son, Isaac. Schaalman believes that Abraham's real test was not the extent to which he carried out God's request, but the extent to which he should have resisted it.

Schaalman thinks the Book of Exodus is also a story of God's failures. God frees the Israelites from Egyptian bondage and sends them under Moses' leadership off to the Promised Land. The journey, however, is fraught with challenges. Repeatedly, the Israelites complain bitterly about their circumstances and lament that they ever left Egypt, where, despite the fact that they were slaves, they believe they were better off. These actions enrage God, who sends them on a forty-year journey into the wilderness until the last adult over twenty years of age at the time of Exodus has perished. Instead of the Israelites becoming the Holy People He envisioned, God has to wipe out the adult generation. Throughout the journey, the Israelites continue to anger God. To head off the various calamitous punishments God decrees—including annihilation—Moses contends with Him in an effort to avert or, at least, mitigate them. Not always successful, Moses manages at least to convince God not to destroy the people. Even Moses, God's favorite, disappoints Him. When Moses strikes the rock in a fit of anger to bring forth water for the thirsty Israelites, he fails to follow God's instruction that he speak to the rock (Numbers 20: 8–12). Not only is God disappointed, but angry. He tells Moses that because he did not carry out his instructions, he would not be allowed to enter the Promised Land.[405]

Beyond the early history of Israel as represented in the Torah, despite God's commitments to defend Israel, Schaalman argues, He has been a near total failure. He ticks off major Jewish catastrophes when God might have helped the Jewish people. First, He failed to protect His people when, in 721 BCE, the Assyrians destroyed the Northern Kingdom of Israel, resulting in the elimination from history of the major portion of the Jewish people. One hundred and fifty years later, when the Babylonians attacked the remnants of the Israelites in the Kingdom of Judah, God did not intervene. Nor did He assist the Jews when the Romans destroyed the Temple in 70 CE and massacred the people, nor during the Bar Kochba revolt in 132 CE, when the Romans killed a higher percentage of Jews than did the Nazis.[406]

In more recent times, during the Crusades God did nothing to prevent the Crusaders from destroying Jewish communities in the Rhineland. When the Jews were expelled from Spain in 1492, God did not protect them either, or when they were expelled from England, France, and Portugal. God did not rise in the defense of the Jews when Chelmnicki and the Cossacks ravaged the local Jewish communities in southern Poland and wiped out a quarter of a million men, women, and children. More recently, or course, is the example of the *Shoah*. Schaalman sums up this history by concluding that Jews have lived for centuries with the God who has failed to live up to his partnership in the covenant as the protector of his people. "Only once," Schaalman asserts, "in Egypt, did God come to their aid."

Pillar #8: The Suffering God

The eighth pillar of Schaalman's theology is his belief that God is a suffering God. God's limitations, Schaalman believes, makes Him vulnerable to hurt from the failures of His humans to be what He intended them to be. Moreover, the covenantal relationship between God and Israel means that God is vulnerable in all the ways that relationship entails. It opens Him to suffering as a result of human behavior. Given humankind's frequent transgressions in small and in historic proportions, Schaalman argues that God's suffering is immense and cumulative. In an effort to substantiate his position, he points to Exodus 34: 6–7 where God speaks of Himself as "long suffering" (p. 170).[407] "One could and should read the Exodus saga," Schaalman argues, "as a near disaster for God, who profoundly misread the character of this people who had now become God's stake in the future of humanity" (p. 169).

God responds to the Israelites' lack of trust in Him and their failure to follow His commandments by threatening to destroy them. Throughout Israel's history, in Chronicles and the books of the Prophets, God threatens imminent destruction of Israel for violating His commandments. Schaalman understands the severity of God's punishments as a measure of the extent of His suffering (pp. 67–68).[408]

Schaalman no longer expects anything from God: "I think of the billions of words that must have been said [by those in the concentration camps] asking God for help and none came." The gravest disappointment and suffering God has known, according to Schaalman, may well be the fact that He could do nothing to prevent this tragedy. To make peace with this idea, Schaalman is left with only one answer to where God was during the Holocaust: God must have been in the camps suffering with his people.

Pillar #9: God Needs Partners

The ninth pillar is Schaalman's idea that God needs partners, an idea consistent with Jewish tradition.[409] Having "withdrawn" from His Totality to create something new, "God was perhaps expecting a partner, a respondent, an 'other,' who could be a joy to the Creator, who could provide an additional capacity for fulfillment, enrichment" (p. 135). In Schaalman's view, God needs an "other" to validate His existence, for God to be God: "Where would God be without his Jews," he asks? God's expectation is that this partner, made in His image, will be righteous and holy and will assist Him in completing creation: "Clearly, no matter how impressive, how infinite, the results of creation had been before Adam, it is only when a human appears that God is finished with the work" (p. 78). God transfers to Adam the responsibility of finishing creation:

> The created order derives from Adam. From the very first moments of reality, as depicted in the biblical record, the human is involved radically, indispensably. ... Even the most obvious and necessary consequences of the divine initiative invite—need— human assistance, involvement, collaboration. (p. 81)

Schaalman maintains that God created Adam as "His" partner and His caretaker of creation, including dominion over the animals, and "hands over ... the created order to Adam and his descendants" (p. 139). An important element of this partnership is clearly established when God enlists Adam's help in naming and differentiating the creatures in Eden: "There would be no world as we understand it without human participation, without human language to distinguish, designate, and thus render creation intelligible" (p. 81). Schaalman concludes that the assignment of taxonomy to the human means that humans are "involved radically, indispensably" as partners in creation.[410] Adam, however, proves to be a disappointment when he violates God's one prohibition not to eat from the Tree of Knowledge. Because he is no longer a desirable partner, God expels him from Eden and begins a search for another human whom He can trust to help complete creation.

From this point forward, Schaalman writes that God needs a human partner to prove to Himself that his creation has not been a failure. Many generations pass before God finds a new partner in Abraham, a man willing to obey and with whom God is willing to enter into a lasting covenant. He promises Abraham that he will be the father of a new nation, a nation of Holy People and "a light to the nations" and as numerous as the stars (p. 110).

Abraham is Schaalman's hero, the prototypical Jew, the man who argues with God. Schaalman's position is that this mutual interchange between God and Abraham allows God to be actualized: "Something happened to God through this interaction. God found something that He had not found in humans before, His completion through dialogue." So totally is Schaalman committed to Buber's sense of the fundamental reality of being that he believes God's being or existence requires relationship, and relationship by definition is two-way in which both partners are actively involved. To make the point, Schaalman claims that God's relationship with Adam was not of this kind. Adam is a passive partner, and, thus, not actually a partner. Abraham, however, is an active participant in his relationship with God. He "argues" with God over the fate of Sodom and Gomorrah and attempts to dissuade God from acting on his anger against the inhabitants, the innocent and the guilty, which God intends to exterminate.

This experience creates for God a need and a love for Abraham that is reciprocal, a relationship carried over to Abraham's descendants. Says Schaalman, "God is forever hooked on Abraham; His own survival is ultimately tied into the survival of Abraham's descendants." The relationship allows God to escape from "His self-destructive isolation." God in isolation is no God; God needs someone to say, "You are my God." If the creature does not understand that his "creatureness is related to a creator," then God has no partner and continues in His isolation.

For a while, God appears to be pleased with His new partner. Yet, to test Abraham's fitness as a partner, God engineers several major tests.[411] One of them is to see how Abraham responds to Sara's demand that he send his first and beloved son Ishmael into the desert, where he is likely to die (p. 117). Though heartbroken, Abraham accedes to the request. God tests Abraham again by requesting that he sacrifice his other son, Isaac. Again, Abraham complies without protest. For Schaalman, these tests represent major failures for Abraham: "It is plausible to conclude that God may now have been doubtful, disappointed, surprised" by Abraham's docile responses. This compliance may have given God pause to consider whether "Abraham was the right person to be the covenant partner" (p. 118). Although God apparently welcomes challenges to His authority that promote peace and justice, God cannot abide mindless conformity.

Later, in the story of the Binding of Isaac, Schaalman claims that God is disappointed in Abraham because of his willingness to sacrifice his son. He "views this willingness as a failure." For that reason, Schaalman claims, God distanced Himself from Abraham's unquestioning compliance to His request.[412] Therefore, instead of speaking to Abraham himself to tell him not to kill Isaac, he sends an angel. "God had hoped," Schaalman argues, "that Abraham would do another Sodom and

Gomorrah." The story leads Schaalman to the radical conclusion: "Were Isaac to die, it would have meant Abraham's suicide and the end of the promises God made to establish a new people."

After Abraham's death, the stories of his descendants move inexorably to the creation of the people Israel. Isaac and Jacob become instrumental in helping God realize this new plan. The implementation of the plan, however, does not proceed smoothly. After Jacob's descendants settle in Egypt, the Pharaohs eventually enslave them. For reasons unknown, God chooses to absent himself for four hundred years before deciding it is time to rescue His Jews.

When He comes out of seclusion, He chooses Moses as His partner to achieve the end He envisions. Disappointed as He is with the world He created, he tries again to develop a plan to make it better, to fix it.[413] It is a threefold plan: first, He has to free the Israelites, transform them into a Holy People, and finally to get them to the Promised Land, where they and their descendents will help God finish creation.[414]

From these stories, Schaalman concludes that God, no longer self-sufficient, "depends on us to be known, sought, probed, rejected, loved" (p. 49). This relationship is not only reciprocal but also covenantal, specifically with the Israelites. Through this covenant, God confers on Israel the obligation to be a "holy people" and "a light to the nations." In return, God promises them prosperity and everlasting title to the Holy Land. This collaboration was totally new territory for God and part of an ongoing process of learning.

Pillar #10: Witnesses

The tenth pillar is Schaalman's belief that God needs witnesses to reassure Him that creation was not a mistake, that human beings are redeemable, and that we have not abandoned the path to *tikkun olam*. "Witnessing," he writes, "is the fundamental redemptive act." Schaalman's personal mission is to reassure God that at least one person, though imperfect and flawed, recognizes and acts in accordance with His wishes and respects the covenant. As he remarked to his Torah Study, "I am willing to see myself as a representative of humanity, a stand-in, a model of what God wants from humanity. I am continually challenged and tested in this role in which I have failed too often." Schaalman believes that to lead a good and moral life requires, in part, that we help God cope with this pain and disappointment, that we "be a comforter." By this, he means bearing witness to the covenant, to make the statement, "*Hineni*," here I am (pp. 136, 188). Assuming this responsibility, Schaalman writes, is part of his prescription for helping a beleaguered God "in terrible need of reassurance" after the "excruciating, maybe unstoppable, pain" produced by the *Shoah*. "My motivation for prayer," he told this interviewer, "is to let God know that I am here. *My* God needs company."[415]

Pillar #11: I-Thou

Not only does God need our company, Schaalman explains, in what we may understand as the eleventh pillar, but our relationship with God must consist in what Buber described as I-Thou, a meeting on common ground (p. 47). The path to such a meeting is not directly to God, but through human relationships. The experience of the divine is in our relationship with others, or to an other. It means giving oneself totally to the experience of the other. This relationship requires that we rid ourselves of preconceptions, prejudgments, and, in place of them, wholeheartedly listen and respond to the other. It is through this means that the other is transformed from an "it" to a "thou." To be fully human is to enter into a "dialogic relationship with the world, its people," even its objects (p. 48). The willingness to be fully open and to experience the other is an act of love that needs to be the basis of all human relations and is the gateway to God.[416]

Pillar #12: God Is Who We Perceive God to Be

The twelfth pillar supporting Schaalman's theology is that God is whom we perceive God to be. The God of Torah, Schaalman argues, is the creation of a people living in a far distant land and time. Their needs were different from those of today; their mentality was fashioned by the world they lived in. Their God was vengeful, angry, and "needy"—a loving yet suffering God. A thousand years later, in the Rabbinic Period, the circumstances for Jews had changed dramatically. As a result, the God of the rabbis was a different God. Under the strong influence of Greek culture and philosophy, their God was omniscient and omnipotent, a kind and loving God, the protector and salvation of "His" people.[417]

Such is the tradition in which Schaalman grew up. After the experience of the *Shoah*, however, that rendering of God no longer made sense. Schaalman explains that his radical reappraisal of God as limited and vulnerable is justified by new experience that requires a new understanding of God (p. 168). His analysis of the changing perception of God based on the experience of the times, led him to propose that God's being exists in proportion and direct relation to humanity's ability to perceive "Him," and that ability is determined by the times in which we live (p. 177).

Pillar #13: A Loving God

In what may be considered the thirteenth pillar, Schaalman believes God is a loving God. In Exodus 34: 6–7, God describes Himself as a "compassionate, gracious, long-suffering, [and] full of love and truth … [Who] shows love to thousands [and] forgives transgressions and sin and holds guiltless, but not totally" (p. 170). God's attachment to the Israelites, according to Schaalman, was predicated on his love for the patriarchs, Abraham, Isaac, and Jacob. As Schaalman put it in a Torah Study, "God fell in love with our ancestors." Schaalman went on to explain that love is the basis of relationship between God and Israel. In the *Shema*, Israel is instructed to love God with all "your heart and all your might." That is the first requirement of belief. So fundamental is this love relationship, that it constitutes a marriage. The Torah is the *ketubah*. Such an understanding of love as the foundation for the relationship between Israel and God helps explain the inclusion of the Song of Songs as part of the Tanach. It is first a love song in which sensuality and eroticism are part of the transcendent and mystical relationship of the people and their God. For Schaalman this relationship carries over into human relationships: "Have I told Lotte enough times that I love her," he asked out loud? "We are going to be married sixty-eight years."

Pillar #14: A Holy Life

The last pillar of Schaalman's theology is his belief that life is holy. It is the proposition toward which his theology has been directed: how to infuse a sense of God's wholeness and holiness into everyday life.[418] Schaalman's God, though limited and vulnerable, is, nevertheless, the indispensable fact of life, a reality that gives it meaning and substance. His belief in God allows him to think that everything around him is sacred and holy. From this holiness, Schaalman derives his raison d'être, his "ground of being." It is the basis of his engagement in the world and his commitment to achieve what he believes is God's plan, the fixing of the world, *tikkun olam*. To the extent that "we are made in God's image," we need to imitate as far as possible the example God sets for us.[419]

As God relates to us, we need to relate to other human beings. "What is necessary," Schaalman argues, "is for us to wake up to our responsi-bilities" (p. 154). By "responsibilities" he means the "answer we give to something that may have long been known and taught." His point is that the question of whether God exists or not should not be the basis on which we develop our sense of individual or collective morality. "The failure in our world," he maintains, "is not the absence of God or the lack of communication by God; rather the failure is our own unreadi-ness, lack of capacity, and lack of will to do what we all know we are 'commanded' to do, are meant to do. We can even go further and say what we all know we *need* to do" (p. 154).

Performing mitzvot or commandments is Schaalman's way of prac-ticing Judaism, of participating with God in the ongoing improvement of the world. [420] The performance of mitzvot is infused also with a sense of religious purpose, a reason for being. [421] Schaalman, nevertheless, makes no pretense to performing all mitzvot. When asked how he deals with living up to the commandments, Schaalman refers to Buber and Rosenzweig as his models:

> Martin Buber made the point that he wanted to perform those mitzvot that spoke to him, that elicited from him a response at a given moment and occasion in his life. Of course, there is also the approach of Franz Rosenzweig, who held that he was "on the way" to performing the mitzvot, but had not yet reached the whole panoply of mitzvot that he hoped someday to perform. For him, it was a process with progressive stages. (pp. 16–17)

Because it is impossible for him to practice all of the mitzvot, Schaal-man has resolved the issue by concluding that, because the covenant was a contract between unequals, humans have to decide how to interpret and live by it. Its obligations clash with the autonomy of the individual and produce an ethical tension resulting in an ethical divide. To bridge this divide, Schaalman believes he is required to make a personal commitment to choose which of the commandments he will practice: "This perilous position is the existential nature of modern life."[422]

Fundamental to the performance of mitzvot for Schaalman is his commitment to promote interfaith understanding and dialogue. Insofar as he has accomplished this goal, he is living out Buber's (1966) ideal that each of us is "called upon to fulfill [our] particularity in this world" and to actualize our "unique, unprecedented and never-recurring potentialities" (p. 16). One of the ways in which Schaalman is living his "particularity and uniqueness" is through his efforts to improve relations among the world's religions and to bring peace and harmony to this world. Schaalman (2007) explains his activities as his way of fulfilling the teaching of the *Pirke Avot*: "It is not up to you to complete the work [of *tikkun olam*], but neither are you free to desist from it" (p. 131). His aim is to give back to the world something of the many gifts he has received: "I have already been given much more than I ever knew I would receive and certainly did nothing to deserve: my very life; the universe in which I meet God as Creator and other human beings; the whole, virtually infinite list of gifts of which I am conscious. ... *Hineni* represents my gratitude, my willingness to do, my awareness of being graced" (p. 133).

Hineni is part of that giving back. Yet, for Schaalman, there is much more to be done, not only alone, but also in partnership with others who need not be Jewish. Anyone who leads a moral and ethical life is a "partner" with God. One such person was the late Cardinal Bernardin, Archbishop of Chicago (1982–1996). Schaalman considered him one of his closest friends. As we have discussed in detail Chapter 7, "Post-retirement," during the seventeen years that they knew each other, they worked to improve relations between Catholics and Jews and to develop interreligious understanding in the Chicago metropolitan area.

Final thoughts on *Hineni*: as radical and unique as it is, the book should not be read as Schaalman's last words on theology. Instead, it is part of an ongoing exploration, of a lifetime search for the meaning and purpose of his being. His caution that the written word does not do justice to the thinking of its writer is particularly important in light of developments after the book was published. Only two months later, Schaalman was already pushing his view of the suffering God to new limits.

At an extended adult weekend retreat at OSRUI, he told his audience, "Christianity understood that, in place of the disembodied and unknowable God of Israel, it needed to give God human form and substance. Jesus is a being of flesh and blood to which humans can relate." Christianity had made flesh the idea that God suffers: "It reached its epitome in Christianity, which recognized that God's suffering is so great that, in order to get the people's attention to it, He committed suicide, the ultimate sacrifice." Christians understand that God sacrificed Himself to redeem humanity. This new perspective coming from Schaalman was an awakening for some of his students. By the end of the retreat, they could only wonder what might be in store for them at their next encounter with him.

They did not have to wait long. A few months later, Schaalman used the occasion of his 2007 Yom Kippur sermon to tell Emanuel's congregation of his latest insight into the Torah. He said, "Despite having read *Bereshit* for more than sixty years, I had never recognized that God's first words to humans came only after Adam had disobeyed Him. God calls out to Adam, 'Where are you?'" Aware of his nakedness and his shame, Adam had hidden himself in the Garden. "This question," Schaalman continued, "is God's first direct 'conversation' with Adam, and, as such, establishes the quintessential relationship between God and His humans." On one level, the question is an attempt to find where Adam is hiding. On another, Schaalman offered, "The meaning of the words depends on the tone in which God utters them. Were they uttered in anger or in love? Harshly or lovingly? In either case, they reveal a God seeking man."

This insight is critical to Schaalman's understanding of the relationship of God and His creatures. Not only is God asking Adam where he is physically, but also, and, more profoundly, where he is spiritually. It is a question, Schaalman suggests, and that echoes down the millennia, the ultimate human question that all God's people need to answer.[423] The publication of *Hineni* in 2007 was Schaalman's attempt to provide his own answer.

Two years later Schaalman took the idea of the suffering God and its ramifications in Christianity a step further. The day before his Yom Kippur sermon in 2009, Schaalman surprised his Torah Study students with a new and even more radical insight: "Although Jews think of themselves as a covenantal people, a reliable partner in God's great enterprise, the question remains, is [God] really satisfied with us, whether we have been that kind of partner that encourages God to be satisfied?" His answer was not only a surprise, but a shock: "In Christian understanding, God came to the conclusion that the Jewish people just wasn't working out sufficiently and tried another experiment, an experiment named Jesus and Paul and then ... Christianity." Of course, he hastened to add, God was no more satisfied with Christians and Christianity than with Jews: "Christianity may be just as deep a failure to God as were His Jews." Nor does this new "covenant" mean that the old covenant has been dissolved.

Seeking to define himself in relation to tradition and to modern Orthodoxy, Schaalman reminded his students of his strong objection to the characterization of God as Father and King, so basic to Orthodox Judaism. It was a mistake made during the rabbinic period: "In the Torah, the Israelites did not bow down to God, but struggled with Him [one of the meanings of "Israel" is to struggle with God]. In the Torah, the patriarchs speak directly to God, often arguing with and contradicting Him." He cited the examples of Abraham and Moses, who challenged God to reconsider his actions. Abraham objected to the injustice to killing the innocents along with the guilty that would result in the destruction of Sodom and Gomorrah. Moses defended the Israelites when God wanted to destroy them. Schaalman understands these events to mean that the relationship of God to his humans is dialogic, not one of lawgiver to servant or slave. At no point in the Torah, he claims, does God expect His people to bow before him. Instead, God welcomes dissent and argument. For Schaalman this dialogic relationship is his model for a relationship with God.

It is this understanding of his relationship with God that brings him to the conclusion that he is a biblical Jew. He argues that this view of the dialogic relationship to God is what separates him from Orthodox Judaism. Orthodoxy, he maintains, requires slavish adherence to God's laws. For them, God is God the Father and they His children. Schaalman thinks of the Orthodox relationship to God as analogous to the way God was presented to him when he was a child. "Children in a German household," he reminisced, "were expected to be seen and not heard. By contrast, today in the American household the situation is reversed. Children have become the center of attention; their parents and relatives dote on every new word their children speak. At an early age, they frequently know more than their parents, particularly about technology." During Schaalman's childhood, such a situation was inconceivable and impossible: "The father could not be contradicted but only obeyed."

Schaalman's theological liberation can be tied to his setting aside parental authority. Over the last half century, he has struggled to overcome his early indoctrination in the idea of the all-powerful, omniscient, and protecting God the Father. The death of the idea of God the Father allows Schaalman to establish a new relationship with Him in which he becomes an indispensable partner. At the age of ninety-six, however, still standing in his way is his inability to totally forgive God for allowing the *Shoah*, which remains "a shadow at his heel." Unable to rest, "I am still working toward a new understanding that will give me peace."

Critical Assessment of Schaalman's Theology

Schaalman's decision to reconstruct his theology around the *Shoah* has set him apart from the mainstream of contemporary Judaism. Although Judaism acknowledges the importance of the event, it does not see it as transformative or a starting place for theological discussion. No matter how deep its wounds on the Jewish psyche, for the most part, Judaism has decided it does not require a major reassessment in response to it.

A brief overview of the response of Reform Judaism to the Holocaust will clarify the extent to which Schaalman's views are heretical. The noted historian of Reform Judaism, Michael A. Meyer (1988), observed that, although the Holocaust may have shattered many illusions, it did not signify the end of faith or belief in revelation as an "incipient messianic consummation" (p. 9). The Jewish response to the Holocaust must be to remember it as "a sacred obligation," but certainly not to overthrow traditional and Reform Jewish belief.

When in 1991, Schaalman published his ideas on the transformational meaning of the Holocaust ("God of Auschwitz?"), the influential

Reform theologian, Eugene Borowitz (1991), published his view that the Holocaust does not require a reassessment of Jewish theology. Although he did not mention Schaalman, he might just as well have been criticizing him in his rejection of Fackenheim and Wiesel's assertions that the Holocaust is qualitatively different from other catastrophes in the Jewish experience and unique in human history (p. 36).[424] The Holocaust "must fundamentally figure in our view of Jewish identity, [but] it does not faithfully teach us the reality of Jewish existence. ... Most Jewish thinkers consider the Holocaust a most egregious human evil ... but one that needs to be considered on the continuum of other human evils, not in a realm of its own" (p. 38). Except for a handful of Jewish theologians, he maintained, the large majority of Jews did not see the need to make radical adjustments in their theology. In fact, even the movement by Jewish thinkers to deal with the issue of human evil (what Christians identified as "sin") was short-lived. Schaalman, however, was not persuaded to follow the majority and continued his efforts to convince Reform Judaism that the *Shoah* had to be understood as more than just another catastrophe in the Jewish experience.

In 1996, the editors of *Commentary* (August 1996) followed up their 1966 symposium on the attitudes and thinking of Jewish leaders across the spectrum of Jewish affiliation, but, this time, did not ask Schaalman to participate. Unlike the 1966 symposium, this one included a specific question on the Holocaust: "How have, respectively, the Holocaust and the existence of the state of Israel influenced your faith, your religious identity, your observance" (p. 19)? The responses make clear that Schaalman's views on God, Torah, and the Holocaust stand outside the mainstream. Most of the respondents to the 1996 survey stressed that the Holocaust, shattering as it was to the modern Jew, is only one more event in the chain of Jewish catastrophes. The lone exception to this view came from Reform Rabbi Joshua O. Haberman (also a survivor) who wrote that the catastrophic nature of the Holocaust changed his beliefs. He called the idea that God is our protector "childish." Instead, we need to understand the idea more as a hope: "God should not be expected to do for us what we are able to do for ourselves" (p. 7). He attributes God's failure to protect Jews during the Holocaust to the idea that at creation God turned it over to His humans. He finds confirmation for his idea in Psalms 115.16:

"The heavens are the heavens of the LORD, But the earth He has given to the sons of men."[425]

The most recent blow to Schaalman's desire to see Reform Judaism make the *Shoah* the centerpiece of its theology is CCAR's "1999 Pittsburgh Statement of Principles." Its reassertion of the traditional position of an all-powerful and all merciful God and its reference and its treatment of the *Shoah* as a nontransformational historical event is hurtful to Schaalman. Finding himself isolated from his colleagues and his beloved Reform movement, he feels like a prophet crying in the wilderness

Complementary Theologies

Although the *Shoah* has not had the transformational impact on Jewish theology that Schaalman would like, he is not completely alone in his thinking. Ironically, many Christian theologians consider the *Shoah* a turning point, a critically decisive moment in human experience that requires a complete rethinking of Christianity's history, its principles, and relationship to others, particularly to Jews.[426]

Among Jewish thinkers, a few may be identified whose thinking parallels Schaalman's. The Jewish philosopher, Hans Jonas, also thinks that the enormity of the *Shoah* requires a complete rethinking of the heritage of traditional Judaism.[427] Like Schaalman, Jonas is a refugee from Germany, deeply and personally affected by the *Shoah*. His 1996 essay, "The Concept of God after Auschwitz: A Jewish Voice," is an effort to answer the question: "How did God let it happen?"

After his mother died in a concentration camp, Jonas put aside his philosophical writings in order to work out a satisfactory explanation of why God failed to save the Jews. The question, he maintains, challenges traditional Judaism's belief in a compassionate and loving God, full of kindness, the Redeemer of Israel, and a participant in history. How could such a God fail to protect his people from this catastrophe? To answer the question, Jonas admits that he has to create "a *myth* of my invention ... a credible, if imaginative conjecture allowed by Plato to venture beyond the world of the knowable" (p. 134). He resorts to mythmaking because words are inadequate to articulate the mystery of being: "All this, let it be said at the end, is but stammering. ... [Even the great sages and prophets] were stammerers before the eternal mystery" (p. 142).

Like Schaalman's, Jonas's myth begins with God's decision to create a world outside of and separate from him. Although we cannot know the reason for this decision, Jonas speculates that, in order to achieve this act of creation, God, as understood in the Kabbalah, withdrew, contracted, and limited himself in order to make room for the world. The contraction of being results in a limitation on divine power. In Jonas's thinking, "having given himself whole to the becoming world, God had no more to give: it is man's now to give to him" (p. 142). By giving over causality in the world of the finite, God gave up His power "to direct, correct, and alternately guarantee its destiny in creation" (p. 134). He also risked exposing Himself to a process of "endless variety of becoming," expecting that in the fullness of time, He would experience himself *in* time. Being in time, posed the risk that He might be "transfigured or possibly even disfigured by it." By entering the world, God submitted himself to mutability and the process of change and development (p. 138).

Jonas also believes that the stories in the Torah show that God is learning and evolving. He comes to this conclusion by observing that the Torah depicts God as being affected, altered, and made different through his interaction with humans. The very nature of the relationship of God and his creation dictates a mutual interaction and consequent response that results in change. As part of being in the world, God experiences the emotions of his humans: suffering, "rejoicing, grieving, approving and frowning" (p. 137). God, he wrote, began to suffer from the moment of creation, "certainly from the creation of man" (p. 136).

Although God may not be omnipotent, Jonas thinks that to view God as anything less than good is to entertain the idea that God may be evil, a concept unacceptable to reason. How, then, to justify God's goodness in the face of Auschwitz? Auschwitz must be understood in terms of the existence of evil in the world and a confirmation of God's inability to alter the course of human events. This is the price God paid by endowing humans with freedom of action. God's only alternative, according to Jonas, is the mute and "insistent appeal of his unfulfilled goal" (p. 141). To fulfill that goal, God needs our help.

Other complementary theological perspectives can be found in the work of Elie Wiesel and Emil Fackenheim. We have already noted

Fackenheim's influence on Schaalman and his view that Judaism must make a place for the Holocaust in its theology. Rabbi Harold Kushner shares their sense of a limited and vulnerable God who could not prevent the Holocaust. In *When Bad Things Happen to Good People* (1981), he raises critical questions about God's apparent absence during the Holocaust: "Why did he not intervene to stop it? Why did he not strike Hitler dead in 1939 and spare millions of lives and untold suffering ..." (p. 84). Like Schaalman and Fackenheim, Kushner concludes that God must have been one of the victims. He argues that once God gave humans the freedom to act, He gave up the ability to control their behavior. On the other hand, he does not accept the idea that God suffers: "I do not know what it means for God to suffer. I do not believe that God is a person like me, with real eyes and real tear ducts to cry. ..." (p. 85). Nevertheless, he thinks that God *must* [italics added] feel anguish in the presence of humanity's enormous and undeserved suffering. To answer the question why God did nothing to prevent the Holocaust, Kushner cites the testimony of a survivor of Auschwitz: "It never occurred to me to associate the calamity we were experiencing with God, to blame him, or to believe in him less, or cease believing in him at all because he did not come to our aid" (as cited in Kushner, 1981, p. 85).

To his surprise and pleasure, Schaalman discovered that his colleague, Rabbi Jack Bloom, shares his theological views, although neither of them knew it.[428] Like Schaalman, Bloom (2008) thinks of the God of Torah as continually wounded by humans, who are unreliable partners, even competitors, rivals, and betrayers. Once expelled from Eden for disobeying God, human behavior continued a downward spiral. An enraged God responds by flooding the world and nearly wiping out His creation. Because of the behavior of His humans, God is continually wounded but, at the same time, needs their help to heal His wounds: "Though it may seem audacious to presume that we mere humans can help heal God, that is an essential part of our covenantal relationship," one that offers the possibility of healing in both directions (p. 6).

Bloom also believes that the divine partnership means that God "teaches" humans, and that humans have a role in "teaching" God. The Midrash *Bamidbar Rabbah*[429] notes three occasions on which Moses contends with God, and God responds, "'By your life! You have spoken well. You have taught me. From now on, I will. ...'" (p. 6).[430]

The Ongoing Quest to Find the Unknowable God

Despite his sense of isolation, Schaalman's fertile mind continues to seek answers to fundamental theological questions. In introducing this chapter, we noted that in 2007, the highlight of Schaalman's Yom Kippur sermon was the question he directed to the congregation: "Where *are* you?" His challenge was "where are you in relation to God and to the mitzvah of *Tikkun olam*?" Then, he turned the spotlight on himself: "Where am I?" His answer: "I will continue to search." His response was a reflection of his own existential quandary.[431]

Another issue Schaalman had been wrestling with for some time was the meaning of the word *Echad* as it appears in the *Shema*, the most powerful prayer in Jewish life.[432] In 2007, he explained to his Torah Study,

> The prayer is said to have been on the lips of martyred Jews in ancient and modern times when Jews were entering the crematoria. ... By reaffirming the basic tenets of Jewish faith, the *Shema* represents the centrality of the Jewish understanding of God. Usually translated as, "Hear O Israel, the Lord is our God, the Lord is One" (*Shema Yisrael Adonai eloheinu Adonai Echad*), this statement is understood to mean that God is one, a unity, and that there is no other. The whole structure of Judaism is based on this premise.

Schaalman, however, is not content to accept this understanding. "No one knows," he stated, "what the word *Echad* meant to the ancient Israelites. Whether it meant what tradition says it meant can never be confirmed."

Paradoxicality

Three years later, Schaalman achieved a breakthrough in understanding the word's meaning. He found it in the story of Rabbi Akiba whom the Romans flayed alive because he violated their prohibition against teaching Torah. The question that haunted Schaalman was how, under such excruciating pain, Akiba could hold onto his belief in God. In a Yom Kippur sermon in 2010, Schaalman explained to Emanuel's congregation,

> As clumps of his flesh were peeled from his body and thrown to the dogs, with his final breath Akiba recited the *Shema*. His disciples, who were present at the flaying, asked, "Rabbi, even now?" Akiba responded, "Until now, I have never understood what it meant to love the Lord your God with all your heart, with all your might, and all your soul."

In an attempt to convey his sense of the power and mystery of that final moment that had been haunting him for a long time, Schaalman drew out Akiba's final word "*Echaaaaad*" and then let his voice trail off into silence. [433]

A few months later, Schaalman told his Torah Study that he had come to see that *Echad* referred to something without substance, a *concept*, and, as such, a "warning to his disciples not to attempt to go any further. The word is meant to tell us that God is unknowable, an admission that I do not know who or what God is."

> Judaism, then, is the ultimate paradox, the ultimate statement of the impossible. At the heart of the paradox is a consciousness that strives for something else, a certainty that it can never attain As a Jew, I am not satisfied with something I can't know, feel, or contemplate. ... But when it comes to God, that is exactly where I am, the unknowable God—*Echad*. Why it took me so long to achieve this understanding is a puzzle to me. Had I died five years ago, I would never have come to this understanding.

He went on to explain that Jewish tradition compensates for this inability to know God by substituting *Adonai* for God's name. "But," he insists,

> *Adonai* is not God's name. In the Torah, God's name is the unpronounceable "YHVH." Its pronunciation was lost with the death of the last surviving High Priest in 70 AD. God's name, therefore, is unspeakable. I know of no other religion where the name of God is unspeakable, unwordable.

The idea that, at bottom, reality could only be understood in terms of paradox became the basis for his presentation the following year at the 2011 Annual Meeting of the National Association of Retired Reform Rabbis (NAORRR). Soon after the conclusion of the 2010 Annual Meeting, the organization reached out to Schaalman to present the keynote address at its next annual meeting. "The normal process of selection of an outside speaker is to bring in a famous personality or a professor from HUC-JIR. By inviting me," Schaalman notes, "I understood that my colleagues were paying me a high compliment and that I would have to come up with something original and profound that they would find interesting."

At first, he reports, "I struggled with what I might say and, when nothing came, I stopped thinking about it for the next two months." He needed time for an idea to develop; the conference, after all, was almost a year away. He comforted himself with the thought that his talk need not be the final word on something, that, instead, he could talk about something he already knew well, such as a particular passage in Torah: "It would have been good enough. I could say something like 'Hello' and that would be enough."

By April or May of 2010, he remembered the sermon he had given the year before, which began, "I have a confession to make ..." He knew he wanted to begin the address with these words, but he was not sure what he wanted to confess. He had been thinking about God's words to Moses, "I forgive because of your words," which had been part of last year's sermon. (The line refers to Moses' efforts to dissuade God from annihilating the Israelites who had provoked Him by their lack of faith in Him. Moses convinced Him otherwise.) Schaalman explained that he was unhappy with his interpretation of this line:

> Over the last year, I was troubled about my rendering of the words and now realized that I had been incorrect. I had always understood the line as the basis for Yom Kippur, a ritualized way of requesting forgiveness. Now, I knew this understanding was totally wrong and that his new understanding placed a radical new light on a sacred text. This new realization gave me an insight into what I might say in my address.

One thought led to another and, over the next several months, the structure of his talk became clear, "The process of developing it was relatively easy. I decided to open myself up as never before and risk the consequences." The risk was that his colleagues would not understand him.

He remembered a Midrash that told of a discussion involving four rabbis and a problem they were trying to decide. One of them, who was always right, appeals to God for an answer. When God responds, the other three reject God's intervention, arguing God's Torah is not in heaven but rather on earth and that whatever He says about earthly matters has no bearing. In the Midrash, God acknowledged this rejection and said, "My creatures have defeated me." In researching the story further, Schaalman found a passage in the Talmud in which the rabbis had declared that, once the last prophet had died, there would be no further prophecy because, they asserted, the "holy spirit" had left Israel. "What I found almost by accident was so profoundly disturbing and, at the same time, confirmative: the centrality of paradox in Judaism."

The idea of paradox also resonated as an explanation of his own life. The discovery allowed him to make paradox a *leitmotiv* of his talk. He remembered that Jews went to their deaths during the Holocaust singing of the coming of the *Meshiach.* For Schaalman, this connection was all the confirmation he needed to see that paradox was at the heart of Judaism: "I was home free; I knew what I would say to my colleagues."

When the time had come for Schaalman to give his talk at the 2011 NAORRR Annual Meeting, he began by telling his colleagues that his speech is, in part, a "confession" of a puzzling experience he had during the last year. Schaalman revealed the "shock" he experienced when he discovered that the Kol Nidre liturgy did not mean what he thought it had. He had always thought that *solachti kidvorecha* meant that God was granting forgiveness to the supplicant. "What a shock it was to discover that the liturgy was not talking about me and my words, but about Moses' daring intercession on behalf of an otherwise doomed people." Another shock was his discovery that the Israelites survived not through God's agency, but because Moses convinced Him to allow them to survive: "We are Jews today because the man Moses managed to change God's mind so that a remnant survived. It was a most shocking discovery that the desert would be an unattended cemetery for over 600,000 Jewish males." His new understanding was "a severe test of credulity of the understanding of that man Moses' relation to his newly found God. It is an unrelieved paradox."

Schaalman explained that for him the ultimate theological issue is that behind the veil of reality is the impenetrable mystery of God.[434] His inability to penetrate the veil had troubled him in ways he has never revealed. As he groped for an explanation, he led the rabbis further into the depths of his perplexity. He turned their attention to the rabbinic decision to declare the Torah closed, a decision that came after the deaths of the last of the three prophets, Haggi, Zechariah, and Malachi, sometime around 500 BCE. With their deaths, the "masters" declared, "The holy spirit was removed from Israel." Not only, Schaalman pointed out, did that mean the end of the prophetic age, but that "God has not spoken to a Jew now for 2,500 years!"

Schaalman attempted to explain his efforts to cope with this reality and the mental anguish it was causing him. For the last several months, he had been struggling with the meaning of four words from the Kol Nidre service, "*solachti kidvorecha*: I forgive because of your words." When he realized that he could not "get them out of [his] head," he sought their meaning in the Torah. He discovered that they came from the story in the book of Numbers in which God threatens to destroy the Israelites when the twelve scouts whom Moses had sent to survey the Promised Land come back and report that it is unlikely that the Israelites will be able to conquer the land. The people panic and threaten to revolt. God becomes enraged at their lack of faith and tells Moses He will destroy them. Moses, however, talks God out of this rash decision. What puzzled and perplexed Schaalman was that God listened to and responded to Moses's argument. Such was the relationship of our ancestors, he suggested, but since then, God has not spoken to the Jewish people.

At the end of his speech, Schaalman referred to the work of the renowned post-World War II German poet, Paul Celan. Schaalman had been profoundly moved by the "enormous power of his words," "the boldness of his imagery, [and] his effort to push the German language to its extreme to express the depths of his despair." One of his poems, "Todesfuge, the Death Fugue," had made a lasting impression on him, especially the line, "Schwarze Milch, wir drinken sie am Morgen, wir drinken sie am Mittag" (Black milk we drink it in the morning, we drink it at noon). Although the poem had overwhelmed him in the past, now he understood it differently: "The words take us to the limits of language, to the very frontier of insanity." When the language ultimately failed him, Celan made up his own words that no one else can understand, perhaps not even himself. Unable to speak any longer, at the age of forty-nine, he drowned himself in the Seine.

"The paradox of his being," Schaalman continued, "finished him off." Then without a pause, Schaalman concluded his talk:

> And so, this is my God, a God whose name I can spell: ה - י - ו - ה [Yod He Wav He] but never pronounce. The God who for two thousand years has been unnamable, unpronounceable, nameless, the un-speakable God. This is my God, here in my very high age as always beckoning but never attained; here in nearing my end my God, mysterious, infinitely fascinating, but never owned perhaps, just perhaps, the God of some of my students; hopefully, the God of my children, and of theirs, of theirs, of theirs. ...

In his best sermonic style, his final words faded out to convey that he could not say anymore.

When he finished speaking, NAORRR's president, Rabbi Hillel Cohn (2011), was so moved that all he could say as he approached the lectern was, "Wow!" The rest of the audience was speechless. Very likely, they were not used to hearing such a confession from a colleague they had admired for at least the last half century. Several of his colleagues asked for a copy of his presentation. Of course, he had none, but promised to send one once he had written it out.[435]

Schaalman's decision to juxtapose his sense of Celan's pain and despair with his own struggle to know an elusive God represents an insight into the depths of his soul that Schaalman had never shared publically. What he may have meant by these words is difficult to determine. His own daughter confided, "I don't understand it," and neither did he. "The reason," he explains, "is that at bottom, the answers I am seeking come to me only as paradoxes. The mind reels at the impossibility of understanding unequivocally the truths they embody." Instead of enlightening him, they remain puzzles. What makes the speech so difficult to understand is that it is couched in metaphors, analogies, and Midrashic stories that bristle with a kind of energy that is unique to Schaalman's speaking and writing.

Schaalman's mind continued to churn in the months following this speech. He was dissatisfied with his inability to speak about God other than to refer to Him as a "Mystery," his attempt since his earliest days as a rabbi to explain God to himself and the various audiences for his sermons, lectures, and writings. He realized that the word "Mystery" was a stopgap measure, an admission of defeat, rather than an illumination. His way past this limitation was his insight that the God he had been seeking could only be understood in terms of paradox. He told his Torah Study students,

> This discovery opened up new pathways to inquiry and experience. It's a way to talk about God that I had not had before. It increases my ability to live with contradiction and is a more effective way to say what I mean by mystery. I would be far less complete had these ideas not come to me. If I were to identify any one thing, this is what keeps me alive. The expectation of what else there is is what keeps me going.

By placing paradox at the center of his universe, Schaalman finds that he can speak only in analogy, simile, and metaphor. In a recent interview, he pointed to a decade-old sickly-looking plant on the windowsill of his living room and said, "I find it incredible that this form of life that has defied the odds. It had been in the same dirt for years and, despite its weakened condition, is still producing flowers." His explanation: "God exists in the flower." He came to this conclusion after reading an article written by Elisa Margolis, an evolutionary biologist, in which she claimed that all being exists in a symbiotic relationship and that bacteria are the glue that holds them together. Their DNA is the building blocks of all other life and dependent on it. For Schaalman, this discovery reminded him of Buber's "indwelling of the Divine" in all things: "If the Burning Bush can contain God's presence, so can the plant on my window sill. It represents the mystery of being. … It is a symbol of perseverance."

The perpetually changing world of nature and God's indwelling in it leads him back to paradox. The paradox is that in a world that constantly changes, nothing is knowable absolutely. Such a state of existence defies our ability to speak about it, defies language. Yet, "paradox" is, nevertheless, part of language and refers to the mental faculty that can simultaneously entertain the existence of two opposite and contrary ideas. This faculty allows Schaalman to get close to the reality he is seeking but cannot ever know or define. It is the reality of his life that has puzzled and amazed him.[436]

Schaalman continues to be hypercritical of the Torah, a book he loves and profoundly respects. In his Torah Study two weeks before Yom Kippur 2012, he lashed out at the *parashah* of the week, Deuteronomy 28–29. In his final hours on earth, Moses attempts to steer the Israelites away from a direction he is all too certain they will follow. He inveighs against them for the sins they have yet to commit and presents them with a list of curses that they will suffer if they do not obey God's commandments. The list is comprehensive, covering a wide range of human life, from the fertility of the land to the sacredness of the marriage bed. Schaalman calls this list "a judgment" on the Jewish people: "I don't think we are nearly as bad as any of these fifty-six verses of denunciation, these curses that are aimed at us. This is a horrendous indictment of the Jewish people, and I think it's totally unjust, even from Moses' point of view. Much more so from God's point of view."

Schaalman speaks in harsh terms about what he considers "the total lack of capacity of Torah to find language that has resonance to any kind of God that is capable of functioning in my life. I don't want to be this kind of Jew, I don't want to be this kind of a worshipper. This is repugnant for me. In fact, it rejects me." Schaalman understands that this language comes from the earliest stages of the Jewish people who are "trying to understand themselves and trying to deal with whatever God was to them." Yet, his response is fierce:

> To this day, nobody knows what God is. Nobody. And there is no language, any kind of language that has anything to say about God that is defensible or supportable. No one can say they know what God is. If God is describable in human language, He is not God. This is to me an indication of the extreme inability of humans to say anything about God that is ultimately valid.

As he has said many times, this is human language and a projection of our own fears and desires: "We are projecting them into the infinite as though that is the way we have any idea of what God might be."

> This is to me an example of the inadequacy of human language to deal with a problem that they can sense is a problem but ultimately can't deal with. This is primitive in the worst way. This is the earliest striving of the human mind, the human soul, to deal with something we are only beginning to understand now. It is beyond us.

One of his fundamental quarrels with the text is its basis in contractual language: "If you do this you get your reward. If you don't, this is the punishment. This is so primitive a notion of relating to the deity." Ultimately, he is led to question the very nature of Rosh Hashanah and Yom Kippur. At his advanced age, these High Holy Days, "speak for and out of an understanding of the human condition that I really think is so ancient, so dead that it is astounding that we are all doing what we are doing on a regular basis." Schaalman finds this language and this view of the relationship of God to His humans so alien that he finds himself compelled to question its relevance to himself:

> And this really gets me: how do I preserve a feeling for this book, which to me is profound. How can I think of this book as sacred and this language as sacred when it begins to be so totally out of relationship to where I am sitting today, ninety-six years old, sitting in a world that is exploding around me? How in the world? This is my whole problem when I read these passages and when I try to be a Jew today.

And at this point, we must leave him, still struggling to understand who he is in the vastness of the universe, his relationship to the Judaism that he has inherited, and to the God who continues to elude him.

Chapter 10

Teaching Torah

"The more I read Torah, the less certain I am of what the words mean."

Herman E. Schaalman, 2011

"Why has it taken you all these years to develop these new insights into the texts?"

Torah Study student, 2011

"This class pushes me to see nuances that I hadn't seen before, and the Shoah forces me to reevaluate the traditional understanding of Torah. I would be far less complete had these ideas not come to me. If I were to identify any one thing, this is what keeps me alive. The expectation of what else there is what keeps me going."

Herman E. Schaalman, 2011

Torah Study

In 1976, the CCAR issued a statement called the *Centenary Perspective* that affirmed, among other positions, the autonomy of individual belief for Reform Jews. Although the document was careful to substantiate the right of Reform Jews to make individual choices for belief, among the six "unities" binding Reform Jews to their religion is, first and foremost, a belief in God: "We ground our lives, personally and communally, on God's reality." Number 3 of the unities, the only one stated as a *requirement*, a religious obligation, is that the study of Torah is "a religious imperative ... whose practice is our chief means to holiness."

These two foundations for Reform Jewish had long been the basis for Schaalman's rabbinic practice and belief. From his earliest days as a young rabbi in Cedar Rapids, he was committed to a belief in the existence of God and the need to study Torah. Soon after he arrived in Chicago in 1949 to take on the job of Midwest Regional Director of UAHC, he agreed to teach a Torah class in the evenings. Although he lacked a pulpit, a small group of people who had heard him speak at one of his many visits to area synagogues asked him to teach them. In 1956, when he became Emanuel Congregation's rabbi, that group continued to study with him by joining the sessions he offered to its congregants. Two of the original couples, Elliot Blumberg and Robert Cooper and their wives, stayed with the group for decades.

For Schaalman, teaching Torah is a vital part of his role as a rabbi. From the beginning of his rabbinate at Emanuel, Schaalman conducted weekly Torah Study. After he retired in 1986, he negotiated the right to continue these sessions, even when the senior rabbi conducted his own. In 2004, when Rabbi Michael Zedek became Emanuel's new rabbi, he began his own sessions, giving Emanuel the luxury of offering its congregants a choice of two Saturday morning classes in the study of Torah.

Schaalman introduced Saturday morning Torah Study at Emanuel (rather than meeting in the evenings) sometime in the 1960s when students from his Confirmation class wanted to continue their studies. He recalls, "Five or six members of my Confirmation class asked me if they could continue studying with me. I told them to find a few others, and they did. They decided the classes should be Saturday morning sessions and the rest is history." Marc Fenton, one of the students in that class and its chief organizer, even now, considers Schaalman one of the finest teachers he has ever known.[437]

As a way of showing his gratitude, a few years ago, Fenton and his wife Gail established a foundation at the University of Chicago to subsidize study in Jerusalem for students and their faculty. When the Dean suggested that they give it a name, they had no trouble naming it. They named it "The Herman E. Schaalman and Lotte Schaalman Civilization Program in Jerusalem." Fenton's decision was an enduring tribute to the love and respect Schaalman has inspired from one of his first Torah Study students.

Schaalman's method of teaching Torah is unique. He deviates from the Reform method of covering in three years pieces of the weekly portion of the Torah. Instead, he offers a more intense seven-year cycle of study. Each chapter of the Torah is subdivided into seven parts called in Hebrew, *parashah*. The seven-year cycle begins with the first *parashah* of Genesis and proceeds throughout the year with a study of the first *parashah* of each of the chapters of each book of the Torah. The second year the process is repeated, only this time with the second *parashah* of each chapter of each book. Thus, in the seven-year cycle, in succeeding years, he teaches each of the *parashah* in order of their occurrence until he has covered the entire Five Books of Moses. He has been teaching this way since his earliest years as a rabbi and, as of July 2012, he is nearing completion of his eleventh cycle.[438]

The number of students who attend the hour-and-a-half sessions varies, usually around ten. Until his stroke in the summer of 2011, Schaalman had always been very particular about starting sessions at precisely 9:30 and concluding at 11:00 a.m. It was part of his German, or as he prefers to call it, his "Yekke" upbringing.[439] Since his stroke, he has adopted a more casual style and no longer watches the clock for the start or finish of a session.

The sessions begin with Schaalman's announcement of the *parashah* to be studied, its page numbers, and the numbers of its verses in the Kaplan translation. Schaalman has no expectation that his students will have read the section before they arrive and gives them plenty of time to read it before he begins with a brief introduction. Because he is committed to the idea that learning is dialogic and that authentic relationship requires and thrives on interaction, his students know they can interrupt him at any time.

Anyone who has had the pleasure of sitting in one of his classes can attest to the spirit of community and shared learning he generates. He believes that his most important role is to affirm his students:

> The learning environment must promote such a sense of complete security that, no matter how far off the subject, or uninformed the question or comment, the student will always feel affirmed. In my German school experience, I was never asked my opinion, never allowed to ask a question. My response to this

denial of the value of the individual's participation in the learning process is to assure that my students always feel empowered and secure in my classes.

Occasionally, he gets through his introduction without interruption, but, more often, someone raises a hand and Schaalman interrupts his monologue to allow the student to speak. Other times, he asks right off whether anyone has a question or comment about the reading. The response may be directly to what he has said or it may be the prelude to a tangent that often becomes a prolonged digression. Usually Schaalman allows these digressions to go wherever his students want to go, even when they take up most of the session.

One of Schaalman's most important intellectual premises is the notion that everything he thinks is open to review and challenge, especially in his interaction with his students who stimulate him to discover new ideas or insights. Not infrequently, he admits that he is baffled by particular Torah portions and is always pleased when his students open up possibilities of meaning he had not considered. It is not unusual to hear him confess, "I would like to make these texts part of my life, but the older I get, the greater the difficulty I have accepting them as my own." That statement usually is an opening for students to jump in to dissect the text. Before such sessions are over, typically Schaalman's students have led him to a new insight into possible meanings for the passage. In recognition of the eye-opening discussion that he had not expected, Schaalman will comment, "I need all of you to open up the texts for me that otherwise I might not have paid any attention to. Teaching for me is education, my education. In Latin "education" means "being drawn out and the Torah Study has been drawing me out for years." The sessions help keep him intellectually alive: "What I experience in this group allows me to think of ideas I never knew I had. As I listen to you and as I think with you, you have led me into what I certainly didn't expect to talk about today, which is why I come to Torah Study." It is not unusual for his sermons and presentations to reflect the insights that came out of these sessions.

Perhaps the greatest testament to Schaalman as a teacher is the fact that a few of his students have been attending his sessions for nearly forty years. Schaalman is more than their teacher; he is a good friend and an important part of their families. Rabbi Ann Folb (2007) writes, "[the group] has its own subculture, which includes the fact that some of the members have their favored seats, which others do not sit in" (p. 60). Frank Metzger is one of them, having sat in the same chair for the last twenty years. It is not clear who among them has the longest record of attendance, but the five candidates are Mel Abrams, Frank Metzger, Barbara Steinberg, Neil Rest, and Charlotte Hart. Each of their stories is unique and provides insight into Schaalman's effect on his students.

One of the "old-timers" with the longest ongoing history with Schaalman, Mel Abrams (2007), traces his history with Schaalman to his teenage years about the time that Schaalman came to Emanuel.[440] According to Mel, Schaalman has been not only his rabbi and teacher but also his guide and comforter in difficult times. He credits Schaalman for being one of the major shaping influences in his life and thinking. Another of Schaalman's longtime students, Neil Rest, has been studying with Schaalman off and on since 1961 when he was a student in Schaalman's Confirmation class. For the last decade, he rarely misses a session of Torah Study. He is one of the most knowledgeable members of the class, bringing with him a huge reservoir of eclectic facts and information.

Frank Metzger has been Schaalman's student for more than forty years and holds the record for consistency of attendance and total number of sessions attended. With his sharp critical mind and a huge reservoir of facts and information, Frank is the only student capable of taking on Schaalman over derivations or meanings of biblical Hebrew. If he disagrees with anything Schaalman says, he responds in no uncertain terms, "No, that can't be. It isn't true." Sometimes Schaalman backs down, other times it's Frank. It is clear they have a mutually reinforcing intellectual relationship. Hardly a week goes by when Metzger (2006) does not present Schaalman with a book or article that he has saved for him. Occasionally, Schaalman will refer to some insight or information he learned from Metzger. In some small way, they are both student and teacher to each other.

Another of the faithful is artist Charlotte (a. k. a. Charli) Hart (2006), who has been Schaalman's student since 1981. Early on, when the classes began to have a profound intellectual and creative hold on her, she began creating visual art inspired by Schaalman's class and has produced more than 300 highly regarded drawings of Torah portions.

Schaalman's impact does not end there. Charlotte writes poetry based on biblical and rabbinic texts. She notes, "I marvel at my good fortune to have found such a generous, scholarly rabbi and friend. His quest for holiness radiates outward to his students and to many of the people with whom he comes in contact."

Another of Schaalman's long-term devoted students doesn't even live in Chicago yet stays in close touch with the Torah Study. Bernard Rozran (Rozran, B., personal communication, April 15, 2011) is so committed to Schaalman that he calls him from Switzerland nearly every week to discuss the previous week's Torah portion. He says, "I celebrate Shabbat by reading the weekly Torah portion, studying the appropriate Torah commentaries Schaalman has published in the *Sentinel* [a Chicago area Jewish community publication], and listening to the recording of Torah Studies that I receive by email. Through these means, I remain connected with both my rabbi and the Torah study group." Over the last twenty-plus years, Schaalman has been his inspiration with so many new insights and thought-provoking guidance that he says, "I am proud to be counted as one of the many devoted students of Rabbi Schaalman. His evident love of Torah is contagious."

Not all the students are Jewish. Two members of the Torah Study are Catholics, John Delaney and Robert Edwards. They come out of their deep love and respect for Schaalman and because he offers them a profound insight into the Old Testament that they cannot get elsewhere. He also provides them an insight into the relationship of biblical Judaism to early Christianity, as well as to the relationship of contemporary Judaism and Christianity.

John Delaney (2011), a former Jesuit seminary student, joined the Torah Study group after his Jewish wife, Sue, recommended that he might learn more about Judaism by attending her rabbi's Torah Study.[441] "It is the highlight of my week," he says. In the ten years that he has been attending the class, he has come to see Schaalman as not only his teacher, but as his friend. One of the indications of this friendship is that when John goes up to Schaalman at the end of the sessions and thanks him for his insights, Schaalman says to him, "'John, it's so important that you are here. I look forward to your questions. It's just so wonderful having you here.' Being one of Schaalman's students is not like the normal academic relationship in which you thank the professor for the class. It's a warm relationship, and it's obvious that he looks forward to seeing me as much as I look forward to seeing him."

The other Catholic in the class is Robert Edwards, by trade an architectural drafter, whose life was transformed when he went to work for the Jewish architect, Richard Meier, in designing the Church of the Year 2000.[442] "The experience," he says, "transformed my life" (Edwards, R., personal communication, April 13, 2011). Edwards attends class regularly and enjoys the camaraderie with the other students. He thinks of his rabbi as a "master-Architect, a major figure in contemporary American Jewish life, and an essential friend of all Christians and, I dare say, to me." Master-Architect is the highest compliment Edwards can give. "A master-Architect," he explains, "is the drafter, who, once freed, becomes a fully awakened architect, the master-builder of the edifice of the mind and a reshaper of the structure of one's being."[443]

Perhaps the most revealing and comprehensive statement of what happens in Schaalman's Torah Study comes from another of the Schaalman faithful, retired Humanities professor and attorney, Edward Mogul (Mogul, E., personal communication, July 25, 2012). Through his broad reading and study at the University of Chicago, he brings to the sessions unique insights and a wide range of knowledge in theology, philosophy, and ancient civilizations of the near east. About the sessions, he says:

> Every Saturday morning in Rabbi Schaalman's study, thanks to our beloved Rabbi, the Torah text for the week radiates meaning and yields fresh insights. Every session in that special place and time leaves me feeling that another profundity has been uncovered. I like to think that in our sessions we are participating in an eternal and majestic schlep. We're schlepping with our ancestors an ark. We're not sure what's inside the ark (some people doubt that there is anything inside). If there is anything that is special here, it is uniting with people more than two millennia ago who also treasured these texts. We, like the ancient Hebrews, still sense the magic of these words. (July 25, 2012)

Interpreting Torah

The study of the Torah is part of Schaalman's ongoing journey of discovery, and, at the age of ninety-six, he is still making new ones: "These texts," he told his Torah Study, "almost demand that we read them over and over. Each time we read them, they disclose something new. I know that is true for me. On the other hand, had I remained in the Berlin rabbinical school, I doubt that I would have questioned the Torah and subjected it to such critical scrutiny."

Schaalman views the Torah as a series of stories that constitute the "original" Jewish theology. Like all stories, they embody truths that will be understood differently in different times and places: "Every age," he says, "creates a new consciousness, which determines how these stories will be interpreted." The history of Jewish understanding of these stories is the unfolding of the Midrashic tradition. He feels perfectly at home in this tradition, and, like his rabbinic predecessors, feels at liberty to interpret the Torah according to his own experience and insight.[444]

"As a young rabbi," Schaalman says, "I was much more traditional in my approach to the Torah, which I understood as the record of the words God spoke to Moses on Mt. Sinai."[445] Now, he makes no bones about saying that the Torah was written by humans, derived from an oral tradition and transmitted in different written versions with generations of various scribal errors before the Masorites settled on the final text.

Another issue that crops up frequently in Schaalman's class is his preoccupation that some words, phrases, and sentences in the Torah are untranslatable and, therefore, unknowable. As he has said many times, "No one knows what these words mean, nor what they meant to our ancestors. The words might be idiomatic and meaningful only to them." The frequency of these remarks to his students makes Schaalman the ultimate Torah deconstructionist. Pushed to their logical conclusion, the question becomes: how can we be sure we understand any of the Torah *as our ancestors understood it or meant it to be understood*? Our best approach, according to Schaalman, is to understand it in our own terms, and, at the same time, acknowledge that there are portions we will never understand. As an example, he cites the fifth verse in the *parashah HaAzinu*, a verse, he argues, that is "untranslatable." These lines have more "gloss," he argues, than any other passage in Torah.[446] Citing another example of the difficulties posed by the text, Schaalman has observed that in this *parashah* the Hebrew word for "rock" occurs seven times: "What exactly did the word mean to our ancestors? I must tell you I'm baffled."[447]

Directly related to this problem of the "correct" understanding of the words of Torah is the problem of transmission of a message between God and humans. That transmission was interactive, a dialogic event, never an infallible transmission between humans and their God. Once an "other" is introduced into a communication, the hearing or witnessing is always contaminated, understood only through the filter of the mind and hearing of the "other," in this case through the experience and understanding of our ancestors. Schaalman concludes, therefore, that there is no direct message from God to humans.[448] God chooses whom he considers the best human instruments to convey his message, as Schaalman explains: "God is something like a radio station, always broadcasting, 'Who will go for me?'" Until Abraham came along, no one had answered that call. God had failed to find a suitable partner. For Schaalman, that failure is embedded in the Torah and clear from the beginning: "The story of Adam and Eve is the story of the failure of humans and God to understand each other and to reconcile with each other. It is a conflict that remains unresolved."

A larger issue is the validity of the claim that Moses received *the* Torah on Mt. Sinai. Schaalman thinks that this conclusion is based on an incorrect translation of the Hebrew text. A better translation is that "Moses *received* Torah on Mt. Sinai." The Hebrew lacks the definite article signifying "the." "Receiving Torah" means oral transmission, which he argues, means interpretation, and interpretation depends on the individual and the culture in which one lives. A contemporary interpretation of Torah is likely to be different from one produced in Spain 500 years ago, or anywhere else for that matter. Moreover, the interpretation of one contemporary is likely to differ from that of another. "The result," according to Schaalman, "is that there is no one authoritative Torah that God gave to Moses.

Yet, another related issue for comprehension of the Torah Schaalman returns to again and again is that it is based on more than one textual source. He points out that the Masorites, who codified the text as we know it, had to decide the "right" text to include in their edition. Faced with various texts, they decided which was the most authentic and then proceeded to use it as the base for their text. "A reasonable conclusion, then," Schaalman has told his students, "is that all Torah texts are the result of the editors' best efforts to establish an authoritative text and translators' best efforts to translate them as faithfully as their knowledge of the language permitted." In the early months of 2012, he made this remarkable statement about his study of Torah:

> Over the last year, my entire outlook on reading Torah has changed: When I read these texts, I read them so differently than I did when I was ninety-five. I'm now going to be ninety-six next month. ... Increasingly, there seems to be a discontinuity in the major assumptions underlying these texts as I confront them, almost on a daily basis. I confront them as I want to be confronted with new questions that are emerging from the human mind that are now expanded to global proportions that simulate me and point me in new directions.

He explained that he had just finished reading an article in *Discover* magazine, "Faster than the Speed of Light" (January–February 2012), which raised new epistemological questions that challenged his sense of the value of the past. British scientists had recently discovered the existence of new particles of matter, "neutrinos," that move faster than the speed of light. The discovery casts doubt on the validity of Einstein's theory of relativity, for the last 100 years the basis of modern physics. According to the author of the article, "Time could flow in reverse. Neutrino-based messages could reach recipients before they were sent. An effect could precede its cause, which would explode our entire way of thinking about the universe" (Mone, G., 2012). For Schaalman, this new discovery requires that he rethink his basic understanding of Torah as well as his sense of who he is.

By June 2012, Schaalman (June 30, 2012) pushed his deconstruction of the language of the Torah a notch higher. Having reiterated his critique of our ability to know what the words mean, he turned his attention to the text itself:

There were no practices or rules of reproducing faithfully a given text without any changes since then. We know quite the contrary: we know, for instance, that copyists who worked with pen and ink have made vast changes in the material they copied and, I don't have to tell you, that until the invention of movable type in the middle of the fifteenth century that was the only way to transmit a text from one place, one time to another. And therefore the possibility, the certainty, that mistakes and changes were made is a given. To rely on any of these texts as unchangeably proven is simply ignorance. And that, of course, gets us into a discussion that I don't particularly want to get into: What *can* you rely on with this particular sort of text? How much of your own life, your own belief system, your own commitments can you put on a text that is basically subject to so many questions? It's a strange thing, and yet, I remind all of us, we live by this text. It is the single and most frequently used basis of human development, at least in the Western world.

Over and over we have to realize that there are many different interpretations not just possible, but necessary, inevitable. All of which makes this text in one way problematic and, most stimulating, precious in another. If we accept this as the basis of our own identity, we have something with which to deal, something with which to refer, something from which to start. But I would certainly warn myself and you too, if you want, against accepting it as the ultimate truth, not in its totality.

Lehrhaus

Schaalman's Torah Study is not the only means for providing adults with the opportunity to study Torah. In 2001, he piloted a new program at OSRUI called "Lehrhaus" (German for "school"). The idea for the Lehrhaus had been developed in Germany by Franz Rosenzweig.[449] Part of his innovation was to turn the strict formal German education on its head by making dialogue rather than lecture the means for learning. Schaalman not only borrowed the name "Lehrhaus" from Rosenzweig, but his teaching methods as well. During the eight years he conducted

Lehrhaus sessions, he encouraged students to interact with him by asking questions or offering comments at any point in the lecture. As a result, the typical session became a give and take with students on the subject of the talk, which included study of the Torah, Jewish philosophy, and history.

The sessions consisted of three- or four-day summer retreats at OSRUI to give adults an opportunity to develop their Jewish learning. The program was so successful that OSRUI adopted and expanded it to a full summer of sessions with other rabbis on a wide variety of Jewish subjects. Schaalman's sessions continued until 2009 when he and Lotte no longer had the stamina to continue them and after attendance by his "regulars" had dropped off.[450]

The sessions were held in a two-story building that was once the home of the founders of the Carnation milk company. The Bayit, as it was named by the camp, had been renovated to serve as a "conference center" capable of sleeping thirty guests. A short walk from the building is the more recently built Herman and Lotte Schaalman Lodge, which houses visiting rabbis and their families who hold Lehrhaus sessions and/or teach in the camp.

Schaalman's study sessions were intense; three-and a half-hour sessions during the day and another at night. Time-outs were scheduled for meals, an afternoon nap, or for recreational activities. For Schaalman, there was only one recreational activity: tennis. During the 2007 Lehrhaus session, at the age of ninety-one, he played tennis in ninety-degree heat with a twenty-one year-old Israeli tennis pro. He plays only with professionals because he cannot run all over the court as he once did and needs to have the ball hit near him so that he can return it with relative ease: "The professional," he comments, "is capable of controlling the direction of a returned ball and engages in a sustained volley."

The topics Schaalman selected were ones that interested him and that he thought would interest his participants. In June 2006, he and his close friend, Fr. John Pawlikowski, whom he had invited to co-lead sessions, discussed the state of Catholic/Jewish relations. Other years his topics included "My Favorite Torah Passages," "The Bible vs. Darwin: What Role Does Judaism Play in This Controversy?," "What is the Relevance of Judaism to the Modern World?," and "Two Twentieth-Century Jewish Poets: Paul Chelan & Yehuda Amichai."

Monday Night Public Affairs

Another of Schaalman's teaching formats is his Monday night Public Affairs discussion sessions. On the third Monday of every month, a small, but faithful group of *very* senior people, who have been Schaalman's fans for decades, fill the small space of Emanuel's library or, more recently, his office. This group is a holdover from a Sunday night Public Affairs group, which lasted more than thirty years and was held in the homes of its members.

Schaalman selects ten or twelve news events of the previous month that focus mainly on Israel and national and international events affecting Jews.[451] The students listen attentively but feel free to interrupt him at any time with their questions, to add their own commentary or to disagree. Schaalman welcomes these interruptions because he wants the sessions to be a give-and-take, the kind of dialogic teaching he encourages in all of his teaching settings. At the age of ninety-six, he continues to hold these monthly sessions.

We might conclude this chapter by noting that teaching is his substitute for writing. Through oral discourse, Schaalman achieves the interchange that constitutes his originality as a thinker and as a theologian. It is the vehicle through which he has influenced, educated, and inspired generations of his congregants, students, and colleagues. It is the essential Herman Schaalman.

Chapter 11

Schaalman on Modern Israel

"I think there is an ultimate feeling among leaders of the traditionalist camp that they know what God wants, that they're prepared to risk everything including their life for their stand."

Herman E. Schaalman, 1988

"We find ourselves confronted with the same dilemma that power has presented to anybody who enjoyed it. ... How we apply the needs of power politics and the employment of power to safeguard our own integrity and survival really is something to which I think we have not yet found an answer."

Herman E. Schaalman, 1988

"Do we need the land to be Jews? I'm asking myself questions for which I have no answer. For 2,000 years we carried our Torah throughout the world. It is our 'homeland.'"

Herman E. Schaalman, 2008

In 1986, soon after he retired, Schaalman made another trip to Israel only to discover that the country he thought he knew had been transformed. The same youthful enthusiasm and optimism that he had seen on his first trip in 1953 was gone, replaced by a sense of a problematic present and a dire concern for the future. Always on the verge of war after achieving independence in 1948, Israel had been victorious in the three wars it had fought since. The most dramatic was the Six-Day War in 1967, when Israel took control of Jerusalem and the West Bank. Although that war ended in a decisive victory, it was not without great cost, including the occupation of Arab lands and the displacement of tens of thousands of Palestinian civilians. Again in 1973, Israel went to war with its Arab neighbors, a war which shattered Israel's sense of its invulnerability and brought into question its ultimate survival. These developments were troubling to Schaalman. He questioned whether, through these wars, Israel had sacrificed its original moral high ground. In 1988, he told Esta Star: "For the first time in 2,000 years, Jews had acquired political power through the state of Israel, a condition which threatened the soul of the Jewish people" (July 25, 1988, p. 6).

The basis of Schaalman's concern is that the history of Jewish statehood as reflected in the Bible is a history of disasters. Not only did they have to take the land by force, but once they settled in the Promised Land, they discovered that they needed a form of government suitable for "landedness," a term Schaalman coined as shorthand for a people's ownership of land. Landedness came with a new set of priorities and needs that did not exist for a desert people. They demanded a king and got one, and their lives were never the same again; they became subjects owing obedience to the kingly power.

Not long after, the unity of the Israel broke down, and two kingdoms, Israel and Judah, were established. Eventually, some thirty-eight kings, nineteen in each kingdom, ruled the Israelites. The outcome of this royal musical chairs was political instability and the consequent weakness of both kingdoms. Schaalman is particularly critical of the establishment of the priesthood, through which each Israelite lost his/her direct connection to God. He argues that the establishment of the kingdoms and the priesthood resulted in a profound transformation in the lives of a people that led ultimately to their defeat. Israel was destroyed by the Assyrians in 722 BCE and Judah, first by the Babylonians in 578 BCE and then by the Romans in 70 CE. For the next 2,000 years, Jews survived as a remnant living as "Diaspora" Jews.

Schaalman is fearful that that the modern State of Israel is headed down the same path. "For 2,000 years," he offers, "Jews carried their Torah throughout the world and survived. [We] developed a fairly substantial disdain for power, because we never had it, and we always were able to point to others who exercised it as being subject to moral compromise" (p. 7). Now that Jews have power, he says, "we find ourselves confronted with the same dilemma that power has presented to anybody who enjoyed it" (p. 7):

> The situation for Israel is how to exercise it without abusing the rights of others and in accord with the values taught by our rabbis. Becoming a "landed people," imposes responsibilities and behaviors on Jews that they did not have as Diaspora Jews. To survive as a national state has meant that for the first time in 2,000 years Jews have inflicted pain and suffering on other people, specifically, Palestinians. In the name of survival, Israelis have destroyed their homes, killed their children, and tortured innocent civilians as well as combatants. They have occupied land that does not belong to them and are pursuing policies that tread on the national aspirations of the Palestinians.

Remarks like these lead one of the world's most influential Zionists and Schaalman's long-time friend and colleague, Rabbi Richard G. Hirsch (2010), to comment, "Herman is no Zionist. I find that remarkable for a refugee from Nazi Germany."[452] Hirsch admits, however, that Schaalman's view is more characteristic among Reform rabbis than his own, which is that Israel is "the means to keep Judaism alive."

The moral dilemma for Israel, Schaalman identifies, includes the use of power to survive and, at the same time, to protect the rights of others, in this case, the Palestinians. In 1987 and again in 2000, resentment towards Israeli occupation and frustration over their failure to achieve statehood, led Palestinians to revolt (the Intifada) in the Gaza Strip and the West Bank. These revolts created a tension between Israel's need to survive and Judaism's inherited values of justice and respect for the rights of others. Schaalman argues that Israel's actions to insure its survival has meant that Israel has acted in ways that are "painfully unacceptable, maybe objectionable," not only to many Israelis, but to Jews in America, and, as well, to public opinion around the world (Star, E., July 25, 1988, p. 8).

Nevertheless, as early as 1988, Schaalman was skeptical that compromise with the Palestinians was possible, nor was peace likely in the short-term: Perhaps in another fifteen years, assuming that there were no flare-ups in violence, peace would be possible. Nor did he think that ceding territory would achieve a guaranteed peace. Such an act might provide a breathing spell that might last as long as fifty years, but was not likely to produce an enduring peace.

On the other hand, given the political climate in Israel, Schaalman was pessimistic that concessions would be made to the Palestinians: "I think there is really something in the Jewish character, something in the Jewish soul, that is not capable of that kind of forgiveness, the kind of yielding, the kind of accepting a compromise, an absolutely unbending and passionate intransigence on the part of the traditionalists that might make peace based on compromise impossible" (p. 11–12). The traditionalists, he argues, are convinced that they know what God wants and are willing to risk everything, including their lives, to hold on to every inch of the biblically promised land. This position creates a serious divide between Diaspora Jewry and segments of the Israeli political and religious establishment. Despite the risks, however, Schaalman was convinced that negotiations with the Palestinians were a necessary condition to make progress toward some ultimate resolution of the conflict.

In 1993, the government of Israel and the Palestine Liberation Organization (PLO) signed the Oslo Accords, which provided a framework for the resolution of the ongoing Palestinian-Israeli conflict. It was the first direct, face-to-face agreement between the two sides. Despite his earlier pessimism, Schaalman, along with many American and Israeli Jews, was optimistic that an accommodation could be made with the Palestinians that would allow them a separate Palestinian state and create peace between the two peoples.

By the year 2000, together with 300 other liberal rabbis, Schaalman was ready to take the controversial step of signing a petition drafted by the Jewish Peace Lobby calling on Israel to share Jerusalem in a peace settlement. Eric J. Greenberg (2000) reported that this group represented a minority of the 1,100 rabbis who might have signed it. America's leading Orthodox and Conservative rabbinical associations, the Rabbinical Council of America and the Rabbinical Assembly blasted the document, arguing that the decision to present such a position undermined the Israeli effort to negotiate. That same year, the Palestinians again revolted in what became a bloody five-year uprising that resulted in thousands of casualties on both sides, the majority of them Palestinians.

Israelis understood the uprising as an effort to destroy Israel and its Jewish inhabitants. Less than a year later, on June 25, 2006, Palestinian Hamas militants tunneled into Israel, killed two soldiers and kidnapped another. Israel's first response was to demand the return of the kidnapped soldier. Hamas, in return, demanded the release of 1,000 Palestinian prisoners held in Israeli jails. As the situation spun out of control, Israeli armed forces crossed into Gaza to attempt to rescue the kidnapped soldier. For about a month, Israel fought with Palestinian militants in an effort to diminish their capability to inflict further harm on Israel and to free its captured soldier.[453]

Three weeks later, Hezbollah, the Islamic militant group in southern Lebanon, pulled off a similar abduction of two Israeli soldiers and killed five others. In return for the captured Israeli soldiers, Hezbollah demanded the release its fighters held in Israeli jails. Israel responded by demanding the return of its soldiers and, when Hezbollah declined, Israel unleashed massive retaliation against Hezbollah and Lebanon. The war went on for three months before both sides agreed to a ceasefire, but not before they had inflicted huge damage on each other.

Despite these major setbacks in the effort to achieve peace, left-leaning Israelis and progressive American Jews held onto the hope that peace was, and is, still possible. Schaalman, on the other hand, disillusioned by the failure of the Oslo Accords and the ongoing strife between the two peoples, had become even more pessimistic. On July 21, 2006, while Israel was at war with Hezbollah and Hamas, he told an audience at Emanuel that he was more doubtful than ever that a peaceful solution was possible: "It is only a dream, still unrealized and perhaps unrealizable." His emphasis, however, was not on the refusal of the Palestinians to give up their national aspirations, but on the huge loss of life in these wars, both Jewish and non-Jewish. He questioned "the value and the efficacy of these Israeli responses to the terrorist actions."

The next day, he told his Torah Study students that he thought the Israeli responses were excessive:

> The Torah calls for equal justice. An eye for an eye requires equal punishment, not one eye for two or one eye for the death of the offender. On that basis, the killing of hundreds of civilians, including women and children and the displacement of hundreds

of thousands is disproportionate to the provocation. Such actions produce long-term hatreds, first because of the deaths of hundreds of Lebanese and Palestinians and second because of the massive physical destruction in Gaza and Lebanon.

"This hatred," he told his students, "is likely to last for generations, as it is passed from father to son."[454]

Schaalman's disillusionment with Israel led him to join J Street, the progressive pro-Israel/pro-peace American-Jewish lobbying group.[455] He is part of its "Rabbinic Cabinet," a group of more than 600 rabbis representing the spectrum of Jewish denominations and leadership. On September 1, 2010, together with nine former CCAR presidents and nearly 600 other rabbis and Jewish leaders, he signed a J Street letter in support of a two-state solution to the Israeli-Palestinian conflict.[456]

Another of Schaalman's recent concerns about Israel is its secularization. In 1986, he had observed that Israeli society had opted for a life that was "totally comfortable," a way of life that ignored the entire history of the Jews. Throughout that history, Jews have had to struggle to survive. The idea that somehow the modern State of Israel meant that the struggle was over was a serious mistake. This struggle has serious moral and social justice implications. He anguishes over the fact that many, if not the majority, of the Israeli Jewish population has little, if any, identification with Judaism as a religion. "Typically," he contends, "Israelis do not identify themselves as Jews, but as Israelis: If you ask an Israeli who he is, he will respond, 'I am an Israeli.' I would prefer that he say, 'I am a Jew and an Israeli.'" Schaalman thinks this new identification is part of the "new Jew," so different from Jews of the past. (As one Israeli told this writer in response his question of whether he goes to the synagogue, "I don't have to go; I live in the Holy Land.")

Schaalman is also concerned about the Orthodox and ultra-Orthodox control of Israel's political and religious life. As a leader of Reform Judaism, he had direct experience with the difficulties Reform has faced, and still faces, in gaining acceptance and legitimacy in Israel. The lack of tolerance by Israel's Orthodox establishment of non-Orthodox forms of Jewish belief and practice is one of the most troublesome problems in Jewish life. Schaalman has been sharply critical of its control, particularly its denial of the validity of rabbinic conversions in Reform and Conservative Judaism.[457] In the fall of 2008, an Israeli Orthodox rabbi, Abraham Sherman, invalidated thousands of conversions of Israeli Jews that had been performed by Rabbi Haim Drukman, head of the Orthodox Conversion Authority. The verdict rendered the Jewish status of thousands of converts invalid retroactively back to 1999 and required them to convert a second time. According to Schaalman, the ensuing controversy "sent a shock wave through Israeli society."[458] He also points out that the loss of Jewish status means that marriages to individuals converted by Rabbi Drukman are no longer valid and that the children born of women he has converted are not Jewish either. These conversions were delegitimized regardless of how much Jewish education the converts had, how much participation they have had in Jewish ritual observances, or how often they have participated in religious services. "These same Orthodox religious authorities," he remarks, "do not accept as authentic conversions performed by American Reform or Conservative rabbis, or Orthodox rabbis whom they consider not authentically Orthodox."

In January 2009, Schaalman shared with Emanuel's congregation his bleak assessment of the current state of Israeli affairs and apologized for burdening them with it. These developments, he confessed, have shattered his belief that the modern State of Israel is the key to Jewish survival. The root of the problem is Israel's Orthodox establishment:

> It opposes most of the achievements of modern liberal Judaism, is totally opposed to interfaith contact, is unrelenting in its unwillingness to accept forms of Judaism outside its own narrow sphere, and refuses to accept Reform Judaism as Judaism. The Orthodox have defined their positions on religious matters so narrowly that they have rejected decisions made by their own rabbis, whom they have come to see as not sufficiently Orthodox. Such a state of intolerance leads to the denial of Jewish authenticity to Jews who do not practice their brand of Judaism.

Schaalman does not see any hope that these anachronistic positions will change anytime in the near future, if at all.

What Schaalman did not tell his congregants was that his assessment of the situation of the status of worldwide Judaism was even more dire. He is now convinced that the dream of *klal Yisrael* (the sense of shared community and destiny among all Jews) is turning into a nightmare. Aware that his view is so provocative and controversial, he did not want it recorded. "Jews outside of Israel," he states, "need to move away from the hope that Jerusalem will be the center of Judaism's future. Instead, American Judaism must become the new center for the survival of a liberal-based Judaism. It is only in this shift of perspective that the great achievements in interfaith relationships and individual choice will survive."

In this regard, Schaalman is heir to the Enlightenment; he refuses to accept a pre-Enlightenment, medieval form of Judaism:

> There has been too much progress toward the acceptance of Jews in the modern Western world to return to what is, in part, a self-chosen exclusiveness within the Jewish community. Such a position as an attempt to circle the wagons as a kind of last-ditch effort to ensure Jewish survival. It is not necessary, or called for.

Chapter 12

Winding Down
Reaching Ninety and Beyond

"We should be playing, but we don't have time for that"
Lotte Schaalman, March 28, 2006

"I never thought I would live so long. My father died when he was sixty-seven. My mother lived to ninety-three, but, in those days, women always lived longer."
Herman E. Schaalman, April 30, 2010

Turning Ninety

On April 28, 2006, Schaalman celebrated his ninetieth birthday and was feted at two birthday celebrations, one hosted by his Torah Study group, and the other by Emanuel Congregation. The event, however, was tinged with sadness: "When you live this long, you outlive most of your friends; there's nobody alive, and that's a horrible feeling." A major part of the Schaalmans' sense of loss is their awareness that outside of their children and grandchildren, they have no living relatives in America. Lotte's parents and her sister died years ago and Schaalman's brothers and their families, who live far away, are almost out of reach.[459] Visiting them always was a challenge and, in recent years, has become almost impossible. Despite this distance, however, Schaalman's one consolation is, "I'm in daily communication with my two brothers internally and cannot think of myself without thinking of them as part of me."

Life for the Schaalmans in their nineties continues to be both challenging and fulfilling. Despite recent hospitalizations for serious health issues, a quick overview of some of Schaalman's major activities reveals that until recently he has barely slowed down. He teaches, gives sermons, writes, participates in national and international events, conducts funerals, and performs weddings. When he was ninety-one, he published *Hineni*, the result of a lifetime of thinking about the most profound questions of life and Judaism. Since then, his active and fertile mind has refused to rest, and he continues to revise and expand his thinking, so much so that he seems to be experiencing a new spurt of creative energy. In 2007, he made a major presentation at HUC-JIR's ordination ceremony. Because he realizes that time is running out, in 2011 he decided to publish an article on some of his latest insights into Torah. Until the fall of 2011, he continued to serve as scholar-in-residence at Emanu-El B'ne Jeshurun in Milwaukee. In January of 2011, he gave a keynote address to his colleagues at the National Association of Retired Reform Rabbis. He meets regularly with his Torah Study students, continues to hold his monthly Current Events sessions, and teaches part-time at Garrett-Evangelical Theological Seminary.

An Enduring Relationship

Every marriage is, after all, a mutually interdependent relationship in which the well-being of one partner is conditional on the well-being of the other. In the marriage of Herman and Lotte Schaalman, no less is true. In their early years together, they grew into their marriage. They were young and inexperienced and, as refugees, totally out of their element, aliens in a strange new world. Both admit that they had to learn what it meant to be intimate with each other, to be lovers and husband and wife. Apparently, they succeeded. Lotte worships her husband. If he has warts, you will never know it from talking to her; not only does she never complain, she idolizes him—yes, after seventy years of marriage!

As the younger partner and in better health, Herman looks after his wife, who, in the last six years has had serious illnesses. When she is feeling good, they hug and kiss. When she is not, he hovers over her and tries to minister to her needs. That is not easy. After a lifetime of taking care of others, she has no tolerance or desire for anyone to take care of her. At these times, when she rejects his ministrations, he is visibly hurt. Often he will say, "I don't know what to do. She won't let me help her."

He's not perfect, of course: without question, her stubbornness irritates him, and he makes no secret of that fact.

Nevertheless, he has adapted his life to be at her side. Unless Lotte is well enough to go with him, he no longer travels to meetings or conferences as he did in the old days. In fact, to know them today is to see them as Siamese twins joined at the hip. More often than not, either they travel together or they don't travel at all. Typically, they attend services together or they don't go.

After seventy years of marriage, the Schaalmans are still very much in love and not reserved in showing it. Barbara Steinberg, a longtime friend, likes to tell the story of an event she witnessed in the Schaalmans' ongoing love story. One evening in 2001, as she was leaving Emanuel and heading for her car in the parking lot, she saw the Schaalmans locked in what she described as a "clearly romantic embrace. What impressed me was that they had been married sixty years!" (This writer, too, can attest to the intimacy they share. Frequently in their home to conduct interviews, he has seen the two lovingly caress each other without any hint of embarrassment.) At her daughter's wedding, Steinberg toasted daughter and new son-in-law "wishing them a marriage as rewarding and long lasting as Rabbi and Lotte's."

The bond between the Schaalmans goes far beyond personal intimacy. Theirs is a partnership in which Lotte has played a dynamic role, not only as a wife, but also as an aide in her husband's rabbinic career. He has no better publicist. She holds back nothing; she told this writer (2007), "He is one of the most unusual human beings that you would ever meet, and I've held this view throughout the seventy years of our marriage." "Sometimes," she confides, "I feel I wasn't good enough, because he is that special." Nevertheless, from the very beginning of their marriage, she decided, "My job was to watch over him, so that he would have a long time of giving what he has to give." For most of her husband's teaching career, she has accompanied him to his classes and describes with pride, "At the end of the semester so many of his seminary students tell me that the rabbi has made a significant difference in their lives."

As part of her commitment to be a rabbi's wife, or *rebbetzin*, she chose to be a stay-at-home mom: "I managed the household, raised our children, and assisted Herman in ministering to the congregation" (2007).

An indication of how closely Lotte watches over her husband and takes an active role in the development of his career was clear to Rabbi Glaser. He remembered that after the CCAR announced that Schaalman would be its next president, she called him: "'Joe,'" she said, "'if Herman ever gives you any trouble, call me'" (Emanuel Congregation, 1986).

Having devoted herself so completely to this role, Lotte takes issue with the profound changes the women's rights revolution has produced in the way younger rabbis' wives respond to this role of supporting their husbands' careers. She notes, "Since feminism taught women that they no longer needed to accept subservient roles, rabbis' spouses now feel entitled to careers of their own and have achieved equality in the home." Their husbands tend to share this view and are willing to accept household responsibilities, including caring for their children. "Over the last quarter century," Lotte asserts,

> I have attempted, unsuccessfully, to tell these wives that the role of supporting my husband was a blessing. The life of a rebbetzin opened up for me all kinds of possibilities for learning, personal growth, and fulfillment. In my case, I worked in partnership with my husband and got to know most of the important people with whom he interacted. I travelled with him for much of his career and participated in numerous dinners and events across the country and around the world.

The Schaalman Home

The Schaalmans live on the twentieth floor of the Tiara, a high-rise condominium in the Edgewater community on Chicago's north side. They have been there since the building was completed in the 1960s. From their balcony, they have an unobstructed view of beautiful Lake Michigan. The building is located only a block north of Emanuel, and, when the weather permitted, the Schaalmans used to walk to the temple. Now that they are in their nineties, walking has become a challenge for both of them and they usually drive.

Except for the recent addition of a new 32-inch flat-screen TV in the kitchen, the unit has not changed much in the nearly half century they have lived there. Plants, some of which have survived for decades, line

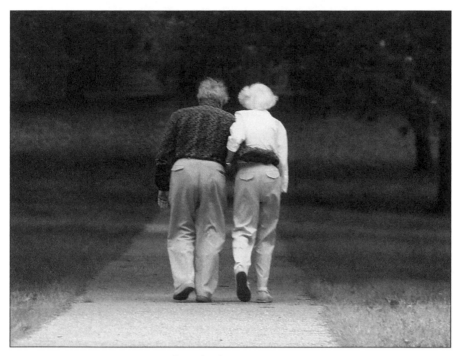

The Schaalmans in 2012

the walls of their living room, many of them gifts from friends and well-wishers. Thanks to the Rabbi's tender loving care, they are all healthy. (Asked what his secret is to keeping them looking so good, he says, "I water them once a week on Sunday mornings and sing to them.") On one side of the dining room against the wall are shelves bearing the awards Schaalman has received over the last seventy years. Several pictures, remnants of the Schaalmans' past lives in Germany, have been hanging in their living room since they moved in. The apartment also has a small study lined floor to ceiling with books that reflect Schaalman's deep love of learning. Next to his desk, Schaalman keeps two pictures, one of his father and the other of Cardinal Bernardin.

Their condo has a master bedroom and a much smaller guest bedroom. When Lotte's mother moved in, they moved into the guest bedroom. Susan was already out the house and Michael was away in college. Furnished with the furniture her parents had sent from Germany in the 1930s, the master bedroom has a private bath and a Murphy bed to allow the room to feel more like a sitting room than a bedroom. After Gussie died, the Schaalmans kept it for their guests, whose comfort is more important to them than their own. On occasion, guests included students who needed temporary housing or friends who were visiting. While Herman and Lotte were recovering from major health issues in 2011 and 2012 (he from a minor stroke, and she from a fractured hip), their son and daughter-in-law slept in the master bedroom during the weekends when they came to Chicago to help care for their parents.

The modest home represents the Schaalmans' decision not to sink money into material things. Despite the fact that they can afford to buy themselves new furniture and appliances, they have chosen to live frugally and to share their limited means with others. When the mail arrives, he opens the many solicitations and evaluates each one to decide whether to send money.

The only luxury he allows himself is his annual rental of a new luxury car, until recently a Lincoln. He reasons that he needs a nice-looking car to represent his position as a rabbi. He loves to drive and drive fast and for that, he reasons, "I need a car with lots of power and one that handles well." Sitting in the car with a ninety-five-year-old driving at dangerously high speeds around the challenging curves of Chicago's Lake Shore Drive is indeed an experience, definitely not for the faint of heart! His stroke in August 2011 prevented him from driving, but only for a few months. By December, he was ready to drive again. After passing the mandatory driving test, he returned to driving, and, according to him, now at moderate speeds.

Torah Scroll Delivered to Hanover

In April 2006, Schaalman traveled to Hanover, Germany, as part of a delegation from Emanuel to deliver a Torah scroll to the city's fledgling Reform synagogue. Led by Rabbi Zedek, the delegation—including long-time friends and temple supporters Bob and Audrey Morris, Jill Gardner, and Rabbi Zedek and his wife, Karen—presented the Torah scroll in Schaalman's honor and in acknowledgement of his survival during the Nazi Holocaust. The gift of the scroll was part of a program created in 1988 by the World Union for Progressive Judaism to donate Torah scrolls that had been rescued from the Holocaust to Reform congregations in the former Soviet Union, Europe, Latin America, and Israel. Thanks to the recent completion of the "Herman and Lotte Schaalman Torah Writing Project," Emanuel had a spare Torah it could "donate." The donation, however, was not a gift, but a long-term loan. In the eventuality that the Hanover congregation might no longer need it, the loan allows Emanuel to reclaim it. Originally, Emanuel had hoped to give the Torah to a congregation in Munich, but missed the opportunity when the Munich congregation received one from another donor.

For Schaalman, the experience was something like a homecoming: he hadn't been in a German synagogue since he left Germany seventy-one years before, nor had he ever expected to be in one again. The young rabbinic student who left his native country to travel to a distant and alien country was now returning after a life of distinguished service as a rabbi. "Had I remained in Germany," he commented, "none of this would have been possible." For the Emanuel delegation, fully aware of this background, the event was a moving experience. They were able to share this precious moment with their beloved rabbi and to realize that in a small but significant way, this was a redemptive historical event.

Chicago Cubs Baseball Game

The following year on May 29, 2007, Schaalman threw out the first ball at a Chicago Cubs home game at Wrigley Field. Ironically, once an ardent Cubs fan who read the sports page of the *Chicago Tribune* daily, he was tired of being disappointed by their failure to win a pennant or the World Series (the last one was in 1908): "I'm a died-in-the-wool mourner. Usually I give up on them by May."

Rabbi Zedek, his close friend and colleague, arranged for him to have the unprecedented honor (for a rabbi) of throwing out the first ball. Although ninety-one at the time, Schaalman's pitch was a respectable performance. The ball he threw from the pitcher's mound arched gracefully over the field toward home plate, took one hop and landed in the catcher's glove. The spectators let out a deafening roar of approval. The catcher signed the ball and gave it to him. Later, the catcher hit a home run. In fact, after this game, the Cubs, who were at the bottom of the National League standings, went on a roll and, within a month, were challengers for first place. Whether there was

Schaalman on his 90th birthday thowing out first pitch
at Chicago Cubs game, April 2006

any connection between the Rabbi's presence and the subsequent winning streak is anyone's guess, but he heard from more than one friend
that there must have been a connection between his appearance and
the Cubs' improved performance.

Ordination Sermon at HUC-JIR, June 2007

Four days after becoming a local celebrity at Wrigley Field, Schaalman
gave the commencement address at the 2007 rabbinic ordination class of
the Hebrew Union College-Jewish Institute of Religion. The address was
the result of an invitation he had received a few months earlier from the
seminary's president, Rabbi David Ellenson. "Never before," Schaalman
confided, "had I been accorded an opportunity to speak at such an important occasion." The invitation had come as a complete surprise, and
it was a great honor. Traditionally, graduating students recommended a

commencement speaker, and, thanks to the recommendation by Ann Folb, a graduating student and his long-time friend, he was selected. Coming sixty-six years after his ordination, the event was a special kind of homecoming.

Schaalman decided to talk about the changes in the rabbinate since his own ordination and the uncertain world the students were about to enter, a world in a state of change unprecedented in human history. In typical Schaalman fashion, he had no text or notes. As he explained to this interviewer, "The contents of the sermon had churned and kept me awake for many nights during the preceding months. I tested certain phrases, but didn't write them down." Uncertain of what he should say, he consulted Lotte. She suggested that he might add his ideas about the role of the rabbi. One night, when she awoke to find him talking in his sleep, she woke him and asked what he was doing: "I'm preaching," he replied, "not now, but for June."

The ordination of twenty rabbinic students began with a Shabbat morning service on June 2, 2007, in the Plum Street Temple in Cincinnati, which, having been designed by the college founder, Isaac Mayer Wise, was steeped in Reform Jewish history. As the guest of honor, Schaalman sat on the bimah between the college president and the vice president of the Board of Governors. Lotte sat in the front row, as befitting the wife of the honoree. (In typical Lotte fashion, however, she reported, "I would rather have been seated in the rear.") Because he wanted the families to be the focus of attention, he was concerned that his sermon should not be the high point of the ordination event.

When it came time for the sermon, Rabbi Ellenson introduced his honored guest as "a rabbi's rabbi, a man of towering intellect" (Hebrew Union College-Jewish Institute of Religion, June 2, 2007). Schaalman began by drawing a historical comparison between the world the ordainees were about to enter and the one he had entered sixty-six years before.[460] At the time of his ordination, he had experienced two major emotions. The first was relief that he had met the challenges of his education; the second was his sense of the loss of his family and country. As an immigrant in a new country, he was about to begin a new life both as a rabbi and a husband and he was unprepared for both: "In one day, I was both a rabbi and a husband. I'm still working in bewilderment in both areas. ... In those early years, I was like a sleep walker."

In his own ordination class, there were only fourteen students, none of them women. The only women on campus were two secretaries, two cooks, and Lillian Waldman, the dorm matron. Black men, who served as their waiters, cleaned their rooms, took care of their laundry, and tended to the students. The new rabbinic students needed and received instruction in what to expect in the social world of Reform Judaism. He remembered that the college president's wife introduced them to artichokes, a delicacy they would likely encounter in their new roles as participants in the leading strata of Reform society.

Since then, Schaalman told the students, the world had changed dramatically. Neither he nor his fellow students had heard of the Big Bang, Genomes, DNA, or Quantum Theory. Although they had heard of Freud and Einstein, they weren't discussed. Nor did the students know about the horrors the Nazis were perpetrating against Jews. Immigrants like him were anxious about the war cables they received and the safety of their families, but, he confessed, "I did not feel engaged" in the war. Like his friends and teachers, he felt protected and sheltered.

Was there anything they could learn from the past that would be of benefit to them? Instead of answering this question directly, Schaalman referred to the biblical account of Abraham's first encounter with God. In the story, God calls to Abraham, "Lech lecha," go, but does not tell him where. "The miracle," Schaalman said, "is that, although he has no certainty who was calling or what the purpose of the message might be, Abraham goes." This was the "call" to which each of them was now responding, and they could not possibly know where it would lead them. "It is the call to which I have devoted my entire rabbinic life," he told them. God's command to Abraham, 'lech lecha,' creates for Abraham a fundamental question, perhaps *the* fundamental question: Go where? Do what? All existence is a response to this question to which we are required to give an answer. The story is the central point of our identity as Jews." It certainly was for him. Without knowing what his future promised or whether he would be able to return home to his family, he left his own country to settle in a new land where he was a stranger. "My destiny was to live without my family and to make my way solely on the merits of who I was."

For his conclusion, Schaalman turned to the biblical story of Adam and Eve's defiance of God's commandment that they not eat from the Tree of Good and Evil. When they violated the commandment, fearful of God's punishment, Adam attempts to hide from Him. God calls to Adam, "Where art thou?" "The question," Schaalman told the students, "means more than where are you hiding? The question is metaphysical: Adam, what is the direction of your life? Where are you along the path to righteous living and holiness?" Schaalman hoped to challenge the ordainees to search for their own answers to these profound questions. It was a challenge he would come back to a few months later in his 2007 Yom Kippur sermon and in a Shabbat sermon in February 2008.

After the ordination, Schaalman received a congratulatory note from his friend, Rabbi Peter Knobel: "You were magnificent at Ordination. It was a very important and deeply moving message. It demonstrates once again why you are one of the 'greats of the generation.' May God grant you many more years of strength and health."

Transitions

When Susan married Rabbi Ira Youdovin, she thought her dream had come true, but, although the marriage lasted nearly twenty years, unfortunately, it did not work out. When Susan and Ira's marriage ended in 2007, the breakup was painful not only for her, but for her parents. The divorce, however, did not end their relationship with Ira's family. Through Susan's marriage, they had acquired two step-grandchildren and two step–great-grandchildren, with whom they have maintained a loving relationship. According to Susan, "When their great-grandfather regales them with stories and asks about their school, the great-grandchildren sit in awe of him." Although they live in Boston, when the children were younger the Schaalmans used to visit several times a year. In December 2010, they flew to Boston so that great-granddad could perform his great-granddaughter's Bat Mitzvah. On May 3, 2009, Susan married Charles Shulkin and, of course, her father performed the wedding, which was held at Emanuel for a small gathering of the bride and groom's families.

Berlin: April 26, 2008

On April 26, 2008, together with representatives of the Jewish Council on Urban Affairs (JCUA), Schaalman flew to Berlin to attend the special fiftieth anniversary conference of the Aktion Sühnezeichen Friedensdienste, or Action Reconciliation Service for Peace (ARSP). Founded in the aftermath of World War II, the ARSP sends German youths over the age of eighteen as volunteers to countries like the United States. The objective is to atone for and remediate the suffering caused by the Nazis, to combat anti-Semitism, and to promote world peace (ARSP, 2008). Together with a host agency such as JCUA, the ARSP supports the volunteers for twelve months to live and work in the host agency. When the JCUA began participating in the program in 1985, the Schaalmans offered to host one of the volunteers for a few weeks. Their volunteer found the relationship so satisfying that he stayed four months. JCUA president, Jane Ramsey (2011), reports that the Schaalmans were so pleased with the outcome of this relationship that they hosted several other volunteers, and Schaalman served as their informal advisor.

Ramsey wanted Schaalman to participate in the conference for the prestige his presence gave to the program; it would "send a message" to ARSP and its volunteers of the program's importance. In addition, because she was well aware of Schaalman's attachment to Munich and that he would be celebrating his ninety-second birthday on the trip, she wanted to give him the opportunity to visit his place of birth. Schaalman was delighted and took the Chicago delegation on a sentimental tour of Munich. He took them to his childhood home on Tengstrasse and walked up the five flights of stairs (!) to look at the apartment door. He was delighted to discover that it was the same as he remembered from his childhood. Other places he took them were his grandmother's grave, the Jewish Museum, and the grammar school he had attended. While they were standing in front of the school, he pointed to a window from which he and his fellow students were compelled to witness the raising of the Nazi flag for the school. One of them, who was also a Nazi, demanded that all his classmates salute it. Schaalman refused, and one of the boys threatened to beat him up. Thanks to Schaalman's martial arts training, he was not intimidated and with one punch knocked the student to the floor, thus ending the episode. According to Jane Ramsey (2011), although the tour tired out the other members of the group, it didn't tire Schaalman, who appeared to have "boundless energy."

Dedication of Holocaust Museum April 26, 2009

On April 26, 2009, Schaalman gave the invocation at the opening ceremony for Skokie's new Holocaust Museum. Held in a huge tent on a cold and rainy April afternoon, the event attracted an estimated 12,000 people. Distinguished guests included Elie Wiesel, the German Ambassador Klaus Scharioth, Illinois Governor Patrick Quinn, President Bill Clinton, Senator Dick Durbin, and members of Congress. President Barack Obama, Secretary of State Hillary Clinton, Israel's President, Shimon Peres, and the ambassadors of ten nations sent videotaped greetings. J. B. Pritzker, longtime friend of the Schaalman family, hosted and served as emcee.

In the preceding months, Schaalman had spent many sleepless nights wrestling with how, in the three minutes allotted to him, he might have the greatest impact on his audience. In his speech, he told them that, because the museum housed the memory of those who had perished, the ground on which they were seated was "sacred ground." He went on to say,

> Despite the fact that many years had passed since the Holocaust, the world still cannot comprehend how or why so many died. The catastrophic and horrendous nature of the event numbed our minds. Nevertheless, what we do know is that we have to be the voices for those who can no longer speak, sing or pray. … Above everything else, it is up to us to make sure that the Jewish people never die.

President Clinton, the keynote speaker, asserted that the Holocaust had set the stage for subsequent genocidal events and apologized for the mistake he made in not doing more to prevent the genocide in Rwanda. Elie Wiesel picked up this theme and remarked that had the message of the Holocaust been learned, the various genocides that have plagued humanity in the intervening years might have been prevented.

Schaalman and Eli Wiesel, opening celebration of Holocaust Museum, Skokie, IL,
April 19, 2009

Right to left. Schaalman, President Clinton, Hillary Clinton,
White House breakfast, 1993

When the ceremony was over, Schaalman had an opportunity to speak privately with his old friend, Elie Wiesel. Schaalman took the opportunity to give him an autographed copy of *Hineni*. Knowing in advance that Clinton would be present at the ceremony, Schaalman also came prepared to give him a copy. Because he knew it would be difficult to get past the Secret Service, as a calling card he brought a picture of himself with the President. It was also his way of reminding Clinton that he had been his guest at the White House. When Schaalman approached Clinton's security detail, he held

Rabbi Schaalman speaks at the dedication ceremony of the Holocaust Museum

up the picture and pointed to the President and himself and said, "I am the one in the picture, and I want to go in and speak to the President." It worked. The guards admitted him to the room where Clinton had been taken after his keynote address. Once inside, Schaalman again held up the picture to remind Clinton of their meeting. When Schaalman handed him an inscribed copy of *Hineni*, which read, "In profound admiration," Clinton promised to read the book. A few days later, he sent Schaalman a note telling him that he was enjoying reading it.

After two hours of being outdoors on this cold and rainy day, Schaalman was chilled to the bone, and he did not feel well. Although he was not aware of it, he was already in the early stages of shingles. He knew something was bothering him but was not sure what it was. Making matters more difficult, getting out of the parking lot was a challenge, and, by the time he got home, he only had time for a short rest before he had to give a major address at the Catholic Theological Seminary (CTS). One can only wonder how a ninety-three year old could have given two speeches under such difficult conditions while in the initial stages of shingles. The next morning he wound up in his doctor's office.

Winter Vacations in Florida: 2010–2012

For the first time since his retirement, in January of 2010 the Schaalmans did something they had not done since the days at Eagle River where they spent their summer vacations. In 2009, Schaalman decided that the Chicago winter was too difficult for Lotte and that spending a part of it in Florida would be good for her. Lotte, one the other hand, thought the expense a waste of money and fought him every step of the way. She confided to this interviewer, "It was too expensive, and we didn't need it. All my life, I have denied myself the luxuries other people take for granted. Why spend money on themselves, when so many others are in greater need?" Schaalman, however, prevailed, and Lotte had to resign herself, as she had done so often throughout their marriage, to accepting his decision. Her rationalization: "It would be good for Herman." Nevertheless, she kept up a steady stream of complaints throughout the trip.

With the help of their close friends, Marvin and Phyllis Goldblatt,[461] in January of 2010, the Schaalmans rented a two-bedroom condominium on Longboat Key, a few miles north of Sarasota. The Goldblatts, who owned a condominium upstairs, served as their guide and chauffeur, taking them to the area's various cultural events, museums, and some of its better restaurants. Despite the fact that Florida was experiencing one of its coldest winters on record, thanks to them, the Schaalman's stay was more enjoyable than it might have been.

The trip gave the entire Schaalman family an opportunity to be together for at least two weeks. Michael and Roberta and Susan and Charlie came for a visit, and so did the grandchildren with their current significant others. Not coincidentally, they came to celebrate Lotte's ninety-fifth birthday. The fact that her family came to visit helped her forget her objections to the trip and convinced her that she should *consider* coming back.

While they were on Longboat Key, Schaalman got the chance to indulge his passion for tennis. He played twice a week with the local professional. Although the younger man pushed him harder than he was used to, Schaalman enjoyed the challenge and the fact that he could keep up with him. Schaalman played what he calls "a more vigorous tennis in which the tennis pros sent me scurrying all over the court." Asked how he felt about these more challenging workouts, he replied,

"It's good for me. It allows me the opportunity to stretch and do more running." He was also happy to report that a woman attendant at the court remarked that she was impressed by the fact that a ninety-year-old was playing tennis on the same court. She was even more impressed when he told her, "I'm not ninety. I'm ninety-three!"

One of Schaalman's challenges during the six weeks in Florida was the fact that he missed the intellectual and spiritual nourishment provided by his Torah Study students. However, he could not escape completely his professional commitments. On two occasions, the Council of Religious Leaders of Metropolitan Chicago called to involve him in conference calls on matters that he thought were trivial.

The fact that the vacation coincided with the annual conference of the National Association of Retired Reform Rabbis (NAORRR) held in nearby Fort Myers helped Schaalman justify his extended Florida vacation. At ninety-three and one of the oldest surviving members of NAORRR, he was known to his colleagues as the "Old Man." Lotte, Susan, and husband Charles went with him. Two months later, Schaalman received a call inviting him to be the keynote speaker at next year's conference in San Diego.

The winter vacation in Longboat Key nearly convinced Lotte that the expenditure was worth it. When her husband proposed that they return the next winter, she was more accepting. She was going to be ninety-six on January 13, 2011, and could look forward to having her family visit to celebrate it with her. Although the Schaalmans did not stay as long as they had the year before, the weather was warmer and they were able to spend more time outside their condominium sunning themselves on the beach.

Returning in 2011, however, was iffy. Lotte was recovering from a hip fracture and Herman from a stroke that that had partially paralyzed his right side. They decided that, as part of their plan for recovery, they should spend part of the winter in what had now become their special winter home. As they had in the previous winters, the family gathered to celebrate their mother's ninety-seventh birthday. Schaalman even managed to play some tennis, though, as he says, "I wouldn't call it tennis. I could only stand still and hit the ball over the net, if it came in my range."

Challenging Health Issues

In the period of their late eighties and nineties, the Schaalmans developed serious health issues. In her eighty-eighth year, Lotte began to experience bouts of uncontrollable coughing, the result of a fluid buildup in her lungs caused by a leaky heart valve. The coughing was particularly severe when she tried to speak. She underwent a series of treatments to reduce the fluid, but her condition continued to deteriorate. In August of 2005, while the Schaalmans were away at OSRUI, Lotte had difficulty breathing. Schaalman cut short his teaching and returned to Chicago. At one point, the coughing and difficulty breathing became so severe that he had to drive her to the emergency room of St. Francis Hospital. During the following week, she underwent a variety of tests to determine whether she might be a candidate for surgery. Her cardiologist cleared her for surgery, but she refused to go through with it. Her condition continued to deteriorate.

By the time she reached ninety, she was having difficulty getting through the day. Her frequent coughing fits left her gasping for breath. Although she continued to receive periodic treatments to remove the fluid buildup, she was unwilling to risk the open-heart surgery required to repair her damaged heart valve. By July 2006, her doctor told her that, unless she had the surgery to relieve the fluid buildup, within a few months she would die of suffocation. She accepted the fatal diagnosis and was ready to die. Schaalman, however, convinced her to have the surgery. Nevertheless, he was frightened at the thought that he might lose her. He shared with this interviewer, "I guess I'll have to learn to live in a totally new reality."

Although the surgery was a huge risk, her doctor told her that her heart was sound and that her prognosis was good. On August 28, 2006, when she was ninety-one, Lotte had open-heart surgery. During the operation, her doctor discovered that the more invasive surgery of valve-replacement was unnecessary and that he could repair the damaged valve. Lotte survived that surgery but, in few days, had a serious setback. She developed a mild case of pneumonia and suffered severe bouts of coughing. The problem was that her lungs had been damaged over time because her heart issues had not been treated. Because the operation had sapped her strength, recovery was difficult. When she came home, she complained of side effects from the surgery: her vision was now blurry, and she was having difficulty reading. She also continued to have coughing fits, though they were less severe than before. Finding the energy to get through the day was another problem. A year later, however, she was nearly fully recovered, and though she still had an occasional cough, she was as feisty as ever. That is until the summer of 2011, when she broke her hip. Although assisted living appears to be their best option, they insist that they will remain in their home, if necessary with caretakers. And so they do, and for the moment, at least, Herman Schaalman continues to march into the future, slowed, but not stilled.

Schaalman's serious health issues began when he was much younger than his wife. In 1970, he discovered that he had skin cancer. After his daughter noticed a growth on his back and recommended that he do something about it, he went to a dermatologist who told him the growth was cancerous and would have to be removed. It was the size of a slice of grapefruit and deep enough that the doctor had to cut out a piece of Schaalman's back to remove it. Ever since, he has been diligent about getting biannual checkups, limiting himself to one hour in the sun and applying lots of sunscreen.

In 1994 or 1995, Schaalman developed a serious case of leukemia. Remarkably, after one series of chemotherapy infusions, the cancer went into remission and has not reoccurred. A side effect of the treatment, however, is that it compromised his immune system and left him vulnerable to severe bronchial infections that take weeks to run their course. When these infections strike, he has difficulty breathing and suffers prolonged and painful fits of coughing. On these occasions, the only way he can sleep at night is to sit upright in a living room chair. As soon as he can, and before he is fully recovered, he returns to teach his classes at Garrett and his beloved Torah Study at Emanuel.

In March of 2009, one of these episodes sent him to the hospital. Although he was sent home after a few nights, his coughing was so intense that he had to sleep upright in a chair for the next two weeks. By the third week, although he had barely slept the night before, he not only taught his Torah Study but also treated his students to one of his best sessions. "Downtime," he explained to his students, "means lots of time to think."

Two months later, he developed a painful rash and lesions on the upper part of his body. The diagnosis was shingles, which stayed with him three months. Although he tried not to scratch them, the itching was an ongoing torment. These two illnesses, first the bronchitis and then the shingles, left him weaker and more susceptible to the next illness.

His discomfort, however, did not keep him from maintaining a busy and challenging schedule. He held each of his weekly Torah Study, attended various luncheons, including one with Chicago's Cardinal George, participated in Emanuel's annual Memorial Day Retreat at OS-RUI, and returned to OSRUI a few weeks later to lead a four-day Lehrhaus seminar.

Over the next two years, his health began to deteriorate. As his ninety-fifth birthday approached in April of 2011, he was on his way to renew his driver's license when he had intense pain in his chest and difficulty breathing. Luckily, Lotte was with him and he had his cell phone. He called his doctor who told him to get to the nearest emergency room, which happened to be St. Francis Hospital in Evanston. When the nurses saw how he looked, they admitted him immediately. Lotte called Susan, and she called Rabbi Zedek. This writer happened to be talking to Zedek when the call came in. Fearing the worst, they left immediately for the hospital. When they arrived, they found their beloved rabbi lying on a bed in the emergency room. He lay there, barely awake, looking pale and drawn. Lotte was at his side and very frightened. The hospital performed various tests but could find nothing wrong. The next day, he was feeling well enough to be discharged. Two days later, he was teaching his Torah Study as if nothing had happened; he appeared well rested and full of energy and gave his students one of the best sessions they could remember.

This hospitalization, however, was a prelude of what was to come. On August 11, 2011, Schaalman suffered a stroke that left him partially paralyzed on his right side. Again, he was hospitalized in St. Francis Hospital, and, a few days later, transferred to the Rehabilitation Institute of Chicago (RIC), one of the best rehabilitation facilities in the country. Fortunately, the stroke did not affect his speech or mental abilities. However, it did render him incapable of walking or using his right hand for simple tasks such as writing or feeding himself. Thanks to the excellent care provided by the RIC and Schaalman's determination to recover, he fought his way back. After six weeks of therapy, he was able to go home, a lot weaker but still able to function.

In the preceding months, Lotte had been suffering from an excruciating pain in her lower back. Although she saw two specialists, neither of them was able to relieve the pain. During this time, she could not take care of herself, and Schaalman had to assume many of the household chores that she had been doing for the last seventy years. Now that her husband was in the hospital, the usually capable and feisty ninety-six year old woman, who had taken excellent care of her husband, was now in need of a caretaker herself.

The children, their spouses, and the grandchildren came to the rescue and took charge of their parents' lives, providing them constant attention. Granddaughter Keren, a senior medical student at the University of Wisconsin, came to help. Susan and Charlie convinced Lotte to move in with them until they could find a capable caretaker. In the mornings, they brought her to the RIC to be with her husband, who, as Susan said, "sweated through three hours of therapy, plus 'homework' in his room."

With the help of the RIC staff, Schaalman continued to make steady progress in recovering his motor skills on his right side. Within two weeks, he was able to feed himself and make markings on paper that, according to Susan, "resembled writing." His main challenge was walking and balance. After five weeks, Schaalman was discharged but was required to follow a rigorous treatment plan that included intense physical therapy several hours a day at a nearby RIC satellite site. Three days a week, a van picked him up at 8:00 a.m. and brought him home three hours later. By that time, he was so exhausted from the strenuous exercises that all he could do was sleep.

Under such a handicap, any other normal ninety-five year old would have decided to cut back on his activities. Not Schaalman. He insisted on teaching his course at Garrett, which had begun September 6, the day of his discharge. Grudgingly, he gave up meeting his first class, but, thanks to what Susan calls his "Teutonic determination," showed up for his next session. He also resumed teaching his Saturday morning Torah Study. For his first day back after a six-week hiatus, nearly everyone showed up to see their beloved Rabbi. His recovery to this point had been remarkable.

Just as life for the Schaalmans seemed to be improving, Lotte broke her hip. It happened suddenly as the couple was getting ready to leave their apartment. For no apparent reason, Lotte fell over and hit the floor. Schaalman called an ambulance and Lotte was rushed to the hospital. A day later, she was operated on to repair the fracture. Remarkably, she survived and, two days later, was able to get out of bed with the aid of her walker.

Lotte's hip fracture was only the latest of various bone fractures she has suffered in the last twenty years. She has broken bones in her legs, arms, and ribs. In 1993, she had knee and hip replacement surgery. "She has enough metallic implants," her husband says, "to make it difficult for her to get past the security machines in airports." During her various illnesses, Schaalman stayed home to take care of her: "Lotte took care of me most of my life, and now it was my turn to take care of her."

Michael and Bobbie come to Chicago almost every weekend to look after their parents. Although she was in her last year of medical school at the University of Wisconsin, Keren came as often as she could to help. Typically, in the first few weeks of her grandmother's hospitalization when she was suffering intense pain, Keren climbed into bed with her to comfort her and help talk her through the most difficult moments. Bobbie threw herself into the role of helper. "For the first time in my marriage," she confided, "I was able to give back some of the attentions that my in-laws had lavished on me. They always took care of us. Now we're taking care of them."

Not only did Bobbie come from Milwaukee almost every weekend during Schaalman's hospitalization, but she also played an important role in Lotte's recovery. Early on, she participated in Lotte's physical therapy so that she could experience firsthand what her mother-in-law was going through and how she might best help her. When Lotte went home, she took charge of the household during the time she spent there. She helped interview prospective homecare workers and made sure that her in-laws were eating well.

The Schaalman children have been indispensable to their parents' recovery. Susan and Charlie are the first line helpers, but on most weekends, they get a reprieve when Michael and Bobbie arrive. It is now nearly a year since Schaalman suffered his stroke and close to that since Lotte suffered her hip fracture. Bobbie and Michael continue to spend most of their weekends in Chicago to be near their parents and to help in any way they can. The fact that together with Susan they are giving so much of their time and energy to their parents is a mark of their character and the impact their parents had on them.

Having a caretaker in the house was a difficult adjustment for the Schaalmans. All their lives, they had taken care of themselves. Both were, and still are, fiercely independent and, now, no longer capable of caring for themselves, they have nearly around-the-clock assistance. It is one of their most difficult adjustments. Their caretakers shop, cook, clean, do their laundry, assist Lotte in bathing, tend to their guests, and help in any other way they can. Not only do the Schaalmans have difficulty with the fact that they had lost their independence, but the cost of this ongoing care is a huge financial burden. Fortunately, "angels" have appeared to help pay for the care, which Schaalman says they could not do without. Although assisted living appears to be their best option, they insist that they will remain in their home, if necessary with caretakers. And so they do, and for the moment, at least, Herman Schaalman continues to march into the future, slowed, but not stilled.

Chapter 13

Conclusion
A Life of Rewards and Challenges

*"When everything is said and done in my life, aside from my own children
and whatever I can be for my grandchildren, that may well prove to have
been the single most important creation ... .In the longest run, I guess I
will be remembered as a grandfather. That's really the only hope I have.
That's what I am working on, maybe the most, in a conscious way."*

Herman E. Schaalman, 1988

*"I'd like to be, I guess, remembered as whatever people could see in me as a
human being, to try to draw their conclusions from this curious history of a
Jew in the twentieth century."*

Herman E. Schaalman, 1988

A t an early age, Schaalman decided that his life's purpose was to
be God's helper to heal a broken world. Out of the darkness
of the Holocaust, he sought and found a way to build a new
and better relationship with his God and with other human beings, a
relationship based on mutual trust, tolerance, and respect. Through his
viewpoint that the fundamental nature of being is relational, he forged
partnerships with others to make this world a better place.

By leaving Germany in 1935, he escaped what might have been his
death at the hands of the Nazis. In the years that followed, he rose from
an obscure immigrant rabbi in Cedar Rapids, Iowa, to become one of
the foremost rabbis in the Reform movement. According to his friend
and rabbinic colleague, Rabbi Marc Berkson (2007), Schaalman's most
significant achievement is the fact that he and four other refugee rabbinic

students from Germany went on to become some of the most influential leaders in American Reform Judaism.[462]

During the 1970s, from his position as committee chair of two of the most critical committees of the CCAR, he put his stamp on two of modern Reform Judaism's most challenging issues, mixed marriage and patrilineal descent. His subsequent election to the presidency of the CCAR was the apogee of his career. From this post, he oversaw and directed important developments in worldwide Reform Judaism at a time when it was experiencing enormous change.

Although retirement meant that he gave up his pulpit and his authority, Schaalman used his prodigious energy to participate in various educational, civic, and religious organizations where he believed he could make a meaningful contribution. Soon after his retirement, the world in which he functioned began to show its gratitude, and the rewards for his lifetime of service began to pour in from areas of his public and religious life, including awards from local, state, national, and international bodies. He has collected so many over the course of his professional life that he has run out of space to accommodate them. They line the walls of his living room and study and spill over into his emeritus office at Emanuel.

Among the more important recognitions in his home are the Laureate from Cardinal Bernardin (1995), the Rosenwald Memorial Award from Jewish Federation of Chicago (1998), the Governor of Illinois Lincoln Academy Medal (2002), and an award from the president of Germany, Order of First Class Merit (1995). He takes great pride in showing off the signed pictures of him and Presidents John Kennedy, Ronald Reagan, and Bill Clinton. He's also justifiably proud of the doctoral hoods conferred on him by Spertus Institute of Jewish Studies, Hebrew Union College, and Garrett-Evangelical Theological Seminary. The City of Chicago gave the Schaalmans a special honor by naming a new park it had built kitty-corner to Emanuel on Sheridan Avenue and Thorndale—"The Herman and Lotte Schaalman Park. (The reader can find a complete list of his Awards and Recognitions in Appendix A.)

Rabbi Emeritus Recognition

On April 3, 2008, the Hebrew Union College-Jewish Institute of Religion announced the creation of a new scholarship fund for rabbinic students from the Chicago area (Hebrew Union College, March 3, 2008).[463] The announcement was part of a ceremony to honor the contributions of fourteen emeritus Reform rabbis to Chicago metropolitan's Jewish life and the life of the community at large. Schaalman, at ninety-one the eldest of this distinguished group, was invited to speak for them. The president of HUC-JIR, David Ellenson, presided and spoke of the lifetime of achievements of this distinguished group. Due to poor health and physical disability, not all of the honorees were able to attend.

Despite a serious leg injury that was the result of a fall several weeks before, Schaalman mounted the podium as spry as the youngest of the honorees. He began his remarks by stating frankly, "I had my doubts about the value of the event. However, after listening to the long list of accomplishments of my retired colleagues, I realized that the event served an important purpose, namely not only the recognition of their accomplishments but the fact that collectively we had prepared a solid foundation for the development of the Reform movement in the Chicago area and for the world."

In 2005, Emanuel Congregation decided to honor the Schaalmans and to raise funds by establishing the Herman and Lotte Schaalman Torah Writing Project. When the fund was established, Herman Schaalman was eighty-nine and Lotte ninety. As he told Emanuel's congregation on the morning of the presentation of the new Torah, "When the fund was established I had no idea that I or Lotte would be alive at the conclusion of the project. To still be alive at the age of ninety-four was more of a blessing than I could have asked for, and the event itself is one of the most meaningful of my long and productive life" (Emanuel Congregation, May 23, 2010).

As part of the many honors that had begun to pile up in Schaalman's later years, in 2002, the 92nd Illinois House of Representatives passed resolution HR0870 awarding him the prestigious Order of Lincoln Award from the Lincoln Academy of Illinois. The award, introduced into the House of Representatives by Harry Osterman, a local state representative from Schaalman's district, was given in recognition "for his lifelong devotion and dedication to the betterment of mankind and for his leadership and humanitarian efforts for the residents of Illinois" (HR 0870). The Resolution also congratulated him for the "kindness to all that he has come in contact with," and the many lives he has enriched "through his divine leadership and human compassion" (HR 0870).

The Herman E. Schaalman Chair of Jewish Studies

In the spring of 2008, the Chicago Theological Seminary (CTS) established "The Herman E. Schaalman Chair in Jewish Studies," of which he says "is perhaps the greatest honor of my career. The Chair was meant to recognize his lifetime involvement in interfaith activities and contribution to CTS.

When asked by this writer how the project originated, Schaalman replied, "It's a mystery to me. I know that the CTS president was aware of my friendship with the Pritzkers and that the CTS has a Jewish Board member named Grossman who may have hatched the idea that the Seminary should have a Jewish chair." According to Schaalman's daughter, Susan, the idea to create the chair must have been made when CTS decided to give Schaalman the Graham Taylor Award. Rev. Thistlethwaite, president of CTS, had called to ask her whether she would contact Cindy Pritzker to invite her to be the main speaker at the Graham Taylor Award ceremony: "The reason Thistlethwaite called me (we had never met or spoken before) was that she learned of the Pritzker connection though my father. I didn't realize at the time that the invitation was the first step in an effort to solicit funds from the Pritzker family for a Chair in Jewish Studies." Cindy Pritzker agreed to speak at the event.

The story of how the Chair came to be established began sometime around 1998 soon after Schaalman had come home from the hospital and was recuperating from pneumonia. He received a surprise visit from his good friends Cindy and Bob Pritzker and Rev. Susan Thistlethwaite and assumed they had come to make a sick call. What he did not realize was that they had come to tell him that the Pritzkers had agreed to a challenge grant of one million dollars to establish a Chair in Jewish Studies at the CTS in his honor. CTS had committed to raising another million to recruit and maintain a major scholar in Jewish studies as part of its faculty. Raising the funds, however, was not easy; it took the CTS nearly a decade to come up with the money. "My concern during that time," Schaalman confided, was that I might not live to see the Chair created during my lifetime. As the years went by and I heard nothing further about it, I assumed that the project had fallen through."

> In January 2008, President Thistlethwaite called to tell him that she had the money and that she was planning a ceremony in April to announce that the Chair had been established. The CTS press release stated that the Chair "will be filled by an esteemed Jewish scholar and teacher [who] will have an impact on the Christian world."[464] It would be directed toward teaching both Master's and PhD seminary students the history and interpretation of the Hebrew Scriptures and the "theological and cultural development of Judaism from the destruction of the temple in 70 CE to the present (Chicago Theological Seminary, 2008)."

The CTS also announced that it would use the funds to develop an annual lecture series called "The Herman Schaalman Lecture in Jewish Studies." The purpose of the series is to develop understanding and increase its students' knowledge of the integral relationship of the Jewish and Christian religious traditions. Another goal is show how the history of Christianity led inevitably to the attempt to annihilate the Jews during the *Shoah*. With these new understandings, seminarians will be able to promote a new awareness among their congregants that will "create a warmer and more fruitful relationship between Judaism and Christianity" (Chicago Theological Seminary, 2008).

On April 15, 2008, CTS held a ceremony on its campus to celebrate the establishment of the new Chair. Rev. Thistlethwaite introduced the program by explaining its importance to the seminary, the fact that it was the first ever for a freestanding Protestant seminary and a testament to Schaalman's contribution to interfaith dialogue and Jewish studies. "The Chair" she added, "will carry forward and expand on the center's pioneering work in bringing to the Christian community the treasures of Judaic thought and scripture. ... [By] establishing this chair in perpetuity, we are promoting the continuation of an honest and authentic dialogue between the Christian and Jewish faith traditions" (Chicago Theological Seminary, 2008).

Following her introduction, the distinguished historian, Paula Fredriksen, who presented the Inaugural Address, reinforced the president's assessment of the importance of the Chair, calling it "revolutionary" and long overdue as Christianity's recognition of its interconnection with Judaism. Although other Protestant seminaries in the United States offered Jewish studies, none had a Chair in Jewish studies.

When it was his turn to speak, Schaalman told the assembled guests that the Chair in Jewish Studies was an "historic" event, one that he never thought possible in his lifetime. It was a sign that Christianity had accepted Judaism as a legitimate and valued partner. The creation of the Chair reflected the enormous progress in interfaith relations that had been made since he and his family had narrowly escaped from the Nazi effort to exterminate the Jews.

After more than a half century of receiving accolades, Schaalman, however, continues to maintain that his life has been a surprise to him. He never expected, nor sought, the positions or honors that have been bestowed upon him: "Unlike many others, I have never had any ambition or plan to achieve the status and stature which are now mine." Never sure of his abilities ("I was a B student in Germany and in the seminary"), he was more surprised than anyone else when he was rising on a trajectory that made him one of the most distinguished and honored rabbis of his generation.

Surveying the Course of a Life: Successes and Regrets

So much for the public man. The private man is a son, husband, father, grandfather, and great-grandfather. Schaalman is the firstborn son of parents who inculcated in him the values of Judaism, respect for others, a love of learning, and a desire to teach. Most importantly, they taught him how to be a parent and to create a caring and loving family. They also taught him how to love, not in the grand sense of loving humanity, but how to love an individual: a wife and children and grandchildren. In fact, at the age of ninety-six, he and Lotte are as tender and loving to each other as if they were newlyweds and are not inhibited by modesty from expressing in public the profound love they have for each other.

Reared in Germany before World War II in a distinctly Jewish household, Herman Schaalman was subject to a set of expectations and values that helped form the person he is. Truly, in his case, character is destiny. Although he long ago gave up identifying himself as a German, he still considers himself a "Yekke" because of his penchant for order and punctuality. He is also stubborn and, when pushed, combative, characteristics he learned from his father. At the same time, he is the most gifted of teachers and a gentle and caring human being.

He learned from his parents to be self-effacing and to put the needs of others first. This early training has made it difficult for him to think of himself as a person of importance. He said to this writer many times, "I don't understand why you would be willing to waste so much time and attention on my life." Now, after a lifetime of self-denial, he questions whether he has earned the right to be more assertive. Because Lotte's upbringing is similar, she opposes this self-assertion; she thinks he has no right to draw attention to himself, any more than she will allow it with her own qualities. Schaalman explains, "She believes everything, always, is to be done for what she considers her assignment, her duty." Although she will not take credit for anything she has done, when it comes to touting her husband's achievements, there is no stronger advocate.

Although Schaalman considers himself a modern Reform Jew, he finds that he resonates to aspects of the Torah's Priestly Code, particularly its emphasis on the need to live in a state of ritual purity, *tahor*. Modern readers, Schaalman says, may understand the emphasis on *tahor* as a need to purify our own lives:

> These texts, which are otherwise archaic, are still capable of evoking in the modern reader something wholly unexpected, namely the awareness of the sacredness of life. The original purpose of the rituals of cleansing was to raise awareness of the sacredness of life and to participate in a ritual act that embodies that awareness. They are a way of separating the sacred from the profane and making us conscious that leading a life that partakes of the sacred requires that we behave in certain ways and live according to strict religious values.

In his own effort to lead a life that is *tahor*, he reviews his day to consider how he might have lived it better before he goes to sleep. He sees himself as continually involved in "imperfections" (e. g., "anger and gossip"), events that happen several times a day: "This introspection is a way of understanding my own place in reality, a way of restoring my integrity ... an act of 'untouchness.'" In this way, Schaalman attempts to return to *tahor*, if not fully, which may be impossible, then at least partially. He credits his rabbinic predecessor at Emanuel, Rabbi Felix Levy, for making him aware of the fact that the act of eating means killing something that had life and that when he eats something he needs to thank God for the food:

> Reciting the blessing over food is an acknowledgement of the sacredness of life. I cannot help but be aware that much of the time I am thoughtless of the holiness of life around me. Even in responding to unwanted telephone solicitations or the way I talk to my wife, I am aware that I might have been more considerate.

Another aspect of living in a state of righteousness is facing up to the daily requests for assistance he receives in the mail: "Every year I receive hundreds of requests from organizations I have never heard of. I don't even open them but throw them in the trash." "The entire process," he says, "is commercialized, and the people who send the mail do not even know to whom they are sent. After more than fifty years of getting these envelopes, I can feel whether the envelope contains mail specifically addressed to me." Despite the fact that he knows there is nothing personal about the solicitation, he is still troubled that he cannot be responsive to all the requests: "I have a sense of not doing the right thing, the way we were intended to do the right thing." Although he gives nearly $10,000 annually to about fifty charities, an act that he feels helps "justify" his existence, he is painfully aware that his effort might not be good enough: "I feel sinful when I turn my back on someone who has asked for my help. The only way I can protect myself from this feeling is to desensitize myself. It is a price that is difficult to pay."

To live in a state of *tahor* means to be aware of the positive values of life: "Judaism teaches us that our world is imperfect and to be Jewish is to give intentionality to our lives by participating with God in the ongoing creation of the world. Our tiny sliver of life, however, severely limits the good we can do." This recognition raises questions: "Who am I? What am I doing?" His answer is to remember the *Pirke Avot*[465] and the injunction that we not despair because we can do so little to repair the world; we are required, however, to keep trying.

Schaalman does not think of the many awards he has received as his greatest accomplishment: "If for nothing else, I would like to be remembered for founding OSRUI. When everything is said and done in my life, aside from my own children and whatever I can be for my grandchildren, that may well prove to have been the single most important creation. ... In the longest run, I guess I will be remembered as a grandfather. That's really the only hope I have. That's what I am working on, maybe the most, in a conscious way."

He also hopes to be remembered for his work as Emanuel's rabbi. In 1988, he thought that others might carry on where he left off and might even exceed his contribution: "I wanted to be remembered as a caring, knowledgeable, expounder of Torah. More than that I'd like to be, I guess, remembered as whatever people could see in me as a human being, to try to draw their conclusions from this curious history of a Jew in the twentieth century." Another, though minor achievement, is that his friend and one of the twentieth century's most influential philosophers, Emil Fackenheim, dedicated his book, *Quest for Past and Future* (1967), to him, which Schaalman says, "That I consider to be a real achievement." Another honor he cherishes is the festschrift *The Life of the Covenant* (1987), a collection of essays in his honor by some of the most influential thinkers in Reform Judaism.

In 1987, when he was asked whether he had fulfilled his parents' aspirations and dreams for him, he told Esta Star (1987):

> I think, no, more than think, I know that both my parents were deeply satisfied with the life I led. They had encouraged me to become a rabbi and if not actively, certainly in a way to not point me to any other choice. Although they did not get the opportunity to witness their son's rise in the ranks of Reform Judaism, nor were they aware of his accomplishments, they were proud that their son was a rabbi.

No life is lived without disappointments, and Schaalman's is no exceptions. The early death of his fiancée, Lotte Strauss, who was barely out of her teens, was a major tragedy that altered his life. He still feels the pain of her loss. The greatest disappointment, however, was the fragmentation of his family. When Schaalman left Germany in 1935, he expected he would return when he completed his rabbinic studies.

Soon after he arrived in America, he realized, however, that his survival and that of his family depended on escaping from Germany. After he tried and failed to get them into the United States, they went to Brazil. This separation destroyed his closeness to them, and, to this day, he still feels its effects. The early death of his father, the inspiration and model for his life, was another major blow. Because Adolf had become an Orthodox Jew, it was necessary that he be buried within two days. In the 1950s when long distance travel would have taken days, it was impossible for Schaalman to attend his funeral; far removed from the immediate comfort and consolation of his mother and brothers, he had to go through the grieving process alone.

Another disappointment for Schaalman is that he believes he has not lived up to his potential. "When I was younger," he explains, "I might have played a significant role in shaping the direction of changes that were occurring in the movement. The opportunity to do so came when I was selected to be the CCAR president. From that position, I could have challenged the members early in the 1980s, but I did not." Despite the radical transformation occurring inside him, he said nothing to them about it: "Now, I'm in the evening hours of my life and of my rabbinate. Frankly, had I known what I know now, I might have become a voice beyond what my reach is now."

A major disappointment for him is the fact that he was not able to convince the Reform rabbinate to incorporate the *Shoah* as a foundational experience for Jews in the twentieth century: "Twentieth century Judaism looked at the *Shoah* and decided that it was part of the historical tragedy of the Jewish people. Rabbis and theologians chose not to understand it as a new Sinai." Schaalman refuses to let go of it: "I cannot understand how Judaism can accept it as one more tragedy and not as the basis for a major revision of Judaism." He is equally frustrated by the fact that younger rabbis, those born after 1940, do not address the *Shoah* as the central fact of modern life. "Not to do so," he believes, "is to mislead their congregations." Although his realm of influence on the movement has diminished, Schaalman continues to talk about these issues in his various speaking engagements, his sermons, and to his beloved Torah Study students.

The Schaalmans have one major regret regarding their sense of success as grandparents. As Schaalman puts it, "We did not have an immediate,

Herman (93) and Lotte (94)

traceable influence on their growth that would have allowed us to transmit our values. This difficulty is part of the cost of living in two different communities, particularly during their formative years when I was a
busy professional and could only visit occasionally." The grandchildren
grew up in Milwaukee, some ninety miles from Chicago, and, during
this time, Schaalman's demanding rabbinic responsibilities severely limited his involvement in their lives.

The Schaalmans want to pass on the value of living for the benefit of
others, "a value that is based on an inner reserve that allows one to sub-
jugate one's own desires and wants to the needs and desires of others."
Although the Schaalmans speak of this value as part of their German
upbringing, it is part of their acceptance of their religious calling. In
practicing this value, they have given a lifetime of service not only to the
local Jewish community but also to people who have entered their lives
regardless of their religious affiliation or belief.

As grandparents, the Schaalmans want their grandchildren to know
the names of their ancestors and whatever information they have about

them. Schaalman does not want to make the same mistake he made with his own parents by not asking them questions about their backgrounds, relatives, and ancestors. His only memory of his father's attempt to share family background with him was an excursion to a cemetery in Pappenheim where his grandparents and great-grandparents are buried. Schaalman's father made this trip with his son only when he realized that, once Herman left Germany, he might not return, and he must have felt the need to show his son the burial places of the nine immediate members of his family. It was a lesson his son would not forget. In July 1988, Schaalman took seven-year-old Keren and eleven-year-old Johanna to Germany to visit the graves of his great-grandparents.

One of the Schaalmans' most important concerns is that they are successful in transmitting the larger history of the Jewish people, particularly the *Shoah*: "Having lived through the experience and suffered from its impact, we desperately want to communicate its meaning to our children and grandchildren." Schaalman is all too aware that he has failed to pass his experience along to his younger rabbinic colleagues, whose life experiences have been completely different from his own.[466]

Schaalman's ultimate concern is his doubt that his great, great, great-grandchildren will visit his grave. "Jewish history," he says, "demonstrates that there are no guarantees that geography is sacred. Jewish life in the twentieth century has been so radically dislocated that few Jewish children have the opportunity to visit the graves of their great grandparents. Where my grandchildren are likely to live is anybody's guess." His great grandparents likely would have been puzzled and shocked to learn that their great, great, great-grandchildren would come from Milwaukee to say Kaddish at their graves.

Having said all this about the Schaalmans' sense of their failings as grandparents, this account would not be complete without adding that they are hugely proud of their grandchildren and seem never to tire of boasting about their accomplishments. On many occasions, this writer has heard the Schaalmans speak lovingly of their grandchildren and their career choices. Most important to the Schaalmans is their sense of their grandchildren's abilities and character, and they are confident that they are maturing into adults who are a credit to their family.[467]

Two months after reaching his ninety-fifth birthday Schaalman told his interviewer, "Now that I am approaching the end, it is time for me to reflect on my legacy:"

Will my name and accomplishments survive more than three generations? *Hineni* is an anchor in the float of time. It might stick, perhaps, for some, but only for a generation or two. My children and grandchildren are another anchor, but they are not a community. After them, what? Oblivion? I have a chair in the Christian seminary, but twenty years from now will it have any meaning? It is simply true that we come and we go. Most religions cosmetize this fact. Throughout my career, I have been very conscious of the names on the Yahrzeit list that I held in my hands during every Sabbath service. Who in the congregation knows who these people are? In the brevity of our appearance in the tsunami of time, there is the forlorn hope that something will stick … for a while.

He recalls the fate of Rabbi Felix Levy, his predecessor at Emanuel, who, during his lifetime, was well respected by his congregation and a vital member of the Reform movement. "Now, who among Emanuel's congregants remembers him? From time to time, I mention him in my sermons at Emanuel, but were it not for me, Levy would be forgotten." What will become of his legacy?

His recent stroke and Lotte's hip fracture have seriously compromised their independence. The fact that they require a full-time home-care worker has led Schaalman to a new awareness of his life. On Yom Kippur October 7, 2011, when few were expecting that after his recent stroke he would have the strength to give a sermon, he, nonetheless, delivered it to an alert and expectant congregation. The sermon was a variation of "Where are You?" only this time, Schaalman exposed himself more fully than he ever had before. As if he were speaking to himself, he posed the question: "Have I lived up to the potential of who I might have been?" Of course, the congregation recognized that it was also a question they would have to answer for themselves.

He told the congregation that he remembered having read a story about Rabbi Zusya, a highly respected and well-loved sage, and teacher of Torah.[468] Then he began to speak softly in a voice that had been weakened by his stroke:

> When Rabbi Zusya was lying on his deathbed, as was the custom in those days, his best students were gathered around his bed in order to ease his way out of life and to accompany him in these last moments. … One student noticed something totally unexpected, Zusya was weeping. The students were totally unprepared to see their beloved master in his last moments on earth in tears.
>
> One of his students asked, "Reb Zusya, *are* you weeping?"
>
> Reb Zusya looks at him and says, "Yes, my beloved, I am weeping."
>
> The student asked, "Reb Zusya, *why* are you weeping?"
>
> And Zusya answered, "I am weeping, my beloved son, because I am afraid."
>
> "Reb Zusya, you cannot be afraid; you've lived such a remarkably good life, taught so many students … what are you afraid of?"
>
> "My son, I'm afraid of the question they will ask me before the Tribunal on High."
>
> The student was totally taken aback.
>
> "Reb Zusya, what could possibly frighten *you*? You've lived such a pure and exemplary life."
>
> And Reb Zusya said to him, "I'm not afraid that they will ask me, 'Why were you not like Moses? Why were you not Akiba?' I'm afraid they will ask me, 'Reb Zusya, why weren't you Reb Zusya?'"
>
> And with that he died.

"Why weren't you," Schaalman repeated, "Reb Zusya?" Then he said, "My name is Herman Ezra Schaalman, the son of Adolf and Regina Schaalman, named after two grandfathers." With these intensely personal revelations, he paused to allow the congregation to get the full sense of where he might be taking them. With Zusya's final words, fresh in their minds, they could not help but feel the impact of Schaalman's closing remarks: "Herman Ezra, who are you? Why aren't you Herman Ezra? Why aren't you Herman Ezra?" Then, in ever-lower voice, he asked, "Why not? Why not? Why not?"

It is impossible to capture the sadness of these words. Those of us who have known him for many years could not hide from their meaning: Schaalman was taking stock of who he is and what he has been, and, in the presence of the congregation, questioning whether he had been the person he could have been. Although the sermon was a personal confession, it was designed to stimulate his congregants to ask themselves the same question: have I been, am I, the person I might have been, should have been?

Throughout the sermon, the congregation was riveted to his words, possibly as they never had been before. It is fair to say that the congregants, possibly fearful that this was the last sermon they would hear from their beloved rabbi, wanted and needed to hear his words. They may have identified with Reb Zusya's students, expecting at any moment to hear his master's last words. Rabbi Zedek, who had descended the bimah to hear Schaalman, was so affected by the sermon that he had to excuse himself from resuming the service as he struggled to hold back his tears. Congregants in the front rows were crying, as was Schaalman's daughter Susan, who had been listening to her father's sermons her entire life.

Schaalman was not done reviewing the course of his life and searching for its meaning. As discussed briefly in Chapter 10, "Teaching Torah," the *Discover* magazine article had led him to reconsider everything he knows.[469] In March 2012, Schaalman told his Torah Study students:

> Whatever is considered true today, ten years from now will be considered untrue. A whole new group of physicists in England has concluded that Einstein was wrong and that a whole new vision of reality is necessary. Einstein is only 100 years old and here we are in 2012 questioning his truth and a whole new theory has been developed. If this can happen in a hundred years, the next one will happen in forty years and the next one after that in ten years or maybe three. These new discoveries open up new possibilities of understanding reality that is so utterly foreign to anything we have known, and they call into question our most basic understandings of ourselves. I don't know how to think of myself. If I think of myself as 146 pounds, ninety-six years old next month, as having come out of a microscopic ball and

microscopic wiggler, I just don't understand it. I can say it because I have finally gotten myself to understand my beginning, but does it really say anything?"

Then, changing course, he raised the question of whether science ultimately tells us the answers to our most important truths, our most important values:

Science gives no answers. It describes what is there. It doesn't tell you how it is, why it is. I think of the big bang, this huge, huge new discovery that overwhelmed us all. We now know when the universe began. *Do we?* Although science tells us that the universe came into being through an initial explosion, it doesn't tell us what happened before the explosion … what caused the explosion?

The more I read, the more I get of this tangential information, I try to digest it to see what it does for me. But I'm just bewildered. There was a time when I knew what everything was. I was invited to bless the young Bar Mitzvah boy today, and, as I was thinking about it, I thought of saying, 'Eighty-three years ago I stood in a similar place, and I knew that I was going to be a rabbi. It was an important and major event in my life. The world was so simple then. When I think back I knew how to prepare myself for my Bar Mitzvah. I knew what my teacher was like, my cantor. I knew why I was chanting. I knew why my parents thought I should do this. I was the oldest of three boys and they all had to undergo this same ritual eventually. I knew what it meant to my extended family, my father's brothers and sisters, my mother's family. I knew all that and the world was so solid and so totally predictable. I knew there would be sixty people coming to lunch on Shabbos because my parents had evacuated the furniture in their bedroom because they had to accommodate so many people. The world was simple.

One of the real paradoxes we face is how to use the past. We have the past in us. It has not simply passed away. I remember what it was like when I was thirteen years old standing on the bimah, how my knees shook. I can't just be in this moment. I have all this past in me and I have this past [Torah Study] in me too. And I want to have this past in me because without a past I'm not really much of a human. I'm trying to live with a valid past, which made me who I am. I can't step out of it; I don't want to step out of it. Fortunately, some of my past is so precious to me that I think of it often, incessantly, it seems. And yet, I'm confronted with a present that seems so frequently to be unrelatable to this past.

Concluding Observations

As this book ends, Herman Schaalman is ninety-six and Lotte ninety-seven. Their health is deteriorating, but they are fighting to survive. Unlike so many other couples who have spent a lifetime together and long ago saw the flame of their passion slowly fade out, the Schaalmans' burns bright. To see them share an affectionate kiss or hug is to see two people for whom that flame is very much alive.

He and his brothers have had the good fortune of living long and successful lives. Although his brother Freddie died in November 2011, Schaalman is blessed that his brother Ernst is still alive and that he has many nieces and nephews in Israel and Brazil. Lotte is not so fortunate; she has no surviving family and feels the pain of their absence. Her loving and attentive children and grandchildren help make up for that loss. She and Susan talk by phone daily and see each other frequently. Michael and Bobbi now visit almost every weekend. The family celebrates all the major Jewish holidays together. Although Lotte used to make all the family holiday dinners, in the last few years, she has turned over that responsibility to her daughter-in-law. The grandchildren, who now live in Denver, visit their parents and grandparents several times a year. When they are not in town, they speak to their grandparents by phone.

As Rabbi Emeritus, Schaalman still leads services at Emanuel when Rabbi Zedek is out of town, gives occasional sermons, and shares the bimah with Zedek for all major and minor holidays. Zedek, as a sign of his love and respect for his senior colleague, also gives Schaalman the responsibility for the Yom Kippur sermon, the most important sermon of the year. Schaalman continues to teach a regular Saturday morning Torah Study, even while Zedek conducts his own session. Not only is Zedek not threatened that Schaalman is infringing on his turf, he is delighted that Schaalman is willing and able to continue to make meaningful contributions to Emanuel.

Although in the 1950s and '60s, Schaalman played an important role in promoting theological discussion in the Reform movement, he occupies only a peripheral position in its theological revival. Instead of publishing his views, he chose to offer them through dialogue, lecture, and sermon. Occasionally, he puts his evolving thoughts on paper, but, typically, only in response to a specific request. Were it not for Anita Rifkin, who insisted on recording his thinking late in his life, there would be no substantial written record of his ideas. However, once he turned ninety, a rabbinic student and longtime friend, Ann Folb, chose him as the subject for her rabbinic thesis.

Schaalman is recognized as one of the leading figures in Reform Judaism. Here at home in Chicago, he is one of the most respected rabbis ever to serve the Jewish community in the more than sixty years he has been here, and, despite his issues with contemporary Reform Judaism, he is held in high esteem by its leaders. Rabbi Richard G. Hirsch, retired president of the World Union of Progressive Judaism and one of the most respected Reform rabbis, offered that Schaalman was someone he respected for his interest in scholarship and his rock-solid ethical principles: "These characteristics not only made Schaalman an outstanding rabbi but also had a significant influence on my own rabbinic values" (Hirsch, R. G., 2010). Rabbi Steven Hart called Schaalman "a rabbi's rabbi," by which he meant that when rabbis look for rabbinic models, Schaalman is the go-to rabbi (Hart, S., June 6, 2006). Rabbi Hart's evaluation echoes a wide chorus of similar claims stretching back to Howard Hall, the non-Jewish business tycoon in Cedar Rapids, who adopted the young rabbi as "his rabbi" to Cardinal Bernardin's statement, "Herman, when you are in the room with me, I feel particularly at peace" (Schaalman, H. E., 2007, p. 262).

As of 2012, he continues to be solicited as a scholar-in-residence or a keynote speaker at important conferences. His creativity is in full bloom. At the age of ninety-six, he continues to have new insights into theological matters and to refine his theology. In the last few years, he has taken his already radical theology beyond bounds that astonish him and his most devoted students. He has even left some of his retired rabbinic colleagues wanting to know more about the direction in which he is going.

To appreciate Schaalman as a rabbi and a theologian, it is helpful to refer to Rabbi Eugene Borowitz's (1998) notion of what it means to be an authentic and credible theologian. After the Holocaust, he writes, theology can only be meaningful if it represents a commitment to both thought and action. Theologians can no longer speak and write about theology if they are not living it: "Not all men who think bright thoughts ... actually live by them ... the Jewish theologian should live his understanding of Judaism" (p. 56). Although not written with Borowitz's words in mind, *Hineni* and Schaalman's subsequent theological insights exemplify the fusing of a way of thinking with a way of life. They reflect not only the life he has lived in the shadow of the Holocaust but also the remarkable person and rabbi that he is.

A basic premise of Judaism is that the world is imperfect, that the meaning and purpose of our existence is to complete creation, to fix it, as it were. It is the end toward which Schaalman has directed his entire life, the source of his commitment, his teaching, and, most importantly of all, his relationship with others. It is his *raison d'être*. Perhaps, there is no better way to convey Schaalman's sense of life than to hear it in his own words:

> To me, life is a continuous excitement, and so far, an unalloyed joy to live, not saying that there aren't times and incidents and events that deeply grieve or challenge everything I am committed to do or to be, but over and over again, I know that I am in the total stance of unremitting gratitude to the fact that the miracle that I am operates and lives within the miracle that the world is and that therefore that mystery that I sense behind it all and through it all which we call God is beckoning, asking for more, never satisfied that I've done all that I could do or should do. And so it goes on I hope, as long as there is strength and life. (Tichenor, L., 2002)

Epilogue

"This book [Deuteronomy] has never impressed me this way.
Maybe, at the age of ninety-six, I'm just waking up."
Rabbi Herman E. Schaalman, September 29, 2012

Just as I thought I had put the finishing touches on this book, Rabbi Schaalman surprised me again. It was no ordinary surprise but one that would recast his theology in a way that is more radical than anything he has offered so far. In my effort to represent his theology, I have argued that he is at the fringe of mainstream Reform Judaism. In this Epilogue, I need to say that he has taken a giant leap and is no longer on its fringe.

In his Torah Study sessions a few weeks prior to Yom Kippur 2012, Schaalman revealed to his students a new insight into the Blessings and Curses spelled out in Deuteronomy 27:15—28:69. In Moses' last few hours of life, he lashes out at the people for what he perceives are their vices and sins and heaps on them a torrent of dreadful curses. Never before, Schaalman told his students so personally, had he read these passages as a devastating critique of the character of the Israelites and, by extension, their descendants—one so devastating that he now rejects it categorically: "Seventy-five percent of this text is no longer meaningful to me."

This new understanding set the stage for Schaalman's Yom Kippur sermon. On September 25, 2012, he told his beloved Emanuel Congregation that he rejects the tone and substance of the holiday and all it stands for. It does not reflect the Judaism he has embraced. We live in a constantly changing and ever-evolving world, and, in order to remain relevant to that world, Judaism needs to open itself to its miraculous nature and embrace its mysteries: "There is so much of the miraculous, of the mysterious that beckons us to be open to it, and by openness to be shaped and become a new kind of humans who are living at this cutting-edge civilization of ours." He proposed that this day of lamentation should be completely revised as a day of celebration that would be given to reflection and enlightenment.

Here's what he said:

KOL NIDRE. Two words that have the strange evocative power to summon us to attendance and to attention … [whose music] penetrates deeply our inner life … and evoke within us depths that we are totally usually unaware of. The melody of Kol Nidre is one of the most beautiful and significant expressions of Jewish chanting. Its text, however, is forgettable. Its authorship is unknown. Over the centuries it was a matter of dispute among our sages, any number of whom refused to allow this text to be chanted or read in their congregations or communities, and which often had been used by those who hate us as proof texts of the unworthiness of the Jews who could not be relied on, who could not be trusted, who were not fit to be part of the human community.

I've often wondered how this text got into a Reform Machzor and why we use it to this day, even though we are protected. Fortunately, most of us don't understand the Aramaic texts in their original meaning.

But you know it gets worse. You and I have read part of the liturgy here tonight whose leitmotif is: we are so bad, we are sinners, we need to plead for mercy and forgiveness. I don't know about you; I'm not that kind of sinner. I don't need to plead to someone else for forgiveness. I do lots of things wrong, and I'm aware of them, and I try to do good or to atone for them in my own way every day.

Why do we need 10 days in the Jewish year, starting with Rosh Hashanah for forgiveness, of repentance? What's the matter with us? Are we so sinful? Yes, of course. There was a group of ultra-Orthodox rabbis who a few years ago took out a full page ad in the *New York Times*, in which they clearly stated that the Jewish people were so bad that God did right in killing a million-and-a-half Jewish children and four-and-a-half people, women and men. A despicable statement. A repulsive statement. That's not who we are.

Of course, that leads to the question, how come these kind of ideas, this tone, rooted itself so deeply in our tradition? Where does it come from? Well, we don't have to look far. Just pick up the Torah, as you should regularly. And there in *Bereshit*, in Genesis, you will read that barely ten generations after the Creation of the world and its climactic achievement in the creation of Adam, God came to the conclusion that the people were so rotten, so evil, that He sent the Flood to destroy them all, allowing only a small group of questionable Jewish characters to survive, together with a passel of animals.

There is a strange kind of a tone in many passages, particularly in *Devarim*, in Deuteronomy, that are so enormously intense in their curses of the Jewish people, simply because it is assumed we deserve them because we will never live up to the program that has been set for us. It was, apparently and still is, unworkable, unattainable, too idealistic.

In the beginning of the Rabbinic, Talmudic period, the rabbis had the absolutely unbelievable task of trying to rebuild and somehow heal the Jewish community, the Jewish people, that had been torn apart, that had no more country, no more capital, no more temple, no government, no judges, no structures left. And the people soon spread all over the globe, as far as India, Great Britain, the Rhineland, and the southern tip of Africa.

Two of the greats of that period of rebuilding were Hillel and Shammai. Two of the greatest of rabbinic teachers that our tradition had produced and whose works and teachings have been enshrined in the teachings of the Talmud. They were such famous and attractive teachers that there were many students who flocked to them and so they are known by the special terms, Beit Shammai and Beit Hillel, the house, the community of Hillel and Shammai.

Now the two of them were totally different characters: Hillel gentle, conciliatory, sensitive; Shammai rather rough and rejectionist, but they talked to each other. They studied with each other. They argued with each other. And so we learn from the

Talmud that the schools of these rabbis engaged in the very special proposition, the proposition that somebody proposed: Did God do right in creating Adam? Just think of the chutzpah of asking that question when you think of the traditional background from which they came: Did God do right in creating the human species?

And the story goes that they discussed this subject, not every day, for two years. And since they had not come to an agreement, they decided to take a vote. Very Jewish. And so they took a vote on the proposition: was God right in having created the human species or did He make a mistake? And you will be surprised: the vote was negative. They agreed that God would have done better not to have created humans. But then I suppose they were aware of how radical this conclusion was so they added a postscript: *yepashpesh b'ma'asov*, "let us be meticulous in our actions."

And now another Jewish story, which on first hearing sounds charming, really one of those lovely stories that was first told and then became part of the traditional lore that has come down to this day. It's the story of the *lamed vov-niks*. You may not remember that there were no numbers in the Hebrew alphabet, only letters. Therefore, every letter became a number. So "*lamed*" is the number thirty, "*vov*" is number six. And this story deals with thirty-six, in this instance, saintly Jews. They are so saintly that they do not know themselves that they are part of this elite group. Nor does anybody else, but because of them, so the story goes, the world continues to exist. If they were not there, there wouldn't be a world anymore.

And that story of the thirty-six saintly, unknown, unknowable saintly people in every generation existed down to this time of ours when, according to Andre Schwartzbart, the writer of *Last of the Just*, almost unreadable because of its depth of misery and pain, the last of these *lamed vov-niks* was killed by the Nazis. And so according to Schwartzbart there is no more protection. The charm is gone. We of the world are now on our own. There are no more *lamed vov-niks* around who guarantee that we can last and give us a hope and a future. But, again, we are not worthy to survive; we are so bad that we are doomed. That is the inescapable condemnation of us, as the implication of this tale of the thirty-six. Well, if that is so, you will perhaps understand why I so totally reject the tone of Yom Kippur, the text of Yom Kippur, and of this whole period of selechot, of prayers of forgiveness.

So what would I do? Obviously, if you think of such a radical thought that I put before you, you want to have a little help, a backup if possible. Well, I found a word in one of the books of that great sage, Abraham Joshua Heschel, a survivor of the *Shoah*, whom the Hebrew Union College brought to this country, thus saving him from death. Heschel had an extraordinary felicity of using the English language, which was not his mother tongue, and coined this, to me, unforgettable phrase, "Radical Amazement." Radical Amazement, amazement that goes to the to the root, not just a casual amazement, not just an occasional amazement, but really a total attitude, a total devotion to amazement, amazement to the *radix*.

And so, I look at myself and there are my nails. They already grew when I was in the womb of my mother, and they are still growing. Why? In fact, they grow in such a way that, according to our custom, I have to have them trimmed regularly. My hair, I also was born with hair, so it was already in my mother's womb. So I also have to have it trimmed on a regular basis. And what about the trillions of bacteria in my intestinal tract that make sure that I function day after day? And what about this muscle that was shaped in the sixth or seventh week when I was formed in my mother's body, that has pumped billions of times ever since—and so far— without fail to make sure that even the outermost aspects of my physical being will receive liquid in channels of various sizes, some so tiny that only a molecule can get through. Radical amazement, indeed.

I am, and of course not just I, everyone sitting here and everyone you ever knew or met, and all humans are living miracles, mysterious agglomerations of powers and functions, and I didn't even talk about my brain. Two and a half pounds of mass, with billions of events of electro-chemical nature, continuing all the time, every second whether I'm awake or asleep.

And then we learned in the 19th century that light travels at 186,000 miles per second, which means that in a second light travels seven-and-a-half times around the equator of our globe. And about a year or so ago our instruments received light that had travelled 12.3 billion years to get to us. Radical amazement.

Or of course even equally unbelievable is the fact that tiny emanations of limitless power were released from an explosion, a Big Bang, creating as a side effect the universe in which we find ourselves, in which we know only about fifteen to twenty percent because it is visible, because the vast mass it is made of has not yet become known to us. It's "dark mass," a joke, isn't it? "Dark mass," "dark energy," but it's the best we can do because we live within a totally, so far, unknowable agglomeration of functions and relationships of elements.

Why tell you all of this, when perhaps most of you know all this anyway? Because I would like to see Reform Judaism reform the tradition and have a day of reflection, reorientation, redirection, a day when we get together, and not for twelve hours either, because nobody today has the *sitzfleisch* to sit on a chair that long. Nor is it necessary. Nor do most of you stay for twelve hours anyway, as you yourselves know. Tomorrow, in the afternoon there will be an exodus here, and after Yiskor the same phenomenon.

But a day devoted to this reflection of who we are, and where we are and what is happening in us, around us. We could summon the best talents. The most exquisite thinkers and researchers and creators to bring us up to date. We could get the best artists to tell us about their music. We could have poets come and read us their latest or best poems that bring insight into the human condition. This could be done nationally by a commission that would have access to anyone and everyone in this country, whether it's Pearlstein, Spielberg, or Elie Wiesel, or whomever you can think of. And we can be given all of this with the modern means of electronic communication. There is so much that this modern life of ours gives to us and the questions it poses for us that somehow or other all of us would be fascinated to be instructed in. That is the kind of a major religious holiday that I would like to see us have.

And if anybody were to do that, why not Reform Judaism? Aren't we supposedly the cutting edge? Maybe. Yes, there is so much of the miraculous, of the mysterious that beckons us to be open to it, and by openness to be shaped and become a new kind of humans who are living at this cutting-edge civilization of ours. Just think of what your great grandchildren will know and how they will think of us as cavemen because the progress of the human mind and human capacity is so astonishing, so rapid, so extensive in our time. Radical amazement, indeed.

Amen.

Endnotes

Chapter 1: The Early Years

1 Frank Metzger, the longest continuing member of the class, told me that in the forty years he had been attending Schaalman's Torah Study, he had never seen any of Rabbi Zedek's predecessors as friendly and collegial toward Schaalman or his students. Metzger's observation points to the deep love and affection Zedek has for Schaalman, which this writer has witnessed on many occasions over the last decade.

2 Since 1950, when Hebrew Union College merged with the Jewish Institute of Religion, it has been known as Hebrew Union College-Jewish Institute of Religion (HUC-JIR). When reference is made to the seminary after 1950, it will be referred to as HUC-JIR.

3 According to Michael Meyer (1988), by the end of the nineteenth century, German Reform Judaism had not spread beyond Berlin where it was confined to Berlin's Reform Congregation (p. 225). In the United States, however, Reform had taken hold and was spreading in major cities and surrounding suburbs. By the end of the twentieth century, it had become that largest denomination of American Jews. The *Encyclopaedia Judaica*, however, tells a different story of Reform Judaism in Germany. Far from being confined in Berlin, by 1908 the movement had created the Union for Liberal Judaism in Germany (*Vereiningung Fuer Das Liberale Judentum in Deutschland*), which included Reform communities in Germany's major cities and rabbis from the Union of Liberal Rabbis in Germany, an organization that had been founded in 1899. In its early days, the Union for Liberal Judaism had 6,000 members, but by 1933, it had grown to 10,000.

4 "Shlomo" is a common male name that in Hebrew means "God's peace."

5 In Simpletoremember.com, this pogrom is referred to as an "expulsion."

6 Schaalman found out about him through a strange coincidence. When he was elected president of the Central Conference of American Rabbis in 1981, an announcement of his election appeared in the *Aufbau*, a

German-Jewish newspaper published in New York City. A woman who read the paper wrote to Schaalman to ask whether he was related to another Schaalman, a Hebrew teacher in the German town of Eichstadt, a small community in Bavaria of no more than 5,000 to 8,000 people. Her parents had brought this teacher to the town to educate her and her sisters and brothers.

7 Cf. the *Gedenkbuch— Opfer der Verfolgung der Juden unter der nationalsozialistischen Gewaltherrschaft in Deutschland 1933-1945*, Bundesarchiv, German National Archives, Koblenz (1986); and Yad Vashem: *The Central Database of Shoah Victims' Names* (2012). A different account of Melania's birthplace comes from a "List of Deportation from France," which states that she was born in Muggensturm, Germany. The List gives these additional details: "During the war she was in France. Deported with Transport 17 from Drancy, Camp, France to Auschwitz Birkenau, Camp on 10/08/1942." The "List of Deportation from France" is found in *Le Memorial de la deportation des juifs de france, Beate et Serge Klarsfeld*, Paris 1978 (Yad Vashem: *The Central Database of Shoah Victims' Names*, 2012). Schaalman, when he filled out his "Page of Testimony" for Yad Vashem, had a slightly different account. He wrote that she died in Gurs in 1943.

8 The term "*Shoah*" will be used interchangeably with "Holocaust." Schaalman prefers the term "*Shoah*," which more fully represents the horror the Nazis inflicted on the Jews. According to Yad Vashem's *Shoah* Resource Center (2003), "*Shoah*" is a biblical word, which, since the Middle Ages, has been used to mean "destruction." As early as the 1940s, "*Shoah*" became the standard Hebrew term for the murder of European Jewry. The word "Holocaust" did not come into use until the 1950s. In its Greek derivation, it means the "whole burnt sacrificial offering to a god." Schaalman refuses to use the term because, "in no sense, is the murder of more than one million children under the age of ten, a sacrifice to the gods."

9 Nor was either grandfather still living by the time of Herman's Bar Mitzvah.

10 Schaalman compares their situation to that of Germans in the United States who, during World War II, were afraid to speak German on the streets because they might draw attention to themselves.

11 Michael A. Meyer (1998), Adolph S. Ochs Professor of Jewish History, HUC-JIR/Cincinnati, writes that by 1925, ninety percent of the 108,000 foreign-born Jews in Germany were from Eastern Europe. Most of them, approximately 75,000, had settled in major cities.

12 Yad Vashem The Holocaust Martyrs' and Heroes' Remembrance Authority. (2012).

13 Although many German Jews were enthusiastic about the war and fought for Germany, others were critical. History records the futile efforts of Walter Rathenau, an influential Jewish citizen, to persuade the German Chancellor, Theobald von Bethmann-Hollweg, that Germany's participation in the war would not be in its best interests, that it would have disastrous consequences for Germany (Folb, 2007). His advice was ignored. Later, he was assassinated by right-wing extremists as part of their extensive effort to eliminate left wing voices from political discussion. He was accused of being "the Jewish prince" who had sabotaged the war effort (Folb, 2007).

14 Interesting is the fact that the Jewish community had no Jewish neighborhoods.

15 The document, which Schaalman has in his possession, does not identify the student by name.

16 Egon Friedell was a key figure in the extraordinary flowering of Viennese culture between the two world wars. Written during the 1920s, *A Cultural History of the Modern Age* describes events from the Renaissance to the age of imperialism. It demonstrated the intellectual universality that Friedell saw as guarantor of the continuity and regeneration of European civilization. The book has been translated into seven languages (Janik, A., 2009).

17 SA in German "*Sturmabteilung*" and translated as "Storm Detachment." "Also known as Storm Troopers and Brown Shirts, they were the uniformed and armed political combat troops of the Nazi Party. The SA was the predominant Nazi terror and propaganda arm from 1923 until the 'Night of the Long Knives' in 1934, when the leadership was killed off on Hitler's orders. They continued to exist throughout the Third Reich but were of little political significance after 1934. The SA numbered 15,000 in 1923, 400,000 by 1933, and 2.5 million by 1934" (Michael and Doerr, 2002, p. 391).

18 In 1933, von Epp became governor of Bavaria and in 1935 was promoted to the rank of general. Although a close ally of Hitler, he later participated in an uprising against him.

19 When in 1931, the Nazis moved into this building, Hitler named it "the Brown House." Formerly known as the Barlow Palace, the building "quickly became known throughout the world as a symbol for the *Fuehrer* and his movement" (Bouhler, 1938, p. 4).

20 The Nazis called the celebration *"Machtergreifung"* (Stern, 1983, p. 15).

21 Although Jews were suffering economically, they were relatively better off financially than their German counterparts, a fact did not escape the notice of the non-Jewish population (Barkai, 1998c). According to Alon (2002), "anti-Semitism was even more ferocious in the years of hyperinflation 1919–1923 than in 1933, the year Hitler finally came to power" (p. 368). The increasing anti-Semitism produced mounting anti-Semitic boycotts that affected Jewish business owners who in return had to lay off Jewish office and factory workers and white-collar workers. These skilled and unskilled workers, along with university graduates, were experiencing higher rates of unemployment than their German counterparts.

22 The influence of his rigorous education is apparent today. His study of classical Greek and Latin enables him to impress his Torah Study students with etymological derivations of English words.

23 According to Barkai (1998,1998b), in 1925, thirty-two percent of Jewish women between the ages of 15 and 65 were in the workforce, a rate higher than that of their German counterparts in the same age group.

24 Freddie also reported having memories of a "wonderful" childhood (Schaalman, F. L., 2008).

25 Most of Munich was Catholic, followed by Baptists and Lutherans; Jews were a small minority.

26 Many years later, he faced this same issue when his close friend, Cardinal Bernardin, who was dying of cancer, told him that he was happy to return home to his Lord.

27 Ernst may have been born with breathing problems. Schaalman remembers one incident when Ernst was still an infant. He turned blue while he was in his crib.

28 Adolf frequently used a walking stick, as most gentlemen did, and had a collection of four or five of them of varying elegance.

29 Freddie Schaalman (2008) reported that she was studying medicine.

30 Jewish women were not admitted to German universities until the beginning of the twentieth century. Before that, education was seen as unfeminine. Women could audit courses if the professor and the Ministry of Education gave their assent. In 1901, Baden was the first state to

officially allow women to matriculate. In 1904, Munich, Erlangen, and Würzburg admitted women, Tübingen in 1905, and Leipzig in 1907. Prussia, the last state to admit women, did not allow them to matriculate until 1908 (Kaplan, M. A., 1991, footnote, p. 137).

31 The fact that the Schaalmans celebrated Shabbat was not unusual. According to Barkai (1998c), for Liberal German families Shabbat "was often spent in the bosom of the family" (p. 67).

32 Although it was a historically significant landmark, as one of his first acts when he came to power, Hitler had the synagogue torn down. He could not tolerate it because it blocked his view from the artists club to which he belonged.

33 Schaalman suggests that this practice may have been related to the Lutheran practice of Bible study at home, though Bavaria was largely Catholic and the Schaalmans had no Lutheran friends.

34 *Shavuot* commemorates the anniversary of the day God gave the Torah to the entire Israelite nation assembled at Mount Sinai. It comes seven weeks after the second day of Passover. This counting of days and weeks (the counting of the *Omer*) expresses the anticipation and desire of the Israelites for the Giving of the Torah. On Passover, the Jewish people were freed from their enslavement to Pharaoh and on *Shavuot* they were given the Torah and became a nation committed to serving God (Richman, C., 2000–2011).

35 The last time Schaalman visited his mother in 1986, prior to her death at the age of ninety-three, she prepared his much-beloved potato salad. Schaalman is proud of the fact that his wife Lotte now makes potato salad that rivals his mother's.

36 Although Reform Judaism originated in Germany, for the Schaalmans "there was no such thing as Reform Judaism."

37 "*Balabatim*" is a Yiddish word meaning persons of high standing.

38 Freddie remembers being asked to fill in as Chazzan after his Bar Mitzvah, typically on short notice. He might be called on Friday to lead services that evening. Other possible substitutes needed several days to prepare the Torah reading, but for him, "it was no problem" (Schaalman, F. L., May 13, 2008).

39 According to Folb (2007), he would be following in the footsteps of the other rabbis on his mother's side.

40 Barkai (1998b) maintains that German-Jewish families that had lived in Germany for hundreds of years had developed strong family traditions, and this was certainly true of the Schaalmans and one that Schaalman attempted to transplant to America as part of his own family life.

41 Founded in 1870 as the *Hochschule für die Wissenschaft des Judentums*, the school was dedicated to scientific work. Later, it became a seminary for Liberal Judaism and changed its name to *Lehranstalt Für Die Wissenschaft Des Judentums*. Nonetheless, it maintained its scientific orientation, which meant that Judaism was studied from a "scientific" perspective, "freed as far as possible from the rancor of theological disputes and practical politics" (Deutsch & Magnes, p. 1). According to Barkai (1998c), the school was part of a nineteenth century development of similar institutions of higher learning designed to meet the needs of Jews seeking a secularized, scientific basis for their religion. It also had the distinction as the only German Jewish seminary for Liberal Jewish rabbis.

42 Early in the 1930s, the Nazis had infiltrated the universities. At many of them, the majority of students were Nazis sympathizers. Their associations frequently "terrorized the lecture halls with anti-Semitic disturbances." To protect their careers, many of their professors joined the Nazi party (Folb, 2007, p. 52).

43 According to M. A. Meyer (2000), from 1935 to 1942 HUC in Cincinnati rescued eleven Jewish scholars from Nazi persecution, had revived the careers for some who had already left Germany, and had saved the lives of a few others. Meyer (1988) also claims that the "number of refugees from the Liberal Seminary in Berlin … made up 12 percent" of HUC's student body (p. 312).

44 According to one of today's foremost liturgical scholars, Rabbi Lawrence A. Hoffman (2003), Elbogen's 1913 publication, *Jewish Liturgy: A Comprehensive History*, was a "landmark volume … [that] has yet to be equaled, and probably never will be."

45 Very likely, Fruedenthal's advice was based on his visit to Hebrew Union College in 1927 that was part of a trip to Cincinnati to attend his sister's wedding. Like Herman's parents, Fruedenthal was a "Liberal Jew" and more open to Reform Judaism. He may also have been more aware of the dangers of Nazism than Herman's father, who continued to deny the seriousness of the situation.

46 Alfred Wolf (1986) offers a slightly different account, "As I remember it, Professor Elbogen was preparing to have you and me draw lots. Before

he was able to complete the task, Heinz Schneemann burst into the room with the news that he was unable to accept the scholarship."

47 According Lorge and Zola (2006), while Schaalman was a student at the *Hochschule für die Wissenschaft des Judentums,* he "was one of several rabbinical students whom Rabbi Leo Baeck sent to Cincinnati, Ohio, to study at Hebrew Union College in 1936" (p. 57). This information contradicts Schaalman's own account of the year (1935) and the means by which he was selected to come to America and attend HUC.

48 The video is available on Youtube at http://www.youtube.com/ watch?v=tqZSFVe3NEo. Asked who did the recording, Schaalman was surprised to learn it was there and could not recall the event.

Chapter 2: Coming to America

49 Although May had never been to America, his many novels about the country were read worldwide. As a result, his writing helped shape the way the world thought about America, and particularly the way Germans thought about it (Tutush, p. 1). In his autobiography, *More Unfinished Business,* Plaut (1997) reported that May's books provided him the same view of "the mysterious continent" full of "untamed Indians" (pp. 108–109). An interesting side note is that when Hitler was a boy, he was "overwhelmed" by May's novels. The books had such a powerful claim on his attention that his grades suffered (Ryback, December 24, 2008). During the war, he told his generals to study May's books and even had a special edition issued for soldiers at the front. He considered Winnetou, the Indian chief of May's tales, a master of "tactical finesse and circumspection" and a model for his own love of cunning tactics and surprises. He told Albert Speer that, when he was "faced by seemingly hopeless situations, he would still reach for these stories [because] they gave him courage [much as] works of philosophy for others or the Bible for elderly people" (Ryback, December 24, 2008).

50 The *Nuremburg Laws* were a turning point in the downward spiral for German Jews. Kaelter, who returned to Germany for a visit a year later, wrote that radical changes had taken place: "more restrictions on Jews, rampant storm trooper violence, concentration camps growing in numbers and in atrocities. It was a totally different country" (p. 58). Nevertheless, he did not detect "pervasive" fear in the Jewish community: "We believed that Nazism would pass" (p. 58). This was the same perspective that kept Adolf Schaalman from believing that the end had come for

German Jews and accounts, in part, for his refusal to leave the following year when his son returned for a visit.

51 Kaelter (1997) and Plaut (1981) report that they sailed from Le Havre (Plaut, p. 47).

52 Plaut (1981) wrote that he went on the *Aquitania*. His father bought him a roundtrip ticket for $148 (p. 47).

53 Plaut (1981) claimed that four of them had a "smattering of English," but Leo had none (p. 48).

54 Kaelter (1997) referred to this group of Irish young people as "wonderful [and] livened up the place with lots of singing" (p. 45).

55 Plaut (1981) wrote of his surprise when he saw a man casually throw away the newspaper he had been reading. Concerned that the man had absentmindedly discarded the paper, Plaut picked it up and ran after him to return it. The man realized that Plaut must have been a "green-horn" and laughed at the gesture. He left Plaut standing there holding the paper. This experience, Plaut wrote, was his introduction to the "world of waste and obsolescence" (p. 51). In Germany, the paper would have been "recycled" for a variety of uses such as a wrapping, a lining for shoes and windows in cold weather, kindling for stoves, and toilet paper.

56 Kaelter (1997) explains that Glueck had studied in Germany and therefore spoke a "well-accented" version of the language. Kaelter (1997) identifies the host as Dr. and Mrs. Iglauer. Plaut (1981) writes that they were served breakfast by Glueck's wife Helen (p. 52).

57 In his autobiography, *Unfinished Business*, Plaut (1981) gives a different account. He claimed that reporters met them at the train station. Because the students were the first immigrants to arrive in Cincinnati, they were "news." Plaut also confirms that they were afraid to give the reporters much information because of the potential repercussions at home (p. 51).

58 During the school year, the dormitory served as the center of student life. The college provided the students with the luxury of "servants," black men, who worked as waiters, cleaned their rooms, and took care of their laundry.

59 By virtue of his superior English language skills, Plaut served as spokesperson for the other student refugees.

60 Cf. Endnote 3.

61 HUC records show Schaalman's name with the German spelling of a double "n."

62 Folb (2007) mistakenly identifies this woman as Rabbi Philipson's wife. The difficulty here is that by 1935, she and her husband had been married nearly 50 years, and both must have been at least 70!

63 Plaut (1981) described them as communities of hope and "places of instruction and spiritual security" for people who otherwise led "constricted lives" (p. 55).

64 Kaelter (1997) writes that the situation of Jews in large numbers turning up for High Holy Day services was also true in Berlin: "There were always more Jews on Rosh Hashanah and Yom Kippur than the synagogues could accommodate …." (p. 58).

65 Rabbi Richard G. Hirsch (2010) told this writer that when he entered HUC in 1944, he "felt it was goyish: the Classical Reform services were goyish and the food service was not kosher."

66 At a dinner in the home of this writer, he asked Schaalman if he would reveal the word. The rabbi turned to his wife and said, "It's a word you never heard before." The biographer then asked if he would divulge the first letter of the word. The letter was "c." Kaelter (1997) relates one of his comical experiences involving a mix up of English words. Lillian Waldman had discovered him in the hall with a pocketbook he had taken from a young woman who was visiting a friend. He had taken the purse as a joke, but when Waldman confronted him, he said, "Oh, Mrs. Waldman, I just raped her" (p. 50). He intended to say "I just robbed her. When I discovered my error, I was so mortified that I hid in my room for the next two hours" (p. 50).

67 In 1941, Silberman, who had only been ordained the day before Schaalman, officiated at Schaalman's wedding. Their friendship continued when both rabbis were in Chicago. When their schedules permitted, they studied together and became best friends. Many years later, when Schaalman called him in 2008, he discovered that the phone had been disconnected. "When I found out that Silberman had died, I was shocked that none of the many Jewish publications I receive had made any mention of it."

68 Cohon was chair of HUC's Theology Department from 1923-1956. He was a prolific lecturer and author of numerous articles, monographs and books, including *The Theology of the Union Prayer Book* (1928), *The Place of Jesus in the Religious Life of His Day* (1929), *Christianity and Judaism*

Compare Notes (with Dr. Harris Franklin Rall, 1928), *What We Jews Believe* (1931), and *Judaism-A Way of Life* (1948). Under the auspices of the Central Conference of American Rabbis, he also edited the *Revised Union Haggadah* (1923) and the *Rabbi's Manual* (1928). In 1937, he formulated the *Guiding Principles of Reform Judaism*; from 1940 to 1945 served on the committee for the revision of the two volumes of the *Union Prayer Book* and, in 1951, was on the committee for the revision of the *Union Home Prayer Book* (Samuel S. Cohon Papers: Manuscript Collection No. 276, n.d.).

69 Kaelter (1997) tells a similar story of making the rounds of the various departments. Because the department heads did not understand the grades on his transcript ("*gut,*" "*sehr gut*" or "*genüngend*"), they approved transfer credit for all of his courses (p. 47). Because he had never been good at mathematics, he had a grade of "*nicht genüngend,*" meaning "insufficient." The professor evaluating his transcript thought *nicht genüngend* was a higher grade than *genüngend* and gave him credit. For the first time in his life, he got credit for passing mathematics! By the time he finished counting the credits that transferred, he had 112 of the 124 needed for graduation. All he needed were credits for English and to meet the requirement for a major and minor.

70 Davenning without a *kippah* was not only an issue for Herman, but also for his immigrant colleagues. Plaut (1981) wrote that none of them had ever davenned without one, nor, at first, could they conceive of doing so. By the time of their ordinations, however, except for Kaelter, the other students had given up wearing them (p. 59).

71 In 1940, Plaut (1981) published an essay in the HUC student publication, *H.U.C Monthly,* describing the differences between rabbinic students at HUC and rabbinic students in Berlin. One of the major differences was that HUC students were a product of American culture and "more worldly" than their German counterparts. On the other hand, due to the pressure under which German Jews were living and because the German student recognized the importance of this period of Jewish history, Plant described the German student as "more earnest than he used to be ... [and] feels responsible for the future of German Jewry" (p. 64). Plant observed that the American student had no such weight on his shoulders and could take life more easily. The chief difference was one of attitude.

72 In Schaalman's thinking, God has no gender, but for the sake of stylistic simplicity and familiarity, in this text the masculine pronouns "He," "Him," "Himself" will be used. The use of the noun "God" whenever a pronominal reference is required is awkward to the English-speaking ear.

73 Schaalman was not the only one of the refugees to be called into Morgenstern's office. Plaut (1981) reported that Morgenstern called him in to warn him about promoting too many of his "orthodox customs" and to tone down his support for Zionism (p. 66).

74 Later, however, Morgenstern criticized the rational approach to religion as inadequate and argued, "No creed can exist entirely without ceremony" (Folb, 2007, p. 33). One practice that he apparently endorsed was a mealtime prayer to express thankfulness to God. At the same time, he did not accept the traditional *motzi* and *birkat hamazon*, but proposed a simple English prayer in their place.

75 According to Weiman (2006), this infusion of a post-Enlightenment German voice to the American Reform movement has not been fully explored, but its meaning is significant.

76 According to Schaalman, as greater respect is paid to the art of storytelling, the trend is reversing. "Scholars have concluded that the art of verbal communication may have been very different from today. As a result, the attempt to apply contemporary standards to biblical text may be misleading. The acceleration of translations of ancient texts in the last century has given scholars a sense of a very different style of ancient writing that opens up the possibility of an entirely new way to understand Torah. This new approach is very different from the understandings developed by Wellhausen and his nineteenth-century German followers. Wellhausen, the renowned German biblical scholar who pioneered the study of the Bible from a critical perspective of textual styles, based his work on the study of style. He and his followers developed the theory that the Bible was written by four different authors in different periods of time."

77 One of its leading thinkers, Rabbi Samuel Solomon Cohon, was one of Herman's teachers at HUC.

78 Rabbi Richard L. Rubenstein (1968) wrote that, when he was a student at HUC in the early 1950s and had decided on a career in Jewish theology, he had to pursue his studies at a Protestant seminary: "[At the time] there was simply no tradition of the study of contemporary theology worthy of its name in the rabbinical seminaries" (p. 59). According to Borowitz (2002), "The Hebrew Union College itself was unable to bring to its students a realization of theology's function and significance" (p. 14). He cites a 1920s HUC graduate who stated that in his day at HUC almost everyone was "for religion and against theology" (p. 14).

79 Kaplan's views stood in stark contrast to those of the early twentieth century philosopher Leo Baeck, who, in 1917, had argued that Jews were not simply a nation or a community of faith, but a historical people founded on belief in the Revelation on Sinai and grounded spiritually in an ongoing relationship to God (Meyer, 1988, p. 208). Baeck had been one of Schaalman's professors at *Lehranstalt Für Die Wissenschaft Des Judentums* in Berlin. Surprisingly, Schaalman makes no reference to him or any influence he might have had on his thinking.

80 Schaalman's embrace of Kaplan's views indicate that he must have had serious doubts about the existence of a supernatural being that responded to human needs. Moreover, Kaplan's idea that Judaism was a way of life that included art, music, dancing, and food, must have caught the attention of this young, highly cultured German immigrant.

81 A little more than a decade later, Herman's friend and renowned Jewish philosopher, Emil Fackenheim, shattered Herman's Kaplanesque ideas and destroyed his theological certainty. However, more of that in a later chapter.

82 Rabbi Lichtenberg's widow, Hilde L. Weltman (1986), remembers that the bedroom they shared was always an obstacle course with shoes, underwear, and socks littering the floor.

83 Silberman (1914–2006), who became a university professor, taught Jewish Theology at Vanderbilt University. Dudley Weinberg went on to a career in the rabbinate and served as senior rabbi at Congregation Emanu-El B'Ne in Milwaukee. Like Silberman, he too was an intellectual, but his life took a tragic turn when he had a nervous breakdown and committed suicide.

84 Egelson had come to know and like Schaalman from having met him at various meetings and having had him as a Shabbat dinner guest in his home. Schaalman remembers that at this dinner he was offered celery as one of the vegetables served with dinner. Because he had never eaten a stalk of celery before, he did not know what to do with it. When he began eating the leaves, Egelson said to him, "Herman, in America we eat the stalk, not the leaves."

85 Folb (2007) reports that the faculty allowed Schaalman to officiate at the High Holy Day services but stipulated that the other German refugee students also had the opportunity to serve that congregation (p. 33).

86 In Munich, sermons were not part of the service. Rabbis gave sermons a few times a year in conjunction with the High Holy Days.

87 One of the two students was W. Gunther Plaut, who had been warned by one of his HUC professors, Dr. Jacob Marcus, not to take the chance of going home because the Nazis might not let him return to America (Plaut, G. W, 1981, p. 71). Like Schaalman, Plaut had promised his family that he would only stay away for two years and come home to attend his brother William's high school graduation. Plaut characterized his decision to make this risky journey as "one of the most stupid chances I have ever taken" (p. 72).

88 Jacob Lestchinsky, *Der Wirtschaftliche Zusammenbruch der Juden in Deutschland und Polen* (Geneva and Paris, 1936).

89 Plaut (1981) writes that his father told him "that the Nazi idiocy will soon come to an end. 'I still believe we have a future in this country'" (p. 40).

90 Ulm is located in Wittenberg near Bavaria. In 1933, the Nazis took control of the city and established a concentration camp nearby primarily for political opponents of the regime.

91 Schaalman relates another story of a harrowing escape with family valuables involving one of his professors, Julius Levi, the world's foremost Assyrianologist. Before he and his wife attempted to cross the German border, his wife sewed all of her jewelry into the bottom of her cat's kennel. She starved her cat for three days prior to departing. When she and her husband reached the border and the guard demanded that she open the cage for his inspection, she told him that she had a "bad cat." Nevertheless, the guard insisted, and when she did, the desperate cat snarled at him. He backed off immediately, enabling the Levis to get out of Germany with their jewels.

92 The Jews responded through the Jewish Community Organization by establishing their own hospitals, welfare services, schools, an orchestra and theater, clubs, and an adult education institute. This defensive posture, however, did little to stop many Jews from leaving the city. The relatively small Jewish population of slightly over 9,000 declined rapidly. From March 1933 to May 1938, about a third (3,574) left the city, the majority (3,130), went abroad (Yad Vashem, 2006). Further harassment came in June 1938 when Hitler decided to tear down Munich's Great Synagogue.

93 The SS were Storm Troopers who replaced the first organization of Storm Troopers, the SA, created in 1921 (St. George, M. & Dennis, L., 1946, p. 192).

94 During the next three years, the Nazis tightened their noose in their process of aryanization and elimination of the Jews from the German economy. By the fall of 1941, in Munich they confiscated 1,500 Jewish homes, and conscripted their occupants to build an assembly and transit camp for Jews awaiting deportation (Yad Vashem, 2006). Beginning in 1942, they began exporting Munich's Jews to various cities outside of Germany, including Riga in Latvia, Lublin in Poland. During the summer or 1942, they began sending Munich's Jews to Theresienstadt. Of the approximately 4,200 Jews sent to Theresienstadt between 1942 and 1945, only 297 survived the war (Yad Vashem, 2006).

95 Even in Brazil, there were no opportunities for him to attend school. He took some commercial courses in English, but the family's dire economic condition (they arrived with only twenty German marks) required that he work.

96 As Stern points out, "Jews were slow to emigrate even when opportunities existed ..." (p. 19). This reluctance came from various motives: "the hope for amelioration, the fear of the unknown, considerations of age, family, health, spirit. Reluctance to leave one's home, to acknowledge that one is no longer wanted in a society in which one feels at home, to abandon one's mother tongue—all this is perfectly human ..." (p. 19).

97 "For reasons of prudence and because the brutality of National Socialism needed time to ripen, the Hitler regime gave most 'non-political' Jews time to leave, a possibility to escape, even though under increasingly difficult circumstances." (Stern, F., 1983, p. 18). Between 1937 and 1938, as Jewish life became more and more unbearable, nearly 120,000 Jews fled Germany. Until 1942, the Nazis plan was to cleanse Germany of Jews, not exterminate them.

98 Schaalman remembers her as a passionate and cultured woman: "Among her passions, she recited poetry and composed songs, which she performed at family gatherings."

99 This generous pension was part of Germany's safety net for its citizens. Although the country suffered heavy damage during the war, it was a wealthy country. Areas like Munich were untouched by the war's devastation.

100 Adolf's income was sufficient for the family to have live-in help. The family always employed one and sometimes two maids. The house no longer exists, having been razed, along with the rest of the houses on the block, to make way for a modern development.

101 The term *"aliyah"* refers to the ancient Jewish yearning to return to live in the land of Israel.

102 Unlike her future husband, Lotte did not come empty-handed. Her well-off family made sure that she came with a dowry, including various pieces of family furniture, which are still part of the Schaalman household.

103 Not completely assimilated, Lotte remembers being confirmed and having a crush on her rabbi. Apparently, her parents were well aware of their Jewish roots and wanted their daughter to know she was Jewish.

104 The Schaalmans report that when they visited with Miele, Schaalman was so impressed with her that he asked Lotte why she did not get her to be the governess for their own children.

105 In 1851, Simon Lazarus opened a men's clothing store in Columbus, Ohio. After prospering from the mass manufacturing of uniforms for the Union army during the Civil War, Lazarus expanded into mass manufacturing of men's clothing and eventually sold a complete line of merchandise (Findsen, 1997). When Simon's sons joined the business, they helped develop it through their astute and innovative marketing strategies. In 1928, the company acquired the prestigious and revered John Shillito Company, a Cincinnati landmark that was established in 1830. As late as 2005, Federated Department Stores consisted of Macy's, Lord & Taylor, Famous-Barr, Filene's, Foley's, Hecht's, The Jones Store, L. S. Ayres, Marshall Field's, Meier & Frank, and Robinsons-May.

106 In 1936, Jews could still leave Germany if they had a place to go, though they were not allowed to take out any money. To obtain an American visa, foreigners needed a sponsor with means to prove that the immigrant would not become a financial burden on the country.

107 At one point, Lotte traveled to Anderson, Indiana, to talk to the son of Uncle Morris to ask for his help in getting her parents into America. She described him as enormously wealthy, but despite the fact that he had visited her parents, he declined. In retrospect, Lotte explains that the Weilers had no concept of the dangers facing Jews in Germany; in fact, neither did she.

108 In later years, whenever the Schaalmans were able to travel to Europe, they stopped in London to visit his grave.

109 Rabbinic students were allowed to date only on Saturdays.

110 An interesting footnote to this story is that, in his capacity of chairman of the HUC Board of Trustees, Simon Lazarus signed Schaalman's diploma and handed it to him at the graduation ceremony.

Chapter 3: Cedar Rapids 1941-1949

111 By September 2008, the congregation had increased to 150 Jewish families and was the only synagogue left in Cedar Rapids (Levin, M. *The Joy of Cedar Rapids*, 2008).

112 To get some perspective on the finances of the congregation, it is worth noting that at a board meeting on September 9, 1941, the treasurer reported a balance of $96.00 (Temple Judah, September 9, 1941).

113 Schaalman comments that Morgenstern did not like Rabbi David Polish and had sent him to Temple Judah. Polish was Schaalman's predecessor (December 18, 2008).

114 Because of this strong industrial base and with its sound industries and its strong workforce, Cedar Rapids was able to make a substantial contribution to the war effort (Ossian, L., L., 2009, p. 73). When, in the 1920s, radio was a cutting edge technology, the Collins Radio Company was established and soon became a pioneer in the development of radio. The company helped propel Cedar Rapids into a leadership role in technology. During World War II, the company supplied electronic equipment to all branches of the armed services (Cedar Rapids Convention and Tourism Bureau, 2010).

115 The city also has the distinction of having been the home of several major American historical figures, including Orville and Wilbur Wright, Mamie Doud, who later became First Lady Mamie Eisenhower, and the famous American artist Grant Wood. While he lived in the city, he painted his most famous work, "American Gothic" (City-Data, n. d.).

116 According to the *American Jewish Year Book: 1942–1943*, the fact that the war drained off much of the younger male leadership meant that the older members had to take on additional responsibilities. Another consequence of this reduction in available leaders was that synagogues established programs to train their younger members for leadership (p. 96).

117 As to be expected, not everyone was happy with this merger. Rosanne Klass, who was a teenager in Schaalman's congregation, wrote many years later that when the two congregations merged because "men might be

allowed to wear yarmulkes in the Temple, her mother was outraged ....
She NEVER ceased to be outraged by the slightest concession at Temple
Judah to more traditional religious rituals and practices" (Schaalman, H.
E., First edit: September 13, 1996, p. 5).

118 During Schaalman's convalescence following his automobile accident in
1945, the congregation used the event to raise funds to add an addition
to the bungalow that provided new classroom space and an office for
the rabbi. Previously, the rabbi's office and the classrooms had been in
the basement.

119 The professional paths of Rabbi Polish and Schaalman later crossed
when both were rabbis in Chicago and when each became major figures
in the Reform movement (cf. Chapter 4, "Chicago: 1949–1955").

120 The Carneys and the Schaalmans later became lifelong friends (Schaalman, H. E., 1999, p. 9).

121 Schaalman adds that had they been part of a later generation, they might
have had different expectations about having a child right away.

122 According to Bindy Bitterman, a longtime member of Emanuel Congregation, "Present day members of Emanuel will confirm that Lotte has
never changed."

123 In 1965, the Central Conference of American Rabbis produced a revised
Rabbi's Manual, which provided HUC graduates instruction in how to
perform life-cycle events and rituals, including prayers and meditations.

124 Plaut (1997) wrote that he encountered the same problem of the lack of
knowledge of his congregants and attributed it to "Reform's neglect of
Jewish knowledge" (p. 109).

125 Once he became confident in his English skills, he discarded written
texts and delivered sermons, lectures, and workshops without notes or
written text. In response to his admirers who speak highly of the depth
and eloquence of his remarks, he explains: "The words just come. I don't
know from where."

126 Holding adult education in the homes of congregants became the
prototype of Schaalman's adult education offerings after he moved
to Chicago.

127 Mays, located on Second Street between Second and Third Avenues, was
the first large, modern drug store in Cedar Rapids (Schaalman, H. E.,
1999, p. 21).

128 In 1948, Schaalman told a Cedar Rapids reporter that for the 130 Jewish families in Cedar Rapids anti-Semitic acts were of "relatively minor importance" (Meek, 1948, p. 11).

129 When Hall died in 1971, his widow, Margaret, asked Schaalman, who had moved to Chicago in 1949, to conduct the funeral, but he had barely returned from a trip to Israel and was too exhausted to make the trip. It was a difficult decision for him, but he declined.

130 Built in the 1880s, the "cottage" had been home to three prominent Cedar Rapids families: the Sinclairs of the T. M. Sinclair Company, the Douglasses of Quaker Oats, and finally the Halls. Brucemore had been the home in which Margaret Douglas grew up. She and her sister had named it Brucemore. It also had a Wagnerian mural, rich woodwork and a magnificent pipe organ (National Trust for Historic Preservation, 2009). When Howard Hall died in 1971, Margaret survived him by ten years, and, on her death at the age of 84, bequeathed Brucemore to the National Trust for Historic Preservation for use as a historic site and community cultural center (Brucemore, 2005).

131 The sense of the Hollywood environment was not far off. Hall was fascinated by Hollywood and its stars. On his frequent business trips to California, he mingled with Hollywood personalities, including Clark Gable, Errol Flynn, Olivia DeHaviland, and Vivien Leigh. He also met Billy Richards, the Vice-President of World Jungle Compound, the company that handled Jackie, the MGM lion, and very likely the inspiration for Hall's purchase of his own lions (Brucemore, 2005).

132 Roy A. was president of the Fruehauf Trailer Co. that in 1951 had eight plants around the United States and Canada. The company produced more trailers (i.e., freight vans pulled behind trucks or "truck-tractors") than any other trailer-maker (*Time Magazine*, 1951). *Time* (1951) reported that "Fruehauf's company 'invented' the modern trailer and has paced the trailer industry for thirty-six years."

133 Despite their wealth, even the Halls were affected by shortages. While Mrs. Hall was wintering in Florida, she wrote to her husband about the food scarcity in the region and thanked him for "sending her staples such as butter and bacon" (Brucemore, 2005).

134 "Entered Apprentice" is the first degree of entry into freemasonry and represents youth. "Fellowcraft" is the second degree and symbolizes man in adulthood and represents work. The third degree is "Master Mason," representing man in old age and relates to wisdom. To attain these stages, a member must pass a prescribed examination, as a test of proficiency,

corresponding to the "essays" of the operative period (Masonic Lodge of Education, 2007–2012).

135 After his trip home to Germany in 1937, he had to reenter the United States by way of Cuba. That's when the clock started ticking for the five-year waiting period for him to become a U.S. citizen.

136 Schaalman remembers the show as "Three Men on a Horse."

137 According to *The Coe Cosmos* (February 2, 1949), in 1948 the Jewish Chautauqua Society, an affiliate of the National Federation of Temple Brotherhoods, had sent speakers to 400 colleges. The large number of speaking engagements suggests that the Jewish community was very active in attempting to promote the acceptance of Judaism.

138 An interesting and amusing anecdote relating to Schaalman's reputation as a public speaker comes from his friend and fellow German refugee, Wolli Kaelter. In his autobiography (1997), Kaelter describes an encounter he had in 1941 after he had taken a job as rabbi in Lebanon, Pennsylvania. A young woman he was counseling about her upcoming wedding told him that he reminded her of Rabbi Schaalman. "Schaalman? That's very funny; he and I shared the same ship coming to this country. We are good friends and he has just visited here" (p. 92). When he asked her how she knew Schaalman, she told him that she had been a student at the University of Iowa and, at the time, Schaalman had been the rabbi in nearby Cedar Rapids. She must have heard him speak on the campus.

139 Two of these speaking engagements are part of the public record. In January of 1945, Schaalman addressed a group at the local YMCA on the subject of Judaism (*Coe Cosmos*, January 17, 1945). In February 1949, he addressed a Coe College chapel gathering on the subject of modern Jewish beliefs. These two speaking events are representative of his many opportunities to speak about Judaism to audiences that knew next to nothing about it.

140 Schaalman's good friend and classmate, Wolli Kaelter, was also intimately involved in interfaith activity. In 1945 in Hot Springs, Pennsylvania, Kaelter began an annual series of institutes on Judaism in which "clergymen from the Catholic, Presbyterian, Methodist, Episcopal, and other Christian churches participated" (Kaelter, 1997, p. 104).

141 Schaalman tells a funny and revealing story of his pariah status: "In a speaking engagement in a Cedar Rapids public school, one of the children had "sneaked in to see the talking 'rabbit.'"

142 Today, Cornell College prides itself as being a liberal arts college.

143 He soon discovered that he was not the only Jewish faculty member. One of his colleagues was a Jewish refugee from Vienna, Eric Kohlman (Star, E., November 13, 1987, p. 11).

144 Schaalman recognized the need for American Jews to promote interfaith activities twenty-five years before Rabbi Eugene Borowitz. In 1969, Borowitz had argued that it was imperative for Jews to develop interfaith dialogue. After the Holocaust, he wrote, Jews have a greater need than ever to speak to Christians to express their grievances at their mistreatment. In a shrinking world that was becoming more a neighborhood or global village, Jewish survival depended on finding partners from other faiths who would welcome dialogue and would join together to create a climate of understanding and tolerance (Borowitz, 1969).

145 An interesting coincidence in the life of the Schaalman family is that they get to celebrate most of their important family events in a one-month period: Michael's birthday on April 25, his father's on April 28, and, on May 28, Susan's birthday, her parents' wedding anniversary, and her father's ordination.

146 Schaalman had been told that the automobile club of Minneapolis would not allow Jews to become members.

147 The Kirschner wire is a surgical steel wire of heavy gauge with pointed ends used for the reduction and fixation of bone fragments (Dorland's Medical Dictionary, 2007).

148   When the United States entered the war, Jewish leaders asked their member congregations to give their rabbis leaves of absence for the duration of the war. HUC even accelerated its rabbinic studies program to prepare students to take over for rabbis who went into the service. By the end of 1943, the army had 58 Jewish chaplains on active duty and the navy had six (*American Jewish Year Book, 1942–1943*, p. 97).

149 The modern reader may be surprised to learn that the cost for the room was a mere $6 a day. As Schaalman points out, "Today, you can't even get an aspirin in the hospital for that amount."

150 Dr. Thaler, a Polish refugee, was a new arrival in Cedar Rapids with whom the Schaalmans became good friends.

151 A "mohel" is a Jewish person trained in performing circumcision.

152 The writer does not know why Lotte's mother Gussie was not available.

153 The story comes from a 1988 interview. In *Hineni* (2007), Schaalman tells a different story: "In 1946, a former classmate of mine living out west called to tell me that there was a congregation forming in Culver City, California. He wanted me to come and interest myself in that congregation. So I was invited to speak to the biggest congregation out there, and people from the new congregation had come to listen to me. They were very much impressed, and they offered me the job. I said, 'Give me a few days to think about it.' On the flight back, I said to myself, 'This congregation in Cedar Rapids has been so good to me and my family, especially during recovery from a serious automobile accident, [sic] I just can't leave this congregation.' In those days, right after the war, there was such a shortage of rabbis that I knew they would not find anyone to come to Cedar Rapids. I turned down the Culver City congregation" (pp. 53-54). Because the 1987 account is closer to the event, I suspect it is the more accurate one.

154 At the time, most synagogues were not air conditioned and closed down during the summer because of the stifling heat and because so many congregants were away on vacation.

155 Because Jews in Chicago were not admitted to non-Jewish social clubs, they founded their own. Such clubs conferred considerable status on their members and provided access to strong social and business contacts. German Jews founded the Standard Club and their Eastern European cousins the Covenant Club.

156 In subsequent visits, Schaalman saw skyscrapers half finished because their investors had gone broke. Inflation destroyed the value of their capital, and, until new money was available, these buildings remained incomplete for several years.

157 As it turned out, when Schaalman discussed this issue with Esta Star in 1988, Rabbi Pinkus had not yet retired.

158 Two surveys on rabbinic ordination had been conducted prior to 1947. In 1937, Louis Mann conducted the first that focused exclusively on interfaith marriage (*CCAR Yearbook* 47, 1937, p. 313). He sent out 325 surveys and received 240 valid responses (74% of the CCAR). The survey revealed that 161 rabbis (67%) did not officiate at interfaith marriages, and that 79 rabbis (33%) would officiate, 62 of them (26%) with some conditions and 17 (7%) without conditions (*CCAR Yearbook* 47, 1937, pp. 314-15). In 1943, Leo Stillpass sent out a second survey to 437 rabbis and found that his results were similar to Mann's: 181 rabbis (65%) do not officiate at interfaith marriages; 95 rabbis (34%) will officiate, 47 (17%) with condition that the children would be raised as Jews

and 48 (17%) with other conditions or no conditions at all (*CCAR Year-book* 57, 1947, p. 183). Based on these statistics, the author concluded that Reform rabbis were opposed to officiation, but that most rabbis wanted a greater role for the CCAR in deciding an official attitude on the subject (pp. 128–29).

159 Schaalman is not clear about the exact year. Folb (2007), in her HUC rabbinic thesis, places the event in 1946 at the annual CCAR conference. However, the list of attendees does not include Schaalman, nor do CCAR conference documents from prior years. The 1947 conference proceedings are the first to list him as an attendee.

160 An indication of the extent of this friendship is apparent in Fackenheim's dedication of his book, *Quest for Past and Future* (1968): "To Herman E. Schaalman *after more than three decades.*"

161 On Kristallnacht, November 9, 1938, Fackenheim was arrested by the Nazis and sent to the Sachsenhausen concentration camp (Fackenheim, 1994). Soon after, he escaped and fled to Great Britain, and, once the war broke out in 1939, the British arrested him as an enemy alien. A year later, they sent him to Canada and, within four years, he was graduated from the University of Toronto with a PhD. Soon after, he began a career at the university as Professor of Philosophy.

162 In the 1960s, Schaalman and Fackenheim were beginning to come to grips with the enormity of the Holocaust. Fackenheim made it the cornerstone of his thinking. He began to assert the centrality of God for Judaism and the importance of the Zionist Movement as the salvation of the Jewish People. He argued that Judaism must survive so that Hitler would not gain a posthumous victory over the Jews.

163 Dr. Deborah E. Lipstadt, author of the widely acclaimed *Beyond Belief: The American Press and the Coming of the Holocaust*, observed that believing the stories required a "leap of the imagination" that too few people could or were willing to make (University of St. Thomas, 1992, p. 17). People had not had experience with evil on such an enormous scale. For some, belief was not convenient. Others were indifferent, uninterested. For those who were concerned, they could not make that leap of imagination (p. 17). When Chief Justice Felix Frankfurter was told by an eyewitness of the atrocities, he responded, "I can't believe you" (as quoted by Lipstadt, p. 17).

164 In his UAHC Report for 1949, he claimed nineteen congregations (p. 249).

165 To get some perspective on how low that salary was, the reader should know that six years later Emanuel Congregation offered him a salary of $20,000 and a housing stipend. Clearly, living costs in Chicago were higher than in Cedar Rapids, but the tenfold increase must have made a significant improvement in the Schaalmans' material circumstances.

166 In 1948, he told a reporter from *The Cedar Rapids Gazette*, that his hobbies included tennis (which became a lifelong love), swimming, music, traveling, chess, and public speaking (Meek, L., January 4, 1948, p. 11). Many years later, his son Michael became an excellent swimmer and won awards for it in high school and college. A family tradition developed when Schaalman's granddaughters won awards for their performance on their colleges' swimming teams.

167 It is not clear whether Schaalman was aware of the existence of the Parliament of the World's Religions, established in 1893, in which he later became an active and influential member.

168 The other panelists included the narrator, Dr. Daniel Day Williams, professor of Christian theology at the Chicago Theological Seminary, and Sheikh Hussein Dabour, teacher of Arabic in the State Department's Foreign Service Institute and the Islamic Center in Washington, D. C.

Chapter 4: Chicago 1949-1955

169 In the 1950s, Hyde Park was considered one of Chicago's most prestigious neighborhoods. It also had a large Jewish population and was the home of several of the city's major synagogues and temples.

170 So persuasive is she that she convinced this writer's non-Jewish wife to attend both functions. For the ten years prior to joining Emanuel, she had refused to go on similar outings sponsored by her husband's temple in Long Grove. To get her to come to the Lehrhaus event, Lotte told her that she could have the Schaalmans' bedroom in the guesthouse, which was the best in the building. She also told her about the amenities: horseback riding, tennis courts, swimming, beautiful natural surroundings, and, above all, the learning experience. Sold!

171 The Sloans had four children, all of them sons, who would later establish themselves in various professions.

172 Over the years, whenever the Schaalmans traveled to California, they made sure to visit the Sloans and, when possible, to celebrate Lotte's

and Polly's birthdays together (Polly and Lotte were born on the same day—Lotte, January 13, 1915, and Polly January 13, 1925). When the Schaalmans visited in 2008, Polly gave them copies of the Samfield family documents and pictures.

173 Not long after he took up residence in Chicago, Schaalman became an ardent baseball fan. His team, like that of most Northside Chicagoans, was the Chicago Cubs, a team he remained faithful to until his later years, when the Cubs continual failure to win a World Series finally became too disappointing. Not that he switched allegiance to another team, but he lost interest in them.

174 Some years later, he became friends with the Pritzker family, one of the most prestigious and wealthiest families in America.

175 Rabbi Richard G. Hirsch (2010), who was Schaalman's replacement as Midwest Regional Director of the UAHC and who claims to have known Eisendrath well, states, "Eisendrath didn't give a damn about youth. Sam Cook, who was head of NFTY, told me that Eisendrath, who had no children of his own, only cared about social issues. Schaalman as the main force behind the camp." Schaalman's sense that his interviewers were skeptical might have been their way of testing him on the issue. Moreover, his emphasis on developing a camp might have been at odds with the responsibilities the Union assigned to its Regional Director. Even before Schaalman served as the Union Institute camp director for its first summer, J. S. Ackerman (1952), the president of the Chicago Federation of the UAHC, expressed concern that this additional responsibility might be too much for him physically and impair his ability to do both jobs well.

176 On April 13, 1951, he gave an address at Emanuel Congregation, the earliest recorded record of his involvement with that congregation (Schaalman to Talk, April 12, 1951).

177 In succeeding years, his negotiating skill earned him the title of "peacemaker" for his role in defusing housing and racial conflicts in Chicago's north side Edgewater neighborhood, the neighborhood where he lived and served as Emanuel Congregation's senior rabbi.

178 On the national level of UAHC, Schrayer attempted to lead a revolt against the Union hierarchy. Because he did not believe a rabbi should be head of the Union, he attempted to dethrone rabbinic leadership. He ran for president of UAHC against Eisendrath but lost.

179 Fifty years later, the movement toward lay leadership in Reform synagogues had become the rule, rather than the exception, and, according
to Kaplan (2003), "plays a major role in the direction of the movement"
(p. 261).

180 Schaalman remembers a time when to be an usher at a service required
knowledge of the prayer book because a key function of the usher was to
hand it to latecomers opened to the correct page. To be an usher meant
that the usher had to study liturgy, a requirement initiated by Schrayer.

181 One of Schaalman's former students and current friend, the newly ordained Rabbi Marc Berkson, became assistant rabbi in 1977 and then
senior rabbi after the death of its founding rabbi, Karl Weiner. Later,
after Berkson became senior rabbi at Emanu-El B'ne Jeshurun in Milwaukee, Wisconsin, he invited Schaalman to be scholar-in-residence and
to teach classes and give sermons on the High Holy Days.

182 Among his most famous compositions are his "Jewish Cycle" and
"America, an Epic Rhapsody" (Upton, G. P., and Borowski, F., 2005,
pp. 93–96).

183 The next year, Eisendrath (1955) called for the creation of several new
regional positions, including one for the Great Lakes Region and the
Midwest Region, which he considered "dire necessities". He cited
Schaalman's "heroic but nonetheless necessarily humanly limited efforts"
to adequately serve the congregations in this region (p. 600).

184 Formed by Reform rabbis during the 1930s who opposed a growing
trend in Reform Judaism to support the creation of a Jewish state, the
organization vigorously fought the Zionist movement in America. It had
many supporters in the State Department and among left-wing intellectuals (Kolsky, T. A., 1990, p. 57ff.)

185 For Eisendrath, Sussman's position must have reminded him of his own
former position on Zionism during the 1940s. According to his biographer, Avi Schulman (1993), Eisendrath challenged Zionism as a "focal
point" of Jewish identity and called it "an ethnic and national chauvin-
ism, a loyalty to the peoplehood of Israel rather than to its soul or teachings or moral *mitzvot* that motivate our identification" (p. 42).

186 The lure of living in a Jewish state also influenced Schaalman's sister-in-
law, Ilse Stern, and his brother, Freddie. Ilse made aliyah in the 1930s
and Freddie in the 1970s. He settled in an Orthodox section of Jerusalem and lived there until his death in November 2011.

187 In *Can Faith Survive* (1964), Eisendrath wrote, "Just as my own position on Zionism has changed through the years, so has the official posture of Reform Judaism" (p. 51). However, that change did not come overnight. Into the late 1940s, the "body of Reform congregations still retained its generally anti-Zionist disposition" (p. 60). Schulman (1993) cites Eisendrath's efforts to quell dissent in Reform Judaism during the 1940s over the issue of Jewish nationalism. His victory was to neutralize the polarizing issue (p. 35).

Chapter 5: Reform Jewish Camping: OSRUI

188 According to Lorge and Zola (2006) in their comprehensive anthology on the history of Jewish camping in America, the idea of Jewish camping can be traced to the early years of the twentieth century. They cite a 1929 publication stating that Jewish camping was the most successful "'instrument for inspiring and remaking individual young Jewish lives'" (p. 17). By the 1940s, leaders of the various branches of American Judaism saw in summer camps the potential to "augment Jewish learning, develop leadership skills, and concomitantly strengthen ideological ties to their respective religious movements" (p. 19).

189 He claims to have "pleaded for the acquisition of a Union camp to serve 'not only for youth conclaves but for many additional functions of our Liberal Jewish cause'" (Eisendrath, M. N., April 19, 1953, p. 544).

190 According to Rabbi Hirsch (2010), Schaalman's job as Midwest Regional Director of the UAHC meant that he had the responsibility to lead the effort to establish the camp.

191 Emanuel Congregation was represented by Rabbi Levy's assistant, Rabbi Arnold Wolf and Mrs. Herman Manheim (Combined Committee for Camp Project Minutes, March 29, 1951).

192 Originally, the Carnation milk family had built the lodge in 1903 as a private residence. In 1934, it was converted into a private camp facility for Jewish boys (Lorge and Zola, 2006, p. 60).

193 In his annual report to the Union, Schaalman refers to the 1953–54 year of the Institute and the success of its year-round program, the first of its kind in the Union (Schaalman's report, n.d.)

194 Through a process of negotiations, the final price was $63,000, $15,000 down and the remaining $48,000 to be paid at $4,800 annually for ten

years at 4% interest (Ackerman, 1951, Oct. 4). Lorge and Zola (2006) mistakenly write that the down payment was $16,000 (p. 60).

195 Rabbi Hirsch adds an interesting sidelight to this emerging story. In the spring of 1951, when he was assistant rabbi at Emanuel Congregation, he formed a youth group called "EGAD," Emanuel Guys and Dolls. Hirsch notes that this group was the first youth group to use the camp site (Hirsch, R.G., 2010).

196 Jake Guzik (1887–1956), known as "Greasy Thumb," was the trusted treasurer and financial wizard for the Al Capone gang. Early in his career, he was involved in prostitution and white slavery. He also was notorious for paying off politicians and police. He got his nickname from his effective and efficient work as Capone's "bagman" (Jake "Greasy Thumb," August 2003).

197 Born less than a month apart (Lorge, May 26, 1916; Schaalman, April 28, 1916), Lorge also came to HUC on scholarship and got a BA from the University of Cincinnati. In 1947, he came to Chicago to become the rabbi at Chicago's Temple Beth Israel where he remained until his retirement in 1985 (The Jacob Rader Marcus Center of the American Jewish Archives, Ernst M. Lorge Papers, 2003). The Union Institute was only one of the many projects on which the two rabbis worked together.

198 Schaalman tells an interesting and humorous story about the founding of the camp. Before it opened in the summer of 1952, Schaalman and Emanuel Congregation's Rabbi Levy used the grounds to hold a New Year's Retreat. The two rabbis occupied the same room, and, to Schaalman's complete surprise and dismay, the seventy-year old Levy opened the windows despite the fact that the air was freezing cold and lay in bed with his chest exposed, obviously enjoying the bitter cold. Schaalman asked him how he could stand it. Levy replied, "'It's perfectly fine; you should try it.'" Not wanting to appear less hardy, Schaalman stated, "I put on my winter coat, hat and gloves and crawled into bed."

199 Although the camp could accommodate eighty youth, only half that number came during the first summer (Schaalman, H.E., Interview, December 16, 2008).

200 The naming of the camp was the result of a combining of the name of the Union of American Hebrew Congregations, the camp's primary sponsor, and the concept of "institutes" that had been held for Jewish youth prior to the establishment of the camp (Lorge and Zola, 2006, p. 52). In 1967, it was changed to Olin-Sang to acknowledge the two

families that were its primary benefactors. In 1972, because of ongoing support from the Ruby family, the camp became the Olin-Sang-Ruby Union Institute, or OSRUI, as it is known today (Lorge and Zola, 2006, p. 52).

201 An interesting historical note related to the development of a "comprehensive" program for the summer camps was the violent condemnation of the use of Hebrew in some quarters of the Reform movement (Eisendrath, M. N., Semi-Annual Report to Executive Board, June 21–22, 1952, p. 155).

202 By June 1952, the Union had established a second camp on the West coast, Camp Swig.

203 According to Rabbi Richard G. Hirsch (2010), in the spring of 1952, "The camp was a mess" and needed substantial work before it was ready to open.

204 Schaalman's remarks came back to haunt him when the camps produced future leaders of Reform Judaism, who made substantial changes in Reform liturgy that he cannot accept. These changes will be discussed in Chapter 8, "The Reform of Reform."

205 Rabbi Richard G. Hirsch (2010) claims, "There is no question that Schaalman was the prime mover and that the camp was his initiative and that he brought the camp into the UAHC."

206 An interesting sidelight in the history of OSRUI was the interaction of Schaalman and Rabbi Arnold Wolf when they were together at the camp. According to Kaye (2006), it was not unusual for their ongoing conflict to assert itself during a camp service. Either one of them might interrupt a Shabbat service during the singing of a song and say, "No, that's not how it's done." They would disagree about the "intention" of the song. Kaye remembers a specific event that occurred in the 1970s when the group was singing a version of L'Chah Dodi that was rock and roll-laced. According to Kaye, Schaalman blurted out, "This is an outrage. This is a prayer. You can't do that. How dare you?" (as reported by Kaye, 2006)

207 What helped make her music become so popular was that it was inspired by folk singers and composers such as Joan Baez and Peter, Paul, and Mary, who were revered by liberal Jews (Klug, L., A., 2004). Her music emphasized congregational participation in sing-along folk-style music. This liturgical music was so much more appealing to Jewish children and adults than the grand operatic style that was performed in a "high

church" style by cantors, accompanied by organs and choirs (Klug, L., A., 2004). In 2007, after recording nineteen albums and performing in hundreds of concerts, Friedman's music had made such an enormous impact on Reform liturgy, that the HUC-JIR School of Sacred Music in New York hired her as a faculty member to teach cantorial students. She had already been named an honorary member of the Reform movement's American Conference of Cantors (Fishkoff, S., July 13, 2007). When she died at the beginning of 2011, Reform Jews around the world held memorial events to celebrate her contribution to Jewish music, and HUC-JIR renamed the School of Sacred Music in her memory.

Chapter 6: Emanuel Congregation and Leadership in Reform Judaism 1956-1986

208 The congregation's history notes that during World War II the congregation helped new German refugees overcome the barriers of language and customs ("History of Emanuel Congregation," 2009).

209 Emanuel was not the only congregation that sought Schaalman's services. He had received another offer from B'nai Torah, a Chicago North Shore congregation, a synagogue he had helped launch in his role as director of the Union. He made weekly trips to conduct services that were housed temporarily in a local school in Highland Park. A few years later, the congregation was sufficiently established to seek its own rabbi and offered the position to Schaalman.

210 An indication of Emanuel's prestige was the fact that Dr. Samuel Hollender, president of Emanuel's Board of Trustees from in the late 1950s, was the immediate past president of the national and international Union of Reform Judaism, president of Chicago's prestigious Standard Club, and president of the Chicago Jewish Federation. Schaalman claims Hollender was one of Chicago's best fundraisers for Jewish causes and "one of the top laymen in the country, a man from whom I learned a lot: I became his student, his apprentice."

211 The congregation's previous home on Buckingham Place was typical of Conservative and Reform synagogues built in the early part of the twentieth century. Classical in design, it had a rich interior with expensive and beautiful stained glass windows, which Schaalman would have liked to relocate to the new Emanuel building. Instead, the Board decided to donate them to a new congregation on Chicago's North Shore. According to Mel Abrams (2006), who was a teenager at the time, the interior

of the Buckingham Temple reminded him of a church. People dressed formally, sat in the pews, and listened quietly to the Rabbi or the choir. When the congregation moved to its new home on Sheridan Road, it sold the building on Buckingham to a Chinese group that wanted to open a church. Later, the building was converted to condominiums.

212 Wolf never forgave Schaalman for getting the job as Emanuel's senior rabbi, a job he fully expected to get as the nephew of its Rabbi Levy and his assistant. In 2005, at a meeting of the International Conference of Christians and Jews, Rabbi Wolf told this writer, "I would be willing to discuss anything about the history of Reform Judaism in Chicago, but would not discuss Herman Schaalman."

213 In Rabbi Hirsch's (2010) telling, he and the Schaalmans became good friends soon after he met them in 1951. He remembers being invited to their home for dinner and that Lotte helped fix him up with dates.

214 Schaalman said that he had never seen the document before or no longer remembered it. When he saw a copy of it in September 2007, he was surprised and moved. He had no idea the trustees held him in such high esteem. In his mind, those first few years at Emanuel were a struggle for acceptance by the board and the congregation.

215 Meyer (1988) called the move to suburbia "the synagogue's new frontier" (p. 354). This movement was not unique to Emanuel but part of a larger migration of Jewish families to the northern suburbs. The movement was precipitated by a variety of factors: a desire for a healthier and safer life; more spacious and affordable housing; better schools; more green space; a desire to move out of the "lower class" neighborhoods where they were born and raised; and, not least of all, a desire to escape from the encroachment of minorities. Some also left so that they could put space between themselves and parents, who could not afford to move with them, or simply preferred to remain in the city close to their friends and the way of life they had become accustomed to. Another major factor contributing to the migration to the suburbs was the opening of the Edens Expressway linking Chicago to the northern suburbs. In its first few years, it made commuting into the city a relatively easy trip. Because of this migration, clusters of Jewish life in Chicago began to break up, including such solidly Jewish communities on Chicago's west side, Hyde Park, and Rogers Park.

216 Soon after Schaalman become senior rabbi, Ronnie Harlow became president of the congregation. Like Schaalman, he was a German refugee who had prospered through a business selling phones. He and Schaalman became good friends, and Harlow proved to be an excellent administrator.

217 A major mishap in the busing program nearly scuttled it. Sometime in the 1970s, a school bus ran over and killed a child who was waiting in Emanuel's parking lot for his ride home. The event rocked the congregation, which came close to shutting down its busing program.

218 Meyer (1988) concludes that the Jewish exodus to the suburbs had a positive effect on institutional Conservative and Reform Judaism (pp. 354–355). Not only did it increase their outreach beyond the city, but became a source of new revenue.

219 Over the years, Schaalman officiated at many of the Pritzker life-cycle events, including weddings, first and second marriages, B'nai Mitzvot, and funerals. Robert Pritzker (1926–2011), son of A. N. Pritzker, and his first wife, Audrey, were members of Emanuel congregation. Col. Jim Pritzker (2009), son of Robert and Audrey, remembers going to Hebrew school at Emanuel for several years between 1959 and 1961. He also remembers that Schaalman performed the marriage of his younger sister, Karen, and in 1990, his second marriage to Lisa Gorin.

In 1970, Schaalman officiated at the funeral of Fanny Pritzker and, two years later in 1972, at the funeral for Donald Pritzker, one of Abram Nicholas (A. N.) Pritzker's three sons. In the years that followed, Schaalman officiated at the funerals of A. N.'s other two sons, Jay in 1999 and Robert in 2011. In 1974, Linda Pritzker, sister of Col. Jim Pritzker, asked Schaalman to perform her marriage. However, according to Jim, because her spouse was not Jewish, Schaalman politely refused. Pritzker (2009) remembers that Schaalman told her, "Who you want to marry is your business. I hope you have a long and happy marriage, but I personally do not feel comfortable performing a mixed marriage." However, he did help find a rabbi who would.

When A. N. Pritzker died in 1986, Schaalman officiated at his funeral. In his eulogy, Schaalman revealed that he and Abram had disagreed about God and Judaism. According to Susan, her father "scored a triumph of the eulogist's art at Abram's funeral when he related some of their conversations in which Abram made a skeptical and dismissive remark about God and Judaism." The Pritzkers thanked Schaalman for not pretending that Abram was something he was not. Schaalman had learned this lesson well from his first eulogy for one of Cedar Rapid's leading citizens.

On October 27, 2011, Schaalman also officiated at the funeral of Robert Pritzker. The funeral took place at Emanuel Congregation. Friends, family, business associates, politicians, and well-wishers filled the hall. The fact that the family chose Emanuel is a testament to Schaalman and part of the temple's ongoing prestige as an important institution in American Judaism. Although Schaalman was in fragile health after a recent stroke, he delivered a eulogy that Susan described as a "home run." Having attended the funerals of other Pritzker family members, she had a good basis to evaluate her father's performance. Schaalman, who had known Robert for sixty years, spoke eloquently of his humanness and his dedication to making the world a better place.

A measure of Schaalman's relationship to the Pritzker family comes from the testimony of Col. Jim Pritzker, who told this writer that Schaalman is the primary face for his contacts with Jewish institutions. According to Pritzker (2009), one of Schaalman's most admirable qualities "is that he stands up for his principles and never offends anybody and, for that reason, has been an important influence on my life."

220 Beginning in late 1990s, the Schaalmans vacationed seven or eight summers at the Pritzker home in Vail, Colorado. The house was empty during the summer because the Pritzkers used it only during the winter ski season. Sometime around 2002, the Schaalmans stopped going to Vail although the home continued to be available to them. During the summer of 2007, their granddaughter, Keren was allowed to stay at the mansion.

221 The extent of the Conservation Committee's recommendations can be seen in the following list: increase publicity, especially about Shabbat services and the topic of the rabbi's sermon; organize a telephone committee to contact members regularly; establish an evaluation committee to define the activities of the various committees; organize professional, business and golden age groups; create a "continuous indoctrination" program on the principles of Reform Judaism; attempt to sign up non-members who attended Friday night services; and initiate a publication describing Emanuel, including advantages of membership (Emanuel Congregation, November 30, 1957).

222 In 1988, Schaalman told Esta Star (1988) that several hundred people served on temple committees.

223 As of 2012, the board continues to feel responsible for promoting Jewish awareness in its youth. Thanks to the generosity of the Abrams family, the board maintains a special scholarship program to send one or two of them each summer to OSRUI.

224 Some even held Shabbat services on Sunday. C. A. Kroloff (1990) explains that the decision to hold services on Sunday became an issue for the CCAR from its very beginning. Rabbi Stephen Wise recognized that the reality of American life was that congregants worked six days a week, especially if they were professionals or owned businesses. Wise accepted

that reality and, though he did not recommend it, allowed congregations to hold services on Sunday. He concluded that it was better to have more Jews attend weekly services than to have them show up only for the High Holy Days. According to Michael Meyer (1988), the idea of holding Sabbath services on Sunday had been one of Hermann Cohen's proposals, which sought to make nineteenth-century German Judaism more compatible with Christianity (p. 205).

225 Until that time, the tradition in Reform temples was that the laity played little role in temple life. All that was required was that they attend temple services. Even in that role, they were largely passive. The service was performed for them by the rabbi and the choir and/or the chazzan.

226 A rabbi by the name of Franklin had written a book in which he argued that singing in the synagogue was forbidden. Although singing was permitted in Reform temples, it had not entered "center stage." Only in the last half century, have congregations been willing to take that step.

227 In the nineteenth century, scorning the idea that a thirteen-year-old was an adult, the Reform movement tried to do away with the Bar Mitzvah and replaced it with a Confirmation ceremony when the teenager reached sixteen or eighteen. When the movement recognized that the Bar Mitzvah was a way to keep Jewish adolescents involved in Jewish education and that it was so very popular, it revived the practice (Jewish Virtual Library, 2007).

228 Reform Judaism developed the Confirmation ceremony in the nineteenth century as an alternative to the Bar Mitzvah and that also included girls. Both constituted a "rite of passage" and were generally preceded by a period of study, but each involved a different understanding of Jewish maturity. The Bar Mitzvah "focused on a child's newfound responsibility for performing Jewish rituals and commandments; the Confirmation signified his or her understanding of Jewish religious principles. Significantly, the Confirmation began relatively early to include girls and as such was a precursor of the bat mitzvah ceremony" (Blank, D., 2007). According to Schaalman, "When I was Regional Director of UAHC, I organized a group of fifteen or sixteen Reform rabbis to introduce Bar Mitzvah into Chicago's Reform synagogues."

229 In 2007, the name was changed to Men of Reform Judaism.

230 Morris is a long-time member of the Brotherhood and part of its national executive Board. Since the late 1950s, he has been a member of Emanuel Congregation. He served as a board member for many years and as a

board president and treasurer. He is also a member of the Mecklen-burger family that for many years during Schaalman's rabbinate played an influential role in Emanuel and is one of its major donors.

231 Although he had great admiration for Eisenhower as a general, Schaal-man did not vote for him. From his first voting opportunity, he always voted Democratic. Had he been able to vote for Roosevelt, he would have, but he had not yet become a citizen.

232 Schaalman may have adopted this method from Martin Buber. In *I-Thou*, originally published in 1923, Buber (1970) wrote, "Our students teach us. … The relationship is reciprocal. My You acts on me as I act on it" (p.67).

233 Schaalman first met Rabbi Greenberg when they were both attending a conference in Canada in the 1960s. According to Rabbi Greenberg, the conference brought together Reform, Conservative, and Orthodox rabbis to study and learn together. Subsequently, Schaalman invited Greenberg to speak at Emanuel. Having developed a warm relationship, they participated together in several interfaith dialogues.

234 The non-Jewish population was mainly Iowa farm boys. In his third week at Grinnell, Michael received a call from the pastor of the local Methodist church, who had heard that his father was a rabbi. The pastor invited Michael to come to the church to speak about Judaism. After the pastor introduced him and walked out, Michael spoke without having prepared anything and then was barraged by hostile questions that he thought were expressions of bigotry.

235 The God Squad is a religious advice column through which Rabbi Gellman answers readers' questions on a variety of topical and spiritual issues, from interfaith marriage to news events.

236 Quarles & Brady (2011) provides broad-based, national-level legal services through a strong network of regional practices and local offices. In its 118-year history, the firm has grown from a small, well-respected local Milwaukee law firm to become one of the leading firms in the country serving major national and multinational corporations, educational and research institutions, municipalities and government agencies, nonprofits, charitable organizations, industry executives, and high-net-worth individuals. With a staff of 450 attorneys, the firm has offices in Chicago, Madison, Milwaukee, Naples, Florida, Phoenix and Tucson, Shanghai, and Washington, D.C. (Quarles & Brady, 2011).

237 Civil rights activist Medgar Evers, June 12, 1963; President John F. Kennedy, November 22, 1963; Kennedy's suspected assassin, Lee Harvey Oswald, November 24, 1963; Black Muslim leader, Malcolm X, February 21, 1965; Martin Luther King, Jr. April 4, 1968; and Robert F. Kennedy, June 5, 1968.

238 Schaalman did not have a personal relationship with King and had only met him once in Chicago where he spoke at a meeting. As one of the dignitaries seated at the speaker's table, Schaalman had the opportunity to talk to him briefly. Unlike some of his colleagues, Schaalman had never participated in any of King's marches. During the civil rights movement, he preferred to work quietly in addressing those issues as they affected Chicago.

239 Rabbi Ira Youdovin (1986), who at the time was Schaalman's son-in-law, wrote that Schaalman is an "idealist" who does not easily get involved in political process" (p. 252).

240 Jack Wertheimer (1993), Professor of American Jewish History at the Jewish Theological Seminary of America, writes that in 1959, Eisendrath made the passionate declaration that he saw no distinction between religion and social action. Because of its focus on relationship between people, social action was the "heart of religion." Two years later, under his leadership, the UAHC established the Religious Action Center in Washington, D.C. Its main target was the elimination of segregation in the South. By setting up the Center, Eisendrath had committed Reform rabbis to the work of transforming American social life.

241 During the civil rights movement of the 1950s and 1960s, Reform rabbis worked together with the leaders of the movement such as Martin Luther King, Jr. to abolish segregation and discrimination in America. At the same time, they were becoming actively involved in other social justice struggles. Rabbis went to jail in St. Augustine, Florida, for promoting desegregation, were beaten by racists in Mississippi while registering voters, and bombed in Atlanta. They participated in marches opposing the war in Vietnam and "boycotted grapes harvested under unjust conditions and unfair labor practices" (Wertheimer, 1993, p. 93).

242 Michael Schaalman (2006) remembers Heschel coming to their home, only a few blocks from the conference. As a young, pre-Bar Mitzvah boy, his meeting Heschel was not only a special occasion, but, at his father's encouragement, he got into the conversation.

243 He commanded such respect and influence that he was one of the major Jewish leaders invited to Vatican II to help draft *Nostra Aetate*, the

breakthrough document acknowledging the Church's responsibility for its injustice to the Jews. It committed the Church to change its theology and teachings toward Judaism and acknowledge its own Jewish roots (Spruch, March, 2008).

244 The Board's decision not to hire an assistant for Schaalman may have been based on the lingering resentment of some of its members over the decision to hire him rather than Rabbi Wolf. Another possible explanation is that Levy had leverage over the board and Schaalman did not.

245 In an interview in 2005, Weinberg remembered that after he had his own pulpit at Skokie's Temple Beth Israel, he used to invite Schaalman to substitute for him on the Friday nights when he was absent. Schaalman jokingly said, "'I may tell them things that will get you in trouble,'" to which Friedman responded, "Oh, don't worry. I'll straighten them out when I return."

246 Founded in 1889 by Rabbi Isaac Mayer Wise, it was one of three organizations he set up as the foundation for Reform Judaism. Its counterparts are the Hebrew Union College-Jewish Institute of Religion (Reform Judaism's rabbinic seminary) and the Union of American Hebrew Congregations.

247 Schaalman began attending these meetings in 1942 and for the next decade was present at almost every meeting except one in 1945, the year he was hospitalized because of his automobile accident.

248 D. E. Kaplan (2003) writes that because there was no agreed upon set of conditions, each rabbi made his or her own (p. 178).

249 In a conversation with this author, Rabbi Hillel Cohn (2011) pointed out that a secondary issue for rabbis who performed mixed marriages was that they might be precluded by synagogue policy from having such ceremonies take place in their synagogues.

250 Already in the mid-1970s, Rabbi S. L. Wolf (1976) had concluded that mixed marriage was "the most crucial issue that the CCAR deliberated and acted upon during the period 1960 to 1975 (p. 273). What gave it this stature was that it went right to the heart of the nature of Reform and to the question of authority and discipline. It raised the issue that was central in the Reform rabbinate, namely freedom of conscience. It had always been understood that Reform rabbis had the freedom to make decisions relative to the circumstances in which they found themselves. Many believed the CCAR's position on mixed marriage was an attempt to legislate behavior and establish a fixed position to which all

rabbis must conform (p. 274). During the years that followed, the issue became a frequent and highly emotional subject at annual meetings.

251 Schaalman credits his selection to the fact that Rabbi Polish had seen firsthand how effective Schaalman could be when he worked as Midwest Regional Director of UAHC. Schaalman had developed a reputation, as he himself admitted, "as someone who was capable of bringing people together in an atmosphere where each side could be heard" (as cited in Folb, 2007, p. 57). During his six years as full-time regional director, he had maneuvered skillfully among the minefields of several congregational schisms that tore apart the fabric of rabbinic associations and families.

252 Herman E. Schaalman, Paper, Feb. 10, 1971, CCAR Archives, 1. In *Intermarriage and Rabbinic Officiation*, sociology professor Egon Mayer (1989) referred to Schaalman's position as part of Reform's concern that "all efforts must be made to avoid driving the liberal and traditional segments of Judaism apart."

253 Orthodox Rabbi Irving Greenberg (1966), raises another issue that CCAR seems to have ignored: "Now the rising divorce and remarriage, intermarriage, and assimilation rates are creating the real possibility that Halachically loyal Jews will be unable to intermarry with this segment of the Jewish people. Aside from the psychic and religious wounds that such a situation will open, this will condemn the bulk of the Jews to eventual assimilation. And they will undoubtedly take a number of committed Jews with them, for love rules paramount in our society" (p. 136).

254 According to Rabbi Richard G. Hirsch (2010), as of 2010, most Reform rabbis perform interfaith marriages, though he will not: "Even rabbis who don't want to perform these marriages are trying to figure out how to do them."

255 When the daughter of his brother Ernst married a Sephardic Jew, the Schaalman family faced a situation almost as serious as if she had married a non-Jew. The marriage outside the clan for this "ur Ashkenazi family," shook up the family, which had to adjust to the new reality of a Sephardic intrusion.

256 Although the issue was contentious for the Reform rabbinate, apparently it was not an issue for most American Jews. In 1988, Schaalman told Esta Star that Rabbi Alex Schindler had just completed a survey in which ninety percent of those surveyed did not consider patrilineality a serious problem (Star, E., April 5, 1988, p. 7).

257 Dr. Leonard Kravitz, one of the Committee members, told Folb (2007) that Schaalman's leadership had been "first rate." As Committee chair, he maintained his calm during often-heated discussions. He gave the impression that he was not leading, but facilitating the meetings. Much of the time, committee members were "not aware of being led" (p. 70).

258 Marmur (2002) argues that through this resolution on patrilineal descent, the CCAR was attempting "to hold onto as many Jews as possible [by casting] a much wider net" (p. 287).

259 As he reveals in his autobiography, *More Unfinished Business* (1997), Plaut was strongly opposed to this new direction of Reform Judaism. He saw it as creating an unbridgeable chasm between Reform and Conservative and Orthodox Judaism. By eliminating the *Halachic* ruling that the offspring of a Jewish mother was automatically Jewish, Reform Judaism set up a new issue for Judaism. For Conservative and Orthodox Judaism, Jewish lineage could no longer be assured in respect to marriage of a Conservative or Orthodox Jew to a Reform Jew. He writes of a meeting he convened with Conservative and Orthodox leadership to discuss the issue of patrilineal descent and was told that these other branches of Judaism might have to set up a table of Jewish lineage as a reference for their members seeking to marry a Reform Jew.

260 Rabbi Richard G. Hirsch (2010) thought he had an opportunity to strike back at his Reform Jewish colleagues when he got a call from the CCAR Executive Director, Joe Glaser, who told him the CCAR wanted to meet with Conservative rabbis to see what their attitude was about the proposed changes to patrilineal descent. Hirsch called Rabbi Wolfe Kelman, a friend since the days when Hirsch was an assistant to Rabbi Levy. "Wolfe," Hirsch (2010) admonished, "you have to be very angry when they pass this resolution, and you'll speak out publically and say that the change would have impact on them." Kelman responded, "Dick, I don't think I can do that because I don't think it's such a bad idea." According to Hirsch (2010), he was very angry: "I thought they would blast the Reform movement." Hirsch (2010) was angry because the proposed policy change meant that for the first time in history a person could be considered a Jew without converting. After consulting the latest surveys on Jewish demographics, he discovered that in 1980, only twenty percent of non-Jews who were marrying Jews were converting and, by 1990, the percentage had dropped to five percent. What made the matter worse, in his view, was that the requirement of granting Jewish status to the offspring of an interfaith marriage had not been carried out. The resolution stated that rabbis would require interfaith parents to

commit to various actions that demonstrated their willingness to raise their children Jewishly, i.e., attendance in Hebrew school, membership in a synagogue, or training for Bar or Bat Mitzvah, actions that would be considered the equivalent of conversion. According to Hirsch (2010), these requirements were never carried out. "Today," Hirsch contends, "even rabbis who do not want to officiate at interfaith marriage are now looking for ways to do it."

261 Perhaps, one somewhat mitigating factor in the increasing number of interfaiths is the fact that twenty-five percent of these marriages result in the conversion of the non-Jewish spouse (Raphael, 2000).

262 In his autobiography, *More Unfinished Business* (1997), Plaut explained that CCAR presidential succession was determined by the "order of their ordination years" of its rabbinic members. "Presidents would be succeeded either by members of their own graduating class or by younger ordainees. Two of my classmates, Arthur Lelyveld and Elie Pilchik, had already served as presidents, and now the choice fell on Herman Schaalman, who had been ordained two years later than I" (pp. 114–115). Plaut was passed over, he claimed, because he had retired from the rabbinate and no other retired rabbi had ever been CCAR president. Another reason he thought was the unpopular stands he took in the movement (p. 114).

263 Only a few months later, on October 27, he became automatically a member of the Hebrew Union College-Jewish Institute of Religion highly prestigious Board of Governors.

264 The location could not have been more meaningful for Schaalman, who would be installed during CCAR's next meeting as its new president. The CCAR had chosen the site to demonstrate the movement's commitment to Israel and, very likely, to publicize its own existence.

265 Anyone who has been close to the Schaalmans knows that this compliment was well earned, that a more supportive and loving wife and rebbetzin would be difficult to find. Schaalman claims that he never met her equal: "The woman who thought she could never be a rabbi's wife wrote the book on it. When a congregation invited me to be its rabbi, they got a two-for-one deal."

266 This chapter of Proverbs describes the attributes of the ideal wife: maintaining a clean house, care of husband and children, as well as providing a living for the family and tending to the charitable needs of the community.

267 The "might have been" is so typically Schaalman, revealing a humility he has expressed at each stage of his life and for the recognition he has received for his many accomplishments. He might have been consciously echoing Heschel (1966) who considered himself a survivor of the Holocaust, "a brand plucked from the fire" (p. 282), or Zechariah 3:2 where God speaks of Joshua (who represents Jerusalem) as "a brand plucked from the fire."

268 ARZA was organized to strengthen and enrich the Jewish identity of Reform Jews in the United States. Its aim was to accomplish this goal by helping Reform Jews become aware of and connected to Israel as a fundamental part of their identity. According to Rabbi Richard G. Hirsch (2010), when he left New York for Jerusalem to establish the headquarters of the World Union of Progressive Zionism, he hired Youdovin to run its New York office.

269 Youdovin's (1986) first impression of Schaalman, who was then sixty-five, "was that he was distant and foreboding, a man with a mane of brown hair that stubbornly refused to gray and an affectation for white turtleneck sweaters worn under a blue blazer" (p. 251).

270 When Susan was a child, she wanted to be a rabbi just like her dad, but in those days, women were not accepted into the rabbinate (Schaalman Youdovin, S., 2006). The next best thing was to become a rebbetzin, like her mother. "On August 21, 1981, my dream came true when I married Rabbi Ira Youdovin" (Schaalman Youdovin, S., 2006). One can only imagine the pride and joy of her parents when her father had the pleasure of performing their wedding. "For the next twenty-five years, I lived out my dream. My marriage to a rabbi helped bring me closer to my parents" (Schaalman Youdovin, S., 2006).

271 S. E. Karff (1990) writes that the issue of the place of spirituality in Reform had not been raised at a CCAR Convention for the last sixty years when Rabbi Samuel H. Goldenson urged his colleagues to affirm the "spiritual content" of Reform (p. 72). Goldenson's challenge to his peers was an effort to persuade them to move beyond Reform's formulaic religious services and its strict rational theology. He was uncomfortable with the fact that Reform congregations had shed the trappings of traditional ritual practices, particularly its physicality, and offered, instead, a rational form of liberal humanism (p. 72). Goldenson's challenge went unanswered for decades. A review of the CCAR proceedings during these years reveals that the Reform rabbinate felt embarrassed about discussing spiritual thoughts and feelings (p. 72). Following World War II, the Reform rabbinate was forced to acknowledge the "monstrous evil"

that human beings were capable of and the reality of the murder of six million Jews (p. 72). At the CCAR convention in 1953, Rabbi Jacob Weinstein was already heralding a return to religion (Karff, S., E., 1990, p. 73). Weinstein, a Labor-Zionist and social activist, told the assembly that an understanding of Judaism that denied the mystery of its destination was a "misunderstanding" idea. After the Holocaust, many of his non-religious colleagues had "reclaimed their religious birthright" (p. 74). Although Weinstein's effort to reclaim religious faith was not widely endorsed by the majority of the Reform rabbinate, it was another early movement in that direction. By the end of the 1970s, Reform was moving toward "a deepening spiritual and religious identity" that included more intense ritual celebration (Rubinstein, P. J., 1989, p. 143).

272 In *American Reform Judaism* (2003), Dana Kaplan argues that by the 1937 Columbus Platform, American Reform had moved away from the more unified theological position of the 1885 Pittsburgh Platform and had become more pluralistic, more accepting of a wide range of theological positions and liturgical practices (p. 62). He cites Plaut's *Liberal Judaism* (1984) for confirmation of this openness of Reform to religious diversity in the latter part of the twentieth century.

273 Schaalman's understanding of the importance of the covenant as the "bedrock" of Jewish existence appears in *Commentary* (1966) where he was speaking as a Covenant Theologian (pp. 201–207). The group had its own unique and revisionary view of Reform Judaism and a course for its future development. Cf. Chapter 6, "Emanuel Congregation and Leadership in Reform Judaism: 1956-1986" for a more detailed examination of the history of the development of Covenant Theology and Schaalman's role in it.

274 Ironically, nearly thirty years later, Schaalman became one of the people he was criticizing. He had come to see the Torah as the product of human hands, replete with duplications and scribal errors, and many untranslatable words and passages. For further discussion, see Chapter 9, "Schaalman's Theology."

275 Although he no longer argues that the laws of Torah must be obeyed, Schaalman believes that God is in the Torah.

276 In *Quest for Past and Future* (1968), Fackenheim had quoted a Midrash on Isaiah 43:12, "Ye are My witnesses, saith the Lord, and I am God." The rabbis understood this statement to mean "when ye are My witnesses, I am God, and when ye are not My witnesses, I am, as it were, not God" (p. 39). The Midrash goes further by asserting that when the Israelites do God's will, they add to God's power, and it follows, that if

they do not, God's power is weakened. The same year that Schaalman made his CCAR speech, Fackenheim published *To Mend the World*, in which he returned to the same theme, this time citing a Midrash on Psalms 123:1, "'You are My witnesses, says the Lord.'—that is, if you are My witnesses, I am God, and if you are not My witnesses, I am, as it were, not God" (p. 331).

277 To appreciate Schaalman's views on the role of the rabbi, it is helpful to understand the changes in the Reform movement. According to Borowitz (1969), in the nineteenth century, Reform Judaism moved away from traditional liturgical practice. In the traditional service, the emphasis was on the individual, not the rabbi. The individual had a firm command of the liturgy and engaged in an emotional recitation of the prayers. The emotion was expressed through body movements and, sometimes, in silent and, other times, vocal appeals to, and praises of, God. In contrast, Reform Jews preferred a religious service that was quiet and dignified. In such a service, the individual delegated the central responsibility of individual prayer to the professional prayer leader, the rabbi or cantor (Borowitz, 1969). Borowitz criticized this form of worship almost universally practiced in Reform congregations. The worshiper in these services, he wrote, "has been aesthetically cowed and emotionally neutralized" (Borowitz, 1969). The service becomes a "form of entertainment" in which the worshiper is largely passive, and the individual's spiritual experience comes from the enjoyment of the music and the sermon of the rabbi (Borowitz, 1969). The typical service incorporates modern folk-like music, a choice of several abbreviated liturgies, mostly in English, a sprinkling of Hebrew and an inspirational sermon. The rabbi not only leads these services but also produces and directs them (Karff, S., E., 1990). Borowitz (1969) maintains that a more authentic prayer service for individuals who believe in God requires that they "speak to him, seek him, [and] commune with him regularly" (p. 118). God wants us to pray, writes Borowitz (1969), not out of a sense of obligation, but as an expression of our awareness and our gratitude that God exists and provides a moral and ethical framework for living (p. 118).

278 The members included Alfred Goodman, Meyer Heller, Robert Lehman, Eugene Lipman, Ernst Lorge and W. Gunther Plaut (ex officio).

279 On a more personal level, he also realized that the culture of the organization had been changing; it had become more family oriented with the result that rabbis did not attend annual conferences by themselves or with their wives, but now brought their children. These new circumstances had an impact on the organization's ability to get its business done.

280 The CCAR did call on Schaalman in the 1990s to help with a new project. In the charged atmosphere created by the sexual abuse scandals in the Catholic Church, before they became public, the CCAR stepped up its own efforts to address problems its rabbis were facing. It established regional Rapid Response Teams and asked Schaalman to chair one of them. When a rabbi in crisis contacted the team chair, the chair would then match the rabbi with one of the team members who would provide local support and advice. However, as of 2011, Schaalman's team had not been activated.

281 At first, the Rabbinic Pension Board sent him $1,000/month. Later it was reduced to $700. When in 2010 it was reduced to $420, Schaalman sent the board an appeal that the monthly allotment remain at $700.

282 In contrast, Handwerger's replacement taught adult education classes, occasionally performed burial services when Schaalman was not available, and was also present at evening minyans. The result for Schaalman was that he was no longer alone in providing necessary services for the congregation (Star, E., January 27, 1988, p. 27).

283 The rabbis "brought a *Shoah* Torah from the Czech Memorial Skoll Trust to OSRUI in honor of Schaalman. The scroll, number 1506, came from Gevay, Moravia, Czechoslovakia" (Emanuel Congregation, May 30, 1986). Three of the rabbis had been Schaalman's assistants: John Friedman, David Mersky and Michael Weinberg. Four came from Emanuel Congregation under Schaalman's leadership: Jay Sangerman, Fred Reiner, Joseph Weinberg, David Levy. Three of these rabbis had been his students at Beloit College: Marc Berkson, Michael Weinberg, and Bennett Greenspan. The tenth was Rabbi Richard Edelson, who had emerged from Schaalman's Saturday morning Torah Study (Emanuel, May 30, 1986).

284 *Pirkei Avot* (Hebrew: פרקי אבות), known in English as "Ethics of the Fathers," is a compilation of the ethical teachings and maxims of the Rabbis of the early rabbinic period.

285 Ironically, although Schaalman got the gist of Glaser's glowing presentation, he could not hear all the details. Schaalman was seated on the podium behind the rostrum where hearing was difficult at best. When he read this account of Glaser's remarks, he had tears in his eyes: "I had no idea Joe harbored such fine sentiments about me."

286 Rabbi John Friedman, one of Schaalman's former assistants, attributes this ongoing commitment in part to Schaalman's "larger than life personality" (as cited in Folb, 2007, p. 57).

287 According to Lotte, her husband "feels distraught if he doesn't get a chance to study for one day. And that's what makes him such a desired speaker ... ."

288 A *festschrift* is a volume of writings by different authors presented as a tribute or memorial especially to a scholar.

289 Late in the 1990s and again in 2006 and 2007, Edelheit wrote to Schaalman seeking to repair the breach between them. In 2006, Edelheit wrote: "I cannot imagine myself as a 'rabbi' without thinking of you and the model you set for me. I am profoundly grateful that we worked together. I learned more about 'being' a rabbi—for good or ill—from you." Although at the time the Schaalmans were deeply offended, they eventually made peace with Edelheit.

290 Morris and Schaalman have been tennis partners for years and have traveled extensively together. Until his death in 2012, Morris and his wife Audrey continue to provide financial support for the congregation.

291 In an effort to stem this drain on the congregation's endowment, a new president, Marlene Dodinval, pushed the board to discard the "fair share" dues policy and return to the former set amount by type of membership. She also convinced the board to eliminate the practice by which individual board members could "make a deal" with a member for dues relief. The board established a new policy of dues relief that would involve it in a more thorough vetting of the request.

292 Rickie Jacobs, one of Emanuel's former presidents and a board member during Sofian's final years, reports that he was well aware of how badly off the congregation was and skeptical of the board's ability to rescue it. According to Jacobs, "Although he was reluctant to leave Emanuel and the Chicago Jewish community, his first commitment was to his family and to providing them the best life he could. He chose to seek a better paying position in a more stable and financially secure congregation."

293 As Folb (2007) points out, Emanuel's decline may not have been the result of the succession of rabbis who followed Schaalman. The reasons, she claims are "undoubtedly quite complex" (p. 61). Popular rabbis are not easy to follow. For example, when Schaalman replaced the renowned Rabbi Levy, he ran into significant opposition from Levy followers. It took him years to win them over and prove himself as a worthy successor (p. 61).

Chapter 7: Post Retirement

294 Two of the most important presentations have been his 2010 keynote address to the Council of Religious Leaders of Metropolitan Chicago and, in 2011, his keynote address to the National Association of Retired Reform Rabbis.

295 In an interview on October 16, 2008, Marx stated that he had no memory of asking for Schaalman's help to restore funding to JCUA. However, he did confirm the events and the difficulties he encountered with continued Chicago Federation funding.

296 According to Dirk Johnson, *New York Times* reporter, Farrakhan praised Cokely "and said Jews were offended because 'the truth hurts.' After Mr. Cokely lost his job, Mr. Farrakhan contributed $1,000 to the Cokely family" (July 28, 1988).

297 Cokely criticized Jackson and Washington "as subservient 'niggers' who catered to Jewish advisers. ... [He] had been especially critical of Mr. Washington's expression of outrage over a series of window-breakings at synagogues and Jewish-operated stores on the North side ...." (Johnson, D., July 28, 1988).

298 Cf. the *Chicago Sun-Times* article (Lehmann, D. J., May 12, 1988): "Three noted clergymen Wednesday agreed to lead a religious task force sought by Mayor Sawyer to soothe tensions arising from the Steve Cokely furor. They are Joseph Cardinal Bernardin, archbishop of the Roman Catholic Archdiocese of Chicago; the Rev. W. Sterling Cary, head of the Illinois conference of the United Church of Christ, and Rabbi Herman Schaalman, president of the Chicago Board of Rabbis."

299 These attacks on Jews are a strange irony given the enormous support Jews gave to blacks during the civil rights movement. This support can be measured in the sacrifice of the lives of Goodman and Cheney, two young Jewish civil rights workers in Mississippi; the large sums of money Jewish individuals and organizations gave to support the movement; the support of Jewish clergy and congregations; and the advocacy of national Jewish organizations such as the Anti-Defamation League, the American Jewish Congress, and the American Jewish Committee. During this period, the civil rights movement spawned a new phenomenon in American life, the radical leftist African American group known at the Black Panthers that advocated violence in the pursuit of justice and equality. Together with the Black Muslims, they attacked Jews and whites with a viciousness only matched by the KKK and the Nazis. They objected strongly to having Jews as partners in their struggle. This backlash was

part of the process of the maturation of the movement as black America sought to separate itself from white society. The worst of the anti-Semitic harangues came from leaders of the Black Muslims such as Malcolm X and Louis Farrakhan, who called Jews a variety of obscene names and identified them with white people who were the source of the injustice they suffered.

300 No racial conflict in Chicago could be ignored by Reverend Jesse Jackson, who, by this time was perhaps the most powerful African American leader in America. When he was asked for his response to Cokely's remarks, he redirected the discussion to the failure of Jews to criticize New York's mayor, Ed Koch, for attacking him. Other black politicians unwilling to criticize Cokely cited three major issues dividing blacks and Jews: remarks like Koch's; the differences between blacks and Jews over the right of Palestinians to statehood; and Israel's sale of weapons to South Africa. Another obstacle in the attempt to create racial harmony was the longtime resentment of Chicago's poor blacks towards Jewish landlords and shopkeepers. Jewish leaders were confounded by these attitudes. After all, hadn't the Jewish community supported Mayor Washington in far greater numbers than any other white ethnic group? Jewish leaders expected that the black community would at least repudiate Cokely's and other black leaders' anti-Semitic remarks.

301 Founded in Detroit in 1930, the Black Muslims split in 1976 into the American Muslim Mission and the Nation of Islam (NOI). Elijah Muhammad, leader of the NOI, transferred the movement's headquarters to Chicago's Southside (Black Muslims, 2001–2007). The NOI was a black separatist movement that appealed to poor blacks and prison populations and, though it never achieved anything like the membership of the mainline black advocacy groups such as the NAACP or the Urban League, it grew rapidly during the 1950s and '60s. The growth has been attributed in large part to the movement's charismatic Minister Malcolm X. In the 1950s, he recruited Louis Farrakhan, who, later became his successor. In 1963, after tensions had developed between Elijah Muhammad and Malcolm X, Muhammad suspended Malcolm X. Two years later, Malcolm was assassinated, and, in 1977, Louis Farrakhan, together with a group of Black Muslims, split off from the parent group, which, under Elijah Muhammad's son, Wallace Dean Muhammad, had embraced traditional Islam. Unwilling to give up the doctrines of the founders, Farrakhan and his supporters called his new organization the Nation of Islam (Black Muslims, 2001–2007).

302 The Anti-Defamation League has cataloged many of Farrakhan's anti-Semitic remarks on its website, www.adl.org.

303 According to Magida (1996), when Farrakhan was before TV cameras or large crowds, "he was obsessed with Jews" but treated them respectfully when he encountered them face-to-face. [Farrakhan] needed this handful of Jews to remind him that they were not a cardboard, one-dimensional people—just as they discovered, to their surprise, that he was not the cardboard, one-dimensional character about whom they had heard—and whom they dreaded—so much" (p. 162). The discrepancy between his public rage about Jews and his congenial affability toward them in private suggested that he practiced a "pragmatic anti-Semitism" (p. 161).

304 The sponsoring agencies were the Anti-Defamation League, the American Jewish Committee, the American Jewish Congress, and the Jewish Community Relations Council of the Jewish United Fund of Metropolitan Chicago.

305 Despite his effort to appease the Jewish community, Jewish leaders were suspicious. Michael Kotzin, at the time, Director of the Jewish Community Relations Council, stated that Farrakhan liked to complain to the media that he had been misunderstood when he had been criticized for his apparent anti-Semitic rhetoric, but, to make his denials credible, he needed to follow up with concrete actions. The acting director of the B'nai Brith Anti-Defamation League, Nina Kavin, also questioned Farrakhan's sincerity. Her position was that, unless he made a public announcement that he had changed his position on Jews, most of the Jewish community would see the concert as "nothing more than a publicity ploy" (Johnson, M. A., 1993, p. 5).

306 According to the renowned Catholic scholar Thomas A. Baima (1996), the change in relations can be traced to 1893 with the creation of the first World's Parliament of Religions. As a result of this first interfaith national and international meeting, a new dynamic began to form between Protestants, Catholics, and Jews. However, it took nearly fifty years before further dialogue among equals within the faith communities could emerge (p. 9). The stimulus was the reaction to the Holocaust and the founding of the state of Israel. Greenberg (1997), reflecting on the new acceptance of pluralism, claims that "we are living in an age of great religious breakthroughs" (p. 8).

307 Major private universities had quotas for the admission of Jewish students, including nearby Northwestern University.

308 Catholics were discovering the Jewish roots to their own rites and prayers. According to Athans (2008), "Already in 1928, Frank Gavin had written

in *The Jewish Antecedents of the Christian Sacraments* that the *berakah* (Hebrew blessing) was a source of the Eucharistic prayer" (p. 53). Athans also noted that the Hebrew blessing before a meal, *Baruch atah Adonai, eloheynu melech ha-olam, hamotsi lchem min ha-aretz* (Blessed are You, O Lord our God, Ruler of the universe, who brings forth bread from the earth) is similar to the Eucharist, "Blessed are You, Lord God of all creation, through your goodness we have this bread to offer, which earth has given, and human hands have made. It will become for us the bread of life" (as quoted in Athans, 2008, p. 56). Athans speculates that the similarity of the blessings is the result of the fact that the Hebrew blessings "were very likely the prayers that Jesus might have said when he sat down to have a meal with his friends" (p. 56).

309 Founded in 1929 by the Sisters of the Charity of the Blessed Virgin Mary, Mundelein College was a small, independent, all-women's Catholic college in Chicago. Currently, it has been incorporated into Loyola University.

310 Schaalman remembers that when Eliezar Berkovits, Orthodox rabbi and renowned Jewish scholar, had been invited as Emanuel Congregation's Scholar-in-Residence, he would not enter the sanctuary during a Shabbat service. Only when it was over, was he willing to come to the bimah to give his lecture (Schaalman, October 11, 2010).

311 According to its mission statement, "Divine Word Missionaries preach the Gospel and share the Word of God by living, working, teaching, and sharing with others in many areas of global ministry. We are the largest international missionary congregation in the Catholic Church. Our mission is 'a giving of ourselves to others'. ... Working among the poor, neglected and disadvantaged, we fulfill a unique cross-cultural and worldwide mission. We strive to perpetuate the vision of St. Arnold when he said, "'To proclaim the Good News is the first and greatest act of love of neighbor'" (Divine Word, 2008). The Society has established missions in seventy countries, including the continents of Africa, Asia, North and South America, and Europe. More recently, because of a decline in students, Techny closed as a seminary and was converted into a convent and convention center.

312 At the time, he had no idea that thirty-five years later the Protestant Chicago Theological Seminary would create a Chair in Jewish Studies named after him. That event may be understood as the fulfillment of the dream of a lifetime.

313 During a session of his Torah Study in 2008, when he was discussing the ritual of prostration of the ancient Israelite priests in front of the

Holy of Holies, he compared it to what he had witnessed at Techny. He pointed out that the ritual of prostration, which had been abandoned by the Jews as a regular practice after the destruction of the Second Temple, had been adopted by the Catholic Church. He recalled having seen Cardinal Bernardin perform the same rite while he was Bernardin's guest at an assembly of Catholic Bishops. Perhaps the most prominent use of prostration, he reminded his students, is in Islam. Muslims are required to worship five times a day, during which they prostrate themselves as a sign of their total submission to their God. In response to this practice and its implication of the relationship of the worshipper to God, Schaalman asserted his own view: "My God does not want me on my belly. My God does not demand my submission but that I be His partner."

314 African Methodist Episcopal Church, African Methodist Episcopal Zion Church, American Baptist Churches of Metro Chicago, Armenian Orthodox Church, Baptist General Convention of Illinois, Chicago Board of Rabbis, Church of God in Christ, Church of the Brethren, Council of Islamic Organizations of Greater Chicago, Episcopal Church (USA), Evangelical Lutheran Church in America, Greek Orthodox Church, International Council of Community Churches, Jain Society of Metropolitan Chicago, Orthodox Church in America, Presbyterian Church (USA), Religious Society of Friends (Quakers), Roman Catholic Church, Salvation Army, Serbian Orthodox Church, Sikh Religious Society of Chicago, Spiritual Assembly of the Baha'is of Chicago, Ukrainian Catholic Church, Ukrainian Orthodox Church, Unitarian Universalist Association, United Baptist State Convention, United Church of Christ, United Methodist Church, Vivekananda Vedanta Society of Chicago, Zoroastrian Association of Metropolitan Chicago, Catholic Theological Union, Chicago Theological Seminary, Lutheran School of Theology at Chicago, McCormick Theological Seminary, Meadville-Lombard Theological School, Chicago Center for Cultural Connections, Community Renewal Society (Council of Religious Leaders of Metropolitan Chicago, 2010).

315 Over the years of Schaalman's involvement, when Ficca asked his help in raising funds for the organization, Schaalman respectfully declined. He told Ficca that he had spent thirty years as a fundraiser and was now "tapped out" (as quoted by Ficca, 2010). Nevertheless, Ficca (2010) remembers that, when Schaalman addressed audiences about the need for funds for the Parliament, he spoke of the act of giving as a "religious or spiritual act."

316 Founded in 1853 as a school to train Methodist ministers, Garrett-Evangelical is a graduate school of theology related to The United Methodist Church.

317 Established in 1855, CTS is an ecumenical seminary of the United Church of Christ, preparing women and men for leadership in the church and society (Chicago Theological Seminary, 2011).

318 On the other hand, Schaalman is shocked by the fact that his students have not been required to learn classical languages such as Greek and Latin or Hebrew: "Not a single one of my students [at Garrett] knows Latin nor, for that matter, Greek or Hebrew. The same situation applies to my students at Chicago Theological Seminary at the University of Chicago.... There was a time when Hebrew was a language of the educated class. Now, even students preparing for the ministry are not required to take these subjects."

319 As with Schaalman, the Holocaust shattered Pawlikowski's (2001) view of the omnipotence of God: "The Holocaust has destroyed simplistic notions of a 'commanding,' all powerful God" (p. 168).

320 A list of his books includes: *Onslaught Against Innocence: Cain, Abel, and the Yahwist; Ruth: A Continental Commentary; The Captivity of Innocence: Babel and the Yahwist; Romance, She Wrote: A Hermeneutical Essay on Song of Songs; The Trial of Innocence: Adam, Eve, and the Yahwist; The Yahwist and Primeval Innocence Collection; The Feminine Unconventional: Four Subversive Figures in Israel's Tradition.*

321 Currently, Pawlikowski is the Director of the Catholic-Jewish Studies Program at Catholic Theological Union and is the immediate past president of the International Council of Christians and Jews. An expert in Holocaust studies, he is well known for his study of the theological and ethical aspects of the Christian-Jewish relationship. For more than forty years, Pawlikowski had been urging Catholics and others to confront the long history of Christian anti-Semitism.

322 When it was established in 1968, CTU hired Rabbi Hayim Goren Perelmutter as one of its faculty. Working closely with CTU, Perelmutter made major contributions to Chicago's Catholic-Jewish dialogue.

323 The succession of Popes from John XXIII (1958–1963) through Benedict XVI (2005–) has been a period of radical liberalization in the relationship of the Church to other major religions. From the time of the Second Vatican Council (1963–1965), the Church, first under the leadership of Pope John XXIII and then Pope Paul VI, redefined its relationship to the other major world religions.

324 When the Council opened, Pope John XXIII welcomed a Jewish delegation with the words, "I am Joseph, your brother" (Gen. 45:3–4). The

significance of this greeting lay in the fact that the Pope's name, Giuseppe, was the Italian equivalent of "Joseph." By his choice of the few simple words from the story of Joseph in the book of Genesis, Pope John attempted to establish a familial bond with the members of the Jewish delegation. If nothing else, they created an atmosphere of warmth and welcome that opened the door to dialogue.

325 In this same year, the Chicago office of the American Jewish Committee and the Archdiocese Office of Human Relations and Ecumenism organized and supported several lay dialogue groups that paired neighborhood parish churches and synagogues (Baima, T. A., 1996, p. 11). The goal of the project was to break down old stereotypes and to reduce tensions between religious communities.

326 Schaalman relates one humorous anecdote about his relationship with the Cardinal. Sometime in the 1990s when Lotte was hospitalized in St. Francis Hospital in Evanston, Bernardin paid her an unexpected visit. Schaalman had gone out to get something to eat and, when he returned, heard voices coming from Lotte's room. When he came to the door, he saw his friend and his driver visiting with his wife. When Bernardin left the room, Schaalman recounted, "All the doors in the hallway flew open and staff and patients came out to ask the Cardinal for his blessing and to kiss his ring. It took the Cardinal another 45 minutes to reach the elevator!"

327 Included among them were Fr. Michael Place and Thomas Baima, both of whom were key members of the planning group, Michael Kotzin, Executive Vice President of the Chicago Jewish Federation, and Maynard Wishner, Chairman of Chicago's Jewish United Fund.

328 Knobel (2006) had known Schaalman since the early 1970s when they worked together on the CCAR's Committee on Reform Religious Practices. They also worked together on the Committee on Patrilineal Descent. At the time, he [Knobel] "was a young pup of a Rabbi and looked on Schaalman as one of the "greats" of the Reform movement."

329 Rabbi Peter Knobel, president of the Chicago Board of Rabbis, possibly reflecting the feelings of the Jewish members of the delegation, said, "We were pleased to be there with the cardinal and the Catholic clergy and the sisters because we knew it was something which was meaningful and important to them. ... But it's not our story. It's not a story that we can fully participate in. Certainly to appreciate the meaning of that story for Christians and Christianity is an important aspect of dialogue" (as quoted in Galloway, March 26, 1996).

330 Pawlikowski (2007) wrote that "the Vatican II's Nostra Aetate, together with many parallel Protestant documents, fundamentally changed Christianity's theological posture relative to Jews and Judaism that had permeated its theology, art, and practice for nearly eighteen hundred years. Jews were now to be seen as integral to the ongoing divine covenant" (p. 71). The Canadian theologian Gregory Baum told the 1986 annual meeting of the Catholic Theological Society that "the Church's recognition of the spiritual status of the Jewish religion is the most dramatic example of doctrinal turn–about in the age ... to occur at the Council" (pp. 70–71).

331 The document put forth eight statements about how Jews and Christians may relate to one another: (1) Jews and Christians worship the same God, (2) share the same bible, though understanding it differently, (3) accept and support Israel as the homeland of the Jewish people, (4) share the moral principles of Torah, (5) recognize that Nazism was not a Christian phenomenon, (6) that the irreconcilable difference between Jews and Christians will not be settled until God redeems the entire world as promised in Scripture, (7) that a new relationship between Jews and Christians will not weaken Jewish practice, and (8) that Jews and Christians must work together for justice and peace (National Jewish Scholars' Project, n.d.).

332 Cf. According to Pawlikowski (2006), the best book on the subject is by J. M. Sanchez, *Pius XII and the Holocaust: Understanding Controversy* (2002).

333 Schaalman's concern is echoed in the formal protest to the action by the Christian-Jewish Dialogue of Montreal (CJDM). Sponsored by the International Council of Jewish and Christian Relations, the Council's position is that "this prayer stands in contradiction with the important change of attitude towards the Jewish people that the Church expressed in *Nostra Aetate* ... [and] to the new Missal promulgated by Pope Paul VI in 1970" (International Council of Christians and Jews, 2009). In response to this and other protests, the Pope issued a replacement prayer in 2008, which, although it did not call for the conversion of the Jews, asked God to "enlighten their hearts so that they recognize Jesus Christ, the Saviour of all men ... [and that] all Israel may be saved. Through Christ our Lord. Amen" (as quoted in International Council of Jewish Christian Relations, 2009). The CJDM concluded that this revision did not go far enough. Instead, the group proposed that the 1962 Prayer for the Jews (Oremus et pro Iudaeis) be replaced "by the prayer of the 1970 Missal of Pope Paul VI already in use by most Roman Catholics throughout the world" (International Council of Jewish Christian Relations, 2009).

334 Dr. Michael Kotzin (2007), Executive Vice President of the Jewish Federation of Metropolitan Chicago, writes that despite all the progress that has been made in Catholic-Jewish relations, "wounds continue to fester and memories of the past continue to impact on many people's sense of the current state of affairs (p. 7). In the Catholic community, fatigue has set in with its efforts to heal the wounds: "There are those inclined to think, haven't we done enough, and why do we have to continue to be the ones to make the overtures, to hear the complaints, to be told about the steps that we need to take?" (p. 16) And, though the dialogue continues and high ranking Church officials like Cardinal George want to strengthen the dialogue, Kotzin (2007) questions whether "the generation formed in the post-*Nostra Aetate* era … recognize and appreciate the nature and the importance of sustaining such work" (p. 7).

335 Together with the National Conference for Community and Justice (NCCJ), the Council of Centres for Jewish-Christian Relations (CCJCR) the ICCJ is a network of national organizations in thirty-two countries.

336 The program was part of the seminary's long history of interfaith commitments dating back to its founding charter. Billed as a "kickoff" for the seminary's next 150 years and a celebration of its first 150 years, the music program was designed as an interfaith dialogue focusing on various aspects of interfaith relations: Unity, Transformation, Encounter, Risk, Resurrection, and Hope (Chicago Theological Seminary, 2006). CTS president, Reverend Susan Thistlethwaite, told the audience that the concert served to highlight "the profound urgency of interfaith work" and the role of music in promoting that work: "Music is a wonderful way to speak soul to soul of the mystery of God. It has the capacity to lift us beyond ourselves to a vision of what could be, what should be" (Chicago Theological Seminary, 2006).

Chapter 8: The Reform of Reform

337 For a meaningful analysis of the *Shoah* to take place, Braiterman (1998) insists, a "discursive context" had to be developed through which to frame an idea, no less to propose an argument. Only after a public vocabulary developed—words that quickly assumed iconic status: i.e., "Holocaust," "Auschwitz," *Arbeit macht frei*—were intellectuals able to conceptualize the horror and give shape to its possible meanings (p. 7). Braiterman (1998) lists various developments in the early years after the Holocaust that contributed to the development of a discourse context for its theological discussion: the release of the documentary "Night and

Fog" (1955), the Eichmann trial (1961), Hannah Arendt's formulation of the banality of evil in her book, *Eichmann in Jerusalem: A Report on the Banality of Evil*, the work of Elie Wiesel, and various thinkers, including Primo Levi, Alexander Donat, Terence DePree, Elie Cohen, Victor Frankl, and Bruno Bettelheim (p. 7).

338   Borowitz (2002) identifies Christian theologians such as Karl Barth and Paul Tillich who, directly challenged by the Holocaust, directed their reassessment of their own beliefs toward a new interest in original sin, the power of human evil, and the theological consequences.

339   Rabbi Marc Berkson points out that there were other rabbis who were refugees from Germany that should be noted: Karl Richter, Karl Miller, Frank Rosenthal, and Karl Schwartz.

340   Meyer (1988) claims "awareness of the Holocaust actually declined in the early years of the 1950s (p. 354). Greenberg (2006) attempts to qualify this assessment by citing lists of materials written in Hebrew that chronicle Jewish responses to the Holocaust during and immediately afterwards (cf. his footnote 3, p. 232).

341   Among the major scientific discoveries were relativity and quantum mechanics, atomic structure, nuclear reactions, radiocarbon dating, the Big Bang, the planet Pluto, extrasolar planets, the structure of DNA, and the ability to clone mammals.

342   The Pittsburgh Platform of 1885 included a disavowal of God as a separate being and substituted in its place the "God-idea." It stripped the Bible of its divine origin, identifying it as a reflection of the "primitive ideas of its own age." It asserted that there was no conflict in Judaism with modern science and did away with Mosaic and dietary law as outmoded and unsuited to modern times. It dismissed the idea that Jews were a nation and rejected the idea that Jews expected to return to Palestine or to restore "any of the laws concerning the Jewish state." It also dismissed the belief in bodily resurrection (Meyer, 1988, pp. 387–388).

343   The Columbus Platform reintroduced the idea of God as "the One, living God, who rules the world through law and love" and reasserted that God was the creative source of all existence, "transcending time and space, and the indwelling Presence of the world." This God was to be worshiped "as the Lord of the universe and as our merciful Father." The Platform also brought back the idea that man is created in the Divine image and a "co-worker with God." The Platform reasserted the traditional idea that the Torah is both oral and written, the product of

God's revealing Himself. Other concepts that it brought back were that revelation is a continuous process; that Judaism "is the body" and "soul" of Israel; that Palestine is the Jewish homeland and that it is every Jew's responsibility to help rebuild it." It also restored the synagogue and the home as the center of religious practice and prayer as the vehicle for reaching God. It called for intensification of Jewish religious education, the restoration of the Sabbath, Festivals and Holy Days, and the "retention and development of such customs, symbols and ceremonies as possess inspirational value" (Meyer, 1988, pp. 388–394).

344 Schaalman remembers having a lunch with Greenberg that "went on for hours." This meeting, Schaalman believes, "was the first with a Reform rabbi that Greenberg ever had and resulted in broadening Greenberg's view of the Reform movement (Folb, 2007, p. 87). According to Greenberg, Schaalman helped "move me further toward pluralism, a position I grew into over decades." For Greenberg, this meeting was his "first encounter with serious Reform rabbis with strong principles, deeper religious/theological foundations and passionate commitment to the totality of the Jewish people. They had built vital religious communities which helped me realize that Reform was here to stay." From Schaalman, he came to understand the importance of the Holocaust in terms of his theological development.

345 It is unclear from Meyer's account (1988) what the Conservative and Orthodox rabbis contributed.

346 Cf. Borowitz's 1959 essay, "Existentialism's Meaning for Judaism: a Contemporary Midrash," reprinted in his *Studies in the meaning of Judaism* (2002).

347 Hasia Diner, Paul S. and Sylvia Steinberg Professor of American Jewish History at NYU, attempts to debunk the idea that American Jews were not active in dealing with the consequences of the Holocaust. In her book, *We remember with reverence and love: American Jews and the myth of silence after the Holocaust, 1945–1962*, Professor Diner presents a wealth of data to support her thesis that American Jews were overwhelmingly engaged in addressing them. Her book, however, does not address the issue of the failure of Jewish theology to discuss the Holocaust.

348 A "Death of God" movement was emerging in radical theological discussions among Protestant Christian theologians such as Gabriel Vahanian, Paul Van Buren, William Hamilton, and Thomas J. J. Altizer. Among those Protestants, the discussions centered on modern secular unbelief, the collapse of the belief in any transcendent order to the universe, and their implications for Christianity. During the 1960s, the "Death of

God" movement achieved considerable notoriety and was featured as the cover story of the April 8, 1966, edition of *Time* magazine. Two years later, Fackenheim (1968) observed that the "God-is-dead theologies, proclaimed as epoch-making only a few years ago, are already dead themselves" (p. 60).

349 Noticeably absent from the respondents were Wiesel and Fackenheim.

350 He might well have said that Christianity was in the throes of a major reassessment of its teachings about Jews and reaching out for a new relationship based on respect for Judaism and its Jewish roots. In the preceding year, Vatican II had just been completed with its far-reaching reappraisal of the relationship of the Church with Judaism.

351 In his 1982 article, "Revelation," Schaalman wrote, "Torah speaks human language and human language only, for language is quintessentially human" (p. 88). More recently, he told his Torah Study students, "The only language available to the Israelites was a polytheistic language. How is it possible for a language without a word for one god to represent that god? Jewish existence, then, is not based on an understanding of God who is beyond human understanding but on a system of behavior, on mitzvot, down to the meanest of behaviors."

352 According to Meyer (1988), although Covenant Theology took center stage in Reform during the sixties and seventies, theologians were beginning to realize that their failure "to deal explicitly with the Holocaust … [was] a critical theological omission" (p. 363).

353 Rubenstein's book appeared at a time when the Death of God movement was at its height (cf. John Warwick Montgomery and Thomas J. J. Altizer, 1967, *The Altizer-Montgomery Dialogue: A Chapter in the God is Dead Controversy* where Altizer observed that Rubenstein had joined with Christian theologians in the Death of God theology (p. 7).

354 David Weiss Halivni (2007), renowned for his Talmud scholarship, provides an extensive bibliography of Orthodox rabbis and scholars who regarded the *Shoah* as God's punishment for various sins: the sin of Zionism (Satmar Rebbe); the sin of anti-Zionism and the failure to make aliyah to Israel (Rabbis Y. S. Taichtal and Menachem Emmanuel Chartum); and several categories of sin: Zionism, assimilation, and secularism (Rabbi B. Maza). For a full account of Halivni's discussion of *Shoah* scholarship, cf. pp. 38–39.

355 Arthur Green,1994, as quoted in H. Diner (2009, footnote 37, p. 458).

356 These conferences continued until Hartman made aliyah to Israel in 1971 (Folb, 2007, p. 87). Over the years, Schaalman kept in touch with Hartman and visited with him during his trips to Israel where Hartman had established the Hartman Institute.

357 Schaalman did not want to keep his discovery of this new writer and intellectual to himself. Sometime in either 1966 or 1967, he brought Wiesel to OSRUI to expose the campers to this powerful new force in Jewish life. According to one of the people who heard his talk, it was mesmerizing (Yearwood, 2000).

358 Like Schaalman and Fackenheim, Borowitz admits that his own recognition of the profound meaning of the *Shoah* did not come until twenty years after the end of World War II. The *Shoah* destroyed the belief in the perfectibility of humanity and its salvation through scientific and technological development (Samuelson, 2000, p. 94).

359 It is surprising that Schaalman did not mention Richard Rubenstein or his good friend Emil Fackenheim, who were struggling mightily to understand the meaning of the Holocaust (Rubenstein, in *After Auschwitz: Radical Theology and Contemporary Judaism* (1966) and Fackenheim's (1967) "Jewish Values in the Post-Holocaust Future: A Symposium." Later, Fackenheim (2001) wrote that most of the greatest Jewish and Christian thinkers of the modern age failed to come to grips with the Holocaust, among them Karl Barth, Leo Baeck, and Martin Buber (p. 438).

360 Borowitz (1991) argued that Rubenstein's critique of the retributive God of traditional Judaism and his conclusion that this God was dead had already been "addressed by modernized, non-Orthodox Jews" (p. 36). By the end of the nineteenth century, they no longer believed in a God responsible for history and, in His place, substituted "human agency—ethics—and so saw secular causation adequately explaining specific events. Every major Jewish philosopher of the twentieth century reinforced this more reticent view of God's role in history; surely rationalism permitted little else" (p. 36). Greenberg (2006) observed that Rubenstein's initial complaint that the Holocaust was not receiving the attention it deserved eventually did get attention. It produced "an important body of religious thought ... offering an impressive range of treatments of the religious implications of the Holocaust" (p. 213). To validate Greenberg's conclusion, this author surveyed the publication of books and articles on the Holocaust. The Spertus Institute library's catalog of books on the Holocaust reveals that it contained seventy-four

books published between 1965 and 1979. By comparison, the catalog shows 517 volumes published during the period 2000-2008, the largest number of them (308) from 2000 to 2003. Another source for records of Holocaust publications, the catalog of Garfield Library at the University of Pennsylvania, reveals that for the period 1962 to 1969 only twenty-one (21) books and articles. In the following decades, the number gradually increases: 1970–1979, 153 books and articles; 1980–1989, 663 non-book publications; and 1990–1999, 994 articles. In one year alone, 1999, the catalog included 167 non-book publications, the largest number of publications for any year up to 2008 the year this survey was concluded.

361 Fackenheim (1982) noted that, although early historians of the Second World War tended to bury the Holocaust in footnotes, an "army of Holocaust specialists" was now at work on the subject (xii). Various influential Jewish theologians argued that God was not responsible for the Holocaust because He is in the process of becoming and not yet fully actualized. Mordecai Kaplan, for example, explained that God is always evolving, in a state of becoming, moving toward an "actualization … that has not yet occurred but is deferred to some point in the far distant future." Disasters [such as the Holocaust] are phases "of the universe which have not yet been completely penetrated by godhood" (as cited in Sicker, 2001, p. 208). Evil can occur during this process because God has not yet been actualized. When that event occurs, evil will ultimately be eliminated. Sicker (2001) cites Henry Slominsky, who also found a way to acquit God of responsibility for the Holocaust. The world, according to him, may be in an ongoing state of creation in which humans and God continue to grow toward some distant goal of "perfection." To be fully realized in the sense of creating a perfect world, God needs help while undergoing a process of maturation along with man (p. 208). Therefore, God has entered into a partnership with humans as "helpers and co-creators … in process of gradual realization" (p. 208). In this mutually dependent relationship, God needs human "strength to carry out his designs," and humans need God's strength as a support and comfort. Such a God will not be "perfect" until the end of time (p. 208). (As we shall see later, these views are similar to Schaalman's who also exonerates God from responsibility for the Holocaust.)

362 "Homeland and Holocaust" provoked a vigorous response from four of the most prestigious Jewish theologians of the time whom Rubenstein had attacked in this article: Milton Himmelfarb, Zalman Schacter, Arthur Cohen, and Irving Greenberg (cf. their "Commentaries" following Rubenstein's essay in D. R. Cutler (1968), *The Religious Situation: 1968*, pp. 64–102).

363 The term "Death of God" was introduced in the 1960s by Gabriel Vahanian in *The Death of God: The Culture of Our Post-Christian Era* (1961), pp. 144–145. The Christian theological response to the gruesome reality of the Holocaust was in part a response to the "Death of God" movement, which insisted that the lesson of the Holocaust was that God was dead. However, rather than accept this conclusion, the theologians found in the Holocaust cause to reconsider the nature of God in the modern world. One of their conclusions was that God was powerless to affect historical events. Because God created a new, time-bound reality out of a timeless world and endowed humans the freedom to act, God could not be held responsible for his creatures' behavior. Yet, to account for God's continuing presence in the world, the theologians reinterpreted the Christian traditional understanding of the suffering God.

364 Rabbi Marc Saperstein (1990), head of Judaic Studies at George Washington University, wrote that *Gates of Prayer* also included the restoration of liturgical language that "conveyed the sense of the centrality of Israel and Jerusalem in traditional worship" that had been eliminated in the Union Prayer Book (p. 109).

365 For an interesting discussion of the idea of God as father and parent, cf. Jack Bloom, "Hide and Seek" (2008). Bloom makes the point that the image of God as parent is inculcated in us when we are children and is based on the sense of our inadequacy and need for protection. He labels this understanding of our relationship to God "pediatric," a level of understanding that too many adults never outgrow.

366 Schaalman must have forgotten that in 1981 the CCAR Executive Committee did in fact "commission the Israeli poet T. Carmi to begin searching through the corpus of post-biblical Hebrew poetic materials for texts that might one day lend themselves to liturgical incorporation in a new CCAR prayer book" (Stevens, 1990, p. 26). The five-year project, known as the "Carmi Project," identified hundreds of texts, which were thematically organized and presented to the Liturgy Committee [and] subsequently submitted to the *Journal of Reform Judaism* for publication. The *Journal* published them in 1989 as part of its critique of *Gates of Prayer* (Stevens, 1990). Also included in this tenth anniversary issue of the *Journal* was a review of the model of a new prayer book produced in 1971. After considering the matter for seven years, the CCAR, at its centennial meeting in 1989, approved a long-term project to develop a new prayer book (Stevens, 1990). Not until the latest revision of the prayer book, *Mishkan T'filah* (officially adopted in 2007), have there been significant efforts to include more "poetic" language, though not enough to please Schaalman.

367 Wertheimer (1993) argued that this movement toward tradition and its once abandoned rituals produced a negative reaction among older Reform rabbis who formed the "elite" of the movement. Like Schaalman, they resented the pressure to reintroduce rituals that, to them, were appeals to the lowest common denominator of Judaism. This turn toward tradition meant a rejection of the Classical Reform movement, the Judaism in which they had been trained and had practiced throughout most of their rabbinical careers.

One of the major forces pushing change in Reform was the retirement of older members of its leadership who were being replaced by younger rabbis. Born after World War II and raised in a Reform movement very different from that of their predecessors, they were more comfortable than their parents in their Jewishness and acceptance in American life. According to Rabbi Peter J. Hass (2002), they "felt empowered to turn unabashedly to the tradition for guidance regarding personal lifestyle," as well as a source of "ethnic identity and moral standards" (p. 241). Many older congregations saw this development as reactionary and a violation of Reform principles (pp. 241–242).

Perhaps the most significant change was that for the first time in Jewish history women were becoming rabbis and, in 2002, outnumbered men in Reform seminaries. According to Hoffman (2003), by challenging the traditional male understanding of academic disciplines and interpretations of Torah, they created a new consciousness in the rabbinic community and a radical change in the Reform community's sense of itself. When the Reform movement issued its newest prayer book, *Mishkan T'filah* (2007), two of its editors were women. Born in the 1950s and ordained in 1980, they were relatively new to the rabbinate (Knobel, 2002). In marked contrast, the editor of *The Gates of Prayer*, Rabbi Chaim Stern, was of a different generation. Born a decade before World War II and ordained in 1958, he was part of a Reform Judaism that was very different from what it became a half century later (Knobel, 2002). Women also had become full partners in synagogue leadership, frequently dominating their boards. (These changes are evident in Emanuel Congregation; when Schaalman became its rabbi in 1956, women did not sit on its board. By 2012, counting the WRJ and brotherhood representatives on the board, as well as the immediate past president who is an officer, eight of the seventeen members of the Board of Trustees are women.)

Another major factor in the transformation of Reform Judaism is the inclusion of Jews by Choice, which, according to Hoffman (2003), eventually will constitute half of the Reform Jewish population and have the greatest impact on the movement in its history. According to Rabbi Dana Kaplan (2003), these new congregants are typically younger and less willing to sit passively and listen while a rabbi, cantor, or choir prays for them. Instead, they are seeking participation in a "common spiritual quest," one that has pushed the Reform movement to revitalize itself by embracing more traditional beliefs, rituals, and practices (p. 63).

A sign of the ferment in the movement was the practice of rabbinic students praying with tallitot and kippot. Hass (2002) sees this development as not only a cultural, but also a generational shift: "the new generation of rabbis feels a much stronger affinity to the Halachic tradition" than the lay leadership in many of the movement's institutions and synagogues (p. 243). In this rightward turn, Reform Jews are seeking more security in tradition, rather than a radical overhaul that might put it at risk. Kaplan (2003) argues that, although these changes are, in a sense, anachronistic, they appear to be a response to the needs of the majority of contemporary Reform congregants; they want "to situate themselves within a historical religion that allows them to explore a range of spiritual paths not limited to artificial boundaries" (p. 64). Hass (2002) writes that this reformation of Reform is likely to prevail for a long time, at least until the next centennial when Reform will have gone "'full circle;' [and] will see itself as the reform movement within Halacha, rather than ... a religion working beyond the Halacha'" (p. 244).

Another force at work in producing these changes was the result of the yearlong experience of rabbinic students studying in Israel, where they had been exposed to more traditional Jewish practice and became more comfortable with it. They saw in this experience a way to respond to their congregants' desire for a richer Jewish life. Their college-age counterparts were also a factor in promoting change in Reform. Through their involvement with campus Hillel groups, where the religious services tend to be inclusive of all branches of Judaism, they came in contact with Jews who were more observant. As a result, some of these Reform Jewish students gained a new respect for, and tolerance of, the more traditional service in which they participated.

Rabbi E. H. Yoffie (2003), on the other hand, warned against concluding that the reintroduction of discarded traditional elements in the prayer service is a sign that Reform is becoming more traditional, as common wisdom would have it. Reform, he wrote, is more complex than a claim of this sort recognizes, and this development is only one strand that coexists with Reform's "theological radicalism" (p. 260).

368 Interesting in this context is that Rabbi Michael Friedman (2005), who was Schaalman's assistant rabbi during this period, later moved in the direction of his many of his Reform peers in adopting more traditional practices. As he observed, "Rabbi Schaalman is probably not happy with me because I put on tefillin every day and wear a kippah."

369 D. E. Kaplan (2003) remarks that, during the period of the 1990s, theology was not a major concern for Reform Judaism (p. 64). Its focus
was on a variety of social issues, mainly inclusion of gays and lesbians,
interfaith couples, and rabbinic officiation at interfaith marriages. Insofar as Reform was successful in its outreach efforts, it gained strength by
exploring "a range of spiritual paths not limited by artificial boundaries"
(p. 64). Rabbi Irving Greenberg (2006) goes further in his view of the
lack of theological discussion in all branches of Judaism. He claims that,
in the fifteen years from 1991 to 2006, Judaism had not given theology
much attention. Holocaust studies and commemorations, on the other
hand, dominated discussion of Jewish issues.

370 When Yoffie spoke before a large assembly of over 5,000 delegates at the
1999 UAHC biennial assembly, he outlined a plan for a major overhaul
of Reform Judaism, including a plan for a "worship revolution" that
would be based on a partnership of congregants, cantors, and rabbis
(Kaplan, D. E., 2003, p. 65). The aim of this partnership was inclusion,
a way to help the laity feel more involved in religious experience within
the context of the synagogue. Yoffie highlighted the well-known situation of Reform where the large majority of its congregants were "two day
a year" Jews (p. 65). The reason for this lack of participation was that
they could not relate to the services and did not experience the spiritual
nourishment they were seeking.

371 The change was necessary, according to the CCAR's past president, Rabbi
Peter Knobel (2002), because many Jews, who were uncomfortable with
the liturgy and the *siddur*, had stopped coming to the synagogue. Others that did come could not reconcile themselves to the prayer texts,
particularly with the language of "divine perfection and omnipotence
along with divine transcendence, [which] did not correspond to their
spiritual reality" (p. 167). The traditional paradigm of subject and
master that has informed Judaism throughout the ages had no meaning
for them.

372 David Ellenson, president of the Hebrew Union College-Jewish Institute
of Religion, makes the same point. Though he does not share Schaalman's criticism, he writes, "There is no question that this [inclusion]
represents a move towards tradition in the Reform movement" (Harris,
B., 2007).

373 It should be noted, that on several recent occasions in his Torah Study,
Schaalman has raised the question, "Why are there so few Jews? If in
the last 2,000 years, the Jewish population had multiplied the way
the Chinese did, the three million Jews existing then would today be
50 million." The reason, he thinks, Jews never reached this number is

because, over this span of time, "most Jews gave up. Being Jewish was too onerous."

374 The challenge of this new world is for rabbis, Jewish educators and Jewish lay leaders to promote Judaism not because it is noble to be a Jew in the face of an inhospitable environment, but to be Jews "because being Jewish is one of the great ways of being human, … [of] understanding the world" and serving God (Star, E., July 25, 1988, p. 23).

375 The section on Patrilineal Descent contained a reference to the fact that twenty-five percent of mixed marriages result in the conversion of the non-Jewish spouse (Raphael, 2000). For a more detailed discussion of the demographic issues related to mixed marriage at the end of the twentieth century, refer to the closing discussion of Patrilineal Descent.

376 He questioned whether numbers are as important as quality when it comes to political influence. He cited as an example the fact that in 1988 eight Jews served in the US Senate, or eight percent of the 100 senators in Congress, a percent far exceeding the two percent of the total population (Star, E., July 25, 1988, p. 19). By 2009, although the percent of the Jewish population remained stable, Jews now represented eleven percent of the 111th U.S. Congress. The number of Jewish senators had risen to fourteen (fourteen percent), and the number of representatives to thirty-three (seven percent), JTA, July 1, 2009.

377 Schaalman was not alone in admonishing the students to think of their rabbinic role as more than a career. Dr. Richard Sarason (2007), HUC-JIR Professor of Rabbinic Literature and Thought, also told them that "Judaism is not a commodity and the synagogue is not a business, even though the consumerist and corporate models continue to spread throughout the not-for-profit sectors of society" (p. 7). Sarason told the students, "Judaism is a way of life, a discipline, a way of being in the world, a life philosophy that cannot be compartmentalized and must engage our total being" (p. 7). By implication, he was saying that such a life could not be commodified and made contractual.

Chapter 9: Schaalman's Theology

378 Still, Schaalman held onto Kaplan's view that God had limited power. Borowitz (1991) writes, "Kaplan considered the notion of God intervening in human affairs to be the kind of carryover supernaturalism that made moderns reject Jewish belief" (p. 35).

379 Rabbi Edward Zerin (July 24, 2012) observes that he and other rabbis and thinkers had also reached the same conclusion but not from the experience of the Holocaust. Their understanding of modern science had led them to abandon the idea of an omniscient and omnipotent God.

380 Fackenheim may have helped him come to this new realization. In *Quest for Past and Future* (1968), he argued that the lesson of Jewish history is that, although God could not save Israel from calamity, He was still active in history. Jews could take comfort in the assurance that He had not abandoned them and could hope for an eventual redemption. It is unlikely that Schaalman, to whom the book was dedicated, was unaware of his friend's conclusions.

381 His comment is another indication of Fackenheim's influence. The words are the same as those used by Fackenheim (1967) almost two decades earlier in "Jewish values in the post-Holocaust future: A symposium," cited above in Chapter 8, "The Reform of Reform." Rabbi Michael Weinberg, Schaalman's assistant rabbi from 1980–1985, remembers that when he came to Emanuel in 1980, Schaalman had not yet come to this more radical explanation for God's role in the Holocaust or the idea that God is vulnerable or that He needs us. On the other hand, he remembers that Schaalman would not include in the worship services the blessing after the reading of the Torah when it is lifted up for the congregation to see and to recite: "*V'Zot haTorah Asher Sam Mosheh liPh'nei V'nei Yisra'el*: This is the Torah that Moses placed before the Israelites." Schaalman's objection then and now is he doesn't believe that the Torah is the "words of Moses.

382 By the time he published *Hineni* in 2007, the spelling of the word became *Shoah*.

383 Rabbi Eliezar Berkovits, a more traditional rabbi, draws a completely different lesson about the meaning of the Holocaust. Aware of the historical record of Jewish survival in the face of persecution, and the fact that Jews have maintained their faith through these events, Berkovits concludes that the *Shoah*, though different in magnitude, could not be considered a foundational experience. In *Faith after the Holocaust* (1973), he argues that this event could only be understood by God's absence. Berkovits assumes there is a Divine Plan and that this event somehow fits in it. To understand the reason for God's absence, it is necessary to invoke the ancient biblical concept of *hester panim*, "the veiling of the Face," the concept that God, on occasion, turns away from humanity in order to enable humans to be moral creatures. God had to remove himself, to step back from history to allow for human

freedom and, as a consequence, could not prevent human beings from engaging in evil. Nevertheless, God maintains a presence to keep creation from ultimately destroying itself. Unlike many of his Orthodox colleagues, Berkovits argued vehemently against the conclusion that the *Shoah* was God's punishment for the sins of His people, a conclusion he considered blasphemous.

384 Although his most developed thinking on this subject did not appear until 2007 in the publication of *Hineni*, the article reveals striking similarities to passages in it, some almost verbatim. When asked about them, Schaalman could not explain them. This author has concluded that once Schaalman decided on the appropriate language to describe his views on the *Shoah*, it became his standard text for sermons and lectures over the next fifteen years.

385 For perspective on how radical this new insight was for him, we need only refer to a radio address he made in 1967 in when he told his audience, [Torah] "envelops everything. It is our study, our prayer, our yearning for God, our *obedience* to Him [italics added]" (Schaalman, H. E., "Judaism's Window on the Divine," November 5, 1967).

386 The only book Schaalman published prior to *Hineni* was *Preaching Biblical Texts* (1995), a book of essays by Christian and Jewish scholars on biblical texts, which was designed to provide preachers with a stimulating source for their sermons or for study, and co-authored with his friend, Prof. Fred Holmgren of North Park Theological Seminary.

387 Soon after *Hineni* was published, Schaalman told his Torah Study students that he should have included a small section on their role in the development of his thinking: "The dialogue between us has led me to many of the changes in my thinking."

388 Schaalman's commitment to truth as dialogic means that he often does not know what he knows until he articulates it in the presence of another or a group of others. In July 2007, a few hours prior to giving a talk on Judaism, this writer asked him what we would be discussing that afternoon: "I don't know yet," he said. "It depends on my audience, what they know, and what they want to hear."

389 Amazon.com lists a copy at the incredible price of $718.54. By June, 2012 a copy was priced at $322.62.

390 Schaalman claims that in the Torah words are the fundamental creative act. In Genesis, "God speaks" and the world is created as in "Let there be light; and there was light" (Genesis 1:3). Fackenheim (1968) writes that

the primacy of speech in the creation story is a human interpretation of the nameless experience and that the Divine call and its human response are the basis of the "divine-human covenant" (p. 116).

391 As of August, 2012, the presentation was available on www.naorrr.org.

392 This personal autobiographical style connects him to a "school" of theology that Borowitz (1991) identified as "personalist" and existential, a theology derived from lived experience rather than from theoretical considerations or abstract thought (p. 168).

393 Schaalman raises other questions about biblical language: "Abraham's journey from Mesopotamia to Canaan raises the question of what language was spoken by the Canaanites and, in particular, whether Abraham or anyone else spoke Hebrew. In other words, who was the first Hebrew speaker? How did Hebrew arise? The fact that the Torah has Abraham and others before him speak Hebrew is clearly anachronistic" and raises the question of what language God used to speak to Abraham or his descendents, to Moses, or to the Israelites.

394 During Torah Study in July 2012, Schaalman raised the question, "How do we know what God says?" Does God speak human language? Human language is the only language we have. All language is human. There is no Divine language and if there is, we don't know it. Language is the great triumph in the developing human story, in our ability to articulate."

395 When Schaalman uses the term "fantasy" for the Torah, he means it in the Greek sense of *phantasía*, an idea, notion, image, literally, a making visible."

396 Borowitz explains that for Leo Baeck God is "the mystery we sense behind our ethics, not an independent agent dominating history" (Borowitz, 1991, p. 35). In his chapter on "Faith in God," Leo Baeck (1936) wrote that such a perception of God as mystery is an "act of faith: In Judaism faith is nothing but the living consciousness of the Omnipresent," by which he meant an act of consciousness that is not based on reason or subject to logical proof (pp. 118–119). Schaalman, however, does not accept the word "faith," which he understands as a Christian word and part of our Christian culture. For him, the word means a kind of unquestioning, irrational commitment. He prefers to use the term "belief." The difference between the two terms is that "belief" is based on trust.

397 Cf. Fackenheim's essay, "Jewish Existence and the Living God" (1959), in which he wrote that God is the "Nameless" One, and the experience

of the Nameless as also nameless. Of necessity, human beings must relate this awareness of an ineffable being to something "familiar and nameable … This awareness, he maintains, is the basis for all religious experience, not only that of the Jews (p. 115).

398 Arthur Green (1996), a well-known Jewish scholar and professor at Hebrew College in Boston, identifies this difficulty as the fundamental theological challenge. It consists of the attempt to give expression to the ineffable experience of divinity and to articulate a series of beliefs around the relationships of God, world and person. Like Schaalman, Green (1996) acknowledges this limitation: "In this we are heirs to both the prophet and the mystical teacher who rail against their inability to refrain from speaking," but by resorting to "sacred" speech, we find a way to speak about the mystery of God (p. 49). After all, "It was God," Green (1996) argues, "who spoke the world into being" (p. 49).

399 Cf. Schaalman's 1967 article on Rosenzweig and Rosenzweig's *The Star of Redemption*, 1971, p. 233–236.

400 An even earlier source for Schaalman's idea of "ground" may have been Hermann Cohen's idea that, as Michael Meyer (1988) states, God is "apart from nature of which God is *ground* [italics added] not substance" (p. 206).

401 In "Creation as a Divine-Human Collaboration," Schaalman (2004) argued that the creation of Adam and Eve is not only the ultimate achievement, it is also the end of the process of creation. Only then, on the seventh day, does God rest. For Schaalman, there is a direct connection between the two events, the creation of Adam and Eve and the day of rest. He states emphatically, "Does God's Shabbat then depend on us? Why not! God does not appear to be totally, radically self-sufficient … [but] inherently, unavoidably linked to us, beginning with the divine rest of Shabbat" (p. 49).

402 Like Schaalman, Green (2006) claims that God's discovery that Adam, too, needs a partner is a projection from His own experience of loneliness. God's creation is the result of His need to break out of his aloneness. Before monotheism, gods always had partners, lovers, wives, and children. With the introduction of monotheism, the essential erotic situation of God changes: He is left without a partner. "God," Green maintains, "has no one to love" (p. 10). God's need for love expresses itself through his creation of a human partner. However, this relationship comes with a cost. God has to learn what it means to be dependent on His relationship to humans "as His only love-partners" (p. 11). God has to take on the role of parent to His wayward children or, to use

another analogy, as "the husband of an unfaithful wife." Green (2006) contends that if God had other outlets for relationship, He might have given up on humans. This dependency is an indication that the condition of aloneness was intolerable to God and, because of it, He could not give up on the human enterprise. In this state of affairs, God can be counted on to remain engaged with humans no matter how difficult the relationship becomes.

403 The view that God learns is not unique to Schaalman. Irving Greenberg (1997) observes that God changes in His interaction with humans. Originally, he argues, God was an absolutist. He wanted a perfect world, but when he discovered that humans were capable of disobeying his commands, he did not wipe them out as he had threatened, but gave them another chance. In fact, the Bible is a record of successive disappointments for God and His willingness to allow humans the right to make bad choices (p. 7). After the Flood, "God renounced the demand for absolute perfection and instead entered into the covenant which guaranteed human freedom, even when it led to bad choices" (p. 7). This freedom allows for humans to develop their full capability, both for good and for evil. Arthur Green (2006) also concludes that the Torah is the story of God's encounter with humans and what He learns from it (p. 10). He cites various stories in which God comes down from the heights to learn what it means to enter into relationship with humans—the stories of Cain and Abel, the Tower of Babel, Noah, and Abraham—in which God discovers that His humans do not, and, apparently, will not, behave as He intended. He learns that his creatures are fatally flawed (pp. 10–11). Nevertheless, he allows humans the freedom to engage with him, to dialogue, and, even, argue. In this give and take, humans "teach" God that some of His decisions are wrong. Green (2006) maintains that these learning experiences are ongoing and that God continues to underestimate and misjudge how His people will react to His commandments. When He enters into a covenant with Abraham, and, later, with Moses and the Israelites, He discovers that His people continue to disappoint him. Later, when the Israelites fail to follow His commandments, He threatens to destroy them, but when Moses intercedes on their behalf, God backs down. He accepts Moses' argument that by annihilating the Jews, He would be admitting defeat, a defeat that would undermine His credibility among other peoples.

404 Cf. Genesis 12: 8-20 and 20: 1–7, both are accounts of Abraham passing off his wife as his sister to hide his identity. Sarah was so beautiful that he thought if he were known to be her husband, he would be killed so that the ruler of the land could take her as his own wife.

405 Although Schaalman does not mention it, in a curious and inexplicable chapter, Exodus 4: 24, God even seeks to kill Moses. Only the quick and astute intervention of his wife, Zipporah, saves him from certain death. Is this action part of God's larger frustration over His failure to create a holy people? Has God concluded that His second experiment has come to naught? Has God suffered enough at the hands of His people? The Torah does not answer these critical questions.

406 According to A. Bein (1990), the number of Jews living in Palestine in the second century CE is uncertain, but probably one to two million. The contemporary Roman historian, Cassio Dio, wrote that 580,000 Jews were killed during the Bar Kochba revolt, perhaps as much as 50 percent of the Jewish population ("Texts on Bar Kochba: Cassius Dio," n.d.). The Nazi slaughtered 6 million Jews, nearly one-third of the number of Jews in the world.

407 Also, cf. Numbers 14:18, "The Lord is longsuffering, and of great mercy, forgiving iniquity and transgression, and by no means clearing the guilty, visiting the iniquity of the fathers upon the children unto the third and fourth generation"; and Psalms 86:15, "But thou, O Lord, art a God full of compassion, and gracious, longsuffering, and plenteous in mercy and truth."

408 Fackenheim (1994) makes the case for a direct connection between the cosmological and the human reality. It is through this connection that he concluded: when His people suffer, God suffers. Green (2006) argues that during the Israelite bondage in Egypt, when God sees His people suffering, Torah tells us that He "knows" (Ex. 2:25). Green interprets "know" to mean "as though He too had taken part in their bondage" (p. 11).

409 Borowitz (1991) contends that Jews believe God "needs" Jews—or that God "wants Jews to be Jews and not simply Noahides [followers of Noah] with a Hebraic ethnic coloration (p. 45). Irving Greenberg (1997) writes that the divine-human relationship was a partnership "in the perfection of the world" (p. 8).

410 In "Creation as a Divine-Human Collaboration," Schaalman (2004) had written, "the structure of the nonhuman biomass, while created by God, becomes only manageable, orderly, structured by the only-then-human, Adam. Or, to put it differently, the created 'order' does not emanate from God. *It derives from Adam* [italics added]" (p. 51).

411 Kurtz (2001) refers to Jewish tradition (*Mishnah Avot* 5:3) which mentions ten tests during the course of Abraham's lifetime.

412 So fundamental is the story to Schaalman and such a major theological challenge that, according to him, "I have shared my thoughts about the *Akeda* [the story of the binding of Isaac] at least twenty-seven times during High Holy Days services. Over the years, not all my congregants have been pleased to hear that sermon again. One irate congregant sent me an anonymous letter stating, 'If you preach one more time on the *Akeda*, I'll quit the congregation.'"

413 Jonas (1996) also makes the case that by entering the world, God submitted himself to mutability and the process of change and development (p. 138). To ascribe to God omniscience is illogical: "the existence of another object limits the power of the most powerful agent at the same time that it allows it to be an agent" (p. 139).

414 He might have been echoing Fackenheim (1994), who goes further in making a case for the interdependence of the human and divine. Relying on both Midrashic and Kabalistic sources, Fackenheim writes that the "exile of the Shekhinah" is a cosmological condition in which God is in retreat from the world (p. 253). Together with "fracture of the vessels," the scattering of the divine light, this notion suggests an interaction between the divine and the human historical reality. If God is in exile, and if the world is broken, it becomes part of the human responsibility to help repair the world through Tikkun (p. 253).

415 Borowitz (1977) makes the point that Judaism is based on "an effort to build a strong relationship with God" (as cited in Meyer and Plaut, 2001, p. 44).

416 By "it" Buber means an object. To treat others as an "it" is to treat them as objects, something to be manipulated, exploited. "Thou," on the other hand, is the "other" as subject, to be encountered on its own terms, to be fully "there" for the other, to be in the moment and open to the other person. Schaalman might have been echoing Buber when Buber (1966) wrote, "God dwells wherever man lets him in. This is the ultimate purpose: to let God in. But we can let him in only where we really stand, where we live, where we live a true life ... if we help the holy spiritual substance to accomplish itself in that section of Creation in which we are living, then we are establishing, in this our place, a dwelling for the Divine Presence (p. 41).

417 Green (2006) claims that the ancient rabbis seem to have realized that our image of God changes according to the needs of the time. When God appeared before the Israelites as they were being pursued by the Egyptians and had their backs up against the Sea, He "'appeared to them as a youth'" (as cited in Green, 2006, p. 8). Green interprets this change

to mean that "on the day of battle one has no use for a tottering old God" (p. 8). On the other hand, when God gave Moses the commandments on Sinai, "'He appeared as an elder'" (as cited in Green, p. 8). An elder, rather than a younger God was needed. The rabbis also transformed "the fierce God of Israel's wanderings who demanded that they slay every man, woman, and child of their foes … into the loving Father of all His creatures" (p. 9). In the process, they "feminized" Him by making Him the "bearer of *rahamim*, womb-like compassion, unfailing nurturer, lover of peace" (p. 9). This evolution of the image of God may also be viewed as an effort on the part of a developing civilization to tame human, and "perhaps especially male violence" (p. 9).

418 In Leviticus 11:45, God says, "For I am the LORD that brought you up out of the land of Egypt, to be your God; ye shall therefore be holy, for I am holy" (JPS, 1917).

419 He learned from Buber (1966), "The task of man, of every man, according to Hasidic teaching, is to affirm for God's sake the world and himself and by this very means to transform both" (p. 6).

420 The term "mitzvot" is preferred here because, unlike "commandments," it conveys a sense of an act expressing human kindness.

421 Arthur Green (1996) writes that a holy life is based on the performance of mitzvot, which is a way "of knowing God" (p. 49). This process of awareness "is the intimate and consciousness-transforming knowledge" that is "infused with the presence of the One" (p. 49). Such awareness is theological, the "religious attempt to help the Jewish people understand the meaning of human life and Jewish existence out of the store of texts, symbols, and historical experience that are the shared inheritance of all Jews" (p. 48). To be a Jewish theologian is to work to affect the continuity of the Jewish people and to be part of that community. Surely, Schaalman's life has been part of that effort.

422 Schaalman refers to Rosenzweig who thought that mitzvot needed to be examined and confronted to see whether they made sense to a twentieth-century intellectual and provided "something that would elicit something from him that even tradition expects." This "something" is Rosenzweig's compliance with traditional expectations. If that were not possible, then Rosenzweig would create "his own response that was different from" the traditional understanding of the purpose of the mitzvah, [though] not necessarily its exact content."

423 In his article, "God!" published in *European Judaism*, Arthur Green (2006) offers his own insight into God's question to Adam. The first is

"Where are you in helping Me to carry this project forward?' Are you extending My work of self-manifestation, participating as you should in the ongoing evolutionary process, the eternal reaching toward the One that is all of life's goal" (p. 2)? The question is God's appeal to humanity to become more aware of His imminence. The question 'Where are you?' is an effort to penetrate the self-imposed barriers that protect us from "our own vulnerability and dependence on forces beyond ourselves" (p. 3). These defenses are "walls behind which we barricade ourselves" so that we can live with the "illusions of our strength and immortality" (p. 3). The question asks that we consider the over importance we give to our egos and "the superficial pursuits toward which most of our lives have somehow become devoted" (p. 3). The question is also God's attempt to awaken our awareness of the need to extend beyond ourselves in our treatment of others. Because every human being is made in the image of God, we are required to treat them as such. We are obligated in our relations with others to help them "to discover the image of God within themselves ...." (p. 3).

424 Borowitz (1991) also rejects what he considers their other major assertions: that the unprecedented uniqueness of the Holocaust negates the possibility of formulating questions about it and precludes the possibility of finding answers, and that it exposed humankind to an utterly new dimension of evil that no previous philosophic or Jewish religious response is remotely adequate to explain (p. 36).

425 Also in 1996, Jacob Neusner (1996) published *Judaism Transcends Catastrophe: God, Torah, and Israel beyond the Holocaust*, an anthology of major Jewish theologians' views on the impact of the Holocaust on Judaism. In his introduction, he claimed that mainstream Jewish theology transcended the Holocaust and, rather than destroying faith in God and Torah, actually revitalized it. He asserted that Conservative and even Reform Jews turned toward Judaism that is more traditional. As if responding directly to Schaalman, he argued that the difficulty with Holocaust theology is that it begins with Auschwitz and ends with it. Holocaust theologians, Neusner contends, fail to see beyond the parameters of the event and, as a result, are unable to consider it in the context of Jewish history and theology. Although the Holocaust casts a shadow on Sinai, it does not obliterate it. Sinai's status as revelation is an eternal covenant between God and his people (p. 11).

   More recently, in his article "Theology after the Shoah: The transformation of the core paradigm," Rabbi Irving Greenberg (2006) argues that the more characteristic theological response to the Holocaust was to incorporate it into "classic paradigms of meaning" and to see it as part of the ongoing tragedies of the Jewish people and not a theological game-changer (p. 213). Like Neusner, Greenberg (2006) argues that mainstream Judaism refused to consider the Holocaust as transformative of Jewish theology because it was "death centered or … an ersatz substitute for observance and learning" (p. 232, footnote #3). As a result, the Holocaust has been dismissed in a "turn to spirituality as the appropriate or credible focus for theology. … These developments are a reprise of the incomprehension and blindness to the unprecedented and shattering nature of the Shoah that marked many bystanders' responses during as well as after the event" (footnote 3, p. 232).

426 In his article "Christology After the Shoah" (2001), Fr. John Pawlikowski, cites more than a dozen Christian scholars and theologians who share this perspective. Included in his list are such famous Christian theologians as Andre LaCocque (a friend of Schaalman's), Johannes Baptist Metz, Gregory Baum, and Marcel Dubois (pp. 158–178).

427 Hans Jonas (1903–1993) pioneered the philosophy of bioethics. The cosmos, he writes, is an organic unity constantly expanding and evolving toward some ultimate unrealized end. He makes no distinction between this process and God. Rather than a fixed and eternal being, Jonas proposes that God is in a state of becoming and that evolution is the process of an evolving God. Ethics arose from the human involvement in this developing process. From this basic understanding, he offers an explanation of the *Shoah* and how God could have allowed it to happen.

428 In conversation with both rabbis, this writer ascertained that neither Schaalman nor Bloom was aware of each other's thinking. Schaalman remembers that the last contact they had was at a meeting in the early 1990s in Jackson, Mississippi, when they co-officiated at a counseling institute for troubled Reform rabbis. Two years after this writer told Rabbi Bloom about *Hineni*, he reviewed it in *The Jewish Ledger*. In 2010, he wrote: "If you want to read a book this summer that will challenge, educate and respect your sophisticated, adult commitment to our tradition, *Hineni Here I Am* by Rabbi Herman Schaalman is meant for you. It certainly was for me. It is a great book, thoroughly thought through, magnificently presented and very readable. A book that will introduce you to the best in Jewish thought, astonish you and make you proud to be a Jew. That Herman is a gift to American Jewry from Adolf Hitler is one of history's ironies. He was one of the 'Berlin 5' saved in 1935 from Nazi Germany by Hebrew Union College. The 5 were astonishing gifts to U.S. Jewry. Herman remains perhaps the greatest gift of all. A rabbi who could shepherd a congregation superbly and teach and write impeccably. And be understood by one and all. And at 94, remains sharp as a tack. *Here I Am* is an introduction for Jews educated in western civilization

to the very best in modern Jewish thought. Discover that Herman is special, that you are special, and we are all part of a very special people as you realize that Jewish theology, miracle of miracles, can be read and appreciated by you and other regular folks, just like you. Get it!"

429 "Numbers Rabbah (or "*Bamidbar Rabbah*" in Hebrew) is a religious text holy to classical Judaism … a midrash comprising a collection of ancient rabbinical homiletic interpretations of the book of Numbers" ("Numbers," 2007).

430 Even more audaciously, Bloom proposes that humans taught God the quality of forgiveness, teshuvah. God has difficulty learning this lesson; He seems to ignore it when he tells Moses that He will pass along punishment for transgressions unto the third or fourth generation. This reaction, writes Bloom, violates the central premise of a covenantal relationship. Teshuvah is, after all, a necessary condition for the healing that must take place in the fragmented world of which both God and His humans are a part.

431 Cf. Arthur Green's (2006) article, "God," for a similar analysis of the creation story.

432 The *Shema* is recited "throughout the prayer services … in the morning blessings, in the *Musaf Amidah* of Shabbat and holidays, when the Torah is taken out of the Ark on Shabbat and holidays, as a bedtime prayer, as part of the deathbed confessional, and at various other times" (Schoenberg, 2007).

433 Schaalman's long-term interest in the story might be compared to two other stories he likes to tell and that are discussed in Chapter 1, "The Early Years." Cf. the story of the young Spartan soldier, who, in order to maintain strict military discipline while in troop formation, stood at attention while the fox he was hiding under his tunic ate out his guts. The other story involves Countess Spee, the wife of a German admiral who commanded the German Atlantic Fleet. During World War I, while she was a volunteer in a hospital for the wounded, an officer informed her that her husband and two sons had been killed in a battle with the British fleet. She thanked him and continued with her rounds. Schaalman was fascinated by these two stories because they revealed the power of inner discipline and adherence to a system of values that transcended the value of human life. A reasonable supposition is to see in Schaalman's obsession with Akiba's story his need to discover for himself how far he is willing to go to defend his beliefs. Akiba's martyrdom, in a sense, is a standard by which he measures his own religious commitments.

434 Thanks to his Torah Study student, Frank Metzger, he had read Wolfson's *Open Secret* (2006), which is an attempt to explore the paradox that the coming of the Messiah, while an 'open secret,' can be revealed in the world only by way of concealment. This book reinforced Schaalman's discovery that his own life might be understood as paradoxical.

435 A copy of Schaalman's presentation can be found at on the NAORRR website: http://www.naorrr.org/From_the_Convention.html/.

436 He had referred to this sense in his presidential address to the CCAR (1981) when he told his colleagues that he saw himself as "a brand plucked from the fire from among the dozens who were equally prepared, equally worthy (perhaps more so)" (p. 166). Because he had been given the gift of life, he felt responsible for giving back to society, for using his talents and abilities "to prove to [himself] and to the God Whom I seek to serve *that it might have been* worthwhile to rescue this brand from the conflagration" (p. 166).

Chapter 10: Teaching Torah

437 Later, as an undergraduate at the University of Chicago, Fenton talked Schaalman into offering a special tutorial on Buber for himself and a fellow student. Despite the fact that Fenton lived nearly an hour away from Emanuel, he came by train to meet with his Rabbi every other week, an experience he says "was transformative" (Fenton, M., personal communication, April 18, 2012).

438 Schaalman explains that when he began his rabbinate in Cedar Rapids, the Reform practice was to study only those portions of the Torah that were seen as relevant to modern life. To him, that was a mistake; he thought the entire Torah should be taught and that's what he set out to do.

439 "The Yekke" (Jecke), a nickname for German Jews who were described as utterly punctual, polite, honest, correctly dressed, but at the same time having no sense of humor, very strict, very formal, inflexible.

440 Mel (2007) notes that his Bar Mitzvah in September of 1955 was the last Rabbi Felix Levy performed at Emanuel. Many years later after becoming a successful attorney, Mel worked with Schaalman to plan trips abroad for the congregation. When it came time for Mel's daughter to marry in 2009, there was no question who should officiate. Mel arranged for Schaalman to fly to New York to conduct the wedding (Schaalman, H. E., personal communication, December 15, 2009).

441 Sue is the great-granddaughter of the same Hollenders who helped Schaalman get his job at Emanuel. At first, Sue and John came to class together, but she soon dropped out. John stayed.

442 As it happens, Meier is the first Jewish architect in the history of the Holy See to design a church, which is recognized as a masterpiece of contemporary architecture. The fact that the Pope John Paul II chose a Jewish architect to build a church reflects the new ecumenical spirit in the Church and is a testimony to the Pope's desire to change the 2,000-year history of the Church's relationship to the Jews.

443 This account of Schaalman's Torah Study would not be sufficient without mentioning another old-timer who no longer attends the class, Barbara Steinberg. She began attending his class sometime around 1987–89 and attended regularly until she became ill in 2008. In her telling, one of the main reasons she attended the class was because "Schaalman never asked us to abandon our reason and take Torah or Judaism on faith. The only exception for him was a belief in God's existence; the rest was open to debate and question." As his student, she felt safe to express her doubts, to ask questions, and to present her own ideas, occasionally in opposition to his own. She always felt that he treated her and the other students with "profound kindness ... no matter how ignorant, irrelevant, or nearly idiotic, their comments might be." When he says something he admits is a "stretch," he always adds, "You don't have to believe it. It's only my opinion."

444 Arthur Green (1996), Jewish scholar and professor at Hebrew College, writes that theologians of any age must build their own commentaries on the original stories, as well as on the Midrashic tradition that followed (p. 51).

445 In 1967, for example, he told a radio audience that Torah is "a divine act ... the process of God's communicating with man as well as to the record of that communication .... [It] is the expression of God's concern for his creation, a gift of love and a guide by which to live."

446 The Kaplan edition of the Torah text Schaalman uses in his class is replete with various possibilities for translation and interpretation, including several medieval rabbinic sources and modern scholarship. None of them is the same.

447 Leviticus 13: 6–17, a section dealing with what has become known as leprosy, diagnosis and treatment, is another example of biblical Hebrew that is untranslatable. Schaalman maintains, as do various translators

(e.g., Kaplan, 1981; Plaut, 1985), that no one knows the meaning of the Hebrew word that has been translated as "leprosy." The origin of the translation can be traced to the Septuagint, an early Greek translation, where the Hebrew is rendered as "lepor." In English, the word morphed to "leper." No medical validation exists, however, to substantiate that the skin disease described in the Torah is in fact what medicine identifies as leprosy.

448 As early as 1982, Schaalman had criticized the idea that the Torah is an infallible text, the "unmediated direct word of God … and that there is only one licit, authentic path of understanding and interpretation" (Schaalman, H. E., "Revelation," 1982, p. 91). His argument was that, as long as there is a hearer, there is mediation.

449 Rosenzweig's Lehrhaus, the first of its kind, became the model for the Lehrhaus movement that spread to major cities in Germany. Established in Frankfort in 1920, his school, *Das Freie Jüdische Lehrhaus* [The Free Jewish House of Teaching] was designed for Jewish adult education, but open to Jews and non-Jews. Its goal was to provide a comprehensive Jewish education. This commitment to a recovery of Jewishness meant that the curriculum had to be comprehensive and embrace "the whole spectrum of Jewish life: philosophy and politics, law and ethics, art and metaphysics" (Lux, 1986). Another critical part of the curriculum was the focus on "the experience of God in everyday life and the experience of personal liberation" (Lux, 1986). When Rosenzweig became ill and could no longer carry on, the Lehrhaus continued without him until 1930, a year after his death. However, without his dynamism the institution closed. It was reopened in 1933 by no less a luminary than Martin Buber.

450 Participants in Lehrhaus came from a variety of professions and repre-sented various interests. For the first session, the small group included Bill Schindler, a ninety-three-year old retired businessman and German immigrant who had been Schaalman's friend for over fifty years; Mel Abrams, a lawyer; Richard Strauss, a retired financial advisor; and Bernie Rozran, who came from Switzerland to attend Lehrhaus. In the succeed-ing years until its demise in 2009, Lehrhaus drew an eclectic group of adults.

451 During the year 2010–2011, he discussed an array of topics, including the seventh-century cleavage between the Sunni and Shia branches in Islam, the impact of the Jews on the silk trade in China, Israel's economy and education system, the Prague Conference on restoration of property stolen the Nazis during WWII, turmoil in Tehran, and the G8 economic conference.

Chapter 11: Schaalman on Modern Israel

452 In his teens, Schaalman had been a member of a Zionist youth group. A fascinating sidelight of this interviewer's conversation with Rabbi Hirsch (2010) is the story he told about his own early conversion to Zionism and the state of mind of Reform Judaism of the time. In 1950, he gave what he described as a passionate speech at HUC-JIR advocating Zionism and American aliyah. After the speech, Rabbi Leo Baeck, himself a survivor of Theresienstadt, a leading figure in Reform Judaism and one of Hirsch's teachers, came up to him and tried to explain how wrong he was. "It was inconceivable to me," Hirsch states, "that Leo Baeck was not a Zionist."

453 Five years later, in October 2011, a compromise between Israel and Hamas resulted in his release and the release of the 1,000 Palestinian prisoners Hamas had demanded.

454 Schaalman argues that there is a direct connection between this issue and Arab resistance to Israel. Arabs view Israel as an outpost of Western civilization and a direct threat to their values and way of life. This enmity, he says, goes back more than a thousand years to the first Crusade, when Christian Europe attempted to wrest the Holy Land from the Muslims. President George W. Bush further exacerbated the current situation by referring to the war against Saddam Hussein as a "crusade," a remark widely interpreted in Muslim countries as a war against Islam: "With its Western values, the very fact of Israel's existence is like a dagger pointed at the heart of Islam." Schaalman believes that the tension generated by this reality is irreconcilable and that peace for the short-term is impossible.

455 J Street describes itself as a counterpoint to the American Israel Public Affairs Committee (AIPAC), the most influential of Jewish-American pro-Israel lobbies. The major difference between the two organizations is that that the non-partisan AIPAC, although it is independent of the Israeli government, represents its position regardless of which Israeli party is in power. J Street, on the other hand, represents the liberal or "progressive" voice of American Judaism. Its major position is that a "two-state solution … is essential to Israel's survival as the national home of the Jewish people" (jstreet.org, n.d.).

456 Released on the eve of Rosh Hashanah 2010, the letter was a response to the long-awaited resumption of direct talks between Israel and the Palestinian Authority. It called on American officials to exercise "bold American diplomatic leadership to urgently achieve two states" and announced its intention to promote "a robust conversation in the American

Jewish community about Israel and the conflict." In putting their names to the letter, the signers made clear that, though they reserved the right to differ on the details of any policy statement, they agreed unanimously "that J Street is an effective catalyst for coming together, [offering] a public forum to engage in dialogue and explore opportunities to advance the cause of peace" (jstreet.org). Concerned that the "window of opportunity was rapidly closing" to achieving a viable two-state solution, the rabbis pointed out that the peace process is threatened by continued settlement expansion, "a growing movement in support of a one-state outcome" and "rejectionists on both sides" including "terrorists who use violence in a vain attempt to challenge Israel's very existence." Peace with security, they acknowledged, "Demands difficult compromises and mutual sacrifice. We ask those who have influence to join us in publicly advocating for a two-state solution and in emphasizing the need for reciprocal moves toward the ultimate goal of safe, peaceful coexistence" (jstreet.org).

457 In the 1990s, the ultra-Orthodox initiated a campaign in both the United States and Israel to label as "not Jewish" both the liberal governments of Yitzhak Rabin and Shimon Peres, and Reform and Conservative Judaism (Ochs, 2000, p. 21). In 1996, the Orthodox introduced legislation in the Knesset to delegitimize non-Orthodox conversions performed in Israel. This action threatened to reignite the 1988 battle over "Who is a Jew" that threatened to tear apart the tenuous fabric of Jewish unity. That struggle resulted from a legislative effort to recognize as legitimate only Orthodox conversions in the Diaspora and that only these conversions would assure automatic Israeli citizenship under the Law of Return.

458 Rabbi Alan Yuter (2008), a modern Orthodox Rabbi and a faculty member at the Institute for Traditional Judaism, wrote that the resulting crisis also had a "searing" effect on the Orthodox community (p. 1).

Chapter 12: Winding Down: Reaching Ninety and Beyond

459 Freddie died in November 2011.

460 The full sermon is available on DVD from HUC-JIR.

461 The Goldblatts had been friends for decades. Marvin had been very active in Emanuel congregation, and for several years, president of its board.

Chapter 13: Conclusion

462 W. Gunther Plaut succeeded Schaalman as President of the Central Conference of Reform Rabbis. He was rabbi of Holy Blossom in Toronto; Alfred Wolf was an associate rabbi at Wilshire Boulevard Temple in Los Angeles and, for a short period of time, became senior rabbi and subsequently employed by the American Jewish Committee; Wolli Kaelter became a rabbi in Long Beach, California; and Leo Lichtenberg was Director of Hillel at Adelphi College.

463 The other emeritus rabbis who were honored were: Howard Berman, Herbert Bronstein, Hillel Gamoran, Donald Gluckman, Harold Kudan, Robert Marx, Robert Schreibmen, Frederick Schwartz, Joseph Strauss, Victor Weissberg, Arnold Jacob Wolf, and Leo Wolkow.

464 On March 16, 2009, the CTS appointed Rabbi Dr. Rachel S. Mikva to fill the position. Rabbi Mikva is a well-known scholar and Reform rabbi and the daughter of former Illinois Congressman Abner Mikva. Two years later, she called Schaalman to ask whether he would agree to team-teach a course on Judaism during the next academic year. He agreed but remarked, "At my age, next year was a long way off." When he hung up the phone, he said to this interviewer, "As old as I am, I still welcome these invitations. They help me feel like I'm still wanted. Lotte and Michael do not understand this. They always tell me 'You've done enough.'"

465 General moral and religious sayings in the *Mishnah*, the first work of Rabbinic Judaism, a redaction of the Jewish oral traditions called the "Oral Torah."

466 The Schaalman grandchildren declare emphatically that their grandparents have been successful and believe that their values and family history have become part of their lives. Jeremy remembers that, when he was a teenager, his grandparents took him to visit the Holocaust Museum in Washington, D.C., and looked at the records of Schaalman family members who were killed by the Nazis. He reports, "I was deeply moved by the experience and hold it as a very special memory I shared with my grandparents."

467 Lotte tells a story that might be interpreted as a successful effort of the grandparents to transmit their Judaism to their grandchildren. On a Friday in July 2006, Keren and her boyfriend had arrived from Denver to visit the Schaalmans. As a favor to Rabbi Zedek, Schaalman had agreed to lead Shabbat services. In addition to making Shabbat dinner for Keren and her boyfriend, Lotte had invited her daughter and son-in-

law and his family. Because of all the arrangements she had to make for these guests, she had forgotten to enlist the help of a congregant to read the Torah blessings. From her earliest days as a rebbetzin, she had taken on the responsibility to find congregants willing to come to a Shabbat service and perform an aliyah, an honor such as opening the ark, carrying the Torah, or reciting the blessings over the Torah. She did not realize her mistake until the service had begun. Whom could she ask at the last moment? The problem resolved itself quickly when Keren, who was sitting at her side, volunteered. When she went up to the bimah, her grandfather lit up with evident pride, not only because of his granddaughter's presence, but because she could assist him in the service. She recited the blessings effortlessly, an indication that she was experienced and well educated in Temple liturgy.

468 The story comes from Buber's *The Tales of the Hasidim: Early Masters* (1958).

469 According to the article, Einstein's theory of relativity and much of twentieth-century physics have come under assault as a result of an experiment by 174 physicists who "fired bursts of neutrinos from the headquarters of CERN, the European Organization for Nuclear Research, in Geneva, Switzerland, to a detector in Gran Sasso, Italy. They tracked 16,111 of the ghostlike particles and measured how long they took to complete the trip…. [The experiment] seems to indicate that the neutrinos were traveling faster than light, violating what has long been regarded as an ironclad cosmic law." (Mone, G., 2012).

Appendix

Major Honors and Awards 1991–2008

1986 *The Life of the Covenant*, a festschrift honoring Schaalman

1991 Honoree for its Hall of Fame, the Jewish Community Centers of Chicago, for years of service to the Jewish community and superb leadership and total commitment to our people and our faith

1994 Richard Alschuler Award from the American Jewish Congress, for years of service on behalf of interfaith understanding and collaboration

1995 Award of Laureate in Ecumenical and Inter-religious Affairs, conferred by Cardinal Joseph Bernardin for Schaalman's efforts to address inter-religious understanding and Chicago's serious social issues

1995 Order of First Class Merit, "the highest tribute the Federal Republic of Germany can pay to individuals for services to the nation, for efforts to foster peaceful interaction and mutual tolerance between different religions and cultures"

1998 Julius Rosenwald Memorial Award from the Jewish Federation of Chicago, given for outstanding and long-term contributions to the advancement of the purposes of the Jewish Federation and to the welfare of the Jewish community

1999 "The Herman and Lotte Schaalman Park," on Sheridan Road, dedicated to the Schaalmans by the City of Chicago

2000 Honorary Doctorate from Chicago's Catholic Theological Union

2000 Graham Taylor Award, Chicago Theological Seminary, for outstanding lifetime dedication to a life of "selfless service, mercy and justice for all"

2001 Honoree, the Hebrew University in Jerusalem and the Israel Cancer Research Association

2001 Hall of Fame, the Jewish Community Centers

2001 Doctor of Hebrew Letters, *honoris causa*, Spertus Institute of Jewish Studies, in recognition of contributions in fostering strong Jewish participation in interfaith dialogue and activity and in pioneering the Jewish camping experience.

2001 Honoree of the Year, Jewish Council on Urban Affairs

2002 Order of Lincoln Award, Lincoln Academy of Illinois, given "to honor individuals whose exceptional effort to advance religious knowledge and understanding among citizens of different religious persuasions, thereby fostering interfaith harmony, religious tolerance, and community goodwill."

2002 Illinois House of the 92nd General Assembly passed Resolution 92_ HR0870, to acknowledge the Order of Lincoln Award, and to confer on him its own recognition for lifelong devotion and dedication to the betterment of mankind and for his leadership and humanitarian efforts for the residents of Illinois and for his accomplishments in or on behalf of the State of Illinois and for his dedication to those principles of democracy and humanity as exemplified by Abraham Lincoln

2003 Doctor of Humane Letters, Garrett Theological Seminary

2005 Interfaith Gold Medallion—Peace Through Dialogue, International Council of Christians and Jews, "given to notable world leaders who have worked tirelessly to promote understanding and peaceful relations between people of different faiths. (Past recipients include HM Queen Elizabeth the Second, Federal German President Dr. Johannes Rau, and Bishop Krister Stendahl.)

2008 Emanuel Congregation's Temple Brotherhood, an award in recognition of Schaalman's contribution to the Jewish Chautauqua Society

2008 Herman E. Schaalman Chair in Jewish Studies, established by the Chicago Theological Seminary (CTS), in recognition of his lifetime involvement in interfaith activities and contribution to CTS

2011 95th Birthday Concert, The Stradivari Society of Chicago

2012 "The Herman E. Schaalman and Lotte Schaalman Civilization Program in Jerusalem," a foundation at the University of Chicago to subsidize study in Jerusalem for students and their faculty

Bibliography

Abrams, Mel. (2007). (Speaker). Interview with Richard Damashek [Cassette Recording]. Cincinnati: American Jewish Archives.

Ackerman, J. S. (1951, October 4). Letter to Harry Lawner. Jacob Rader Marcus Center of the American Jewish Archives MS Collection No. 648. Cincinnati: American Jewish Archives.

Ackerman, J. S. (1952, March 12). Letter to Harry Lawner. Jacob Rader Marcus Center of the American Jewish Archives. MS Collection No. 648. Cincinnati: American Jewish Archives.

Adolf Schaalman. (n.d.). Unpublished manuscript. Author unknown. Cincinnati: American Congregation Archives.

Allen, J. L. Jr. (2007, February 23). Interwoven DNA of Catholics, Jews The Free Library. Retrieved September 24, 2010 from http://www .thefreelibrary.com/Interwoven DNA of Catholics, Jews-a01592162

American Jewish Archives. (n.d.). Olin-Sang-Ruby Union Institute records. Jacob Rader Marcus Center of the American Jewish Archives. Manuscript collection no. 648. Retrieved June 20, 2008, from http://www .americanjewisharchives.org/aja/FindingAids/olin-sang.htm

Archdiocese of Chicago. (1996). *A blessing to each other: Cardinal Joseph Bernardin and Jewish-Catholic Dialogue.* Chicago: Archdiocese of Chicago: Liturgy Training Publications.

Archdiocese of Chicago. (1996, November 19). Jewish readers' memorial service: Opening remarks of Rabbi Herman C. [sic] Schaalman. Chicago: Archdiocese.

Archdiocese of Chicago: Office for Ecumenical & Interreligious Affairs. (n.d.). Ecumenical, interfaith, & interreligious relations. Retrieved April 5, 2009, from http://www.archchicago.org/departments/ecumenical/eia_ relations.shtm

Athans, M. C. (2006). A dictionary of Jewish-Christian relations. *Theological Studies*, 67(4), 897+. Retrieved September 22, 2010, from Questia database: http://www.questia.com/PM.qst?a=o&d=5018378577

Athans, M. C. (2008, November). "Judaism and Catholic prayer: A new horizon for the liturgy," *New Theology Review*, 21 (4), 48-58.

Athans, M. C., Gannon, A. I. & Jegen, C. F. (Speakers), (2010, July 15). Interview with Richard Damashek [Digital Recording]. Cincinnati: American Jewish Archives.

Baeck, L. (1936). *The essence of Judaism.* New York: Macmillan.

Baima, T. A. (1996). Catholic-Jewish relations in Chicago. In Archdiocese of Chicago (Ed.), *A blessing to each other: Cardinal Joseph Bernardin and Jewish-Catholic dialogue* (pp. 9-16). Chicago: Archdiocese of Chicago: Liturgy Training Publications.

Barkai, A. (1998a). Exclusion and persecution: 1933-1938. In M. A. Meyer & M. Brenner (Eds.), *German-Jewish history in modern times: Renewal and destruction 1918-1945.* NY: Columbia University Press, 197-230.

Barkai, A. (1998b). Jewish life under persecution. In M. A. Meyer & M. Brenner (Eds.), *German-Jewish history in modern times: Renewal and destruction 1918-1945.* NY: Columbia University Press, 231-257.

Barkai, A. (1998c). Population decline and economic stagnation." In M. A. Meyer & M. Brenner (Eds.), *German-Jewish history in modern times: Renewal and destruction 1918-1945.* NY: Columbia University Press, 30-103.

Baron Maurice de Hirsch. (2008). Jewish Virtual Library. Retrieved August 14, 2008, from http://www.jewishvirtuallibrary.org/jsource/biography/Baronhirsch.html

Bayme, S. & Gordis, D. M. (1997, July). Preface. In B. A. Phillips, *Re-examining intermarriage: Trends, textures and strategies.* The Susan and David Wilstein Institute of Jewish Policy Studies and American Jewish Committee.

Bein, A. (1990). *The Jewish question: Biography of a world problem.* (Zohn, H., Trans.). Cranbury, NJ: Associated University Presses.

Beller, S. (2001). Renewal and destruction: 1918-1945. *German Politics and Society 19*(2).

Berkovits, E. *Faith after the Holocaust.* New York: KTAV Publishing House, Inc.

Berkson, M. (2007, July 7). Interview with Richard Damashek [Digital Recording]. Cincinnati: American Jewish Archives.

Bernardin, J. (1996). Anti-Semitism: The historical legacy and continuing challenge for Christians. In Archdiocese of Chicago (Ed.), *A blessing to each other* (145-163). Chicago: Liturgy Training Publications.

Besdin, A. R. (1992). The Holocaust and the State of Israel: Are they related? In B. H. Rosenberg and F. S. Heuman (Eds.) *Theological and Halakhic reflections on the Holocaust* (pp. 137-143). Hoboken, NJ: KTAV Publishing House, Inc.

Biography of Joseph Cardinal Bernardin. (n.d.). Retrieved October 11, 2010, from http://archives.archchicago.org/jcbbio.htm

Blank, D. (2007). History of Confirmation. Retrieved September 20, 2007, from http://www.myjewishlearning.com/lifecycle/Bar_Bat_Mitzvah/History/HistoryConfirmation.htm

Bloom, J. (2008, Winter). What God can learn from us: A conversation with Jack Bloom. *Reform Judaism online.* Retrieved December 11, 2008, from http://reformjudaismmag.org/Articles/index.cfm?id=1426

Bloom, J. (2010, May 19). Summer page turners. *The Jewish Ledger.* Retrieved June 22, 2012, from http://www.jewishledger.com/2010/05/summer-page-turners/

Borowitz, E. B. (1959, November). Existentialism's meaning for Judaism: a contemporary Midrash. Retrieved July 12, 2012, from http://www.commentarymagazine.com/article/existentialisms-meaning-for-judaisma-contemporary-midrash/

Borowitz, E. B. (1968). *A new Jewish theology in the making.* Philadelphia: The Westminster Press.

Borowitz, E. B. (1969). *Choosing a sexual ethic.* New York: Schocken Books.

Borowitz, E. B. (1969). *How can a Jew speak of faith today?* Philadelphia: The Westminster Press.

Borowitz, E. B. (1983). *Choices in modern Jewish thought, a partisan guide,* 2nd edition. West Orange, NJ: Behrman House.

Borowitz, E. B. (1991). *Renewing the Covenant: A theology for the postmodern Jew.* Philadelphia: Jewish Publication Society.

Borowitz, E.B. (1991, Fall). Rethinking our Holocaust consciousness. *Judaism, 40(4), 389.* Retrieved December 9, 2008, from Academic Search Premier database.

Borowitz, E. B. (2000). Postmodern Judaism: One theologian's view. In P. Ochs (Ed.), *Reviewing the Covenant* (35-48). Albany, NY: State University of New York Press.

Borowitz, E. B. (2002). *Studies in the meaning of Judaism.* Philadelphia: Jewish Publication Society.

Bouhler, Phillip. (1938). Kampf um Deutschland. Ein lesebuch fur die Deutsche Jugend. Reprinted in *The Battle for Germany.* German Propaganda Archive. Retrieved December 4, 2006. http://calvin.edu/academic/cas/gpa/bouhler6.htm

Braiterman, Z. (1998). *(God) After Auschwitz.* Princeton: Princeton University Press.

Brenner, R. R. (1980). *Faith and doubt of Holocaust survivors.* New York: Macmillan Publishing Co.

Brent, J. (1988, August 8). Political perversity in Chicago. *New Republic, 199(6/7),* 16-19. Retrieved February 18, 2008, from Academic Search Premier database.

Brucemore. (2005). Welcome to Brucemore: History - The Hall era 1937-1981. Retrieved June 3, 2010, from http://www.brucemore.org/pdf/hall_essay.pdf

Buber, M. (1970). *I and Thou* (W. Kaufman, Trans.). New York: Charles Scribner's Sons. (Original work published 1923).

Buber, M. (1958). *The tales of the Hasidim.* New York: Schocken Books.

Buber, M. (1966). *The way of man according to the teaching of Hasidism.* New York: The Citadel Press.

Campolo, T. (2007, May). God as the suffering servant. *Tikkun, 22(3),* 17-19. Retrieved September 30, 2009, from Academic Search Premier database.

Catholic Theological Union. (2008). People. Retrieved January 16, 2009, from http://www.ctu.edu/Bernardin_Center/The_People/Board_of_Advisors.html

Catholic Theological Union. (2008). Public events: The legacy of Joseph Cardinal Bernardin: A living gift to the Church. Retrieved January 16, 2009, from http://www.ctu.edu/News_and_Events/Public_Events/2006-2007_Academic_Year

CeaseFire.org. (n.d.). About. Retrieved November 3, 2010, from http://www.ceasefirechicago.org/cpvp.shtml

Cedar Rapids Tourist Bureau. (2010). History. Retrieved May 30, 2010, from http://www.cedar-rapids.com/about/history/

Central Conference of American Rabbis (CCAR). (1950). *CCAR Yearbook*, (82). Columbus, Ohio: CCAR.

Central Conference of American Rabbis (CCAR). (1972). *CCAR Yearbook*, (82). Columbus, Ohio: CCAR.

Central Conference of American Rabbis (CCAR). (1972, January 23-25). Minutes of the Committee on Mixed Marriage. Cincinnati: American Jewish Archives.

Central Conference of American Rabbis (CCAR). (1977). *CCAR Yearbook*, (87). Columbus, Ohio: CCAR.

Central Conference of American Rabbis (CCAR). (1979). *CCAR Yearbook*, (90). Columbus, Ohio: CCAR.

Central Conference of American Rabbis. (1976). Reform Judaism: A centenary perspective. Retrieved June 11, 2012 from http://ccarnet.org/rabbis-speak/platforms/reform-judaism-centenary-perspective/

Central Conference of American Rabbis. (1980). Reform Judaism and mixed marriage. American Reform Responsa, XC, 86-102. Retrieved July 15, 2008, from http://data.ccarnet.org/cgi-bin/respdisp.pl?file=146&year=arr

Central Conference of American Rabbis (CCAR). (1981). *CCAR Yearbook*, (91). Columbus, Ohio: CCAR.

Central Conference of American Rabbis (CCAR). (1982). *CCAR Yearbook*, (92). Columbus, Ohio: CCAR.

Central Conference of American Rabbis (CCAR). (1983). Report of the committee on patrilineal descent on the status of children of mixed marriages. *CCAR Yearbook*, (93). Columbus, Ohio: CCAR.

Central Conference of American Rabbis (CCAR). (1983). The status of children of mixed marriages. *CCAR Yearbook,* (93). Retrieved July 21, 2008, from http://data.ccarnet.org/cgi-bin/resodisp.pl?file=mm&year=1983

Central Conference of American Rabbis (CCAR). (2008). CCAR creating dialogue instead of debate over intermarriage issues. Retrieved July 18, 2008, from http://ccarnet.org/_kd/Items/actions.cfm?action=Show&item_id=1311&destination=ShowItem

Central Conference of American Rabbis (CCAR). (2008, January 17). Mission statement. Retrieved October 20, 2008, from http://ccarnet.org/aboutus/ccar_mission/#cprCCAR%20Mission%20Statement

Chester, M. A. (2001). Heschel and the Christians. 246+. Retrieved March 5, 2009, from Questia database: http://www.questia.com/PM.qst?a=o&d=5000604673

Chicago Archdiocese Office of Ecumenical and Religious Affairs. (n.d.). Ecumenical, Interfaith, and Interreligious Relations. Retrieved October 11, 2010 from http://www.archchicago.org/departments/ecumenical/eia_relations.shtm

Chicago Federation UAHC. (1951, March 29). Minutes of the Combined Committee for Camp Project. Cincinnati: Jacob Rader Marcus Center of the American Jewish Archives.

Chicago Theological Seminary. (n.d.). CTS: About us. Retrieved May 5, 2009, from http://www.ctschicago.edu/about/index.php

Chicago Theological Seminary. (2000, Fall). A timely celebration. *Tower News,* p. 5.

Chicago Theological Seminary. (2006, Fall). A timely celebration. *Tower News: Making new history,* p. 5.

Chicago Theological Seminary. (2008). CTS establishes Jewish studies chair. Retrieved April 29, 2008 from http://www.ctschicago.edu/general/schaalman-news.php

Chicago Theological Seminary. (2008, April 15). Chicago Theological Seminary presents the inaugural Herman Schaalman Lecture in Jewish Studies. Chicago: The Chicago Theological Seminary.

Chicago Theological Seminary. (2009, March 16). Rabbi Dr. Rachel S. Mikva to fill newly established Rabbi Herman E. Schaalman Chair in Jewish Studies at CTS. *Chicago Theological Seminary News.* Retrieved May 5, 2009, from http://www.ctschicago.edu/general/news.php#RachelSMikva

Chicago Theological Seminary. (2011). Statement of commitments. Retrieved February 22, 2011, from http://www.ctschicago.edu/index.php/mnuaboutus/58-statement-of-commitments

"Cincinnati, Ohio -- Congregation Bene Israel (Rockdale Temple) Records: Manuscript Collection No. 24 American Jewish Archives." (1999). Retrieved August 21, 2012, from http://americanjewisharchives.org/aja/FindingAids/Rockdale.htm

City Council needs anti-bigot policing [Editorial]. (1988, September 17). The Chicago Tribune, p. 12.

City-Data.com. (n.d.). Cedar Rapids: History. Retrieved May 30, 2010, from http://www.city-data.com/us-cities/The-Midwest/Cedar-Rapids-History.html

Cohen, M. (1979). The Idea of the sanctity of the Biblical text and the science of textual criticism. (I. B. Gottlieb, Trans.) In U. Simon (Ed.), *HaMikrah V'anachnu*. Tel-Aviv. Retrieved April 18, 2008, from http://cs.anu.edu.au/~bdm/dilugim/CohenArt/

Cohen, S. M. (2006). Steven Cohen responds. *New Jersey Jewish News.* Retrieved September 7, 2008, from http://www.njjewishnews.com/njjn.com/033006/nbtHolyVsWholly.html

Cohen, S. M. (2006, November). A tale of two Jewries: The 'inconvenient truth' for American Jews. *Jewish Life Network/Steinhardt Foundation.*

Cohen, S. M. (2008, March 21). Seeking a third way to respond to the challenge of intermarriage. Paper presented at the meeting of the Central Conference of American Rabbis 2008 Convention.

Cohen, S. M. & Wertheimer, J. (2006, June). Whatever happened to the Jewish people. *Commentary.* Retrieved July 16, 2008, from http://www.huc.edu/faculty/faculty/pubs/StevenCohen/CohenWertheimer.pdf

Cohn, H. (Speaker). (2011, March 21). Interview with Richard Damashek [Digital Recording]. Cincinnati: American Jewish Archives.

Cohon, S. S. (1950, March 20). Reform Jewish theology: Introductory words to Institute on Reform Jewish Theology Today. Cincinnati: American Jewish Archives.

Combined Committee for Camp Project. (1951, March 29). Minutes. Jacob Rader Marcus Center of the American Jewish Archives MS Collection No. 648. Cincinnati: American Jewish Archives.

Coe Cosmos, The (1947, October 29). p. 5.

Council of Religious Leaders of Metropolitan Chicago. (1988, November). ECUMENICAL/INTERFAITH PRAYER ON RACISM: An Open Letter to the People of Chicago. Retrieved June 23, 2010, from http://www.crlmc.org/1988Thanksgiving.php

Cutler, D. R. (Ed.). (1968). *The religious situation:1968*. Boston: Beacon Press.

Dashefsky, A., & Heller, Z. I. (2008). *Intermarriage and Jewish journeys in the United States*. Newton Centre, MA: The National Center for Jewish Policy Studies at Hebrew College.

David Philipson Papers: Manuscript Collection No. 35. (n. d.). American Jewish Archives. Retrieved August 21, 2012, from http://americanjewisharchives.org/aja/FindingAids/Philipso.htm

Deaths. (1951, March 2). *The Cedar Rapids Gazette*, p. 8.

Deutsch, G. & Magnes, L. (n.d.). *Lehranstalt für die Wissenschaft Des Judentums*. Retrieved March 22, 2006, from http://www.jewishencyclopedia.com/view_friendly.jsp?artid=156&letter=L

Diemert, B. (2005). Uncontainable metaphor: George F. Kennan's "X" article and Cold War discourse. *Canadian Review of American Studies*, Vol. 35 Issue 1, p21-55, 35p Retrieved April 21, 2008, from MasterFILE Premier database.

Diner, H. (2009). *We remember with reverence and love: American Jews and the myth of silence after the Holocaust, 1945-1962*. New York: New York U. Press.

Donation documents Des Moines' Jewish community. (2007, March-April). *Iowa Historian: The newsletter of the State Historical Society of Iowa*. Retrieved May 27, 2010, from http://www.iowahistory.org/publications/iowa-historian/2007/historian_march-april_07.htm

Dorland's Medical Dictionary for Health Consumers. (2007). wire, Kirschner. Retrieved January 4, 2011, from www.medical-dictionary.thefreedictionary.com/_/dict.aspx?word=K+wire

Drake to hear Malcolm Boyd. (1965, February 13). *Des Moines Register*, p. 6.

Edelheit, J. (Ed.). (1986). *The life of Covenant: The challenge of contemporary Judaism*. Chicago: Spertus College of Judaica Press.

Edelheit, J. (2006, November 11). Letter to Rabbi Herman Schaalman. Cincinnati: American Jewish Archives.

Edwards, R. (2011, April 12). Drawing and reading. Unpublished manuscript.

Egelson, L. I. (Ed.). (1956). *Proceedings of the Union of American Hebrew Congregations Seventy seventh–eightieth Annual Reports: July 1, 1950 – June 30, 1955.* Boston: UAHC Press.

Eichhorn, D. M. (1974). *Jewish intermarriages: Fact and fiction.* Satellite Beach, FL: Satellite Books.

Eisendrath, M. N. (1951, October 25). President's report to the executive board of the Union of American Hebrew Congregations. In L. I. Egelson (Ed.), *Proceedings of the Union of American Hebrew Congregations Seventy seventh–eightieth Annual Reports: July 1, 1950 – June 30, 1955*: Appendix A (90-102). Boston: UAHC Press.

Eisendrath, M. N. (1952, June 21-22). President's semi-annual report to the executive board of the Union of American Hebrew Congregations: June 21-22, 1952. In L. I. Egelson (Ed.), *Proceedings of the Union of American Hebrew Congregations Seventy seventh–eightieth Annual Reports: July 1, 1950 – June 30, 1955* (146-165). Boston: UAHC Press.

Eisendrath, M. N. (1953, April 19). The report of the president: The state of our Union. In L. I. Egelson (Ed.), *Proceedings of the Union of American Hebrew Congregations Seventy seventh–eightieth Annual Reports: July 1, 1950 – June 30, 1955*: Appendix A (536-564). Boston: UAHC Press.

Eisendrath, M. N. (1956). President's report to the executive board of the Union of American Hebrew Congregations. In L. I. Egelson (Ed.), *Proceedings of the Union of American Hebrew Congregations Seventy seventh–eightieth Annual Reports: July 1, 1950 – June 30, 1955*: Appendix A (257-261). Boston: UAHC Press.

Eisendrath, M. N. (1956). *The report of the president: The state of our union. In L. I. Egelson (Ed.) Proceedings of the Untion of American Hebrew Congregations (Seventy-Seventh-Eightieth Annual Reports: July 1, 1950 – June 30, 1955.* Boston: UAHC Press.

Eisendrath, M. N. (1964). *Can faith survive?* New York: McGraw Hill.

Elazar, D. J. (1995). *Community and polity: The organizational dynamics of American Jewry* (Revised ed.). Philadelphia: Jewish Publication Society. Retrieved April 28, 2010, from Questia database: http://www.questia.com/PM.qst?a=o&d=16329173

Elbogen, I. (1993). *Jewish liturgy: A comprehensive history* (R. P. Scheindlin, Trans.). Jerusalem: The Jewish Publication Society and The Jewish Theological Seminary of America (Original work published 1913).

Elon, A. (2002). *The pity of it all.* New York: Picador.

Emanu-El B'ne Jeshurun. (2009). Welcome to Congregation Emanu-El B'Ne Jeshurun. Retrieved September 16, 2009, from http://www.ceebj.org/about_us/staff_list/

Emanuel Congregation. (1957, February 26). Minutes of the Board of Trustees. Cincinnati: Emanuel Congregation Archives.

Emanuel Congregation. (1957, March 27). Minutes of the Board of Trustees. Chicago: Emanuel Congregation Archives.

Emanuel Congregation. (1957, November 30). Minutes of the Board of Trustees. Chicago: Emanuel Congregation Archives.

Emanuel Congregation. (1957, December 10). Minutes of the Board of Trustees Meeting Chicago: Emanuel Congregation Archives.

Emanuel Congregation. (1958, May 27). Proposed budget for the fiscal year from July 1, 1958 to June 30, 1959. Minutes of the Board of Trustees. Chicago: Emanuel Congregation Archives.

Emanuel Congregation. (1960, May 24). Minutes of the Board of Trustees. Chicago: Emanuel Congregation Archives.

Emanuel Congregation. (1971, January 30). Minutes of the Board of Trustees. Chicago: Emanuel Congregation Archives.

Emanuel Congregation. (1986, May 30). A Year of Tribute [Cassette Recording]. Chicago: Emanuel Congregation Archives.

Emanuel Congregation. (2007, January 22). Minutes of the Board of Trustees. Chicago: Emanuel Congregation Archives.

Emanuel Congregation. (2010). Staff. Retrieved December 22, 2010, from http://www.emanuelcong.org/aboutus/staff/

Emanuel Congregation. (Producer). (2010, May 23). Herman and Lotte Schaalman Torah Writing Project [Video Recording]. Chicago: Emanuel Congregation Archives.

Epstein, L. J. (1992, Summer). The patrilineal principle: A time for clarification. *CCAR Journal: A Reform Quarterly*, XXXIX(2), 57-62.

Essrig, H. (1973, February 28). Letter to Rabbi Jacob Shankman. Cincinnati: American Jewish Archives.

Evaluation Committee of Union Institute. (1955, October 3). Report of meeting of Evaluation Committee of Union Institute. Jacob Rader Marcus Center of the American Jewish Archives. MS Collection No. 648. Cincinnati: American Jewish Archives.

Evans, R. J. (2004). *The coming of the Third Reich*. New York: Penguin Press.

Fackenheim, E. L. (1967, Summer). Jewish values in the post-Holocaust future: A symposium, *Judaism 16* (3), 293-4.

Fackenheim, E. L. (1968). *God's presence in history: Jewish affirmations and philosophical reflections*. New York: Harper and Row, Publishers.

Fackenheim, E. L. (1968). *Quest for past and future*. Scarborough, Ontario: Fitzhenry & Whiteside, Ltd.

Fackenheim, E. L. (1994). *To mend the world*. Bloomington: University of Indiana Press.

Fackenheim, E. L. (2001, Fall). Why the Holocaust is unique. *Judaism*, 50, 438-447.

Fackenheim, E. L. (2002). Faith in God and man after Auschwitz: Theological implications. Holocaust Teacher Resource Center. Retrieved September 22, 2009, from http://www.holocaust-trc.org/fackenheim.htm

Faith in conversation. (2005, July). *U.S. Catholic*. Retrieved May 5, 2008, from Academic Search Premier database.

Fendel, H. (2009). Chief Rabbi: Decision to overturn conversions won't stand. Israel National News.com. Retrieved February 5, 2009, from http://www.israelnationalnews.com/News/News.aspx/126074

Ficca, D. (Speaker). (2010, November 30). Interview with Richard Damashek [Digital Recording]. Cincinnati: American Jewish Archives.

Financial aid for mental hygiene clinic requested. (1949, May 31). *The Cedar Rapids Gazette,* pp. 1, 4.

Findsen, O. (1997, October 12). Lazarus store has long, rich lineage. *The Cincinnati Enquirer*. Retrieved December 6, 2009, from http://www.enquirer.com/editions/1997/10/12/bus_wwlazarus.html

Fishbein, I. H. (n.d.). List of rabbis who officiate at interfaith marriages. Rabbinic Center for Research and Counseling. Retrieved August 28, 2008, from http://www.rcrconline.org/rabbi.bylocation.htm

Fishbein, I. H. (2003, December 29). Summary of Rabbinic Center for Research and Counseling 2003 Survey. Rabbinic Center for Research and Counseling. Retrieved August 28, 2008, from http://www.rcrconline.org/research.htm

Fishbein, I. H. (1973, June 19). Central Conference of American Rabbis: Report of Committee on Mixed Marriage: Minority Report. Rabbinic Center for Research and Counseling. Retrieved June 19, 2008, from http://www.rcrconline.org/resourc2.htm

Fisher, E. J. (2004, September 17). Pope John Paul II and the Jews. The Tidings.com. Retrieved February 28, 2008 from http://www.the-tidings.com/2004/0917/fisher_text.htm

Fisher, E. J. (2010). Jewish-Christian relations 1989 - 1993: A bibliographic update. Jewish-Christian relations. Retrieved November 3, 2010, from http://www.jcrelations.net/en/?id=809

Fishkoff, S. (2007, February 6). Latest salvo in intermarriage debate suggests a split in Jewish community, JTA. Retrieved July 16, 2008, from http://www.huc.edu/newspubs/pressroom/07/2/cohen.shtml

Fishkoff, S. (2007, July 13). 70s rebel takes job at cantorial school. Retrieved November 29, 2009, from http://jta.org/news/article/2007/07/13/103003/friedman

Folb, A. (2007). *An intellectual and historical biography of Rabbi Herman Schaalman.* Unpublished master's thesis. Hebrew Union College-Jewish Institute of Religion, Cincinnati, Ohio.

Foto Facts. (1949, September 8). *The Cedar Rapids Gazette*, p. 12.

Friedman, M. (Speaker). (2005, June 10). Interview with Richard Damashek [Cassette Recording]. Cincinnati: American Jewish Archives.

Frymer-Kensky, T. Novak, D. Ochs, P., & Signer, M. (2002, April). Jewish-Christian dialogue. *Commentary*, 113(4), 8. Retrieved June 4, 2009, from Academic Search Premier database.

Fuellenbach, J. (2004, October 3). The reign of God: The mission of the Church. In God's missionary people: A new way of being Church. Symposium conducted at the National Mission Annual Symposium of the Glenmary Home Missioners, Louisville, Kentucky.

Galloway, P. (1995, March 19). Bernardin heading Jewish-Christian tour of Holy Land: [Chicagoland Edition]. *Chicago Tribune*, p. 3. Retrieved April 1, 2010, from *Chicago Tribune*. (Document ID: 20954024).

Galloway, P. (1995, March 26). Chicago pilgrims share the Sabbath Cardinal Bernardin, Rabbi Peter Knobel worship in Holy city: [Chicagoland Final Edition]. *Chicago Tribune*, p. 10. Retrieved October 15, 2010, from *Chicago Tribune*. (Document ID: 20961121).

Galloway, P. (1995, March 29). Arafat gives Bernardin some gentle chiding on gift: [North Sports Final Edition]. *Chicago Tribune*, p. 3. Retrieved October 15, 2010, from *Chicago Tribune*. (Document ID: 20963216).

Garfield Library: University of Pennsylvania. (2009). Holocaust title search. Retrieved March 9, 2009, from http://www.garfield.library.upenn.edu/histcomp/holocaust_ti/list/py-name.html

Garrett-Evangelical Theological Seminary. (2007). Who we are. Retrieved 21 October 2007 from http://www.garrett.edu/content.asp?A=6&C=20001

Gellman, M. (n.d.). The God Squad. Retrieved March 28, 2011, from http://www.tmsfeatures.com/columns/religion/the-god-squad/

George, F. C. (2010, June 21). Remarks Twenty-Fifth Anniversary Celebration Council of Religious Leaders of Metropolitan Chicago. Archdiocese of Chicago.

George Mason University. (n.d.). Paul Celan Biography. Retrieved March 18, 2011, from mason.gmu.edu/~lsmithg/celan.html

Gerald Hiland presented 1948 Civic Service Award. (1949, May 27). *The Cedar Rapids Gazette*, p. 1.

Gergely, T. (2006). Was the *Shoah* the "Sanctification of God?" In E. Ben-Rafael & Y. Gorny (Eds.), *Jewish identities in a changing world* (Vol. 6, 289-304). Leiden and Boston: Brill.

Gibbons, T. (1988, May 8). Cokely flap spotlights old rift – Black-Jewish tensions hark back to '60s. *Chicago Sun-Times*, p. 8.

Glaser, J. B. (1971, August 16). Letter to Rabbi Herman E. Schaalman. On file at the New York office of the CCAR.

Glaser, J. B. (1971, September 8). Letter to Rabbi Herman E. Schaalman. On file at the New York office of the CCAR.

Glaser, J. B. (1971, September 21). Letter to Rabbi Herman E. Schaalman. On file at the New York office of the CCAR.

Glaser, J. B. (1982, July 8). Letter to Rabbi Herman E. Schaalman. On file at the New York office of the CCAR.

Glaser, J. B. (1983). Presentation to the outgoing president. *CCAR Yearbook.* Columbus: CCAR.

Glaser, J. B. (1983, March 25). Letter to Rabbi Herman E. Schaalman. On file at the New York office of the CCAR.

Glaser, J. B. (1988, December 23). Letter to Rabbi Herman E. Schaalman. On file at the New York office of the CCAR.

Glaser, J. B. (1991, July 3). Letter to Rabbi Herman E. Schaalman. On file at the New York office of the CCAR.

Glenmary Home Missioners. (2004, Oct. 12). National Mission Symposium challenges U. S. Church to be about the "Kingdom business" not Church business. Retrieved June 1, 2009, from http://www.glenmary .org/Whats_new/2004/0410/symposium_wrapup.htm

Gordis, D. M. (2008). Preface. In A. Dashefsky & Z. I. Heller, *Intermarriage and Jewish journeys in the United States.* Newton Centre, MA: The National Center for Jewish Policy Studies at Hebrew College.

Gravelle, S. (2003, November 7). Haven from Holocaust. *The Gazette*, section B, edition F, p. 1. Retrieved June 8, 2010 from http://nl .news-bank.com/nl-search/we/Archives?p_action=doc&p_docid= 0FEB001861081BC0&p_docnum=4

Green, A. (1996). What is Jewish theology? In Neusner, *Judaism transcends catastrophe: God, Torah, and Israel beyond the Holocaust.* Macon, GA: Mercer University press.

Green, A. (2006). God! *European Judaism, 39*(2), 83+. Retrieved November 20, 2008, from Questia database: http://www.questia.com/ PM.qst?a=o&d=5019494422

Greenberg, E. J. (2000, January 28). Split on Jerusalem. *The Jewish week.* Retrieved July 16, 2009, from http://www.thejewishweek.com/viewArticle /c36_a4672/News/New_York.html

Greenberg, I. (1966, Spring). Symposium toward Jewish religious unity. *Judaism* 15, 2, 31-163.

Greenberg, I. (1997). Seeking the religious roots of pluralism: In the image of God and Covenant. *Journal of ecumenical studies, 34*(3), 385+. Retrieved August 28, 2009, from Questia database: http://www.questia.com/PM.qst?a=o&d=5000581611

Greenberg, I. (2006). Theology after the *Shoah*: The transformation of the core paradigm. *Modern Judaism: A Journal of Jewish Ideas and Experience, 26* (3), 213-239.

Greenberg, Y. K. (2000). A theology for the postmodern Jew. In P. Ochs (Ed.) *Reviewing the Covenant* (pp. 49-59). Albany, NY: State University of New York Press.

Haas, P. J. (2002). Reform and Halacha: A rapprochement? In D. E. Kaplan (Ed.), *Platform and prayer books* (pp. 233-246). Lanham, MD: Rowman & Littlefield Publishers.

Halivni, D. W. (2007). Prayer in the *Shoah*. In P. Ochs (Ed.), *Breaking the tablets* (pp. 15-41). New York: Rowman & Littlefield Publishers, Inc.

Harris, B. (2007, September 20). Reform *siddur* revives resurrection prayer. JTA News Service. Retrieved January 6, 2008 from www.jta.org/cgi-bin/iowa/news/print/20070920reformprayerbook.html

Hart, C. (2011). Charlotte Hart. Retrieved April 20, 2012, from http://www.charlotte-hart.com/biography.html

Hart, S. (Speaker). (2006, June 6). Interview with Richard Damashek [Cassette Recording]. Cincinnati: American Jewish Archives.

Hebrew Union College-Jewish Institute of Religion-Jewish Institute of Religion. (2007, June 2). Ordination ceremony: 2007. (DVD). Cincinnati: Hebrew Union College-Jewish Institute of Religion.

Hebrew Union College-Jewish Institute of Religion-Jewish Institute of Religion. (2008, March 3). Reception honoring fourteen Chicago-area rabbis with new HUC-JIR student scholarship on April 3, 2008: Rabbi David Ellenson, Ph.D. to present. Retrieved April 6, 2008, from www.huc.edu/news/08/3/reception

Henry, G. T. (2001). *Images of America: Cedar Rapids, Iowa*. Chicago: Arcadia Publishing.

Henry, G. T. and Hunter, M. W. (2005). *Then & now: Cedar Rapids: Downtown and beyond*. Charleston, SC: Arcadia Publishing.

Hepburn, M. A. (1990, July/August). Educating for democracy. *Social Studies*, Vol. 81, Issue 4 Database: MasterFILE Premier.

Heschel, A. J. (1966). *The insecurity of freedom*. New York: Farrar, Straus & Giroux.

Himmelfarb, M. (Ed.). (1966, August). What do American Jews believe? A symposium. *Commentary*, 102, 2, 18-79.

Hirsch, R. G. (2010, March 26). Interview with Richard Damashek [Digital Recording]. Cincinnati: American Jewish Archives.

History of Emanuel Congregation. (2009). *Emanuel Congregation*. Retrieved July 8, 2009, from http://www.emanuelcong.org/aboutus/history/

Hoffman, L. A. (2003). Searching for a second course inaugural address: Founder's day address. Hebrew Union College-Jewish Institute of Religion. Retrieved August 26, 2008, from http://www.huc.edu/faculty/faculty/pubs/hoffman.shtml

Hollinshead to speak at installation. (1949, October 16). *The Cedar Rapids Gazette*, p. 10.

Howard Hall, C. R. industrialist, dies. (1971, May 17). *The Cedar Rapids Gazette*, p. 3.

Interfaith Awards. (1995, January 29). Joseph Cardinal Bernardin Archbishop of Chicago confers upon Rabbi Herman Schaalman the award of Laureate in ecumenical and interreligious affairs. Chicago: The Archdiocese of Chicago.

International Council of Christians and Jews: Chicago ICCJ Conference. (2005). Invitation. Retrieved July 19, 2006 from http://www.iccj.org/en/index.php?item=229

International Council of Jewish-Christian Relations. (2009, February 1). Resolution on the Revised 1962 Good Friday "Prayer for the Jews." Retrieved July 18, 2010, from http://www.jcrelations.net/en/?item=3054

International Council of Christians and Jews. (2010). Retrieved October 6, 2010, from http://www.jcrelations.net/en/

Iowa Pathways. (2005). Jewish settlers in Iowa. Retrieved June 9, 2010, from http://www.iptv.org/iowapathways/mypath.cfm?ounid=ob_000156

Jacob Rader Marcus Center of the American Jewish Archives. (2003). Ernst M. Lorge Papers: Manuscript Collection No. 672. Retrieved February 14, 2012, from http://americanjewisharchives.org/aja/FindingAids/ErnstLorge.htm

Jacobs, L. (1995). *The Jewish religion: A companion.* Oxford: Oxford University Press.

Jake "Greasy Thumb" Guzik (1887-1956): Capone Financial Brain. (2003, August). Seize the Night. Retrieved \May 4, 2010, from http://www.carpenoctem.tv/mafia/guzik.html

Janik, A. (2009). "Introduction to the Transaction Edition." In E. Friedell, *The cultural history of the modern age.* New Brunswick, N.J.: Transaction Publishers.

Jaques, D. (Speaker). (2005, July 8). Interview with Richard Damashek [Cassette Recording]. Cincinnati: American Jewish Archives.

Jewish Council on Urban Affairs. (n.d.). Outreach and education: Accomplishments and challenges, 1991-1993. Chicago: Jewish Council on Urban Affairs.

Jewish Council on Urban Affairs. (1985, February 26). Board Minutes. Chicago: Jewish Council on Urban Affairs.

Jewish Council on Urban Affairs. (1985, October 21). Board Minutes. Chicago: Jewish Council on Urban Affairs.

Jewish Council on Urban Affairs. (1987, July 16). Board Minutes. Chicago: Jewish Council on Urban Affairs.

Jewish Council on Urban Affairs. (1992). Education Sub-Committee Report to the Board. Chicago: Jewish Council on Urban Affairs.

Jewish Council on Urban Affairs. (1993, April 26). Position Statement: A wholistic approach to economic development in Chicago. Chicago: Jewish Council on Urban Affairs.

Jewish Council on Urban Affairs. (2001). Annual Report. Chicago: Jewish Council on Urban Affairs.

Jewish Council on Urban Affairs. (2008). Mission statement. Retrieved February 11, 2008 from http://www.jcua.org/site/News2?page=NewsArticle&id=5055

Jewish Virtual Library. (2007). "Bar Mitzvah, Bat Mitzvah and Confirmation." Retrieved September 20, 2007 from http://www.jewishvirtuallibrary. org/jsource/Judaism/barmitz.html

Jewish Virtual Library. (2008). Rabbi Mordecai Kaplan. Retrieved September 23, 2008, from http://www.jewishvirtuallibrary.org/jsource/biography/ kaplan.html

Johnson, D. (1988, July 29). Black-Jewish hostility rouses leaders in Chicago to action. *New York Times*, Retrieved February 24, 2008, from http:// query.nytimes.com/gst/fullpage.html?res=940DEFDB1E3FF93AA157 54C0A96E948260&sec=&spon=

Johnson, M. A. (1993, May 14). Farrakhan tries tune of harmony with Jews. *Chicago Sun-Times*, p. 5.

Jonas, H. (1996). *Mortality and morality: The search for the good after Auschwitz.* Evanston: Northwestern University Press.

jstreet.org. (n.d.). About us. Retrieved October 31, 2010 from http://jstreet. org/about/about-us

JTA. (2009, July 1). The chosen: Jewish members in the 111th U.S. Congress. http://www.ask.com/bar?q=Jews+in+111+congress&page=1&qsrc=24 17&ab=1&u=http%3A%2F%2Fjta.org%2Fnews%2Farticle%2F200 9%2F07%2F01%2F1000795%2Fthe-chosen-jewish-members-in-the-111th-us-congress

Judaism to be topic of Rabbi Schaalman at YWCA meeting. (1945, January 17). *The Coe Cosmos*, p. 1.

Kaelter, W. (1997). *From Danzig: An American rabbi's journey.* Malibu, CA: Pangloss Press.

Kaiserman, M. (1997). *A historical analysis of rabbinical officiation at interfaith marriages in the Reform Movement.* Cincinnati: HUC Press.

Kaplan, D. E. (2003). *American Reform Judaism: An introduction.* New Brunswick, NJ: Rutgers University Press.

Kaplan, M. A. (1991). *The making of the Jewish middle class: Women, family, and identity in Imperial Germany.* New York: Oxford University Press, 1991.

Kaplan, M. A. (Ed.). (2005). *Jewish daily life in Germany, 1618-1945.* New York: Oxford University Press.

Kaplan, M. M. (1934). *Judaism as a civilization.* New York: The Macmillan Company.

Kaplan, M. M. (1936). *Judaism in transition.* New York: Covici Friede Publishers.

Karff, S. E. (1990). The rabbi as religious figure. In J. B. Glaser (Ed.), *Tannu Rabbanan: Our rabbis taught: Essays in commemoration of the centennial of the Central Conference of American Rabbis* (71-88). New York: Central Conference of American Rabbis.

Karp, A. J., Jacobs, L., Dimitrovsky, C. Z. (Eds). (1991). *Threescore and ten: Essays in honor of Rabbi Semour J. Cohen on the occasion of his seventieth birthday.* Hoboken, N.J. KTAV Publishing House.

Katz, S. T. (1992). *Historicism, the Holocaust, and Zionism.* New York: New York University Press.

Kaye, G. (2006, July 1). Interview with Richard Damashek [Digital Recording]. Cincinnati: American Jewish Archives.

Kimelman, R. (1983, Winter). Leadership: Portraits of challenge, vision and responsibility. *Melton Journal,* No. 15. Retrieved October 21, 2008, from http://www.crosscurrents.org/heschel.htm

Kloehn, B. (1999, Oct. 27). 2 rabbis offer differing views of Holocaust's continuing impact on American Jews. *Chicago Tribune* (IL), Retrieved September 16, 2009, from Newspaper Source database.

Klug, L. A. (2004, December 12). Debbie Friedman's spiritual undertaking. *The Jerusalem Post.* Retrieved November 29, 2009 from http://jta.org/news/article/2007/07/13/103003/friedman

Knobel, P. S. (2002). The challenge of a single prayer book. In D. E. Kaplan (Ed.), *Platform and prayer books* (155-172). Lanham, MD: Rowman & Littlefield Publishers.

Knobel, P. S. (Speaker). (2006, December 18). Interview with Richard Damashek [Cassette Recording]. Cincinnati: American Jewish Archives.

Knobel, P. S. (2007, June 16). Letter to Rabbi Herman E. Schaalman. Cincinnati: American Jewish Archives.

Kohler, K. (2001). The origin and functions of ceremonies in Judaism. In M. A. Meyer and W. G. Plaut, *The Reform Jewish reader* (104-105). New York: UAHC Press.

Kolsky, T. A. (1990). Jews against Zionism: The American Council for Judaism, 1942-1948. Philadelphia: Temple University Press. Retrieved May 16, 2010, from Questia database: http://www.questia.com/PM.qst?a=o&d=34693620

Komerofsky, D. (1999). *Julian Morgenstern: A personal and intellectual biography* (Thesis, Hebrew Union College-Jewish Institute of Religion, 1999).

Korn, B. W. (1974). Preface. In D. M. Eichhorn, *Jewish intermarriages: Fact and fiction.* Satellite Beach, FL: Satellite Books.

Kosmin, B. A. (2008). *The changing population profile of American Jews 1990-2008.* Paper presented at the Fifteenth World Congress of Jewish Studies. Hartford, CT.: Trinity College.

Kotzin, M. (2007, February 4). The Catholic-Jewish Scholars Dialogue of Chicago: A model of interreligious dialogue. *JUF News.* Retrieved October 18, 2010, from www.juf.org/news/local.aspx?id-12866

Kraut, A. M. (2007). Frankland's History of the 1873 Yellow Fever Epidemic in Memphis, Tennessee. *American Jewish Archives Journal, LIX,* 1 & 2, 89–98.

Kroloff, C. A. (1990). Unity within diversity. In J. B. Glaser (Ed.), *Tanu Rabbanan: Our rabbis taught: Essays on the occasion of the centennial of the Central Conference of American Rabbis, 1989 Yearbook, II,* (89-103). NY: Central Conference of American Rabbis.

Kroloff, C. A. (2008, September 15). Interview with Richard Damashek [Digital Recording]. Cincinnati: American Jewish Archives.

Kurtz, V. (2001). Three biblical portraits of the Divine-human encounter. In W. D. Edgerton (Ed.), *The honeycomb of the word.* Chicago: Exploration Press.

Kushner, H. *When bad things happen to good people.* New York: Schocken Books.

Lama Gangchen Peace Times. (n.d.). Chicago, USA, 19th & 20th November 1995: The Council of the Parliament of World Religions and the Millennium Institute at North Shore Congregation Israel. Retrieved November 4, 2010, from http://www.lgpt.net/Forum/cron_list_it.htm

Lampman, J. (2000, September 14). Catholics and Jews show different faces toward interfaith dialogue. *Christian Science Monitor,* 92(206), 14. Retrieved June 4, 2009, from Academic Search Premier database.

Laqueur, W. (2001). *Generation Exodus.* Hanover and London: Brandeis University Press.

Lawner, H. L. (1951, September 6). Letter to Hollender. In L. I. Egelson (Ed.), *Proceedings of the Union of American Hebrew Congregations Seventy seventh–eightieth Annual Reports: July 1, 1950 – June 30, 1955: Appendix A* (78-79). Boston: UAHC Press.

Lawner, H. L. (1952, March 25). Letter to Ackerman. Jacob Rader Marcus Center of the American Jewish Archives MS Collection No. 648. Cincinnati: American Jewish Archives.

Layton announces record enrollment in evening college. (1948, October 20). *The Coe Cosmos,* p. 1.

Lefebure, L. D. (1993, September 22). Global encounter: At the Parliament of Religions. *The Christian Century,* 110, (26), 886-889.

Lefebure, L. D. (1998). Encounters among the World's Religions. Retrieved September 25, 2008 from http://www.urbandharma.org/bcdialog/bcd1/conflict.html

Lefebure, L. D. (2002, February 13). Interreligious impact. *Christian Century,* 119(4), 19. Retrieved May 5, 2008, from Academic Search Premier database.

Lehmann, D. J., Hanania, R. (1988, May 12). 3 clerics seek calm in Cokely aftermath. *Chicago Sun-Times.* Retrieved February 21, 2012, from http://infoweb.newsbank.com.covers.chipublib.org/iw-search/we/InfoWeb?p_product=NewsBank&p_theme=aggregated5&p_action=doc&p_docid=0EB36DD366D86195&p_docnum=1&p_queryname=1

Leighton, C. (2005, June 28). For the sake of heaven and earth: The new encounter between Judaism and Christianity. *Christian Century,* 122(13), 38-39. Retrieved June 4, 2009, from Academic Search Premier database.

Lerner, M. (1994). *Jewish renewal: A path to healing and transformation.* New York: G. P. Putnam's and Sons.

Levenson, J. D. (2001, December). How not to conduct Jewish-Christian Relations. *Commentary,* Vol. 112 (5), 31-37.

Levenson, J. D. (2004, February). The agenda of Dabru Emet. *Review of Rabbinic Judaism,* 7(1), 1-26. Retrieved June 4, 2009, doi:10.1163/1570070041960893

Levin, J. (2008). The joy of Cedar Rapids. Retrieved September 18, 2008, from http://templejudah.org/index.php?option=com_content&task=view&id=87&Itemid=136

Lipman, E. J. (1990). *Tanu Rabbanan*: Our masters have taught us. In J. B. Glaser (Ed.), *Tanu Rabbanan: Our rabbis taught: Essays on the occasion of the centennial of the Central Conference of American Rabbis, 1989 Yearbook, II* (39-70). NY: Central Conference of American Rabbis.

Lorge, M. M., & Zola, G. P. (2006). The beginnings of Union Institute in Oconomowoc, Wisconsin, 1952-1970. In M. M. Lorge & G. P. Zola (Eds.). *A Place of their own: The rise of Reform Jewish camping* (52-84). Tuscaloosa, AL: The University of Alabama Press.

Lux, R. (1986). Franz Rosenzweig: (1886-1929). *Jewish Virtual Library.* Retrieved June 6, 2008, from http://www.jewishvirtuallibrary.org/jsource/biography/Rosenzweig.html?event_id=9185&schema_id=6&q=lehrhaus

Magida, A. J. (1996). *Prophet of rage: A life of Louis Farrakhan and his nation.* New York: HarperCollins.

Many corporate officials to C. R. for Hall funeral. (1971, May 18). *The Cedar Rapids Gazette*, p. 3.

Marendy, P. (2005, Spring). Anti-Semitism, Christianity, and the Catholic Church: Origins, consequences, and responses. *Journal of Church & State*, 47(2), 289-307. Retrieved June 4, 2009, from Academic Search Premier database.

Marmur, D. (2002). American Reform: Observations from the margin. In D. E. Kaplan (Ed.), *Platforms and prayer books* (285-296). New York: Rowman & Littlefield Publishers, Inc.

Marx, R. (Seaker). (2008, October 16). Interview with Richard Damashek [Digital Recording]. Cincinnati: American Jewish Archives.

Marx, R. (2008). *The excluded middle.* Unpublished manuscript.

Masonic Lodge of Education. (2007-2012). Freemason ritual: The fastest way to learn Degree Ritual. Retrieved March 14, 2012, from http://www.masonic-lodge-of-education.com/freemason-ritual.html

Mayer, E. (1989). *Intermarriage and rabbinic officiation.* New York: American Jewish Committee, Institute of Human Relations.

McCabe, M. (1979, September 24). Scroll destroyed in temple burglary. *Chicago Tribune* (1963-Current file), p. 3. Retrieved April 1, 2010, from ProQuest Historical Newspapers *Chicago Tribune* (1849 - 1986). (Document ID: 620826932).

McQuiston, E. (1989). *A history of Temple Judah of Cedar Rapids.* Cedar Rapids: Temple Judah.

Meek, L. (1948, January 4). Think you are busy? Then try following Schaalman's routine. *Cedar Rapids Gazette*, 11.

Mendes-Flohr, P. (1998). In the shadow of the World War. In M. A. Meyer & M. Brenner (Eds.), *German-Jewish history in modern times: Renewal and destruction 1918-1945* (7-29). NY: Columbia University Press.

Mendes-Flohr, P. (1998). Jewish cultural and spiritual life. In M. A. Meyer & M. Brenner (Eds.), *German-Jewish history in modern times: Renewal and destruction 1918-1945* (127-156). NY: Columbia University Press.

Mental health makes second visit to board. (1949, June 20). *The Cedar Rapids Gazette,* pp. 1, 4.

Metzger, F. (2006, November 17). Interview with Richard Damashek [Cassette Recording]. Cincinnati: American Jewish Archives.

Meyer, M. A. (1976). *Hebrew Union College-Jewish Institute of Religion: A centennial history 1875-1975,* Cincinnati: Hebrew Union College-Jewish Institute of Religion Press.

Meyer, M. A. (1988). *Response to modernity: A history of the Reform movement in Judaism.* New York: Oxford University Press.

Michael, R., and Doerr, K. (2002). *Nazi-Deutsch/Nazi-German: An English lexicon of the language of the Third Reich.* Westport, CT: Greenwood Press.

Miss Gasway is married to A. S. Malmon. (1959, March 23). *The Cedar Rapids Gazette,* p. 10.

Modern Jewish beliefs: Tuesday chapel subject. (1949, February 2). *The Coe Cosmos*, p. 1.

Mone, G. (2012). Top 100 stories of 2011 #1: Faster than the speed of light. *Discover* (January-February special issue). Retrieved March 10, 2012, from http://discovermagazine.com/2012/jan-feb/01

Morgenstern, J. (1945, June 8). Letter to Herman E. Schaalman. Cincinnati: American Jewish Archives.

Morgenstern, J. (1946, February 15). Letter to Herman E. Schaalman. Cincinnati: American Jewish Archives.

Morgenstern, J. (1947, January 10). Letter to Herman E. Schaalman. Cincinnati: American Jewish Archives.

Morgenstern, J. (1947, March 17). Letter to Herman E. Schaalman. Cincinnati: American Jewish Archives.

Morgenstern, J. (1947, May 23). Letter to Herman E. Schaalman. Cincinnati: American Jewish Archives.

Morris, M. D. (1993, November). The turbulent friendship: Black-Jewish relations in the 1990s. *Annals of the American Academy of Political and Social Science*, Vol. 530, Interminority Affairs in the U. S.: Pluralism at the Crossroads, 42-60. Retrieved February 11, 2008 from http://links.jstor.org/sici?sici=0002-7162%281993 11%29530%3C42%3ATTFBRI%3E2.0.CO%3B2-J&size=SMALL&origin=JSTOR-reducePage

Murray, J. S. Murray, F. G. (1950). *The story of Cedar Rapids.* New York: Stratford House.

National American Federation of Temple Youth (NFTY.org). (2010). History. Retrieved March 2, 2010, from http://www.nfty.org/about/history/

National Jewish Scholars' Project. (n. d). Dabru Emet: A Jewish statement on Christians and Christianity. Retrieved October 3, 2010, from http://www.icjs.org/programs/ongoing/njsp/dabruemet.php

National Trust for Historic Preservation. (2009). Brucemore. Retrieved June 3, 2010, from http://www.preservationnation.org/travel-and-sites/sites/midwest-region/brucemore.html

Nesuner, J. (1996). *Judaism transcends catastrophe: God, Torah, and Israel beyond the Holocaust.* Macon, GA: Mercer University Press.

New York Times. (1915, September 29). Rabbi Max Samfield. Retrieved December 8, 2009, from http://query.nytimes.com/mem/archive-free/pdf?res=9F02E1D71138E633A2575AC2A96F9C946496D6CF

Niagara Foundation. (2008). About us. Retrieved May 23, 2009, from http://www.niagarafoundation.org/niagara/about.php

Niagara Foundation. (2006, June). Niagara Foundation awarding the individuals and organization who have committed their time, energy, expertise, and leadership skills to peace, community service, education, dialogue, and understanding here in Chicago. Retrieved September 25, 2008, from http://www.niagarafoundation.org/niagara/newsroom .php?file=pr_peaceaward06052006

North American Federation of Temple Brotherhoods—Jewish Chautauqua Society. (2008). JCS Programs: Scholar in Residence—Rabbinic Reflections. Retrieved September 13, 2008, from http://menrj.org/jcs_ programs_scholar.html

Ochs, P. (Ed.). (2000). *Reviewing the Covenant.* Albany, NY: State University of New York Press.

Ochs, P. (2000). The emergence of postmodern Jewish theology and philosophy. In P. Ochs (Ed.) *Reviewing the Covenant.* Albany, NY: State University of New York Press.

Ochs, P. (2007). Editor's introduction (xii-xxix). In P. Ochs (Ed.), *Breaking the tablets.* New York: Rowman & Littlefield Publishers, Inc.

Ohio History Central: An online encyclopedia of Ohio history. (2009). Federated Department Stores. Retrieved December 2, 2009 from http://www .ohiohistorycentral.org/entry.php?rec=888

Olitzky, K., & Golin, P. What is an "in-marriage" initiative? Jewish Outreach Institute Blog. Retrieved September 6, 2008, from http://joi.org/blog/ index.php?p=92

One world religion proposed on Coe panel. (1954, Feb. 16). *The Cedar Rapids Gazette*, p. 2.

Park dedicated to rabbi known as a peacemaker [Chicagoland Final, CN Edition]. (2004, September 20). Chicago Tribune, p. 3. Retrieved April 1, 2010, from Chicago Tribune. (Document ID: 695217791).

Parker, R. (2010). An overview of the Great Depression. EH.Net. Retrieved March 28, 2012, from http://eh.net/encyclopedia/article/parker .depression

Parliament of World Religions. (1993, September 4). Declaration toward a global ethic. Retrieved November 1, 2010, from http://www.parliamen tofreligions.org/_includes/FCKcontent/File/TowardsAGlobalEthic.pdf

Parliament of the World's Religions. (1999). *1999 Parliament of the World's Religions Summary Report.* Retrieved October 27, 2010, from http://www.parliamentofreligions.org/_includes/FCKcontent/File/1999report.pdf

Parliament of the World's Religions. (2007-2010). Retrieved October 27, 2010, from http://www.parliamentofreligions.org/index.cfm?n=1&sn=1

Pawlikowski, J. T. (1986, May 11). *The state of the Christian-Jewish dialogue today—twenty Years after Nostra Aetate.* Paper presented at a Colloquium on Interfaith Relations, Temple B'rith Shalom, Springfield, Illinois

Pawlikowski, J. T. (1996). Covenantal partnership—Cardinal Bernardin's theological approach to Christian-Jewish relations. In Archdiocese of Chicago (Ed), *A blessing to each other: Cardinal Joseph Bernardin and Jewish-Catholic dialogue* (17-22). Chicago: Archdiocese of Chicago: Liturgy Training Publications.

Pawlikowski, J. T. (2001). Christology after the *Shoah.* In W. D. Edgerton (Ed.), *The honeycomb of the word.* Chicago: Exploration Press,158-178.

Pawlikowski, J. T. (2006). Developments in Catholic-Jewish relations: 1990 and beyond. *Judaism: A Quarterly Journal of Jewish Life and Thought,* 55(3-4), 97+. Retrieved March 5, 2009, from Questia database: http://www.questia.com/PM.qst?a=o&d=5028581414

Pawlikowski, J. T. (2006, June 26). Interview with Richard Damashek [Digital Recording]. Cincinnati: American Jewish Archives.

Pawlikowski, J. T. (2007, January 1). Reflections on Covenant and mission forty years after Nostra Aetate. The Free Library. Retrieved June 01, 2009 from http://www.thefreelibrary.com/Reflections on Covenant and Mission forty years after Nostra Aetate-a0160168128

Phillips, B. A. (1997, July). *Re-examining intermarriage: Trends, textures and strategies.* The Susan and David Wilstein Institute of Jewish Policy Studies and The American Jewish Committee.

Pittsburgh Platform. (1885). Jewish Virtual Library. Retrieved July 10, 2008, from http://www.jewishvirtuallibrary.org/jsource/Judaism/pittsburgh_program.html

Plaut, W. G. (1965). *The growth of Reform Judaism.* New York: World Union for Progressive Judaism.

Plaut, W. G. (1981). *Unfinished business: An autobiography.* N. P.: Lester & Orpen Dennys Publishers.

Plaut, W. G. (Ed.). (1985). *The Torah: A modern commentary* (4th ed.). New York: Union of American Hebrew Congregations.

Plaut, W. G. (1997). *More unfinished business.* Toronto: University of Toronto Press.

Poetry Portal. (n.d.). Paul Celan. Retrieved March 18, 2011, from http://www.poetry-portal.com/poets43.html

Pritzker, J. (Speaker). (2009, June 11). Interview with Richard Damashek [Digital Recording]. Cincinnati: American Jewish Archives.

Quarles & Brady. (2011). About us. Retrieved March 29, 2012, from http://www.quarles.com/About/Overview/

Rabbi Schaalman departs. (1949, July 17). *The Cedar Rapids Gazette*, p.1.

Rabbi Schaalman to talk at Emanuel tomorrow. (1951, April 12). *Chicago Daily Tribune* (1923-1963), p. n_a4. Retrieved April 1, 2010, from ProQuest Historical Newspapers *Chicago Tribune* (1849 - 1986). (Document ID: 503740602).

Radio Council Committee gives buffet supper. (1949, June 16). *The Cedar Rapids Gazette*, p.18.

Ramsey, J. (2011, April 15). Interview with Richard Damashek [Digital Recording]. Cincinnati: American Jewish Archives.

Raphael, M. L. (2000, Summer). Reform Jewish congregants and intermarriage, 1998. *CCAR Journal: A Reform Jewish Quarterly*, 49-55.

Raphael, M. L. (2003). *Judaism in America.* New York: Columbia University Press.

Reardon, C. (1996, April 17). African-Americans and Jews rebuild a tattered alliance. *Christian Science Monitor*, 88(99), 1. Retrieved February 11, 2008, from Newspaper Source database.

Regner, S. L. (1990). The history of the Conference, Part I: 1889-1964. In J. B. Glaser (Ed.), *Tanu Rabbanan: Our rabbis taught: Essays on the occasion of the centennial of the Central Conference of American Rabbis, 1989 Yearbook, II* (3-15). NY: Central Conference of American Rabbis.

Reisman, B. (2002, May 20). Cincinnati graduation address. Cincinnati: Hebrew Union College-Jewish Institute of Religion. Retrieved August 28, 2008, from http://www.huc.edu/faculty/faculty/pubs/reisman.shtml

Religion in life week will open at Coe on Sunday. (1954, February 16). *The Cedar Rapids Gazette*, p. 2.

Richman, C. & The Temple Institute. (2000-2011). Shavuot. Retrieved January 12, 2012, from http://www.templeinstitute.org/shavuot.htm

Rivkin, E. (1986). The revealing and concealing God of Israel and humankind." In Joseph A. Edelheit (Ed), *The life of Covenant: The challenge of contemporary Judaism,* (155–171). Chicago: Spertus College of Judaica Press.

Rodin-Novak, S. (2001, November 26). Interview with Rabbi Herman E. Schaalman. *Chicago Jewish Historical Society.*

Rosen, D. (2001, November 6). An address given at the 20th anniversary celebration of the Dutch Council of Christians and Jews (OJEC) at Tilburg, The Netherlands. Retrieved June 1, 2009, from http://rabbidavidrosen .net/doc/Dabru%20Emet%20Presentation.doc

Rosenzweig, F. (1971). *The star of redemption.* (Translated from the 2d ed. of 1930 by William W. Hallo). New York: Holt, Rinehart and Winston.

Rubinstein, P. J. (1989). The next century. In J. B. Glaser (Ed.), *Tanu Rabbanan: Our rabbis taught: Essays on the occasion of the centennial of the Central Conference of American Rabbis, 1989 Yearbook, II* (133-155). NY: Central Conference of American Rabbis.

Rubenstein, R. L. (1966). *After Auschwitz: Radical theology and contemporary Judaism.* Indianapolis: Bobbs-Merrill.

Rubenstein, R. L. (1968). Homeland and Holocaust: Issues in the Jewish religious situation. In D. R. Cutler (Ed.), *The Religious Situation: 1968* (39-64). Boston: Beacon Press.

Ryback, T. W. (2008, December 24). Hitler's private library: The books that shaped his life. *The New Republic.* Retrieved January 12, 2009, from http://www.tnr.com/politics/story.html?id=1fb48fe8-1d1c-4088-a435-f72087238c07

Samuel, S. Cohon Papers. (n.d.). Cincinnati: American Jewish Archives. Retrieved December16, 2008, from http://www.americanjewisharchives .org/aja/FindingAids/Cohon.htm

Samuelson, N. M. (2000). A critique of Borowitz's postmodern Jewish theology. In P. Ochs (Ed.) *Reviewing the Covenant* (49-59). Albany, NY: State University of New York Press.

Saperstein, M. (1990). Israel and the Reform Rabbinate. In J. B. Glaser (Ed.), *Tanu Rabbanan: Our rabbis taught: Essays on the occasion of the centennial of the Central Conference of American Rabbis, 1989 Yearbook, II* (105-131). NY: Central Conference of American Rabbis.

Sarna, J. D. (2006). The crucial decade in Jewish camping. In M. M. Lorge & G. P. Zola (Eds.), *A place of our own* (27-51). Tuscaloosa, AL: University of Alabama Press.

Sarna, J. D. & Golden, J. (2000, October). The American Jewish experience in the twentieth century: Antisemitism and assimilation. National Humanities Center.org. Retrieved June 20, 2008, from http://nationalhumanitiescenter.org/tserve/twenty/tkeyinfo/jewishexpb.htm

Sarna, J. D. & Klein, N. H. (1989). *The Jews of Cincinnati.* Cincinnati: Hebrew Union College.

Schaalman, F. L. (Speaker). (2008, May 13). Interview with Richard Damashek [Digital Recording]. Cincinnati: American Jewish Archives.

Schaalman, H. E. (n.d.). Rabbi Schaalman's Report (1953-54). Jacob Rader Marcus Center of the American Jewish Archives MS Collection No. 648. Cincinnati: American Jewish Archives.

Schaalman, H. E. (n.d.). Recording on Youtube.com. Retrieved October 19, 2011, from http://www.youtube.com/watch?v=tqZSFVe3NEo

Schaalman, H. E. (1946, January 15). Letter to Dr. Julian Morgenstern. Cincinnati: American Jewish Archives.

Schaalman, H. E. (1946, January 22). Letter to Dr. Julian Morgenstern. Cincinnati: American Jewish Archives.

Schaalman, H. E. (1946, February 6). Letter to Dr. Julian Morgenstern. Cincinnati: American Jewish Archives.

Schaalman, H. E. (1947, January 4). Letter to Dr. Julian Morgenstern. Cincinnati: American Jewish Archives.

Schaalman, H. E. (1947, March 10). Letter to Dr. Julian Morgenstern. Cincinnati: American Jewish Archives.

Schaalman, H. E. (1947, May 20). Letter to Dr. Julian Morgenstern. Cincinnati: American Jewish Archives.

Schaalman, H. E. (1949). Report—Midwest Region. *Union of American He-brew Congregations Bi-Annual Report: 1948-1949* (p. 249). Boston: Union of American Hebrew Congregations.

Schaalman, H. E. (1951, July 9). Memorandum to J. S. Ackerman. Jacob Rader Marcus Center of the American Jewish Archives MS Collection No. 648. Cincinnati: American Jewish Archives.

Schaalman, H. E. (1951, October 11). Memorandum to J. S. Ackerman. Jacob Rader Marcus Center of the American Jewish Archives MS Collection No. 648. Cincinnati: American Jewish Archives.

Schaalman, H. E. (1951, October 11). Letter to Ernst Lorge. Jacob Rader Marcus Center of the American Jewish Archives. Cincinnati: American Jewish Archives.

Schaalman, H. E. (1952, February 26). Memo to: All rabbis in the Midwest-ern, Rocky Mountain, & Great Lakes Regions of the Union including all the Rabbis of Chicago. Jacob Rader Marcus Center of the American Jewish Archives. Cincinnati: American Jewish Archives.

Schaalman, H. E. (1963, April). Introduction. In Schaalman, H. E. (ED.) *The goals of Jewish religious education: A symposium* (p. 68). New York: Cen-tral Conference of American Rabbis.

Schaalman, H. E. (1967, February 22). Franz Rosenzweig: a voice for today. *Christian Century,* 84(8), 233-236.

Schaalman, H. E. (1967, November 5). Judaism's window on the divine. *Mes-sage of Israel.*

Schaalman, H. E. (1971, February 10). Paper. Cincinnati: CCAR Archives.

Schaalman, H. E. (1972, June 16). Letter to Rabbi Joseph B. Glaser. In Schaal-man file at the New York office of the CCAR.

Schaalman, H. E. (1981). Melanie Schaalman. *Pages of testimony. The Central Da-tabase of Shoah Victims' Names.* Retrieved May 10, 2006, from Yad Vashem The Holocaust Martyrs' and Heroes' Remembrance Authority. (2006). http://www.yadvashem.org/lwp/workplace/!ut/p/_s.7_0_A/7_0_2BS/ .cmd/acd/.ar/sa.portlet.FromDetailsSubmitAction/.c/6_0_VF/.ce/7_0 _2CQ/.p/5_0_12I/.d/5?related_key=&DTsearchQuery=&todo=2&im ages=%5B%5C25032001_349_5895%5C37.JPG%5D&imagedescs= %5B%5C25032001_349_5895%5C37.JPG%5D&itemid=1463105 &q1=haiqwxpVZCE%3D&q2=cTtw%2FWls0Pm9WrzI4Jts9pnVVC HfkmfQ&q3=7hnu1H%2F7D%2Bo%3D&q4=7hnu1H%2F7D%2

Bo%3D&q5=%2BarbpY0ZQ0k%3D&q6=oD5EfnvLBDg%3D&q7
=fIeAdJlFtiI%3D&npage=&zoomdesc=%5C25032001_349_5895%
5C37.JPG&victim_details_name=Schaalman+Melanie%3BSchaalma
n+%D7%9E%D7%9C%D7%A0%D7%99%D7%94%3B%D0%A8
%D0%B0%D0%BB%D1%8C%D0%BC%D0%B0%D0%BD+%D
0%9C%D0%B5%D0%BB%D0%B0%D0%BD%D0%B8&victim_
details_id=1463105&imagenum=0&searchfor=0

Schaalman, H. E. (1981). Herman E. Schaalman: Remarks of the new president. *CCAR Yearbook, XCI*, 164-166.

Schaalman, H. E. (1982, February 2). President's message. *CCAR Newsletter.* Columbus, Ohio.

Schaalman, H. E. (1982, April). Minutes of the CCAR Executive Committee. Cincinnati: The American Jewish Archives.

Schaalman, H. E. (1982, September). From the president. *CCAR Newsletter.* New York: Central Conference of American Rabbis.

Schaalman, H. E. (1982, Fall). An agenda for Reform Judaism in Israel. *Judaism*, 31(4), 438. Retrieved May 5, 2008, from Academic Search Premier database.

Schaalman, H. E. (1983). Installation of the new president. *CCAR Yearbook*: Columbus: CCAR.

Schaalman, H. E. (1983, Summer). The Key is the Covenant. *Judaism, 32*(3), p. 292. Retrieved May 5, 2008, from Academic Search Premier database.

Schaalman, H. E. (1985, Winter). History and Halakhah are related and inseparable. *Judaism, 34*(1), 74. Retrieved May 5, 2008, from Academic Search Premier database.

Schaalman, H. E. (1986). An autobiographical reflection." In J. A. Edelheit (Ed.), *The life of Covenant* (xiii-xvii). Chicago: Spertus College of Judaica Press.

Schaalman, H. E. (1986, May 11). The state of the Christian-Jewish dialogue today—twenty years after *Nostra Aetate*. Symposium including Rabbi Herman E. Schaalman, Rev. John T. Pawlikowski and Rev. Clark Williamson and conducted at B'rith Shalom, Springfield, Illinois.

Schaalman, H. E. (1989, July 18). Note to Rabbi Joseph Edelheit. Cincinnati: American Jewish Archives.

Schaalman, H. E. (1990, October 25). Letter to Rabbi Joseph B. Glaser. On file at the New York Office of the Central Conference of American Rabbis.

Schaalman, H. E. (1991). God of Auschwitz? In Karp, A. J., Jacobs, L., & Dimitrovsky, C. Z. (Eds.). *Threescore and ten: Essays in honor of Rabbi Seymour J. Cohen on the occasion of his seventieth birthday* (293-301). Hoboken, NJ: KTAV.

Schaalman, H. E. (1992, Summer). The patrilineal principle: A time for clarification. *CCAR Journal, XXXIX*(2), 62-64.

Schaalman, H. E. (1993). The life of the Covenant [Cassette Recording]. Parliament of the World's Religions, 1993. Chicago: DePaul University Archives.

Schaalman, H. E. (1995). The binding of Isaac. *Preaching biblical texts* (36-45). Grand Rapids: Eerdmans. Retrieved May 5, 2008, from ATLA Religion Database with ATLASerials database.

Schaalman, H. E. (1996). To herald and create a new day. *A blessing to each other: Cardinal Joseph Bernardin and Jewish-Catholic dialogue* (5-8). Chicago: Archdiocese of Chicago: Liturgy Training Publications.

Schaalman, H. E. (1996, September 13). First edit: September 13, 1996. Cincinnati: American Jewish Archives.

Schaalman, H. E. (1996, November 19). Jewish readers Memorial Service: Opening remarks of Rabbi Herman C. Schaalman [sic]. Chicago Archdiocese.

Schaalman, H. E. (1997, May). What's in a Name? *Covenant Quarterly, 55*(2-3), 69-74. Retrieved May 5, 2008, from ATLA Religion Database with ATLASerials database.

Schaalman, H. E. (1999, January 9). *Speech to National Association of Retired Reform Rabbis (NAORRR)*. Unpublished manuscript. Cincinnati: American Jewish Archives.

Schaalman, H. E. (1999, November 18). *Cedar Rapids history.* Unpublished manuscript. Cincinnati: American Jewish Archives.

Schaalman, H. E. (2000, July 21-27). *Chicago Jewish News*, p. 11.

Schaalman, H. E. (2001). God of the future. In W. D. Edgerton (Ed.), *The honeycomb of the world* (pp. 228-235). Chicago: Exploration Press.

Schaalman, H. E. (2004). Creation as a divine-human collaboration. In E. Foley, & R. Schreiter (Eds.), *The wisdom of creation* (48-52). Collegeville, Minn.: Liturgical Press.

Schaalman, H. E. (Speaker). (2005, July 1). Faith in conversation. *The Free Library.* Retrieved February 10, 2008 from http://www.thefreelibrary .com/Faith in conversation-a0133705116

Schaalman, H. E. (2005, October 4). Ayekah-Where are you? [Sermon] Congregation Emanu-El B'ne Jeshurun. Retrieved March 7, 2011, from http://www.ceebj.org/our_staff/rabbi/sermons/5766-rh-morning-day-1/

Schaalman, H. E. (Speaker). (2005, October 31). Interview with Richard Damashek [Cassette Recording]. Cincinnati: American Jewish Archives.

Schaalman, H. E. (Speaker). (2005, December 3). Interview with Richard Damashek [Cassette Recording]. Cincinnati: American Jewish Archives.

Schaalman, H. E. (Speaker). (2005, December 8). Interview with Richard Damashek [Cassette Recording]. Cincinnati: American Jewish Archives.

Schaalman, H. E. (Speaker). (2005, December 15). Interview with Richard Damashek (Cassette Recording #1). Cincinnati: American Jewish Archives.

Schaalman, H. E. (Speaker). (2005, December 15). Interview with Richard Damashek [Cassette Recording #2]. Cincinnati: American Jewish Archives.

Schaalman, H. E. (Speaker). (2005, December 20). Interview with Richard Damashek [Cassette Recording]. Cincinnati: American Jewish Archives.

Schaalman, H. E. (Speaker). (2005, December 23). Interview with Richard Damashek [Cassette Recording]. Cincinnati: American Jewish Archives.

Schaalman, H. E. (2006, February). Indelible image. *You May Be Right, U.S. Catholic, 71*(2), 5-6. Retrieved May 5, 2008, from Academic Search Premier database.

Schaalman, H. E. (Speaker). (2006, January 20). Interview with Richard Damashek [Digital Recording]. Cincinnati: American Jewish Archives.

Schaalman, H. E. (Speaker). (2006, February 14). Interview with Richard Damashek [Digital Recording]. Cincinnati: American Jewish Archives.

Schaalman, H. E. (Speaker). (2006, February 27). Interview with Richard Damashek [Digital Recording]. Cincinnati: American Jewish Archives.

Schaalman, H. E. (Speaker). (2006, April 1). Interview with Richard Damashek [Digital Recording]. Cincinnati: American Jewish Archives.

Schaalman, H. E. (Speaker). (2006, April 8). Interview with Richard Damashek [Digital Recording. Cincinnati: American Jewish Archives.

Schaalman, H. E. (Speaker). (2006, April 15). Interview with Richard Damashek [Digital Recording]. Cincinnati: American Jewish Archives.

Schaalman, H. E. (Speaker). (2006, April 21). Interview with Richard Damashek [Digital Recording]. Cincinnati: American Jewish Archives.

Schaalman, H. E. (Speaker). (2006, April 30). Interview with Richard Damashek [Digital Recording]. Cincinnati: American Jewish Archives.

Schaalman, H. E. (Speaker). (2006, May 2). Interview with Richard Damashek [Digital Recording]. Cincinnati: American Jewish Archives.

Schaalman, H. E. (Speaker). (2006, May 6). Interview with Richard Damashek [Digital Recording]. Cincinnati: American Jewish Archives.

Schaalman, H. E. (Speaker). (2006, May 25). Interview with Richard Damashek [Digital Recording]. Cincinnati: American Jewish Archives.

Schaalman, H. E. (Speaker). (2006, May 30). Interview with Richard Damashek [Digital Recording]. Cincinnati: American Jewish Archives.

Schaalman, H. E. (Speaker). (2006, June 27). Lehrhaus Presentation [Digital Recording]. Cincinnati: American Jewish Archives.

Schaalman, H. E. (Speaker). (2006, June 29). Lehrhaus Presentation [Digital Recording]. Cincinnati: American Jewish Archives.

Schaalman, H. E. (Speaker). (2006, June 31). Lehrhaus Presentation [Digital Recording]. Cincinnati: American Jewish Archives.

Schaalman, H. E. (Speaker). (2006, July 8). Torah Study [Digital Recording]. Cincinnati: American Jewish Archives.

Schaalman, H. E. (Speaker). (2006, August 26). Torah Study [Digital Recording]. Cincinnati: American Jewish Archives.

Schaalman, H. E. (2006, September 23). Where are your children? [Sermon]. Emanu-El B'ne Jeshurun. Retrieved March 3, 2011, from http://www.ceebj.org/our_staff/rabbi/sermons/5767-rh-morning-day-1/

Schaalman, H. E. (Speaker). (2006, November 8). Interview with Richard Damashek [Digital Recording]. Cincinnati: American Jewish Archives.

Schaalman, H. E. (Speaker). (2006, November 20). Interview with Richard Damashek [Digital Recording]. Cincinnati: American Jewish Archives.

Schaalman, H. E. (Speaker). (2006, November 22). Interview with Richard Damashek [Digital Recording]. Cincinnati: American Jewish Archives.

Schaalman, H. E. (Speaker). (2006, December 11). Interview with Richard Damashek [Digital Recording]. Cincinnati: American Jewish Archives.

Schaalman, H. E. (2007). *Hineni.* Jersey City, NJ: KTAV Publishing House, Inc.

Schaalman, H. E. (Speaker). (2007, May 11). Interview with Richard Damashek [Digital Recording]. Cincinnati: American Jewish Archives.

Schaalman, H. E. (Speaker). (2007, May 25). Interview with Richard Damashek [Digital Recording]. Cincinnati: American Jewish Archives.

Schaalman, H. E. (Speaker). (2007, June 28). Interview with Richard Damashek [Digital Recording]. Cincinnati: American Jewish Archives.

Schaalman, H. E. (Speaker). (2007, July 4). Interview with Richard Damashek [Digital Recording]. Cincinnati: American Jewish Archives.

Schaalman, H. E. (Speaker). (2007, July 5). Lehrhaus presentation [Digital Recording]. Cincinnati: American Jewish Archives.

Schaalman, H. E. (Speaker). (2007, July 7). Lehrhaus presentation [Digital Recording]. Cincinnati: American Jewish Archives..

Schaalman, H. E. (Speaker). (2007, July 16). Interview with Richard Damashek [Digital Recording]. Cincinnati: American Jewish Archives.

Schaalman, H. E. (Speaker). (2007, August 16). Interview with Richard Damashek [Digital Recording]. Cincinnati: American Jewish Archives.

Schaalman, H. E. (Speaker). (2007, September 1). Interview with Richard Damashek [Digital Recording]. Cincinnati: American Jewish Archives.

Schaalman, H. E. (Speaker). (2007, September 15). Interview with Richard Damashek [Digital Recording]. Cincinnati: American Jewish Archives.

Schaalman, H. E. (Speaker). (2007, September 24). Interview with Richard Damashek [Digital Recording]. Cincinnati: American Jewish Archives.

Schaalman, H. E. (Speaker). (2007, October 2). Interview with Richard Damashek [Digital Recording]. Cincinnati: American Jewish Archives.

Schaalman, H. E. (2007, October 4). Where are our children? Retrieved September 25, 2008, from http://www.ceebj.org/Articles/index.cfm?id=1034&pge_prg_id=6008&pge_id=1099

Schaalman, H. E. (Speaker). (2007, October 20). Interview with Richard Damashek [Digital Recording]. Cincinnati: American Jewish Archives.

Schaalman, H. E. (Speaker). (2008, January 17). Interview with Richard Damashek [Digital Recording]. Cincinnati: American Jewish Archives.

Schaalman, H. E. (2008, February 9). Torah Study [Digital Recording]. Cincinnati: American Jewish Archives.

Schaalman, H. E. (Speaker). (2008, February 12). Interview with Richard Damashek [Digital Recording]. Cincinnati: American Jewish Archives.

Schaalman, H. E. (2008, February 16). Torah Study [Digital Recording]. Cincinnati: American Jewish Archives.

Schaalman, H. E. (2008, February 23). Torah Study [Digital Recording]. Cincinnati: American Jewish Archives.

Schaalman, H. E. (2008, March 1). Torah Study [Digital Recording]. Cincinnati: American Jewish Archives.

Schaalman, H. E. (2008, March 8). Torah Study [Digital Recording]. Cincinnati: American Jewish Archives.

Schaalman, H. E. (2008, March 15). Torah Study [Digital Recording]. Cincinnati: American Jewish Archives.

Schaalman, H. E. (Speaker). (2008, March 17). Interview with Richard Damashek [Digital Recording]. Cincinnati: American Jewish Archives.

Schaalman, H. E. (2008, March 22). Torah Study [Digital Recording]. Cincinnati: American Jewish Archives.

Schaalman, H. E. (2008, April 5). Torah Study [Digital Recording]. Cincinnati: American Jewish Archives.

Schaalman, H. E. (2008, April 12). Torah Study [Digital Recording]. Cincinnati: American Jewish Archives.

Schaalman, H. E. (2008, April 13). Interview with Emanuel Congregation Confirmation Class [Videotape]. Cincinnati: American Jewish Archives.

Schaalman, H. E. (2008, April 15). The inaugural Herman Schaalman lecture in Jewish Studies [Video Recording]. Chicago: Chicago Theological Seminary.

Schaalman, H. E. (Speaker). (2008, April 20). Interview with Emanuel Congregation Confirmation Class [Digital Recording]. Cincinnati: American Jewish Archives.

Schaalman, H. E. (Speaker). (2008, April 23). Interview with Richard Damashek [Digital Recording]. Cincinnati: American Jewish Archives.

Schaalman, H. E. (Speaker). (2008, July 6). Lehrhaus [Digital Recording]. Cincinnati: American Jewish Archives.

Schaalman, H. E. (Speaker). [2008, August 25]. Interview with Richard Damashek [Digital Recording]. Cincinnati: American Jewish Archives.

Schaalman, H. E. (2008, September 13). Torah Study [Digital Recording]. Cincinnati: American Jewish Archives.

Schaalman, H. E. (Speaker). (2008, December 10). Interview with Richard Damashek [Digital Recording]. Cincinnati: American Jewish Archives.

Schaalman, H. E. (Speaker). (2008, December 13). Torah Study [Digital Recording]. Cincinnati: American Jewish Archives.

Schaalman, H. E. (Speaker). (2008, December 18, 2008). Interview with Richard Damashek [Digital Recording]. Cincinnati: American Jewish Archives.

Schaalman, H. E. (Speaker). (2009, February 4, 2009). Interview with Richard Damashek [Digital Recording]. Cincinnati: American Jewish Archives.

Schaalman, H. E. (2009, February 14). Torah Study [Digital Recording]. Cincinnati: American Jewish Archives.

Schaalman, H. E. (2009, March 15). Torah Study [Digital Recording]. Cincinnati: American Jewish Archives.

Schaalman, H. E. (2009, April 4). Torah Study [Digital Recording]. Cincinnati: American Jewish Archives.

Schaalman, H. E. (Speaker). (2009, April 16). Interview with Richard Damashek [Digital Recording]. Cincinnati: American Jewish Archives.

Schaalman, H. E. (Speaker). (2009, April 30). Interview with Richard Damashek [Digital Recording]. Cincinnati: American Jewish Archives.

Schaalman, H. E. (2009, May 2). Torah Study [Digital Recording]. Cincinnati: American Jewish Archives.

Schaalman, H. E. (2009, May 16). Torah Study [Digital Recording]. Cincinnati: American Jewish Archives.

Schaalman, H. E. (2009, May 23). Torah Study [Digital Recording]. Cincinnati: American Jewish Archives.

Schaalman, H. E. (2009, June 27). Torah Study [Digital Recording]. Cincinnati: American Jewish Archives.

Schaalman, H. E. (2009, July 25). Torah Study [Digital Recording]. Cincinnati: American Jewish Archives.

Schaalman, H. E. (2009, August 8). Torah Study [Digital Recording]. Cincinnati: American Jewish Archives.

Schaalman, H. E. (2009, September 26). Torah Study [Digital Recording]. Cincinnati: American Jewish Archives.

Schaalman, H. E. (2010, January 26). Letter to Richard Damashek. Cincinnati: American Jewish Archives.

Schaalman, H. E. (2010, March 18). Interview with Richard Damashek [Digital Recording]. Cincinnati: American Jewish Archives.

Schaalman, H. E. (2010, June 21). Keynote address at the 25th Anniversary Program of the Council of Religious Leaders of Metropolitan Chicago [Digital Recording]. Cincinnati: American Jewish Archives.

Schaalman, H. E. (Speaker). (2010, June 28). Interview with Richard Damashek [Digital Recording]. Cincinnati: American Jewish Archives.

Schaalman, H. E. (2010, July 31). Torah Study [Digital Recording]. Cincinnati: American Jewish Archives.

Schaalman, H. E. (2010, September 25). Torah Study [Digital Recording]. Chicago Jewish Archives.

Schaalman, H. E. (Speaker). (2010, October 7). Interview with Richard Damashek [Digital Recording]. Cincinnati: American Jewish Archives.

Schaalman, H. E. (Speaker). (2010, October 11). Interview with Richard Damashek [Digital Recording]. Cincinnati: American Jewish Archives.

Schaalman, H. E. (2011, January 10). Keynote speech to the National Association of Retired Rabbis. San Diego. Unpublished manuscript. Cincinnati: American Jewish Archives.

Schaalman, H. E. (2011, March 12). Torah Study [Digital Recording]. Cincinnati: American Jewish Archives.

Schaalman, H. E. (Speaker). (2011, March 15). Interview with Richard Damashek [Digital Recording]. Cincinnati: American Jewish Archives.

Schaalman, H. E. (2011, March 19). Torah Study [Digital Recording]. Cincinnati: American Jewish Archives.

Schaalman, H. E. (2011, April 2). Torah Study [Digital Recording]. Cincinnati: American Jewish Archives.

Schaalman, H. E. (2011, April 16). Torah Study [Digital Recording]. Cincinnati: American Jewish Archives.

Schaalman, H. E. (2011, July 15). Jewish survival: Herman Schaalman. USC Shoah Foundation. Retrieved September 30, 2012, from http://www.youtube.com/watch?v=d1jLkHAepF4

Schaalman, H. E. (2011, December 17). Torah Study [Digital Recording]. Cincinnati: American Jewish Archives.

Schaalman, H. E. (2012, March 10). Torah Study [Digital Recording]. Cincinnati: American Jewish Archives.

Schaalman, H. E. (2012, June 23). Torah Study [Digital Recording]. Cincinnati: American Jewish Archives.

Schaalman, H. E. (2012, June 30). Torah Study [Digital Recording]. Cincinnati: American Jewish Archives.

Schaalman, H. E. (2012, September 22). Torah Study [Digital Recording]. Cincinnati: American Jewish Archives.

Schaalman, H. E. (2012, September 25). Sermon: Emanuel Congregation [Digital Recording]. Cincinnati: American Jewish Archives.

Schaalman, H. E. (2012, September, 29). Torah Study [Digital Recording]. Cincinnati: American Jewish Archives.

Schaalman, H. E., & Schaalman, L. (2006, December 6). Interview with Richard Damashek [Digital Recording]. Cincinnati: American Jewish Archives.

Schaalman, H. E., & Schaalman, L. (2009, October 7). Interview with Richard Damashek [Digital Recording]. Cincinnati: American Jewish Archives.

Schaalman, K., Schaalman, Jeremy & Schaalman, Johanna. (Speakers). (2006). Interview with Richard Damashek [Digital Recording]. Cincinnati: American Jewish Archives.

Schaalman, L. (Speaker). (2006, April 30). Interview with Richard Damashek [Digital Recording]. Cincinnati: American Jewish Archives.

Schaalman, L. (Speaker). (2006, December 12). Interview with Richard Damashek [Digital Recording]. Cincinnati: American Jewish Archives.

Schaalman, L. (Speaker). (2007, August 16). Interview with Richard Damashek [Digital Recording]. Cincinnati: American Jewish Archives.

Schaalman, L. (Speaker). (2009, December 1). Interview with Richard Damashek [Digital Recording]. Cincinnati: American Jewish Archives.

Schaalman, M. (Speaker). (2006, March 13). Interview with Richard Damashek [Digital Recording]. Cincinnati: American Jewish Archives.

Schaalman, R. (Speaker). (2011, October 29). Interview with Richard Damashek [Digital Recording]. Cincinnati: American Jewish Archives.

Schaalman to lecture Northwestern students. (1961, September 20). *The Cedar Rapids Gazette*, p. 3.

Schaalman Youdovin, S. (1986). A kid's eye view: Remembering our family. In J. Edelheit (Ed.), *The life of Covenant: The challenge of contemporary Judaism* (259-263). Chicago: Spertus College of Judaica Press.

Schaalman Youdovin, S. (Speaker). (2006, April 6). Interview with Richard Damashek [Digital Recording]. Cincinnati: American Jewish Archives.

Schaalman Youdovin, S. (2009, February 20). *Susan's first wedding: December 26, 1966.* Unpublished manuscript. Cincinnati: American Jewish Archives.

Schoenberg, S. (2007). *The Shema.* Jewish Virtual Library. Retrieved August 15, 2007. http://www.jewishvirtuallibrary.org/jsource/Judaism/shema.html

Schulweis, H. M. (1984). *Evil and the morality of God.* Cincinnati: Hebrew Union College-Jewish Institute of Religion Press.

Schulweis, H. M. (2003). Beyond interfaith marriage. Retrieved September 2, 2008 from http://wws.vbs.org/rabbi/hshulw/interfa.htm

Schulman, A.M. (1993). *Like a raging fire.* New York: Union of American Hebrew Congregations.

Sicker, M. (2001). *Between man and God: Issues in Judaic thought.* Westport, CT: Greenwood Press.

Smothers, R. (1989, April 9). Black-Jewish talks produce angry clash but some hope. Retrieved February 11, 2008, from http://query.nytimes.com/gst/fullpage.html?res=950DEFDB1F3FF93AA35757C0A96F948260&sec=&spon=&pagewanted=all

Sofian, D. (2005, June 5). Interview with Richard Damashek [Digital Recording]. Cincinnati: American Jewish Archives.

Sonsino, R. (2004). *The Many Faces of God: A Reader of Modern Jewish Theologies.* New York. UJR Press.

Spilly, A. (n.d.). *As those who serve: Tributes to Joseph Cardinal Bernardin at his wake and funeral rites.* Chicago: Mission Press.

Spruch, G. (2008, March). *Wide horizons: Abraham Joshua Heschel, AJC, and the spirit of Nostra Aetate.* New York: The American Jewish Committee.

St. George, M. & Dennis, L. (1946). A trial on trial: The great sedition trial of 1944. Washington, D. C.: National Civil Rights Committee.

Star, E. (1987, February 25). American Jewish Committee Oral History of Rabbi Schaalman [Interview transcript]. American Jewish Committee.

Star, E. (1987, July 13). American Jewish Committee Oral History of Rabbi Schaalman [Interview transcript]. American Jewish Committee.

Star, E. (1987, November 13). American Jewish Committee Oral History of Rabbi Schaalman [Interview transcript]. American Jewish Committee.

Star, E. (1988, January 27). American Jewish Committee Oral History of Rabbi Schaalman [Interview transcript]. American Jewish Committee.

Star, E. (1988, April 5). American Jewish Committee Oral History of Rabbi Schaalman [Interview transcript]. American Jewish Committee.

Star, E. (1988, July 25). American Jewish Committee Oral History of Rabbi Schaalman [Interview transcript]. American Jewish Committee.

Steinfels, P. (1996, November 21). Chicago, Joined by an array of dignitaries, bids farewell to Cardinal Bernardin. *New York Times.com.* Retrieved July 2, 2010, from http://www.nytimes.com/1996/11/21/us/chicago-joined-by-an-array-of-dignitaries-bids-farewell-to-cardinal-bernardin.html?pagewanted=print

Stern, F. (1983). Germany 1933: Fifty years later. *The Leo Baeck Memorial Lecture #27.* New York: The Leo Beck Institute.

Stevens, E. L. (1990). History of the Conference, Part II: 1964-1989. In J. B. Glaser (Ed.), *Tanu Rabbanan: Our rabbis taught: Essays on the occasion of the centennial of the Central Conference of American Rabbis, 1989 Yearbook, II* (15-38). NY: Central Conference of American Rabbis.

Stevens, E. L. (2006, Summer). The prayer books, they are a 'changin.' *Reform Jewish Magazine.* Retrieved November 13, 2008 from http://reformjudaismmag.org/PrintItem/index.cfm?id=1150&type=Articles

Sullivan, M., Venuti, J., Schaalman, R., Pawlikowski, J., Fitzpatrick, M., & Pilney, R. (2006, February). You may be right. *U.S. Catholic, 71* (2), 5-6. Retrieved May 5, 2008, from Academic Search Premier database.

Sweet, L, & Hanania, R. (1988, May 4). Sawyer hedges on Cokely-Sees self as aide's 'father figure.' *Chicago Sun-Times,* p. 3.

Swift, I. L. (1992). Mourning and consolation. In B. H. Rosenberg and F. S. Heuman (Eds.) *Theological and Halakhic reflections on the Holocaust* (3-8). Hoboken, NJ: KTAV Publishing House, Inc.

Telushkin, J. (1991). *Jewish literacy.* NY: William Morrow and Co.

Temple Judah. (1941, April 25). Minutes. Cedar Rapids: Temple Judah Archives.

Temple Judah. (1941, May 9). Minutes. Cedar Rapids: Temple Judah Archives.

Temple Judah. (1941, June 6). Minutes. Cedar Rapids: Temple Judah Archives.

Temple Judah. (1941, September 9). Minutes. Cedar Rapids: Temple Judah Archives.

Temple Judah. (1942, April 15). Minutes. Cedar Rapids: Temple Judah Archives.

Temple Judah. (1943, April 12). Minutes. Cedar Rapids: Temple Judah Archives.

Temple Judea Mizpah. (2008, September 25). *History of Temple Judea Mizpah.* Retrieved September 25, 2008, from http://www.templejm.org/aboutus/history/

Terex/Cedar Rapids. (2006, January 20). History. Retrieved June 10, 2010, from http://www.cedarapids.com/about_cr/history.htm

Texts on Bar Kochba: Cassius Dio. (n.d.). Cassius Dio, Roman history 69.12.1-14.3. Retrieved June 1, 2012, from http://www.livius.org/ja-jn/jewish_wars/bk05.html

The state of Jewish belief: A symposium. (1966, August). *Commentary 42*(2), 71-160.

This day 10 years ago. (1954, November 17). *The Cedar Rapids Gazette.*

This day 10 years ago. (1956, September 28). *The Cedar Rapids Gazette,* p. 10.

This day 10 years ago. (1957, March 9). *The Cedar Rapids Gazette.*

This day 10-20-30 years ago. (1967, December 18). *The Cedar Rapids Gazette,* p. 6.

This day 10-20-30 years ago. (1968, September 2). *The Cedar Rapids Gazette.*

Thrope, S. (n.d.). Emil Fackenheim: The last interview. *Habitus: A diaspora journal.* Retrieved January 14, 2009, from http://www.habitusmag.com/index.php?section=article&id=16

Tichenor, L. (Producer) & Suski, R. (Director). (2002). Unedited Interview [Rabbi Herman E. Schaalman] for Lincoln Academy Public Television Program (Videotape). (Available from WSIU Public Television Southern Illinois University Carbondale.

Time Magazine. (1951, May 21). Corporations: Trailer king. Retrieved May 3, 2010, from http://www.time.com/time/magazine/article/0,9171,859221,00.html

To speak at Temple Judah. (1963, June 5). *The Cedar Rapids Gazette,* p. 16.

Tobin, G. A., & Simon, K. C. (1999). *Rabbis talk about intermarriage.* San Francisco: Institute for Jewish and Community Research

Tutush, Danica. (1999, September). The strange life and legacy of Karl May. Retrieved December 2, 2005, from http://www.cowboysindians.com/articles/archives/0999/karl_may.html

Union of Reform Judaism. (2007). *Newsletter.* Retrieved November 13, 2007, from http://urj.org/glc/

United Press International. (1982, July 1). Rabbis defining Jewishness. *New York Times* (Late Edition (east Coast)), p. C.5. Retrieved April 1, 2010, from ProQuest National Newspapers Premier. (Document ID: 946927901).

United States Holocaust Museum (n.d.). Baden-Baden. Retrieved May 12, 2006, from   http://www.ushmm.org/museum/exhibit/online/kristallnacht /issues/k-night2.htm.

University of St. Thomas. (1997, Spring). Proceedings of the Center for Jewish-Christian Learning: Lest we forget: The Holocaust and the 21st century…Reflections of a Jew, a Catholic and a Protestant. St. Paul, Minn.: University of St. Thomas.

Upton, G. P., and Borowski, F. (2005). *The standard opera and concert guide, part two.* Whitefish, MT: Kessinger Publishing, p. 93.

Vatican Commission for Religious Relations with the Jews. (1998, March 16). We remember: A reflection on the *Shoah.* Retrieved June 3, 2009, from http://www.vatican.va/roman_curia/pontifical_councils/chrstuni/ documents/rc_pc_chrstuni_doc_16031998_Shoah_en.html

Vatican Archives. (1965, October 28). Declaration on the relation of the church to non-Christian religions: *Nostra Aetate.* Retrieved May 31, 2009, from http://www.vatican.va/archive/hist_councils/ii_vatican_council/docu ments/vat-ii_decl_19651028_nostra-aetate_en.html

Wagner, M. (2008, May 5). Amar calms converts after decision. *The Online Jerusalem Post.* Retrieved, February 5, 2009, from http://www.jpost .com/servlet/Satellite?pagename=JPost%2FJPArticle%2FShowFull& cid=1209627010371

Weber, J. (2003). The House of Pritzker. *Business Week,* (3824), 58-65. Retrieved October 31, 2011, from EBSCOhost.

Weiman, R. R. (2006, February 7). Putting the fragments together. *Ten minutes of Torah.* Union of Reform Judaism. Retrieved December 28, 2008, from http://tmt.urj.net/archives/2socialaction/020706.htm

Wertheimer, J. (1993). *A people divided: Judaism in contemporary America.* NY: Basic Books.

Weintraub, L. (1993, May 21). Farrakhan meets with area Jewish leaders. *Chicago-Sun Times*, p. 21.

Who was Heschel? (n.d.). The Heschel Center for Environmental Thinking and Leadership. Retrieved May 6, 2008, from http://www.heschel.org .il/eng/Heschel

Wollaston, I. (2000). The possibility and plausibility of divine abusiveness or sadism as the premise for a religious response to the Holocaust. *Journal of Religion and Society, 2*, 1-13.

Wolf, S. L. (1976). *Reform Judaism as process: A study of the Central Conference of American Rabbis 1960-1975* (Doctoral dissertation, Saint Louis University, 1976).

Wurzburger, W. (1985, Winter). Patrilineal descent and the Jewish identity crisis. *Judaism,* 34(1), p. 119. Retrieved April 22, 2009, from Academic Search Premier database.

Wyman, D. S. (1998). *The abandonment of the Jews.* NY: The New Press.

Wyschograd, E. (2000). Reading the Covenant: Some postmodern reflections. In P. Ochs, *Reviewing the covenant* (60-68). Albany: State University of New York Press.

Yad Vashem. Kristallnacht. (n.d.). Retrieved May 27, 2008, from http://www1 .yadvashem.org.il/odot_pdf/Microsoft%20Word%20-%206461.pdf

Yad Vashem: *Shoah* Resource Center. (2003). The Holocaust definition and preliminary discussion. Retrieved May 20, 2009, from http://www1 .yadvashem.org/Odot/prog/index_before_change_table.asp?gate=0-2

Yad Vashem. The Holocaust Martyrs' and Heroes' Remembrance Authority (2006). Gurs. Retrieved May 10, 2006, from http://www.yadvashem .org/lwp/workplace/!ut/p/.cmd/cs/.ce/7_0_A/.s/7_0_2C4/_s.7_0_A/7 _0_2C4?New_WCM_Context=http://namescm.yadvashem.org/wps/ wcm/connect/Yad+VaShem/Hall+Of+Names/Lexicon/en/Gurs

Yad Vashem: *The Central Database of Shoah Victims' Names.* (2012). Retrieved August 17, 2012, from http://db.yadvashem.org/names/nameResults .html?language=en&applid=SAPIR7&queryId=JAGUAR27-VM _2784_074422&page=2

Yad Vashem: *The Central Database of Shoah Victims' Names.* (2012). Retrieved August 17, 2012, from http://db.yadvashem.org/names/nameDetails .html?itemId=3216244&language=en

Yad Vashem The Holocaust Martyrs' and Heroes' Remembrance Authority. (2012). *This month in Holocaust history.* Retrieved February 7, 2012, from http://www1.yadvashem.org/yv/en/exhibitions/this_month/april/01.asp

Yearwood, P. D. (2008, April 4). Heschel at 100: Applying the great rabbi's lessons to Jewish life today. *The Chicago Jewish News Online.* Retrieved May 1, 2008 from http://www.chicagojewishnews.com/story.htm?sid=1&id=251849

Yoffie, E. H. (2003). Afterword. In D. E. Kaplan *American Reform Judaism* (259-262). New Brunswick, NJ: Rutgers University Press.

Youdovin, I. (1986). Reform Zionism and Reform Judaism: A creative encounter waiting to happen. In J. Edelheit (Ed.), *The life of Covenant: The challenge of contemporary Judaism* (251-256). Chicago: Spertus College of Judaica Press.

Yuter, A. (2008, November 24). Conversions, covenant and conscience. *Institute for Jewish Ideas and Ideals.* Retrieved February 19, 2009 from http://www.jewishideas.org/articles/conversions-covenant-and-conscience

Zedek, M. (Speaker). (2005, May 27). Interview with Richard Damashek [Cassette Recording]. Cincinnati: American Jewish Archives.

Zenger, E. (2009, March 2). The churches between renewal and regression with specific reference to the Second Vatican Council (1962-1965). International Council of Christian and Jews. Retrieved July 16, 2010, from http://jcrelations.net/en/?item=3068

Zola, G. P. (2006). Jewish camping and its relationship to the organized camping movement in America. In M. M. Lorge & G. P. Zola (Eds.), *A Place of their own: The rise of Reform Jewish camping* (1-26). Tuscaloosa, AL: The University of Alabama Press.

Index

E

Eastern Europe, 4, 121, 367, 512n11
Eastern European, 9, 12, 531n155
Echad, 428-429. *See also* Schaalman,
    Herman E., theology
Edelheit, Rabbi Joseph, x, 262,
    289-290, 296, 298, 554n289
Eden, 24, 414, 427. *See also*
    Schaalman, Herman E.,
    theology 24, 414, 427
Edwards, Robert, x, 442-443.
    See also Torah Study
Egan, Msg. John, 307
Egelson, Rabbi L. I., 84, 522n84
Egypt, xix, 403, 410-412, 416,
    579n408, 581n418
Eichstadt (Germany), 512n6
Einstein, Albert, 3-4, 61, 446,
    468, 497, 591n469
Eisendrath, Rabbi Maurice N.,
    173-175, 191, 195-199, 202,
    206-208, 210, 214, 256,
    534n175, 534n178, 535n183,
    535n185, 536n187, 545n240
Elbogen, Ismar, 52-53,
    516n44, 516n46
Ellenson, Rabbi David, 466-467,
    485, 572n372
Elon, A., 604
Emanu-El B'ne Jeshurun (Milwaukee),
    295-296, 460, 535n181
Emanuel Congregation (Chicago),
    xv, xviii, 133, 182-193, 192, 208,
    213-237, 240-241, 244-246, 248,
    250, 254, 257-263, 278, 287-303,
    319, 321, 438, 459, 485, 503,
    527n122, 533n165, 534n176-177,
    536n191, 537n195, 537n198,
    541n219, 543n230, 553n283,
    558n310, 570n367, 589n461, 594
Enlightenment, 387, 458, 521n75
Episcopal Diocese of Chicago, 326
Episcopalians, 120, 388
Essrig, H., 605
Ethical Humanism, 367-368

Ethics and Appeals Committee,
    296. *See also* Schaalman,
    Herman E., theology
European Jewry, 123, 179,
    368, 375, 512n8
Eve, 408, 445, 469, 577n401. *See also*
    Schaalman, Herman E., theology
Exodus, 379, 409-411, 413, 418,
    579n405. *See also* Schaalman,
    Herman E., theology

F

Fackenheim, Emil, 76, 171-172,
    240, 366, 368-369, 371, 373-374,
    376, 392, 395, 424, 426-427, 491,
    522n81, 532n160-162, 551n276,
    566n348-349, 567n358-359,
    568n361, 574n380-381, 575n390,
    576n397, 579n408, 580n414
Faith after the Holocaust, 574n383.
    See also Fackenheim, Emil
"Faith in God and man after
    Auschwitz: Theological
    implications," 605. *See also*
    Fackenheim, Emil
Fascism, 189, 365, 368
Father Coughlin, 59
Feinsinger, Professor, 68
Fenton, Marc and Gail, xi, 438,
    585n437
Ficca, Dirk, x, 332, 559n315
Fierman, Morton, 67
Fisher, Eugene, 357
Fishbein, Rabbi I. H., x, 269. *See also*
    Committee on Mixed Marriage
Fishkoff, S., 606
Fleischman, David, x, 237.
Flood, The, 408, 478, 505. *See also*
    Schaalman, Herman E., theology
Folb, Rabbi Ann, xi, 51, 75, 262,
    269, 274, 286, 289, 440, 467,
    500, 515n39, 519n62, 522n85,
    532n159, 548n257, 554n293
Franzblau, Abraham N., 80